Entrepreneurship

Entrepreneurship

Venture Initiation, Management, and Development

Second Edition

George S. Vozikis
Chaminade University of Honolulu
and Reighard Chair of Management (ret.)
California State University, Fresno

Timothy S. Mescon
Columbus State University

Howard D. Feldman
University of Portland

Eric W. Liguori
California State University, Fresno

M.E.Sharpe
Armonk, New York
London, England

The EuroSlavic fonts used to create this work are © 1986–2013 Payne Loving Trust.
EuroSlavic is available from Linguist's Software, Inc.,
www.linguistsoftware.com, P.O. Box 580, Edmonds, WA 98020-0580 USA
tel (425) 775-1130.

Library of Congress Cataloging-in-Publication Data

Vozikis, George S. (George Soterios), 1948–
  Entrepreneurship : venture initiation, management, and development / by George S. Vozikis,
Timothy S. Mescon, Howard D. Feldman, and Eric W. Liguori.—Second edition.
    pages cm
Includes bibliographical references and index.
ISBN 978-0-7656-3113-8 (hardcover : alk. paper)
1. Entrepreneurship. I. Mescon, Timothy S. II. Feldman, Howard D., 1948– III. Title.

HB615.V84 2013
658.1′1—dc23   2013003778

Printed in the United States of America

The paper used in this publication meets the minimum requirements of
American National Standard for Information Sciences
Permanence of Paper for Printed Library Materials,
ANSI Z 39.48-1984.

EB (c)   10   9   8   7   6   5   4   3   2   1

To our parents, who always thought we were better than we really are. . . .

To our mentors, Bill Glueck, Mike Mescon, Craig Aronoff, and Mark Weaver who made us what our parents thought we were . . . .

And to our families, who support us despite our shenanigans. . . .

"Viva la revolucion!"
—Emiliano Zapata, Mexican Revolutionary
—William R. Bartmann, Tulsa Serial Entrepreneur

Contents

Preface

We four share a common passion for entrepreneurship and a strong desire to improve the likelihood of success for students as they embark on their entrepreneurial careers. We have tried to leverage our strengths and bring what we know, have experienced, and have read to this project. We hope that we have been successful in this endeavor and that it will result in students' having better theoretical and applied backgrounds to draw upon and to enrich their entrepreneurial experiences—both within and outside of the classroom.

Venture initiation and development are key components of this book. We have used these two key elements as the foundation for a discussion that bridges the gap between theory and practice, between talking and doing. The book focuses upon the activities comprising a venture's launch, growth, and management. At the same time, we have provided the reader a deeper understanding of the research conducted in entrepreneurship beyond anecdotal stories of success.

ORGANIZATION

The overall framework of the book follows our "Enterprising Model." It consists of four parts, each germane to understanding the entrepreneurial process and venturing (and discussed in greater detail in Chapter 1).

"Part I: Introduction to Entrepreneurship and Intrapreneurship" discusses the evolution of the entrepreneur and intrapreneur and examines the feasibility of a venture's value concept. It shows the student how to "put it all together" in a business plan and provides a conceptual framework for success.

"Part II: Venture Initiation" presents the development of a framework for the venture's value concept or "niche" idea. These chapters cover the topics of value opportunity in strategic target markets, financial analysis and returns, and designing the framework for the venture's infrastructure, i.e., product and marketing considerations, organizational and operational considerations, and legal issues.

"Part III: Venture Management" cites the "ability to execute" once the venture is launched. The venture must be organized and staffed with skilled individuals, and they must be provided with competent managerial leadership with FAKTS, and with solid financial money management and control.

"Part IV: Venture Development" discusses how to determine whether the venture can protect, improve upon, and expand its value concept and sustain a competitive advantage through effective growth management, development, and/or "harvesting," and by examining future expansion possibilities of the venture's value concept by looking, in particular, at international opportunities.

Throughout the development of this book, we considered the very different facets of entrepreneurship and its overwhelmingly worldwide appeal. It is our hope that this textbook will be a portal for students to succeed in launching new ventures.

ADDITIONAL FEATURES

Several other features within the book enhance the students' learning experience, including key terms, learning objectives, topic outlines for each chapter, references, and review questions. In addition, at the end of each chapter is a section entitled "Reflections from the Front Lines of LifeGuard America." These sections provide a bridge between theory and practice that presents the actual thoughts and contemplations of a nascent but very successful entrepreneur regarding his real-life venture startup. John R. Fitzpatrick, III, the founding president and CEO of LifeGuard America, an organization in the organ procurement and transplant industry, has substantial experience in corporate America. He graciously wrote these sections himself as a reflection of his experiences in launching and developing his venture and as an expression of his sincere devotion to entrepreneurship education.

Supplementing these tools are the "Magnificent Seven Conceptual Hooks" (chapter 3), an innovative framework to be used by students in analyzing and writing their business plans. The Business Plan Hooks that we call "The Magnificent Seven" are labeled after the classic 1960 American Western film directed by John Sturges, which itself was based on Akira Kurosawa's 1954 movie masterpiece "The Seven Samurai." The "Magnificent Seven Hooks" comprise an evolutionary approach to writing a business plan. They focus the student's attention on distinct chapter topics and facilitate the gradual and progressive formulation of a plan, as these topics themselves actually represent the conceptualized elements of a business plan.

Agriculture (also known as "ag" in the world of economics) and related businesses are the foundation of many communities throughout the United States and around the globe. "Ag" industries employ hundreds of thousands of individuals, represent billions in revenues, and help drive the global economy. In some areas, like the Central Valley of California, agriculture and related businesses comprise over 90 percent of the region's economic base. In addition, agriculture is experiencing a "tech boom" and daily advancements are making the agricultural world an ever-changing business. As entrepreneurs, this creates opportunities for you, and we want to challenge you to recognize opportunities in this evolving industry. To this end, some chapters of this text are supplemented with agriculturally focused questions, forcing you to do some additional research on your own community and the industry as a whole.

ACKNOWLEDGMENTS

Many individuals assisted in the processes of developing, writing, reviewing, and editing this text, and they deserve our appreciation and recognition. We thank Dr. K. Mark Weaver (University of South Alabama) and Dr. Gary Selden (Kennesaw State University) for their helpful input in revising this textbook. We are also especially thankful to Josh Bendickson for his work in developing the business model generation portion of Chapter 3. Finally, we thank our many, many colleagues and students with whom we have worked, "argued," and collaborated, in some cases for decades. You inspire us, you motivate us, and you advocate for us. Thank you.

George S. Vozikis
(vozikis@sbcglobal.net)

Timothy S. Mescon
(tmescon@columbusstate.edu)

Howard D. Feldman
(Feldman@up.edu)

Eric W. Liguori
(eliguori@csufresno.edu)

Introduction to Entrepreneurship and Intrapreneurship

1 Entrepreneurship and the Entrepreneur

LEARNING OBJECTIVES

1. To understand the essence of entrepreneurship.

2. To identify the major characteristics of the entrepreneur.

3. To be able to relate and integrate the process of venture initiation and development into a workable action model.

TOPIC OUTLINE

"We say here that everybody wants to be a chicken's head, not a bull's toenail."

(Chien-Shien Wang, Taiwan's former vice minister for economic affairs, on why there are so many small businesses in his country.)

___

INTRODUCTION

"Twenty years ago, *Fortune* 500 companies in the U.S. hired over 70% of college graduates. Today, *Fortune* 500 companies hire less than 7% of college graduates and the entrepreneurial enterprises hire over 80%. More than 40% of students start a business within one year of graduation" (*Houston Business Journal*, 2000). These businesses employ 55% of the total American work force. When we think of the entrepreneur, we often visualize the small business. While most, if not all, business ideas begin "small," a great deal of focus is placed upon entrepreneurial ideas that have grown into sizable corporations. In examining the entrepreneur, we should not get entwined in the small vs. large argument; rather, we should focus on the individual that made his or her dream come true. The individual who is able, through painstaking effort, to transform a simple idea into a moneymaking, successful venture is the real, classical entrepreneur.

HISTORY OF ENTREPRENEURSHIP

In the beginning of human history, mankind was an agrarian society, and the first entrepreneurs were farmers, artisans, or craftsmen. True entrepreneurial recognition came much later, during the mercantilism period in Louis XIV's France in the eighteenth century, which created merchant entrepreneurs. The word **entrepreneur** evolved from the French *"entreprendre,"* meaning "to undertake." This meaning was first introduced by Richard Cantillon (1697–1734), an Irish economist of French descent whose *Essai sur la Nature de Commerce* preceded Adam Smith's *Wealth of Nations* by more than 20 years. He characterized an entrepreneur as a "specialist in taking on risk," in terms of "insuring" workers by buying their products or labor services for resale long before consumers indicated how much they are willing to pay for them. In other words, according to Cantillon, the entrepreneur is the agent who purchases the various means of production for ultimate assembly or combination into marketable products. He recognized that a degree of uncertainty and risk entered into the entrepreneurial activity. The workers receive an assured income (in the short run, at least), while the entrepreneur bears the risk caused by price fluctuation in consumer markets.

Until then, the prevalent theory on wealth accumulation was the one advocated by Jean-Baptiste Colbert (1619–1683), who served as the French Minister of Finance from 1665 to 1683 under King Louis XIV. He coined the term **mercantilism**, in which the wealth of a nation is ensured by relentlessly exporting and hoarding gold rather than importing, which had left the French people impoverished and hastened the French Revolution. But the fate of the East India Company, which personified mercantilism, showed that the mercantilists might have been too optimistic about a state company's ability to avoid being corrupted by politics. Later, Adam Smith (1723–1790) denounced the East India Company as a "bloodstained, burdensome, and useless monopoly" (*The Economist*, 2011). Today's global, Chinese state-owned companies are the most similar in concept to the East India Company, which was finally put out of its misery in 1874.

In an attempt to refute mercantilism and to explain how nations accumulate wealth, Adam Smith credited the entrepreneur and his or her *invisible entrepreneurial hand,* unrestrained and seemingly chaotic, to determine resource allocations that produce wealth rather than merely export it. Adam Smith, the father of private enterprise, influenced heavily by Cantillon, viewed the entrepreneur as a contributor to the workings of the economic system. According to Smith, the businessman who funded entrepreneurial ventures provided capital and nothing else to the productive process. The role can be likened to that of the catalyst that serves to initiate and incite a chemical reaction but serves no useful subsequent function (Schumpeter, 1939).

Of course, this relates to the undertaking of a business and translating words into action in the same way that we view today's entrepreneur. The Webster's definition of entrepreneur is "One who organizes, manages, and assumes the risks of a business or enterprise" (Merriam-Webster, 1999). This definition applies to an entrepreneur's desire to undertake an idea and implement it through a business plan, with the essential goal of making a profit. The word itself expresses the dynamic nature of entrepreneurship and the inherent contradictions in the attempt to balance the need for a venture's flexibility with the need for coordination.

Additionally, the word entrepreneurship also reflects the inherent difficulties in balancing three seemingly impossible acts: (a) the **entrepreneurial problem** as far as the choice of products and markets are concerned; (b) the **engineering problem** in terms of the development of a production process for these products and their distribution in the targeted markets; and (c) the **administrative problem** of designing the appropriate managerial structures and processes to ensure the venture's effective organization, in anticipation of the next entrepreneurial problem, as the venture grows and evolves.

Entrepreneurs come in all shapes, sizes, and colors. They are young and old, male and female. Some are successful in their endeavors, while many are not. However, one common bond exists among all entrepreneurs: they have implemented their thoughts in a cohesive, concerted effort. Words become action, and hopes become realities.

Joseph A. Schumpeter (1883–1950) an acclaimed Austrian economist, labeled entrepreneurship as "the perennial gale of creative destruction" (1939). He viewed the entrepreneur as an innovator as well as a manager. Schumpeter continues this line of reasoning by arguing that entrepreneurial profit evolves from innovation or from procuring a commodity at a lower unit cost than any competitor. However, subsequent statements in his seminal work titled *Business Cycles: A Theoretical, Historical, and Statistical Analysis of the Capitalist Process* (1939) serve as a caveat to any entrepreneur hoping to rest upon past accomplishments. Schumpeter warned of the continuous prospect of creative destruction, because once their enterprise is in existence, almost all entrepreneurs feel threatened and put on the defensive. As a matter of fact, he warned that successful businesses conspire with politicians through lobbying to preserve the status quo! Entrepreneurs and business people, therefore, are unsung heroes and are responsible for the most benign development in human history: the spread of mass affluence by moving resources, however painfully, to areas where they can be used more innovatively and productively. Schumpeter said: "The capitalist achievement does not typically consist in providing more silk stockings for queens but in bringing them within the reach of factory girls, in return for steadily decreasing amount of effort!"

Chester I. Barnard advanced the belief that a relationship exists between the entrepreneur and innovation. To Barnard, the entrepreneur was the one who conceives, discovers, and promotes innovative activities in business operation. Innovation is essential to all formal organizations. In an environment that is constantly changing, it is crucial to have the capacity to sense and affect change if an organization is to survive.

Harbison and Myers (1959) developed the notion of the organization builder. To them, the organization builder is "the catalytic agent in the process of industrialization, that is, he/she acts and reacts with economic and social environment to bring about economic change" (Harbison & Myers, 1959, p. 17). On the other hand, Collins, Moore, and Unwalla (1964) concluded, after an exhaustive review of conflicting terminologies, that when utilizing the term entrepreneur, "We shall (only) mean the innovating entrepreneur who has developed an ongoing business activity where none existed before" (p. 20).

Exhibit 1.1   The Evolution of the Entrepreneur

Cantillon	A specialist in taking on risk
Smith	Catalyst initiating a chemical reaction
Schumpeter	Innovator who engages in creative destruction
Barnard	One who conceives, discovers, and promotes innovative action
Harbison & Myers	Organization builder who brings economic change
Collins, Moore, & Unwalla	Developer of a business activity where none existed before
Ronstadt	One who infuses value into a product or service
Today's entrepreneur	Undertakes, implements, and transforms dreams into realities by creating value where none was perceived to exist before

Perhaps the most candid and frank views and definitions of the entrepreneur were provided first by Schöllhammer and Kuriloff (1979, pp. 8–12), who wrote that entrepreneurs, in the modern sense, are the self-starters and doers who have organized and built successful enterprises since the Industrial Revolution. Robert Ronstadt, as quoted by Kuratko and Hodgetts (1989), furthered the description:

> Entrepreneurship therefore is the dynamic process of creating incremental wealth. This wealth is created by individuals who assume the major risks in terms of equity, time, and/or career commitment of providing value for some product or service. The product or service itself may or may not be new or unique, but value must somehow be infused by the entrepreneur by securing and allocating the necessary skills and resources. (222–223)

In this context, we reserve the term **enterprise** for actions that entail carrying out innovations. For the individuals who carry them out, we reserve the term entrepreneurs. This terminological decision is based on a historical fact and a theoretical proposition, namely, that carrying out innovations is the only function that is fundamental in history and essential in theory to the type of activity usually designated by that term. To prosper in the long run, the entrepreneur must continually initiate innovative actions and reactions in a competitive economic system (Dale, 1970, p. 28).

What has historically separated the entrepreneurs from the masses is the fact that they undertook a business idea. They implemented where others dreamed. They transformed dreams into realities. They tried, and perhaps even failed, where others merely weighed their options. Entrepreneurs charge, while others hesitate. They run when others walk, and they leap when others hope. Cantillon, as mentioned earlier, was the first to associate the risk-bearing activities of the economy with the term entrepreneur. The **industrial revolution** in England brought forth entrepreneur/industrialists, and later, entrepreneurial service industries developed. Many similarities can be drawn between entrepreneurs at the end of nineteenth century and **Internet entrepreneurs** at the beginning of twenty-first century. A success manual from the late nineteenth century advocated that "never before in the world's history was competition in every calling and pursuit as fierce as now in this latter half of the (nineteenth) century. Those who don't play by the new rules would be trampled underfoot in the rush and roar of the nineteenth century" (Useem, 1999, pp. 159–160). For example, people during the 1890s started shopping from Sears and Montgomery Ward catalogs, whereas much shopping is now done from the Internet. What these periods have in common is the kind of people who shaped the new way of "doing things" and who recognized the value of

- The fundamental changes in the world that presented new opportunities.
- The new strategies that were needed to take advantage of these changes.
- The new kinds of organizational structures that were needed to execute those strategies.
- The implementation of a value-creating vision into action.

Another historical perspective of entrepreneurship is the more recent revolution of a business firm's organizational structure. There have been four distinct phases of organizational transformation. The first phase was the evolutionary development of professional managers. The second phase started when these professional managers determined that their companies could operate many different conglomerate businesses, such as an oil firm owning and operating a retail store, or a sugar company owning and operating hotels. Over time, the weaknesses of this model became more pronounced, and during the 1970s a third phase emerged when most conglomerates started unraveling. As the conglomerates proved their inefficiency, this third entrepreneurial phase became a true force. These entrepreneurs, such as Sam Walton, Bill Gates, and Charles Schwab, emerged by undertaking financial ventures and turnaround improvements of old businesses, or by building up businesses from nothing. Their entrepreneurial creations have ushered a new wave of alliances of competing and noncompeting companies with entrepreneurial roots, without, of course, negating the entrepreneurial phase, which is far from over, especially with the advent and continued expansion of the Internet (Chakravarty, 1998). The future of entrepreneurship is indeed today, and the opportunities are limitless because the bricks-and-mortar days have been replaced with bricks and "clicks."

CHARACTERIZING THE ENTREPRENEUR

Jean Baptiste Say in the early nineteenth century, and the economic genius Joseph Schumpeter in the twentieth-century, began writing about entrepreneurship and its impact on the economic development of a country. For many years psychologist David C. McClelland studied a particular human motive, the need to achieve. In his landmark effort, *The Achieving Society* (1961), McClelland tested the hypothesis "that a society with a generally high level of [need for] achievement will produce more energetic entrepreneurs, who in turn produce more rapid economic development" (p. 205). According to McClelland, the need for achievement is the most dominant among the psychological drives that motivate the entrepreneur and this need can be classified into three broad categories:

1. Entrepreneurs like to set goals for themselves and measure their performance against stringent standards of excellence. They want to succeed and compare themselves only to their own specifically conceived criteria.

2. Entrepreneurs are interested and actively involved in unique accomplishments. They want to be distinctive, to protrude, and to stand out among others.

3. Entrepreneurs are not "buck passers." Coinciding with their achievement motivation is the acceptance of responsibility for all their actions. (pp. 36–46)

McClelland and his associates also provided a more comprehensive list of tested entrepreneurial characteristics, some of which are listed here:

- Individuals high in **need for achievement** are moderate risk takers.
- Entrepreneurs wish to operate in situations in which they can obtain a sense of personal achievement.
- Entrepreneurs perceive their probability of succeeding to be very high.
- Entrepreneurs are not strongly motivated by material rewards.

- Entrepreneurs desire and need constant progress reports and personal performance assessments. (pp. 36–46)

One additional entrepreneurial personality characteristic deserves mention here. Shapero (1978) conducted a number of research efforts focusing on the concept of **locus of control**. Shapero's observations emphasize the fact that entrepreneurs, in general, feel that they can influence events to their own benefit or detriment. Their strong internal locus of control contrasts with that of those whose locus of control is external and who believe that rewards or punishments in life come through fate, luck, or chance (ibid.).

Economic breakdowns should be blamed precisely on the lack of entrepreneurship and lack of entrepreneurial-type decision making. A basic characteristic of most entrepreneurial decision making is its ongoing nature and the entrepreneurial desire to see things through (Cole, 1959, p. 14). An entrepreneur's work is not over until the decision he or she made has been implemented and executed. In such circumstances, while most of us would probably settle for the status quo, entrepreneurs act. Reasons for this stem from the very heart of human creativity and can rarely be expressed in anything other than terms such as animal spirit, instinct, drive, purpose, or sheer self-righteousness; the entrepreneur believes he or she is right, while everyone else is wrong (Casson, 1991, p. 14).

ENTREPRENEURS: BORN OR MADE?

While entrepreneurs have many unique characteristics, a main idea is still missing. Previous research in entrepreneurship has often focused on identifying the personal characteristics or traits that distinguish entrepreneurs from the general population, rather than adopting a process-oriented approach (Low & Macmillan, 1988; Boyd & Vozikis, 1994). Additionally, many of these identified characteristics are not exclusively held by entrepreneurs but rather are possessed by many successful individuals (Brockhaus, 1982; Brockhaus & Horwitz, 1986; Gartner, 1985). The one important characteristic that is missing is the trait of self-efficacy, which has been defined as a person's belief in his or her capability to perform a task (Gist, 1987; Boyd & Vozikis, 1994). Self-efficacy plays a very important role in the development of entrepreneurial intentions and actions and confirms that the main entrepreneurial drive comes from inside the individual, because individuals will not be successful entrepreneurs if they do not believe in themselves. Through education or actual work experience, one can readily acquire specific attitudes, knowledge, and skills in the business functions of accounting, finance, marketing, etc., but the spark needed to fire the entrepreneurial spirit must come from within.

Whereas we can easily identify a number of individuals who exhibit "inborn" entrepreneurial characteristics, theory leans toward the position that anyone can develop, refine, and emerge as a *bona fide*, successful entrepreneur. Minniti and Bygrave (1999) advocate the idea that people who are alert to an entrepreneurial environment where "disequilibrium" exists, in the sense of continuous change, and have the ability to cope with uncertainty can be "made" into entrepreneurs. Of course, this idea complements Schumpeter's ideas, in which the entrepreneur is the one who *creates* the disequilibrium, rather than merely *reacts* to changes. Alert individuals can react to market opportunities and act upon them when they are convinced that the utility received from undertaking an entrepreneurial venture exceeds the utility received from any alternative income-producing activity. Some detect these marketing opportunities, and some do not. Those who do can be labeled entrepreneurs, and those who do not cannot be labeled entrepreneurs. Minniti and Bygrave further identify three simultaneous elements that reinforce the label of entrepreneur:

- The subjective initial personal endowment of the entrepreneur, such as family background, education, and personal history;

- The institutional and economic state of the specific economic setting of an entrepreneurial venture, such as property rights, taxes, inflation rate, and opportunity cost of engaging in entrepreneurial activities; and

- The existing level of entrepreneurial activity in that specific economic setting as perceived and evaluated by the individual entrepreneur, such as networking, and support system for entrepreneurial activities. (p. 3)

Furthermore, some specific events in one's lifetime increase or decrease the prospect of becoming an entrepreneur. An inheritance or a sudden gift, for example, increases the probability of becoming self-employed, especially since most entrepreneurial ventures begin not with bank loans but with one's own or family funds (Blanchflower & Oswald, 1998).

Can entrepreneurship be taught? This is debatable unless the characteristics of an entrepreneur are separated, conceptually speaking, from the entrepreneurship process. The basic assumption guiding this text is that entrepreneurship cannot be "forcefully" taught and that nobody can be forced to become an entrepreneur. Rather, this course endeavors to transpose the student into the mind frame of an entrepreneur or intrapreneur! This requires the creation of worthwhile and positive outcomes as a result of hard work and initiative on the part of the student. To accomplish these positive outcomes, the entrepreneurial process can be taught in terms of

1. **Analysis of facts** by collecting information and evaluating knowledge on the possibility of the existence of a value concept.

2. **Active thinking** by synthesizing, planning, integrating, and assigning meaning to the knowledge related to this value concept.

3. **Application of the knowledge** by initiating the venture and validating the value concept.

4. **Active doing** by the effective management and development of the venture, thus advancing the relevance of the knowledge about the value concept by ensuring its growth and survival.

Hopefully, this initial exposure will inspire you, the student, to create and implement your own business ideas by building your confidence. As our old friend, the late Jeff Bracker, an entrepreneurship professor at the University of Louisville used to say: "Competence can be bought or acquired; confidence, never!" The atmosphere provided by our free market economy is most amenable for budding entrepreneurs. However, the spark needed to fire that entrepreneurial spirit must come from within. Through schooling or actual work experience, you can readily acquire and become truly confident about the required **FAKTS** of entrepreneurship, the building blocks of venture development:

- Financials
- Attitude
- Knowledge
- Timing
- Skills

THE ENTERPRISING MODEL

Every plan needs structure, and the complex task of determining what needs to be accomplished requires a course of action that will bring structure and lay the foundations for the transformation of a plan into a real-life firm. The enterprising model offered here is composed of four parts, which are outlined below in more detail.

Part I: Introduction to Entrepreneurship and Intrapreneurship

Part I delineates the evolution of the entrepreneur as an individual with distinctive characteristics through the application of individual entrepreneurial efforts (Chapter 1) or entrepreneurial activities and processes in a corporate setting. These efforts develop entrepreneurial pockets of corporate innovation (Chapter 2) and fulfill the essential role of entrepreneurship by (a) evaluating the feasibility of the venture's value concept, (b) "putting it all together" in a business plan (Chapter 3), and (c) developing a success framework by identifying overall success requirements (Chapter 4).

Part II: Venture Initiation

Part II presents the development of a framework for the venture's value concept "niche" idea. This development begins by systematically seeking and conceptualizing the value opportunity concept (Chapter 5) in a demand-driven, strategic, target market (Chapter 6). Then the potential returns and the timetables for the venture's financial prospects are projected (Chapter 7), and the need for personal and additional financial and overall commitment is specified (Chapter 8). Finally, the framework for the venture's infrastructure is designed; it consists of the product and marketing considerations (Chapter 9), organizational and operational considerations (Chapter 10), and legal considerations (Chapter 11).

Part III: Venture Management

The entrepreneurial or intrapreneurial venture's "ability to execute" once the venture is launched is ensured only by organizing and staffing the venture with skilled individuals and providing them with competent managerial leadership with FAKTS (Chapter 12) and by providing solid financial money management and control (Chapter 13).

Part IV: Venture Development

Whether a venture proposal constitutes a real "deal" depends on whether its survival and growth is ensured by *protecting, improving,* and *expanding* the venture's value concept and sustainable competitive advantage through effective growth management, development, and/or "harvesting" (Chapter 14), and finally, by examining future expansion possibilities of the venture's value concept by assessing its growth and development prospects through internationalization (Chapter 15).

In addition to the text and the material that it highlights, at the end of each chapter is a section titled "Reflections from the Front Lines of LifeGuard." This section provides a bridge between theory and practice; it presents the thoughts and contemplations of a nascent entrepreneur in the process of a real-life venture startup. These sections are written by John R. Fitzpatrick III, founding president and CEO of LifeGuard America, a venture aimed at dramatically improving the organ procurement and transplant industry and consequently saving the lives of many who are waiting for transplant organs around the country. John has more than 15 years of senior leadership experience in such companies as Hewlett-Packard and Harley-Davidson and as president and CEO of Indian Motorcycle Company in Gilroy, California. In May of 2001 he returned to Tulsa, Oklahoma, to start LifeGuard America and bring the company to a point where the management team, strategic partners, and the value concept itself were fully tested and ready to deliver services. John is a 1978 graduate of the University of Tulsa's Electrical Engineering College and served 12 years as a fighter pilot with Tulsa's 125th Tactical Fighter Squadron while working at FlightSafety (1980–1981), Hewlett Packard (1981–1987), and Advanced Graphics Systems (1987–1994). John and his wife, Luanne, have two wonderful daughters, Kelli Kathleen and Ashlee Anne.

CONCLUSION

The characteristics of the entrepreneur and the intrapreneur and their impact on the venture's performance have long been a subject of academic debate. However, they inherently rely on several **FAKTS** that seem to be universally accepted. Entrepreneurs and intrapreneurs possess **F**inancial skills to help them avoid strategic and financial pitfalls. They have a compelling but realistic **A**ttitude about their venture's possibilities. They are the world's experts on the potential of their products and services because they **K**now their specific product, market, and industry. They have a clear vision of the enterprise's current and future state of affairs because their **T**iming is perfect at the juncture of economic, financial, competitive, and personal circumstances when everything has come together. This enables them to provide direction and effective communication to other organizational members as well as convey confidence to investors. Finally, entrepreneurs and intrapreneurs possess the organizational, communication, and competence **S**kills to effectively manage operational processes and to formulate and implement strategies. These **FAKTS** constitute the fundamental blocks of venture initiation and development.

Additional Website Information

Topic	Web Address	Description
History of the Entrepreneur	www.technopreneurial.com/articles/history.asp	Gives a brief overview of the history of the entrepreneur.
Characteristics of the Entrepreneur	www.cbsc.org.alberta/tbl.cfm?fn=cutout	Lists characteristics of successful entrepreneurs, personal qualities of successful entrepreneurs, skills of successful entrepreneurs, external factors involved in success, and, reasons for starting a business.
Characteristics of the Entrepreneur	http://www.entrepreneur.com/article/200730	Links to a profile of the entrepreneur, myths about entrepreneurs, and self-analysis.
General Entrepreneur Information	www.startupjournal.com/	*Wall Street Journal's* center for entrepreneurs includes recent articles about entrepreneurship.
Fortune 500 Companies	www.inc.com/inc500/	Lists of America's fastest-growing private companies, and information on each.
Sam Walton, Charles Schwab, Bill Gates, etc.	www.iusb.edu/~mfox1/w100/cnn2.htm	Brief biographies of the people who had a profound impact on business in the twentieth century.
Achieving Society	http://www.businessballs.com/davidmcclelland.htm	In-depth information about the study carried out by David McClelland.
Locus of Control	http://www.careerdiagnostics.com/surveys/locus_control.htm	Provides a brief survey to test your own locus of control as well as other websites that give information about locus of control.

Key Terms

Active doing: The effective management and development of the venture that advances the relevance of the knowledge about the value concept and ensures its growth and survival.

Active thinking: Synthesizing, planning, integrating, and assigning meaning to the knowledge related to this value concept.

Administrative problem: Concerned with designing the appropriate managerial structures and processes to ensure the venture's effective organization, in anticipation of the next entrepreneurial problem, as the venture grows and evolves.

Analysis of facts: Collecting information and evaluating knowledge on the possibility of the existence of a value concept.

Application of knowledge: Initiating the venture and validating the value concept.

Engineering problem: Concerned with the development of a production process for products and their distribution in the targeted markets.

Enterprise: A term reserved for action, which entails carrying out innovations.

Entrepreneurial problem: Concerned with the choice of products and markets.

Entrepreneurs: From the French, to undertake, a term reserved for the individuals who carry out the action of an enterprise.

FAKTS of entrepreneurship: Financials, Attitude, Knowledge, Timing, Skills.

Industrial Revolution: A period in England that brought forth entrepreneur/industrialists.

Internet entrepreneurs: A title given to entrepreneurs of the twentieth century.

Locus of control: The distinct feeling that one can either influence events to their own benefit or detriment or can hold the belief that that rewards or punishments in life come through fate, luck, or chance.

Mercantilism: A period during Louis XIV's eighteenth-century France that created merchant entrepreneurs.

Need for achievement: The most dominant among the psychological drives that motivate the entrepreneur.

Review Questions

1. In what ways are the FAKTS of entrepreneurship universally accepted by each entrepreneur?

2. Are entrepreneurs born or made?

3. Discuss the concept of self-efficacy.

4. What does the word "entrepreneur" mean to you?

5. Can entrepreneurship be taught?

6. Briefly describe the evolution of the entrepreneur through the ages.

7. Consider the evolution of the entrepreneur presented in Exhibit 1.1 and do some research on your local agriculture industry. Where in this evolution do you see the current industry, and why? Has it evolved to the same extent as other industries in your area?

Reflections from the Front Lines of LifeGuard America

How does one become an "entrepreneur"? Are entrepreneurs born, raised, or converted from some other stock? Looking back, I must confess that my entrepreneurship began at a very young age. My father was a genius, period. It doesn't hurt, I guess, that he graduated from Berkeley in the 1940s with honors, had Enrico Fermi as a physics professor, and sat in on monthly breakfast talks with Mr. Fermi and Albert Einstein at a local Berkeley café. I have met few people that have the ability to conceive, process, and design in three-dimensional space while at the same time have the ability to communicate effectively to those of us who cannot. His incredible abilities led him to a path of entrepreneurship in the oil and gas industry that is, to this day, without equal. In 25 years, he amassed more than seventeen patents and started seven different companies with products that remain state-of-the-art 21 years after his all-too-early death. It was in the shadow of this giant that I watched, learned, and "apprenticed" for thirty-some years.

It is hard to say whether I actually learned from or just came to appreciate and imitate my father's actions. I believe that by witnessing his undaunted spirit while launching a new company with products that were groundbreaking in their field, I came to appreciate and to aspire to that same goal: to make a difference. His words still ring in my ears, "Be good at something first; then and only then can you extend yourself into the world making it a better place." Born, raised, or converted? I guess it doesn't much matter. Once entrepreneurism gets into your blood, it becomes a way of life, and good or bad, there is no turning back.

Discussion Questions on LifeGuard America

1. Does it appear that Mr. Fitzpatrick was unknowingly an apprentice to entrepreneurship?

2. How would an apprenticeship differ from being "taught" entrepreneurship?

3. What do you think is meant by Mr. Fitzpatrick's reference to conversion?

References

Blanchflower, D. G., & Oswald, A. J. (1998, January). What makes an entrepreneur. *Journal of Labor Economics, 16*(1), 26–60.

Boyd, N. G., & Vozikis, G. S. (1994, Summer). The influence of self-efficacy on the development of entrepreneurial intentions and actions. *Entrepreneurship Theory and Practice, 18*(4), 63–77.

Brockhaus, R. H. (1982). The psychology of the entrepreneur. In C. A. Kent, D. L. Sexton, & R. W. Smilor (Eds.), *Encyclopedia of entrepreneurship* (pp. 288–307). Englewood Cliffs, NJ: Prentice Hall.

Brockhaus, R. H., & Horwitz, P. S. (1986). The psychology of the entrepreneur. In D. L. Sexton & R. W. Smilor (Eds.), *The art and science of entrepreneurship* (pp. 25–48). Cambridge, MA: Ballinger.

Casson, M. (1991). *The entrepreneur: An economic theory.* Aldershot, England: Gregg Revivals.

Chakravarty, S. N. (1998, January 12). Greatness is made not bought. *Forbes, 161*(1), 98–99.

Cole, A. H. (1959). *Business enterprise in a social setting.* Cambridge, MA: Harvard University Press.

Collins, O. F., Moore, D. G., & Unwalla, D. B. (1964). *The enterprising man.* East Lansing, MI: MSU Business Studies.

Dale, E. (1970). *Readings in management* (2nd ed.). New York: McGraw-Hill.

Economist, The. (2011, December 17). The company that ruled the waves. *401*(8764), 109–111.

Gartner, W. B. (1985). A conceptual framework for describing the phenomenon of new venture creation. *Academy of Management Review, 10*(4), 696–706.

Gist, M. E. (1987). Self-efficacy: Implications for organizational behavior and human resource management. *Academy of Management Review, 12*(3), 472–485.

Harbison, F., & Myers, C. A. (1959). *Management in the industrial world.* New York: McGraw-Hill.

Houston Business Journal. (2000). History of the center. *31*(12), S-2.

Kuratko, D. F., & Hodgetts, R. M. (1989). *Entrepreneurship: A contemporary approach.* Orlando, FL: The Dryden Press.

Low, M. B., & MacMillan, I. C. (1988). Entrepreneurship: Past research and future challenges. *Journal of Management, 14*(2), 139–161.

McClelland, D. C. (1961). *The achieving society.* New York: Free Press.

Merriam-Webster Online Dictionary. (1999). Retrieved October 13, 1999, from http://www.m-w.com.

Minniti, M., & Bygrave, W. (1999, Summer). The microfoundations of entrepreneurship. *Entrepreneurship Theory and Practice, 23*(4), 1–16.

Schöllhammer, H., & Kuriloff, A. H. (1979). *Entrepreneurship and small business management.* New York: John Wiley & Sons.

Schumpeter, J. A. (1939). *Business cycles: A theoretical, historical, and statistical analysis of the capitalist process* (Vol. 1). New York: McGraw-Hill.

Shapero, A. (1978, Fall). Corporate heroes or lousy managers? *Wharton Magazine, 3*(1), 32–37.

Useem, J. (1999, May 18). Entrepreneur of the century: Who changed things? Who's changing them now? And exactly what makes an entrepreneur great, anyway? Hint: It's not about the money. *Inc. Magazine, 21*(7), 158–169.

Wolf, William B. (1974). *The basic Barnard: An introduction to Chester I. Barnard and his theories of organization and management.* Ithaca: New York State School of Industrial and Labor Relations.

2 Corporate Entrepreneurship and Intrapreneurs

LEARNING OBJECTIVES

1. To explain why corporate entrepreneurship or intrapreneurship is a real source of new businesses and an activity encouraged by many larger firms.
2. To compare and contrast the advantages and disadvantages of corporate venturing efforts.
3. To identify the primary characteristics, attitudes, and philosophies usually attributed to corporate entrepreneurs.
4. To identify the four stages of the corporate entrepreneurship process and the various activities comprising each stage.
5. To identify the challenges faced by corporate management during the corporate entrepreneurship process and how their resolution can contribute to the success of a corporate venture.

TOPIC OUTLINE

Introduction

Corporate Venturing, Entrepreneurship, and Intrapreneurship
- Benefits of Corporate Entrepreneurship
- Popularizing the Concept of Corporate Entrepreneurship
- The Advantages Offered by Larger Firms to Venturing Efforts

The Corporate Entrepreneur
- The Trials and Tribulations of the Corporate Entrepreneur
- Some Additional Costs and Benefits to Consider

The Corporate Entrepreneurship Process
- Initiating the Process: Choosing an Idea
- Planning the Venture
- Managing the Venture from Survival to Growth
- Integrating the Venture into the Organization

Conclusion

Website Information

Key Terms

Review Questions

Case Study

References

"Every time you put a new idea into action, you find ten people who thought of it first, but they only thought of it."

(Unknown)

———

INTRODUCTION

Individual entrepreneurs have become our mythic heroes, and their success, as well as the excitement, action, and dynamism surrounding their ventures, is broadcast daily in business journals, newspapers, and other forms of news media. Entrepreneurship, as a legitimate alternative career path, has captured the imagination of the American public and educational institutions like at no other time in our business history, and it has traveled as a concept to other countries to promote economic development (Lado & Vozikis, 1997).

Discussions of entrepreneurship, however, cannot afford to focus simply on smaller or emerging ventures and to ignore larger firms. Only 3–4% of the millions of businesses in the United States employ more than 500 workers. Together, however, they account for more than 38% of the total working population (Birch, 1987). This is a substantial number of workers, without a doubt, but can they play a role in entrepreneurship? Can senior managers turn corporate employees into *bona fide* entrepreneurs? Can organizations, generally perceived as bureaucratic and conservative, adjust to the radically different mindset needed for corporate entrepreneurship? Can these large firms, which need to depend on coordination and centralization for sheer survival reasons, create conditions of flexibility from within, so entrepreneurial activities can spring up and flourish?

If organizations can make this paradigm shift, corporate entrepreneurship or intrapreneurship becomes another alternative mode of entry for potential entrepreneurs. But this type of entry strategy differs significantly from the more traditional methods of independent entrepreneurship. For one thing, ownership is typically not part of the bargain between the parent firm and the corporate entrepreneur, and even if it is, it is generally a token share provided as an incentive to engage in intrapreneurial activities. Ownership usually remains firmly in the hands of the corporation that provides the intrapreneurial environment. Furthermore, the corporate entrepreneur's personal wealth is not at risk, nor are financial resources as difficult to obtain. Even with these differences, however, bringing a new product or service to market within the context of a larger firm offers many of the same challenges as independent entrepreneurship. Aspiring entrepreneurs working for a corporation are unable or not yet willing to experience some of the same highs and lows that independent entrepreneurs do; they engage in entrepreneurial activities that add value to the organization that employs them.

CORPORATE VENTURING, ENTREPRENEURSHIP, AND INTRAPRENEURSHIP

Corporate entrepreneurs, corporate venturers, intrapreneurs, product or business champions, business innovators. . . . At one time or another, all of these terms have been used to describe individuals or teams employed by a large organization or their subsidiary that undertake the broad range of entrepreneurial activities within the framework of the larger organization. For example, Kolchin and Hyclak (1987) define **intrapreneurship** not as a concept, but rather as a "managerial philosophy." Invariably, researchers and authors have drawn distinctions between these labels, but these terms can safely be used interchangeably, as long as they engage, as Covin and Miles (1999) argue, in some sustained regeneration, organizational rejuvenation, strategic renewal, or strategic domain redefinition. It follows then, that the responsibility of intrapreneurs, as individuals or groups, is to identify a new business opportunity from various venture ideas that constitutes a process of renewal or innovation within a large organization and ultimately bring it to market (Sharma & Chrisman, 1999). Corporate resources may or may not be used, but because the intrapreneurs are employed by the corporation, the ownership of the venture idea and the potential benefits from its commercialization remain predominantly in the hands of the firm.

Not surprisingly, ownership is a critical issue. There are many examples of entrepreneurs who worked for substantial periods of time in their companies and originated new business ideas. But their ideas were frequently developed outside the confines of their employers' organizations, and at the right "timing" juncture, they left to start their own firms. Howard Head, the developer of metal skis and the metal tennis racket, as well as Chester Carlson, the founder of xerography, typify these individuals. Both men identified potential business opportunities while working with established firms, but they chose not to use their employers' resources and risk losing ownership of their ideas. Instead, they left their companies, took their vision and ideas with them, and followed their respective entrepreneurial strategies to success. This type of "latent entrepreneur" does not fit the model of the corporate entrepreneur but resembles the independent entrepreneur discussed earlier.

Adding confusion to these definitions is the fact that the process of corporate entrepreneurship is frequently customized to fit each firm's unique characteristics. There are distinct differences in generalized processes of corporate venturing. Some firms use a deliberate and highly structured corporate entrepreneurship framework, while other firms pursue a relatively unstructured approach in their intrapreneurial activities. Neither approach is better than the other; most firms modify their intrapreneurial activities to fit their own unique circumstances. For example, a systematic intrapreneurial opportunity search process may be intentionally designed by a firm's senior management to ensure that any new business opportunities reflect the firm's core strategy and mission. In contrast, other firms may follow the "anything goes" approach and leave things somewhat unstructured. Accordingly, employees either have relatively few guidelines, with plenty of free time to work on their intrapreneurial projects, or because of corporate restrictions, they may have to circumvent the system to find the time and resources needed to develop their ideas.

In the introduction of the 1990 *Strategic Management Journal* issue devoted to corporate entrepreneurship, Guth and Ginsberg (1990, p. 5) break down the concept into two parts: (a) the development of new business ventures inside an already established business, and (b) the further development and renewal of an organization's existing underlying key ideas.

Benefits of Corporate Entrepreneurship

Advocates of corporate entrepreneurship profess that our larger and more established organizations have little choice but to encourage entrepreneurial behavior. They claim that corporate entrepreneurship increases innovation, productivity, and morale; that it provides employees with a better feel for their markets; and that it enables firms to retain their most talented workers. If these claims are true, a sense of entrepreneurial spirit should be encouraged among employees, if only to maintain a firm's competitive position in their marketplace. To date, however, the purported benefits of corporate entrepreneurship are based, for the most part, on anecdotal evidence rather than good exploratory research. While this does not negate the value of corporate entrepreneurship, it reinforces the need to understand its pros and cons before committing the firm to corporate venturing efforts.

This has resulted in a substantial number of medium- and larger-size firms working to overcome the traditional perception that "big" is necessarily "bad" as far as entrepreneurial activities are concerned. What these firms realize is that many of their employees possess the kinds of ideas and entrepreneurial skills on which both parties can capitalize. If enough ideas can be generated, it is a good bet that some will be cultivated into significant new business ventures. The trick is to find these people and foster that potential. To do so, firms are trying hard to overcome the traditional obstacles to implementing innovative ideas. They are learning how to recognize and accommodate the differences between standard corporate practices and the procedures, philosophies, and systems (or lack of the same) that a venturing effort requires. In other words, businesses serious about setting up internal venturing efforts cannot just tell their employees to go out and be creative. Instead, they first must do some serious soul-searching about their ability to implement programs often incompatible with their usual methods. If they choose to go ahead, changes in their practices and philosophies will be necessary. Obviously, trying to mobilize an entire firm to accommodate new ventures is an ambitious task, but if successful, the financial and psychological rewards from a successful new business can be substantial for both the company and the corporate entrepreneur.

Popularizing the Concept of Corporate Entrepreneurship

The idea of corporate entrepreneurship gained momentum with the publication of Gifford Pinchot's (1985) book, *Intrapreneuring*. Media coverage, along with the "pop" aspect of the term, made intrapreneuring one of the buzzwords of the 1980s. While the term was new, the idea was not. Larger firms have long acknowledged the need for entrepreneurship within their boundaries, but only recently have they made such highly publicized attempts to encourage it in their organizations. This shift in thinking can be traced to four causes, detailed below.

Increasingly Poor Competitive Positions in Dynamic Marketplaces

The flexibility, quality, and rapid response offered by smaller businesses has led to the erosion of significant competitive positions in key markets traditionally dominated by more established firms. On occasion, the markets claimed by larger firms have been stolen away by smaller, more aggressive entrepreneurial companies. As a reaction, some firms have initiated intrapreneurial efforts in an attempt to restructure themselves into smaller units possessing characteristics similar to those of their more innovative competitors. In his revolutionary book *The Innovator's Dilemma* (2013), Professor Clayton Christensen of Harvard Business School describes a theory about how large, outstanding firms can fail "by doing everything right." The firm's successes and capabilities can actually become obstacles in the face of changing markets and technologies. Christensen describes two types of technologies: sustaining technologies and disruptive technologies. Sustaining technologies are technologies that improve product performance. Most large companies are familiar with these technologies; they involve improving a product that has an established role in the market. Most large companies are adept at turning the challenges of sustaining technology into achievements. However, large companies have problems dealing with disruptive technologies. Disruptive technologies are "innovations that result in worse product performance, at least in the near term." They are generally "cheaper, simpler, smaller, and, frequently, more convenient to use." Disruptive technologies occur less frequently, but when they do, they can cause the failure of highly successful companies that are only prepared for sustaining technologies (Christensen, 2013).

Inability to Implement Innovative Ideas

Most often, firms find themselves with no shortage of innovative ideas; they are hobbled, however, by their inability to implement them, to bring them to market. Businesses are questioning the effectiveness of their centralized management structures—Can they adapt to changes in the marketplace as needed? Can they stay in touch with their customers and state-of-the-art technology? Circumventing their tried-and-true systems of analysis and control to accommodate new business ideas is one response. Reorganizing into smaller, more entrepreneurial units is another. In her study of the working habits of more than 9,000 people, Teresa Amabile of the Harvard Business School found that focus and creativity are connected. People are more likely to be creative if they are allowed to focus on something for some time without interruptions or being forced to attend meetings (*The Economist*, 2011a).

"Vulture" Capitalists

Without an infrastructure set up to encourage and reward creative ideas, the best talent and the newest technologies are being lured away by venture or, as some call them, **"vulture" capitalists** possessing abundant resources and the promise of making entrepreneurial dreams come true. Competition is no longer isolated to products and services but instead has shifted to a struggle to retain the firms' best employees. If dissatisfaction with their firms' procedures and philosophies become too much to bear, talented employees find it easy to locate better opportunities. In some firms, product development efforts are slowed down, short-circuited, or completely derailed by a lack of talented secondary personnel able to step in and replace technical specialists who depart for greener pastures and their own entrepreneurial dreams.

Unproductive Mergers and Acquisitions

Firms believing that mergers and acquisitions are a cheap way of obtaining assets and technologies often find their strategies counterproductive. Participants in the merger mania craze of the 1970s, 1980s, and 1990s frequently encountered difficulties in integrating dissimilar cultures and resources. Not only did firms lose key people, but they also lost many newly acquired entrepreneurial businesses, their competitive advantages were squandered, and their highly prized freedom was more constrained than originally thought. As problems and costs multiplied with acquired firms, internal venturing efforts became a more acceptable alternative.

By pointing to the reasons outlined above, advocates of corporate entrepreneurship are able to convince senior management (in many companies, they *are* senior management) of the benefits of venturing. Other firms jump on the bandwagon because it is "fashionable" or because their competitors are doing it. Some firms choose to set up elaborate internal systems to promote venturing, while others are satisfied with more freewheeling and unstructured approaches. Peters and Waterman (1982) described the latter:

> All of these companies were making a purposeful trade-off. They were creating almost radical decentralization and autonomy, with its attendant overlap, messiness around the edges, lack of coordination, internal competition, and somewhat chaotic conditions, in order to breed the entrepreneurial spirit. They had forsworn a measure of tidiness in order to achieve regular innovation. (p. 201)

Another group of businesses use consultants and/or intrapreneurship "schools" to educate their employees. For example, in the mid-1970s, a Swedish firm, Foresight Inc., set up one of the first schools to teach intrapreneurship. Companies using their services were required to select from a group of volunteers those employees felt to have the greatest intrapreneurial potential and the most promising new business ideas. Selected individuals were sent to Foresight, Inc., and were instructed in the fundamentals of intrapreneurship and implementing their ideas. On returning to their firms, participants were expected to resume their normal activities. Whatever free time they had was used to develop their ideas into business plans, which were subsequently presented to their senior management staffs. If an idea was deemed feasible, start-up capital was supplied to get the new venture off the ground and the project was either integrated into the firm as a new product or service or spun off into a subsidiary business (Arbose, 1982).

The Advantages Offered by Larger Firms to Venturing Efforts

Corporate entrepreneurship has become more popular with the realization that a large firm's size, expertise, and resources can provide significant advantages over the independent entrepreneurship process. Pinchot (1985), for instance, identifies four potential advantages provided by the larger firm: (a) **marketing clout**, (b) a **technology base**, (c) **financial resources**, and (d) **personnel resources**.

Marketing Clout

Unlike the entrepreneur who must start from scratch convincing potential customers of the value of a new product or service, the intrapreneur comes equipped with an established company name. More often than not, this implies staying power in the marketplace, the ability to pay bills, prior successes, and organizational expertise. Legitimacy is accorded the venture right from the start, which is particularly handy when attempting to secure and negotiate initial contracts with suppliers and distributors.

Technology Base

The intrapreneur is provided access to substantial technological resources, including people with technical skills and proprietary knowledge. Technical facilities, including laboratories for start-up and prototype work, and manufacturing pilot plants may also be available to cut overhead and scale-up costs. Fortunately, proprietary knowledge can be exchanged freely within the firm because an implied (and sometimes explicit) trust exists among company personnel. On the other hand, independent entrepreneurs who frequently come into contact with consultants, suppliers, distributors, potential customers, and others, undoubtedly must be more concerned about the possible theft of proprietary knowledge.

Financial Resources

While it is easy to view a parent firm as an ever-reliable source of funding, the reality for most companies is that development funds are generally limited by the number and variety of potential investments available. Hence, internal competition for resources is often vigorous. Even with the prospects of strong competition, however, the internal fund-raising process pales in comparison to the independent entrepreneur's plight in raising capital. Undoubtedly, capital is more easily accessible when a venture starts off with senior-level support and a budget for venturing efforts. Sometimes the venture may even benefit from the corporate mentality of throwing money at problems until they are resolved. The venture may actually get more funds than needed—usually an entrepreneur's dream come true.

But a word of caution. Although the cliché reads, "Never look a gift horse in the mouth," overfunding can work against a start-up venture. Many have failed for the unusual reason that they had too much money. Just how they manage to do this is not well researched, but some experts suggest that ventures with too much money never learn how to conserve their resources for the tougher times ahead. They lose their "hunger" and get lazy. They stop finding ways to shave costs, they lose their competitive edge, and they begin to settle for second-best. Indeed, Fashion Portfolio, a venture begun by Levi Strauss and Co., Inc., was given twice as much space as it seemingly needed, had 58 employees when 16–20 would probably have been sufficient, and was provided a constant flow of money from the parent firm. Shortly after they began the venture, Levi's abandoned it due to poor performance and a lack of fit with their corporate strategy.

Personnel Resources

Skilled personnel, familiar with their firm's corporate strategy and resources, may be available to help build and develop the new venture. They already understand the firm's capabilities, and perhaps even more importantly, they know the "ins and outs" of getting things done in a large firm. Skills such as cannibalizing, scavenging, and bootlegging, among others, can help in successfully circumventing the normal corporate control systems that often block innovative efforts.

Organizations may benefit from the venturing process in other, more intangible ways. For example, Shapero (1985) asserts:

> Entrepreneurship benefits organizations by bringing out or generating behaviors valuable to organizational survival and successful performance. For an organization, an increase in the tolerance of ambiguity among its managers means the ability to deal with uncertainty in a positive way. An increase in optimism, creativity, and the ability to take initiative and act independently means an increase in behaviors highly appropriate to the task of dealing with today's tough international marketplace. The greatest benefit from entrepreneurship for an organization is achievement of focused motivation that cannot be realized through other means. Entrepreneurship acts as a powerful lens focusing individual motivation and energy in a way unmatched by all the manipulations of industrial psychologists and organization developers. (p. 4)

Although big companies often excel at incremental innovation (i.e., adding more and different features to existing products), they are less comfortable with disruptive innovation, the kind that changes the rules of the game and brings forth conditions for Schumpeter's "creative destruction." Furthermore, what matters is not so much whether companies are big or small but whether they grow through the benefits of innovation. For example, companies like Amazon and Google, known for their innovations, have become huge creators of jobs. In the United States, it is estimated that innovative companies constitute 1% of all companies yet generate roughly 40% of new jobs (*The Economist*, 2011b).

THE CORPORATE ENTREPRENEUR

Regardless of the approach used to foster corporate venturing, a necessary early step is to identify employees possessing entrepreneurial capabilities. Unfortunately, no existing tests can be considered valid indicators of entrepreneurial potential. Neither are psychological profiles of the prototypical corporate entrepreneur of much use. What researchers do agree upon, however, is that the manager of an entrepreneurial unit requires skills different from the manager of an existing operating unit. Pinchot's (1985) comparison of the characteristics and traits of traditional managers, traditional entrepreneurs, and intrapreneurs found wide discrepancies between the manager and the intrapreneur. At the same time, however, he recognized many similarities between the entrepreneur and the intrapreneur. Pinchot's work provides some interesting insights into the intrapreneur as an individual, but it reflects his bias toward a solo entrepreneur, initially working on his/her own initiative to develop new business ideas for their own companies. The characteristics possessed by his intrapreneurs are those necessary to successfully navigate his view of the intrapreneurial process: networking the idea, bootlegging resources, and team-building.

Pinchot's (1985) view of intrapreneurship is not the only model available. Slightly different approaches to corporate entrepreneurship exist in some firms in which a more deliberate search process to generate new opportunities is used. In this case, firms often look for individuals possessing a mixture of characteristics: the independence and networking qualities of Pinchot's solo intrapreneurs and the discipline and administrative skills of more traditional corporate managers.

Carrier (1996) found that intrapreneurs have similar psychological profiles, even though the contexts within which they operate are different. For example, intrapreneurs are motivated by promotion rather than independence, even though they value the freedom and the extra resources that promotion will bring them, as well as the ability, authority, and power to take further entrepreneurial initiatives into other areas of the organization. Another reward valued by the intrapreneur, identified in Carrier's study, was ownership of capital stock as additional compensation and incentive. Not surprisingly, this type of corporate entrepreneur must recognize the advantages offered by a large company in terms of marketing and financial clout as well as personnel and technological resources, and he or she learns to capitalize upon them within the constraints established by a firm's philosophy toward risk and return. To this end, autonomy must be accommodated, but at the same time, it has to be tempered by the reality of getting things done through a usually bureaucratic organization.

Beyond the characteristics mentioned above, corporate entrepreneurs must have an extraordinary capacity to learn from failure. Thomas Edison, perhaps more the inventor than entrepreneur, may best exemplify this philosophy. He is reputed to have said to someone asking about the 2,000-plus failures he had while developing the lightbulb: "They were not failures but successes. I now know over 2,000 ways that the lightbulb will not work." Turning every setback into a learning experience is critical to long-term success.

The Trials and Tribulations of the Corporate Entrepreneur

At every step of the way lie pitfalls, traps, and obstacles waiting to bog down the corporate entrepreneur in endless mazes of red tape and untold frustration. Coalitions formed by groups and individuals around the issues in which they have vested interests may either support or endanger entrepreneurial ventures. It pays for corporate entrepreneurs to know how to minimize their political exposure and how to maneuver politically within their firms when necessary. One way of doing this is to secure senior-level corporate sponsors who can protect and shelter the venture from those unsympathetic to the entrepreneurial effort.

Another way is to recognize supporters and detractors for who and what they are and the stakes for which they are playing. Appropriate responses can then be made to reduce the venture's exposure and to effectively protect it from any detractors.

Almost invariably, corporate entrepreneurs start with little more than their ideas and a position in their organizations. The issue then becomes how to persuade senior management that their projects are viable business opportunities rather than just good ideas. Persuasion and team-building skills are a necessity. Corporate entrepreneurs have to be able to share their visions with other employees, to sell them on their ideas, and to get them to join their venturing teams. No easy task, this requires substantial interpersonal skills. But more firms are insisting that employees joining venture teams put their careers at risk, that is, that they link their future with their venture's performance. Giving up job security makes corporate entrepreneurs much more committed to attaining success with their own ideas, but it also makes the recruiting process much more difficult.

Considerable danger faces venture managers unable to secure internal support and/or convince key supporters of the worth of their projects (George & MacMillan, 1986). Therefore, without the commitment and support of critical players, such as other executives, workers, suppliers, distributors, and potential customers, essential resources may be delayed or denied, and projects may die a fast death. It is crucial, therefore, that all risks be identified. Not only those of the venture team but also those of the venture's various support groups. For instance, what are the risks for the customer? What if the venture cannot comply with delivery dates? What if the new product does not perform as promised? What risks are assumed by suppliers? How about distributors? Will the new venture threaten in any way their supporters' current businesses, and if so, how? All of these concerns and more must be considered in advance or the venture faces the possible loss of critical members of its support group.

As the venture progresses, corporate entrepreneurs frequently face new problems with their firms' control and reporting mechanisms. Finding a balance between the freedom and autonomy needed by the venture and corporate requirements for controlling and safeguarding company resources is often difficult. Parent firms requiring even petty decisions to be justified to corporate management are a prime example of a stumbling block. Corporate interference can cause agonizing and frustrating delays for corporate entrepreneurs who need to make rapid decisions and who can seldom take no for an answer. Unfortunately, second-guessing and corporate obstruction have terminated many new ventures. Consider, for example, the problems faced by Exxon's information-processing ventures in the 1970s. Exxon executives shackled their ventures by requiring corporate approval for such trivial decisions as advertising campaigns. Undoubtedly, the lack of autonomy contributed to the ventures' poor performance, which ultimately led to Exxon's decision to eliminate many of these entrepreneurial efforts.

Corporate entrepreneurs must possess the highest level of self-confidence in both their abilities and their ventures. They must live with the uncertainty of companies who struggle to have patience for one year, much less the five years it might take to prove that a venture is indeed a success. Not surprisingly, many corporate venturers face the threat of less-than-supportive senior managers. Unsympathetic to the venturing effort, these senior managers wait for the one mistake that will let them politic against the venture, and if successful, they pick up the leftovers for their own operations. Even with a corporate sponsor protecting the venture, and no matter how hard the corporate venturer may try to convince detractors of the value of venturing, senior managers are not easily persuaded if the venture does not fit their agenda. In general, the best advice we can offer the corporate entrepreneur to counter this danger is to learn how to move freely across organizational boundaries, to exercise political skills when and where necessary, to obtain resources even when scarcity prevails, and to convince senior managers to empower them with the kinds of freedom and decision-making responsibilities required for successful venturing efforts. In a nutshell, the corporate entrepreneur must protect the venture and learn to personally survive and prosper in the corporate world.

Some Additional Costs and Benefits to Consider

Thus far, we have identified an extensive assortment of potential costs and benefits associated with the venturing process. Of course, other issues can impact either favorably or unfavorably on the organization or the corporate entrepreneur. For example, benefits may be gained from using the venture as a laboratory, such as experimenting with new techniques, structural innovations, cultural changes, etc. Experiments deemed successful in new venture projects can be tried with considerably less risk in other parts of the parent organization. Ventures may also create new jobs and increase the positive economic impact of a firm on the local community. Some firms are, in a sense, "forced" to plan for success, that is, to prepare their second-line employees to eventually step in and take over for individuals targeted for venturing efforts.

The risks for potential corporate entrepreneurs must also be considered. No doubt, pressures to perform financially are substantial, but social pressures may be as much a concern. Because corporate entrepreneurs may be perceived as "risk takers," they may be seen by some as not being team players or rather as mavericks seeking personal gain at the expense of their firms. The hoped-for integration of the new venture into the parent firm can be endangered. Jealousy and resentment toward members of the venture team may also surface, at which point corporate interference is usually just a short step behind. For example, a few years ago, Xerox Corporation announced a new venture product called Yardbird, a low-cost copying machine designed to make 36-inch-wide copies for the technical market. Several executives responsible for all other copier marketing functions attempted to gain control of the Yardbird machine. Until senior management stepped forth and reaffirmed their commitment to this corporate venture, the Yardbird project was in danger of becoming just another item in Xerox's marketing strategy.

Of course, not all venture managers are embattled entrepreneurs confronted by hostile executives on all sides who are waiting to pick up the pieces when their ventures fail. On more occasions than not, the corporate entrepreneur has substantial support within the organization. Support may come not only from senior-level sponsors but also from executives and workers in all parts of the firm. Employees hoping to be part of the next venturing effort recognize their stake in the venture's success and will offer help whenever and wherever possible. As venturing efforts build winning track records, opportunities to be creative and independent become more common. When this happens, claims of improved morale, productivity, and innovation begin to surface.

THE CORPORATE ENTREPRENEURSHIP PROCESS

So far we have discussed corporate entrepreneurship in terms of what it is, who is involved, and what characteristics they possess, as well as the costs and benefits associated with venturing efforts. Now it is time to turn to the venturing process itself to try to make sense of what Peters and Waterman (1982) described as "messiness around the edges, lack of coordination, internal competition, and somewhat chaotic conditions."

Fortunately, the literature on the subject provides some help in organizing a framework to examine the process. Antoncic and Hisrich (2001) propose that in order for the intrapreneurial process to be successful, four dimensions must characterize it: (a) a commitment to new business venturing, (b) innovativeness per se, (c) self-renewal, and (d) proactiveness. Russell (1999) further advocates that any intrapreneurial process should concentrate on the improvement of the firm's competencies and the extension of opportunities to do so through an internally generated innovation process. Cunningham and Lischeron (1991) propose a model of the entrepreneurial process that takes the form of a reiteratively staged process of evaluating, planning, acting and managing, and continuously reassessing the need for change.

It is quite obvious that any intrapreneurial effort should be a process, not merely the identification of new ideas, products, and philosophies (Rule & Irwin, 1988). It should also be a process of problem-solving and teamwork, as well as a structural rearrangement of the organization to promote the vital forces critical to the organization's continued development and success (Reilly & DiAngelo, 1987). By combining the issues advanced by the work of these authors as well as others, four **corporate entrepreneurship process stages** can be identified, characterized by *proactive change, innovation,* and *structural accommodation* of entrepreneurial activities:

1. Initiating the process.

2. Planning the venture.

3. Managing the venture from survival to growth.

4. Integrating the venture into the parent organization.

By no means is the model comprehensive, because each venturing effort has unique features. However, the successful overall implementation of this process and the careful execution of entrepreneurial activities at each of the corporate entrepreneurship stages create added value for the organization by supporting the proactive creation and pursuit of opportunities in the environment. In contrast, neglecting this process causes the organization to be less focused on entrepreneurial activities, ultimately not only causing the failure to produce added value but also the destroying existing value over time (Vozikis, Bruton, Prasad, & Merikas, 1999).

Initiating the Process: Choosing an Idea

Corporate entrepreneurship begins with the idea for a new product or service. Most firms are blessed with an abundance of ideas, thanks to the creativity and talents of their workforces. These ideas emerge through every means possible, from a deliberate search process conducted by the organization, to the individual who observes a need in the marketplace, to simply stumbling upon the creation of a new product and recognizing how to take advantage of it.

Generating good ideas, however, is not the only answer for a firm wanting to begin a corporate venturing effort. In truth, new business ideas are not hard to produce; rather, it is whether or not they represent opportunities that matter. How often have you heard the old adage, "a dime a dozen"? This is exactly what ideas are. If you don't think so, check out the business failure statistics for your community. See how many presumably "good" business ideas have failed for one reason or another.

Successful businesspeople recognize that there is a significant difference between a good idea and a good opportunity. An **opportunity** includes a set of conditions that enhance a firm's chances of success:

• Answers a customer need.

• Holds the promise of a stream of future tie-in products or services.

• Enters an expanding market at the right time, when the window of opportunity is wide open.

• Possesses an inherent "unfair" advantage that enables a company to effectively and profitably compete in the marketplace (Timmons, Smollen, & Dingee, 1985).

On the other hand, a good idea is an opinion, a belief in the validity of a yet-to-be-proven business concept. The conditions surrounding it are unknown, and they may be good or bad, but they have yet to be fully examined. In the best of all worlds, market research may eventually prove that a good idea is a good opportunity. Entrepreneurs, however, frequently get carried away with the excitement of their ideas and often fail to take that extra step to determine whether or not they actually represent an opportunity. Unfortunately, ventures like these more often than not end in failure because the chances of attracting funding, the right people for the team, and the necessary resources decrease if your "homework" is not done. But some ventures are obviously not good opportunities, yet they do not fail, strangely enough, because some businesses succeed in spite of what they do rather than because of what they do. Conditions change rapidly, and over time an idea may evolve into an opportunity. There are plenty of unsophisticated businesspeople out there, who, by their poor decisions, may help keep you in business. In other words, good planning and research is only partly responsible for the success of a venture. Luck, happenstance, timing, and a host of other factors also play important roles in the survival of a business.

Companies sponsoring venturing efforts, however, don't often have the patience to wait for ideas to evolve into opportunities or for luck to strike. They need to be more proactive, while recognizing the constraints of operating within a large firm. Hence, opportunities must be defined in a broader context. For example, Pinchot (1985) contends that good intrapreneurial ideas meet the needs of three parties: the customers, the corporation, and the intrapreneur's personal needs. The first, fulfilling customer needs, has already been mentioned. The second, meeting corporate needs, means that venture ideas must fit the corporation and its purposes. For example, does the idea make sense financially and practically? Will it achieve the corporation's financial performance goals? Is the idea affordable? If not, the chance of attracting a sponsor to support such a venture is not high. What are the upside potentials and the downside risks? Does the venture pose any substantial threats to the rest of the organization? If so, forget it. Does the venture fit in a practical sense with the mix of the company's businesses? Meeting personal needs revolves around the intrapreneurs' wishes. Will their skills match the venture's needs? Do they have experience in their proposed business? Do they like their venture and will they be happy working for it? Obviously, an early but difficult task for the firm is sorting through the variety of business ideas that may be proposed and trying to find the relatively few with the characteristics necessary to make them good opportunities.

Planning the Venture

Once a new business idea is selected, converting it into a viable business enterprise is no simple task. For lack of a better term, we simply call this stage **planning the venture**. It begins more or less with a corporate entrepreneur sharing an idea with colleagues in an attempt to convince them to join a venture team, and it ends when the product is brought to market. To a great extent, forming a team is a type of pre-selling; it is just that the corporate entrepreneur is selling an idea to his/her colleagues, rather than a product to customers.

It is critical that the viability of the idea is conveyed to colleagues. Can the heart of the idea be expressed simply, in a couple of sentences? Do colleagues respond with, "I wish I had thought of that"? If potential team members are not completely convinced of the opportunity, or if they feel uncomfortable with the people involved and the possibility of corporate interference, they aren't going to join the venture. And a corporate venture without a team is doomed to failure more often than not. Team members are needed to contribute complementary skills and to share the pressures and uncertainties of the venturing effort.

George and MacMillan's study (1986) identified several other important steps in the venturing process, that is, building consensus for the venture both inside and outside the firm and obtaining support from a senior-level sponsor. Not surprisingly, these activities go hand-in-hand. Indeed, it is crucial that the venture team builds internal support because, inevitably, there will be groups or individuals resistant to corporate entrepreneurship. At that point, it is incumbent upon senior-level sponsors to step forth and impress upon these groups the importance of not interfering with the venture. The real issue, then, is that supporting new business ideas must be made a goal for the entire organization, not just for isolated venturing efforts.

Outside support also must be garnered for venturing efforts. As noted before, suppliers, distributors, and customers may hold back resources or information at key times if they feel that a venture is not addressing their needs. They may, in fact, have a vested interest in the failure of the venture. They may feel threatened by the disruption of their status quo, or they may be upset by the novel demands made on them by the new venture. Whatever the reason, it is important to the venture's chances of success that the commitment and support of key outside parties is obtained. George and MacMillan (1986) suggest several ways such support can be attained:

- Identify potential risk bearers and their concerns and learn how to accommodate them. Customers, suppliers, and distributors face a variety of very real risks with a new venture, such as nonperformance, late delivery, poor risk/return trade-offs, etc. Once these concerns are recognized, they need to be alleviated.

- Identify risk sharers and the outside parties who stand to benefit if the venture succeeds. Sometimes they can help lower the costs and initial risks of the venture. Remember, if you win, they win, so they should have an interest in helping wherever possible.

- Ensure that all third-party and government concerns, such as product liability, performance guarantees, supplier delivery contracts, government requirements, etc., have been addressed in detail. (pp. 86–88)

Getting permission to proceed may sound relatively easy, but it encompasses a great deal more than a simple decision. To get to this position, the venture team must provide senior management with data and information that will convince them that this project is indeed a good opportunity, not just a good idea. Typically, this begins with the development and submission of a written business plan. If the idea looks promising, the venture team is asked to present their plan to senior management, at which point approval or rejection is given. If approved, capital is formally committed to the project. The acquisition of resources begins in earnest after the venture is given legitimacy, that is, once it is approved by senior management. Financial resources are transferred to the venture, and in some cases, outside organizations also provide funding through joint ventures, strategic alliances, or other forms of partnering. Physical resources, such as office space, equipment, research and development facilities, etc., are provided, as are intellectual resources. New employees are either hired from outside or transferred from other areas within the firm. All of these resources and the energy of the venture team are ultimately focused on developing a prototype of the new product.

An **Enterprise Resource Planning (ERP)** model may be needed at this stage, manned by the Management Information Technology department of the organization, to ensure that resources are directed toward the intrapreneurial effort and that productivity improvements and cost reductions, along with added value outcomes, are forthcoming. ERP systems are necessary because the implementation of intrapreneurial activities is very complex and far-reaching within the organization; many different and novel types of knowledge and input are required. The implementation of intrapreneurial activities may introduce fundamental changes in the way people work (Scott & Vessey, 2000). ERP systems help generate physical models, product designs, testing requirements, product documentation, user's manuals, and a variety of other functions that must be produced before the product is presented to potential customers.

Once the prototype has been developed and the venture moves into the initial selling phase, typical problems are encountered that are common to many businesses, not just corporate venturing efforts. It is usually difficult to create and fill the first orders. In particular, technical intrapreneurs may not have good selling skills. Therefore, the majority of the venture's efforts should be focused on a few critical "deals" to obtain those first sales (George & MacMillan, 1986). Specific action plans for accomplishing the initial sales orders from targeted customers are preferred over broad-range, end-user marketing; many of these targets cost more to develop into good customers than they may initially be worth. For venture teams to progress through this stage, however, senior management must be actively involved in the venturing effort beyond merely championing the new business. Because they do not have the time needed to manage each venturing effort, they must make sure that appropriate guidelines and conditions are in place that will aid the venture in its development. Senior managers must not abdicate their responsibility to the venture. Indeed, there are times when only senior managers can prevent or resolve some of the major problems confronting a venture. The exact roles senior managers play and when are unique to each firm, but MacMillan and George (1985) identify four general challenges during the initial planning stages:

1. Selecting a context.
2. Designing an appropriate structure.
3. Committing to provide support.
4. Using a venture ombudsman.

Selecting a context is the initial role of senior management. If this role is not fulfilled, the firm runs the risk of wasting time and resources by essentially telling their employees to innovate in a vacuum with no concern for what the firm is doing now or should be doing in the future. Therefore, it is the senior management's responsibility to identify the boundaries for their firm's venturing efforts and to ensure that all venturing efforts fit into the corporate strategy and mission. If not, the consequences can be dire.

Another way senior management selects a context for a firm's entrepreneurial efforts is by developing an appropriate assortment of ventures, that is, a portfolio of new businesses. Some companies attempt to spread their risk by supporting many different ventures. All things considered, perhaps the best way to handle the context selection is for senior managers to clearly express a venturing strategy that outlines the firm's strengths and weaknesses as well as their vision of the future. Such a strategy provides venture businesses with a clear reference point for their decision making.

Designing an appropriate structure for a new corporate venture is quite different from the process followed by an independent entrepreneur. By starting the firm, the independent entrepreneur generally becomes the president. Vice-presidential slots tend to be filled, either immediately or as the venture progresses, with members of the venture team. On the other hand, corporate ventures start off within the context of a more established firm; hence, the "structure" must fit into the larger design of the parent organization. Therefore, senior management's challenge is to ensure that conditions encourage and enhance corporate venturing efforts. Senior management must ensure what Pinchot (1985) calls "freedom factors" that establish the conditions needed for a venture to grow to maturity.

Suppose you are trying to design a structure that provides freedom and autonomy to a group yet, at the same time, encourages some adherence to corporate direction, procedures, and policies. Where would you start? Frankly, most people can probably contribute dozens of suggestions, but pulling them all together into a cohesive package is a monumental task, and this is exactly what confronts senior management. Pinchot (1985) offers some suggestions that make good sense for most corporate venturing efforts. For example, does the firm encourage the self-appointed intrapreneur? Will intrapreneurs be as likely to have their ideas funded as the groups whose ideas were developed through the firm's deliberate search process? Does the firm encourage the venture manager to accept "ownership" or responsibility for the project, in essence, providing an internal champion ultimately accountable for the success of the idea? If they do, do they reward this person accordingly?

Who will be the corporate entrepreneur? Choosing a manager for the venture is an area in which the senior manager must sometimes tread lightly. It is not always true that the person who develops the idea is the best venture manager. Although they may be the most committed and enthusiastic team member, they may not have the management, marketing, or financial skills required for the venture to succeed. For instance, AT&T and Exxon learned this lesson the hard way. Respectively, they put the technical specialists who had developed the original business ideas in charge of several ventures. Needless to say, these technicians flopped miserably because they did not possess the requisite business skills. It is crucial that senior management recognize the kinds of challenges presented by a new venture and that they place in charge a manager with the appropriate skills to shepherd it to success.

Senior management must also determine where the venture is best located, that is, within an existing division or in a specialized structure. Every location offers some advantages and disadvantages that must be considered before any decision is made. For instance, if it is isolated in a specialized structure, will the venture generate resentment and jealousy? If it is placed in an existing division, will the venture encounter interference or impede current production?

Are funds available for investigating new ideas? Can the firm ensure that employees will have access to resources when needed, without having to go through a potentially ponderous control system? Can employees use the resources, such as people, equipment, knowledge, etc., found in other areas of the firm? Can they purchase materials from outside vendors if internal suppliers are not competitive? Is trial-and-error acceptable? Error, in particular, needs to be seen as an acceptable pathway to progress, as Edison discovered in his 2,000 "successes" during the development of the electric bulb. Does the firm encourage experimentation? If the firm does not promote risk-taking and does not communicate to its employees that failure is just another learning process, then innovative intrapreneurial activities will be nonexistent.

One interesting approach to structural smoothing in accommodating intrapreneurial activities is a process called "figure-eighting," or ∞, similar to the figure eight that ice-skaters form. This concept was used very successfully in the product development division of the Williams Company in the early 2000s, with consultants serving as liaisons and coordinators between intrapreneurs and line managers. The forward motion of the figure eight (˷) is undertaken during the forward-moving intrapreneurial activity until a certain point at which this forward motion is halted temporarily. Then a backward motion is purposefully implemented to close the figure eight to create a structural "cushion" and to make a strategic fit of the intrapreneurial outcomes. Certain value chain activities may be outsourced. Once this structural accommodation is securely in place, the process resumes its forward motion until it is time to back up again for further structural smoothing. Thus, continuous forward progress of intrapreneurial activities is ensured, while the oppositional complaints of both the intrapreneurs ("you are slowing me down") and the line managers ("you are going too fast") are given serious consideration and are contained. For the figure eight process to be successful, it must run continuously as successive figure-eights creep further forward after each respite. However, if the forward intrapreneurial motion continues unabated for a long period of time, especially if it generates a lot of revenue initially, structural disintegration and lack of connectivity with the rest of the corporation may result. Later, this disintegration may present serious problems for any positive intrapreneurial outcomes. Similarly, if the backward figure-eight motion of structural accommodation takes too long, intrapreneurial activities may atrophy and may never regain momentum, even after the return to forward motion.

Finally, senior management must confront a particularly thorny design issue: the reward system. Unfortunately, the reward systems of most firms are not set up to deal with venturing efforts. Pinchot (1985) contended that firms encourage safe and conservative attitudes rather than risky behavior. With that in mind, why do traditional reward systems fail, and how can senior management resolve their shortcomings?

First, traditional reward systems fail because even when they are successful, their rewards are not commensurate with the risks taken. Corporate entrepreneurs may (or may not) be risking their job security for small-to-moderate financial rewards. Financially, they may do relatively well, but when compared with the successful independent entrepreneur, the compensation gap is fairly wide. Second, employees who achieve success in a firm are typically rewarded with promotions. Promotions are frequently of little interest to the corporate entrepreneur, who prefers autonomy and the opportunity to be innovative to managing old ideas. Having the freedom to spend funds on additional new business ideas is often much more appealing to the corporate entrepreneur than a promotion.

Resolving these problems is not easy. Even when firms have crafted an appropriate reward system, they may have created a weakness elsewhere. For example, Xerox tested the commitment of one of its venture managers by asking him to raise half the seed capital needed to start his proposed project. While his success at raising the money showed Xerox that there was outside validation for his idea, it also created a problem for the employee. Venture capitalists refused to invest in the idea unless the employee left Xerox and its implied job security. He complied, and subsequently he owns 50% of the venture, while Xerox owns 20%. The firm's intent seems reasonable; this arrangement allows the corporate entrepreneur to share the project's risk by owning a substantial portion of the venture. Yet Xerox gave up a good chunk of the venture, along with the services of a talented employee, to get the project off the ground. Was the trade-off worthwhile?

AT&T attempted to resolve financial concerns by placing half of a venture's after-tax profits into a bonus pool for their employees. At the maximum, employees received up to eight times their salary. But the sudden infusion of wealth may have its downside. As corporate entrepreneurs accrue financial resources, they also gain the experience of success. They may leave the parent firm to start as independent entrepreneurs. One way senior management handles this is to simply spread out bonuses and other forms of compensation over time.

What about promotion? How do you reward someone who may not be interested in promotion? Is recognition enough? Perhaps a second career path allowing the corporate entrepreneur to move on to other ventures will suffice. Unfortunately, not many firms are set up to offer this opportunity. Ultimately, senior management has to handle these situations on an individual basis. Designing a reward system in advance to handle these contingencies is admirable, but the unique needs of each member of the venture team dictate that promotion considerations be handled during the management and integration stages, not during initiation and planning.

The third challenge for senior management is the commitment to provide support for the venture. Much has already been said about the importance of finding a sponsor, but without a clear sign of commitment from the firm in both dollars and resources, few employees will risk their careers on a venturing effort. The senior manager must ensure that the venture gets the resources it requires, not only at start-up but also as it continues to develop and grow. Occasionally, this entails some political maneuvering to protect the venture and to keep it from antagonizing those threatened by innovation.

At the same time, senior management has to work hard to keep the interest of other internal venture supporters. As difficult as it is to keep other members of the firm patient, senior management must make them aware of the commitment in time and resources typically required of successful innovation efforts. Pinchot (1985) called this "nervous money," that is, the tendency of executives to pull out of a venture at the first hint of trouble. Senior management must work to counter this attitude. Several firms have had success with the appointment of a venture ombudsman or a venture board. As a middleman, the ombudsman has to be both focused on the corporation's goals and sensitive to the protection and enhancement of the venturing process. MacMillan and George (1985) defined the role of the ombudsman as making certain that key issues are considered, identifying and recruiting venture managers, and in general, keeping the operation moving in the right direction. AT&T, Xerox, IBM, 3M, and Eastman Kodak, among others, have formed venture boards to ensure that ventures have senior-level sponsorship.

In summary, it is obvious that the first two stages of the corporate venturing process hold substantial challenges for senior management. The chances for success of any venturing effort may hinge on the roles assumed by senior managers during the initiation and planning stages of the corporate entrepreneurship process. An old saying applies to the roles these senior managers create and fill: "In business, the most successful person is the one who holds on to the old as long as it is good and grabs the new as soon as it is better."

Managing the Venture from Survival to Growth

Once the venture's product is out the door and the first few sales are made, there is still no time to relax. This is the crucial period during which the venture emerges as either a flash-in-the-pan or a true opportunity with a stream of future products and services. During this period, the corporate entrepreneur's role begins to change. The entrepreneurial characteristics of the venture manager's job begin to diminish and his or her role becomes more administrative in nature. This role shifts from nurturing the venture to making certain that problems related to growth are successfully addressed. Again, George and MacMillan (1986) identified the most important steps in this process: (a) preparing for the inevitable attacks from competitors, (b) ensuring the existence of an adequate infrastructure, and (c) managing the resource squeeze.

As soon as rapid growth commences, the business is assured of competition. If the venture has developed a new technology, competitors are sure to be close behind. After the new venture has already undertaken the lion's share of the development risk, "follower" firms will jump in and try to imitate or improve upon the venture's product, particularly if the potential market size is attractive. Therefore, the venture manager must prepare in advance for the first serious attacks by competitors. Given the burdens of coping with rapid growth, this competition comes at probably the worst time imaginable. If the firm is not prepared for this scenario, it is left extremely vulnerable to competitive threats.

Managing growth means a great deal more than simply taking in more sales dollars. The venture manager cannot assume that growth will take care of itself. Instead, growth requires more clerical staff, more production workers, more of everything. It means more paperwork, more orders, an expanded distribution system, better inventory control procedures, and changes to just about all other systems. In George and MacMillan's (1986) words, "The venture must ensure that its infrastructure is adequately developed to accommodate such growth" (p. 89). Venture managers must understand what is happening with their suppliers and distributors. Will they be capable of servicing the venture if it expands by 30% per year? What if annual growth reaches 50% or more?

In relation to the rest of the organization, the venture is usually a very small part of the overall firm. As the venture grows and the infrastructure expands to accommodate it, and as other divisions of the firm evolve, the overall organization's need for resources continues to increase. Not surprisingly, the "favored" status of the venture may be endangered. Given the increasing demand for resources in all areas of the firm, the venture may be asked to compete for these resources against other internal divisions. Thus, the venture manager may face a resource squeeze, that is, resources may be harder to obtain because the venture is in competition with other parts of the organization. Among other things, this squeeze may result in staffing shortages or in financial resources being more closely monitored and controlled. Unfortunately, competition for resources may occur during the growth stage, when these resources incur substantial financial and personnel costs as they shift from a customized product to a mass-production culture.

Integrating the Venture into the Parent Organization

As the venture continues to evolve, the organization must make choices about what it intends to do with it. Obviously, a variety of exit decisions are possible. The venture can be sold to the venture team or to an outside group; it can be spun off into a separate business or into a subsidiary. Typically, the preferred alternative is to integrate the venture into the parent firm. Doing so, however, requires some substantial adjustments on the part of both the venture team and the parent firm. What should corporate entrepreneurs and their team do next? Move on to another venture? Return to their previous roles as corporate citizens? If they have to give up control of the venture to someone else, how do they avoid losing the commitment, energy, and enthusiasm that originally drove the project? Needless to say, a wide assortment of questions must be asked and answered at this stage, and these issues must be jointly decided by senior management and the venture team.

During the management and integration stages, similar to the initiation and planning stages of the corporate entrepreneurship process, senior management faces four **challenges to integration**:

1. To impose discipline.
2. To fully assess and understand the risks involved.
3. To manage the process rather than the projects.
4. To assure either a smooth integration into the parent firm or a problem-free exit (MacMillan & George, 1985).

Imposing discipline is similar to setting limits for a child. Senior management must ensure that the venture is focused on specific goals and opportunities and that the boundaries are clear. Venture managers must not be allowed to overanalyze; instead, the venture's efforts must be centered on achieving its objectives, such as revenues, profits, growth, etc. Some amount of discipline must be established rather than allowing the venture to continue to expand unchecked. Progressive milestones must be set up to evaluate progress, and if necessary, to give a clear signal when the venture should be terminated. It is very difficult for a venture manager, who proposed and is committed to a new business idea, to objectively define failure. At what point should a venture be terminated? That is a question that is typically better left to senior management.

How objective can venture managers really be about their projects? Can they really assess and understand the financial and nonfinancial risks involved? It may be relatively easy for them to identify what failure would cost them in terms of asset write-offs, but what about their credibility with suppliers, distributors, stockholders, etc.? What about the risks incurred by great success? Can the infrastructure maintain its service capabilities? Undoubtedly, these concerns must be addressed by the venture manager, but at the same time, we believe that the broader corporate view of senior management must also have a say. Contingency plans should be developed by senior management and the venture team in tandem.

If the goal of the venture's management team is to avoid corporate interference at all costs, it misses out on the positive aspects of the relationship with the parent firm. On the other hand, complete neglect by the corporation leaves much to be desired. Therefore, senior management is responsible for providing an appropriate balance between these two extremes and for managing the venturing process, rather than the venture projects. Monitoring strengths, weaknesses, progress, and other problems are ways of checking on the venture. All of these activities require time and attention, but senior management has no choice; they cannot forego their responsibilities, unless they want their venture to fail.

The final challenge for senior management, if this option is chosen, is to assure the smooth integration of the venture into the parent firm. In this case, the venture must become part of the corporation, subject to its policies and procedures. Consider the difficulties in this situation. Successful venture managers may have reaped financial rewards far beyond those of their peers in the larger corporation. What now? If these venturers are brought back into the corporation, is their compensation cut to be comparable to that of the other corporate executives? Where should they be placed? In their old job? In a brand new venture? Or in charge of the newly integrated venture? How do intrapreneurs adjust to the divisional and corporate controls from which corporate venturers typically try to escape? The bottom line is that each situation must be handled on its own merits. But to do so, the venture team and senior management must fully communicate their expectations, concerns, and suggestions. The venture team must realize that integration, or exit, is inevitable. If integration is the definitive outcome, it comes with corporate policies and control systems. The parent firm must understand that the venture's success is an important corporate goal. Even so, the integration process is seldom complete without its share of frustrations on both sides.

CONCLUSION

What does the record show? Has corporate venturing been successful? Actually, the jury is still out. Intuitively, corporate venturing is a way for corporations to sustain their growth while their core businesses are beset with problems of foreign competition, changing technology, and volatile markets. Corporate venturing is also a way for corporations to nurture an innovative climate and to develop badly needed new businesses. Some remarkable successes, such as, 3M's Post-It notes and IBM's 650 computer, among others, are credited to corporate venturing. Hewlett-Packard, Bristol-Myers, Johnson & Johnson, and many other large firms have had outstanding successes with new ventures. On the other hand, disenchantment has increased among some firms regarding corporate venturing. Simulating the culture of an independent start-up is not without its problems. Choosing the right ideas and having the patience to wait for them to mature is not something to which large firms can easily adjust. Many dangers threaten or challenge a corporate venturing effort: (a) obtaining support, (b) fending off corporate interference, (c) managing growth, (d) along with the conflict between the start-up environment of a new venture, and (e) the control-oriented behavior of a larger firm. Not surprisingly, many agree with Hollister Sykes, the former head of Exxon's new ventures program, who said, "It is impossible to preserve completely an independent entrepreneurial environment within a large, multi-product corporate setting" (Sykes, 1986, p. 74). Exxon, Levi Strauss & Co., and others have experienced difficulties in the venturing process, but the attractiveness of the idea keeps it high on many corporations' list of priorities. Firms endeavoring to initiate corporate venturing need to concentrate on the following tasks:

- Paying attention to what constitutes a good opportunity versus a good idea.
- Identifying the qualities needed in a successful venture manager.
- Making good matches between venture projects and venture managers.
- Understanding how to integrate the complementary activities of the venture manager and senior management to achieve the venturing goals.

Website Information

Topic	Web Address	Description
Exxon	http://www.exxonmobil.com/corporate/	Background information on the company as well as current press releases, investor info, and brand info.
Enterprise Resource Planning	http://www.enterpriseresourceplanning.com/index.html	Brief overview of solutions offered by ERP.
Xerox	www.xerox.com	Company, product, and service information.
Company venture boards	www.att.com	Company, product, and service information.
Corporate Venturing	http://www.globalcorporateventuring.com/article.php/5602/nokia-looks-to-future-with-fund	Provides examples of how Nokia was successful in its corporate venturing efforts.

Key Terms

Challenges to integration: The need to impose discipline, to fully assess and understand the risks involved, to manage the process rather than the projects, to assure either a smooth integration into the parent firm or a problem-free exit.

Corporate entrepreneurship stages: Initiating the process, planning the venture, managing the venture from survival to growth, and integrating the venture into the parent organization.

Enterprise Resources Planning (ERP): Ensures that resources are directed toward the intrapreneurial effort and that productivity improvements and cost reductions, along with added value outcomes, are achieved.

Financial resources: Taking into account both outside sources of funding and internal competition for the funds available for distribution.

Intrapreneurship: A managerial philosophy.

Marketing clout: The established company name implies a staying market power that provides an advantage to the intrapreneur.

Opportunity: A set of conditions that enhance a firm's chances of success.

Personnel resources: Skilled workers, familiar with their firm's corporate strategy and resources, available to help build and develop a venture.

Planning the venture: Begins with a corporate entrepreneur sharing their idea with colleagues to convince them to join a venturing team and ends when the product is brought to market.

Technology base: The substantial technological resources to which an intrapreneur has access.

"Vulture" capitalist: An investor with abundant resources and the promise of making entrepreneurial dreams come true.

Review Questions

1. Describe two of the four reasons for the recent shift by organizations toward highly publicizing their attempts to encourage entrepreneurship in their organizations.

2. What is the difference between sustaining and disruptive technologies?

3. List the four potential advantages provided by larger firms to venturing efforts. Briefly describe each.

4. Intrapreneurial ideas must meet the needs of three different parties. Briefly describe the three parties and how their needs can be met.

5. Why do traditional rewards systems fail, and how can senior management resolve these shortcomings?

6. What constitutes an effective integration of the intrapreneurial venture in a firm's organizational structure?

7. Many agricultural entrepreneurs will admit they have not embraced advancements in technology. In part this is because the industry has historically lagged in technology adoption. Some would argue that it's the solo ag-entrepreneur pioneering change, others would argue that it's corporate efforts seeking higher profit margins and shareholder return on investments that are driving the tech boom. Who, in your community, is spearheading this transformation, and why? Is it solo, corporate entrepreneurship, or intrapreneurship?

Reflections from the Front Lines of LifeGuard America

I believe that there are still several companies that incubate entrepreneurs. Sure, there is the story of Steve Jobs, who left Hewlett Packard because "They just don't get it." But on the flip side, I learned a great deal of my skills while working at Hewlett Packard in the early 1980s. Their now-famous MBWA ("Management by Walking Around") was very much a "here is the objective—you create the solution" environment that nurtured the early development of effective entrepreneurial skills. Harley-Davidson Motor Company is another excellent example of a company that has created a corporate environment that truly fosters the development of entrepreneurial skills within the workplace. We created a one-of-a-kind workplace in Kansas City's Harley Plant. And I say *WE* because no one had all the answers when we started in 1994 in Milwaukee, but by the time we opened the plant in 1997, we had created a self-directed workplace unlike any other on earth.

I have also had the privilege of learning about and working with several companies like Nokia. Nokia has taken the logical next step in creating a group within the company that has the sole objective to develop both internal and external entrepreneurs. Their charter reads like a true twenty-first-century organization:

> "*Innovent*" an Insight & Foresight Team, offers a collaborative environment for early stage entrepreneurs in the U.S. working on concepts that facilitate connections between people, their communities, and the things that matter to them. By connecting with Nokia, leading-edge entrepreneurs are offered an opportunity to position themselves at the forefront of developments in the exciting field of communications.

Even their website, www.nokia.com/innovent, is an excellent example of how a company has transformed itself from rubber and wood products in the twentieth century to a state-of-the-art, twenty-first-century telecommunications company in less than a decade. Nokia is clearly one of the best examples of a company that has embraced every element of the corporate entrepreneurship process and is reaping the benefits every day with newborn partnerships and advancing technology relationships.

Discussion Questions on LifeGuard America

1. Do you believe it possible that a company like Hewlett Packard could provide an entrepreneurial environment, as Mr. Fitzpatrick suggests, even in light of the Steve Jobs' story, in which he left to start Apple Computer, only to come back later? Explain why or why not.

2. After reviewing Nokia's *innovent* website, what in your opinion makes Nokia different from any other company that offers an incubation environment for entrepreneurial growth?

References

Antoncic, B., & Hisrich, R. D. (2001, September). Intrapreneurship: Construct refinement and cross-cultural validation. *Journal of Business Venturing, 16*(5), 495–527.

Arbose, J. (1982, March). Intrapreneurship: Holding on to people with ideas. *International Management, 37*(3), 16–20.

Birch, D. (1987). *Job Creation in America.* New York, NY: MacMillan.

Carrier, C. (1996, Fall). Intrapreneurship in small businesses: An exploratory study. *Entrepreneurship Theory and Practice, 21*(1), 5.

Christensen, C. M. (2013). *The Innovator's Dilemma: When New Technologies Cause Great Firms to Fail.* Boston, Mass: Harvard Business Reveiw Press.

Covin, J. G., & Miles, M. P. (1999, Spring). Corporate entrepreneurship and the pursuit of competitive advantage. *Entrepreneurship Theory and Practice, 23*(3), 47.

Cunningham, J. B., & Lischeron, J. (1991, January). Defining entrepreneurship. *Journal of Small Business Management, 29*(1), 45–61.

Economist, The. (2011a, July 2). Too much information: How to cope with data overload. *400*(8740), 59.

Economist, The. (2011b, December 17). Big and clever. *401*(8764), 116.

George, R., & MacMillan, I. (1986). Corporate venturing: venture management challenges. *Journal of Business Strategy, 6*(2), 85–91.

Guth, W. D., & Ginsberg, A. (1990). Guest editors' introduction: corporate entrepreneurship. *Strategic Management Journal, 11*(4), 5–15.

Kolchin, M. G., & Hyclak, T. J. (1987, Summer). The case of the traditional intrapreneur. *SAM Advanced Management Journal, 52*(3), 14–18.

Lado, A., & Vozikis, G. S. (1997, Winter). Transfer of technology to promote entrepreneurship in developing countries: An integration and proposed framework. *Entrepreneurship Theory and Practice, 21*(2), 55–72.

MacMillan, I., & George, R. (1985). Corporate venturing's challenges for senior managers. *Journal of Business Strategy, 5*(3), 34–44.

Peters, T., & Waterman, R. (1982). *In Search of Excellence.* New York: Harper & Row.

Pinchot, G. (1985). *Intrapreneuring.* New York: Harper & Row.

Reilly, B. J., & DiAngelo, J. A. (1987, Summer). Entrepreneurial behavior in large organizations. *SAM Advanced Management Journal, 52*(3), 24–31.

Rule, E. G., & Irwin, D.W. (1988, May/June). Fostering intrapreneurship: The new competitive edge. *The Journal of Business Strategy, 9*(3), 44–47.

Russell, R. D. (1999, Spring). Developing a process model of intrapreneurial systems: A cognitive mapping approach. *Entrepreneurship Theory and Practice, 23*(3), 65–81.

Scott, J. E., & Vessey, I. (2000, August). Implementing enterprise resource planning systems: the role of learning from failure. *Information Systems Frontiers, 2*(2), 213–231.

Shapero, A. (1985, October). Why entrepreneurship? A worldwide perspective. *Journal of Small Business Management, 23*(4), 1–5.

Sharma, P., & Chrisman, J. (1999, Spring). Toward a reconciliation of the definitional issues in the field of corporate entrepreneurship. *Entrepreneurship Theory and Practice, 23*(3), 11.

Timmons, J., Smollen, L., & Dingee, A., Jr. (1985). *New Venture Creation.* Homewood, IL: Richard D. Irwin.

Vozikis, G. S., Bruton, G., Prasad, D., & Merikas, A. (1999, Winter). Linking corporate entrepreneurship to financial theory through additional value creation. *Entrepreneurship Theory and Practice, 24*(2), 33–43.

3 | Feasibility Analysis and Venture Evaluation

Putting It All Together

LEARNING OBJECTIVES

1. To recognize the importance of a feasibility analysis.
2. To understand and integrate the results of the feasibility analysis of a venture idea into a workable action plan.
3. To recognize the critical value and importance of a business plan.
4. To provide a credible framework for the launching of the new venture.

TOPIC OUTLINE

Introduction

Preparing a Feasibility Analysis: The FAKTS

F for Financial Considerations
- What Bankers and Investors Want to See: Putting It All Together

A for Attitude and Self-Analysis Considerations

K for Knowledge Considerations
- Knowing the Venture's Business
- Knowing the Venture's Market
- Knowing the Venture's Competition
- Knowing the Venture's Location
- Knowing the Venture's Legal and Governmental Requirements

T for Timing Considerations

S for Management Skill Considerations

Business Plans and Business Model Generation
- Business Model Generation
- Written Business Plan
- The Conceptual Essentials of a Business Plan
- A Sample Written Business Plan Outline
- A Conceptual and Operationalized Oral Presentation Business Plan Outline

Conclusion

Website Information

Key Terms

Review Questions

Case Study

References

"It wasn't the president of the Bank of England who came over on the Mayflower. It was the members of the genetic pool who desired change, adventure. They were able to live on the edge of a frontier. America, therefore, has been selected genetically as the agent of change."

(The late Dr. Timothy Leary, in an interview with *The Chicago Tribune*, "Notables," 1980).

INTRODUCTION

The word **feasibility** merely implies the possibility of an idea becoming a success. Feasibility studies are conducted by entrepreneurs as well as by the largest multinational corporations. While in-depth feasibility studies are time-consuming and occasionally even tedious, they represent a source of potential savings and assistance to the individuals preparing them. When the City University of Hong Kong began their virtual education initiative, they undertook just such a study to help ensure the success of their program (Ma, Vogel, & Wagner, 2000). Based upon the conclusions drawn from a feasibility study, it will become obvious whether or not it is financially advisable to commit funds, time, and energy to a given venture idea. The feasibility study provides the entrepreneur or the corporate intrapreneur with an enormous amount of flexibility that is not available if the business idea has been hastily conceived. The feasibility study provides a "go, no-go" conclusion based on sophisticated data collection by answering the question: Is it possible for this idea to succeed and to be profitable? Or in simpler terms: *Can we make it? Can we sell it? Can we make money out of it?* The successful evaluation of any business venture requires attention and care. Even though half of the *Inc. Magazine* 500 companies did not have a formal plan when they started (Olson & Bokor, 1995), planning, revenue, and expense control should be given careful consideration in evaluating the financial potential of a venture idea. An example of this type of feasibility study is the Analytic Hierarchy Process (AHP), which is primarily used for small- and medium-sized firms considering a start-up business (Lee & Osteryoung, 2002). Most of the entrepreneurial literature exploring the relationship between pre-startup planning and the venture's actual performance confirms that there is indeed a high correlation between planning and the survival of a new business (Castrogiovanni, 1996). A critical self-analysis of the individual responsible for initiating the venture as well as an analysis of the essential business plan are also needed to "put it all together." A master plan can detect potential problems long before a loan application or, even worse, before the doors of the firm have opened and funds have been committed. The preparation of a master plan also enhances the confidence of the entrepreneur or intrapreneur in the potential success of the business and its stability, and the venture avoids wasting substantial investments of talent, time, and money because of insufficient attention to the feasibility, evaluation, and requirements of the venture.

PREPARING A FEASIBILITY ANALYSIS: THE "FAKTS"

The feasibility analysis is the operationalization of the entrepreneur's idea. In analyzing a venture idea, the following **FAKTS** will determine its feasibility:

F for **Financial** considerations
A for **Attitude** and self-analysis considerations
K for **Knowledge** considerations
T for **Timing** considerations, and
S for **Skill** considerations

Careful consideration and validation of these FAKTS is critical. They represent written and unwritten prerequisites of the venture's framework of success, as well as philosophical credos for the business venture that will provide both stability and direction. In outlining the feasibility analysis, the rule of the three Cs—be *candid, concise,* and *clear*—should be observed in evaluating and organizing the outcomes of this very critical process. If the idea cannot be described simply and clearly, it has not been thought through, and the preparation of a solid business plan cannot be initiated if the feasibility analysis proves that the venture undertaking would be indeed a waste of time, money, and energy. The time and energy expended in a feasibility analysis is an investment that should be quickly recovered if the venture idea proves feasible and reaches its potential.

"F" FOR FINANCIAL CONSIDERATIONS

The most important components of the feasibility analysis and evaluation of a venture idea are the expected financial result, the venture's growth potential, and its capital needs. For anyone investing or lending money to the venture, including the individual entrepreneur, the analysis should make abundantly clear why an investor or creditor should provide funds, when they can expect a return, and how large that return is expected to be. A business plan is a plan for the future, and consequently, the presentation of financial information about the business venture and its product(s) or service(s) must be future oriented.

The ability to obtain money is as necessary to the operation of the business venture as a good location, the right equipment, reliable sources of supplies and materials, or an adequate workforce. The amount of money needed depends on its proposed purpose. Calculating the amount of money required for a new venture start-up business, be it construction, conversion, or expansion, is relatively easy.

To plan working capital requirements, it is important to know the *cash flow* that the business will generate. This involves simply a consideration of all elements of cash receipts and disbursements at the time they occur. Similarly, if a heavy capital investment is required, it may be difficult for an entrepreneur to assemble the needed financial resources. For example, we see very few new automobile manufacturing businesses being planned. An employee of a steel mill, no matter how motivated, would find it difficult to start a similar business because of the capital requirements.

By contrast, in growing industries with low capital requirements, many new firms are being organized; examples include companies producing computer software and solar power equipment. Likewise, an experienced real-estate salesman in a growing metropolitan area might find it relatively easy to spin off from his employer and start a new firm.

Financial projections should be realistic, with reasonable margins that conform to experience and industry standards. Assumptions in the business plan concerning necessary or possible capital requirements such as increased personnel, expanded manufacturing facilities, or equipment needs should be clearly stated and identified as such. Otherwise, the business plan will create an overly optimistic picture for management, which will later create difficulties in the budgeting process and plan evaluation. Excessive optimism can also create skepticism for potential investors.

The budgetary process is the monetary portion of the business plan, and it is integral to the plan, not separate from it. The budget should be the last step in the planning process, undertaken only after the feasibility information has been gathered and analyzed and after objectives have been set. Then budget needs can be realistically formulated. Later, the budget can also serve as a tool for determining the sensitivity impact of any necessary changes in objectives, action steps, or timetable.

What Bankers and Investors Want to See: Putting It All Together

It should be obvious by now that the successful evaluation of a business venture is the most important aspect of the business plan; it requires attention to all the items that have been extensively discussed so far. The feasibility analysis, planning, revenue and expense levels, as well as the future prospects of the proposed venture, are the factors that should be given careful consideration in evaluating the potential of a venture idea because they will strengthen the credibility of the business plan. The financial history of the entrepreneur and the requirements of the business plan are usually intertwined and should take precedence over the formulation of a business plan. The first step in starting a business is to get personal finances in order (Bailey, 2001). Sometimes, for entrepreneurs to put together their financial credentials and history, they have to start from scratch:

1. Find records, receipts, checkbook stubs, etc., and sort them in a "shoebox" manner, according to type (revenue or expense) and according to the timing involved (day, month, and year).

2. Prepare a *current* balance sheet to see where you stand now.

3. Prepare a *current* income statement (if pre-startup operations have already begun).

4. Once the price and profit margins are set, there is a need to identify and determine the following essential operating data:

   — Projected sales increases.

   — Sales revenue breakdown between cash sales and accounts receivable.

   — Ratios and the accounts receivable turnover.

   — Estimated current and projected allowance for bad debt.

   — Estimated current and projected inventory needs and corresponding levels.

   — Estimate of the proportion of accounts payable that has to be paid in cash.

   — Method and amount of depreciation expense.

   — Tax implications of your expenditures.

5. Prepare a *projected* income statement taking into consideration optimistic, pessimistic, and realistic projections (preferably for 2 or 3 years).

6. Prepare a *projected* cash flow statement on a monthly basis and for the next two years, to identify the venture's cash needs.

7. Prepare a *projected* balance sheet for the next two years. If there are problems in cash solvency during certain months in the cash flow statement, either revise pricing, cut costs, or make preparations for cash infusion in the future (via loan, stock sale, etc.), and then readjust the projected balance sheet.

Prospective entrepreneurs should be absolutely honest with their bankers and investors after they have been honest with themselves, and they should provide accurate and detailed information to answer three fundamental questions:

- Can the entrepreneur *make* the product or service?

- Can the entrepreneur *sell* the product or service?

- Can the entrepreneur *make money* from the product or service, so it can repay the loan and the investors get their money back?

A sound business plan can satisfy the first question, the entrepreneur's experience addresses the second, and the entrepreneur's credit history and collateral assures the lender about the third. The banker should be briefed regularly in good and bad times. It is better for the bank to know trouble is coming than to be surprised when a payment cannot be met. A banker or an investor should not be treated like a doctor, and the entrepreneurs should not only pay a visit when the firm's health is in bad shape. In good times, they should stop by and say "hello," and offer reassurances that everything is going well. Bankers and investors have human traits, too, and good relations between borrowers and lenders, or between investors and entrepreneurs, are important so that all are on the same side in times of trouble as well as times of great success and opportunity.

Because a good relationship is important, entrepreneurs need to look for bank officers and investors who meet these specifications:

- Is likeable and respectable as a person.

- Likes and respects you as a person.

- Has a genuine interest in the venture.

- Has respect and authority within the bank or the investment community so their superiors, as well as others, will respect their opinion of you.

- In addition the entrepreneur and the investor should have mutual trust and should find each other to be predictable.

"A" FOR ATTITUDE AND SELF-ANALYSIS CONSIDERATIONS

While the scope, history, and essence of entrepreneurship from a theoretical perspective have already been covered, it is most important, for the development of any sound feasible business idea, to step back and assess one's own abilities and interests. The ultimate success of any venture lies with the entrepreneur. Certainly, other factors (which are examined later) are also of great importance, but none—not a single one—is as critical as the input, involvement, energy, attitude, and resolve of the individual that will spearhead the effort.

So what is an entrepreneur, anyway? Many definitions have been listed and analyzed in the previous chapters. One way to understand the entrepreneur is to read the writings of theorists and researchers. As mentioned earlier, the word "entrepreneurship" is derived from the French, but if you ask the French what they mean by "an entrepreneur," they usually mean a building contractor. Others have defined an entrepreneur as anyone who "talks fast and breathes fast."

The attitude of an entrepreneur plays a large part in the decision to start a business. It is believed by some that a true entrepreneur is a person who has decided to start a business and then looks to find a niche (Krueger, Reilly, & Carsrud, 2000). Entrepreneurial start-ups do not necessarily result from a good idea that a person happens to stumble upon. An entrepreneur is looking for good ideas that can be put to use.

Thus, a good way to define an entrepreneur is to spend time with the entrepreneurs of this world. The definition, of course, does not concentrate on heroic people with special genes but rather on leadership qualities and the events that occur as a result of entrepreneurial leadership, that is, the *entrepreneurial events*. President Truman once said that a leader is a person who gets other people to do what they do not want to do, and *like it!*

When an **entrepreneurial event** happens, the following conditions are present:

- An individual or group takes initiative.

- They bring together resources and form an organization to accomplish something.

- They run it with relative autonomy.
- They succeed or fail with the event (Goldstein, 1984).

There are, of course, more practical questions that a prospective entrepreneur must address. One important issue in academic literature deals with the intentions vs. actions paradox. It is widely known that many persons with bright ideas never cross the bridge between having an idea and putting forth the effort to implement it. Research on this subject in both management and cognitive psychology has centered on the relationship between such traits as the need for achievement, locus of control, risk-taking propensity, tolerance for ambiguity, and entrepreneurial intentions. One of the most important notions that contribute to understanding entrepreneurial intentionality is that of self-efficacy, a person's belief in his/her ability to perform a certain task that can be mastered and developed into stronger levels (Boyd & Vozikis, 1994).

The following worksheet provides a simple yet insightful checklist of many of the necessary components for defining one's self-efficacy to determine whether entrepreneurial intentionality, which will hopefully engage into successful entrepreneurship, is present in the individual's psyche. While weaknesses need to be acknowledged, entrepreneurs should concentrate on their strengths. Strengths are related to what one likes and enjoys doing, therefore one will work hard to improve. Under each question, check the answer that comes closest to what you really feel. Be honest with yourself.

- **Are you a self-starter?**

    _____ I do things on my own. Nobody has to tell me to get going.

    _____ If someone gets me started, I keep going.

    _____ Easy-does-it! I don't put myself out until I really have to.

- **Why are you interested in entrepreneurship or intrapreneurship?**

    _____ Self-employment?

    _____ Profit?

    _____ Service to my family or loyalty to the company?

- **How do you feel about other people?**

    _____ I like people and I can get along with just about anybody.

    _____ I have plenty of friends and I don't need anyone else.

    _____ Most people bug me.

- **Can you lead others?**

    _____ I can get most people to go along when I start something.

    _____ I can give the orders if someone tells me what we should do.

    _____ I let someone else get things moving. Then I go along if I feel like it.

- **Can you take responsibility?**

    _____ I like to take charge of things and see them through.

    _____ I'll take over if I have to, but I'd rather let someone else be responsible.

    _____ Always some "eager beaver" around wants to show how smart he is. Let him!

- How good an organizer are you?

  _____ I like to have a plan before I start. I'm usually the one to get things lined up.

  _____ I do all right unless things get too messed up. Then I cop out.

  _____ I just take things as they come.

- How good a worker are you?

  _____ I don't mind working hard for something I want.

  _____ I'll work hard for a while, but when I've had enough, that's it!

  _____ I can't see that hard work gets you anywhere.

- Can you make decisions?

  _____ I can make up my mind in a hurry if I have to. It usually turns out OK.

  _____ I can, if I have plenty of time.

  _____ I don't like to be the one who has to decide things. I'd probably blow it.

- Can people trust what you say?

  _____ You bet they can! I don't say things I don't mean, and I always mean what I say.

  _____ I try to be on the level most of the time, but sometimes I just say what's easiest.

  _____ What's the sweat if the other fellow doesn't know the difference?

- Can you stick with it?

  _____ If I make up my mind to do something, I don't let anything stop me.

  _____ I usually finish what I start, if it doesn't get messed up.

  _____ If something doesn't pan out right away, why beat your brains out?

- How good is your health?

  _____ I never run down!

  _____ I have enough energy for most things I want to do.

  _____ I run out of steam sooner than most of my friends or colleagues.

- Is it easy for you to get up in the morning and go to work?

  _____ I'm up and out of the house before the alarm goes off!

  _____ Most of the time, I can get up all right.

  _____ I really like to sleep.

- When you're working on a project, does time seem to fly by unnoticed?

  _____ When I am interested in something I could care less about the time involved.

  _____ I try to work on a semi-regular schedule.

  _____ I go in at 9:00 and leave by 5:00, and that's it!

- Do business ideas frequently come to mind?

  _____ I always come up with the greatest ideas everywhere, even when I just watch TV.

  _____ Sometimes I come up with flashes of brilliance.

  _____ Every so often I think of something I consider a good idea.

- Do you really want to start an entrepreneurial venture for yourself or at your job?

  _____ It has been my lifelong dream and ambition.

  _____ It would be great but if it didn't happen, it wouldn't be the end of the world.

  _____ Truthfully, I like the security of corporate life.

If most checks are beside the first answers, you probably have what it takes to be an individual or corporate entrepreneur. If not, you are likely to have more trouble than you can handle if you venture into uncharted waters. If you still want to get involved in entrepreneurial activities, it would be better to find a partner who is strong in the areas where you are weak. However, if most checks are beside the third answer, not even a good partner will be able to shore you up. (For an analysis of your brain's entrepreneurial preferences, visit http://mindmedia.com/braintest.html)

"K" FOR KNOWLEDGE CONSIDERATIONS

Many people may wish to start a business venture, but they are unable to do so. They lack the knowledge, the experience, the contacts, or the resources needed. An entrepreneurial venture, whether independent or corporate, is built around the individual entrepreneur, who must be able to perform those key activities required for success. If it is a clothing store, the entrepreneur must be good at buying the right merchandise, as well as displaying, advertising, and pricing it. The entrepreneur as a manager must also be able to do the selling, handle the record keeping, identify suppliers, and train employees. An alert employee of a clothing store can learn many of these needed skills and can become capable of starting a successful clothing store. People often start businesses in fields they already know in order to draw upon their previous knowledge and backgrounds. Thus, one might think of established organizations as "incubators," providing their employees with experiences that make them more or less prepared to become entrepreneurs. However, companies vary widely in the extent to which they provide an environment conducive to entrepreneurial activity.

Notably, even within the same organization, employees develop different kinds of knowledge and experience. Some stay in the same job and never achieve much breadth in work experience or contacts. Others become specialists; they are good in their jobs, but they lack the basic skills needed to produce or sell a product and get a company started. Still others are in better positions to develop external contacts and to learn about market opportunities. Thus, an industrial salesperson may learn that customers would buy a particular product that is not currently available. The salesperson may conclude that a new company could get started by offering that product.

However, an entrepreneur may start a firm in a field in which he or she has no experience. It happens every day. If the founder gets started by buying an existing business or by entering into an agreement with a franchisor, then previous experience is less important. However, available evidence suggests that more than 50% of all entrepreneurs start businesses in industries they know intimately and in which they already have a great deal of experience. The previous educational and job choices a person has made help determine what kind of business, if any, he or she might someday be in a position to start (Cooper, 1980).

Knowing the Venture's Business

The overwhelming majority of fast-rising entrepreneurial ventures are single-product or single-service, single-market firms, or more recently, e-commerce firms. The founding entrepreneurs have gone to great trouble to define their businesses as narrowly as possible. While the task of defining a business seems exceptionally elementary, businesses have, at times, great difficulty defining what business they are in. A blurred image results in customer confusion. Interestingly, when W. T. Grant Co. closed back in 1975, many argued that the retail industry had finally learned some valuable lessons in defining its business. However, the subsequent and more recent failures of Woolco, Fed Mart, and others prove that lack of definition of the business is still a very serious problem.

Most entrepreneurial ventures find themselves in a similar bind, often caused by lack of foresight. Quite frequently, entrepreneurs do not envision where they would like their businesses to be one year, one month, one week, or even one day in advance. Deciding what a business will look like in one, two, or even five years is no easy task. To succeed initially, many businesses become involved in a variety of activities. Opening a new grocery store may require that the entrepreneur sell not only groceries but also books, magazines, lawn furniture, cookout grills, and health and beauty aids. But there has to be a central core activity that the business performs. The plans that ultimately develop into successful businesses are based on *someone's specific perception* of just what business he or she is in. If the importance of this single activity is overestimated or underestimated, the chances for eventual business success are limited. The prospective entrepreneur needs to take time, work with friends and associates, listen, and then respond concisely to the following questions:

1. What is the central activity of the proposed or existing venture?
2. What type of business will it be? Will it primarily be involved in merchandising, manufacturing, or providing a service?
3. Does anyone want the product/services it will provide?
4. Have you studied surveys and/or sought advice and counsel to find out what fields of business may be expected to expand?
5. Are general business conditions good?
6. Are business conditions good in the city and neighborhood where the venture will locate?
7. Are current conditions good in the proposed venture's line of business?
8. Does the venture constitute a unique business?
9. Is the business a seasonal one? If so, is there a need for adjustments in business operations, and why? Can sales fluctuations be reduced to reduce uncertainty?
10. Why is this business going to be profitable?
11. What are the chances for the venture's success?

Responding to these questions should provide important and necessary clarity to the entrepreneur's business mission.

Knowing the Venture's Market

The importance of defining the business cannot be overemphasized. To succeed, however, the individual or corporate entrepreneur must also be knowledgeable about the venture's market. When the new *Life* magazine was introduced, the publisher, Time, Inc., had thoroughly identified and researched its target market. The publisher knew the number of potential subscribers in the target market, the age group it wanted to attract, the average income, the average education of its market, as well as a number of other factors. By first identifying these crucial characteristics, Time, Inc., was then able to develop a product and a marketing program designed to appeal to this *particular* target market. Even this thorough analysis, however, did not prevent *Life*'s ultimate demise; markets shift, and what was valid yesterday may not be valid today.

Market research is not a one-time project. It should be a continuous process because companies operate in a dynamic and changing world. One of the critical capabilities identified by George Day (1994) was **market sensing**. Systematic gathering, interpretation, and use of market information gives the company a significant advantage over its rivals, which may be more internally focused. In today's environment, an ever-increasing amount of knowledge is available about the potential customers for a start-up business. Customer profiling has increased in quantity and accuracy over the past two decades. Information is so sophisticated that marketers can spot individuals in every household and can target each separately (Berwick, 2002).

Another important aspect of knowing the market is customers. Because entrepreneurial companies usually choose an unfilled niche, drawing the exact customer profile is critical. After all, customers are the source of real cash inflow that keeps the company functioning. Because customers tend to be very specific to each business, we will mention only two general types of customer. Currently, with the advent of the e-commerce terminology, these two types are described by today's popular terms as B2B (business to business) and B2C (business to consumer). The questions that need to be answered about the *specific venture's* market and customers include the following:

- Who is the typical customer of the venture's market?

- Where is the market?

- What is the size of the total U.S. market for the venture's product or service in numbers and dollars?

- Are there plans to appeal to local, regional, or national segments of this market?

- Are there any new customer market segments that the venture would want to attract?

- What is the venture's market growth potential?

- What trends could be projected for the venture's market?

- What market share should the venture gain?

- Is brand name important to the venture's market?

One of the greatest needs of prospective individual and corporate entrepreneurs is adequate, accurate, and current information they can use to make knowledgeable decisions concerning the market for their products and/or services. Market research is the means by which information about the various elements that comprise buying and selling is obtained and evaluated. Good market research can be costly and time-consuming, but poor research is even more costly when the answers obtained cause an entrepreneur to make a wrong decision. Because financial resources are usually limited, the entrepreneur's margin of error is quite often very narrow. However, in some cases, inference analysis using related products, markets, and/or environmental variables can provide a certain degree of accuracy and confidence in the results of the market research (Jeannet & Hennessey, 1998, p. 254).

Knowing the Venture's Competition

Once the issues described above have been settled, another important factor must be considered: competition. To be successful in a start-up operation, it is important to identify and understand the competition. If an entrepreneur claims to have no competition, he or she will lose credibility. If there are no identifiable competitors, it could be a result of not having a market (Shah, 2002). Regardless, if no direct competitors can be found, an analysis should be done that encompasses all of the businesses selling anything close to the same product and all of the businesses addressing the same market. The entrepreneur should use this information to outline a plan to stay ahead of the competition and to maintain a competitive advantage.

Two factors distinguish the company from its rivals: product/service uniqueness and low price. In a study of Inc. 500 companies, Olson and Bokor (1995) found that 56% of firms used the innovativeness of a new product or idea to distinguish themselves from the competition, while 44% decided to duplicate competition. While the definition of "duplicating the competition" is arguable because the companies could have merely added some inconsequential distinguishing features to their products, we can also safely assume that many of these new ventures hope to beat competition with lower prices. Charging a price that is too low in the attempt to position themselves as low-cost providers is considered one of the most common mistakes made by entrepreneurs (Stern, 1993). In determining price, the entrepreneur should consider such variables as industry trends, the competition's pricing, and the niche for the product. If the product is unique, the company may consider a skimming or penetration strategy, rather than direct competition based on price. In evaluating competition, entrepreneurs should address the following questions:

- Who are the nearest competitors, and how long have they been in business?
- Where are they located in relationship to the business site?
- What prices do the competitors charge for their products or services?
- Have their businesses been steadily improving? If yes, why? If not, why not?
- Why and how will the business be able to compete with existing competitors?
- What can we learn from the competition?
- Do we regularly review competitors' ads to obtain information on their prices?

Knowing the Venture's Location

The questions concerning competition in the preceding section have a direct bearing on selecting a proper location for the business venture and estimating the value of the investment in the chosen location. The maximum return on investment must be considered when deciding the best location in which to establish the business. The return on investment can be determined by comparing the total cost for a specific location with the cost of the existing location (Brimberg & ReVelle, 2000).

Proper site location can help the business make money. Even if the entrepreneur has ample financial resources and above-average managerial skills are available, they cannot offset the handicap of a poor location. Moving is costly, and legal complications of a lease can be difficult to untangle, not to mention other location-related problems that may arise. Clearly, a careful examination of alternative sites is a worthwhile endeavor. By studying the relevant *Bureau of the Census* reports, valuable insights about the characteristics of prospective customers, as well as knowledge about the economic strengths and weaknesses of the trading area, can be developed. Every business has a trading area, that is, the geographic region from which it draws its potential customers. Data for trading areas, regardless of size, generally can be assembled by combining a number of census tract tables, and these tables may be the best single source of information, supplemented with other material.

The main concern of a prospective owner of a retail store, for example, should be the factors that have direct relevance to the store's trading area. Far too many small retailers select a store site by chance. In fact, the most common reason is "noticed vacancy." Their high failure rate would be considerably lower had they analyzed in advance the trading area's population characteristics, the housing characteristics, the nature and quality of competition, the traffic count, and accessibility. It is also of fundamental importance to determine total consumer purchasing power and the store's expected share of this total. Each location analysis must be customized, concentrating on a particular line of business. Some of the questions that should be addressed regarding the location include the following:

1. Have at least three possible locations for the business been selected?

2. Weighing the benefits of rent vs. actual location of the business, what is the most *feasible* site for the business firm?

3. Are water, electricity, gas, and sewer facilities available at the site?

4. How good is police and fire protection in the area?

5. Are there any particular zoning laws in the area that must be considered?

6. Is the location near schools, libraries, recreational facilities, residential or commercial neighborhoods, and is this important?

7. What kind of people will want to buy what is being sold? What is the makeup of the population in the city or town where the firm plans to locate? Do potential customers live in the area?

8. What are the specific makeup, number, type, and size of competitors in the area?

9. Does the area need another business like that?

10. Are potential employees available in the area?

11. If parking is an essential part of doing business, are there adequate parking facilities?

12. Is the cost of the prospective location reasonable in terms of taxes and average rents?

13. Is there sufficient opportunity, prospect, and room for growth and expansion?

When it comes to choosing the most favorable specific street site, certain factors should be considered. For example a retail firm may wish to locate on the side of the street

- With the highest pedestrian traffic count.

- Where major department stores and other "business attractors" are located.

- Nearest the community's primary area of population growth.

- That protects customers from extreme weather conditions.

- With shade in the afternoon.

- With the fewest alleys, loading zones, fire hydrants, and the like.

Additionally, there are many advantages to opening shop in a mall, shopping center, or office complex because small ventures benefit from the overflow of the traffic of major stores or businesses. Furthermore, there is prestige involved in being part of a modern, cosmopolitan shopping mall or office tower. However, in a mall location, many leases require small shops to remain open when department stores are open. Therefore, on Sundays and major holidays when foot traffic is slow, the small owner is stuck with the high overhead and low sales volume that do not justify remaining open.

In a downtown area, rent hikes threaten small businesses as the market for commercial space tightens. For instance, in places like San Francisco or Boston's Back Bay area, where land space is scarce and demand for office and store space is enormous, the supply of retail and office space is very small, resulting in the entrepreneur being at the mercy of the landlord. Ten important potential trouble spots must be negotiated carefully before signing a lease:

1. How long will the lease run?
2. How much is the rent?
3. How much will the rent go up?
4. Can I sublease?
5. Can I renew?
6. What happens if my landlord goes broke?
7. Who is responsible for insurance?
8. What building services (electricity, heating-ventilation-air conditioning [HVAC], cleaning services) do I get?
9. Who else can move next door or nearby?
10. Who pays for improvements? (Cunningham, 1982).

Finally, all prospective entrepreneurs must determine the long-range quality of the site and the general trade area. Relocation can be very expensive. Sophisticated initial site work can save a great deal of trouble later.

Knowing the Venture's Legal and Governmental Requirements

The legal requirement for a business varies from location to location. For example, if an entrepreneur is starting a venture in Oklahoma, there may be dramatically different tax laws and other requirements that might not be required in another state or outside of the United States altogether. Various incentives may be offered by local and federal governments to attract a company to a certain area (Cochineas & Argent, 2002). In gathering the comprehensive information needed to prepare a business plan, certain mundane but extremely important considerations must also be examined:

- What licenses (if any) are needed to operate the business?
- What police and health regulations apply to the business?
- Will the firm's operations be subject to interstate commerce regulations? If so, which?
- Has advice from a lawyer been obtained regarding responsibilities under federal and state laws and local ordinances?
- Is there a system in place for handling the withholding tax for employees?
- Is there a system in place for handling sales taxes? Excise taxes?
- Is there an adequate record system in place for efficient and accurate tax form preparation?
- Is there a worksheet system in place for meeting tax obligations?
- Has advice from an insurance agent been obtained about what kinds of insurance the business will need and how much it will cost?

"T" FOR TIMING CONSIDERATIONS

Today, unlike some years ago, widespread changes in technology and globalization present many opportunities for entrepreneurial ventures, especially for the e-commerce–oriented entrepreneur or the corporate intrapreneur, who can put together a solution much faster than in the past. While technological or international trends may not bear any relation to a venture's plans, other trends and events will certainly affect the "go/no-go" decision.

Many well-conceived, sound ideas fail because of improper *timing*. For example, even conservative predictors suggest that most Americans are eating at least one of every three meals away from home at a restaurant. What will this trend do to grocery stores? The current average price for an American car keeps increasing. If this figure continues to climb, many car owners will be forced to repair and repaint rather than replace their older vehicles. What do these consumer trends mean? Will they have any impact on the business idea? Can it still be successful? The idea may be great, but its timing may be lousy.

The timing of the business entry is one essential, critical variable that is too often overlooked. Timing corresponds to what philosopher and psychologist Karl Jung called **synchronicity**, that is, when all opportune psychological and environmental conditions, circumstances, and favorable state of affairs come into a juncture to form a good timing nexus. He specifically defined synchronicity as an "acausal connecting principle," that is, an essentially mysterious connection between the personal psyche and the material world, based on the fact that both are only different forms of energy. Jung associated synchronistic experiences with the relativity of space and time and a degree of unconsciousness in two junctures. First, an unconscious conceptual image content comes into consciousness either directly (i.e., literally) or indirectly (symbolized or suggested) in the form of a dream, idea, or premonition, and then in a synchronous fashion, an objective situation coincides with this conceptual content. As soon as psychic content crosses the threshold of consciousness, the synchronistic marginal phenomena disappear, time and space resume their accustomed sway, and consciousness is once more isolated in its subjectivity. The one is as puzzling as the other (Sharp, 2001).

Prospective individual or corporate entrepreneurs researching the feasibility of a proposed venture should be cognizant of the ever-changing trends in themselves and in the environment of many prospective industries that may trigger conditions for *synchronicity* and opportunistic *timing*. They must pay close attention to the following issues:

1. What has been the growth and stability of the industry in question?
2. What are the major technological changes or advances within the industry?
3. Are consumer preferences changing, or are they fairly steady and predictable?
4. What is the nature and intensity of competition in the industry?
5. Has there been an excessive amount of regulatory activity directed at that specific industry?
6. Is franchising making significant inroads into the industry?
7. What does it take to be successful in the specific industry, and do I have it, or can I get it?
8. Is a great deal of experience needed for success in that industry?

Even though "luck" is an important element of the timing factor, it is quite interesting that luck has a peculiar habit of favoring those who do not really depend on it. "Lucky" individuals are usually those that applied the extra ounce of care and due diligence in their feasibility study and are quite oblivious of the concept of "bad luck." They are not as vulnerable to misfortune as are the individuals who did not exercise care and due diligence in the conceptualization of their business venture idea.

"S" FOR MANAGEMENT SKILL CONSIDERATIONS

According to various studies of factors involved in the failures of small businesses, roughly 98% of businesses fail because of managerial weakness. Less than 2% of failures are due to factors beyond the control of the individuals involved. This points to one very important fact: successful entrepreneurs build their businesses upon their own *personal* strengths, experiences, and hobbies. In addition to having a good deal of knowledge about their product or service, they also *enjoy* the business. This factor is too frequently overlooked and too critical to ignore. It is much easier for entrepreneurs to commit tremendous amounts of managerial time and energy to an activity they enjoy rather than one they dislike or that bores them. The following questions must be addressed and emphasized in the management section of a business plan *prior* to the operationalization of ideas:

1. Are the right people in place and properly organized to implement the plan?

2. Who will make things happen? The entrepreneur himself or herself, or some other enthusiastic, experienced, and committed individuals? The experience, talent, and integrity of those responsible for enacting the business venture's proposals are of primary concern.

3. What will be the total number of employees hired? How will their work be scheduled?

4. What form will the organizational structure and the organizational chart take?

5. Who will report to whom?

6. Which other members of management are officers and directors?

7. Are there outside board members?

8. What are the business histories and experiences of the people involved in your business? What will be their duties and responsibilities?

9. What are the job descriptions for key personnel?

10. What growth opportunities will be provided for key, non-family personnel?

11. How will salaries in the business compare with the competition?

12. Will the business require skills taught in a local vocational technical program? If so, could students be used as interns in the business?

Although details of the personnel manual are not a necessary portion of a feasibility study or a business plan, a brief discussion of employee policies and benefits may be a helpful indication of the general management approach. Curriculum vitae or other details of the personal backgrounds of management may be left to an appendix.

By answering these questions, key areas of potential weakness in the required *skill* part of the feasibility study can be identified *before* problems arise.

BUSINESS PLANS AND BUSINESS MODEL GENERATION

By this point in the planning process, the feasibility of a business venture idea or a potential acquisition of a going concern has been thoroughly defined, outlined, and conceptualized. The final obstacles that must be overcome include "putting it all together" and obtaining start-up capital to get the business going. Once all of the in-depth questions, such as those outlined above on feasibility, have been considered and an enterprise idea has been thoroughly evaluated, much information has been gathered and analyzed. Entrepreneurs should then turn their attention to organizing all pertinent information into a core business model and spelling out a formal business plan. Next, we begin by providing an overview of Osterwalder & Pigneur's (2010) business model canvas and conceptualization, then we turn to the process of formalizing the written business plan.

Business Model Generation

In the past few years, a new trend in business planning has emerged, coined **business model generation**. These models do not center solely on traditional business planning but rather on describing "the rationale of how an organization creates, delivers, and captures value" (Osterwalder & Pigneur, 2010). Thus, they follow a more holistic approach to doing business. The crux of the business model is developed according to nine building blocks (as seen below in Exhibits 3.1 and 3.2):

1. Customer segments (CS),
2. Value propositions (VP),
3. Channels (CH),
4. Customer relationships (CR),
5. Revenue streams (R$),
6. Key resources (KR),
7. Key activities (KA),
8. Key partnerships (KP), and
9. Cost structure (C$)

Accordingly, these elements shape the business canvas and establish the fundamental language with which the business models progress throughout various phases: canvas, patterns, design, strategy, and process.

The canvas is the language of business model generation. Business models are ideally developed on a large surface; Post-It notes are utilized to sketch out business models fulfilling components for each of the nine building blocks. As the canvas is developed, patterns are discovered in the business model which give depth and insight into the business model by comparing it with similar business types (e.g., patterns) according to the nine building blocks. An example of a pattern utilizing the popular web-based television and movie-viewing business is Hulu. Hulu patterns itself similarly to many other organizations (i.e., Flickr, Skype, and Dropbox), in that the basics are free but the advanced or extended content is provided at a cost using various patterns: unbundling, long tail, multi-sided, free, and open. The "Freemium" pattern on the canvas is illustrated in Exhibit 3.3.

Following the pattern analysis, business model generation shifts its focus toward design through various outlets, such as customer insights, ideation, visual thinking, prototyping, storytelling, and scenarios. This is a creative process in which ideas are explored to best suit the elements of the business in accordance with the nine items on the canvas. Here, traditional business planning differs from business model generation in that business plans often follow a very particular path, whereas business models encourage design variation for more innovative business models. Through these design variations, value can be created, delivered, and captured.

Exhibit 3.1 — The Nine Building Blocks Defined

Customer segments (CS)	Who to reach and serve
Value propositions (VP)	What products/services to bundle for your CS
Channels (CH)	How to communicate with your CS and deliver your VP
Customer relationships (CR)	What types of relationships are built with your CS
Revenue streams (R$)	Cash generated from each CS
Key resources (KR)	Necessary assets for the business model
Key activities (KA)	What must be done to make the business model work
Key partnerships (KP)	Suppliers and partners which the business model relies on
Cost structure (C$)	Costs incurred

Exhibit 3.2 — The Business Model Canvas

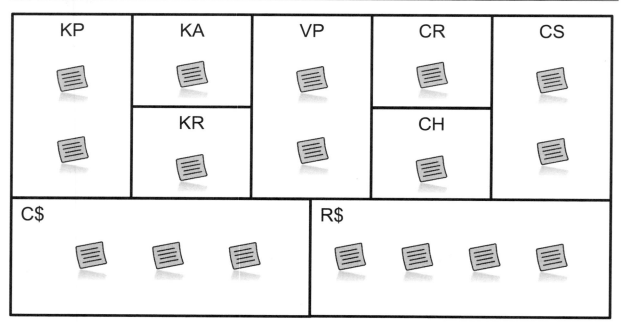

Once the canvas, patterns, and design are established, business models provide a lens for macro-level lending considerations according to four strategic foci: environment, evaluation, blue ocean strategy, and multiple-model management. Within these realms, environmental forces will push a canvas to evolve over time. Then SWOT (strengths, weaknesses, opportunities, and threats) analysis can be used to guide amendments in specific portions or across all of the business canvas. The *Blue Ocean Strategy* (Kim & Mauborgne, 2005) blends with business model generation, adding the consideration of cost reductions and the omnipresent value creation of the business. Consideration of multiple models is a key component of macro-level lending considerations in that overlap of the business unit models may provide cost reductions and/or value creation within organizations containing multiple business models.

Exhibit 3.3	Hulu Sketched on the Canvas

KP	KA	VP	CR	CS
Television stations Movie industry	Platform management	Direct access to multiple networks Free basic viewing	Self-service Mass customized	Casual users High volume users
	KR Copyrights Platform	Hulu Plus: Extra content and mobile application	**CH** Hulu.com	

C$	R$
Platform development and maintenance Storage costs	Free limited basic account: Advertising Subscriptions to Hulu Plus account

Lastly, as organizations undertake business model generation, much uncertainty is generated, and design is up for debate. But once design is established and uncertainty is resolved to the greatest extent possible, a narrowed focus will enable implementation. Although some lack of clarity may remain in the mobilization, understanding, and design phases, implementation and continuous management of the model's evolution should become more deliberate. Undertaking the business model generation is no easy feat, but it is a revolutionary and thought-provoking alternative to traditional business plans. Individuals seeking to learn more about business model generation should see *Business Model Generation* (2010) by Osterwalder and Pigneur.

Written Business Plan

Once your core model is fleshed out, it is time to create your written business plan. Why go through the trouble of creating a formal written business plan? There are two major reasons:

1. The process of putting a business plan together, including the conceptual thought and analysis before actually writing the business plan, forces the entrepreneur to take an objective, critical, and unemotional look at the venture project in its entirety.

2. The completed business plan is an operating tool that, if properly used, will guide the management of the business and contribute to its success.

The importance of planning cannot be overemphasized. By taking an objective look at the proposed business venture, areas of strengths and weaknesses can be identified and needs can be pinpointed that might have been overlooked otherwise. As an operating tool, the business plan helps establish reasonable objectives; it guides the entrepreneur in determining how best to accomplish them. It helps to identify "red flag" problems as they arise, it assists in identifying their source, and it also suggests ways to resolve them. The business plan can even help avoid some problems altogether.

However, the business plan should not create an overly optimistic picture, because this will create difficulties in the budgeting process and in the plan's evaluation by investors, creating skepticism on the part of the potential investor. Internet sales forecasts, especially, give outlooks that are too rosy, and these are often tossed about without an explanation of their methodology. Therefore, even though they may be easy to find, they can be difficult to analyze and validate ("Business Bulletin: Internet Sales," 2000, p. A1).

The budgetary process and the resulting budget should be the last steps in the business plan process. Only after gathering all pertinent information, setting objectives, assessing the venture's needs, and determining its feasibility can the budget be realistically formulated. The budget can then steer any necessary changes in objectives, action steps, or timetables.

Finally, a business plan is written primarily for the purpose of clarifying in the mind of the entrepreneur, in a crystal clear manner, where the venture is headed. Secondarily, it serves to convince outsiders that the business venture is promising and not doomed to failure. If the proposals in the business plan turn out to be marginal at best, it is far cheaper *not* to embark on an ill-fated venture at all. A few hours of concentrated and hard work in putting together an honest, crystal clear business plan are imperative in determining the short- and long-term prospects for the new venture at the earliest (and least expensive) point in its development.

Potential entrepreneurs are sometimes too enthusiastic; they are often sidetracked when it comes to practical matters by the potential success of their new venture. Bankers and investors, however, want to be assured that the proposed venture's financial, managerial, operational, and marketing plans are more than adequate. Loan requests from entrepreneurs are frequently rejected because of poor preparation, inadequate presentation, or because the entrepreneur is unsure of the precise capital requirements of the business. They can also be rejected because of some tangible or intangible element of Murphy's Law that appear suddenly:

- Nothing is as simple as it seems.

- Everything takes longer than it should.

- The more innocuous a change appears, the further its influence will extend.

- All warranty and guarantee clauses become void upon payment of the invoice.

- The necessity of making a major design change increases as the fabrication of the system approaches completion.

- Firmness of delivery dates is inversely proportional to the tightness of the schedule.

- Dimensions will always be expressed in the least usable term. Velocity, for example, will be expressed in furlongs per fortnight.

- An important Instruction or Operating Manual will have been discarded.

- Suggestions made by the Value Analysis group will increase costs and reduce capabilities.

- Original drawings will be mangled by the copying machine or the printer.

- In any given miscalculation, the fault will never be placed if it involves more than one person.

- In any given situation, the factor that is most obviously above suspicion will be the source of error.

- Any wire cut to length will be too short.

- Tolerances will accumulate unidirectionally toward maximum difficulty of assembly.

- Identical units tested under identical conditions will not be identical in the field.

- The availability of a component is inversely proportional to the need for that component.

- If a project requires n components, there will be $n - 1$ units in stock.

- Left to themselves, things always go from bad to worse.

- Nature always sides with the hidden flaw.

- If everything seems to be going well, you have obviously overlooked something.

The Conceptual Essentials of a Business Plan

A proposed sequential method for "putting it all together" using a critical thinking approach to the preparation of the business plan is presented in Exhibit 3.4. It constitutes the basic foundation for the meticulous analysis of the concepts related to the entrepreneurial venture's business plan. Although the thorough and comprehensive formulation of a business plan entails a great deal of effort, time, and money, it is essential for the future of the new business. This approach can convincingly crystallize the merits of the venture in the entrepreneur's mind, further convincing the entrepreneur that the venture is worth pursuing.

This critical thinking approach and conceptual analysis of the essentials of the business plan enable the prospective entrepreneur or intrapreneur to identify the current and future needs of the venture in terms of type, amount, and timing. At the same time, they greatly increase the probability of securing funds on favorable terms by presenting a clear and persuasive argument to bankers or investors. To ensure this objective, the **concepts of the business plan** shown in Exhibit 3.5 need to be re-conceptualized and reconfigured in terms of seven "hooks" that will convey to bankers and investors that you do, indeed, "know what you're talking about." Additionally, another strong message will be conveyed to the interested parties that this is not a random exercise in futility but rather a well-thought-out business plan. Exhibit 3.5 presents the actually **conceptualized business plan** in terms we have labeled the **Magnificent Seven conceptual hooks**. Of course, this approach was named after the classic 1960 American Western film of this name directed by John Sturges, which itself was based on Akira Kurosawa's 1954 movie masterpiece *The Seven Samurai.*

These Magnificent Seven serve to put everything into perspective and to crystallize the reasons that the entrepreneur is engaging in this long but rewarding journey toward financial and personal independence.

A Sample Written Business Plan Outline

After in-depth conceptual and critical-thinking questions have been considered and analyzed, and the necessary information to answer them has been collected, attention should be focused on organizing the mechanical structure of each specific section of the business plan to enhance its readability and straightforwardness.

The suggested format of a written business plan outline presented in Exhibit 3.6 on pages 60–61 is helpful in constructing a complete written version of the business plan that can be used as a blueprint for launching the venture.

Exhibit 3.4   The Concepts of a Business Plan

The Niche	The value concept for the customer	Why buy?
The Market	The demand-driven strategic opportunity target	Who buys, how many, when, how, where?
The Return	The financial projections and their time-tables	How much can we profit and when?
The Need	Success, personal investment, and additional financial need requirements	How much we personally contributed, how much more we need, and what does it take to succeed overall?
The Infrastructure	The product and marketing considerations The organizational and operational considerations The legal considerations	What business functional plans need to be in place as the venture's infrastructure?
The Ability to Execute (FAKTS):	The management and leadership of personnel The financial management and control of money	Ability to lead and manage people and money?
The Deal	The external and internal performance risks The growing and sustained competitive advantage edge The future possibilities	Evaluation and contingency plans to *protect* the value concept's performance against any threats? Growth and development plans to *improve* the value concept's sustained competitive advantage edge? International, "harvesting," and/or exit prospects to *expand* the value concept?

Exhibit 3.5   The Conceptualized Business Plan

The Niche Hook #1: Can we **make** it?	The value concept for the customer	Why buy?
The Market Hook #2: Can we **sell** it?	The demand-driven strategic opportunity target	Who buys, how many, when, how, where?
The Return Hook #3: Can we **profit** from it?	The financial projections and their timetables	How much can we profit and when?
The Need Hook #4: Can we **commit** to it?	Success, personal investment, and additional financial requirements	How much we personally contributed, how much more we need, and what does it take to succeed overall?
The Infrastructure Hook #5: Can we **plan** it?	The product and marketing considerations The organizational and operational considerations The legal considerations	What business functional plans need to be in place as the venture's infrastructure?
The People "FAKTS": Financials, Attitude, Knowledge, Timing, and Skills Hook #6: Can we **execute** it?	The management and leadership of people The financial management and control of money	Ability to lead and manage people and money?
The Deal Hook #7: Can we **grow** it?	The external and internal performance risks The growing and sustained competitive advantage edge The future possibilities	Evaluation and contingency plans to *protect* the value concept's performance against any threats? Growth and development plans to *improve* the value concept's sustained competitive advantage edge? International, "harvesting," and/or exit prospects to *expand* the value concept?

A Conceptual and Operationalized Oral Presentation Business Plan Outline

The presentation of a venture proposal and its business plan should not be elaborate and taxing to the intended audience, but rather it should target and give details on the essential "hooks" that will quickly generate enthusiasm and interest in the venture and result in its approval and funding.

The suggested format for a business plan's oral presentation outlined in Exhibit 3.7 on pages 62–63 follows the conceptualized business plan with its *Magnificent Seven Hooks* and should be adaptable in its length depending on the time allotted for its presentation. An oral business plan presentation should never exceed its allocated time.

CONCLUSION

No business plan, no matter how carefully it is constructed or how thoroughly it is understood, will be of any use at all unless it is put into action. Going into business is difficult, and, as mentioned earlier, more than half of all new businesses fail within the first 2 years of operation, while more than 90% fail within the first 10 years.

A major reason for failure is lack of planning, and the best way to enhance the chances of success is to plan and follow through on the business plan. Again, the business plan should be implemented and executed, not placed forgotten in the bottom drawer of a desk.

Website Information

Topic	Web Address	Description
Banking	http://www.theventurebankgroup.com	Venture Banking Group is an operating division of Greater Bay Bancorp, a diversified bank holding company (GBBK-Nasdaq). VBG was started in 1994, and it provides innovative banking solutions to emerging growth technology companies in the Silicon Valley and beyond. VBG serves a broad range of industry segments in both technology and life science. VBG also provides a form for entrepreneurs to fill out to request services.
Knowing the Venture's Market: Life Magazine	http://www.life.com/Life/	Tells about the magazine's current projects as well as a history of the magazine.
Knowing the Venture's Location	http://www.census.gov/main/www/subjects.html	Gives an A–Z list of all current census information.
Business Plans	http://www.business-plans.co.uk	Defines the purpose, necessity, and process of creating a business plan. Includes links to other informational websites about forming a business plan.
Sample Business Plans	http://www.businessplans.org	Excellent variety of sample business plans.

Exhibit 3.6   A Sample Written Business Plan Outline

1. **Cover Sheet**
   - Business name, address, phone and fax numbers, e-mail address
   - Principals
   - Date
2. **Executive Summary**
   - Brief summary of the plan
   - Major objectives
   - Product/service(s) description
   - Marketing strategy
   - Financial projections
   - Personal investment and the description of additional financial needs
3. **Table of Contents** *(each section listed with headings and subheadings)*
4. **History**
   - Background of principals or company origins
   - Value concept, product/service(s) background
   - Organizational structure
   - Brief outline of the owner's past and current successes and experiences
5. **Definition of the Business**
   - The value concept to the customer
   - The added value in the purchasing decision
   - Reasons for buying the product or service
   - Reasons for buying from this specific business
   - Solutions to customer problems
6. **Description of Products or Services**
   - Define what is to be developed or sold
   - Status of research and development
   - Patents, trademarks, copyrights
   - Catalogue sheets, photographs, or technical information in the appendix
7. **Definition of the Industry**
   - Description of the industry and business fit
   - Entry and growth strategy
   - Licenses, regulatory and compliance requirements
   - Barriers to entry for competitors
   - Barriers to exit in case of venture failure
8. **Definition of the Market**
   - Strategic target market: WHAT needs? WHOSE needs? HOW needs are satisfied? HOW MUCH price-wise?
   - Market size and trends
   - Market penetration and market share and sales projections
   - Gross and operating margins and pricing
   - Analysis of competition
9. **The Management Team**
   - The ability to execute: Financials, attitude, knowledge, timing, and skills
   - Key personnel
   - Organizational structure
   - Compensation and incentives
   - Partnerships, agreements, and other employee policies

Exhibit 3.6 *(continued)*

- Supporting external team of professional advisors and services
- Additional details such as resumes in the Appendix

10. Objectives and Goals
- Marketing plans
- Operating plans
- Quality assurance plans and service and warranty policies
- Profit, revenue, and cash goals and potential and profit durability
- Development status and timetable schedule
- Financial plans and future needs

11. Financial Data
- Fixed and variable costs
- Break-even analysis
- Projected income statements
- Projected cash flow analyses
- Projected balance sheets
- Pro-forma ratio analysis
- Projected statements of changes in financial position
- Cost-volume-revenue-profit analyses and tax implications (if applicable)

12. Concluding Remarks: The Deals
- Evaluation of external and internal risks and contingency plans to PROTECT the value concept's performance from any threats.
- Growth and development to IMPROVE the value concept's sustained competitive advantage edge and productivity goals for its continuous renewal and improvement.
- The venture's future possibilities and overall prospects to EXPAND the value concept through internationalization, "harvesting," and/or exit prospects.

13. Appendices
- Narrative history of the company in detail
- Management structure (organizational charts, detailed resumes, etc.)
- Lists, specs, pictures and brochures of products, systems, software
- Detailed objectives and goals
  a. Products and services and technical analysis
  b. Research and development
  c. Marketing
  e. Manufacturing and/or operations and facility layout
  f. Administration
- Finance.
- Historical financial information (3 to 5 years if possible)
- Major assumptions
- Regulatory, environmental, compliance, license, and approval documents
- Reports by independent technical experts and consultants
- Lists of customers and suppliers
- Letters of recommendation or endorsement
- Any other pertinent material that would enhance the business plan's validity and credibility

Source: Adapted from Peat, Marwick, Mitchell & Co., 1984, pp. 22–23.

| Exhibit 3.7 | A Sample Oral Presentation Business Plan Outline |

1. **Cover Sheet**
   - Business name, address, phone and fax numbers, e-mail address
   - Principals
   - Date

2. **Executive Summary** (Hook them with the "Magnificent Seven" early, so they read the written long version of the business plan later!)
   - **Hook 1:** We can MAKE it: The *niche* and the *value* concepts (The way the world IS now, which constitutes a problem.)
   - **Hook 2:** We can SELL it: The strategic target market opportunity (The Solution . . . the way the world *ought to* be, the definition of the Industry, Market, and Business, the Strategic demand or supply-driven opportunity target, added value to the customer's purchasing decisions, etc.)
   - **Hook 3:** We can PROFIT from it: The financial return (How much return on investment will the venture generate for an investor, and when? Credible, substantiated, and realistic, optimistic, and pessimistic scenarios and timetables in a graphic format.)
   - **Hook 4:** We can COMMIT to it: The success, personal investment, and additional financial requirements (The framework of the specific needs that are required for the venture's success, their nature, degree and level, cost, and justification, the amount of personal investment committed and its proportion to overall personal wealth, and finally and as a result of this analysis, the specific needs of additional financial investment. Investors want to know up front how much you need, whether you really know what and how much you need, and how much you put out of pocket, so they "categorize" and measure you as an individual and as a true entrepreneur, as well as your venture as a degree of risk.)
   - **Hook 5:** We can PLAN it: The *infrastructure* plans (Product and marketing plans, organizational and operational plans, and legal structure plans.)
   - **Hook 6:** We can EXECUTE it: The personnel and money management (YOU, the FAKTS, the ability to execute once the venture is launched, plugging the holes by organizing and staffing the venture with skilled individuals and providing them with competent managerial leadership with FAKTS, and if you cannot, with other credible individuals, and the responsible and solid financial management and control of the money.)
   - **Hook 7:** We can GROW it: The deal! (Why is this venture proposal such a deal for an investor? Because its survival is ensured, and by reviewing the venture's threat and performance risks and by making sure that contingency and management plans are in place that will fend off external and internal threats to *protect* the venture's value concept performance, by renewing through growth and development its sustainable competitive advantage edge to *improve* the value concept, and finally, by examining the future possibilities of the venture's value concept by assessing its prospects for internationalization, "harvesting, and/or exit potential in order to *expand* the value concept.)

The remainder of the oral presentation business plan outline should describe in more detail certain of the aforementioned items, if time is not of essence and there is enough interest on the part of the audience to hear more. Never risk taxing the patience of an audience by elaborating on details and covering issues beyond the "Magnificent Seven Hooks" that can be easily covered in the written long version of the business plan!

3. **The Product/Service**
   - The product and its value added (The solution again. . . .)
   - Define what is to be developed or sold
   - Status of research and development
   - Patents, trademarks, copyrights

Exhibit 3.7 *(continued)*

4. **The Marketing Plan and Mix**
   - **Definition of the industry** (given the problem of what *is*, what *could* be done, and finally, what *should* done)
   - **Definition of the market and *target* market** (what needs, whose needs, how to satisfy those needs, and at what price and quality)
   - **Market potential** (market size and strategic fit)
   - **Competitive strengths/advantages** (in the specific industry and the specific market)
   - **Business and marketing strategy**
   - **Entry and growth strategy**
   - **The Four Ps of Marketing:**
        P1: Advertising and promotional strategy
        P2: Distribution channels (positioning)
        P3: Product development strategy
        P4: Price and profit margins

5. **The Company**
   - History (background of successes and failures of the individual and the company)
   - Organizational structure
   - Legal organizational structure

6. **Operations Overview**
   - Production technology and operations
   - Technical qualification and certification program
   - Plant/store layout
   - Hours of operation/service
   - Operations flow
   - Operational timetable

7. **The Management Team**
   - Key personnel (FAKTS)
   - Consultants and advisors
   - Hierarchical organizational structure

8. **The Financial Summary**
   - Financial plans and needs
   - Profit, revenue, cash goals, potential, and durability
   - Summarized financial statements (income statement, balance sheet, and cash flow)
   - Key ratio analysis (margins, profitability, debt/equity)
   - Other important financial considerations (taxes, additional sources of funding, revenue, etc.)
   - Financial timetables

9. **Exit Strategy/Concluding and Reemphasis Remarks**
   - Why this is such a great DEAL for an investor!
   - What kind of contingency plans have been evaluated and are in place to protect the venture's value concept from external and internal risks that could possibly threaten its performance.
   - Emphatically state again about why YOU have a sustainable EDGE over the competition, and how you will grow, develop, and improve the value concept's sustained competitive edge through productivity and renewal.
   - Where do you want to take this "thing," what are the possibilities for future international growth by expanding the value concept, and ultimately how do you intend to "harvest" or exit the venture?
   - Finish by re-emphasizing the "Magnificent Seven Hooks"!

Key Terms

Business model generation: These models do not center solely on traditional business planning but rather on describing "the rationale of how an organization creates, delivers, and captures value."

Concepts of the business plan: The niche, the market, the return, the need, the infrastructure, the ability to execute, and the deal.

Entrepreneurial event: The event in which the individual or group takes an initiative, resources are brought together to form an organization to accomplish something and to run with relative autonomy.

Feasibility: The possibility of an idea becoming a success.

Financial considerations: An analysis of why they should provide funds, when they can expect a return, and how large that return is expected to be.

Magnificent Seven conceptual hooks: The business plan deals with making it, selling it, profiting from it, committing to it, planning it, executing it, and growing.

Market sensing: Systematically gathering, interpreting, and using market information.

Synchronicity: When all opportune psychological and environmental conditions, circumstances, and favorable state of affairs come into a juncture to form a good timing nexus.

Review Questions

1. What are the three fundamental questions that all prospective entrepreneurs should be able to answer when dealing with investors and bankers, and how can these three questions be satisfied?

2. What are the "Magnificent Seven" conceptual hooks, and what questions do these hooks pertain to?

3. What sorts of considerations are included in the "K" of the FAKTS of the feasibility analysis? Give some examples of what these considerations pertain to.

4. Briefly discuss the issues of timing in launching a venture.

5. Why is the "right" attitude important in launching a venture?

6. Select, research, and evaluate an agriculture-related business in your region. Sketch out the nine boxes of their core business model. What opportunities do you see for diversification? What are their strengths and weaknesses?

Reflections from the Front Lines of LifeGuard America

I have written many business plans in my career, and I continue to learn through the use of others to review, critique, and refine the end product. I tend to write operational business plans, which sometimes makes for a lengthier document that must be broken into a more concise core with several addendums. Whatever you do, before you begin the distribution and resulting presentation of your new endeavor, get professional and comprehensive reviews of your documents. I worked for eighteen months on the business plan for LifeGuard America and thought I had it ready to take to the market. Luckily for me, I was introduced to the Oklahoma Technology Commercialization Center and its director,

Tom Walker. Tom took one look at the 97-page business plan and began laughing out loud. Part of the service the OTCC provides its clients is a critical review of their business plans by professional outside reviewers who take the gloves off and "call it like it is." Tom's initial review of my plan was like being hit with a cold bucket of water: basically a grade of "D" on a subject and document about which I considered myself an expert. He and the team at the OTCC were right on target. I had forgotten the fundamental aspect of any business plan: the target audience is the investor. Here I was telling someone how to build a watch when all they really wanted to know was what time it was. Once again, the words of my good friend rang in my ears: "Never say boo who, when boo will do." We immediately tore the business plan apart and created an Executive Summary of six pages—an extremely tough but necessary project. The Executive Summary was followed by a newly organized main section in the following format:

1. Company Overview & Background

2. Services & Technology

3. Market Definition

4. Competitive Landscape

5. Market Plan & Positioning

6. Sales Plan

7. Management Team

8. Implementation Plan

9. Financials

We also created separate documents including a marketing plan, a sales plan, a Private Placement Memorandum, and an operating agreement for our LLC. These documents were, in some manner, all originally bundled into my 97-page phone book of a business plan, but now that they were properly organized after a long three days worth of work, they received an updated grade of "A-"—still not perfect, but ready for serious consideration.

It is also important to note how crucial it is for any entrepreneur to be flexible in the development over time of his original idea. One must always remember that it is indeed a shared vision that is being created. My original concept focused on the high-speed jet transportation of time-critical human organs like the heart and lungs. Over time, however, it has metamorphosed into a logistical support system for transplant teams to assess organ suitability using our Internet Protocol based Virtual Private Network IP/VPN (a term not even invented when I first started working on LifeGuard America). In short, the business plan had evolved into the information age where the demands of the transplant community had progressed to the need for real-time medical information to support rapid decision making in a time-critical business. The old plan of high-speed transportation is now only a footnote to the key element of the business plan. If I had been inflexible to the changing requirements of the environment, I would have missed the opportunity completely. Remember, it is not about you and your ideas, but rather the creation of a shared vision based on a flimsy idea or concept that evolves into a strong, viable business opportunity.

Discussion Questions on LifeGuard America

1. What do you believe is the most important function of your business plan?

2. Why do think Mr. Fitzpatrick is so insistent on being flexible with a business plan?

References

Bailey, J. (2001, June 10). Starting a business? Exercise fiscal fitness. *The Wall Street Journal,* p. E7.

Berwick, I. (2002, February 2). They know all about you: Customer profiling. *Financial Times,* p. 4.

Boyd, N., & Vozikis, G. S. (1994, Summer). The influence of self-efficacy on the development of entrepreneurial intentions and actions. *Entrepreneurship Theory and Practice, 18*(4), 63–77.

Brimberg, J., & ReVelle, C. (2000, June). The maximum return-on-investment plant location problem. *Journal of the Operational Research Society, 51*(6), 729.

Business bulletin: Internet sales forecasts. (2000, May 25). *The Wall Street Journal,* p. A1.

Castrogiovanni, G. (1996). Pre-startup planning and the survival of new small businesses: Theoretical linkages. *Journal of Management, 22*(6), 801–823.

Cochineas, A., & Argent, P. (2002, February 27). Tax break for venture capital investment limits. *Monday Business Briefing,* Article 15508. Retrieved March 18, 2000, from http://www.mondaq.com/article.asp?articleid=15508&searchresults=1.

Cooper, A. C. (1980). *Entrepreneurship: Starting a New Business* [NFIB Public Policy Discussion Series]. San Mateo, CA: National Federation of Independent Business.

Cunningham, R. S. (1982, April). Ten questions to ask before you sign a lease. *Inc. Magazine, 4*(4), 79–82.

Day, G. S. (1994). The capabilities of market-driven organizations. *Journal of Marketing, 58*(4), 37–53.

Goldstein, J. (1984, September/October). So what's an entrepreneur anyway? *In Business, 6*(5), 4.

Jeannet, J. P., & Hennessey, H. D. (1998). *Global marketing strategies* (4th ed.). Boston: Houghton Mifflin.

Kim, W. C., & Mauborgne, R. (2005). *Blue ocean strategy.* Boston, MA: Harvard Business School Press.

Krueger, N. F., Reilly, M. D., & Carsrud, A. L. (2000, September/November). Competing models of entrepreneurial intentions. *Journal of Business Venturing, 15*(5,6), 411–432.

Lee, S., & Osteryoung, J. (2002). Start-up business evaluation model using the Analytic Hierarchy Process: An empirical investigation in the USA and Korea. *The International Journal of Entrepreneurship and Innovation, 3*(3), 211–219.

Ma, L., Vogel, D., & Wagner, C. (2000). Will virtual education initiatives succeed? *Information Technology and Management, 1*(4), 209–227.

Notables and quotables. (1980, April 2). *The Wall Street Journal,* p. 31.

Olson, P. D., & Bokor, D. W. (1995, January). Strategy process-content interaction: Effects on growth performance in small start-up firms. *Journal of Small Business Management, 33*(1), 34–45.

Osterwalder, A., & Pigneur, Y. (2010). *Business model generation.* Hoboken, NJ: John Wiley & Sons.

Peat, Marwick, Mitchell & Co. (1984). *Business planning.* New York: Author.

Shah, S. (2002, July 4). Make your plans investor proof. *New Media Age, 9.*

Sharp, D. (2001). *The Jung lexicon.* Retrieved October 10, 2001, from http://www.cgjungpage.org/jplexicon.html.

Stern, L. (1993). Ten deadly sins that'll wreck your business. *Home Office Computing, 11*(10), 58–60.

4 Venture Success Framework: Overall Success Requirements

LEARNING OBJECTIVES

1. To discuss success and failure.
2. To describe a comprehensive framework of success factors.
3. To identify the factors that lenders and investors seek before deciding to fund a new venture.

TOPIC OUTLINE

Introduction

Income-Oriented Businesses vs. Entrepreneurial Ventures

Success and Failure

Determinants of Success: A Review of the Literature

A Framework for Success

Competitive Strategy

Environmental Factors

Demographic, Psychological, and Behavioral Factors

–Inquisitiveness and Risk Acceptance

–Motivation and Leadership

–Professionalism and Self-Confidence

–Adaptability to the Environment

–Achievement and Action-Oriented Characteristics

Management Practices

Conclusion

Website Information

Key Terms

Review Questions

Case Study

References

"People who try to do something and fail are infinitely better than those who try to do nothing and succeed."

(Lloyd James)

———

INTRODUCTION

Everyone who is at all familiar with the problems of creating new ventures and developing small businesses believes that the majority of these companies could continue to live and prosper if the people at their heads would spend on preventive planning only a fraction of the imagination, care, and work they spent on building up their businesses in the first place. Mario Ieonni, a small business consultant said: "I know how the surgeons in the accident ward down at the hospital must feel when the highway casualties are brought in Saturday nights: frustration at being unable to do much more than make the patient's last hour a bit more comfortable; rage at the needless waste and destruction of so much that could live constructively and productively; and sadness when I ponder what might have been had these friends of mine only started to think about the future of their business a few years sooner."

There is no doubt that the challenges and issues facing entrepreneurs in their quest to develop and sustain their businesses are complex and multiple, but the prospect of pure personal economic gains motivates individuals to pursue sustainable development opportunities with a high probability of success (Dean & McMullen, 2007). The price of failure is high, not only to entrepreneurs and investors but also to society. Entrepreneurs and investors stand to lose their investments; society loses jobs and incurs high social costs such as unemployment insurance, reduced competition, less innovation, and wasted investment capital.

In the start-up stage, the key question is quite simple: Why does one business idea succeed in getting implemented, when others do not? That is, what factors improve the chances of successfully starting a business and overcoming the major obstacles to its survival? Once past the survival stage, however, the manager must make a conscious decision about the future of his/her venture. Will it be entrepreneurial and attempt to grow, or will it be income-oriented, opting for stability or slow growth, maintaining the founder's personal and business lifestyles? With this decision, these questions arise: Why does one existing business succeed and another cease operations, or at best perform marginally? What will improve the firm's chances of maintaining its income orientation, developing into a high-growth company, and sustaining growth and profitability? This chapter provides some insights for avoiding the more common pitfalls that new firms tend to encounter as they are created and as they evolve. The objective is to "stack the deck" in favor of success.

INCOME-ORIENTED BUSINESSES vs. ENTREPRENEURIAL VENTURES

Income-oriented businesses (e.g., flower shops, bowling alleys, hardware stores, etc.) are different from entrepreneurial ventures; therefore, they have different funding needs and success requirements. Income, or lifestyle, businesses are often created to serve as a substitute to working for someone else, and the owner has, in a sense, purchased himself/herself a job. Such businesses tend to grow slower than entrepreneurial ventures and to plateau at some steady employment level.

Birch (2001) differentiated between the two by labeling "small businesses" **income-oriented businesses** while calling entrepreneurial ventures **gazelles**. Gazelles are usually in high-tech sectors. They acquire venture capital. They are young, small, and operate in national or international markets rather than regional markets. The ability of small businesses to grow or decline in terms of employment, what Birch (1988c) called *volatility*, tends to be extremely low. In contrast, gazelles have a different fate:

> Entrepreneurial businesses never *just* grow and rarely *just* decline. They do both sequentially. They stumble onto something, get a big boost out of it, and grow significantly. Then, as soon as they think they're rounding third base, someone always seems to move home plate. Maybe there is a change in their economic world. Other competitors close in on them. A new technology eliminates the value of their market niches. Or perhaps they simply get cocky, or lazy, and lose track of the direction in which they were headed. Whatever the cause, the inescapable fact is that the most likely result of any company's growth is a slowdown or even outright decline. (p. 25)

Almost invariably, entrepreneurial ventures are characterized by high volatility. Their growth patterns are not simple upward curves; over enough time, their growth is a series of peaks and valleys. To recover from the valleys, the firm has to learn from its mistakes and reversals. Once it does, it can get back on the path to success. Large declines tend to be preceded by rapid growth; rapid growth is a frequent precursor of big declines, and either a big decline or no change is often the forerunner of a business closing.

This kind of activity highlights the fact that for most entrepreneurial ventures, rapid growth is inherently volatile. A word of caution is needed here. The growth of many firms simply goes straight up: sales increase year to year by dramatic percentages. But the rule for entrepreneurial ventures tends to be a cyclical peak-and-valley pattern (Richman, 1988).

Companies that increase rapidly often come down fast (Hyatt, 1988), in part because they frequently rely on a single product for their sales, technology, or market. For example, what might be "a pothole" to a bigger company with other revenue sources and a larger capital base may prove to be a large ditch for a small company. Furthermore, explosive sales growth often requires a company to add costly additions, such as personnel, plant, and equipment, at an equally rapid rate. If growth slows abruptly, a company may be caught with excess capacity, personnel, and fixed costs. Growing quickly on the tiny capital base of most young, first-spurt companies leaves little room for even small errors and none for egregious greed (Richman, 1986).

Perhaps by understanding volatility better, firms learn how to cope with it, anticipate it, plan for it, and capitalize on it. After all, volatility is healthy because it eliminates inefficiency and poor ideas from our economic system. Firms that do not learn how to profit from their mistakes may end up forever riding a roller coaster between their peaks and valleys.

SUCCESS AND FAILURE

Statistics indicate that the majority of new ventures are discontinued within five or six years. To say that the odds are not attractive is obviously an understatement, but they can be beaten. It should be recognized that the so-called "failure rates" are plagued by definitional problems and inconsistent measures. Definitions of failure vary from study to study; economists and politicians often quote a widely held belief about the failure of small firms: *Four out of five small firms fail in their first five years.* Spokespersons of the Small Business Administration have used this statement to express their concern about the health of small firms, and mainstream economists have used it to express what they think is the irrelevance of small companies for economic development. However, this claim has no foundation; in fact, no statistical source or any other type of analysis reports such high failure rates. Instead, there is good evidence that more than 50%, rather than the reported 20%, of all new small firms survive for 8 or more years. The rest of the firms either died or failed. To distinguish between death and failure, Dun & Bradstreet defines **business failure** as "business termination with losses to creditors." This is a suitable definition because it differentiates between the firms that fail because of financial distress and the firms whose owners voluntarily terminate operations. This also tells us that the chances for an entrepreneur starting out in the United States are surprisingly good. Therefore, from a lender's perspective, the probability of losses from lending to new businesses is far less than the 80% implied by the statement, "Four out of five firms fail in the first five years." Furthermore, the survival rate of the small firm, including ownership changes, is 50%, with 28% surviving with their original owners at the helm (Bygrave, 1997, pp. 458–459).

Just what are the odds of starting a business that survives? Unfortunately, business mortality records are notoriously poor and only deal with firms that have ceased operations. What about the individual who comes up with an idea and wants to know his/her chances of getting the business off the ground? Of course, there is no way to keep track of failed ideas or business plans that could not be implemented (Birch, 1988b).

Prospective entrepreneurs should understand that many firms that cease operations are started by people lacking the fundamental training and business skills needed to succeed, that is, by people who have never balanced a checkbook before, much less understood a set of accounting books, and by people who let their excitement and enthusiasm outweigh rational considerations about the potential success of their ventures.

Obviously, failure is a most disturbing term, loaded with emotion and negative implications. Yet it has been the operative word for the majority of studies examining firms that go out of business. Failure does not always have a disappointing outcome. There are many ways a firm can cease operations without undergoing real failure. For example, many firms close down without incurring losses; the owner(s) may sell their operations at a profit and reopen under a different name, or owners may move into other occupations with better opportunities. Businesses are also discontinued because of the owner's retirement or illness. They may simply be sold for a profit, rather than because of poor operating performance. Because of the variety of ways businesses can be discontinued, a multitude of competing definitions and measures of small business "failure rates" have been formulated. There is simply no uniformity in conceptualizing the failure of small businesses. That's the good news.

The bad news is that, typically, around 98% of the business plans submitted to venture capitalists are rejected for one reason or another. The odds are probably pretty good that you can start a business, but the more you need outside funding, the more the odds for success get progressively worse. The entrepreneur's capacity to raise money is a result of having the other venture factors stacked in favor of success. Whether the funding materializes or not, these other success factors do not happen automatically. Instead, in most instances, venture funding follows good entrepreneurs with FAKTS, who have spotted good opportunities and who demonstrate a clear grasp of the driving forces that govern success. For this type of venture, there is no serious shortage of risk capital or non-venture capital financing. Increasingly, sophisticated bankers, financial institutions, and informal investors back people who have demonstrated that they understand what is required to succeed in their proposed business (Timmons, Smollen, & Dingee, 1985, p. 16).

Obviously, there is a huge gap between success and failure at the start-up stage. The role of entrepreneurs, therefore, is to identify as many ways as possible to increase the chances for the success of their ideas and to find ways to improve the odds that their ventures are funded if outside capital is needed. In this sense, good opportunities are more likely to get funded and started than good ideas. But what constitutes a good opportunity? Is it the venture's chance of success? Baron and Ensley (2006) argued that opportunities are identified when entrepreneurs, using relevant cognitive frameworks, "connect the dots" between seemingly unrelated events and trends. As a consequence, they identify patterns in these connections that indicate patterns of market failure in terms of new products and services that are needed. Timmons et al. (1985) contended that success in a new venture takes much longer to appear than most people realize; pearls (winners) take 7–8 years to mature, while lemons (losers) ripen much more quickly, in 2.5 years. Before creating an aura of success and gains for investors, entrepreneurs, and the overall economy in general, entrepreneurs must first believe that an entrepreneurial opportunity exists for others (third-person opportunity belief) and that this opportunity is one they are committed to pursuing (first-person opportunity belief) (Shepherd, McMullen, & Jennings, 2008).

Regardless of the statistics used, no one disagrees that the odds of success for an entrepreneurial venture are poor. Failure is definitely more often the rule than the exception, but there are ways to improve the odds. For one thing, the 65% failure rate cannot be generalized across the board. Substantial variation exists between industries, localities, and time periods. The success rate is also considerably improved among firms that receive venture capital. For instance, one study found only an 18% failure rate among 272 ventures financed over a 7-year time period (Dorsey, 1979). But at the same time, venture capitalists do not automatically pick winners. One study of performance found that 40% of venture capital deals resulted in a loss of 50–100% of the total investment. In only slightly more than 10% of their deals did venture capitalists realize their targeted return of five or more times their investment (Timmons et al., 1985).

Perhaps the most comprehensive and insightful examination of company survival and failure was undertaken by Birch (1987). Using a database of 5.6 million firms ranging in size from mom-and-pop grocery stores to Fortune 500 conglomerates, Birch found that smaller firms (0–19 employees) are only slightly less likely to cease operations than larger firms (500+ employees). On the other hand, the odds of survival for intermediate-sized firms (20–499 employees) are better than those for smaller companies. Hence, Birch supports the intuitive belief in a threshold concept up to a certain level of employment, meaning that the odds of survival are, as Timmons et al. (1985) suggested, progressively better as the firm gets larger, or at least until it hits a threshold of 500 or more employees, at which point survival rates get slightly worse.

Can we pinpoint the specific venture opportunities that have the highest survival rates? How about the ones that are easiest to start? And what about survival and growth? Wouldn't it be great if we could find a business that is easy to open, and likely to survive, with a high probability of growing? Unfortunately, we cannot. High survival rates and rapid growth just are not compatible with the most frequently started businesses. The businesses that seem easiest to start tend to grow little or, even worse, they tend to close. Those that easily survive do so because they are difficult businesses to get into. And the ones that can make entrepreneurs and investors rich are hard to start and hard to keep going. Entrepreneurs must think carefully about the kind of venture opportunity they want to undertake, because none is likely to provide easy entry, security, and rewards. Thus, entrepreneurs are forced to choose ventures with those characteristics that matter most to them and their financiers and to forego others (Birch, 1988a).

DETERMINANTS OF SUCCESS: A REVIEW OF THE LITERATURE

As mentioned previously, venture funding mostly follows good entrepreneurs with FAKTS, those who have spotted good opportunities and who have demonstrated a clear grasp of the driving forces that will govern the success of their proposed venture. Perhaps no topic has been researched more often in entrepreneurship and/or small business literature than the determinants of success. Unfortunately, the early literature on the topic of success seldom provided any connection between the various approaches. Some studies advocate personality variables, and others purport demographic characteristics as the key determinants of success. And still another group of studies champions the use of simple rules-of-thumb developed through experience, such as "never get involved in a partnership." A more recent set of studies suggests that entrepreneurial strategy is the major concern. *Innovation and Entrepreneurship* (1985) by Peter Drucker provides several chapters and examples of successful **entrepreneurial strategies**, along with an interesting discussion of the key elements necessary for entrepreneurial management to flourish in a new venture.

Entrepreneurial knowledge is an extremely important factor influencing success. It includes the physical natural environment and its corresponding phenomena and events (Parris & Kates, 2003), as well as knowledge of the communal environment in which people live and from which they derive a sense of history, belonging, and identity (Padua, 2007). Environmental gains (e.g., diminished air pollution, increased quality of drinking water), economic gains (e.g. employment, consumption, economic wealth), and social gains (e.g., education, equal opportunity, better quality of life) comprise a desirable "triple bottom line" (National Research Council, 1999; Leiserowitz, Kates, & Parris, 2006). Economic gains especially can also lead to psychological (Twenge & Campbell, 2002) and physical health (Hanson & Chen, 2007). Entrepreneurial knowledge as a success requirement was also defined by Shane (2000) as simply knowledge of markets, ways to serve the markets, and customer problems; this type of knowledge identifies changes in supply and/or demand (Dew, Sarasvathy, & Venkataraman, 2004).

Entrepreneurial strategy has become a key research topic in new venture performance (e.g., MacMillan & Day, 1987; McDougall & Robinson, 1987; Sandberg, 1986; Stuart & Abetti, 1987). A word of caution here: in several studies purporting to examine entrepreneurial strategies, the researchers have included intrapreneurial ventures. Given the significant resource advantages possessed by large firms, it may not be appropriate to apply their findings to independent entrepreneurs. A second concern is that many strategy studies limit their focus only to entrepreneurial ventures and exclude income-oriented small businesses, which are often content with stability or slow-growth strategies.

Another favored approach to studying success has been to examine the personality, behavior, and demographic characteristics of entrepreneurs and small-business people. The belief here is that successful entrepreneurs possess traits, behaviors, and personality characteristics different than non-entrepreneurial types. One criticism of this segment of the entrepreneurial literature is the lack of a widely accepted definition for an entrepreneur. Because no uniform definition exists, much of this research makes little distinction between an entrepreneur and a small-business person, and the results are somewhat confusing. Still, an enormous amount of literature exists regarding personality traits (e.g., risk-taking, autonomy, locus of control, etc.), behavioral activities related to organization creation, and demographic characteristics (e.g., age, experience, education, and family role models) (Brockhaus, 1982; Carland, Hoy, Boulton, & Carland, 1984; Gartner, Carland, Hoy, & Carland, 1988).

Examining psychological traits is perhaps the most controversial of all approaches to studying success. It reflects the search for a "magic bullet" of the single best psychological profile describing the successful entrepreneur or small-business person (Carland, Hoy, & Carland, 1988; Gartner et al., 1988). Therefore, the search has not been very successful. In fact, the consensus seems to be moving toward accepting that demographic variables may indeed help predict the probability of someone starting a new venture, but they offer little in terms of predicting or improving the odds of succeeding at starting and growing an entrepreneurial venture or a small business (Hofer & Sandberg, 1987, p. 22). Gartner et al. (1988) further criticized the utility of examining personality variables to identify a so-called "entrepreneur." Nevertheless, this remains a fairly controversial, and as yet unsettled, issue.

A final approach (**comprehensive strategy of success**) to discussing success is more comprehensive in nature, because it attempts to identify all the personality, demographic, behavioral, environmental, strategic, and other factors that affect a venture's odds of succeeding. The reality is that any one factor may affect the chances of success, but many others can quickly lead to financial ruin if they are not avoided or addressed. Authors of these studies of entrepreneurial success are trying to cover all the bases in order to make new venture owners sensitive to the multiplicity of factors that can make or break a new venture. These data often take the form of a checklist of factors most responsible for small business failures. The entrepreneurship and small-business journals, such as *The Journal of Business Venturing, The Journal of Small Business Management, Entrepreneurship Theory and Practice,* among others, consistently publish articles that highlight these issues and offer suggestions on how to avoid or resolve them.

Recently, academic research has entered a new and hopefully fruitful phase wherein different success factors are investigated and analyzed simultaneously to determine their impact on success, similar to the FAKTS profile advocated earlier. Though the results are preliminary, progress is being made. For instance, one study found success to be related to four factors: 40% entrepreneurial values or personal traits, 40% managerial skills, 10% interpersonal skills, and 10% environmental dimensions (Goodwin & Ibrahim, 1987).

In a review of the literature on this combination of determinants of new-venture performance, Hofer and Sandberg (1987) suggest that success is most affected by three generic factors, in order of importance:

1. Structure of the industry entered.
2. The business strategy used by the new venture.
3. The behavioral characteristics of the founding entrepreneur.

Another particularly interesting discussion on success and failure factors was presented by Vesper (1980). He cited factors related to the founder, such as choice of business, education and experience, collaboration with other parties, prior choices of employer and geographic location, ability to attract starting capital, and management practices, as affecting the firm's chances for success.

Timmons et al. (1985) took a different view. Rather than explicitly talking about success factors, these authors identified the variables driving a potentially high-growth, new-venture creation process: the founders, the opportunity per se, and the resources required. By paying close attention to all of the elements encompassed by these three categories, it is implied that the venture process will be successful.

A FRAMEWORK FOR SUCCESS

To provide a comprehensive review of the factors linked to small business and entrepreneurial success, the work of previous authors must be synthesized into a framework useful for studying the determinants of success. This comprehensive approach includes several factors that are often noted as key contributors to the failure or success of small ventures but that cannot be controlled by the entrepreneur or small-business person: interest rates, taxes, inflation, and the regulatory climate.

The classification scheme offered here is fundamentally similar to several of the frameworks mentioned previously, but it also differs in certain respects. The venture's competitive strategy is considered to be the most important determinant in the success of both small businesses and entrepreneurial ventures, while personality traits are also considered to be significant factors in determining the odds of success. Instead of attempting to identify a single best psychological profile, certain behaviors, attitudes, and traits been identified that do tend to benefit various entrepreneurial and small-business situations. These characteristics should not be discounted, even though each business situation is unique. This **framework for success** is built around the following aspects:

- Competitive strategy
- Environmental factors
- Demographic, and psychological and behavioral characteristics
- Management practices

This is by no means a complete list. Entrepreneurs and small-business persons need to recognize which of the factors are most appropriate to their own situation; there is no definitive categorization scheme.

COMPETITIVE STRATEGY

As mentioned previously, much of the literature related to success and management practices appears to be more relevant to small businesses after the start-up stage. As far as entrepreneurial start-ups are concerned, a "think big" strategy is essential for entrepreneurial start-ups. Furthermore, firms funded with venture capital command a better success rate. As many as 98% of all submitted business plans are rejected by venture capital firms because the odds of success of their competitive strategy are not great to begin with.

A fair amount of research has been conducted on venture capitalist criteria (e.g., MacMillan, Siegel, & SubbaNarasimha, 1985; MacMillan & SubbaNarasimha, 1986; MacMillan, Zemann, & SubbaNarasimha, 1987; Robinson, 1987; Sandberg, Schweiger, & Hofer, 1987; Tyebjee & Bruno, 1984). These studies provide some good insights into (a) the criteria used by venture capitalists in evaluating proposals; (b) the differences between funded and non-funded plans; and (c) the differences between successful and unsuccessful ventures that had previously received funding from venture capitalists.

One way of improving the success rate with venture capitalists is to know the criteria they use in judging a proposal. Unfortunately, venture capitalists tend to weigh their various criteria differently, depending on (a) the characteristics of the associated industry; (b) the quality of the proposed management team; and (c) the strategy identified for the venture.

Even considering the unique characteristics of each venture and venture capital firm, there are some generalizations that can be made regarding the criteria used to evaluate proposals. Three studies (i.e., MacMillan, Siegel, et al., 1987; Robinson, 1987; Tyebjee & Bruno, 1984) yielded somewhat similar results, except regarding the importance of the entrepreneur's vs. the team's characteristics. A quality team is believed to be the best foundation for a successful competitive strategy. In contrast to the conventional wisdom of the venture capital industry, Tyebjee and Bruno found market attractiveness to be the most important criterion. Outside of this one issue, the results among studies were relatively similar. A fourth study by MacMillan, Zemann, et al. (1987) examined the kinds of criteria used to screen ventures but not the specific criteria per se. For comparative purposes, the criteria venture capitalists use to evaluate venture business proposals according to these four studies are shown in Exhibit 4.1; they illustrate the components of the venture's competitive strategy that contribute to future success and survival.

Addressing the criteria used by venture capitalists is one way to enhance the chances for funding. Another way is to understand some of the differences between funded and

Exhibit 4.1	Competitive Strategy Criteria Used by Venture Capitalists in Evaluating Business Proposals

Tyebjee & Bruno (1984)

- *Market attractiveness:* Is there a market and how attractive is it?
- *Product differentiation:* Does the entrepreneur have technical skills and is the product unique and patentable?
- *Profitability potential:* Can we realistically expect high profits?
- *Managerial capabilities:* Demonstrable skills in management, marketing, and finance.
- Environmental threat resistance: Venture's protection against competitive and non-competitive threats.
- Cash-out potential and ease of exit.

MacMillan, Siegel, et al. (1987)

- *Competitive risk:* Product market threats.
- *Bail-out risk:* Financial potential.
- *Investment risk:* Prospect of attractive returns.
- *Management risk:* Entrepreneur's risk management abilities, capacity for sustained effort, and market familiarity.
- *Implementation risk:* Developing a prototype, market acceptance, and ability to articulate the venture.
- *Leadership risk:* Leadership talent of the entrepreneur.

Robinson (1987)

- Management team.
- Fit between management's technical skills and industry's requirements.
- Resource needs vs. personal skills and motivation of management.
- Venture's financial history.
- Professional references.

MacMillan, Zemann, et al. (1987)

- Criteria that screen out ventures where there is a risk of failure due to unqualified management.
- Criteria that screen out management that may be well qualified but lack experience.
- Criteria that screen out ventures where the basic viability of the project is in doubt.
- Criteria that screen out ventures where there is high exposure to competitive attack and profit erosion before the investment can be recouped.
- Criteria that avoid ventures locking up the investment so that it cannot be cashed out for long periods of time.

non-funded plans. MacMillan and SubbaNarasimha (1986) examined this topic and found that plans that were not funded typically projected extremely optimistic performance results for their venture's competitive strategy. Apparently, venture capitalists identify an upper and lower boundary of acceptable results. Anything outside these limits tends not to impress venture capitalists, which prevents the plan from being funded. Unfortunately, these limits cannot really be identified because they are unique to each venture capital firm; each situation is different. Funded plans tended to have a balance in terms of the material devoted to each functional area of the business (e.g., marketing, finance, production, etc.), that is, the necessary ingredients for a successful competitive strategy, while plans that were not funded did not demonstrate this balance.

Another study highlighted just how difficult it is to evaluate new venture proposals. Examining businesses that had already received venture capital funding, MacMillan, Zemann, et al. (1987) found that proposed business plans could be classified into three unsuccessful and four successful venture types. Unfortunately, these types are difficult to evaluate because the unsuccessful ventures were virtually mirror images of the successful ventures, with typically only one characteristic separating the successful from the unsuccessful venture. The bottom line is that a proposal might conform to every characteristic and suggestion listed here, but a large component of venture evaluation and acceptance is more an "art" than a "science."

ENVIRONMENTAL FACTORS

Goodwin and Ibrahim's (1987) study specifically identifies three environmental factors that contribute to small-business success, namely, interest rates, taxes, and government assistance. The following factors should also be added: inflation, the founder's choice of geographical location, the regulatory climate, technology transfer programs, incubator and entrepreneurship centers, luck, the structure of the industry in which the business competes, timing, and in the case of high-tech firms, the presence of a cluster of other technology companies (Goss & Vozikis, 1994). Exhibit 4.2 illustrates these factors, plus several others related to these general categories.

Can all of these economic variables be controlled or even affected by an individual entrepreneur or small-business person? Typically not, but they are on every list of factors that most often contribute to small-business failure. Therefore, entrepreneurs or small-business persons who wish to succeed when seeking funding must, at the very least, be educated and aware of these issues, and they must be able to demonstrate that they will be able to capitalize on opportunities when they present themselves and that they are able to avoid pitfalls.

As far as interest rates are concerned, many entrepreneurs believe that they are being unjustly singled out as high credit risks. A congressional report based on a survey of the ten largest US banks found that large banks often issue loans to big companies at interest rates lower than the published prime rate. The small firms are never charged an interest rate near the better rates charged bigger corporations. Banks frequently believe they must charge more for smaller loans to compensate for a higher cost of money. They privately concede that it is usually more advantageous for a bank to extend credit to a larger corporation than to a smaller company, since larger corporations can afford higher interest costs. Large corporations actually reduce a bank's costs; it is usually advantageous for a bank to receive "service charges" on accounts with larger businesses because they are able to consolidate a wide variety of the company's banking functions. The small-business mentality is different than that of larger firms, and the entrepreneurial mentality is different from that of the small-business person. Unfortunately, the majority of bankers seldom relate to either because their job is to make loans that do not go bad, not to take excessive risks on someone starting a new venture. Another reason small businesses suffer disproportionately from higher interest rates is that they typically have less equity than larger companies. Their needs have to be met by short-term debt, which again makes them less attractive to both long-term lenders and investors.

Inflation, while no longer at the high levels of the late 1970s, is an often-misunderstood phenomenon in relation to small business. As damaging as inflation may seem, the truth is that inflation results in increased prices, which can help to keep a lot of poorly run companies above water. Alan Greenspan, Chairman of the Federal Reserve Bank,

| Exhibit 4.2 | Environmental Factors Contributing to Venture Success |

Interest Rates, Inflation, and Taxes

Choice of Location

- Trained Business Professionals and Consultants
- Community Networking Opportunities
- Proximity to a Good University
- Labor Supply

Transportation

Utilities

Industry Structure

Regulatory Climate

Federal, State, and Local Government Assistance

Technology Transfer Programs

Incubator and Entrepreneurship Centers

Presence of a Cluster of Other Technology Firms

Timing

Luck

labeled inflation as "clearly the number one reason that a higher percentage of businesses managed to survive in the late '70s." This unusual effect occurs because borderline businesses may run up large debts. In this case, inflation makes such debts cheaper and cheaper to repay, because in the long run, lenders may charge fixed interest rates that prove to be lower than the inflation rate. For borrowers, this is a splendid arrangement because they are able to repay loans with dollars that are depreciating at a higher rate than their interest charges (Malabre, 1980, p. 40). High inflation also helps smaller businesses because it fosters a climate in which badly managed companies can more easily survive by continuing to sell goods and services of inferior quality with widely expected price increases. Similarly, inflation bolsters profits, though in an unsound manner, by exaggerating the value of assets, by producing inventory profits, and by creating earnings write-offs for the depreciation of equipment that are unrealistically low (i.e., that do not reflect true replacement costs) (ibid.).

The federal tax structure includes a big-business bias: it is unduly complex and fails to take into account the special needs and problems of the small firm. Such problems include understanding and complying with the tax system at all levels of government; retaining needed capital for operations and growth; acquiring long-term financing and equity capital; maintaining the independence of the small business as a viable objective; and providing financial security for the entrepreneur. Small firms that are capital-intensive enough to benefit from depreciation schemes and investment tax credits must assemble a battery of high-paid accountants, lawyers, and tax consultants to understand the complex array of today's tax laws. Complicated exemptions, record-keeping requirements, and other complex features combine to produce a heavy compliance burden for the small business.

Location choice is another critical consideration for new ventures seeking funding, because it contributes to success in a variety of ways. For example, today's emphasis on economic development by state and local officials is a bonanza to entrepreneurial ventures able to take advantage of the incentives and subsidies being offered. Some locations can provide a community infrastructure that enhances the chances of developing new ventures, such as the existence of local venture capital, Chamber of Commerce support, and workshops (e.g., on financing, marketing, etc., for small-businesses, by trained professionals in law, accounting, insurance, or banking). The choice of location can also reinforce the validity of an entrepreneurial effort by providing psychological support and solid networking from nearby successful entrepreneurs and small-business owners. Some locations are much more supportive of start-ups and young growth companies and every year; many financial publications and magazines produce rankings of cities with business-friendly climates. Typically, locations with both a high frequency of start-ups and excellent support for growth companies have a mix of characteristics, including close proximity to a university with a strong graduate program that can facilitate technology transfer, a good labor supply, excellent transportation facilities, a superior educational system, good and inexpensive utility services, access to suppliers, and professional assistance.

The industry structure sometimes takes on a life of its own in a particular location. For instance, Atlanta's excellent transportation facilities and centralized regional location makes it a home base for numerous distribution companies. Omaha, Nebraska, has 25 telemarketing centers employing 10,000 people. Why has Omaha become the national center for this industry? It is a centrally located in the United States, and the midwestern population has no noticeable accent. Thus, there is less chance of insulting someone when contacting them by telephone. Socorro, New Mexico, has become the center of expertise in explosives technology because it offers huge chunks of vacant land right outside the New Mexico Institute of Mining and Technology. Anyone working with explosives knows that transporting experimental explosive devices long distances is not particularly safe.

The regulatory climate is another element that can influence the success of start-ups and existing small businesses. For instance, Arizona, which has been consistently ranked at or near the top in new jobs, business births, and growth climate, offers a very favorable regulatory environment, a pro-business attitude, reasonable tax rates, moderate labor laws, and the presence of a large number of high-tech companies, which spin off many new ventures. New jobs in Arizona originate from three sources: (a) 5% from out-of-state recruiting; (b) 49% from expanding existing firms already in the state; and (c) 55% from new businesses from local industry (Charland, 1988). Recognizing the favorable regulatory environment on a state level can benefit the entrepreneur seeking subsidies, inexpensive financing, and/or a core group of skilled personnel.

Government assistance on all levels, federal, state, and local, also takes many different forms. Government-financed and government-backed loans are available through a number of sources. In Colorado, for example, the Colorado Department of Local Affairs, the Colorado Housing and Finance Authority, and the Farmers Home Administration all offer such loans. Similar programs exist in other states.

Technology transfer programs like Pennsylvania's Ben Franklin Partnership, Ohio's Thomas Edison Incubator Program, Virginia's Center for Innovative Technology, and Oklahoma's Technology Commercialization Center try to bridge the gap between academic research and industry by finding ways to facilitate the commercialization of technical research. Potential entrepreneurs with an idea for a technology-related business based on technology transfer, or individuals looking for a technically oriented partner, can enhance their chances of success by locating near technology transfer centers and by becoming familiar with technical personnel working in related areas. These centers tend to attract a core mass of expertise, where state-of-the-art technology and knowledge can serve as a good potential source for qualified partners for a venture team.

Incubators, like holding companies, help ventures and especially e-commerce sites get off the ground, nurturing them with sound advice and then "unloading" them when they become profitable. Incubators grow by finding companies with promising business ideas and prospects, but lacking a key ingredient or two, such as office space or technical and legal help, and supplying these missing elements; they most often invest in these companies. They also introduce them to customers of other "incubates," or help them recruit talent, or ultimately help them find prospects for other companies to acquire, or even point them to the right direction of possibly being "harvested" themselves. However, strong companies already have what an incubator provides because they have strong managerial skills, a good business plan, and are already attracting investment and venture capital. Consequently, an incubator is not the right location for strong companies ("Incubators Lay," 2000). Universities, through research parks and Centers of Entrepreneurship, also provide useful services (i.e., housing) and technical assistance to businesses by establishing cooperative research projects among academia and industry. These services may include consulting services and information, often free of charge, through the Service Corps of Retired Executives (*SCORE*), the Small Business Administration (SBA), the Small Business Development and Assistance Centers (*SBDC and SBAC*), Minority Business Development Centers (*MBDC*), and a host of other federal, state, and local government or quasi-government organizations.

Technology firms also tend to prefer to gather around high-technology clusters such as California's Silicon Valley, North Carolina's Research Triangle, Texas's Austin, and Alabama's Huntsville in order to take advantage of the technology climate, and the possibility of "cannibalizing" other firms' technical personnel. Most importantly, tech firms benefit from what the economic literature calls **agglomeration economies**, that is, the benefits of just being in an environment that is conducive to high-tech opportunities and being associated with other similarly minded entrepreneurs and high-tech firms (Goss & Vozikis, 1994).

Finally, timing and luck are issues that are always present and could have a tremendous impact. However, as mentioned earlier, timing and luck need to be treated in a way that ensures that the venture's success relies upon them as little as possible.

Much of what has been discussed regarding the environmental factors contributing to a venture's success appears to benefit the venture entrepreneur because the prospective entrepreneurial venture has more to gain from favorable environmental factors than a small business. This is because small-business persons generally begin their businesses within a short distance of their home city; they rarely move to start a business. Small businesses are often started to enact a profession or to pursue a personal interest, often a craft or a trade whose success depends on the businessperson's knowledge of the local area. They trade in a much more restricted region, and they are more interested in maintaining their business and their personal lifestyle than being bothered with growth. They strive for personal income and security. Because of their more limited objectives and focus, the small-business person often finds that the support mechanisms offered by the government and other organizations are of little use, or worse, are completely irrelevant for their purposes, because such programs tend to be heavily oriented to assisting growth firms.

DEMOGRAPHIC, PSYCHOLOGICAL, AND BEHAVIORAL FACTORS

Much research in the entrepreneurship field has focused on the person of the entrepreneur, asking the question: Why do certain individuals start ventures successfully when others, under similar conditions, do not? Asking *why* here leads to the question of *who*. Certain inner qualities and traits differentiate entrepreneurs from non-entrepreneurs.

However, a startling number of traits and characteristics have been attributed to the entrepreneur, and an entrepreneurial "psychological profile" assembled from these research studies tends to portray someone larger than life, full of contradictions, and conversely, someone so full of "traits" that the term dissolves into a generic "Everyman" (Gartner et al., 1988). Importantly, being a successful entrepreneur is not equivalent to being a modern-day Renaissance person.

The focus in this section, however, is not to define who is an entrepreneur but rather to identify the variety of characteristics that have been considered important for success by investors, lenders, and venture capitalists during the funding evaluation process in entrepreneurial ventures and/or small businesses. Psychological and behavioral factors are inextricably bound; to understand behavior, one has to understand why the person behaves in a particular manner, because personality cannot be separated from other aspects of life (Carland et al., 1988, p. 35).

Successful venture performance is determined by events before, during, and after the creation of the venture. Many of the key behavioral determinants of successful entrepreneurship can be learned from experience, from education, from workshops and seminars, from role models, and from a variety of other sources of knowledge and information.

In this sense, an entrepreneur is not only born but can be made better. In other words, it is not only about traits; entrepreneurs *somehow* have learned to take the steps required to set up a successful business. This could settle the argument whether entrepreneurship can be taught, because, as Gartner advocates, "It's like tennis, I cannot guarantee how good you will be if you take a course, but we can pretty much get you up to speed. We can provide the skill sets" ("Where Are We Now," 2001).

Exhibit 4.3 lists a number of demographic as well as behavioral and psychological variables that investors and potential team members seek in entrepreneurs. Five groups combining both psychological and behavioral characteristics have been identified, but this is by no means a definitive categorization; rather, it is one of many possible frameworks.

The demographic characteristics pertain to gender, age, household income/net worth, education, role models, and experience, while the groups of psychological and behavioral characteristics, not necessarily in any ranking order, are as follows:

1. Inquisitiveness and risk acceptance
2. Motivation and leadership
3. Professionalism and self-confidence
4. Adaptability to their environment
5. Achievement and action-orientation

Virtually every study of entrepreneurs and/or small-business people has found consistent conclusions regarding demographic variables. Entrepreneurs are more likely to be males and to be better educated as a whole ("Today's Self-employed," 2001). Age is irrelevant to starting a business, but certain characteristics related to age are considerations. For example, in most cases, the younger entrepreneur the less business experience, but at the same time, younger entrepreneurs tend to have more energy and enthusiasm. Every so often, the latter makes up for the former.

Family role models influence the likelihood of starting a business, and they provide psychological support and background for venturing efforts. Education, life, and job

| Exhibit 4.3 | Demographic, Psychological, and Behavioral Characteristics Contributing to New Venture Performance |

Demographic Variables

- Gender
- Age
- Household Income/Net worth
- Education
- Role Models
- Experience

Psychological and Behavioral Variables

Inquisitiveness and Risk Acceptance
- Willingness to learn about and invest in new techniques
- Propensity to take calculated risks
- Team building
- Overcoming the fear of failure

Motivation and Leadership
- Ability to activate vision and instill it in others
- Sense of humility
- Leading by example
- Sensitivity and respect for employees
- Builds and sustains an entrepreneurial culture
- Positive role model
- Encourages people to do their best
- Shares rewards

Professionalism and Self-Confidence
- Projects a successful image
- Interested in and enjoying business
- Has discipline to sit down and plan
- Good physical health, energy, stamina
- Emotional stability
- Positive mental attitude
- A sense of optimism and self-confidence
- Pays attention to details
- Not afraid to stand out from the crowd
- Internal locus of control
- Integrity and reliability

Adaptability to Environment
- Flexibility and adaptation to change
- Learns from mistakes
- Emphasizes tolerance
- Able to conceive the environment accurately
- Keeps things in perspective between business and personal life
- Seeks and uses feedback to develop innovative ways to exploit opportunities
- Focuses mostly on opportunities, not problems
- Tolerance for ambiguity and uncertainty
- Creative and innovative

Achievement and Action-Orientation
- Taking personal initiative
- Ambitious
- Patience with people, but impatient with obstacles
- Goal-oriented and goal-directed
- Total commitment and determination to succeed
- Achievement-oriented
- Tenacity, perseverance, and desire to overcome hurdles
- Low need for status and power
- Decisiveness

experiences, which shape personalities and attitudes toward risk-taking, achievement, control, etc., alert the entrepreneur to particular opportunities. In fact, the National Panel Study of U.S. Business Start-ups conducted a large-scale study that compared nascent entrepreneurs to a control group of Americans who were not starting a business. The results indicated that more than 90% of business founders *already* had prior experience in the line of business in which they created their new venture and/or that they ran another business of their own when they started a new company ("The Founder," 2001).

Prior management and marketing experience plus a proven prior success record tend to enhance the entrepreneur's chances of obtaining outside funding. How does experience work? Not surprisingly, experience provides a set of rules-of-thumb to guide the entrepreneur. It allows entrepreneurs and small-business people to operate in familiar territory and with familiar people, suppliers, distributors, customers, etc. But to truly enhance the chances for success, experience needs to be combined with education. One without the other is no guarantee of failure, but whem combined the odds of success improve. Education plays a key role in determining success because entrepreneurs can be made better. Numerous programs on the fundamentals of starting, developing, and growing a business are available at colleges and universities, Chambers of Commerce, SBA workshops, and many other sources.

In contrast, psychological and behavioral variables describe *who* the entrepreneur is (psychological or personality traits) and *what* the entrepreneur *actually does* (behavioral activities). As Exhibit 4.3 indicated, this covers a lot of ground; to group these variables into a more manageable set and discuss them in some logical fashion, they were classified into five categories, with each category having its own differentiating logic that separates it from the others. While each category of these attributes may contribute to success in a certain way, it should be emphasized that their absence also provides the entrepreneur with an opportunity to seek these characteristics among potential partners, business associates, and team members. Having a team whose whole exceeds the sum of its parts is attractive to investors, lenders, potential customers, team members, and many other stakeholders.

Inquisitiveness and Risk Acceptance

The propensity of entrepreneurs to take calculated risks and be sensitive to risks within certain limits, or in other terms, **inquisitiveness and risk acceptance**, has been well researched by academics. Unfortunately, the myth that entrepreneurs are gamblers or big risk-takers still exists. The research, however, proves otherwise; it indicates that successful entrepreneurs minimize their risks by consciously following strategies where risk is clearly defined and managed and by buffering themselves personally and financially from the dire consequences of excessive risk. Additionally, learning how to share the risks with partners, investors, customers, suppliers, distributors, and others is a critical requirement for a successful venture. Mitton (1984) found that successful entrepreneurs do the following:

- They initiate and orchestrate actions, which, while not risky to themselves, have risk consequences. And while they shun risk, they sustain their courage by the clarity and optimism with which they see the future.

- They limit the risks they initiate by carefully defining and strategizing their ends, controlling and monitoring their means, and tailoring them both to what they see the future to be.

- They manage risk by transferring it to others. This way they leverage their position by using resources other than their own, and, in so doing, the rewards of success far outdistance the penalties of falling short. (p. 427)

Motivation and Leadership

It is seldom that a single individual starts any successful business undertaking alone. Instead, a team of individuals is critical not only for their complementary skills but also to demonstrate that the idea is sellable and that the venture's founder has been able to communicate and instill his or her vision in other people. Simply put, for the venture to achieve success, the team's individual members need to be as committed and enthusiastic about the opportunity's value concept as the founder. Certainly this is a critical issue, but once the venture is past start-up, founders have just as difficult a task confronting them. They must continue to build the firm, but at the same time they must sustain an entrepreneurial culture that enables new products and services to continually be developed and improved. To accomplish this, the successful entrepreneurs must motivate, lead, understand, and respect the people they come in contact with, such as customers, employees, investors, suppliers, etc., and they must encourage the team to continue to excel. Entrepreneurs must be positive role models, leading by example rather than by telling. Simultaneously, they must exert relatively tight financial, managerial, and communication controls during the early stages of the venture. This last characteristic contradicts the popular literature concept that emphasizes independence, informal management styles, limited controls, etc.. Stuart and Abetti's (1987) research, however, contradicts this popular view: they found success positively linked to the entrepreneur's strong control and guidance during the formative stages.

Professionalism and Self-Confidence

Much of the entrepreneur and small-business person's success is tied to their ability to market their ideas, themselves, and their products or services. Since many of them lack a proven "track record" when they first start out, they must find some other way to communicate their enthusiasm and professional competency (Dible, 1986). They must be able persuade people to join their team, persuade investors to fund their ideas, and persuade customers to buy. One of the keys to doing this is to project a professional image and to exude self-confidence to gain the confidence of others. Successful entrepreneurs believe in themselves and their abilities. They tend to be internally directed and to have an internal locus of control. Success or failure is not a random event determined by timing, luck, or happenstance, it can be controlled and influenced by the entrepreneur's actions or inactions. These desirable characteristics are further solidified by the individual's ability to make time to carefully plan for the future, while giving attention to the daily myriad of details that, if left unattended, can easily turn a winner into a loser.

Establishing a successful image should also be tied to high ethical standards and good physical and emotional health. These characteristics convey the ability to combat the pressures of starting and growing a business as well as fully participating in the business world's network. In addition to these characteristics, the entrepreneurial leader must also demonstrate a positive mental attitude, optimism, and a sense of confidence in both the business venture and the people involved.

Adaptability to the Environment

The ability to adapt to their environment is clearly a skill that entrepreneurs must possess if they desire to be both successful in their start-up efforts and to maintain their venture's viability as they grow. This behavior appears to revolve around four characteristics. First, they seem to have an ability to perceive the realities of their environment relatively accurately, and at the same time, they not only adapt to the changes in the environment, but they also focus on the opportunities that these changes represent. Secondly, they learn from their mistakes, and they are not afraid of criticism. Instead, they seek feedback and use it to develop innovative methods to take advantage of their opportunities. Third, they are able to keep a balance between their personal and their business lives. They stress tolerance of the ambiguity, complexity, and uncertainty surrounding them, and they try to keep everything in perspective, emphasizing what really matters. Those who do not often find themselves plagued with unhappy personal and family lives. Finally, entrepreneurs bring creative and innovative approaches to bear on new opportunities, instead of using the same old tactics and *modus operandi.*

Achievement and Action-Oriented Characteristics

Much has been written about the entrepreneur's need for achievement. It is perhaps the primary motivational force at work within the entrepreneur. Indeed, the very act of starting a new business personifies the need for achievement (McClelland, 1961). Successful entrepreneurs tend to be self-motivated individuals with a strong desire to overcome challenges. Obviously, an attractive challenge to entrepreneurs is the ability to start and succeed in their own business. They set high but realistic goals, and they compete against self-imposed standards. They look for moderate risks and use feedback when possible to gauge their progress. They use money to keep score, rather than as an end in itself.

Along with the traditional need for achievement behaviors, some other action-oriented characteristics are important in determining performance, such as the need to take personal initiative, to be ambitious and to take action, to be patient with people but impatient with obstacles, to be totally committed and determined to succeed, and to be tenacious and persevering in pursuing an opportunity's value concept. Finally, entrepreneurs have a low need for status and power, because it is the need for achievement that drives them, rather than the desire for power and control over others (Timmons et al., 1985).

MANAGEMENT PRACTICES

A lack of superior management practices is consistently cited as one of the primary reasons for the failure of small venture firms. Unfortunately, the degree to which management practices are a cause versus a symptom of failure is much more difficult to assess (Vesper, 1980).

Nevertheless, an extensive body of literature exists that has identified the types of problems, critical issues, and causes of failure encountered by small firms, as they relate to inadequate and ineffectual managerial practices. Exhibit 4.4 is such a list, compiled from a review of the literature. These studies lead to one fundamental conclusion: most small-firm managerial problems are essentially problems of poor managerial practices, even problems of other functional business areas, such as finance or marketing. They are generally internal to the firm (i.e., within the scope of responsibility of the manager), and they appear to play a much more important role after the start-up phase is completed.

CONCLUSION

An enormous number of success factors, if addressed properly, can significantly improve the odds for survival, growth, and overall success. These factors are many and complicated. Indeed, many are firm or industry specific, but many others are considerably easier to generalize. Some result from rigorous research studies; others originate from the anecdotes and experiences of successful entrepreneurs.

Unfortunately, they do not all contribute equally to success, nor do they contribute in every situation. Indeed, several of the factors have produced contradictory results. For example, in one study they are identified as prime determinants of success, and in another they may be minor considerations or even completely immaterial. Rather than try to settle the debate by critiquing the research, we preferred to cast our net as broadly as possible and to identify the factors that have been considered important in determining the odds of success for either entrepreneurial ventures or small businesses.

The key to success lies in the venture's value concept idea, its strategic target market, the original feasibility study, the venture's formal business plan, the financial statements, and

Exhibit 4.4	Critical Problems of Small Firms

General Management

1. Dependence for survival on a principal manager or a "one-man show."
2. Neglect of selection and supervision of personnel.
3. Lack of planning and information.
4. Lack of management development.
5. Lack of management and coordination.
6. Lack or misuse of time.

Operations

1. Lack of operating experience in product buying, pricing, and handling finances.
2. Poor record keeping and control.
3. Inventory mismanagement—not the right kind or amount.
4. Wrong location.
5. Competitive weakness and diseconomies of scale in purchasing, operating, etc.
6. Heavy operating expenses and overhead.
7. Wrong overall attitudes of avoiding hard work and responsibility for the firm's operations.

Finance

1. Lack of total capital.
2. Lack of financial planning and use of financial information and ratios.
3. Lack of working capital.
4. Poor credit practices and overextension of credit and bad debts.
5. Slow collection of accounts receivable.
6. High debt level.
7. Improper application of capital.

Marketing

1. Non-aggressive selling, promotion, and advertising.
2. Inadequate sales.
3. Lack of concentration on result areas of products, markets, and technology.
4. Lack of research and development and product upgrading.
5. Poor knowledge of markets.
6. Poor knowledge of competition.

Source: Vozikis, 1979.

the quality of the management of the firm proving the ability to "execute." Information pertaining to all these factors should be thoroughly examined and reexamined to allay any fears of failure, because entrepreneurs will be doing both themselves and their investors or lenders a tremendous disservice if they enter into any new venture ill prepared. However, once the venture's success framework is ready, the enormous possibilities of the venture should justify a very optimistic outlook for its success.

Website Information

Topic	Web Address	Description
Entrepreneurship Theory and Practice	http://business.baylor.edu/entrepreneur/default.aspx?pageID=241	Subscription information, links to other entrepreneurial sites, back issues, history of the journal.
Incubator and Entrepreneurship Centers	http://www.entrepreneur.com/article/201228	Contemporary perspectives on business incubators.
Financial Environmental Factors	http://www.bls.gov/cpi	Helpful site for researching statistics about current and past economic trends, tables, graphs, and other websites.
Technology Transfer Programs	http://www.benfranklin.org	Informative website about what the Ben Franklin Partnership does, where it is located, and the companies it supports.
Minority Business Development Centers	http://www.mbda.gov	Stories about new businesses, home businesses, small, medium, and large businesses, as well as start-up tools and services.

Key Terms

Agglomeration economies: The benefits of being in an environment conducive to similar businesses and opportunities.

Business failure: Business termination with losses to creditors.

Comprehensive strategy of success: Identifies all the personality, demographic, behavioral, environmental, strategic, and other factors affecting a venture's odds of succeeding.

Demographic factors: Where a business is located and what kinds of people (both customers and associates) are in close proximity.

Entrepreneurial strategies: Different set of rules and tactics to help secure the survival and success of a venture.

Environmental factors: Outside factors contributing to a firm's success, such as interest rates, taxes, and government assistance.

Framework for success: Competitive strategy, environmental factors, demographic and psychological behavioral characteristics, and management practices.

Gazelles: Young, high-tech, and venture-capital-focused entrepreneurial ventures, which operate in national or international markets rather than regional ones.

Income-oriented businesses ("small businesses"): Created to serve as a substitute to working for someone else, and the owner has, in a sense, purchased himself/herself a job.

Incubator: A company that helps ventures, especially e-commerce sites, get off the ground, nurturing them with sound advice and then "unloading" them when they become profitable.

Inquisitiveness and risk acceptance: The propensity of entrepreneurs to take calculated risks and be sensitive to risks within certain limits.

Review Questions

1. Describe a few of the ways that a firm can cease operations without experiencing real failure.

2. Entrepreneurial strategies have become a key research topic in new-venture performance. Entrepreneurs should be aware of a few things when looking at this literature. What are they?

3. Identify the reasons that smaller firms are charged higher interest rates than larger firms.

4. Describe the ways in which successful entrepreneurs deal with risk.

5. Critical problems of small firms typically arise out of four main sources. What are they? List some of the problems associated with each source.

6. Evaluate a local agricultural entrepreneur. Would you say they are income oriented or entrepreneurial?

Reflections from the Front Lines of LifeGuard America

The difference between being good and being great is ultimately determined by those whom you surround yourself and how well and how far you are able to project your shared vision. True success, in my book, is measured not in dollars but in the amount of greater good done by a group of individuals acting as one. One of my first endeavors fell prey to the most fundamental of all mistakes an entrepreneur can make: underfunding. TeamwareTM was a software company that developed a solution for the amateur sports enthusiast who managed a league or just wanted to keep track of individual statistics. We had a grand exit strategy of selling to Microsoft, as well as being added to the Microsoft At-Home product line. We badly underestimated the amount of marketing and advertising required to break into the already-established league management software environment. It was the first real lesson in Entrepreneurship 101: take what you think you will need in funding and multiply it by at least 1.5.

I have been blessed, lately, to have the opportunity to pull a group of highly talented people together around a shared vision that saves hundreds of lives every year and is profitable enough to support having fun getting the job done. LifeGuard America, as you will learn later in the book, has a rare opportunity to create a business environment of self-directed work teams with a collaborative approach to R&D. It utilizes the strengths of local higher education to deliver services that saves lives and improves the human condition starting here in America and moving into the international community.

Long ago, I also read what Mark Twain once wrote: "Great people are those who can make others feel that they, too, can become great." I have always believed that you should find a way to help others reach their goals, and in the process you will find that your reward is a byproduct of your actions. I found this to be true in business and the military, whether I was selling to a customer, technically supporting a sales team, or leading a group of fighters to a distant target: find out what will make the other guy successful and help him/her get there. I also have come to realize that this manner of work ethic builds trust and loyalty, which are absolutely required when building a successful venture around a shared vision.

The fear of failure is not a driver for me, but rather the desire to succeed is. It is also important for me to be a part a something bigger than myself. I have always felt most successful in my business life when I was around a group of talented people who were highly driven by the objective at hand. Base your endeavor's success factors on meaningful objectives that make your customers more successful, and I will guarantee that revenue will follow. Do not become consumed by the fear of failing but rather driven by the absolute need to successfully implement your business plan for the sake of your customers. This focus will see you through the tough times when everything appears to be going against you and your plans. The words of Michael Jordan are timeless and always pertinent: "I have missed more than 9,000 shots in my career. I have lost almost 300 games. On 26 occasions, I have been entrusted to take the game winning shot . . . and I missed. I have failed over and over and over again in my life. And that's precisely why I succeed."

Discussion Questions on LifeGuard America

1. How do you think entrepreneurs can best protect themselves from the most basic of mistakes when they are first starting out?

2. Mr. Fitzpatrick sounds like an idealist. Do you believe that success is really a function of the people who are a part of your venture?

3. What are your fears? Is failure one of them? How important do you think not having a real fear of failure is when it comes to starting a new business venture?

References

Baron, R. A. & Ensley, M. D. (2006). Opportunity recognition as the detection of meaningful patterns: Evidence from comparisons of novice and experienced entrepreneurs. *Management Science, 52,* 1331–1344.

Birch, D. (1987). *Job creation in America.* New York: MacMillan, Inc.

Birch, D. (1988a, January). The truth about start-ups. *Inc. Magazine, 10*(1), 14–15.

Birch, D. (1988b, February). RFD Inc. *Inc. Magazine, 10*(2), 14–15.

Birch, D. (1988c, July). What goes up. *Inc. Magazine, 10*(7), 25–26.

Birch, D. (2001, May 29). The gazelle theory. *Inc. Magazine, 23*(7), 28–29.

Brockhaus, R. (1982). The psychology of the entrepreneur. In C. A. Kent, D. L. Sexton, & K. H. Vesper (Eds.), *Encyclopedia of entrepreneurship* (pp. 39–57). Englewood Cliffs, NJ: Prentice-Hall.

Bygrave, W. D. (1997). *The portable MBA in entrepreneurship* (2nd ed.). Hoboken, NJ: John Wiley & Sons.

Carland, J., Hoy, F., Boulton, W., & Carland, J. (1984, April). Differentiating entrepreneurs from small business owners: A conceptualization. *Academy of Management Review, 9*(2), 354–359.

Carland, J., Hoy, F., & Carland, J. (1988, Spring). "Who is an entrepreneur?" Is a question worth asking. *American Journal of Small Business, 12*(4), 33–39.

Charland, W. (1988, July 17). Colorado's shotgun approach to development misses mark. *Denver Post,* p. 1-F.

Dean, T. J. & McMullen, J. S. (2007). Toward a theory of sustainable entrepreneurship: Reducing environmental degradation through entrepreneurial action. *Journal of Business Venturing, 22,* 50–76.

Dew, N., Sarasvathy, S. D., & Venkataraman, S. (2004). The economic implications of exaptation. *Journal of Evolutionary Economics,* 14, 69–84.

Dible, D. (1986). *Up your own organization!* Reston, VA: Reston.

Dorsey, T. (1979). *Operating guidelines for effective venture capital funds management.* Austin: University of Texas.

Drucker, P. (1985*). Innovation and entrepreneurship*. New York: Perennial Library.

The founder next door. (2001, May 29*). Inc. Magazine, 23*(7), 72–73.

Gartner, W., Carland, J. W., Hoy, F., & Carland, J. C. (1988, Spring). "Who is an entrepreneur?" Is the wrong question. *American Journal of Small Business, 12*(4), 11–32.

Goodwin, J., & Ibrahim, A. B. (1987). *Small business success factors*: An empirical study. Unpublished manuscript.

Goss, E. P., & Vozikis, G. S. (1994, August). High-tech manufacturing: Firm size, industry size, and population density. *Small Business Economics, 6*(4), 291–297.

Hanson, M. & Chen, E. (2007). Socioeconomic status and health behaviors in adolescence: A review of the literature. *Journal of Behavioral Medicine, 30,* 263–285.

Hofer, C., & Sandberg, W. (1987, Summer). Improving new venture performance: Some guidelines for success. *American Journal of Small Business, 12*(1), 11–25.

Hyatt, J. (1988, May). The Inc. 100 portfolio. *Inc. Magazine, 10*(5), 102–104.

Incubators lay an egg financially. (2000, December 10). *Honolulu Advertiser*, p. 16.

Leiserowitz, A. A., Kates, R. W., & Parris, T. M. (2006). Sustainability values, attitudes, and behaviors: A review of multinational and global trends. *Annual Review of Environment and Resources, 31,* 413–444.

MacMillan, I., & Day, D. (1987, Winter). Corporate ventures into industrial markets: Dynamics of aggressive entry. *Journal of Business Venturing, 2*(1), 29–40.

MacMillan, I. C., Siegel, R., & SubbaNarasimha, P. N. (1985). Criteria used by venture capitalists to evaluate new venture proposals. In J. A. Hornaday, et al. (Eds.), *Frontiers of Entrepreneurship Research* (pp. 126–141). Wellesley, MA: Babson College.

MacMillan, I., & SubbaNarasimha, P. N. (1986). Characteristics distinguishing funded from unfunded business plans evaluated by venture capitalists. In R. Ronstadt, et al. (Eds.), *Frontiers of Entrepreneurship Research* (pp. 404–413). Wellesley, MA: Babson College.

MacMillan, I., Zemann, L., & SubbaNarasimha, P. N. (1987, Spring). Criteria distinguishing successful from unsuccessful ventures in the venture screening process. *Journal of Business Venturing, 2*(2), 123–137.

Malabre, A., Jr. (1980, March 12). Despite a worrisome rise, far fewer firms fail nowadays then before inflation roared. *The Wall Street Journal*, p. 40.

McClelland, D. (1961). *The achieving society*. Princeton, NJ: Van Nostrand.

McDougall, P., and Robinson, R., Jr. (1987). New venture strategies: An empirical identification of eight distinct strategic orientations. In F. Hoy (Ed.), *Academy of management proceedings* (pp. 73–77). Briarcliff Manor, NY: Academy of Management.

Mitton, D. (1984). No money, know-how, know-who: Formula for managing venture success and personal wealth. In J. A. Hornaday, et al. (Eds.), *Frontiers of entrepreneurship research* (pp. 414–428). Wellesley, MA: Babson College.

National Research Council. (1999*). Our common journal. A transition toward sustainability*. Washington, DC: National Academy Press.

Padua, M. G. (2007). Designing an identity: The synthesis of a post-traditional landscape vocabulary in Hong Kong. *Landscape Research, 32,* 225–240.

Parris, T. M. & Kates, R. W. (2003). Characterizing and measuring sustainable development. *Annual Review of Environment and Resources, 28,* 559–586.

Richman, T. (1986, May). Seeing red. *Inc. Magazine, 8*(5), 77–79.

Richman, T. (1988, May). In the black. *Inc. Magazine, 10*(5), 116–120.

Robinson, R., Jr. (1987, Winter). Emerging strategies in the venture capital industry. *Journal of Business Venturing, 2*(1), 53–77.

Sandberg, W. (1986). *New venture performance: The role of strategy and industry structure*. Lexington, MA: Lexington Books.

Sandberg, W., Schweiger, D., & Hofer, C. (1987). Determining venture capitalists' decision criteria: The use of verbal protocols. In N. C. Churchill, et al. (Eds.), *Frontiers of business venturing* (pp. 392–407). Wellesley, MA: Babson College.

Shane, S. (2000). Prior knowledge and the discovery of entrepreneurial opportunities. *Organization Science, 11,* 448–469.

Shepherd, D. A., McMullen, J. S., & Jennings, P. D. (2008). The formation of opportunity beliefs: Overcoming ignorance and reducing doubt. *Strategic Entrepreneurship Journal, 1,* 75–95.

Stuart, R., & Abetti, P. (1987, Summer). Start-up ventures: Towards the prediction of initial success. *Journal of Business Venturing, 2*(3), 215–230.

Timmons, J., Smollen, L., & Dingee, A., Jr. (1985). *New venture creation.* Homewood, IL: Richard D. Irwin.

Today's self-employed American. (2001, May 29). *Inc. Magazine, 23*(7), 45.

Twenge, J. M. & Campbell, W. K. (2002). Self-esteem and socioeconomic status: A meta-analytic review. *Personality and Social Psychology Review, 6,* 59–71.

Tyebjee, T., & Bruno, A. (1984, September). A model of venture capitalist investment activity. *Management Science,* 30(9), 1051–1066.

Vesper, K. H. (1980). *New venture strategies.* Englewood Cliffs, NJ: Prentice-Hall.

Vozikis, G. S. (1979). *A strategic disadvantage profile of the stages of development of small business: The experience of retail and service small business in Georgia.* Unpublished doctoral dissertation, The University of Georgia, Athens.

Where are we now. (2001, May 29). *Inc. Magazine, 23*(7), 18–19.

Venture Initiation

5 Venture Idea Sources and Opportunities

Can We Make a Value Concept Niche for the Customer? Why Buy?

LEARNING OBJECTIVES

1. To understand that there are almost limitless sources of ideas.
2. To identify these sources of ideas.
3. To learn how to systematically pursue the opportunities presented by the sources of ideas.
4. To be able to distinguish the most promising ideas and relate them to a specific entrepreneurial situation.

TOPIC OUTLINE

Introduction
Creativity
Intuition
Innovation
– Dos
– Don'ts
Ideas from Education
The Most Popular Idea: The Family Business
Invention
Hobby
Home-Based Businesses
Moonlighting

Buying an Existing Firm
– Financial Evaluation of an Existing Business
Direct Mail
"Unincorporated" Executives
Starting Up Again
Franchising
Conclusion
Website Information
Key Terms
Review Questions
Case Study
References

"Imagine . . ."
(John Lennon)

———

INTRODUCTION

Ken Paulson, Executive Director of the First Amendment Center, encapsulated the American spirit in a newspaper editorial published across the nation in September 2003 with the following words:

> "This nation was founded by hell-raisers, dissenters, and rebels. That willingness to raise issues, question authority, and take risks has served us well for more than 200 years. That spirit can be summed up in a few words and can even fit on the front of a T-shirt: *DARE TO BE FREE!*"

Entrepreneurs apparently are not averse to dissent, creative maneuvering, and starting something out of nothing in the pursuit of happiness, independence, and freedom. According to one survey, when asked how they came to own their firms, 42% of business owners said they started their business from nothing, 23% said they purchased it, 22% said the business was passed on to them from the family, 5% reported it was a spin-off from another business, and the remainder 8% was "other" (Laventhol & Horvath, 1987). As Thurow writes, "Take two guys just graduating from the same business school: The bureaucrat among the two will figure out the odds of the new venture objectively, while the other guy, the entrepreneur, will say, 'These are the odds the way I'm going to make them. I'm going to do whatever it takes to make it work. If my dumb uncle can do it, then I can certainly do it!'" (Thurow, 1980, p. 7).

The essence of entrepreneurship is creativity. Products, customers, and start-up costs of ideas that entrepreneurs turn into businesses vary, but they all share the spirit of creativity and innovation. Creative "balloons" rise until one pops and bathes the prospective entrepreneurs in creative "juices." Suddenly you know, *this is it !* Whether introducing a new technology or offering a better product, ideas start with an inspiration that gets developed into a value concept and then into an opportunity that fills a customer need. For success, ultimately the 1% inspiration is as critical as the 1% market timing, or as the 98% of perspiration and hard work (Robinett, 1985).

How important is the original idea to the development of a significant business? By itself, not very important, but with hindsight it appears critical. The original inspirational idea is likely to endure and become a business only if it is anchored in a niche serving a specific customer and market need with real benefits derived from a value concept.

The word **niche** is a French word meaning "bird's nest." This bird's nest safeguards, incubates, and nurtures the entrepreneurial idea and ultimately ensures the survival of the value concept by providing answers to these fundamental questions: Why is the idea concept of any value? Why should a customer buy it? And why from your niche? How does the value idea concept provide added value to a customer's buying decision? How does the customer's decision to buy this particular value idea concept compare to similar and/or other purchasing decisions?

Good ideas do not always look very good at first glance or even at a second glance; rather, they may sound strange, crazy, or obscure. As a matter of fact, if people say you have a wonderful idea, you may be in trouble: an idea everybody acknowledges as wonderful has probably arrived at the scene too late (Hawken, 1987).

CREATIVITY

Creativity is often confused with innovation. Creativity deals with the invention of something new. Innovation involves putting this new idea into use. Consequently, an innovator may or may not be the creative force behind an innovation, but he or she is always the actual originator of the idea (Fonvielle, 1987). Creativity is the mental process that leads to solutions, ideas, conceptualizations, artistic forms, theories or products that are unique or novel. Creative thought calls for the use of the right side of the brain or "soft" thinking, as opposed to logical, left-brain, "hard" thinking (Duncan, 1992).

Creativity can be defined as the production of novel ideas that are useful and appropriate to the situation, regardless of the type of idea, as the reasons behind its production, or as the starting point of the process. Why do people engage in creative activity? What is the initial trigger? The first question involves the drivers for idea generation, whereas the second involves the degree of problem-finding effort to trigger the process (Unsworth, 2001).

Creativity is a vital ingredient for any new venture. Entrepreneurs must think outside of the creative norms to improve the chance of success. They must also be creative enough to foresee potential problems for the new venture and to develop a contingency plan to make it work. Even after the new venture begins operation, this creative spirit needs to be maintained. It is common for a firm to lose creativity as it ages for entirely good reasons, such as maximizing business imperatives of coordination, productivity, and control (Amabile, 1998). One suggestion for maintaining workplace creativity is to hire at least a small percentage of oddballs, or smart people who "don't get" how they are supposed to act or think. This may cause difficulty in social interaction, but the differences of opinion will foster creativity (Sutton, 2002).

Research has shown that creativity can be taught, especially in terms of "mental gymnastics engaging the conscious and subconscious parts of the brain" (Smith, 1985, p. 81). It is a mix of logic, intuition, imagination, and knowledge as they all relate to the ability to see connections, contrasts, distinctions, and relationships among people, ideas, things, and processes. Creativity is simply the ability to use different modes of thought.

Two basic types of creativity are internal and external creativity. Internal creativity involves finding new ways of doing things or new things to implement from our own thinking. External creativity means the introduction of new ideas from outside sources. Both of these creativity types are sources for ideas for new businesses (Hemphill & Kuriloff, 1978).

Michael Ray and Rochelle Myers, who teach a course on creativity at Stanford University, offer the following suggestions for developing a springboard for creativity:

- Destroy judgment and create curiosity by attacking barriers to creativity.

- Pay attention by putting your senses to work.

- Do not be afraid to ask dumb questions.

- Do not stress yourself by thinking about creativity.

- Balance concepts by asking yourself if things are "yes" or "no."

- Be creative by being yourself, not someone you are not (Bacas, 1987).

Creativity involves surrounding a problem with a myriad of solutions and dredging up ideas beyond the ordinary. It is like challenging someone to find one hundred uses for a cup. The first twenty are quite obvious, the next batch is farther from ordinary, and the best creative solutions come at the end (Mamis, 1985).

Creative thinkers do not necessarily have the exact characteristics that prescribe their creative traits. Nevertheless, creative individuals share the following common attributes (Smith, 1985):

- *Personality:* Creative types are generally risk takers, independent, highly motivated, skeptics, and hard to get along with. Change and uncertainty do not make them anxious, instead they relish disorder.

- *Childhood:* Creative people were granted unusual freedom and independence during childhood and were exposed to diverse cultural and intellectual possibilities, including financial strain, parental divorce, and a dose of adversity.

- *Social habits:* The creative loner is a myth. In contrast, gifted creators are social "animals," exchanging ideas with friends and colleagues, and talking about their areas of interest with anyone who cares to listen.

- *Education:* School is not a prerequisite for creativity. With its stress on logic and conformity, it may hinder creativity. Tests have shown that a child's creativity plummets 90% between the ages of 5 and 7. By the age of 40, adults possess only 2% of the creative ability they possessed when they were 5. Some creativity may emerge after some degree of college education, but some experts believe that graduate school may actually be detrimental to creative thinking in some fields.

- *Intelligence:* Studies point to approximately 130 IQ as a threshold for creativity. Beyond this level, a higher IQ does not seem to make much difference. Instead, nonintellectual trait differences take over, such as personality and value systems.

- *Know-how:* Mastering a field and developing expertise takes a lot of hard work. Creative inspiration is almost always a product of years of perspiration in a certain field. A 1980 study found that most renowned musicians and painters spent on the average 10 years of hard work before they created a true masterpiece.

Creativity does not happen in a vacuum, and individuals need to create an environment that elicits creativity. Creativity cannot be demanded on the spot, but it can be incorporated as part of the expectations of a task or job (Harris, 2001).

INTUITION

Intuition's role in creativity and innovation is indispensable, yet people frequently discount its value. "It's only a hunch," you've probably said more than once, or "I'm not going to play any hunches." Not trusting hunches may actually impair the ability to make good business decisions. Research shows that business success depends to a large extent on the ability and willingness to make intuitive decisions, frequently with incomplete information and raw data. For entrepreneurs in particular, intuition, combined with the courage to take risks, can be a critical factor in the success of companies.

Long ago, when a paper cup salesman noticed the long lines at a Walgreen Drug's soda fountain, he had a gut feeling that milkshakes should be sold in paper cups that would allow customers to carry them out. Drugstore managers, however, dismissed the salesman's intuitive idea because they claimed that the extra penny and a half for the cup would eat most of their profit on the 15-cent milkshake. The young salesman staked his reputation and personal survival on his intuition and promised the drugstore owners free paper cups for a month if they were willing to try his idea. Sure enough at the end, the take-out milkshake became a big winner. The intuitive salesman, Ray Kroc, made plenty of paper cup commissions, which later helped him start his subsequent venture, McDonald's Corporation (*Inc. Magazine*, 1985).

John Mihalasky, a professor at the New Jersey Institute of Technology, has tested hundreds of business executives for intuitive ability. He found that effective, superior decision making does indeed correlate highly with intuitive ability. In one experiment, Mihalasky chose 25 chief executive officers who had held top positions for at least 5 years in their companies. All came from manufacturing companies with less than $50 million in annual sales. In general, those who scored highest on the intuitive test also reported the greatest increase in company profits. In fact, the high scorer was also the top profit maker, whose company's annual sales had increased from $1.3 million to $19.4 million (Raudsepp, 1981).

The shrewd guess, the fertile hypothesis, the courageous leap to a tentative conclusion, these are the most valuable products of the thinker at work according to Jerome S. Bruner, a visiting scholar in psychology and social relations at Harvard University. Certainly, the history of technology and innovation provides proof that the ideas responsible for great breakthroughs came from intuitive perceptions that were only later tested and verified. Consider, for example, the case of George I. Long, former president of Ampex Corporation. When Long recognized that a product permitting the transcription of TV programs for distribution and rebroadcast had the potential to tap a huge market, others felt that the technical difficulties were too great. They were dubious about the potential market value of the product and considered Ampex too small to tackle the problem. But Long's hunch about the success of the product was so strong that he left another company to join Ampex. The hunch paid off: Videotape established Ampex as an early leader in a booming industry.

But good hunches are not the monopoly of an elite few, like Edwin Land, who followed his hunch that the Polaroid camera would sell despite the ominous forecasts of market surveys. We all know what it feels like when a hunch is born, but often we doubt the trustworthiness of our hunches, and sometimes we do not have the courage to follow through on our insights.

The underlying assumption of intuitive hunches is that entrepreneurs can identify the prospect of a market's failure and recognize and exploit sustainable opportunities by proposing creative solutions to this failure through the application of prior and/or newly acquired entrepreneurial knowledge and thus accumulate economic gain (Cohen & Winn, 2007; Dean & McMullen, 2007). Although hunches can be validated only when acted upon, there are, of course, ways to develop intuitive ability and generate more valid intuitive hunches:

- *Get the facts:* If you are familiar with your business or a particular subject, you are much more likely to intuitively reach an appropriate decision or solution to a problem.

- *Watch out for self-decision:* If a hunch turns out to be wildly wrong, chances are it emerged from wishful or fearful thinking, not from intuition. Be willing to confront your fears and to accept things as they are. That allows intuition to function more freely.

- *Keep a record:* Diary keeping is the best way to determine whether you have genuine intuitive hunches or wishful projections. If you discover that many of your hunches are inaccurate, take stock and try to learn how your personal interests or anxieties distort your perceptions. Jotting down your insights also helps you retain those ideas that often evaporate the moment the phone rings or an impromptu meeting is called.

- *Combine intuition and analysis:* Scientific research shows that the two hemispheres of the human brain process different kinds of information. In most people, the left side controls the analytical, linear, and verbal processes; the right, the intuitive, nonlinear, and nonverbal thought. Effective problem solvers, scientists say, couple right-brain processes with left-brain processes. They transpose intuition into a logical order before implementing ideas.

- *Be patient and don't "force" solutions:* Often the intuitive hunch comes in a flash when the problem is put aside. "Sleeping on it" provides time for ideas to incubate. Many creative people report that they find solutions to apparently intractable problems during periods of relaxation after concentrated intellectual activity. Drawing, music, exercise, and other forms of nonverbal expression provide excellent ways to activate intuition.

- *Don't brush aside your hunches:* Intuition is not irrational or unnatural; it is a normal function of the brain that is probably not related to clairvoyance, mystical precognition, or similar phenomena. R. Buckminster Fuller, developer of the geodesic dome, called intuition "cosmic fishing." "You feel a nibble," he said. "Then you've got to hook the fish." Too many people get a hunch, then light up a cigarette and forget about it. Intuition is no good without the courage to implement a decision based on it (Raudsepp, 1981).

INNOVATION

As mentioned previously, innovation is the process of putting a creative idea to use. Joseph A. Schumpeter viewed innovation as an entrepreneurial tool to profitability because as entrepreneurs succeed in developing and implementing innovations in their respective industries, their dominance in terms of profits, market share, and industry strength increases, while at the same time destroy the existing status quo through their creative activities. Schumpeter's definition identified innovation in five different cases:

1. The introduction of a new good
2. The introduction of a new method of production
3. The opening of a new market
4. The conquest of a new source of supply of new materials, and
5. Carrying out a new organization of any industry by creating a monopoly or by breaking up a monopoly position (McDaniel, 2000).

Peter Drucker (1986) laid out a number of "dos" and few "don'ts" as fundamental principles of innovation.

Dos

- Purposeful innovation starts with a systematic analysis of the opportunities.

- Innovation is both conceptual and perceptual, in the sense that you have to "go out there" and look, ask, and listen. Otherwise you may conceive the right innovation in the wrong perceptual form.

- An innovation, to be effective, has to be made simple and focused, otherwise it confuses. Specific, clear applications address specific, clear needs.

- Effective innovations start small requiring little money, few people, and addressing few needs in a small, limited market, and everything being "almost right."

- A successful innovation always starts and aims at leadership within a given economic environment without necessarily becoming "big business."

Don'ts

- Do not try to be too clever, either in design or execution. Innovations must be handled by and addressed by ordinary human beings.

- Do not diversify, do not splinter, and do not try to do too many things at once; instead stay focused.

- Do not try to innovate for the future, but rather innovate for the present, with current applications and benefits for the user.

Entrepreneurial genius lies more in implementation, that is, turning ideas into innovative, profitable enterprises, rather than merely generating original creative ideas and concepts. Innovators excel at *recognizing* a creative idea as identifying a problem and matching it to a specific solution in the way that is market driven rather than supply driven. In other words, demand for the solution is automatic once the solution is commercially introduced, rather than supplying the education, information, and expensive promotion necessary to educate customers that they have the problem that the proposed product or service solves. Actually, it is sometimes better if you are not the creator of something. Too much creativity usually does not produce results, since innovation is a concept that requires the discipline to create a commercial success out of the creative idea. The innovative entrepreneur "must be more of a critic and an implementer, rather than a creative thinker" (Lener, 1986).

Similarly, entrepreneurs are adjusting their creative business models to deal with the age of austerity and frugal behavior. Some examples are prepaid credit cards, which appeal to consumers with poor credit or prevent their kids from overspending, and wireless services, which can be collaboratively consumed by customers who share or rent rather than own. Swap.com allows customers to swap DVDs and videos with others, while ThredUp.com does the same for children's clothes (*The Economist*, 2011a).

Failure, however, is an integral part of innovation (Farson & Keyes, 2002). IBM's Thomas Watson, Sr., once said, "The fastest way to succeed is to double your failure rate" (Farson & Keyes, p. 64). This lesson is becoming part of the norm in today's marketplace. A truly successful entrepreneur should expect a few failures along the way. Besides, most innovative breakthroughs are unexpected. For example, in 1928, Alexander Fleming was looking at his bacteria experiment under a microscope, trying to identify what had gone wrong. A mysterious mold was forming on the sample, disrupting his experiment. Then Fleming began to notice something interesting. Bacteria would not grow near the mysterious mold. Completely by accident, Fleming made one of the most significant breakthroughs in medicine, the discovery of penicillin (Hillis, 2002).

Innovation can be compared to life's evolution: endless mutation, occasional progress. Through eons, life has undergone uncounted mutations, and once in a while one of these haphazard events produces results that improve the survival prospects of a species. These successful mutations become part of the genome. The only difference between innovation and evolution is that not all the innovation "mutations" are accidental, haphazard, or waiting for a mutation to occur. Individuals can be taught to think unconventionally, and situations can be created that will be conducive to innovation. But what cannot be done is the precise prediction of which apparently worthwhile innovation will be a permanent part of our future and thus will make the greatest contribution toward long-term entrepreneurial success (Hamel, 2001).

Finally, individuals have different levels of needs concerning stability, certainty, and predictability in their lives. Consequently, while there may be more opportunities for creative ideas in an unstable, uncertain environment, some people would prefer to sleep well rather than eat well, and they forego creative and innovative ideas and business opportunities for the sake of stability and a steady job and paycheck. However, when *necessity entrepreneurship* strikes as a result of a threat to one's economic well-being, the creative recognition of sustainable entrepreneurial opportunities, especially opportunities that will counteract these threats, takes precedence, and individuals are called into entrepreneurial action (Henrekson, 2005; Ho & Wong, 2007). Moreover, sometimes empathy, sympathy, and the desire to help others is also a powerful call to arms for altruistic actions in social entrepreneurship that creates social gain and sustainable social developmental opportunities (Austin, Stevenson, Wei-Skillern, 2006; Zahra et al., 2009).

IDEAS FROM EDUCATION

Back in 1945 when he was a senior at Cornell, Donald Berens applied to the university's graduate business school. He wanted to go into business for himself, and, even though Cornell did not have specific courses in entrepreneurship, he figured that anything he learned would help. Cornell, however, figured otherwise, and rejected Berens's application. According to school officials, he did not project enough "success potential." Berens became the multi-millionaire president of Hickory Farms Sales Corporation, a chain of 106 food stores with headquarters in Rochester, New York. He gave Cornell University $1 million to set up graduate small business and entrepreneurial courses, not as a case of sweet revenge, but rather as the fulfillment of a 10-year dream to do something substantial for young people. He believed that by funding a chair in entrepreneurship, he could not only help students sample the entrepreneurial experience but also help the business community benefit from better-educated entrepreneurs (Graham, 1980).

Interest in entrepreneurship among students from elementary school through high school is quite strong (Gallup, 1994). Almost 90% of high school students indicated a desire to learn more about entrepreneurship, while 73% stated that they wanted to be "their own boss." Some 69% of the students wanted to start a business of their own, and among African American youths the percentage was even higher, up to 80%. However, entrepreneurship curricula at that level have been given only nominal attention at best. Despite the strong demand for entrepreneurship among students, 85% reported they were taught "a little about" or "practically nothing about" business and entrepreneurship throughout their years of schooling.

At the post-secondary level, courses in entrepreneurship are a breathtaking innovation in graduate schools of business. A surprising number of young college students possess the spirit of American private enterprise along with their belief in a successful and prosperous future for themselves and their country. This has produced a more pro-business climate on university campuses, and student-owned businesses have spread so quickly that they now have their own trade association (Bock, 1984). This phenomenon is a result of the heavy criticism that American colleges and universities have received for turning out too many people whose sole aspiration is a secure, well-paying job in a large corporation. "The trouble with most of you today," Roger Babson, a pioneer financial forecaster and founder of Babson College, told a group of students late in his life, "is that you are not willing to start at the bottom and create a business" (Rowe, 1986).

One example of the new interest in entrepreneurship is the proliferation of courses on new-venture management at colleges and business schools. Professor Karl H. Vesper, an expert on entrepreneurial education from the University of Washington, reports that in 1969, when he started compiling statistics on the subject, only 16 schools offered courses in entrepreneurship. Today, he says, there are quite a few endowed chairs in the subject, and more than 500 colleges and universities offer courses in new venture management, marketing, and finance. The proliferation of websites and Internet start-ups has also created conditions by which talented and college students are lured away from their studies to work full-time in an e-commerce-related firm, or more likely, to use what they learned in college to start their own entrepreneurial ventures and skip or postpone their education (*Tulsa World*, 2000).

Although Vesper stresses that courses can provide useful assistance, he believes they cannot provide at least five ingredients needed for the successful business:

- The concept for a product or service

- Technical know-how

- Money and facilities

- Personal contacts

- Customer orders

One very successful project is the Small Business and Entrepreneurship program at the University of Texas at Austin Institute for Constructive Capitalism, better known as IC2. This program focuses on initiative and risk-taking behavior, the capital needs of small businesses and entrepreneurs, and the environment best suited to new and small enterprises. To understand the role of the entrepreneur in American society, a database of approximately 35,000 representative companies has been developed at IC2. Information on firm locations, sales, fixed assets, stock, gross profit, long-term obligations, etc., is available to researchers for advanced study and to small businesses for assessing their own firms (Kuhn, 1982).

Similarly, at the University of Tulsa, it has become increasingly apparent in recent years that there are problems in the traditional approaches to the development of innovation, intellectual property, and patents developed by faculty and/or students, especially in the College of Engineering. Innovation centers across the United States have demonstrated that the proper environment can produce successful start-up companies, combining the best of technologies developed at universities and student interests with competent and professional managerial and financial advice. The ultimate purpose of Tulsa University's Innovation Institute (TUI2) program is to determine whether the idea or invention under examination ought to be developed further, in terms of both technical and commercial feasibility. The university's academic programs provide TUI2 participants an in-depth, integrated, and cross-functional education and research opportunities as the focal point for cutting-edge entrepreneurial and innovation activities. The program also provides access to private equity investors and structured mentoring. TUI2 aspires to be an invaluable resource for TU students, faculty, alumni, and the Tulsa business community (Vozikis & Cornell, 2000).

The popularity of such entrepreneurial academic programs stems from the general consensus that the information provided corresponds nicely with that needed to actually start a new business. Generally, entrepreneurship courses show students real business problems by giving them the opportunity to hear and to question people who have gone into business for themselves, as well as accountants, bankers, lawyers, and venture capitalists. Many courses require students to carry out such academic exercises as finding a product and drawing up plans for a company's success (Pappas, 1977).

Education in entrepreneurship/small business covers the entire scope of business administration, and as such, it is the closest approach to the original concept of management education available in universities at the present time. With the continued increasing fragmentation of business education into ever-narrower specializations, it would seem that a field of study that tries to take an overall, integrative, pragmatic, rational approach to business would find itself increasingly popular, even with those who aspire to be top executives (Zeithaml & Rice, 1985).

Others point out that some of the most successful entrepreneurs of the age never attended business school, including Ray Kroc of McDonald's and Edwin Land of Polaroid. "There are some things you just don't teach, such as a person's commitment to his goals, his drive, his dedication to a task," says Lewis A. Shattuck of the Smaller Business Association of New England (Pappas, 1977, p. 1). However, universities should not remain detached from society's needs, they should do the work that needs to be done to train tomorrow's entrepreneurs. They need to do this to maintain the value of higher education as they have in the past—by recognizing that the beginning of wisdom in academia, as in business, is choosing what not to do and doing instead what needs to be done (*The Economist*, 2011e).

Despite the attractions of entrepreneurship, few opportunities are immediately available to the graduating MBA whose emphasis is on entrepreneurship. Small firms are reluctant to take on fresh and seemingly overqualified MBAs because they rarely have staff positions in which to place MBA graduates as trainees. Further, it is quite costly for a small firm to train overqualified individuals only to see them move on to greener pastures.

THE MOST POPULAR IDEA: THE FAMILY BUSINESS

The family-run Mom and Pop store is alive and well. Only now it may be Dad and Daughters, or Mom, Her Nephew, and His Wife. More than just a proprietorship built by one hardworking person, the family-run shop is one in which "Dad starts building toward the future, bringing in daughters-in-law, wives, and cousins." Dreux (1990) suggests that conservatively there are an estimated 1.7 million privately owned business entities in the United States, excluding sole proprietorships, that can be considered family run. In terms of sole proprietorships, the Internal Revenue Service also claims that among more than 9 million non-incorporated proprietorships, most include more than one family member.

Experts see a growing spirit of entrepreneurship in this country, but as many experts point out, a small business or a new business is not the same as a *family business*. It is very difficult to attach numbers to the family business phenomenon because family business is a totally different "animal" than a small business per se or an entrepreneurial venture with a solo-flying entrepreneur. Family business is largely a state of mind, and Wortman (1995) contends that more than 20 definitions of family business are in use in the literature: usually researchers develop one that fits their needs. There is even debate as to whether family business constitutes true entrepreneurship (Hoy & Verser, 1994).

Family firms are considered one of the engines of the post-industrial growth process because they are so important for intergenerational development and transfer of entrepreneurial talent, business success, long-term strategic commitment, and entrepreneurial independence (Poutziouris, 2001), as well as, economic development in local communities (Astrachan, Zahra & Sharma, 2003; Heck & Stafford, 2001).

In the United States alone, family firms represent 90% of all businesses (Dyer 1986), while the global percentage is also high, around 70%. Family firms are viewed as entrepreneurial firms, the ownership and management of which belongs to a family (Burch, 1972; Barnes & Hershon, 1976). Others contend that the classification is valid only when there has been at least one generation of transfer (Ward, 1987), while most recent definitions concentrate on family culture as a dominant attribute (Litz, 1995; Dreux & Brown, 1999). Although some researchers view the family dimension as a constraint to true entrepreneurial endeavors (Holland & Boulton, 1984), the vast majority of the literature asserts that family businesses constantly achieve a better performance than non-family businesses (McConaughy, Matthews & Ftalko, 2001; Vickers, 1997). They maintain a competitive advantage through the preservation of the "idiosyncratic knowledge of family character" (Bjuggren & Sudd, 2001).

Family firms seem to outperform non-family firms both internationally (Stoy Hayward, 1992; Dunn, 1995) and in the United States (Kleiman, Petty, & Martin, 1995) during their average life span, which is approximately 24 to 26 years (roughly the working span of its founder). There is a 50% chance that the family business longevity will stretch beyond this to the second generation. Only about 16–18% of family businesses survive to the third generation, and any one that survives beyond that is a rare commodity. The fact that family businesses do not outlive their founders is owed largely to time bombs planted by the founders at the beginning that make succession difficult or even impossible. A family firm is often considered the patriarch's or matriarch's baby, and nobody can tell them what to do, or make them let go. As a result, there is an overall lack of succession planning in family firms (Dean, 1992). Astrachan and Kolenko (1994) found in a random national sample of family firms that only 21% had a succession plan in writing.

The problem of family succession is often the most acute in family firms when the original founder hangs on while the heirs feel overshadowed and frustrated. For example, an 85-year-old patriarch who had just passed the business along to his son was contending that "the kid's coming along fine." The "kid," however, was in his 60s, and his father still resisted letting go, which seriously constrained the firm's ability to grow. However, family love is the essence of this enterprise: "It's a chance to take something you have created with the people you love and build them a future." It is also a chance to multiply earnings by keeping them in the family. A successful, growing business is one of the best investments anyone can make and one of the best legacies anyone can leave (Churchman, 1982). One of the oldest families in England, the Cliffords, have owned and farmed the same corner of Gloucestershire for almost 1,000 years, emphasizing the values of grace, enterprise, and chivalry (*The Economist*, 2011d).

According to studies on the growth of family businesses, the traditional beliefs that family businesses start and remain small because they are marginal operations are questionable. This perspective stems from the assumption that individual owners with profitable businesses seek to increase profits and reduce losses through firm growth and economies of scale. Daily and Dollinger (1992) found that the majority of family firms they surveyed adopted a "defender" strategy in which growth was not actively sought but was achieved through operating efficiencies and incremental process improvements. This idea has also been supported regarding family firms across the globe (Gallo, 1995; Ouh, 1995). Contrary to theory however, profits of family businesses increase at very small firm sizes, suggesting that the owners may be "profit maximizers" and may elect not to enlarge their operations because of the higher profitability of small size (Kirchhoff & Kirchhoff, 1985).

Large family-run companies such as M&M/Mars and Marriott, for example, usually exclude non-family executives from stock ownership plans and real political power, despite promises made during the professional recruiting process. However, as the business matures, usually during the third generation of family ownership, very few family businesses are still run by family members because they have either lost interest or they have become so wealthy that they do not have to work any longer (Byrne, 1988).

INVENTION

In the early part of the twentieth century, The Animal Trap Company of America sold a 5-cent mousetrap. For years, Chester M. Woolworth, the president of the company, had tried to improve it. Finally, in 1928, he introduced a better mousetrap that he offered to the public for 12 cents because of higher production costs. The better and improved mousetrap proved to be a market disaster. Even though it was clearly better, the higher price caused it to lose its disposable nature. After the husband hurried to work in the morning, even though he was the one who had purchased the mousetrap, it was the wife who had to remove the dead mouse and clean the trap, which was too expensive to throw away. The housewife, who did not want a dead mouse around all day, clearly preferred the old mousetrap that could be disposed along with the dead mouse. This is the story of the "better mousetrap" (Hargadon, 2003).

Inventors love ideas. They always want to know how something works. They adore fixing things and rigging up little gadgets and suggesting how to improve the airflow through the attic, even if nobody asks. The spark that lights an idea comes most often from a problem. Inventors might just as well be called "problem solvers" because they refuse to put up with life's problems in the world as it is today. The best inventors not only solve problems, they also recognize needs and value concepts in a world "the way it ought to be" and that no one else can see. The office copier may be a shrine now, but Chester Carlson had to knock on hundreds of doors before Batelle Labs advanced the money that started Xerox. Everyone else thought the idea was cute, but not necessary: isn't that what carbon paper is for, after all? Carlson was able to knock off the blinders of what one invention expert calls object-centered thinking, or the inability to see anything but what already exists. The act of invention, like all creative endeavors, can be likened to a trip down a sort of mental cafeteria line, taking a piece of one idea, two slices of another, and ending up with a brand-new concept. Inventors must be able to fit together many seemingly disparate pieces of information (Eisenstein, 1987).

When things rattle around a bit, an idea strikes. Typically, inventors say their inventions come to them suddenly. Inventors must be curious and persistent. They must be patient, hardworking, and able to think in both abstract and concrete terms. They must also be a bit impractical: a friend once asked Benjamin Franklin what good was one of his minor inventions. Franklin, miffed, replied, "What good is a newborn baby?" In short, they must be like every other successful person, only more so. Whether these traits are innate or acquired is debatable. Perhaps inventing is a natural, irresistible process, like breathing. Teachable or not, inventing, like writing, is a solitary occupation that breeds emotional attachment to the product. Benjamin Franklin's analogy seems apt: many inventors refer to their ideas as "children." They show off patent drawings as if they were baby pictures, and they believe that their inventions will grow up to be worth a million dollars. Alex Weinstein, who invented a spill-proof spoon ideal for children and adults with cerebral palsy, Parkinson's disease, or other muscular dysfunctions that make a steady hand almost impossible, put it this way: "It goes beyond money. An experience like that, you can't buy" (Divito, 2000, p. H7).

The heart of American technological growth may be the rise of systems, such as mass marketing and mass production, but the spark for this technological growth is still invention. Invention experts view America as a uniquely creative country, where many people refuse to know their place and keep tinkering against all odds, sometimes wondering themselves why they keep doing it, especially when things turn sour. Americans have always considered themselves inventive. Independent inventing formed the basis of computers, lasers, and photocopying. For example, light polarization, used in many sunglasses, was discovered in a rented room by young Edwin Land. According to a National Science Foundation report, many aluminum fabrication techniques were first developed by independents, as were 7 of 13 major advances in steel production during the decade following World War II. Eugene Houdry was unemployed when he invented a practical way to catalytically "crack" crude petroleum in the refining process (Livezey, 1981).

"Yankee ingenuity" may be one of America's most fundamental myths—part truth and part nostalgia. Inventors come from a complete cross section of the population, according to George Lewett, head of the Office of Energy-Related Inventions at the National Bureau of Standards. The only generalization that can be made is that they are all different, with one exception: few women invent. Historically, women have been issued only about 2% of US patents. Experts say that only 1% of those patents ever earn money for the inventor. This was the case with Juanita Donica and Dianne Syme, who came up with the idea of the icicle Christmas lights in 1994 but found that the patent they had obtained was not enough to prevent large competitors from copying their invention and raking in most of the profits. Instead, the mother–daughter invention team concentrated on their next creation, skipping tradeshows and going directly to retailers to avoid copycats (Coleman, 2000).

The number of patent applications in the world rose from around 800,000 in the early 1980s to 1.8 million in 2009, according to the *World Intellectual Report 2011*, published by the World Intellectual Property Organization (*The Economist,* 2011b). There was also a tremendous growth of patents issued in countries other than the United States between 1950 and 2010. The basic idea of patents is a simple: an inventor is granted a limited monopoly (20 years in the United States and elsewhere) for an invention in return for disclosing the details of how it works, so that others can, in time, improve the original invention, rather than having the invention remain a trade secret. In some industries, like pharmaceuticals, without the protection of a patent, the huge research and development expenditures required to develop new drugs would probably not be made (*The Economist,* 2011b). A patent, therefore, is an exclusive property right of an invention that is issued by the Commissioner of Patents and Trademarks of the United States Department of Commerce. This patent gives the inventor the right to prevent others from making, selling, or using that invention for 17 years, and it is valid only in the United States and its territories and possessions. To market and protect a patented product in a foreign country, patent protection should be granted in the particular country.

To be patentable, an invention must satisfy three conditions: (a) it must be "novel," (b) it must be useful, and (c) it must not be obvious to one "skilled in the art." Therefore, an idea, a method of doing business, printed matter, or an improvement that is obvious is not patentable. The requirement of novelty is the most critical and most difficult to establish. The invention must be analyzed on the basis of specific standards. A search of Patent Office files will determine whether anyone else has patented it already and will establish its novelty. The invention is not novel if it known or used by others in this country or if it is described in a publication in any country. Even inventors themselves cannot get a patent if their invention was disclosed and described in a printed publication more than 1 year prior to the date of the patent application. Additionally, a patent cannot be obtained if the invention is in public use or has been for sale for more than 1 year before the patent application.

There are five statutory classes of patents. First, machine patents are primarily mechanical or electrical. Second, process (method) patents cover a process or a series of at least two steps. Third, patents are granted for composition of matter, especially for chemically produced items. Fourth, articles of manufacture patents cover products such as rulers or a bike seat. Lastly, new and useful improvement patents involve a new method or process for using a previously known invention. If, after preliminary analysis and patent search, the invention appears to be patentable, a patent application covering the invention must be prepared and filed in the name of the inventor with the Commissioner of Patents and Trademarks. Seeking the advice, expertise, and experience of a patent attorney is essential at this point, because the patent examiner carefully studies the application and decides whether the patent application needs to be revised and resubmitted. If it is refused, the decision can be appealed to the Board of Appeals of the Patent Office. Patent applications are reviewed in the order they are received; consequently, it may take a long time before a decision for a patent approval is made, but it usually takes between 18 and 24 months. Once the patent is granted, a fee is assessed in addition to printing charges. The patent application must include three items:

- A written document that comprises a petition, a specification, and an oath

- A drawing when appropriate

- A patent fee

After years of indecisiveness, in September 2011 the America Invent Act set the stage for major patent reform in the United States. Instead of a "first to invent" principle, which was used previously, patents began to be awarded to inventors who were the "first to file," a system similar to that already used by most other countries. This change avoids the acrimonious arguments and legal costs during court trials of who was first to come up with an idea, as well as avoiding the rush to apply for a patent before the invention is really complete and ready rather than dubious (*The Economist*, 2011c).

A patent, despite its obvious advantages, is by no means a guarantee of immunity from lawsuits, but rather attracts challenges to its legality, and constitutes merely an interest worth fighting for in a lawsuit regarding patent infringement and interference. Interference occurs when two or more inventors have applications pending for substantially the same invention. In this rare case, evidence regarding priority and time precedence is submitted to a board of examiners. Infringement, on the other hand, constitutes unauthorized manufacture, use, or sale of subject matter protected by a patent. In this quite common case, the patent owner may file suit in a federal court for damages and/or may file an injunction to "cease and desist," which prohibits the continued use or manufacture of the patented article.

Is the purpose of the patents to protect inventors? Most people would say yes, but the framers of the U.S. Constitution provided this protection as a means to a broader end, namely national progress by sharing knowledge, not hoarding it. Thus, they gave Congress "power to promote the progress of science and useful arts by securing for limited times to authors and inventors the exclusive right to their respective writings and discoveries" (Livezey, 1981).

Inventors are proud of their independence and suspicious of those who meddle in their affairs. One day, Sir Robert Peel, then prime minister, visited the 19th-century English inventor Michael Faraday. Peel, spying a prototype of Faraday's famous magneto-electric generator, asked a question that inventors always like to answer: "Of what use is it?" Faraday fixed his prime minister with a cynical stare and said: "I know not. But I wager someday your government will tax it" (*Christian Science Monitor*, 1981).

HOBBY

When Calvin Coolidge proclaimed that the business of America is business, he could scarcely have imagined today's hustling hobbyists: insurance agents who make pots for profit, stockbrokers who cook for cash, banker/musicians, or dentist/stamp collectors. Name the hobby and almost certainly someone is turning it to his part-time profit. People are playing the saxophone, performing magic, taking photographs, tracing genealogies, breeding animals, hybridizing plants, leading charter-travel groups, fixing up old cars, refereeing sports events, trading coins, and more to supplement their day jobs (Main, 1980).

Fads also emerge from a passion for a particular creative hobby. Ken Hakuta is a self-prescribed "Dr. Fad" who some years ago introduced the "Wacky Wallwalker"—a plastic, spiderlike creation that sticks to the wall, then proceeds to slowly walk down the wall to the floor. Hakuta has become a mentor for other fad and hobby enthusiasts, and he has even initiated a fad hot line (1-800-USA-FADS) to help creative hobbyists with free advice. Americans have a special place in their hearts for fads and hobbies, and these kinds of ideas come in any number of sizes, shapes, or forms (Eisenstein, 1987).

A growing number of managers and middle-aged executives are also turning their hobbies into full-time businesses, especially if they are faced with untimely firing or early retirement. Robert L. Swain, chairman of Swain & Swain, Inc., a New York placement firm, estimates that about 20% of fired executives start hobby-based ventures. Madeleine Swain, president of the same firm, has a name for these individuals: **midpreneurs**. An entrepreneur, she says, creates an idea and tries to market it, while a midpreneur takes a hobby, something he or she has experience with, and tries to make it into a profit-making venture (Gottschalk, 1986).

Microsoft founder and CEO Bill Gates represent a clear example of a case of an entrepreneur who started a business as a hobby. Gates, whose vision has been compared to that of Thomas Edison and Henry Ford, considers himself and cofounder Paul Allen as almost accidental entrepreneurs whose computer hobby catapulted them into immense riches (*Chief Executive*, 1994).

During downturns, consumers fill their needs for luxury by buying things made by hand that are beautiful but not too expensive. Regardless of the state of the economy, the basic rule is that only quality sells, and whatever the hobbyists do, they need to do it well. Additionally, even the amateur has to be professional, businesslike, and original. Many truly talented people will not succeed, simply because they fail to grasp the importance of such elementary things as market research, record keeping, and the promotion of one's business.

A profitable pastime does not necessarily pay off right away. Some hobbyists with a comfortable current income from their professions just want to build up their leisure-time activity until they retire or turn it into a full-time enterprise. Others, such as coin or stamp collectors, deal in appreciating assets rather than regular income. Still others may be more interested in generating the tax advantages of their hobby.

Many entrepreneurs, in contrast, outgrow the home office for their hobby business (Strempel, 2002). Real estate investors have begun to offer office space with amenities such as high-speed Internet access and a receptionist for businesses that are becoming more than just a hobby. Many hobby businesses use these leased office spaces before building or purchasing their own building.

HOME-BASED BUSINESSES

Working out of the home is not a novel idea, in fact there is a very old name for it: **cottage industry**. It does take a certain type of person to run a business at home, whether making canoes, computers, or chocolate chip cookies. It is hard to get financing, and the success rate is not high. Few fortunes are made at home. It can be frustrating to understand taxes, government regulations, zoning laws, or accounting practices. And there is no "leaving it all behind" at the end of the day. Yet these small operations are abundant. Nearly a half a million retail businesses exist without a payroll, meaning that just one person or a family runs them. Service industries, which include such work as accountants, typists, and researchers, have more than a million businesses without a payroll. There is no exact count on how many of these are actually at-home businesses (Irwin, 1980).

In recent years, the number of self-employed persons has grown at a faster rate than the number who work for someone else, according to the Bureau of Labor Statistics (2010). Home-based businesses spend about $10 billion annually just in equipment and supplies, and thus they constitute a major target market for companies such as Bell Atlantic's *Call Manager*, Ameritech's *Home Office Telecom* services, and Sprint's *Sprint Sense Home Office* (Dyszel, 1999).

The self-employed work more hours than those who work for others, namely an average of 41.9 hours a week compared with 38.5 hours for other workers. About 54% of home-based businesses fall into the white-collar category; 46% are blue-collar businesses. One in five businesses has home-based origins, including such giants as Ford Motor Company and Apple Computers. Their average earnings are below those who are on someone else's payroll, but the self-employed may fare better because of the things their businesses can provide them that are not counted as income (Biddulph, 1991).

Organizations such as the National Alliance of Home-based Businesswomen provide a local and national network for this relatively unknown part of the workforce. The alliance is a national, nonprofit organization dedicated to the professional, personal, and economic growth of women who work from their homes. NAHB grew out of a survey of local home-based businesswomen conducted by Marion Hehr of Edison, New Jersey, and Wendy Lazar of Norwood, New Jersey. Even before they published their findings in *Women Working Home: The Home-based Guide and Directory*, they met with a few home-based businesswomen to mold the organization. In January 1981, 16 founding members were listed in the board meeting minutes. A year later the organization had members in all but 12 states and chapters starting in more than 25 cities. The alliance encourages members to form local chapters for personal contact and mutual support. Through chapters they exchange information and experiences, create educational programs, make professional contacts, and showcase their goods and services (MacBride, 1982).

People start a business at home for financial reasons. Saving money on overhead is very important at this stage. Another common attraction of home offices is that a parent can stay home with their children. The convenience of a home-based business is also a factor in the decision to work from home: the hours are flexible, there is no need to commute, and those who do not see clients do not have to go to the expense of buying a business wardrobe or commiting to an expensive office overhead. In addition, home-based businesses get tax breaks.

Sometimes, however, the home-based businessperson may seem to have the worst of all possible jobs. The flexible hours are long, sometimes longer than a regular job, and work can stretch into 7-day weeks. Distractions are numerous, and interruptions to do household chores are the rule. Priorities conflict endlessly, and quitting time never comes. Worst of all, perhaps, supplies and equipment that are necessary to conduct business are not as available as they are in a regular office, and paychecks are usually erratic and frequently small. Finally, restrictive zoning laws mean that 90% of home-based businesses may be in violation of zoning ordinances and regulations (Danbom, 1995).

But the home-based businessperson also faces unique challenges. Many questions arise: Are my prices right? My service is good, but how do I develop a professional business identity? Am I keeping the necessary business records? How can I persuade my family and friends to take my business seriously and not treat it as a hobby? When do I devote my time to my family, and when do I demand their cooperation? Owners of a home-based business cannot step into the next office to test a new idea on a co-worker, nor do they learn about new business trends and opportunities over lunch with other businesspersons. To a large extent, they are separated from the business world in which they compete.

But beyond money, beyond talent, and beyond "fun," these individuals also find a renewed sense of self-worth, even though sometimes there is a feeling that work at home is not as important and glamorous as in the "real world," or a feeling of loneliness. The intangible rewards of personal growth, self-esteem, and fulfillment become payment themselves. Even those whose businesses have folded or whose bottom lines are "in the red" speak enthusiastically about this positive experience (Gardner, 1980).

MOONLIGHTING

Moonlighting entrepreneurs are real: when the economy is uncertain, people take action to take care of themselves. Because moonlighters typically want to keep their employers ignorant of such ventures, their ranks cannot be counted. Just how many moonlighters there are is hard to tell, but the U.S. Department of Labor puts the number of "dual jobholders" between 1% and 5% of all employed persons. Their median age is about 43 years, 4 years older than the median age for all workers. Male second-job entrepreneurs outnumber females by 50%, and 70% are married. A sales occupation is the most common nature of their second job, while their first job is usually administrative, executive, managerial, or professional. These characteristics are found at all economic levels (Gruenert, 1999).

For an entrepreneur, moonlighting is a good way to start a new venture while maintaining the safety net of an existing job. Moonlighting may not be viewed in a positive light by the primary employer, especially if the new venture is in a similar field. Primary employers have filed lawsuits against other companies claiming that the company benefited from the proprietary information that was passed along by the moonlighting employee (Anna, 2002). Employees who are considering moonlighting should take into account the business ethics related to their situation: they were hired to do a job for a given amount of money. An employer has the right to expect a full day's work for a full day's pay. Employers should establish the ground rules for employees who moonlight, and they should be prepared to enforce these rules before the profits of the company are affected (Schmitt, 2001).

Moonlighting can be as creative as one chooses to make it. Commonly, part-time workers find a new field so exhilarating that they switch careers. They include part-time carpenters, upholsterers, salesmen, and welders. There are car repair shops in backyard sheds and photography studios in basements. People across the country are also getting imaginative with their computers; they establish a commercial presence by acquiring and registering an Internet domain by paying a nominal fee to the Internet Corporation for Assigned Names and Numbers, or a slightly higher fee to domain registration houses. Then they buy commercial space on the World Wide Web to host their site. With the opening of a "great domain land rush" similar to the one that opened the state of Oklahoma to settlers, new domain names such as .biz, .info, .pro, .name, .aero, .coop, .museum, in addition to the existing ones such as .com, .net, .org, .edu, .int., .mil, .gov, offer many opportunities to moonlighting entrepreneurs engaging in e-commerce with part-time ventures (Hoffman, 2001). Inevitably, there are failures as well as successes. Building a small business "to fall back on" is a practice not a unique to today. Every business cycle and every kind of profession has produced part-time, "hedging," and "moonlighting" entrepreneurial ventures. For many, it is a way to supplement paychecks or social security. For others, it is simply an insurance against job loss, and this sense of job precariousness seems especially strong during troubled economic times (Cox, 1981).

However, moonlighting also provides a hedge against the failure of an entrepreneurial venture. Moonlighters rely on a secure career as a fallback position that allows them to risk starting a part-time business, sometimes at the expense of neglecting their main jobs. If the entrepreneurial venture succeeds, it is not unusual for moonlighters to abandon secure careers to engage in their venture full-time. In the meantime, as Professor Bygrave put it: "The guy who cuts my trees has a very nice tree business. But that doesn't mean he should leave his job with the phone company, with all its benefits and pension plan" (Robichaux, 1990, p. B1).

BUYING AN EXISTING FIRM

Entrepreneurs do not always start a new business from scratch; some purchase a going concern. There are many reasons that some individuals choose to buy an existing business. The major reason is that it is easier to buy a business that is already in operation than to start one. Of course, a going concern must be researched carefully before a decision to purchase can be made. Pre-purchase assessment and due diligence research are a must if an entrepreneur wants to be confident that the firm under consideration has good prospects for survival and success.

Advantages of buying an existing business are numerous. Of course, less time, effort, and pressure are involved in a takeover than in a start-up. There is also the possibility that a good business may be purchased at a bargain low price, and if the firm has performed well in the past, financing for the purchase may be easier as well. Much investigative work is eliminated when an existing business is purchased. Sources of supply as well as customers are already established, and there is less uncertainty about the demand for goods or services. Management information concerning equipment, personnel, and facilities is already available. Often there is a smaller or no time lag involved concerning the initial return on investment, which is generally not the case when starting a brand-new venture.

However, where there are advantages, there are also disadvantages. Purchasing a going concern entails the possibility that a bargain buy is actually a high-priced purchase. Another negative possibility may be poor existing inventory or selection of merchandise. Other negative aspects that should be researched include the possibility of suppliers or customers with ill will toward the business. Buyers may also be forced to have their own ideas and plans set aside in order to conform to the existing goals of the firm. With this possibility comes the difficulty of changing existing policies and practices that may be questionable but are already taken for granted by suppliers, employees, and customers. The new owner faces the possibility that old customers will not accept the change in ownership and will decide not to patronize the business any longer.

From a tax standpoint, buying another company is truly an adventure. Big or small, winner or loser, the company can frequently offer dramatic potential for earning power and tax savings. At the same time, the entire subject is a tax maze because sometimes the tax ramifications themselves determine whether a deal is feasible. For instance, an entrepreneur may have to forgo an acquisition if the tax savings will not compensate for the decreased cash flow needed for the purchase. On the other hand, an acquisition that needs capital might provide special write-offs for the buyer who has had a very profitable year from other ventures or investments.

Prospective buyers of existing firms can also utilize the services of business brokers, who specialize as dealmakers in buying and selling companies. Good brokers, like good real estate agents, can be the key to structuring a good deal for both the buyer and the seller of the firm. A business broker's track record is indicative of the quality of his or her services. Competence in appraising the value of the business and avoidance of "sign first, look later" pressure tactics, benefit the buyer, while discretion about the possibility of the sale of a business to avoid losing employees and customers benefits the seller; all are signs of a reputable business broker.

Financial Evaluation of an Existing Business

Setting a value on an existing business is not an easy task. The problem is compounded because there are many different ways to value a closely held business, with no simple method that covers every business. The intangible factors of the various motives and goals of business buyers and sellers, as well as the difference of interest between a buyer and a seller, can complicate things even further. At the end, what really matters is how badly the seller wants to sell and how badly the buyer wants to buy that particular business. These *qualitative* aspects of the evaluation of an existing business are shown in Exhibit 5.1.

The *quantitative* aspects of setting a value for an existing business involve a variety of approaches and valuation methods. The most commonly used techniques are listed here:

Exhibit 5.1	Qualitative Aspects of the Evaluation of an Existing Business

Breadth of the Business
- How broad is the client base?
- How broad is the product mix?
- How broad is the services mix?

Market of the Business
- Competitive position
- Market characteristics
- Marketing force
- Distribution network

Management of the Business
- Management skills
- Facilities
- Management perks
- Management objectives

- **Fixed price:** The owner, the seller, or both set a value of what they think the business is worth.

- **Value of salable assets or book value:** This technique is set by the company's most recent balance sheet.

- **Adjusted value of salable asset:** This method uses the book value approach, but with certain assets adjusted upward or downward of their reported book value.

- **The gross income multiplier method:** Gross income is determined and then is capitalized using a price-earnings multiple.

- **Discounted cash flow method:** This valuation method implies that the future earning power of the firm is the real value.

- **Replacement value:** The value of each asset is determined by its replacement value.

Of all the methods of valuation, the simplest is the *value of salable assets*. This method involves using the book value of the assets and liabilities of the business to arrive at a specific value. For this reason, this method is sometimes referred to as the *book value* method. However, the simplicity of the method is offset somewhat by its inadequacy to accurately determine the value of a small business.

The problem lies in the fact that the value of the business is influenced more by the use to which the assets are put, rather than their actual book value. If the assets are used effectively, then the business will prosper and provide earnings to the owner(s). However, if the assets are not used effectively, then the returns to the business will be considerable lower. Therefore, the value of salable assets method does not give a true picture of the worth of the business as an income generator. Nevertheless, its simplicity accounts for its continued usage and the method can be beneficial in that it provides a "low" estimate of the value of the business.

Establishing a value is not the same as setting a price for the business. The value is the assessment of the worth of the business by whomever is performing the valuation. Any valuation method will give a value for an existing business firm, and the more alternative methods are used, the better and the more accurate the estimate of that value. The price, on the other hand, is the negotiated value agreed upon by the buyer and seller, which, as mentioned previously, depends on how badly the seller wants to sell and how badly the buyer wants to buy that particular business. Very seldom will the price at which the business changes hands be the same as the value determined by either the buyer or seller. However, for the deal to be a win–win situation, the price should fall within the range of values that were predetermined by the buyer and seller (Carland & White, 1980). There are several exceptional cases, however, in which the traditional valuation methods may be of limited use. Exhibit 5.2 illustrates some of these cases (Howard, 1982).

> *Example 1.* A restaurant, the building, the land where it was located, and an adjacent parking lot owned by one individual were valued separately at $400,000 for the restaurant and $70,000 for the parking lot. On the surface, a total valuation of $470,000 seems correct. But further analysis reveals that the restaurant was worth the full $400,000 only if the parking lot was available. So despite the value of the parking lot as a piece of developable land, it cannot be used for anything other than its present purpose, which is a parking lot for the restaurant. If the restaurant goes out of business, the lot will have very little value, and as a result of this analysis, the parking lot's $70,000 value was eliminated from the final valuation for tax purposes.

The *gross income multiplier* method is favored because it, too, is relatively simple to construct. It is based on the concept that the gross profit margin is the most important number to a small business, and it has the added benefit of considering the efficiency of the firm's asset utilization in the generation of earnings and cash flows. Additionally, the method comes closer to an accurate business valuation than the value of salable assets method because it is calculated without the consideration of operating expenses, which are controllable, to a large extent, by management. Therefore, the actual management practices of one owner compared to another need not be considered in determining the value of the business. The gross income multiplier method can be used in conjunction with other methods to establish a range of values, which can be used in the negotiation of a selling price for the business.

> *Example 2.* A retail clothing store showed a 100% increase in both sales and earnings during the 5 years preceding its owner's death. Initially, these facts gave the impression that the business was booming and that it should command a premium valuation. The first impression, however, turned out to be wrong; subsequent analysis showed that each year's sales growth was directly related to expansion of floor space, while sales per square foot had not increased at all. In short, the former owner had doubled his investment to double his sales and his earnings. A buyer, therefore, would have to invest more than the cost of acquiring the business to continue the growth trend in earnings, and the final valuation confirmed that the business was probably worth less than face value, not more.

The most difficult and probably least-used valuation method is the *discounted cash flow approach.* This approach, by virtue of the subjectivity involved in determining some of the key factors, is likely provide the widest range of values. However, because it considers the cash flows to the owner(s) as the key factor, this method is considered by many to be the most appropriate method of valuation. The discounted cash flow method is more difficult than the value of salable assets or gross income multiplier methods. However, it provides

Exhibit 5.2	Exceptions to the Traditional Valuation Methods

High-tech businesses	These are generally valued by the condition of the acquisition market, which may be exceptionally high if the market is "hot."
"Information" businesses	Very difficult to value. Often based on an initial payment plus future payments depending upon sales and earnings.
"Hobby" businesses	These so-called lifestyle businesses are part business, part fun, and may have unrealistic earnings or losses.
High-leverage businesses	Such businesses have special qualities that make them worth more than a valuation method would indicate. An example would be a business that has exclusive rights or product lines that might be expected to generate much higher earnings if fully exploited.
Professional businesses	Medical, accounting, legal practices, and other professional businesses are generally governed by prevailing practices and the reputation of specific individuals. Their valuation is often based on a percentage of future billings.
Start-ups	Start-ups are hard to value, especially those with exciting high-tech qualities and patents that can be worth much more than what the asset value or the immediate earnings prospects would suggest. The price will be negotiated and will depend on the needs of both parties.

the most realistic measure of value to the owner (or potential owner) because it requires the owner's input for the calculation of the firm's value. Therefore, the calculated value that the discounted cash flow method produces represents the existing or prospective owner's assessment of the firm's prospects.

> *Example 3.* A manufacturing company with a long history of steady earnings was initially valued at $1.1 million on a federal estate tax return. Based on history, the valuation made sense. Inspection of the plant, however, revealed severe physical deterioration, and in fact the building had been condemned. The management had already made plans to acquire a new building elsewhere, but the cost of the new plant, the cost of the move, and the salvage value of the old plant had not been factored into the value of the company. An estimate of $500,000 in net costs to the business as a result of the move led to a reduced valuation of $600,000 ($1.1 million minus $500,000) because no buyer would pay the full value knowing that an additional $500,000 had to be invested immediately for the company to keep earnings at historic rates.

Common sense is the guide in almost all cases, but also of critical importance is the professional appraiser's role in a valuation. Whether it concerns the valuation of a firm for tax purposes, looking at a potential acquisition, or dealing with an estate after death, who prepares the valuation makes all the difference in the world (Blackman, 1981).

DIRECT MAIL

The practice of sending off for goods and goodies goes back to Colonial days, when settlers wrote to England for everything from port to pianos (Morrison, 1981). Since the early twentieth century, more and more people have turned to catalog shopping because they do not have the time to go into a store or because they don't want to put up with parking hassles or a lack of salespeople.

Direct-marketing sales of merchandise and services have grown at twice the rate of overall retail sales. Direct marketing includes not only mail-order catalog sales but also telephone sales and direct-response advertising in newspapers, magazines, television, and radio. Catalog sales are so impressive that the major department stores find their turf getting crowded. Some 10,000 companies rely on mail order for more than 15% of their sales, and independently owned specialty houses appear to be growing even faster than the rest.

Mail-order houses generally operate at least one store as a place to sell off leftover merchandise. Some firms began as specialty shops and found expansion by mail far cheaper and more practical than trying to open a nationwide chain. But a mail-order company, like any retailer, must keep careful rein on costs. Elaborate glossy catalogs are expensive to produce and distribute, and most catalogs get thrown in the trash. Mail-order merchants eagerly buy or rent one another's mailing lists, hoping to reach mail-order consumers who will not only browse through the catalogs but will fire off big orders as well.

"Owners of businesses shouldn't be afraid to decide for themselves what media to use. They usually know more about the market than they think but don't have enough confidence in their own abilities. Unless a product is highly complicated and needs a lot of explanation," advises Richard Thalheimer, owner of the San Francisco-based mail-order firm The Sharper Image, "start with a small ad in several magazines, then put more dollars into the most productive publication. Try to target your audience very narrowly so you're paying only for those you want to reach." For advertising to be effective, Thalheimer feels he must make $2 gross profit for every $1 he spends on advertising. Profit margins on merchandise average about 40% (Kemp, 1982, p. 147).

However, the boom years of the catalog and mail-order business are nearly over. The tremendous boost that mail-order sales received in the 1970s, when many women joined the workforce in large numbers, created a transition phase in shopping habits that is quite complete now. Mail-order sales, which constitute about 40% of consumer sales, will grow at a comparable annual rate to retail sales, about 10%, due to the proliferation of websites by many small firms. These sites, however, in most cases are nothing more than electronic brochures, according to a 2001 National Federation of Independent Business study. Some 65% of small-firm websites do not allow customers to buy online, and that substantially reduces their effectiveness. About 35% of firms (2 million firms) with fewer than 250 employees have websites, while 45% of those without websites expect to launch them in the near future. Small firms still struggle to fully exploit the Web, thus leaving plenty of commercial opportunities for direct mail catalogs and marketing. The reasons for this include lack of technical support in maintaining the website, uncertain payoff, and wrong product. This last issue is quite prominent; the NFIB survey reported that 77% of the small firms claim that their product or service does not lend itself to direct online sales and that their site is limited to promotion only (*The Honolulu Advertiser*, 2001).

Entrepreneurs who speculate on engaging in a mail-order venture should remember that the mail-order business is a continuous series of tests and experiments which requires a certain degree of risk taking. The unique selling niche of a value concept proposition for which customers can hold a catalog in their hands can prove to be very valuable and successful.

"UNINCORPORATED" EXECUTIVES

Sometimes large corporations can be confounding places for talented entrepreneurs to work. The creative flair and aggressive style that make them valuable employees can also make them very unpopular and sometimes even expendable. Most true entrepreneurs sense this in the organizational climate, and if they are too assertive about their beliefs and ideas, they may be let go. Entrepreneurs are often labeled mavericks or troublemakers, and some will job-hop several times before they strike out on their own. For others, it takes only one brush with a bureaucracy to inspire self-employment.

Michael N. Garin, president of Telepictures, Inc., recalled his years with Time, Inc.: "They raised my salary by $15,000 and cut my job in half. I was 32, and I thought I was too young to be paid a high salary and be unhappy. I figured that if I didn't leave then, I'd be chained to a big corporation forever. My partner and I were refugees from big companies who wanted to be on our own" (*Business Week*, 1981). Dallen Peterson, president of Merry Maids, a professional home-cleaning service, claims that his move from a corporate executive position to a business of his own "was like going from renting a house to owning your own home . . . all of a sudden you see dandelions in the front yard" (Bacas, 1987).

Why do entrepreneurs discard high-paying jobs for what is many times an uncertain future? The answer is the same as why they are driven to be their own boss: control over their lives, NOT money, seems to be the motivating factor. Again, control over their lives, NOT money, seems to be the motivating factor.

Researchers who have investigated the entrepreneurial decision-making process have found that displacement, often in the form of firing or mere job dissatisfaction are two of the primary reasons that entrepreneurs make the decision to set up their own shop. Job dissatisfaction and discontentment with the status quo in a large organization can be a trigger for change as dissatisfied individuals come up with new ways to improve current conditions. In an era in which we emphasize the need for change, creativity, and innovation in organizational efforts (Frohman, 1997), it is ironic that employee dissatisfaction, which may actually lead to creative performance, not only is often unrecognized but also may be stifled by the same organization that ultimately might have benefited from creative ideas (Zhou & George, 2001). "That's why I feel these people are pushed, not pulled into it," contends Robert Brockhaus, an entrepreneurship professor at St. Louis University. "An extreme degree of dissatisfaction with the previous job seems not only to push the entrepreneur from the previous place of employment, but it may also convince the entrepreneur that no other place of employment would be a satisfactory alternative. Their need to be in control is so great that they cannot function properly inside other organizations. That's why the successful entrepreneur's resume usually shows they've changed jobs frequently" (Brockhaus, 1980).

It is estimated that a third of all executives who change careers will end up in small, one-person businesses (Wolner, 1977). Small firms are more likely to be breeding grounds for potential entrepreneurs than are larger companies, according to a study sponsored by the National Federation of Independent Business (NFIB), which surveyed owners-managers of 1,805 small companies nationwide. Results show that certain types of jobs act as "incubators" for entrepreneurs, providing them with the knowledge, skills, and motivation to start their own businesses. Smaller firms are especially prone to spin-offs, because they give employees a broad range of job experiences. The study also showed that 70% of entrepreneurs started businesses in a field in which they already had job experience; 36% had 16 or more years of schooling, compared to 13% of the overall population; and 50% had parents who owned their own business. The typical executive looking for his or her own business was a person in their mid to late forties, whose children were finished with school, who had stalled in a career, who were tired of commuting, who were fed up with office routine, and who were looking for new challenges. Finally, this survey showed that entrepreneurs spend an average of 8 years at their previous jobs before striking out on their own and that most of the financing for these ventures comes from personal savings and from financial institutions (*Inc. Magazine*, 1982).

The entrepreneurial spirit is contagious among other professionals as well. For example, large numbers of civil or military service employees retire early from a government career, and many of them have the time, freedom, and capital to start a business venture. A person entering a second career in entrepreneurship must be somewhat of a "Renaissance person." Small-business management requires a keen mind and a desire to learn within a number of different areas. For the second careerist, it often requires a giant step from specialized skills and knowledge to the administration and integration of diverse operative and managerial functions. A former executive with a large company may still encounter serious problems running a small firm. Many managers in large organizations become quite spoiled, specializing to the extent that they fail to keep up in other functional areas. In large companies, these managers had ample resources and they were able to call upon other specialists, such as accountants, salespeople, personnel managers, or legal staff for advice on particular aspects of business problems. In short, selecting a new career, especially one in entrepreneurship, should not be done haphazardly. A career change of this type can be exciting and rewarding. However, if one is not cautious and far-sighted, it may prove to be a major mistake. Thus, if the growing entrepreneurial spirit is to flourish among changing careerists, it is vital to develop in advance a systematic program and plan for starting a new entrepreneurial career (Weinrauch, 1980).

STARTING UP AGAIN

The urge to re-emerge sometimes strikes the entrepreneur who started a company, made a success of it, and then got bored with day-to-day management. Dozens of executives in such circumstances have left comfortable, remunerative jobs in recent years for the excitement and uncertainties of starting over. "Some people like to climb mountains; others like to start companies. Some people are simply 'spawners of companies'," says Professor Karl H. Vesper (Buckley, 1981).

In past years, dozens of well-known entrepreneurs in information processing and other high-technology industries have started their second, third, or even fourth high-tech company. The list of these "high-tech repeaters" is growing longer every year because a great deal of recycling talent occurs in this industry. Entrepreneurs have always been the driving force behind the rapid growth of any industry, and the recycling of talent most likely will help the United States maintain its technological lead.

Of course, people leave companies that they started for a variety of reasons. Some are pushed out when the inventive spirit that launched an enterprise proves inadequate to manage it. Others, who have sold out to bigger companies, grow restless when they lose their proprietary interest. Arguments with co-founders can also spur entrepreneurs to begin thinking about starting a new company. Some entrepreneurs become frustrated after their first companies are acquired by other firms and they are no longer running the show. Others form their second company not only to gain more control but also to retain a greater financial stake. Still others want to return to the cutting edge of technology, and they believe that starting over is the only way to do it (*Business Week*, 1981).

Others still simply prefer small businesses. Former successes have usually endowed their founders with the wealth to retire to a life of luxurious obscurity. Instead, they start all over again in the hope of matching the brilliance of their original start-up. However, a first-time winner by no means guarantees success the second time, although venture capitalists claim that ventures started by someone who did it before have a 35% chance of success, compared with only 5% for original start-ups. However, even if the second company succeeds, the repeater may not, because, as mentioned previously, some repeaters that start over were unable to manage their original companies as they grew or because their temperaments were not suited to running large companies. Many entrepreneurs have the single-mindedness to build but not the breadth and patience to orchestrate and manage growth (Garner, 1997).

"Serial" entrepreneurs have some common characteristics (Cowe, 1998):

- Their parents were businesspeople.
- They have a will to win.
- They love assuming responsibility.
- They need to be in control.
- They have leadership skills and abilities.
- They are networkers, knowing everyone worth knowing in their industry.
- They have a background in a volatile industry.
- They have experience with rapid change and believe that dealing with it is very important.
- They have experienced early successes, leaving with financial independence early in life.
- They already have a success track record.

Experienced "serial" entrepreneurs bring a great deal of knowledge to new ventures. With a track record of success, many repeaters are able to bargain for a larger share of the second company. Frequently, they had too small a portion the first time. They got a taste of getting rich, and they want to get richer or at least to not be poor again. The trend has been further accelerated by changes in the U.S. tax laws and the investment climate. In Europe, where the investment and tax climate is different, entrepreneurs have a tougher time cashing in on their ventures' success because stock markets are less fluid than in the United States, and as a result, there is less venture capital available and practically no second-time entrepreneurs.

FRANCHISING

Franchising, long synonymous with fast-food restaurants and hotel chains, now encompasses every good or service imaginable. It is growing both as a way for companies to do business and as a way for individuals to start businesses. Large corporations increasingly see franchising as a way to distribute products without the problems of managing far-flung operations. Small firms use franchising to grow into large corporations quickly, without great amounts of capital. Franchisees view it as a way to go into business for themselves without the risks faced by independent businesses.

As a word, **franchise** has its origins in French. Originally it meant, "to be free from servitude." Today, franchising appears to mean "something for everyone," at least to both franchisor and franchisee. Technically, franchising is a form of licensing in which the owner of a product, service, or method sells the rights to do business in a prescribed manner over a certain period of time in a known place. The parent company is termed the franchisor, while the receiver of the privilege is the franchisee, and the right to the business itself is the franchise. A universally accepted definition is hard to come by, but the one most often used is that of a continuing relationship between two independent parties based on contractual arrangements whereby a franchisor (producer) grants and provides tangible and non-tangible assets to the franchisor for a fee.

Franchising has proved to be a much-needed business activity capable of creating business opportunities and jobs with a low percentage of failure. Based on data gathered by Justis and Judd (1989), the Small Business Administration (SBA) contends that as many as 33% of all independently owned businesses fail in their first year of operation, and within the first 5 years, up to 65% of these non-franchised businesses discontinued operations. In contrast, according to Department of Commerce estimates, less than 5% of franchises fail each year, and, as a method of distribution, franchising is increasing its stake in the economy, claiming an ever-larger market share by moving into different business categories.

One characteristic that more and more companies find unnecessary in the franchising world of today is "bigness." Although the major corporations still control the majority of franchises, franchising is increasingly becoming the tool that smaller ventures use to expand. Key to the success of franchising is the concept of marketing and market share. Just as the large, vertically integrated chain stores started to grow and prosper after World War II by employing the techniques of mass marketing and advertising, in the 1960s franchisors started to use these same techniques. But with their late start, marketing alone did not account for the success that followed.

The success of franchising is due primarily to the fact that franchisee entrepreneurs invest their own money and, therefore, are more interested in the franchise firm's success than an employee would be. The combination of the modern marketing practices of a large corporation and the entrepreneurial drive of the franchisee is the cornerstone of success for franchised operations. Franchisors and franchisees understand each other because after all, every major franchise company was founded by entrepreneurs. They both have the vision, daring, and interest to streamline an operation to its maximum efficiency (Hayes & Matusky, 1989).

CONCLUSION

"You miss 100% of the shots you don't take."

(Hockey legend Wayne Gretzky, who upon his retirement in 1999 held or shared 61 National Hockey League records)

Opportunities and ideas for businesses are readily available for anyone to capitalize on. The only problem is how to convert ideas into a value concept and, in turn, into a profitable business. Most businesses today are not founded upon truly innovative ideas. Most individuals who start new ventures do not do so from ideas that just "hit" them. They gain specialized knowledge from their occupations and then are able to recognize weaknesses and gaps as value concepts in a niche that is not being filled within a particular market. Business ventures are born whenever entrepreneurs put their ideas together with a financial backbone. When this is done, work can begin to develop the idea and the business (Mancuso, 1974).

Other methods of formulating ideas for business may be derived from capitalizing on the shortcomings of existing products and services, such as finding extraordinary uses for ordinary things, looking for opportunities in social change and trends, and turning technological advances to business advantages. All of these methods can be used to generate new ideas and opportunities for business ventures.

Sometimes a large corporation can be a confounding place for talented entrepreneurs to work. The creative flair and aggressive style that make them a valuable employee can also make them very unpopular and sometimes even expendable. Entrepreneurs are often considered mavericks, and some will change jobs several times before they start their own ventures. For others, the choice for self-employment is more obvious. Why do they discard high-paying jobs for what is many times an uncertain future? They are driven to be their own boss; they want control over their lives more than job security. "There are just certain things you cannot do in a big corporation."

Researchers who have investigated the entrepreneurial decision-making process have found that displacement, unemployment, and job dissatisfaction are the initial motivators of entrepreneurs. Change, creativity, and innovation are often stifled by the parent organization that ultimately might have benefited from them (Frohman, 1997; Zhou & George, 2001).

Finally, Patzelt, & Shepherd (2011) have offered a summary of the factors that lead to the successful recognition of ideas and opportunities and their equally successful exploitation: interdependencies between an individual's entrepreneurial knowledge and their knowledge of the natural and communal environment within which these opportunities lie; the degree of a perceived threat toward one's personal economic status and economic well-being at present and in the future; and finally, in the case of social entrepreneurship, altruism in the sense of a desire to create social gain and sustainable developmental opportunities for society as a whole.

Website Information

Topic	Web Address	Description
Intuition: Ray Kroc	http://www.time.com/time/time100/profile/kroc.html	Tells the story of the founder of McDonald's.
Family business	http://www.inc.com/guides/running-family-business.html	Articles on how to run a family business and links to websites that give information on family businesses.
Patents	http://www.uspto.gov	Official homepage of the United States Patent Office: allows you to check on the status of a patent, tell how to get a patent, and gives information on the Patent Office. itself.

Key Terms

Adjusted value of salable asset: This method uses the book value approach, but with certain assets adjusted upward or downward of their reported book value.

Cottage industry: An outdated name for working out of the home.

Discounted cash flow method: The most difficult (and probably least used) valuation method which, by virtue of the subjectivity involved in determining some of the key factors, will likely provide the widest range of values.

Fixed price: The owner, the seller, or both set a value of what they think the business is worth.

Franchise: A French word originally meaning "to be free from servitude" which now appears to mean "something for everyone," at least to both franchisor and franchisee.

Gross income multiplier method: A valuation method based on the concept that the gross profit margin is the most important number to a small business, which has the added benefit of considering the efficiency of the firm's asset utilization in the generation of earnings and cash flow.

Midpreneurs: A term suggested by Madeline Swain to describe fired executives who start hobby-based ventures.

Niche: A French word literally meaning "bird's nest," a niche is used to safeguard, incubate, and nurture the entrepreneurial idea and ultimately ensure the survival of the value concept.

Replacement value: The value of each asset is determined by its replacement value.

Value of salable assets or book value: This technique is set by the company's most recent balance sheet.

Review Questions

1. Discuss four attributes that creative individuals may have in common.

2. What do we mean by "necessity entrepreneurship"?

3. What is the main problem of family succession in a family-run business?

4. Briefly outline the three conditions that an invention must satisfy to be patentable.

5. What are some of the advantages and disadvantages of working from home?

6. What are some common characteristics of the "serial" entrepreneur?

7. List some of the advantages and disadvantages of buying an existing firm.

8. List and describe some quantitative approaches used in the financial evaluation of an existing business.

9. Why are franchises so successful?

10. The text notes that opportunities are bountiful and exist in almost infinite amounts awaiting discovery and exploitation by the right entrepreneur. Visit http://www.soycorninnovation.com/ to review the past winners of Purdue's Soybean and Corn Product Innovation Competition. Considering the varied products that have emerged, take a few minutes to brainstorm new, innovative product ideas. These can be adaptations of the past winners or new ideas all together.

Reflections from the Front Lines of LifeGuard America

I have learned over a long career in business process improvement that true innovation usually happens when an outsider comes into a business environment and fundamentally redefines the business paradigm. This is an extremely interesting phenomenon that typically happens when someone who is not invested in the way things are begins asking why things are done this way when it makes more sense to do it another way. Or someone asks the all-important question: "What is the one thing that is impossible to do today, that if it became possible, would fundamentally change the way your business is done?" I made a living asking that question to Fortune 500 companies in the 1980s and 1990s and then helping them create the environment necessary to achieve dramatic improvements in their performance. This experience ultimately led me to ask the organ transplant community, "Why do transplant teams travel to procure their own organs?" This line of questioning eventually led to the creation of LifeGuard America's business plan and will redefine the process by which human transplant organs are procured and allocated across America. If you want an interesting read, pick up any of Joel Arthur Barker's publications on the business of paradigms and you will get a better understanding of where to look for innovative ideas and how to predict the future by creating it.

Let's look at the origin of LifeGuard America from the perspective of the current environment of the Organ Procurement and Transplantation Network (OPTN). From the business plan section entitled The Current Environment:

> The United Network for Organ Sharing (UNOS) has developed centralized, information-based system for the notification, acquisition, and assignment of transplant organs. This service is a centralized, computer-based software system that automates the activities of the donor-to-recipient allocation process operated 24 hours a day, 365 days a year by the UNOS Organ Center staff. This process requires *manual coordination,* through the OPO coordinators, of medical procurement teams, transportation, and delivery

of all organs involved. Once a donor is identified and the list of possible matches has been received, the local Organ Procurement Organization (OPO) begins the task of coordinating organ allocation. In a situation where the organs travel out of the local area, the OPO must coordinate the logistics of multiple procurement teams. This involves the scheduling of procurement teams; travel to and from the donor site, and recipient patients. The process to coordinate these events can take 12 to 20 hours. If successful, two to four organs will be procured and that many lives changed. However, statistics show that about 15% of the time, this coordination process takes place and the team arrives only to discover that, due to multiple reasons, the organ is not suitable for the planned recipient. In this scenario, the organ is not procured and therefore wasted.

The business plan continues by answering the call with the next section titled LifeGuard America's Approach:

LifeGuard America's solution is to develop a secure network and services that will dramatically reduce the time it takes for transplant teams to get critical donor information and begin the process of organ assessment. We also allow multiple teams to participate as secondary or tertiary recipients of organs without having to travel to the donor site. In the future, LifeGuard America will use new, faster jet aircraft to increase the distance that a procured organ can travel. Under LifeGuard America's plan, once the donor–recipient matched list has been received, the OPO relays a refined list to the Response Center at LifeGuard America. At this point, the website and communications network is coordinated for the transplant teams to view donor information and/or the organ procurement procedure. Staff at the donor hospital will perform requested procedures related to the assessment and procurement. This option eliminates the transplant team's need to travel, thus reducing the associated cost and lost opportunity. As the procurement is taking place, teams will be able to view the procurement in real time and have interaction with the local team as to the specific characteristics of the organ. If the primary team should reject the organ for any reason, the secondary and tertiary teams would be immediately available to assess the organ, thus increasing the opportunity for organ placement. LifeGuard America's solution has been designed to reduce the critical time and logistical issues of this multitiered approach giving a higher probability that viable organs can be effectively placed.

Discussion Questions on LifeGuard America

1. Mr. Fitzpatrick discusses paradigms. Why are paradigms so important for entrepreneurship and the success of a new venture?

2. What is the paradigm shift in the organ procurement environment that has led to LifeGuard America's opportunity?

References

Amabile, T. (1998, September/October). How to kill creativity. *Harvard Business Review, 76*(5), 77.
Anna, C. (2002, July 15). Internet banking startup sues rival over moonlighting worker. *Austin American-Statesman (via Knight-Ridder/Tribune Business News)*, p. A1.
Astrachan, J. H., & Kolenko, T. A. (1994). A neglected factor explaining family business success: Human resource practices. *Family Business Review, 7*(3), 252–262.
Astrachan, J. H., Zahra, S. A., & Sharma, P. (2003). *Family-sponsored ventures.* Paper presented in New York on April 29, 2003, at the First Annual Global Entrepreneurship Symposium: The

Entrepreneurial Advantage of Nations. Available from: http://www.emkf.org/pdf.UN_family_sponsored_report.pdf.

Austin, J., Stevenson, H., & Wei-Skillern, J. (2006). Social and commercial entrepreneurship: Same, different, or both? *Entrepreneurship Theory and Practice, 30,* 1–22.

Bacas, H. (1987, March). Leaving the corporate nest. *Nation's Business, 75*(3), 19–22.

Barnes, L. B., & Hershon, S. A. (1976). Transferring power in the business. *Harvard Business Review,* July–August, 105–114.

Biddulph, D. (1991, April). An untapped market: The home-based business. *Direct Marketing, 53*(12), 37.

Bjuggren, P. O., & Sudd, L. G. (2001). Strategic decision making in intergenerational succession of small and medium sized family owned businesses. *Family Business Review, 14,* 11–23.

Blackman, I. (1981, November). Valuing a business: More than numbers alone. *Inc. Magazine, 3*(11), 154.

Bock, G. M. (1984, May 28). Capitalists prosper on college campuses. *U.S. News & World Report, 96*(21), 77–78.

Brockhaus, R. H. (1980, April). The effect of job satisfaction on the decision to start a business. *Journal of Small Business Management, 18*(2), 37–43.

Buckley, W. M. (1981, June 9). Second time around: The attractions of starting a new venture prove irresistible to some entrepreneurs. *The Wall Street Journal,* p. 48.

Burch, P. (1972). *Managerial revolution reassessed: Family control in America's largest corporations.* Lexington, MA: Lexington Books.

Business Week (1981, May 4).The thrill of starting up again. 112.

Byrne, J. A. (1988, July 11). Braving a family-run business. *Business Week,* 109.

Carland, J., & White, L. R. (1980, October). Valuing your business. *Journal of Small Business Management, 18*(4), 40–48.

Chief Executive (1994, September). 1994 chief executive of the year: Microsoft founder Bill Gates. *(97),* 20.

Christian Science Monitor, The. (1981, November 16). Backyard inventors. pp. 12–13.

Churchman, D. (1982, May 17). Mom and pop stores: An ongoing tradition. *The Christian Science Monitor,* p. 18.

Cohen, B. & Winn, M. I. (2007). Market imperfections, opportunity and sustainable entrepreneurship. *Journal of Business Venturing, 22,* 29–49.

Coleman, C. (2000, December 21). The cutthroat side of Christmas. *The Wall Street Journal,* p. B1.

Cowe, R. (1998, September). Serial entrepreneurs. *Management Today,* 90.

Cox, M. (1981, September 19). In a quest for security, more employees set up private little ventures. *The Wall Street Journal,* p. 1.

Daily, C. M., & Dollinger, M. J. (1992). An empirical examination of ownership structure in family and professionally managed firms. *Family Business Review, 5*(2), 117–136.

Danbom, D. (1995, May). I gave at the basement. *Communication World, 12*(5), 18.

Dean, S. M. (1992). Characteristics of African-American family-owned businesses in Los Angeles. *Family Business Review, 5*(4), 373–395.

Dean, T. J. & McMullen, J. S. (2007). Toward a theory of sustainable entrepreneurship: Reducing environmental degradation through entrepreneurial action. *Journal of Business Venturing, 22,* 50–76.

Divito, N. P. (2000, August 20). Basic physics at work. *The Tulsa World,* p. H7.

Dreux, D. R., IV. (1990). Financing family business: Alternatives to selling out or going public. *Family Business Review, 3*(3), 225–244.

Dreux, D. R., IV, & Brown, B. M. (1999). *Marketing private banking services to family businesses.* Available from: http://www.genusresources.com/Mark.Priv.Bank.Dreux_5.htm.

Drucker, P. F. (1986, February). Principles of innovation: The do's and don'ts. *Modern Office Technology, 31*(2), 12–16.

Duncan, I. (1992, April). Generating ideas: Explorers and artists wanted. *CMA Magazine, 66*(3), 36.

Dunn, B. (1995, March). Success themes in Scottish family enterprises: Philosophies and practices through generations. *Family Business Review, 8*(1), 17–28.

Dyer, W. G., Jr. (1986). *Cultural change in family firms: anticipating and managing business and family transitions,* San Francisco: Jossey Bass.

Dyszel, B. (1999, April). Home, sweet phone. *Success, 46*(4), 36.

Economist, The. (2011a, June 25). The bottom of the pyramid. *400*(8739), 80.

Economist, The. (2011b, August 20). Patent medicine. *400*(8747), 10.

Economist, The. (2011c, September 10). Many patents, still pending. *401*(8750), 72.

Economist, The. (2011d, December 3). Happy landings. *401*(8762), 103–104.

Economist, The. (2011e, December 10). University challenge. *401*(8763), 74.

Eisenstein, P. A. (1987, February 4). Off-the wall fad turns inventor into mentor for future faddists. *The Christian Science Monitor,* p. 21.

Farson, R., & Keyes, R. (2002, August). The failure-tolerant leader. *Harvard Business Review, 80*(8), 64.

Fonvielle, W. H. (1987, February/March). The rise of the idea entrepreneur. *Management World, 16*(2), 35.

Frohman, A. L. (1997, Winter). Igniting organizational change from below: The power of personal initiative. *Organizational Dynamics, 25*(3), 39–53.

Gallo, M. (1995, June). The role of family business and its distinctive characteristic behavior in industrial activity. *Family Business Review, 8*(2), 83–98.

Gallup Organization and National Center for Research in Economic Education. (1994). *Entrepreneurship and small business in the United States: A survey report on the views of the general public, high school students, and small business owners and managers.* Kansas City, MO: Center for Entrepreneurial Leadership.

Gardner, M. (1980, December 2). Burgeoning businesses: Women working from home. *The Christian Science Monitor,* p. 19.

Garner, R. (1997, September 29). Sequel stories: Why once is not enough. *Computerworld, 31*(39), S10–13.

Gottschalk, E. C., Jr. (1986, December 23). More ex-managers seek to turn hobbies into full-time businesses. *The Wall Street Journal,* p. 23.

Graham, R. (1980, September). Want to be an entrepreneur? Go to college. *Nation's Business, 68*(9), 65.

Gruenert. J. (1999, Fall). Second job entrepreneurs. *Occupational Outlook Quarterly, 43*(3), 18–26.

Hamel, G. (2001, July 9). Innovation's new math. *Fortune, 144*(1), 130.

Hargadon, Andrew (2003). *How Breakthroughs Happen: The Surprising Truth About How Companies Innovate.* Boston, MA: Harvard Business School Press. http://www.amazon.com/books/dp/1578519047.

Harris, E. (2001, May). Keeping a creative current. *Sales and Marketing Management, 153*(5), 71.

Hawken, P. (1987). *Growing a business.* New York: Simon & Schuster.

Hayes, J. P., & Matusky, G. (1989, September). Goodbye to the small fries … hello to the big guys. *Inc. Magazine, 11*(9), 102–107.

Heck, R. K. Z., & Stafford, K. (2001). The vital institution of family business: Economic benefits hidden in plain sight. In G. K. McCann & N. Upton (Eds.), *Destroying myths and creating value in family business* (pp. 9–17). Deland, FL: Stetson University.

Hemphill, J. M., & Kuriloff, A. H. (1978). *How to start your own small business and succeed.* New York: McGraw-Hill.

Henrekson, M. (2005). Entrepreneurship: A weak link in the welfare state? *Industrial and Corporate Change, 14,* 437–467.

Hillis, D. (2002, August). Stumbling into brilliance. *Harvard Business Review, 80*(8), 152.

Ho, Y.-P. & Wong, P.-K. (2007). Financing, regulatory costs and entrepreneurial propensity. *Small Business Economics, 28,* 187–204.

Hoffman, L. (2001, July 22). More "land" opened for Internet users. *Honolulu Star-Bulletin,* p. E14.

Holland, P. G. & Boulton, W. R. (1984). Balancing the family and the business in family business. *Business Horizons, 27*(2), 16–21.

Honolulu Advertiser, The. (2001, August 28). Power of Web lost on small businesses. Retrieved September 21, 2001, from http://the.honoluluadvertiser.com/.

Howard, J. (1982, July). What's it worth to you? *Inc. Magazine, 4*(7), 80.

Hoy, F., & Verser, T. G. (1994, Fall). Emerging business, emerging field: Entrepreneurship and the family firm. *Entrepreneurship Theory and Practice, 19*(1), 9–24.

Inc. Magazine. (1982, April). Small firms can breed other small firms. *4*(4), 33.

Inc. Magazine. (1985, May). When the paper-cup salesman saw ... *7*(5), 15.

Irwin, V. (1980, August 26). Running a business at home requires commitment, savvy. *The Christian Science Monitor,* p. 17.

Justis, R. T., & Judd, R. J. (1989). *Franchising.* Cincinnati, OH: South-Western.

Kemp, D. (1982, May). Hitting the jackpot with direct mail. *Inc. Magazine, 4*(5), 147.

Kirchhoff, B. A., & Kirchhoff, J. J. (1985, December). *Productivity and profitability among the small family businesses* (RS No. 26). Washington, DC: U.S. Small Business Administration, Office of Advocacy.

Kleiman, B., Petty, J. W., & Martin, J. (1995). Family controlled firms: An assessment of performance. *Family Business Annual, 1,* 1–10.

Kuhn, R. L. (1982, April). Partners in profit: The University of Texas's Institute for Constructive Capitalism. *Texas Business, 1,* 112–118.

Laventhol & Horvath. (1987, January 22). In the beginning…[survey graph]. *The Wall Street Journal,* p. 33.

Lener, J. (1986, December). What an idea! *Inc. Magazine, 8*(12), 24–26.

Litz, R. A. (1995). The family business: Toward definitional clarity. *Family Business Review, 8*(2), 71–81.

Livezey, E. T. (1981, February 26). U.S. Patent Office: Why the pats are pending. *The Christian Science Monitor,* pp. B8-B11.

MacBride, M. (1982, April 22). Home-based businesses: The best of both worlds. *The Christian Science Monitor,* p. 15.

Main, J. (1980, July). Hobbyists get down to business. *Money, 9*(7), 38–45.

Mamis, R.A. (1985, October). The gang that doesn't think straight. *Inc. Magazine, 7*(10), 108–111.

Mancuso, J. (1974). *The entrepreneur's handbook.* New York: Artech House.

McConaughy, D., Matthews, C. H., & Ftalko, A.S. (2001). Founding family controlled firms: performance, risk, and value. *Journal of Small Business Management 39*(1), 31–49.

McDaniel, B. (2000, April). A survey of entrepreneurship and innovation. *The Social Science Journal, 37*(2), 277.

Morrison, A. M. (1981, November 16). Santa's mail order elves. *Fortune, 104*(10), 131.

Ouh, Y. (1995). Cultural basis of skills for success in small and medium enterprises: The Korean cases. In W.C. Dunlop & B. Gibson (Eds.), *Proceedings of the ICSB 40th World Conference: Skills for success in small & mediums enterprises* (pp. 77–97). Sydney, Australia: Institute of Industrial Economics.

Pappas, V. (1977, December 9). Colleges are replacing school of hard knocks for some businessmen. *The Wall Street Journal,* p. 1.

Patent applications. (2011, November 19). *The Economist, 401*(8760), 105.

Patzelt, H. & Shepherd, D. A. (2011, July). Recognizing opportunities for sustainable development. *Entrepreneurship Theory and Practice, 35*(4), 631–652.

Poutziouris, P. (2001). The (re)-emergence of growth vis-a-vis control dilemma in a family business growth star: the case of the UK Taramasalata kings. In Poutziouris, P. & Pistrui, D. (Eds.), *Family business research in the third millennium–building bridges between theory and practice,* The Family Firm Institute Publication. Boston, MA, pp. 88–103.

Raudsepp, E. (1981, July). You can trust your hunches. *Inc. Magazine, 3*(7), 89–90.

Robichaux, M. (1990, January 9). Entrepreneur takes a leap without risking a big fall. *The Wall Street Journal,* p. B1.

Robinett, S. (1985, November). Starting with an idea. *Venture, 7*(11), 38–80.

Rowe, J. (1986, January 17). How two colleges fuel entrepreneurs. *The Christian Science Monitor,* pp. 21–22.

Schmitt, J. (2001, November). Don't allow moonlighting by workers to erode profits. *Contractor, 48,* 12.

Smith, E. T. (1985, September 30). Are you creative? *Business Week,* 80–84.

Stoy Hayward (1992). *The Stoy Hayward/BBC family business index.* London: Stoy Hayward.

Strempel, D. (2002, February 25). Life could be "suite-er" for home-based businesses. *Fairfield County Business Journal, 41*(8), 8.

Sutton, R. (2002, February). That'll never work! *Entrepreneur, 30*(2), 62.

Thurow, R. (1980, April 4). Scholars identify qualities that make entrepreneurs tick. *The Wall Street Journal,* p. 7.

Tulsa World (2000, July 29). Careers before college. p. E3.

Unsworth, K. (2001, April). Unpacking creativity. *Academy of Management Review, 26*(2), 289–297.

Vickers, M. (1997). For long-haul performance, considers all the best families; study sees benefits in relatives rule. *The New York Times,* Jan 12. http://www.nytimes.com/1997/01/12/business/for-long-haul-performance-consider-all-the-best-families.html.

Vozikis, G. S., & Cornell, C. (2000). *Tulsa University Innovation Institute proposal.* Unpublished manuscript, University of Tulsa, Tulsa, OK.

Ward, J. L. (1987). *Keeping the family business healthy: How to plan for continuing growth profitability and family leadership.* San Francisco: Jossey-Bass.

Weinrauch, J. D. (1980, January). The second time around: Entrepreneurship as a mid-career alternative. *Journal of Small Business Management 18*(1), 25, 32.

Wolner, W. (Ed.) (1977, December 26). Economic diary/Dec. 5–Dec. 9: The dollar, women, and Carter's deficit. *Business Week,* 23.

Wortman, M. S., Jr. (1995). Critical issues in family business: An international perspective of practice and research. In W. C. Dunlop & B. Gibson (Eds.), *Proceedings of the ICSB 40th World Conference: Skills for success in small & mediums enterprises* (pp. 53–76). Sydney, Australia: Institute of Industrial Economics.

Zahra, S. A., Gedajlovic, E., Neubaum, D. O., & Shulman, J. M. (2009). A typology of social entrepreneurs: Motives, search processes, and ethical challenges. *Journal of Business Venturing, 24,* 519–532.

Zeithaml, C. P., & Rice, G. H. (1985). *Entrepreneurship/small business education in American universities.* Paper presented at the Academy of Management Meeting, San Diego, CA.

Zhou, J., & George, J. M. (2001, August). When job dissatisfaction leads to creativity: Encouraging the expression of voice. *Academy of Management Journal, 44*(4), 682–696.

6 Venture Strategic Market Targeting, Management, and Planning

Can We Sell in a Demand-Driven Strategic-Opportunity Target Market? Who Buys, How Many, When, How, Where?

LEARNING OBJECTIVES

1. To understand the differences in "strategic competence" between small and larger firms.
2. To define the venture's strategic competence in a specific strategic target market.
3. To determine a venture's course of action of acting, reacting, pro-acting, or ignoring, within a preferably demand-driven or a supply-driven opportunity target market of who buys, how many they buy, when they buy, how they buy, and where they buy.

TOPIC OUTLINE

INTRODUCTION

Entrepreneurs are often accused of "seat-of-the-pants" management. When times are good, the entrepreneur's poor planning within its strategic target market or total lack of planning may be tolerable. But when the economy grows weak, mere reaction to the business environment's threats and opportunities, rather than actual planning, may not be adequate. A firm needs to plan fine-tuned adjustments of its target market regularly and to redefine its strategic competence to maintain a winning dimension in the marketplace. A demand-driven opportunity constitutes better circumstances than a supply-driven opportunity. Supply-driven opportunity is a more expensive proposition; the entrepreneur has to educate potential customers about the value concept and convince them that they need to buy the product or service. In contrast, with a demand-driven opportunity, the need to buy has already been established, and the customers cannot wait to "vote" on the legitimacy of the value concept with their purchase. Whether this demand-driven opportunity is real or perceived is almost irrelevant because the demand already exists and is unfulfilled. In this chapter, we address the fundamental controversy over venture planning in the strategic sense. In a small firm, how sophisticated should target market planning and planning in general be? What are the specific advantages and disadvantages for an entrepreneur in dealing with the development of a formal strategy? Specifically, how can an entrepreneur develop strategic competence for a venture through planning and management?

"STRATEGIC COMPETENCE" MARKET TARGETING

In an era when corporate giants are spending millions of dollars marketing their products in 30-second spots to national television audiences during the Super Bowl, can a small business venture possibly compete? Yes. Many entrepreneurs have proven this true by selecting the appropriate strategic target market and plan accordingly. Frieda Caplan is just one example—her story was highlighted in *Inc. Magazine*.

Many years ago, Frieda Caplan started *Frieda's Finest*, a wholesaler of exotic fruit and vegetables in Los Angeles. She nurtured the business into a multimillion-dollar company by relying on instinct, simple marketing tools, and her willingness to keep an open mind as far as her target market was concerned. Hers is a classic case of aiming at just the right strategic market target in order to compete with the corporate giants. Frieda attributes her success to several specific factors:

- *Innovation:* To be successful, you have to be totally open to weird new concepts.

- *Convenience:* Market the firm's wares as product lines, not individual commodities, as well as offer the luxury of one-stop shopping for hard-to-get items.

- *Niche:* Frieda took on business that mainstream wholesalers turned away.

- *Know the industry:* Frieda noticed the national trend toward more variety in grocer produce departments.

- *Definition of the target market:* Frieda virtually reinvented vegetables by adding new exotic items.

- *Quality:* Offer a predictable and consistent standard of quality.

- *Research and development:* Vegetables were tested in the kitchen before they were added to the target market product mix.

- *Use of publicity:* She did have the potential to generate excitement and news coverage.

- *Recognize limitations:* Know that if something takes off, that business will be "alone" for a limited period of time.

- *Position the company as a leader:* Frieda conducted retail supermarket seminars, lectures on produce theory, bulletins for retailers, and newsletters for consumers (Larson, 1989).

What Frieda Caplan's story is about, along with many similar stories, is the ability to effectively implement a market strategy in a competitive environment. It is about growing a thriving venture in an industry otherwise known for being both dull and brutal—the business of selling produce. In a field dominated by generic products and devoid of attention to marketing, she created a brand identity and persuaded millions of Americans to buy fruits and vegetables they had never seen or tasted (Larson, 1989, p. 80).

Most people, when they hear the words market or marketing, invariably relate them to advertising. Peter Drucker (1985a), however, maintains that target marketing relies on innovation as much as product innovation and development do, and it is precisely innovation that connects product marketing and development and establishes a framework for success in a new venture. Drucker suggests that innovation comes from leadership and leadership can be established by being, as he put it, *"the Fastest with the Mostest"* (sic!). This concept of being first does not just mean the first to introduce a product; it can also be characterized by adding a new twist to a product, a new means of distribution, or even an innovative means of promoting its sale.

Most small-venture success stories hinge on satisfied customers and innovation. Four basic premises define an innovative strategic target market to ensure the venture's success (adapted from Peterson, 1989):

1. The entrepreneur defines the company's value concept niche in terms of responding to and fulfilling a specific and identifiable set of wants of an identifiable set of customers (Who buys and how many do they buy?).

2. The entrepreneur realizes that an active market research program must be conducted to satisfy the rapidly fluctuating wants of the consumer (How and when do they buy?).

3. The entrepreneur realizes that all consumer-related activities must be coordinated under a grand strategy aimed at ensuring the delivery of customer satisfaction in their terms and at their convenience (Where do they buy?).

4. The entrepreneur believes that by satisfying customers, loyalty to the firm is created along with repeat business and word-of-mouth promotion (development of strategic competence).

Kotite (1989) expanded on this idea by suggesting that the reasons for this venture success lie in the entrepreneur's ability to recognize niches and to move quickly on a market opportunity, and by adapting larger company strategies without the cumbersome management structure and problems.

Christine Forbes (1989), staff writer for *Entrepreneur* magazine stresses the importance of identifying a venture's niche and strategic target market, especially for service firms:

Businesses need to attend to the different marketing niches by taking more of a personal approach. There's no tangible product in most service fields, so the only way to set oneself apart from the competition is to provide high-quality service and an extra dimension. We need to return to the old adage "The customer is always right." (p. 56)

Strategic Competence: Big vs. Small Business

A small business is not a little big business. A small firm has its own distinctive advantages and disadvantages. In a comparison of strategic disadvantages between small and big business, very few corresponding similarities can be drawn. Theory, research, and practice support this idea, and the entrepreneur that attempts to solve problems or plan according to the conventional wisdom of big business, is in for a big surprise. Small firms have their own strategic competence, their own edge in the business world, their own abilities, fitness, and means for survival.

A small firm has a unique expertise in a narrow segment of the market. If small business is placed on one end of a continuum of organizational characteristics and big business is on the other, certain interesting observations on the differences in strategic competence between small and big business can be derived.

Defining the strategic competence of a business is the most difficult aspect of the firm's target market strategy. Moreover, strategic competence can be extremely deceptive, because it relies on the collection of the strength of the venture, as well as the strengths of the entrepreneur *as perceived* by customers and investors alike.

Coordination

Big business needs a high degree of coordination due to its size and its multiple functions. In a small venture, the task of coordination is much easier.

Flexibility

Flexibility is probably a small firm's "heaviest gun"! Inputs, processes, and outputs can be increased, substituted, eliminated almost at will. Big businesses cannot afford this luxury.

Control

Because of the lower need for coordination and the higher degree of inherent flexibility, a small firm does not require the sophisticated control mechanisms that are absolutely necessary in a large firm.

Sophistication

Quantification, automation, optimization are elements of sophistication in the operation of a large firm. Without sophistication, a big business renders itself vulnerable to its competition. The small firm, however, does not need costly sophistication in its operations; it is not perceived as a threat because it can carve its own niche without disturbing its big competitors.

Environmental Scanning

Operational, day-to-day decisions combined with inherent flexibility do not need sophisticated, future-oriented environmental scanning to identify trends, new areas of activity, and elements of change. Small firms can weather **contingencies** (unpredictable, uncontrollable factors) because of their flexibility; they can withstand **constraints** (predictable but uncontrollable factors) because of their low sophistication; and finally, they can manage their operating **variables** (predictable and controllable factors) because of their low need for control.

Effectiveness

The emphasis of a small firm is on **effectiveness**, to accomplish and achieve its goals. The target of most big firms is **efficiency**, to achieve a goal with the least possible cost. Again, due to the large-scale competition and the high stakes involved, an efficient big firm stands a better chance of survival than an effective but not efficient big firm.

Emphasis on Customer Needs

Effectiveness in a small firm means satisfying the specific needs of customers. People will go to great lengths to get the perfect shoeshine, the perfect quilt, or to spend the night at the bed-and-breakfast inn that is friendly and romantic. Big businesses, while not neglecting customer needs, put more emphasis on which customer groups they serve, how, and at what price and cost. The effectiveness of small firms once again is pitted against the efficiency of a large firm.

Experience Curve Learning Effects

Large firms enjoy economies of scale, or the continuous allocation and distribution of fixed costs and overhead to a larger number of production units. Their large size avails their ability to command quantity discounts from their suppliers, as well as the successful substitution of expensive materials with less costly ones, for example, plastic vs. wood. On the other hand, small firms enjoy advantages from the learning effects of an experience curve. As small-business operators become more familiar with the tasks to produce a value concept, more experience is gained, and planning, tooling, and quality control become more effective.

Time Horizon

A small firm tackles today's problems first, because they are more critical than tomorrow's problems. A large business has to look further into the future, sometimes sacrificing short-term objectives for long-range survival. A small firm cannot afford this luxury. Flexibility, the ability to react to changes quickly, and sometimes luck, are the small firm's weapons for tomorrow's problems.

Experience

A large firm relies on specialized training as a managerial skill, such as an MBA degree. Small firms rely on the experience of their owner/entrepreneurs and their emphasis on general, rather than overspecialized skills. Small-business owners are experienced general managers, whereas managers of large firms are specialized functional managers.

Decentralization

Flexibility entails freedom, and freedom requires a decentralized structure. Small firms have few hierarchical levels; they have broad spans of control, and they rely more on participative management than their larger counterparts do. Big firms are more centralized and more bureaucratic, with coordinating mechanisms such as organizational charts, manuals, policies, and procedures.

Change and Innovation

In any given year, entrepreneurs rarely do what they were doing the year before. They do not ask the question "what if?" as a large firm might; rather, they ask "why not?" Big businesses emphasize the *status quo,* and unless something drastic happens, rarely are any fundamental changes made, other than incremental and sometimes merely cosmetic adjustments to their original strategy.

Intuition

Intuition's role in creativity, innovation, and change is indispensable. John Mihalasky tested hundreds of small-firm executives for intuitive abilities. He found that superior decision-making and profitability indeed correlate highly with intuitive ability (Raudsepp, 1981). This, of course, does not mean that entrepreneurs should not use rational, analytical decision making. Even large-firm executives prefer to use judgment instead of analytical, rational decision making, even though they sometimes try to hide this fact because it may appear professionally disreputable. The larger the relative commitment of resources, the greater the availability of documented and quantitative data and the less time pressure (all big business characteristics more or less), the greater the tendency to use analysis (Mintzberg, Raisinghani, & Theoret, 1976).

Dynamic Nature

A small firm, due to its inherent flexibility, can *act* to seize opportunities, *react* to threats, and *pro-act* to create opportunities and prevent threats from occurring, much faster than a big firm. A constant redefinition of its strategic competence and a relatively wide array of available options provide the small firm with a dynamic character, which is absent in a big firm. This dynamism often counterbalances the small venture's lack of sophistication in operations and planning. The consequences of potentially incorrect decisions because of inadequate screening of market and overall environmental information can be quickly offset by the almost instantaneous and dynamic redefinition of strategic competence.

"Satisficing."

Entrepreneurs cannot operate by quantifying everything. Because of what management theorists have called **bounded rationality** limitations in terms of ability and time, the entrepreneur sets some general minimum criteria that have to be satisfied by a decision. Then a sequential search of alternatives is undertaken until a satisfactory solution is found, one that satisfies those minimum criteria. This **satisficing** alternative may not be the best—the one that maximizes profits or minimizes costs, for example—but given the time and money constraints of a decision, it is better than all alternatives and their consequences.

It is quite obvious that the small, innovative firm has a different nature of distinctive strategic competence than its larger counterpart. Despite the generalizations that were made in this section and the broad overlapping gray area between entrepreneurial and large-firm organizational characteristics, the stage is set to discuss the management of strategic target-market planning, management, and development, strictly in the context of small firms.

Strategic Competence: A "Strategic Window"

Given the small-firm limitations relative to big business, the entrepreneur should concentrate on the advantages that the small firm enjoys, as discussed previously. Relying on flexibility, the most important advantage of all, the small firm should

- Constantly redefine its strategic competence.
- Continuously identify what Abell (1980, p. 224) so perceptively called "strategic windows."

- Emphasize effectiveness rather than efficiency.

- Identify its strategic flexibility tactics:

  - *Act* to seize an opportunity;

  - *React* to avoid a threat;

  - *Proact* to induce drastic changes internally or externally creating opportunities or preventing threats; and

  - *Ignore* a situation presenting itself neither as a threat nor as an opportunity.

Strategic Window Identification

Abell and Hammond (1981, p. 63) advanced the concept of **strategic windows**, which they defined as follows:

> "There are only limited periods during which the 'fit' between the key requirements of a market and the particular competencies of a firm competing in that market are at an optimum."

This concept is a much more dynamic configuration of the strategic competency of the firm as opposed to a static nature. The strategic window concept recognizes the inevitability of changes and forces the firm to focus on what can be changed, improved, enhanced, or reduced to deal with tomorrow, rather than the current market position of the firm (Abell, 1980, p. 224).

Strategic window opportunities aiming at a specific strategic target market may emerge along four dimensions: *customer needs, customer segments, alternative technologies* (or alternative ways of satisfying a customer need in a customer segment), and *alternative prices*. The strategic window identification therefore goes hand in hand with the constant redefinition of strategic competence, taking full advantage of the inherent flexibility of a new entrepreneurial venture. Some alternative dimensions can be used for strategic window identification, such as service (customer needs), industry (technology), or geography (customer segments), or any other dimension that applies to targeting a particular market. As the company grows, the coverage of strategic windows can be extended along each dimension, covering more needs and/or more segments with more alternative technologies and/or more price differentiating levels.

Sexton and Bowman-Upton (1991) argue that the upper limit on the realization of the benefits from a strategic market opportunity is determined by various market constraints. The size of the market niche served by the firm represents the potential volume of sales. The actual sales generated within this niche is constrained by the amount of time the firm has to serve this niche, that is, how long the strategic window will remain open, and by the rate of sales within this niche, as determined by a product's position in its life cycle. Finally, the extent to which the sales potential of a strategic window is realized is a function of the desire for growth on the part of the entrepreneur.

The continuous identification of strategic windows serves to clarify what business, what industry, and what market the venture serves:

- A *business* is defined by a selection of customer groups and functions and is usually based on one primary technology (e.g., producing one engineered plastic serving a variety of customer groups).

- An *industry* is defined by the boundaries of several businesses but is still usually based on a single technology.

- A *market* is defined by the performance of given functions in given customer groups and includes all of the substitute technologies used to perform those functions. Generally speaking, the greater the similarity in manufacturing and marketing requirements across and within customer groups, the more broadly defined the market in terms of customers and functions. However, in all cases, all substitute technologies must be included (Abell, 1980).

Effectiveness over Efficiency

Wright (1983) provided an interesting formula for small firms on the road to effectiveness, growth, development, and profitability:

Uniqueness + Quality + Personal Attention + Flexibility = Profitability

In other words, effectiveness means providing the customer with a *unique* product, of high *quality* and especially reliable service, with *personal attention* to the needs of that customer by the small firm, which is always ready to accommodate the customer with *flexibility* in terms of payment terms, packaging, custom-made fabrication, etc. (Wright, 1983).

Sometimes small firms outperform their big rivals, even in terms of efficiency and economies of scale—an advantage that large companies supposedly enjoy due to their size. In a modest pilot program conducted by the SBA and the Air Force, spare parts were cheaper when small contractors supplied them. A big contractor charged $11,007 for a wing part that a small company made for $7,000 less. A preamplifier that a large contractor priced at $699 cost $174 from a small supplier. Through the program, the Air Force saved $6.7 million on 181 spare parts contracts in 18 months; savings averaged 38.5%. However, less than 8% of the 3.9 million spare parts the Defense Department stocks are open to competitive bidding, and programs that assure small companies more contracts seem to be faltering ("Small Business: What Economies of Scale," 1982, p. 27).

Strategic Flexibility Tactics

Having defined its strategic competence, having identified its strategic windows, and having ensured effectiveness in rendering a product or a service, the small firm has to understand and analyze its strategic options in terms of flexibility and position in the marketplace. These strategic tactics are the result of the values, attitudes, and perceptions of the small-firm owners. They represent the overall *disposition* of the firm toward the market and the competitive, aggressive, defensive, or passive view it holds in relation to its strategic competence. As mentioned previously, a small firm has, broadly speaking, four tactical options:

- *Act* to seize an opportunity.
- *React* to avoid a threat.
- *Pro-act* to induce drastic changes internally or externally by creating opportunities where none existed before or preventing threats before they mushroom into real danger.
- *Ignore* a threat or an opportunity.

These tactics are by no means mutually exclusive or always discrete. A small firm may use a combination or hybrid tactic. For example, as a firm acts to seize an opportunity, it may take some reactive action to directly defend its strategic competence and market position. These tactical distinctions may reflect a difference of degree rather than separate, disassociated courses of action. Nevertheless, these distinctions among tactical responses are quite useful in setting the stage for growth and development.

Act

In practice, firms quite commonly act to seize opportunities. By focusing on a specific customer group, and/or by catering to specific customer needs, a firm aggressively steps toward the development of a strategic target market. The strategic firm disposition to regularly act to seize strategic window opportunities by expanding or contracting along four dimensions (i.e., customer segments, customer needs, alternative technologies, and alternative prices) is a sign that a small firm is predisposed to take full advantage of its target market. If these tactical actions continue to be successful, the firm is destined to grow. Of course, the factors that determine the attractiveness of an opportunity are based on judgments and perceptions of the entrepreneur. Trade-offs among different factors and opportunities, as well as taking into account how competitors will react, influence the decision to act. Strategic competence is an asset that can be exploited to seize opportunities in strategic windows. However, a tactical action seldom automatically yields the desired results without hard work, thorough research, and trade-offs in financial and human costs.

React

Reacting is a tactic in which the small firm builds on its strengths and defends its strategic competence. Reacting to competitive, financial, or other threats on a regular basis instead of acting may characterize a firm predisposed to maintaining the status quo of its strategic target market as originally identified, rather than concentrating on growth. In most cases, it entails a strategic competence loss, because the competitor that attacks first has a significant advantage, and because it takes time for the small firm that is attacked to react. Consequently, a contraction along the four dimensions of strategic window opportunities may be undertaken. However, reacting does not always constitute a concession to a threat. A vigorous defensive reaction can successfully protect the firm's strategic competence and signal to the attacker that it will not be "pushed around," but will fight instead. This is especially true when reacting is less expensive than acting, and when defense is less expensive than attack. However, when the attacked firm makes concessions, loss in the strategic competence should be considered permanent.

Pro-act

With pro-active tactics, a small firm, not only during the venture initiation stage but also on a regular basis, engages in an offensive style of creating opportunities for its strategic target market and prevents threats from becoming real. The firm is constantly advancing and extending along the four strategic window opportunities dimensions, not waiting for the opportunities to show, but creating opportunities where they seemingly do not yet exist. At the same time, measures are taken to ensure that slight disturbances in the internal or external environment of the firm are addressed and prevented before they ever develop into full-scale problems. Such an aggressive tactic can be very expensive and quite dangerous, perhaps to the point of exposing vulnerable areas in the strategic competence of the firm while the firm is occupied with other activities. The pro-active tactic is also unstable because it drains energy from the firm and is not sustainable in the long term. Total victories as well as absolute prevention of problems are unrealistic, as history tells us. However, frequent management audits and regular reassessments of the strategic target market are healthy ways of spotting opportunities, threats, and weaknesses, and they generally anticipate the seemingly unforeseeable events.

Ignore

Ignoring a threat from (or opportunity in) the strategic target market is not generally a desirable tactical option and is usually ruled out, except in situations in which acting or reacting are fairly costly, or when opportunities are not particularly attractive and threats are not very dangerous.

From the previous discussion, certain conclusions in relation to strategic competence and strategic tactics can be drawn:

1. When acting on an opportunity in a strategic target market is fairly inexpensive and reacting is fairly expensive, act on the opportunity.

2. Reacting is appropriate when acting on the strategic target market opportunity is expensive, when reacting later is fairly inexpensive, and when the market has high entry barriers. Thus, the venture gains the relative protection of its existing original strategic target market.

3. Pro-acting is usually expensive and is advisable only for short periods, when it is used to preempt other firms from acting or to prevent a serious internal or external threat from endangering the strategic target market.

4. Ignoring is advisable when the perceived threats or opportunities do not warrant the selection of war over peace in the marketplace.

5. Finally, opportunities and threats, as well as their degree of importance, are all a matter of perception and value judgment. In real life, the players in the entrepreneurial venture are not always perfectly rational or accurate in their perceptions. Emotional involvement, bias, and under- or overestimation of opportunities and/or threats tend to distort tactical formulations.

Constant Redefinition of Strategic Competence

As mentioned previously, small firms do not have the sophistication of large businesses when it comes to environmental scanning and external information screening and processing to identify strategic competence. As a result, very often, responses to identify external threats and opportunities are inadequate.

Additionally, the achievement of a particular level of growth or growth rate of sales through the exploitation of a strategic target market opportunity in a strategic window should not be viewed as evidence of long-term organizational viability. As a matter of fact, many firms reach their greatest size just before they die (Adizes, 1989). Hoy, McDougall, and D'Souza (1992) concluded that a high growth rate in a firm may be minimally or even negatively correlated with firm profitability.

To balance out the consequences of some inevitable wrong decisions in terms of strategic competence, the small firm possesses the formidable weapon of flexibility. Control of the effects of occasional inadequate or incorrect decisions can be exercised through a flexible, dynamic realignment and redefinition of the firm's strategic competence to effect needed transitions in the venture's organizational system (Dodge, Fullerton, & Robbins, 1994).

The *conceptual metamorphosis* of the venture is needed to overcome the many crises that must be resolved to successfully redefine the strategic competence (Mount, Zinger, & Forsyth, 1993). Entrepreneurs need to reduce the tension that builds in the organizational system as a result of the difference between the current strategic competence configuration and the venture's transition needs (Naman & Slevin, 1993). The essential task in maintaining and renewing the venture's strategic competence is to create a new configuration comprised of the venture's organizational attributes and system interrelationships that are more appropriate

(Hanks, 1990). Specifically, the redefinition of the venture's strategic competence can be accomplished with the following:

1. Basic marketing and pricing strategies that flout industry norms.

2. A goal-oriented and rigorously trained sales force with tight parameters and attitudes.

3. A focus on profitability (Taylor, 1979).

STRATEGIC COMPETENCE MANAGEMENT

The strategic competence that results from successfully conceptualized venture target market identification needs to be carefully managed. Successful strategic competence management requires careful consideration of the following managerial skills that contribute to new venture success: (1) industry structure considerations; (2) opportunity identification and evaluation considerations; (3) obtaining, managing, and controlling resources considerations; (4) managing the strategic and operational elements of the business; and (5) professional development skills.

Industry Structure Considerations

In their review of the determinants of new venture performance, Hofer and Sandberg (1987) contended that the most important consideration is the structure of the industry to be entered. Because industry structure can be described by many characteristics, these authors identified the five most critical factors influencing the chances for successfully entering a new market: (1) the degree of stability in the industry entered, (2) the industry's competitive nature, (3) stage of evolution, (4) barriers to entry, and (5) product characteristics.

However, these results must be viewed cautiously. First, the authors' insights dealt predominantly with existing industries rather than markets yet to be developed. Second, much of the research from which the authors drew their conclusions consisted of studies of corporate ventures rather than independent entrepreneurial ventures, which may have biased these suggestions. In the long run, these concerns may not greatly affect their recommendations for our purposes. However, the independent entrepreneur should consider them in the context of his/her situation. Here are five guidelines for enhancing new venture performance.

1. Focus on industries facing substantial technological or regulatory changes, especially those with recent exits by established competitors.

Successful entries are facilitated by unstable industry conditions. Entry is easier, particularly if it occurs relatively early during the unstable period.

2. Seek industries whose smaller firms have relatively weak competitive positions.

Perhaps surprisingly, industries possessing a dominant competitor (> 49% market share) were easier to enter for new ventures than those where the largest competitor had less than a 25% share of the market. The former situation may imply that the remaining competitors are relatively weaker, allowing new ventures easier entry into smaller market niches. The latter situation may support more intense competition.

3. Seek industries in early, high-growth stages of evolution.

Entering rapid-growth markets early contributes to success. Most competitors share this rapid market growth; hence, competition is less intense. Also, mistakes and unsuccessful experiments are easier to overcome when they occur at an early stage, when the market is more forgiving.

4. Seek industries in which it is possible to create high barriers to subsequent entry.

Industries that provide natural entry barriers (e.g., a limited number of customers or captive suppliers of raw material) or allow entry barriers to be erected improve the chances of success by helping new ventures avoid competition.

5. Seek industries with heterogeneous products that are relatively unimportant to the customer's overall success.

Industries with heterogeneous products allow ventures to avoid or lessen competition by following product differentiation strategies or by finding smaller market segments. Entry is easier when the venture's product or service is relatively unimportant to the customer's needs. If the product is important, the customer is less willing to try new sources or to experiment with new approaches (Hofer & Sandberg, 1987, pp. 13–17).

Studying the industry structure as it relates to strategic competence and the new venture's performance is, however, like making decisions in a vacuum, isolated from all of the elements surrounding it. In other words, entrepreneurs must plan and develop an entrepreneurial strategy that successfully matches their strategic competence as well as the unique characteristics of the industry that they intend to enter.

The earliest literature in entrepreneurial strategies recommends the pursuit of *market niche* strategies to avoid direct competition with large firms. Such approaches advise concentrating on one or more of the following market segments: specialized or customized products, local geographic markets, markets that are too small to attract the attention of large-scale firms, and markets in which a competitive advantage can be obtained through service and/or company flexibility.

More recently, the conventional wisdom for new ventures, and particularly for corporate ventures, was to follow an aggressive strategy, that is, to enter on a large scale, to market and promote extensively, and to incur high relative advertising and sales force expenditures. In several studies, this type of strategy resulted in higher performance than in those ventures pursuing less aggressive entry strategies. Recently, however, this "wisdom" has come under fire. New studies have shown that aggressive entry is not appropriate for all firms. Indeed, a number of entrepreneurial strategies have been identified, which, under the right conditions, can lead to success. Even direct competition with industry leaders can be a successful strategy if the venture has positioned itself appropriately.

One study that examined 247 independent start-ups and corporate ventures identified eight distinct entrepreneurial strategies. Of these, only one, controlled growth via premium-priced products sold directly to consumers, had significantly better performance than the other seven strategies, which had relatively similar performance results (McDougall & Robinson, 1987a). With one exception noted previously, these results support the idea that no single strategy always works best. These eight strategies are:

1. Aggressive strategic competence management via commodity-type products to numerous markets with small customer orders.

2. Aggressive strategic competence management via price-competitive new products to large customers.

3. Aggressive entry with narrow, special products priced competitively to a few larger buyers.

4. Controlled growth with broad product range to many markets and extensive backward integration.

5. Controlled growth via premium-priced products sold directly to consumers.

6. Limited growth, in small niches offering a superior product and high customer service.

7. Average growth via steady development of new channels, brand-name identification, and heavy promotion.

8. Limited growth selling infrequently purchased products to numerous markets with some forward integration (McDougall & Robinson, 1987b, pp. 74–76).

In their review of the literature, Hofer and Sandberg (1987) identified five strategy considerations that play important roles in new venture performance: (a) product differentiation; (b) quality, service, and price; (c) market and/or segment domination; (d) innovation; and (e) methods of growth. From these considerations, the authors identified several guidelines for improving the odds of success. Much of what they recommend is similar to but more generalizable than the competence management strategies identified by McDougall and Robinson (1987b). Their recommendations are listed here:

1. Seek to differentiate your products from those of your competitors in ways that are meaningful to your customers. Focus such differentiation efforts on the areas of product quality, marketing approaches, and customer service—and charge enough to cover the costs of doing so. Cost-based focus strategies are not as successful in new ventures because of the lack of scale, expertise, scope, capital, and market power usually associated with a newly developed business.

2. Seek to dominate the market segments in which you compete. If necessary, either segment the market differently or change the nature and focus of your differentiation efforts to increase your domination of the markets you serve.

3. Stress innovation, especially new product innovation built on existing organizational capabilities. To remain successful in the long term, the key is continued innovation. This is especially important immediately after the introduction of a venture's first product; therefore, R&D expenditures are heavier in the first 2 years after start-up in more successful new ventures.

4. Seek natural, organic growth through flexibility and opportunism that builds on existing organizational strengths. Successful new ventures don't pursue growth for growth's sake. They build on their existing strengths and stay with their core skills (Hofer & Sandberg, 1987, pp. 17–19).

The various characteristics representing the competence management strategy and industry structure for an entrepreneurial firm need to be consistent and well matched. As such, Hofer and Sandberg (1987) offer several suggestions. First, they recommend that the venture remain flexible and pursue a broadly defined strategy during the early stages of evolution; there is too much uncertainty at play to do anything else. Customer needs and product characteristics are still changing, and any type of focused strategy might cause the firm to lose attractive segments.

As the industry evolves into later stages, this approach should be revised: competition becomes more significant, and the industry and product characteristics begin to stabilize. Second, follow a differentiation strategy in the early stages, but combine it with other approaches as both the venture and industry mature. Third, follow a differentiated strategy in industries with heterogeneous products and avoid undifferentiated strategies in industries with homogeneous products (Hofer & Sandberg, 1987, pp. 19–21).

A variety of other strategic frameworks exist, but most of them reflect the ideas and issues cited above. Nevertheless, the entrepreneur benefits from his/her familiarity with the various strategies used by new ventures. But familiarity doesn't necessarily mean mastery. Following an entrepreneurial strategy is not a matter of just choosing one and hoping that it will work. Identifying the appropriate strategy for a new venture's target market and implementing it is an extensive and difficult process, but if the entrepreneur is willing to do his/her homework, the right strategy can pay off in the end in terms of sales and profitability.

In summary, industry structure is an important factor to consider when looking at ways to improve the chances of succeeding in a new venture. But the Hofer and Sandberg (1987) recommendations also are more important for the entrepreneur than for the small-business person, who typically enters businesses in which competition is fragmented and virtually impossible to avoid (e.g., hair salons, sewing shops, dry cleaners, etc.).

Opportunity Identification and Evaluation Considerations

The crux of this set of management skills is the importance of recognizing the difference between a good idea and a good opportunity. To accomplish this, Timmons, Smollen, and Dingee (1985) indicate that opportunity identification and evaluation skills entail gathering information, conducting a feasibility study to assess whether an idea is in actuality a good opportunity, writing a business plan, and recognizing the critical success factors that will enable the target market opportunity to produce results and the venture to perform once it is started.

Drucker (1985b) added an interesting perspective to this group of skills. He contended that a market focus is required because when a new venture does succeed, it may be in a market other than the one it was originally intended to serve; that is, it serves these markets with products or services not quite those with which it had set out. These products and services may be purchased in large part by customers it did not even think of when it started, and products may be used for a host of purposes other than the ones for which they were first designed. If a new venture does not anticipate this, does not organize itself to take advantage of unexpected and unseen markets, and finally, if it is not totally market focused and market driven, then it will succeed only in creating an opportunity for a competitor (p. 189).

Since truly new products create markets that have never before existed, how can any form of sophisticated and accurate market research be conducted? Drucker (1985b) provided a number of examples to illustrate this point. For instance, around 1950, the manufacturer of the Univac, the first and most sophisticated computer on the market, concluded from its market research that by the year 2000 only 1,000 computers would be sold. After all, they reasoned, the technical and scientific markets that could use this product were very small. IBM, on the other hand, recognized the expanding utility of the machine for the business world, and the rest is history. To avoid this problem, Drucker suggests that the entrepreneur must search not only for unexpected successes but also for unexpected failures, and then must examine them carefully for potential opportunities, because they are not just exceptions to the rule (p. 192).

Obtaining, Managing, and Controlling Resources Considerations

Being undercapitalized in a specific target market is one problem, but having enough cash and managing it poorly is another. Needless to say, the lack of financial resources is believed to be the most common cause of small business failures. This may be true, but it is probably better to look at cash shortage as more a symptom than a cause of failure. The sad truth is that a lack of financial and accounting skills frequently leads to failure. What can small businesses do to avoid this problem? For one thing, they need to recognize that the ability to obtain sufficient initial capital for their venture is critical to their success. Being well capitalized allows the firm to overcome its early mistakes and to survive long enough to resolve initial challenges in its strategic target market.

After the initial start-up considerations, the focus shifts to skills in managing and controlling financial resources to preserve the emerging strategic competence in the strategic target market. The founder, or a member of the venture team, should know enough about finance and accounting to be able to prepare and use financial statements, keep track of and manage cash flows, reliably forecast the target market's cash needs for the future, understand and be able to calculate break-even analyses, and set up an effective budgetary and control system. Much of this is made easier if the founder also possesses some fundamental accounting skills.

How do these situations differ (assuming they do) between small-business owners and entrepreneurs? The very nature of the entrepreneurial venture requires that either the founder or a financial professional in the management team possesses financial skills. The more the founder understands the rudiments of finance and accounting, the more investors tend to be comfortable with the venture's chances of succeeding. In small businesses, however, founders often lack financial and accounting skills, and far too frequently they end up running out of cash. Yet these skills are not that difficult to master, and they make life with the outside world that much easier. Does it make sense to surrender the control of your business to an accountant or a financial advisor when you've put in all the hard work and effort to build it? Unfortunately, not enough small-business people understand that accounting is the language of business and to effectively communicate in the business world, they must speak this language fluently.

Beyond financial resources, physical, intellectual, and human resources also need to be obtained and managed. To a certain extent, the way an entrepreneur goes about obtaining, controlling, and managing such resources is driven by their philosophy. At the heart of this philosophy is a commitment and ability to use resources belonging to other people, groups, organizations, etc. This way, they not only leverage their risk, but they also learn how to manage resources without having to own them, that is, they subcontract, rent, lease, barter, trade, or whatever else is necessary to get their job done. They do not commit excessive funds they generally do not have to begin with, and they do not retain assets they frequently do not need to own anyway.

Strategic and Operational Considerations

Although the entrepreneur may have creative and innovative ideas, the management team must possess excellent sales, marketing, and operations knowledge to run the day-to-day operations of the firm. Early strategy researchers were predominantly concerned with identifying the *best practices* that contribute to success. Researchers in this stream share an interest in pondering the inner growth engines or "the black box" of the firm; they argue that a firm's continued success is chiefly a function of its internal and unique competitive resources (Hitt, Hoskisson, Wan, & Yiu, 1999). Typically, this covers all the various skills needed to manage, market, and produce a product or service. It encompasses both the short- and long-term elements of managing the venture in the specific target market, including: gaining the trust and commitment of the customer; setting specific goals and time-phased targets; recognizing and using the rules-of-thumb gained from experience in the particular trade, industry, or market; possessing negotiating skills; managing the strategic and daily operations of the business; and effectively managing time. The list could go on and on, but the idea is that solid management of the strategic competence of the venture and its related practices can contribute to success and can keep the venture from failing. However, as argued by Miller (1992), firms with a high degree of strategic fit with their market and customers run the risk of being less attentive to maintaining the needed strategic and operational complementarities among the components of their internal organizational systems.

Additionally, evidence suggests that as the venture's size increases, substantial strategic and operational managerial energies must be expended to sustain the venture's strategic competence in a target market (Slevin & Covin, 1995), especially because these kinds of transitions and their successful management constitute the key to venture growth and success (Ahlbrandt & Slevin, 1992).

Professional Development Considerations

Finally, through professional development, entrepreneurs can enhance their chances for success if they continually update and improve their skills to manage their strategic competence in their target market. Professional development includes management education, continuing education, and a variety of available seminars, workshops, networking, etc., which can keep them abreast of the latest managerial techniques, industry trends, and ideas. Part of this professional development work can be delegated. For example, the shop foreman may have the task of watching for technical changes as reported in trade journals for the industry while the sales manager keeps abreast of significant changes that occur in the firm's target markets. But entrepreneurs cannot delegate the hardest part of this work. They cannot delegate the decisions about the revisions that will be made in the strategic market target plan.

Strategic competence management and planning and their importance are functions of the industry and the technology used, as well as functions of personality. Entrepreneurs with a high internal locus of control seek information categories other than personal sources, such as neighbors or family members. Rigid thinkers, in contrast, seek structure from professional sources, such as bankers, consultants, and institutional sources, such as professional organizations or the IRS, and they may verify this information with their personal sources (Welsch & Young, 1982, p. 57).

CONCLUSION

Having gained an understanding of the specific characteristics of strategic competence in market targeting and management, the issue becomes how to make it work for the small firm. By concentrating on the advantages typically possessed by a small enterprise, a well-designed planning process can bring results. Flexibility in terms of strategic competence, exploitation of the plentiful profitable small value concept niche opportunities, taking advantage of the lower (relative to larger firms) overhead burden, and direct profit orientation focus by the entrepreneur can provide great rewards from planning (Van Kirk & Noonan, 1982). This basic fact makes entrepreneurs carry strategic thinking to the point of actually developing concrete goals and specific objectives for their target market regarding who buys, how many they buy, when they buy, how they buy, and where they buy.

This transition from mere strategic thinking to full-scale strategic competence market targeting is what makes new ventures succeed. When the conceptualization of the strategic competence target market is as near the actual configuration of the target market as possible, the opportunity represented by that specific target market was acted upon. Action is the difference between a plan and a dream.

Thus, entrepreneurs can at least partially control their own destiny. For instance, they can locate in areas conducive to start-up and growth ventures; they can enter industries with traditionally higher survival rates and that possess characteristics on which they can capitalize; and they can become familiar with the wealth of external support groups and organizations whose mission is to help small businesses and entrepreneurial ventures succeed. Founders must examine their own strengths and weaknesses to decide whether they have the capability and the patience to stay with their ventures during a target market's up and down periods. They must educate themselves in the management practices indicative of successful small businesses and growth firms. And finally, they must develop strategies that take advantage of their industry's structural characteristics, their own managerial abilities, and their firm's strengths and weaknesses. Strategic competence targeting and management is a deliberate, value-oriented, time-consuming, specialized function for which entrepreneurs are sometimes ill qualified. Most entrepreneurial efforts are oriented toward problem solving in the present rather than contemplating opportunities in the future. The entrepreneur must deliberately reallocate enough time to accommodate this early identification process, even though present problems make relentless demands on the entrepreneur's time. When a judgment about a seemingly exciting opportunity represented by a target market proves to be wrong, the losses need to be cut as soon as possible, and lessons should be learned from this bad experience. The mental anguish caused by wrong judgments is part of the price an entrepreneur pays for being his or her own boss. The challenges are there, as are the recommendations for improving the odds of succeeding. But remember, as someone once said, the only place where "success comes before work is in the dictionary."

Website Information

Topic	Web Address	Description
Strategic competence market targeting	http://www.friedas.com/	Homepage for Frieda's Finest, Caplan's wholesale exotic fruit and vegetable company.
Strategic competence development	http://www.grundfos.com/web/grfosweb.nsf/Webopslag/FC932C5A898C9489C1256C2B00256669	Grundfos is a company based in Denmark that specializes in water pumps. This section of the website talks about strategic competence. Other links in the site talk about innovation, strategic planning, etc.

Key Terms

Bounded rationality: limitations in terms of ability and time.

Constraints: Predictable but uncontrollable factors that a small firm may overcome because of its low sophistication.

Contingencies: Unpredictable, uncontrollable factors that a small firm may overcome because of its flexibility.

Effectiveness: The ability of a small firm to accomplish and achieve its goals. Effectiveness means providing the customer with a unique product of high quality and especially reliable service, with personal attention to the needs of that customer who is treated with flexibility in terms of payment terms, packaging, custom-made fabrication, etc.

Efficiency: Achieving effectiveness with the least possible cost; the objective of most big firms.

Flexibility: The ability to react quickly to changes.

Satisficing: Satisfying minimum criteria.

Strategic windows: Limited periods during which the "fit" between the key requirements of a market and the particular competencies of a firm competing in that market are at an optimum.

Variables: Predictable and controllable factors.

Review Questions

1. What are the four basic premises that define an innovative strategic market in order to ensure the venture's success?

2. Explain the concepts of contingencies, constraints, and variables in regard to the environmental scanning benefit of a smaller venture.

3. Distinguish between the terms business, industry, and market.

4. Describe four of the eight entrepreneurial strategies used to enhance performance.

5. List and explain a small firm's strategic flexibility tactics.

6. Using the Business Model Canvas presented in Chapter 3, sketch out a business model canvas for an agricultural concept. Use your "intuition" and "experience," as well as the dynamic nature of the well-known entrepreneurs, to guide your thoughts.

Reflections from the Front Lines of LifeGuard America

It is critically important to clearly define your market, and again we return to the business plan section on market definition. The market for LifeGuard America's services consists of three primary institutions governed by the policies and guidelines of the Organ Procurement and Transplantation Network (OPTN) and administrated by the United Network for Organ Sharing (UNOS). The first are the 59 Organ Procurement Organizations responsible for the procurement and allocation of all donated organs in the United States. The second consists of the 259 Transplant Centers, or hospitals, in which all transplant operations are conducted, and the third encompasses the 871 Transplant Programs that make up the organizations that perform the procurement and transplant surgeries. The transplant programs are identified by organ type and number of programs below:

Type of Program	Number
Kidney transplant programs	245
Liver transplant programs	122
Pancreas transplant programs	135
Islet cell transplant programs	30

Intestine transplant programs	39
Heart transplant programs	141
Heart-lung transplant programs	83
Lung transplant programs	76
Total	**871**

This represents our entire market of approximately 1,000 organizations across the United States. The number of transplants that take place is increasing but is currently limited by the number of donors, which has not been growing as rapidly as the number of patients added to the waiting list. There were approximately 22,000 transplants last year, and the number of people on the waiting list eclipsed 80,000. This is the single greatest problem facing the entire OPTN and is a primary driver for services, such as our focus on eliminating wasted organs and ultimately raising the number of organs per donor that are transplanted. The OPTN is organized into 11 UNOS Regions depicted on Map 6.1.

Map 6.1   UNOS Region Map

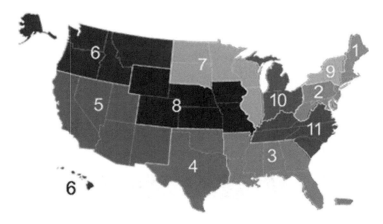

These regions operate in an autonomous way that allows us to approach each region with services that are tailored to meet their individual needs based on geography, demographics, and population density. These regions all have individual meetings, and each region has representation on the UNOS committees that meet regularly in open forums nationwide. These meetings are planned well in advance and are the basis for our marketing plans for the next 3 years.

Our market is based on the regional segmentation defined by UNOS. As depicted above, currently 11 regions defined by UNOS cover all 50 United States. These regions are further segmented into areas served by the Organ Procurement Organizations (OPOs). There are currently 59 OPOs within the 11 UNOS regions. These OPOs are non-profit organizations responsible for the management of procurement and transplantation within their defined geography. Within these 59 OPOs are 259 Transplant Centers that manage 871 organ transplant programs. This segment is in the growth phase of its life cycle. The OPTN as a whole is growing steadily. The number of cadaveric and living donors increased 59% between 1990 and 1999—from 6,633 to 10,561. Cadaveric donors increased 30%

(from 4,509 to 5,849) during the same time period. In 1999, a total of 21,155 organs were recovered from cadaveric donors. This was a 2% increase from the 20,829 organs recovered in 1998. Over the last 10 years, the number of organs recovered has increased 41%. In 1999, 51% of all organs recovered were kidneys, 23% were livers, 11% were hearts, 8% were pancreata, 7% were lungs, and 5% were intestines. Of all organs recovered in 1999, 88% were used for local or shared (outside of the recovering OPO service area) transplants.

We have produced a marketing plan that calls out the UNOS National and Regional meetings that we will attend as we roll out our sales program in Region 4 and then in Region 3. These regions are served by the OPOs, which are all competitive in nature due to the fact that to maintain a viable OPO, Center or Program, you must perform a certain number of procurements and/or transplants, which tends to provide a natural competition for organs in the current environment.

It is equally important to know why your customers will buy and to define clearly what drives demand. Again, from the business plan section titled Demand:

> There are several reasons why the demand for this approach is high. Organ Procurement Organizations generate revenue based on the number of organs they recover. Our services increase their ability to place an organ which, in turn, increases their revenue. The transplant center that receives these otherwise wasted organs generates increased revenue from the resulting transplants that occur. The doctors that perform the transplants receive better information to make their assessments enabling them to make better decisions that lead to more productivity and less wasted time chasing unsuitable organs. The service also allows transplant teams to visually inspect the procurement organs and process while building trust among the teams and confidence that they will receive an organ "*As Advertised.*" This building of trust will perpetuate the paradigm shift toward less travel and better allocation of organs, thus, making this approach the standard within the OPTN community.

Discussion Questions on LifeGuard America

1. What is the business of LifeGuard America?
2. In what industry is LifeGuard America operating?
3. What is the market for LifeGuard America?

References

Abell, D. F. (1980). *Defining the business: The starting point of strategic planning.* Englewood Cliffs, NJ: Prentice Hall.

Abell, D. F., & Hammond, J. S. (1981). *Strategic market planning problems and analytical approaches.* Englewood Cliffs, NJ: Prentice Hall.

Adizes, I. (1989). *Corporate life cycles: How and why corporations grow and die, and what to do about it.* Englewood Cliffs, NJ: Prentice Hall.

Ahlbrandt, R. S., & Slevin, D. P. (1992). *Total competitiveness audit (TCA).* Pittsburgh, PA: University of Pittsburgh Press.

Dodge, H. R., Fullerton, F., & Robbins, J. E. (1994, February). Stage of the organizational life cycle and competition as mediators of problem perception for small business. *Strategic Management Journal, 15*(2), 121–134.

Drucker, P. F. (1985a, Winter). Entrepreneurial strategies. *California Management Review, 27*(2), 9–25.

Drucker, P. F. (1985b). *Innovation and entrepreneurship.* New York: Perennial Library.

Forbes, C. (1989, May). Selling time. *Entrepreneur, 17*(5), 51–56.

Hanks, S. H. (1990). The organization life cycle: Integrating content and process. *Journal of Small Business Strategy, 1*(1), 1–12.

Hitt, M. A., Hoskisson, R., Wan, W. P., & Yiu, D. (1999). Theory and research in strategic management: Swings of a pendulum. *Journal of Management, 25*(3), 417.

Hofer, C., & Sandberg, W. (1987, Summer). Improving new venture performance: Some guidelines for success. *American Journal of Small Business, 12*(1), 11–25.

Hoy, F., McDougall, P. P., & D'Souza, D. E. (1992). Strategies and environments of high-growth firms. In D. L. Sexton & J. D. Kasarda (Eds.), *The state of the art of entrepreneurship* (pp. 341–357). Boston: PWS-Kent.

Kotite, E. (1989, December). Made in the USA. *Entrepreneur, 17*(12), 69–75.

Larson, E. (1989, November). Strange fruits. *Inc. Magazine, 11*(11), 80–90.

McDougall, P., & Robinson, R., Jr. (1987a). *Modeling new venture performance: An analysis of new venture strategy and venture origin.* Unpublished paper.

McDougall, P., & Robinson, R., Jr. (1987b). New venture strategies: An empirical identification of eight distinct strategic orientations. In F. Hoy (Ed.), *Academy of Management proceedings* (pp. 73–77). Briarcliff Manor, NY: Academy of Management.

Miller, D. (1992, May). Environmental fit versus internal fit. *Organization Science, 3*(2), 159–178.

Mintzberg, H., Raisinghani, D., & Theoret, A. (1976, June). The structure of unstructured decision process. *Administrative Science Quarterly, 21*(2), 246–275.

Mount, J., Zinger, J. T., & Forsyth, G. R. (1993, October). Organizing for development in the small business. *Long Range Planning, 26*(5), 111–120.

Naman, J. L., & Slevin, D. P. (1993, February). Entrepreneurship and the concept of fit: A model and empirical tests. *Strategic Management Journal, 14*(2), 137–153.

Peterson, R. T. (1989, January). Small business adoption of the marketing concept vs. other business strategies. *Journal of Small Business Management, 27*(1), 38–46.

Raudsepp, E. (1981, July). You can trust your hunches. *Inc. Magazine, 3*(7), 89.

Sexton, D. L., & Bowman-Upton, N. B. (1991). *Entrepreneurship: Creativity and growth.* New York: MacMillan.

Slevin, K. G., & Covin, J. G. (1995). New ventures and total competitiveness: A conceptual model, empirical results, and case study examples. In W. D. Bygrave et al. (Eds.), *Frontiers of entrepreneurship research* (pp. 574–588). Wellesley, MA: Babson College.

Small business: What economies of scale. (1982, April 26). *The Wall Street Journal* (Western ed.), p. 27.

Taylor, T. C. (1979, May 14). Northern air freight makes big ideas fly. *Sales and Marketing Management, 122*(7), 37–39.

Timmons, J., Smollen, L., & Dingee, A., Jr. (1985). *New venture creation.* Homewood, IL: Richard D. Irwin.

Van Kirk, J. E., & Noonan, K. (1982, July). Key factors in strategic planning. *Journal of Small Business Management, 20*(3), 1–7.

Welsch, H. P., & Young, E. C. (1982, October). The information source selection decision: The role of entrepreneurial personality characteristics. *Journal of Small Business Management, 20*(4), 49–57.

Wright, P. (1983, Spring). Competitive strategies for small business. *The Collegiate Forum,* 3–4.

7 | Venture Financial Analysis and Return Projections

Can We Profit?

LEARNING OBJECTIVES

1. To understand the fundamental premises of the accounting process.
2. To learn the purposes and uses of financial statements.
3. To provide a general framework for the financial evaluation and profit projections for the venture.

TOPIC OUTLINE

Introduction

Financial Analysis

The Accounting Process
- Bookkeeping
- Accounting

Financial Statements
- The Balance Sheet
- The Income Statement
- Sources and Uses of Funds Statement

Financial Analysis Techniques
- Ratio Analysis
- Profit Analysis
- Cash Flow Analysis
- Break-even Analysis

Conclusion

Website Information

Key Terms

Review Questions

Case Study

Reference

INTRODUCTION

Inadequate capital is one of the most acute problems that plague small businesses and new venture start-ups. Adequate financial evaluation of the new firm's capital needs is a *must*, because capital shortage is not only the cause of many new business failures but is also a constant concern for the survivors. Even successful firms with a proven record of sales and profit growth often find themselves with unanticipated shortages of funds. The main causes of these shortages are usually increased inventories, loose credit policies, and investment in overhead that may outpace the growth in income.

Another typical problem with small business finance is the fact that these shortages may not be detected until it is too late. The crisis-management style of the small-firm manager does not allow the constant scrutiny of financial matters that larger firms can afford. The results are bad debts, payroll that cannot be met, bills that are not paid, and/or missed note payment dates. The firm then must seek unanticipated additional funds and usually on the worst possible credit terms.

With adequate planning of capital expenditures, inadequate capital crises can often be avoided. Financial analysis and the development of a financial plan for the new venture help forecast present and future cash requirements. Sources of funds can be evaluated, avoiding excessive interest costs and keeping the debt burden at a minimum. But most importantly, the development of a financial plan and its inherent analysis improves the chances of securing the capital needed for the initiation of the venture. An elaborate financial evaluation of the venture provides the small-business owner with a persuasive argument to lenders and investors, enhancing their confidence in the business as a safe place to put their money.

This chapter provides an overview of financial concepts and techniques, as well as a general framework for the financial evaluation of a venture, with a special emphasis on the preparation of a loan application package.

FINANCIAL ANALYSIS

The term **financial analysis** refers to the systematic study of the current or potential performance of a business enterprise. Managers and small-business owners use financial analysis to assess and improve the profitability of their firm. Investors use financial analysis to evaluate the potential return on their investment. And finally, creditors use financial planning to determine whether their loan is secure and to determine the appropriate term for a loan.

Financial analysis also provides guidelines for all asset and liability accounts, so that actual balances and performances can be compared regularly with the planned or estimated balances and performance. Thus, any gaps between planned and actual performance can be detected early, and corrective measures can be taken promptly and economically.

Financial analysis requires certain basic skills on the part of the small-business owner:

1. Sound understanding of the accounting process.

2. Understanding of the economic significance of the facts and figures contained in the basic financial reports, such as the balance sheet, the income statement, and the sources and uses of funds.

3. Understanding and mastering techniques of financial analysis, such as profit planning, break-even analysis, cash flow analysis, and forecasting, ratio analysis, capital planning, and budgeting.

The task of the prospective small-firm owner is to integrate these basic skills to adequately evaluate the financial prospects of the venture and eventually to achieve the best overall performance.

THE ACCOUNTING PROCESS

At least some of the venture's goals should be stated in quantitative terms. For example, "I want the new business to provide me with at least $30,000 a year, otherwise maybe it is not worth it. . . ." Bookkeeping and accounting are the means to provide an overview of the firm's progress toward that goal. At the same time, bookkeeping and accounting constitute a common language among owners, managers, investors, and accountants.

Owners make all kinds of decisions as they steer the course of the firm. Managers translate these general decisions into the daily activities in the everyday course of the business. Investors want to be informed of the financial impact of those decisions and activities. Finally, the accountant documents and categorizes the results and consequences of the owner's decisions, the manager's activities, and the investor's investment. By examining a financial report, owners can improve their decisions, managers can improve their activities, and investors can increase their investment allocations, all for better overall results.

Bookkeeping

Bookkeeping is the function of keeping books, that is, recording business transactions and information in an organized manner, by type of transaction and by chronological period. For example, when we order merchandise and in due time receive it, there are usually four pieces of paper representing four different pieces of information: a piece of paper to constitute the order, another accompanies the merchandise when it arrives, and an invoice, comes later by mail, billing us for a certain amount. When we pay this invoice, our check constitutes payment of the invoice and is the fourth piece of paper.

All four pieces of information relate to the same category of business transaction, namely, purchase of merchandise. However, all of these separate pieces of information and their documentation, the four pieces of paper, have to be brought to a central location, sorted, and filed into transaction categories (in this case, purchasing), and finally arranged by chronological order: merchandise order first, shipping documents second, invoice third, and payment last.

The overall purchase transaction involves giving up something (money sent by check) in exchange for something else (merchandise). In other words, bookkeeping lists transactions that involve increases or decreases on one side of an imaginary vertical line that equal decreases or increases of the other side of the line:

Increase in Merchandise $1,000   Decrease in Cash $1,000

This business transaction, an increase in merchandise for a decrease in cash, involves two separate accounts: merchandise and cash. An **account** is simply a place in which to record the effects of the business transactions on each item involved in the transaction. The **balance** of that account is the difference between the increases and decreases in the account that have been recorded due to various business transactions, as of some specified date. The file of all the different accounts of the business is known as the **ledger**. The ledger is the final product of bookkeeping and a source for the accountant's analysis, reporting, and interpretation of all financial data.

However, before we talk about accounting, we need to summarize the bookkeeping process:

* Transactions originate during the course of conducting business.

* All pieces of information and documents pertaining to each business transaction are brought to a central location, sorted, and filed into transaction categories, and arranged in chronological order.

* The business transaction is recorded in terms of increases and decreases in the business accounts that it involves.

| Exhibit 7.1 | Bookkeeping |

| Increase in merchandise | $1,000 | | | Decrease in cash | $1,000 |

Cash Account

Date	Description	Increase	Decrease	Balance
July 30	Investment by owner	$10,000		$10,000
July 31	Merchandise purchase		$1,000	$9,000

Merchandise Account

Date	Description	Increase	Decrease	Balance
July 31	Merchandise purchase	$1,000		$1,000

- The balance of the accounts is updated.
- All accounts are filed in the ledger.

A typical bookkeeping transaction is depicted in Exhibit 7.1.

Accounting

The primary function of accounting is to serve the *planning* and *controlling* aspects of the managerial process. It is the procedure of categorizing, analyzing, and interpreting financial data. Before these "raw" financial data are processed into meaningful managerial information, decisions must be made regarding the form and the nature of the data categories. The accountant designs the recording system and deals with non-routine items and transactions that require the exercise of judgment, e.g., tax returns, bank loan applications, etc. In other words, accounting is needed whenever there is a need for an informed financial analysis to reach a sound decision.

From an accountant's perspective, a **business enterprise** is a collection of assets, under common control, aimed at the generation of profit. An **asset** is anything of value that can be claimed as the property of the enterprise: cash, machines, amounts to be collected from customers for goods or services sold to them, but not yet paid (accounts receivable), land, inventory, etc. Even the name of the enterprise can be of value and can carry a hefty price tag for the right to use it, as in the case of a franchise like McDonald's.

The assets of the enterprise are obtained from two sources: creditors and owners. Creditors provide the enterprise with assets in the form of goods or services for which they have a legal claim to receive payment in the future. In other words, the enterprise has a legal obligation and is *liable* to legal sanctions in case it does not repay the creditors the amount of assets they financed. These legal obligations are called liabilities, and they usually take the form of accounts payable (i.e., amounts owed to banks and other creditors that were borrowed for a relatively short period of time) and long-term debt (i.e., amounts borrowed for long periods of time).

The owners of the enterprise contribute the remaining assets, which constitute the firm's **net worth** or the **owner's equity**, that is, the *residual* interest in the enterprise *after* all liabilities are paid to the creditors. A careful examination of these definitions leads us to the fundamental accounting equation:

Total Assets = Total Liabilities + Owner's Equity

In other words, all that the firm owns is owed to the creditors first, and what is left, the residual, belongs to the owners.

FINANCIAL STATEMENTS

In preparing financial statements, the accountant often uses a **worksheet** that can include many accounts, usually taking the form of a capital T, and consequently called *T-accounts*. In the fundamental accounting equation we discussed previously, each asset account as well as each liability or owner's equity account can be represented as a T-account. For assets, *increases* (inflows) are shown on the left side of the T, which is called *debit*, and *decreases* (outflows) in the amount of assets are shown on the right side of the T, which is called *credit*.

CASH

Debit (+)		Credit (−)	
Beginning Balance, July 1	$4,600		
Merchandise sale in cash, July 2	$500	Cash purchase of merchandise, July 5	$300
		Payment of bill for merchandise purchased on credit in June, July 8	$150
Ending Balance, July 31	$4,000	Salary paid to John Clark, July 31	$650

In this example, the cash asset account started with a balance of $4,600, as of July 1. On July 2, merchandise was sold, and there was an inflow or increase of cash in the amount of $500. Merchandise was purchased on July 5, and there was an outflow of cash in the amount of $300. A June bill of $150 was paid, and a salary of $650 was paid to John Clerk. On July 31, the ending balance of the cash T-account was $4,000 reflecting the net effects of a $500 inflow (debit) and a $1,100 outflow (credit): *Beginning balance + debits = Ending balance.*

For *liabilities*, *increases* are shown on the right side of the T-account (*credit*) and *decreases* are shown on the left side (*debit*).

ACCOUNTS PAYABLE

Debit (+)		Credit (−)	
Merchandise bill paid, July 8	$150	Beginning Balance, July 1	$2,100
		Merchandise bought on credit, July 7	$500
		Ending Balance, July 31	$2,450

For *owner's equity*, increases are also shown on the right side of the T-account (*credit*) and *decreases* are shown on the left side (*debit*).

OWNER'S EQUITY

Debit (+)		Credit (–)	
Cost of Goods Sold during *July*	$250	*John Enterprise, Proprietor*	
		Initial Investment, *July 1*	$4,600
Other Expenses		*Revenues from Sales*	
Salary to John Clark		Merchandise Sale	
July 31	$650	*July 2*	$500

The owner's equity account includes one account showing the owner's equity at the beginning of the period, plus a revenue account that *increases* owner's equity when there are credits in it. In addition, owner's equity includes expense accounts, which are negative components of ownership because they *decrease* owner's equity. Because equity decreases are recorded by debiting owner's equity accounts, expense accounts have debit balances.

Both sides of the accounting equation must always balance: if we change one account, we must change another. The accounts must always balance such that total assets equal total liabilities. For instance, we mentioned that sales increase owner's equity by increasing the credit balance. Sales, however, also bring in cash, thus increasing an asset by debiting the corresponding amount in the cash T-account.

In our example, the $500 of the July 2 sales revenue, when credited to owner's equity and debited to cash, became an asset. Payment of the $650 salary, an expense, decreased cash (credit) and also decreased owner's equity (debit). We can increase an asset by decreasing another asset (e.g., increase in inventory for a decrease in cash). Or we can increase an asset by increasing a liability or owner's equity (e.g., increase in cash and an increase in owner's equity). But the two sides of the equation must *always* be equal. (see Exhibit 7.2).

Exhibit 7.2   Table of Debit and Credit Entries

Account type	Account increase	Account decrease	Typical balance
Asset	Debit	Credit	Debit
Liability	Credit	Debit	Credit
Equity/Capital	Credit	Debit	Credit
Revenue Income	Credit	Debit	Credit
Expense	Debit	Credit	Debit

The Balance Sheet

The **balance sheet** is the representation of the fundamental accounting equation: total assets equal total liabilities plus total owner's equity. It is also the result of the adjustments to the balances of all the T-accounts that were included in the worksheet. Consequently, the balance sheet is a statement of financial position on a specific date. It is a snapshot, if you will, of the company in monetary terms, usually as of December 31. It consists of a list of the balances of the assets, a list of the balances of the liabilities, and a list of the balances of the equity.

The balance of these accounts can be listed on a **liquidation basis of measurement**, that is, listing each asset at the amount that could be obtained by selling it. Each liability is listed at the amount that would have to be paid if the business were to liquidate immediately; the residual difference constitutes the owner's equity.

Another possible basis of measurement of the balances of these accounts is the **historical basis**. Using this approach, asset balances are measured at their historical cost (i.e., the cost of acquisition of the asset at the time it was acquired). Liabilities and owner's equity balances are measured at the amounts invested to date by creditors and owners. Regardless of which measurement basis is used, if we assume that the business firm goes out of business on the particular date of the balance sheet, the owners, stockholders, or proprietors will receive the residual, after all assets are liquidated and all liabilities are paid with the proceeds. In other words:

Proceeds from total asset liquidation – The amount required to pay all liabilities
= The residual amount remaining for the owners

Assets

Assets are arranged from top to bottom in order of decreasing liquidity; that is, the further down, the longer the time required for converting these assets into cash, and the greater the likelihood of a loss from the sale.

Current assets are assets that head the list because, if necessary, they can be converted into cash in a relatively short period of time, usually less than 1 year, with minimum loss in the conversion. Current assets include the following:

- **Cash:** Bills, petty cash, and money in the bank.

- **Accounts receivable:** Amounts not yet collected from customers minus a certain allowance (depending on our credit policy) for accounts that experience tells us will turn into bad debt.

- **Merchandise inventories:** Raw materials, partially finished goods still in the process of manufacture, and finished goods ready for shipment.

The **total current assets** therefore are constantly involved in the generation of cash; they constitute the "blood" of the firm circulating throughout the enterprise's "body." They are part of what accountants call **working capital**, which is the current assets remaining after we pay off current liabilities and running expenses. Working capital should be monitored closely because without adequate cash capital to meet its current obligations, the enterprise cannot operate.

Fixed assets are assets that cannot usually be converted to cash in a short period of time. Fixed assets represent long-term investments in assets with long life expectancies, and they are used over and over again to manufacture the product, store it, transport it, and sell it. Fixed assets include the following:

- Land

- Buildings

- Machines and equipment

- Office furniture and fixtures

The generally accepted accounting method of valuation for fixed assets is their *historical acquisition cost minus the depreciation accumulated* by the date of the balance sheet. Thus, the figures posted for fixed assets are neither their real market value nor their replacement cost.

Accumulated depreciation, therefore, is a large accounting "pot" in which we "deposit" the entire decline in useful value of a fixed asset due to wear and tear from use and/or passage of time. This imaginary pot contains all of the yearly value declines (depreciation expenses) of all fixed assets, except for land, which is not subject to depreciation because its value generally remains unchanged from year to year.

The **total fixed assets** statement, therefore, is the net valuation for balance sheet purposes of the firm's investment in land, buildings, machines, and office furniture and fixtures, minus the depreciation accumulated as of the date of the balance sheet.

Before we close the discussion on the assets, we should mention some categories of unusual assets that may follow the list of fixed assets:

- **Prepayments:** Out-of-the-ordinary assets for which the firm has paid in advance, for example, for equipment rental, or for insurance. The benefits from the use of the equipment or the protection from the prepaid insurance premiums have not yet been received and should be listed as prepayments among the assets.

- **Deferred charges:** Out-of-the-ordinary assets similar to prepayments. Deferred charges occur when a major expenditure, such as research and development, is gradually written off over several years instead of being charged in full in the year in which the expenditure was made.

- **Intangibles:** Out-of-the-ordinary assets that do not exist physically, but they may be of substantial value to the firm. For instance, a franchise name like McDonald's, or a license granted for the manufacturing of a product, or even goodwill, can be listed as intangible out-of-the-ordinary assets.

Current assets, fixed assets, and out-of-the-ordinary assets all added together give the figure listed on the balance sheet as *total assets.*

Liabilities

Liabilities are arranged from top to bottom in order of the seniority of claims against earnings and assets.

Current liabilities consist of claims that must be paid off in a relatively short period of time, usually 1 year or less. Current liabilities also represent the first claim against assets in most cases and, in particular, the first claim against current assets. We can now see the intimate relationship between current assets and current liabilities, and how they help form one of the most revealing things to be learned from the balance sheet: *working capital.*

Current liabilities usually include the following:

- **Accounts payable:** accounts owed to regular business creditors resulting from trade and usually subject to a discount if paid in full within a short period of time.

- **Notes payable:** Promissory notes owed to banks or creditors, usually due within a year.

- **Payroll, sales, and withheld taxes:** Amount owed to the Internal Revenue Service.

- **Accrued expenses payable:** Any amount of expense accrued but unpaid as of the date of the balance sheet.

The total current liabilities sum up all these items. Once again, total current liabilities subtracted from current assets give us the most important concept of accounting: the working capital of the firm as of the date of the balance sheet.

Long-term liabilities represent the longer claims against the fixed assets of the company, and they are usually due more than 1 year from the date of the balance sheet. Long-term liabilities include the following:

- Notes payable due in more than 1 year

- Mortgages

- Any other secured of unsecured long-term debt such as bonds

Finally, all liabilities, current and long-term, are added up and listed under total liabilities.

Owner's Equity and Capital

As pointed out previously, this is the residual interest that the owner has in the firm. In other words, it is the firm's net worth after subtracting all liabilities from all assets. The balance sheet in Exhibit 7.3 shows:

- The balance of the proprietor's capital as of the beginning of the fiscal period, the end of which is reported as the balance sheet date.

- The net profit during that period, minus the proprietor's capital withdrawals during that period.

- Equals the net increase in the proprietor's capital during that period. If this final amount is added to the beginning balance of the proprietor's capital, it shows the following balance.

- The balance of the proprietor's capital as of the end of the period, which corresponds to the balance sheet date.

In a corporation, the owner's equity is represented by capital stock, that is, shares in the proprietary interest of the company. These shares take the form of either preferred stock or common stock. Preferred stock has preference over common stock as regards dividends or in the distribution of assets in case of liquidation, but usually preferred stock carries no voting rights in company affairs. Common stocks have no guarantees but also no limits on dividends payable each year. Another corporate equity account is the accumulated retained earnings account, which corresponds to the proprietor's capital account in a proprietorship.

Finally, total liabilities and total owner's equity and capital are added together to always give the same balance as the total assets balance. Again, this explains why the balance sheet is called just that—a balance sheet.

Uses of the Balance Sheet

As mentioned previously, the balance sheet represents the state of the business at a particular point in time by specifying what the firm owns and what it owes. For financial analysis purposes, the balance sheet can be used to do the following:

1. *Determine the overall health of the firm* through the equation of assets and liabilities and owner's equity.

2. *Identify trends* in terms of increases or decreases in assets, liabilities, or owner's equity by comparing the balance sheets of successive months, or years.

Exhibit 7.3	Balance Sheet, XYZ, Co. December 31, 2xx1

	2xx1	2xx0
Assets		
Current Assets		
Cash	$450,000	$300,000
Marketable securities at cost (Market value: 2xx1, $890,000; 2xx0, $480,000)	850,000	460,000
Accounts receivable (Less: Allowance for bad debt: 2xx1, $100,000; 2xx0, $95,000)	2,000,000	1,900,000
Inventories	2,700,000	3,000,000
Total current assets	6,000,000	5,660,000
Fixed assets (property, plant, and equipment)		
Land	$450,000	$450,000
Buildings	3,800,000	3,600,000
Machinery	950,000	850,000
Office equipment	100,000	95,000
Less: Accumulated depreciation	1,800,000	1,500,000
Net fixed assets	3,500,000	3,495,000
Prepaids	100,000	90,000
Intangibles (good will, patents, trademarks)	100,000	100,000
Total Assets	9,700,000	9,345,000
Liabilities		
Current Liabilities		
Accounts payable	$1,000,000	940,000
Notes payable	850,000	1,000,000
Accrued expenses payable	330,000	300,000
Taxes payable	320,000	290,000
Total current liabilities	2,500,000	2,530,000
Long-term liabilities		
First mortgage bonds (5% interest, due 2xx5)	2,700,000	2,700,000
Total Liabilities	5,200,000	5,230,000
Owner's/Stockholders Equity		
Capital stock		
Preferred stock $5 cumulative, $100 par value each authorized, issued, and outstanding 6,000 shares	600,000	600,000
Common stock, $5 par value each, authorized, issued, and outstanding 300,000 shares	1,500,000	1,500,000
Capital surplus	700,000	700,000
Accumulated retained earnings	1,700,000	1,315,000
Total Owner's/stockholders equity	4,500,000	4,115,000
Total Liabilities and Equity	9,700,000	9,345,000

3. Determine the ability of the firm to meet its obligations by *checking its working capital*. Moreover, this year's working capital should be larger than last year's.

4. Provide information to owners and managers for *planning and budgeting*.

5. Provide information to creditors, investors, and government agencies for *tax disclosure, and overall control*.

6. Provide additional information to owners and investors through the *calculation of financial ratios*, such as current ratio or ratio of inventory turnover.

7. *Determine the net book value* (i.e., net asset value) of a corporation's securities of preferred stock, common stock, or long-term debt (bonds).

8. *Determine the capitalization ratios for each of the corporation's securities* in terms of proportion of capital provided by each kind of security issued by the corporation, i.e., bonds, common stock, or preferred stock.

The balance sheet, therefore, along with other financial statements discussed later, can provide the owner or manager a wealth of information. When designing the balance sheets and the other financial statements, the specific information needed and its format should be carefully decided in advance so that later any important information is readily available at the desired level of detail.

The Income Statement

Just as the balance sheet shows the fundamental soundness and health of the company at a *specific* point of time, the **income statement** (sometimes referred to also as a profit and loss statement) reflects what happened *during* a period of time. It shows the record of operating activities, *how* the firm's earnings were derived, what the sales were, and what expenses were incurred to generate these sales during the time period. Of utmost importance also is the historical record of a series of years, quarters, or months of income statements, which tells the owner, the IRS or the potential creditor or investor how the business has performed in the past and in the present, and how it might do in the future.

The income statement matches all the costs and expenses incurred by the company against the amounts received from the sale of goods and services or from any out-of-the-ordinary income source (e.g., interest income). The final outcome of this comparison is net profit or net loss for a particular time period. This outcome is carried to the balance sheet, where profit increases the owner's equity in terms of proprietor's capital or corporate retained earnings and is distributed in terms of owner's withdrawals or corporate dividends. This is how the income statement and the balance sheet are integrated. The source of the information to be used in the income statement is derived from the final product of bookkeeping: the *general ledger*. Balancing the general ledger proves the accuracy of all the bookkeeping entries and sets the stage for the preparation of the income statement. The **net sales** item represents the amount received after taking into consideration returned goods and allowances for reduction of prices.

The **cost of goods sold** item represents the amount of inventory in raw materials that was used to produce the sold finished goods. It is calculated by counting the beginning inventory at the start of the income statement period and adding to it any merchandise purchases during the period to arrive at the total amount of merchandise that is available for sale. If we subtract from this figure our count of the ending inventory at the end of the income statement period we have the total cost of goods sold.

A condensed version of the income statement takes the following form:

Plus Factors	Minus Factors	= Net Profit
Net sales	Cost of sales and operating expenses	
Extraordinary income	Interest expense	
	Depreciation expense	
	Provision for federal income tax	

Basically, the income statement is developed in the manner depicted in Exhibit 7.4. The difference between net sales and the costs of goods sold is the **gross profit margin**, which represents the value the firm added to the purchased raw material or merchandise by processing, packaging, upgrading, and finally selling it as a finished good.

Exhibit 7.4   A Basic Income Statement

Net Sales
Less: Cost of sales (or cost of goods sold), equals:

Gross Profit Margin
Less: Operating expenses and general administrative expenses, equals:

Gross Operating Income (or Loss)
Less: Depreciation for the income statement period, equals:

Net Operating Income (or Loss)
Plus: Out-of-the-ordinary income, equals:

Net Income (or Loss)
Less: Interest expense, equals:

Net Income before Taxes (or Loss)
Less: Income taxes, equals:

Net Income after Taxes (or Net Loss)

Operating and general administrative expenses are costs that include everything but raw materials: labor, and factory overhead (e.g., rent, utilities, repairs, supplies, etc.). Subtracting these costs from the gross profit margin gives us the **gross operating income** (or loss). If we further subtract depreciation (i.e., the yearly/monthly decline in the useful value of an asset due to wear and tear), an expense chargeable to operations or production, we arrive at the **net operating income** (or loss).

Out-of-the-ordinary income (not derived from operations, e.g., dividends and interest received by the firm from savings or investment in marketable securities) is added to the net operating income to give us **total net income** (or loss). From this figure, out-of-the-ordinary expenses, like interest expenses, which are tax deductible, must be subtracted to arrive at the **total net income before taxes**. By setting aside a provision for federal income taxes, we finally arrive at the **total net income after taxes**.

It is a good idea to express every item on the income statement in terms of a percentage of net sales, which of course represents 100%. The percentages are obtained by dividing each amount by the net sales for the period. This way, the expense categories can be closely monitored to see how much of sales revenue they are responsible for "eating up." Any alarming increase from year to year in an expense item is thus clearly noted by the percentage, which is more apparent than with absolute figures.

A slightly varied income statement of a typical small firm is presented in Exhibit 7.5.

Uses of the Income Statement

The income statement, as previously mentioned, shows the result of the operation of the firm during a period of time. A few observations and detailed analysis can tell a lot more:

1. Whether the *firm met its goals* for sales or profit.

2. How effective the firm has been by calculating its *operating profitability*, operating profit over sales, over the years.

3. How efficient the firm has been by calculating its *operating cost*, operating costs over sales, over the years.

4. How profitable the firm has been by calculating its *net profitability*, net profit over sales, over the years.

5. The *ratios of various expense items* in relation to sales: constant, rising, or falling.

Sources and Uses of Funds Statement

The balance sheet, as mentioned previously, is a "snapshot" of an enterprise. In other words, it shows the assets, liabilities, and owner's equity the firm has at a *specific* point of time. The income statement shows the profit made *during* a period of time. The **Sources and Uses of Funds** statement shows the financing and the investing activities of the enterprise, that is, where the funds came from and what they were used for. Another name for this financial statement is the *Statement of Changes in Financial Position.*

The *Sources and Uses of Funds* statement shows how the enterprise works. Like the income statement, it is an explanation of how net working capital (the excess of current assets over current liabilities) has changed *during* a period of time. It provides direct information on the inflow and outflow of funds that could not have been obtained without tedious and makeshift analysis and interpretation of the balance sheet and the income statement.

Typically, sources of funds are provided from the following:

• Net income from operations

• Sale of assets (e.g., plant, equipment, etc.)

• Issuance of debt

• Issuance of capital stock

• Depreciation

Depreciation deserves some special attention. It was stated previously that depreciation constitutes an expense, so why, suddenly, is it treated as a source of funds? The answer lies in the definition of **depreciation**, which is the decline of the useful value of a fixed asset due to wear and tear. This is the price of owning a fixed asset. If the asset were not owned, a certain price had to be paid for leasing or renting a building or a piece of equipment to obtain the *right to use it*. So the right to use a fixed asset for a period of time and the associated value

Exhibit 7.5   Income Statement XYZ Company

Income Statement
Month of _____ 20___, and ___ months ended _____, 20___

		This month		Year to date	
		Amount	% of Sales	Amount	% of Sales
1.	**Net Sales**	$_____	100	$_____	100
	Less: Cost of goods sold				
2.	Beginning inventory	$_____	$_____		
3.	Merchandise purchases	$_____	$_____		
4.	Merchandise available for sale	$_____	$_____		
5.	Less ending inventory	$_____	$_____		
6.	Total Cost of Goods Sold	$_____	_____	$_____	_____
7.	**Gross Profit Margin**	$_____	_____	$_____	_____
	Less: Expenses				
8.	Salaries and wages	$_____	$_____		
9.	Rent	$_____	$_____		
10.	Utilities	$_____	$_____		
11.	Repairs and maintenance	$_____	$_____		
12.	Delivery expenses	$_____	$_____		
13.	Supplies	$_____	$_____		
14.	Advertising	$_____	$_____		
15.	Various taxes and licenses	$_____	$_____		
16.	Bad and uncollectible debt	$_____	$_____		
17.	Insurance	$_____	$_____		
18.	Other expenses	$_____	$_____		
19.	*Total Expenses*	$_____	_____	$_____	_____
20.	**Gross Operating Income (Loss)**	$_____	_____	$_____	_____
21.	*Less: Depreciation for the period*	$_____	_____	$_____	_____
22.	**Net Operating Income (Loss)**	$_____	_____	$_____	_____
23.	*Plus: Out-of-the-ordinary income*	$_____	$_____		
24.	**Net Income (Loss)**	$_____	_____	$_____	_____
25.	*Less: Interest expense*	$_____	_____	$_____	_____
26.	**Net Income before taxes (Loss)**	$_____	_____	$_____	_____
27.	*Less: Income taxes*	$_____	_____	$_____	_____
28.	**Net Income after Taxes (Loss)**	$_____	_____	$_____	_____

from its use is, for accounting purposes, a source of funds. Depreciation frees the funds that would have been paid to rent or lease the fixed assets. The uses of funds include the following:

- Dividend payments (or owner's withdrawals)

- Purchase of assets

- Payment of debt

- Repurchase of outstanding stock

The difference between the sources and uses of funds shows whether the working capital increased or decreased during the year, explaining why this financial statement is also known as the *Statement of Changes in Financial Position.* If the sources exceed uses of funds, there is an increase in working capital. The opposite, a decrease in working capital, occurs when more funds were used than were provided for during a certain period of time.

Further analysis of two consecutive fiscal years and their corresponding balance sheet statements can provide valuable information regarding the *causes* of the changes in working capital. In other words, simple computation of the change in each current asset or current liability item for two consecutive years shows which item is responsible for the increase or decrease in working capital. This comparison reveals how strong the working capital position became from one year to the next. The Sources and Uses of Funds statement of XYZ Company is a direct representation of where funds came from and where they went; it accounts for the changes exhibited by the balance of the two years. XYZ's Sources and Uses of Funds statement in Exhibit 7.6 shows the typical relationship of operations to the production of working capital.

It should be noted that depreciation by itself is not a source of funds. It is treated as such for accounting purposes. If depreciation were a true source of funds, a firm could double or triple its depreciation charges in bad times to "create" funds. Of course this is not possible. As depreciation increases, the net income decreases by the same amount, leaving the net sources of funds total unaffected.

Exhibit 7.6	Sources and Uses of Funds (Cash Flow Statement)		
XYZ, Co., Year 2xx1			
Funds were provided from:			
Net income		$535,000	
Depreciation		300,000	
Total			$835,000
Funds were used for:			
Dividends on preferred stock		$30,000	
Dividends on common stock		120,000	
Plant & equipment		305,000	
Sundry assets		10,000	
Total			$465,000
Increase in working capital			$370,000

Uses of the Sources and Uses of Funds Statement

Valuable information can be obtained from the Sources and Uses of Funds statement. The most important contributions of this financial statement to the overall financial analysis of the firm include the following:

1. The *proportion of funds* applied to plant, dividends, owner's withdrawal, debt retirement, etc.

2. The *financial habits of management* with regard to financing and spending.

3. The *sources of funds* (profitable operations vs. borrowing vs. issuance of capital stock).

4. Indications of the *impact of fund outflows* on the future profitability potential of the firm.

5. A general indication of the firm's trend toward financial strength or weakness.

FINANCIAL ANALYSIS TECHNIQUES

It is absolutely necessary to apply certain techniques of financial analysis, both before the initiation of the venture and after. This helps owners and managers establish targets in sales and profits, and it helps them make periodic evaluations of the enterprise to make sure they never lose sight of these targets.

Ratio Analysis

One of the most important financial analysis techniques for assessing the strength of a firm in the past and the present, and for comparing its performance with that of the industry, is *ratio analysis*. Managers use ratio analysis to determine how well the firm is doing. Investors use it to determine whether the firm will provide an adequate return on their investment. Creditors use financial ratio analysis to determine whether the company is a good credit risk. Typically, four categories of ratios provide four different conclusions about the firm: *liquidity ratios, activity ratios, profitability ratios,* and *leverage ratios.* However, the ratios by themselves do not help in deriving any meaningful information about the firm unless the following occur:

1. Each ratio is compared with the same ratio of past years to detect a certain trend.

2. Each family of ratios is compared with the other families of ratios to draw conclusive information about all aspects of the firm's operations.

3. Each ratio is compared with the industry average for the same ratio, since each industry has its own operational characteristics.

Typically, the balance sheet and the income statement are the two financial statements used for the ratio analysis. It should be remembered, however, that firms may have different accounting practices, a fact that may make comparisons difficult.

Liquidity Ratios

Liquidity demonstrates a firm's ability to meet its short-term obligations. These include any current liabilities, including currently maturing long-term debt. A firm uses current assets to pay off these current liabilities. Therefore, one indication of a firm's liquidity is the *current ratio*, that is, current assets divided by current liabilities:

$$Current\ Ratio = \frac{Current\ assets}{Current\ liabilities}$$

Most analysts suggest a current ratio of 2. A high current ratio is not necessarily a good sign; it may mean that the organization is not making the most efficient use of these assets. The optimum current ratio varies from industry to industry: more volatile industries have higher current ratios. Because slow-moving or obsolete inventories can overstate a firm's ability to meet short-term demands, the quick ratio is sometimes preferred to assess a firm's liquidity. The *quick ratio* is current assets minus inventories, divided by current liabilities:

$$Quick\ Ratio = \frac{Current\ assets - Inventories}{Current\ liabilities}$$

A quick ratio of 1 is typical for American industries. Although there is less variability in the quick ratio than in the current ratio, stable industries can safely operate with a lower ratio.

Activity Ratios

These ratios demonstrate how effectively a firm is using its resources. By comparing revenues and expenses with the resources used to generate them, the efficiency of operation can be established. The asset turnover ratio indicates how efficiently management is employing its assets. Industry figures for asset turnover vary: capital-intensive industries have a much lower ratio.

$$Asset\ Turnover\ Ratio = \frac{Sales}{Total\ assets}$$

Another activity ratio is inventory turnover, which is estimated by dividing cost of goods sold by average inventory for the year. The norm for American industries varies depending upon the product or service sold. Small, inexpensive items usually turn over at a much higher rate than durable goods.

$$Inventory\ Turnover\ Ratio = \frac{Cost\ of\ goods\ sold}{Inventory}$$

The accounts receivable turnover ratio measures the average collection period on credit sales. If the average number of days on credit sales varies widely from the industry norm, this may be an indication of poor management. A low figure may indicate that the firm is losing sales because of a restrictive credit policy. If the ratio is too high, too much capital is being tied up in accounts receivable, and management may be increasing its chance of bad debts. Because of varying industry credit policies, a comparison for the firm over time or within an industry is the only useful analysis.

$$Accounts\ Receivable\ Turnover\ Ratio = \frac{Sales}{Accounts\ receivable}$$

On the basis of a 360-day period (the accountant's year), the average collection period is

$$Average\ Collection\ Period = \frac{360}{Accounts\ receivable\ turnover\ ratio}$$

Profitability Ratios

Profitability is the result of an organization's management, operation, sales, and marketing. The first ratio to compute is the profit margin. This is calculated by dividing net income by sales. There is wide industry variation, but the average for American firms is 5%.

$$Profit\ Margin = \frac{Net\ income}{Sales}$$

A second useful ratio for evaluating profitability is the return on investment or equity, calculated by dividing net income by total assets:

$$Return\ on\ Equity\ (ROE) = \frac{Net\ income}{Total\ equity}$$

It is often difficult to determine causes for lack of profitability. If the return-on-investment ratio is low, it can be broken down into three other key ratios to provide management with clues to the lack of success of the firm.

$$Return\ on\ Equity = \frac{Net\ income}{Sales} \times \frac{Sales}{Total\ assets} \times \frac{Total\ assets}{Total\ equity} = \frac{Net\ income}{Total\ equity}$$

This longer *return on equity* ratio shows more clearly whether the lack of a satisfactory return was a result of a low profit margin (too high expenses or too low a price), low sales generation from assets, too much debit (i.e., low equity), or a combination of these factors.

Leverage Ratios

The last category of ratios identifies who has supplied the firm's capital requirements, owners or outside creditors. These ratios are termed "leverage" because of the effect of the fixed expenses to service debt on profits or losses. The most common ratios computed are debt to equity and debt to total assets.

There are several variations of these ratios, but the ones employed here define debt as long-term liabilities and equity as the total stockholders' equity.

$$Debt\ to\ Equity\ Ratio = \frac{Debt}{Equity}$$

Because of the possible losses in poor years, debt-to-equity ratios over the 0.5 norm are usually considered safe only in the most stable industries.

Profit Analysis

It is absolutely essential during the financial evaluation of a particular idea to have a profit target. Some businesspeople hit their profit target more than others because they keep their operation aimed in that direction and they never lose sight of the bull's-eye.

Ending the year with a profit is reserved for the small-business people who always strive for outstanding performance. To keep the firm pointed toward profit and to achieve this outstanding performance, some principles need to be identified:

Know Your Revenues

Each revenue source must be identified for each of the product lines and for the operation as a whole.

Know Your Costs

All cost items must be known in detail. This way, cost figures can be compared as a percentage of sales (operating ratios). The costs must be itemized so that the costs that seem to be rising or falling can be identified easily, based on the owner's experience and cost figures for the industry. An important thing to remember is that profit is not only a function of revenues but also a function of the cost level (*Profit = Revenues – Costs*).

Know Your Profit

The pricing of products or services must provide an adequate profit to cover costs. Pricing must be monitored closely to adjust prices due to rising costs or to remain competitive. There should be no hesitation to drop a "loser" product from the product lineup. Pricing often remains an art despite claims to the contrary. In some cases, it involves a straightforward equation: material and labor costs, plus overhead and other expenses, plus profit, equals price. But in many cases the price includes sociological and psychological factors that are hard to identify. Thus, the pricing process is sometimes incredibly arbitrary, and, after considering costs and prices of similar products, it very often takes the form of a wild guess. Higher prices seem to suggest higher quality. The relation is at least questionable.

Know the Tax Implications of Your Expenses

Major decisions, such as how to treat pre-opening expenses, must be determined early in order to minimize taxable income during the firm's early years. For example,

- *Investigatory expenses:* When a prospective small-business person examines a venture, such as market surveys, or plant location analysis, these expenses can be amortized.

- *Organization expenses:* Legal fees for professional services used in setting up a new business can be amortized over a period of not less than 5 years, beginning on the date the business starts operations.

- *Start-up costs:* The cost of hiring and training employees is deductible.

- *Ordinary business expenses:* Rent and utilities should be deducted right away.

Some additional steps that may need to be taken, as far as the profit analysis of a prospective venture is concerned, are the following:

1. Analyze the business idea to determine whether it constitutes a brand new business or an expansion of an existing business. If it is an existing business, investigatory and start-up costs can be deducted currently, rather than over 5 years.

2. Determine *when* the business began operations to distinguish between start-up costs and ordinary business expenses.

3. Prepare for the possibility of abandoning the business idea before the firm begins operations. In this case, it is advisable to set up a corporation to claim ordinary loss deductions.

4. Prepare for the possibility of abandoning the business even after it begins operations. If this happens within 5 years after the start-up, the remaining unamortized expenses can be written off as a loss (Stayen, 1982).

Cash Flow Analysis

The **cash flow cycle** defines the period of time beginning with the initial cash outlay for inventories, raw materials, or services, and ending with the collection of funds from the sale of the finished product. That is, in any business there is some time lag before cash is actually received for the goods or services provided. This time lag creates the need for sound cash planning.

As a beginning step, the length of the cash flow cycle for the firm must be determined. If actual production takes 4 weeks, for example, while payment is made 4 weeks after delivery of the goods to the customer, the cash flow cycle is 8 weeks. The firm incurs expenses to produce these goods at the onset of production and receives cash from the sale 8 weeks later. This is the cash flow cycle.

As a further exercise, consider the amount of the cash the firm must have to start this business. The "up-front" cash costs are the cost of the machine, 8 weeks of lease payment, 8 weeks of wages, and the cost of raw materials for two production cycles.

A *cash flow projection* is a forecast of cash receipts that business anticipates receiving, on the one hand, and cash expenditures on the other hand, throughout the course of a given period of time, and the resulting anticipated cash position at specific times during the period being projected.

The purpose of preparing a cash flow projection is to determine deficits or surpluses in cash from that necessary to operate the business during the time for which the projection is prepared. If deficits are revealed in the cash flow, financial plans must be altered either to provide more cash from more equity capital, loans, or increased selling prices of products; from reduced expenditures including inventory; or from less credit sales, until a proper cash flow balance is obtained. If surpluses of cash are revealed, this may be an indication of excessive borrowing or idle money that could be "put to work." The objective is to finally develop a plan, which, if followed, will provide a well-managed flow of cash.

A cash flow projection form (Exhibit 7.7) provides a systematic method of recording estimates of cash receipts and expenditures, which can be compared with actual receipts and expenditures as they become known. This is why the form has two columns: *estimated* and *actual*. The entries listed on the form will not necessarily apply to every business, and some entries pertinent to specific businesses may not be included. It is suggested, therefore, that the form be adapted to the particular business for which the projection is being made, with appropriate changes required.

Before the cash flow projection can be completed and the pricing structure established, it is necessary to know or to estimate various important factors of the business, for example:

- What are the direct costs of the product or services per unit?
- What are the monthly or yearly costs of the operation?
- What is the sales price per unit of the product or service?
- What is a reasonable break-even goal (including a reasonable net profit) when conservative sales goals are met?
- What are the out-of-the-ordinary sources of additional cash, other than income from sales, such as interest income, loans, equity capital, rent, etc.?

Exhibit 7.7 Cash Flow Analysis: A Monthly Cash Flow Projection Form

Year 2xx3	Month:	Pre–Start-up		1		2	
XYZ, Co.		Estimate	Actual	Estimate	Actual	Estimate	Actual
1. Cash on Hand (Beginning of the month)							
2. Cash receipts							
• Cash sales							
• Collections from A/R							
3. Total cash receipts							
4. Total cash available (1 + 3)							
5. Cash paid out							
• Operations							
• **Subtotal**							
• Loan principal payment							
• Capital purchases							
• Reserve and/or escrow							
• Owner's withdrawal							
6. Total cash paid out							
7. Cash Position (4–6) (End of month)							

The cash position at the end of each month should be adequate to meet the cash requirements for the following month. If the cash balance is low, then additional cash will have to be injected or cash paid out must be reduced. If there is too much cash on hand, this money is not working but instead sits idle.

The cash flow projection, the profit and loss projection, the break-even analysis, and good cost control information are tools, which, if used properly, are useful in making decisions that can increase profits to ensure success. These projections become more useful when the estimated information is compared with actual information as it develops. It is important to follow through and complete the actual columns as the information becomes available. The cash flow projection also assists the small-business person in setting new goals and planning operations for future growth.

Break-even Analysis

Imagine a firm, XYZ Company. XYZ has a vacant plant equipped sufficiently to produce a number of products. Fixed costs for this facility are $250,000. Acme is looking at a potential new product for production in this plant. The product, an electric fork, will sell for $10.00 and has variable costs for materials, labor, overhead, and other items of $7.50 per unit. At present, management feels certain that the market for this product is 2 million units per year. The physical capacity of the plant is 15,000 units per month or 180,000 per year. Should Acme make electric forks in its vacant plant? To begin to answer this question, we need to find the *contribution margin* (CM) for the product. The contribution margin is simply what is left of revenue to cover fixed costs and profits after direct out-of-pocket costs have been subtracted, that is,

$$CM = Revenue - Variable\ costs\ (VC)$$

When the *fixed costs* (FC) are subtracted from the *contribution margin* (CM), you get *income* before interest and taxes. Then the break-even volume can be calculated by dividing the fixed costs by the CM. If the CM is expressed on a per unit basis, the break-even volume will be expressed in units. If it is expressed as a percentage of revenue, the break-even volume will be in dollars. Exhibit 7.8 presents some alternative ways of performing a break-even analysis, one as a contribution required on a per unit basis and another as a contribution as a percentage of revenue.

Exhibit 7.8 Break-even Analysis

Contribution on a *per unit* basis	Contribution as a *percent* of revenue
$CM = Revenue\ (Price) - Variable\ costs\ (VC)$	$CM\% = \dfrac{Prices - VC}{Prices}$
$= \$10 - \$7.5$	
$= \mathbf{\$2.50}$	$= \dfrac{\$10 - \$7.50}{\$10} = \dfrac{\$2.50}{\$10}$
	$= \mathbf{25\%}$
$Break\text{-}even\ volume = \dfrac{Fixed\ costs\ (FC)}{CM}$	$Break\text{-}even\ in\ dollars = \dfrac{FC}{CM\%}$
$= \dfrac{\$250,000}{\$2.50}$	$= \dfrac{\$250,000}{25\%}$
$= \mathbf{100,000\ units}$	$= \mathbf{\$1,000,000}$

Break-even analysis is a quick screening device that can indicate whether it is worthwhile to employ more intensive and costly analysis such as discounted cash flow, which requires large amounts of data that are expensive to collect. Break-even analysis also provides a handle for designing product specifications. Because each product design has its own cost implications and because cost obviously affects price and marketing feasibility, break-even analysis permits comparison of alternative product designs with a different cost mix before the specifications are determined.

Break-even analysis also serves as a substitute for estimating an unknown factor in making project decisions. In deciding whether to go ahead with a project or to skip it, there are always many variables to consider, such as demand, costs, price, and other factors. Whereas most expenses can be determined fairly easily, two unknown variables usually remain: *profit* and *demand*. Because demand is usually tougher to estimate, by deciding that profit must at least be zero (the break-even point), demand can then be fairly simply calculated. Of course, this demand figure at break-even needs to be related to the predicted market share to judge the ultimate worthiness of the project. Ultimately, this is a matter of careful evaluation and business sense, but break-even analysis provides a tool for tackling uncertainty.

For example, in many small businesses, a new product with an uncertain volume is often more feasible if it is made with temporary hand tools and jigs rather than with expensive production tooling. The first method typically has higher variable costs but lower fixed costs. This often results in a lower break-even sales volume for the project as well as lower risks and lower potential profits. The more automated approach, on the other hand, raises the break-even level, but it also raises the risks as well as the profit potential for the company. Break-even analysis helps evaluate these trade-offs (Exhibit 7.9).

Exhibit 7.9   Break–even Analysis

Break-even analysis determines how many *units need to be produced/sold* to break even and *cover at least total costs* (fixed and variable costs).

$$BEP = \frac{\$Total\ fixed\ costs}{\$Unit\ price - \$Unit\ VC} = \#\ BEP\ units$$

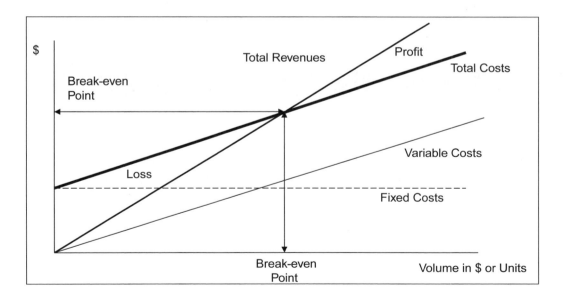

CONCLUSION

One of the most important components of the feasibility analysis and the evaluation of an enterprise idea is the expected financial results of operations, the capital needs, and the growth potential. As has been mentioned repeatedly, for investors and lenders, the analysis should make abundantly clear why they should provide funds, when they can expect a return, and how large that return is anticipated to be. It is a plan for the future. Therefore, any presentation of financial information about the venture and its product or service must be future oriented, regardless how successful the venture may be at present.

The final outcome produced through financial analysis is the reflection of the true financial condition and thus of the venture. Financial analysis is used by the entrepreneur and by individuals both inside and outside the enterprise to make business decisions about the present and the future, whether to invest or not, whether to lend to the firm or not, whether to buy from or sell to the firm. Additionally, financial analysis guides decisions regarding growth and development and decisions about the venture's performance and the performance of the entrepreneurs as managers. If the enterprise's accounting system and the resulting financial statements and analysis are sound and trustworthy, the financial analysis will reflect positively on the venture's management and prospects, and it will make complicated and risky decisions much easier for all concerned.

Financial projections should be realistic, with reasonable margins that conform to experience and industry standards. To plan working capital requirements, it is important to know the cash flow the business will generate. This simply involves the consideration of all elements of cash receipts and disbursements at the time they occur. Assumptions concerning necessary or potential capital requirements, such as additional personnel, expanded manufacturing facilities, or equipment needs, should also be clearly stated. Otherwise, the business plan will create an overly optimistic picture for management as well as subsequent difficulties in the budgeting process and planning evaluation in the future. Worst of all, an overly optimistic business plan can create skepticism for the potential investors and lenders.

Remember that the budgetary and financial analysis processes are the monetary portion of a business plan. They are integral to the business plan, not separate from it. The budget should be the last step in the planning process; only after gathering information for the feasibility analysis can objectives be set and budgetary needs be realistically formulated. The budget and financial analysis can then steer any necessary changes and adjustments in objectives, action steps, or timetables.

Website Information

Topic	Web Address	Description
Financial statements	http://www.ibm.com/investor/ services/new-investor-packet. wss	An online guide on how to read IBM's financial statements, geared toward those who have little or no experience reading financial statements.
Balance sheets	http://www.fool.com/ school/valuation/ howtoreadabalancesheet.htm	More extensive explanation of how to read a balance sheet.
Income statement	http://www.toolkit.cch.com/ text/P06_1578.asp	More extensive explanation of how to read and use an income statement.
Ratio analyses	http://www.investopedia.com/ university/ratios/	Helpful website for understanding and practicing ratio equations. Gives a complete listing of all equations, concepts involved, and practice problems.

Key Terms

Account: A place in which to record the effects of the business transactions on each item involved in the transaction.

Accounts payable: Accounts owed to regular business creditors resulting from trade and usually subject to a discount if paid in full within a short period of time.

Accounts receivable: Amounts not yet collected from customers minus a certain allowance (depending on credit policy) for accounts that experience tells us will turn into bad debt.

Accrued expenses payable: Any amount of expense accrued but unpaid as of the date of the balance sheet.

Asset: Anything of value that can be claimed as the property of the enterprise: cash, machines, amounts to be collected from customers for goods or services (accounts receivable), land, inventory, etc.

Balance: The difference between increases and decreases in the account that have been recorded due to various business transactions, as of some specified date.

Balance sheet: The representation of the fundamental accounting equation: total assets equal total liabilities plus total owner's equity. It is also the result of the adjustments to the balances of all the T-accounts that were included in the worksheet. It is a statement of financial position on a specific date.

Business enterprise: A collection of assets, under common control, aimed at the generation of profit.

Cash: Money bills, petty cash, and money in the bank.

Cash flow cycle: The period of time beginning with the initial cash outlay for inventories, raw materials, or services, and ending with the collection of funds from the sale of the finished product.

Cost of goods sold: Amount of inventory in raw materials that was used to produce the sold finished goods.

Current liabilities: Claims that must be paid off in a relatively short period of time, usually 1 year or less.

Deferred charges: Major expenditures written off over several years rather than charged fully during 1 year (e.g., research and development).

Depreciation: Decline in the useful value of an asset due to wear and tear over time.

Financial analysis: The systematic study of the current or potential performance of a business enterprise.

Fixed assets: Assets that cannot easily be converted to cash in a short period of time, most of which are subject to depreciation.

Gross operating income (loss): The gross profit margin minus operating and general administrative expenses.

Gross profit margin: The value added by a firm to the purchased raw material of merchandise by processing, packaging, upgrading, and finally selling it as a finished good.

Historical basis: An approach to measure balances in which asset balances are measured at their historical cost (i.e., cost of acquisition of the asset at the time it was acquired).

Income statement: The statement that shows the record of operating activities, how the firm's earnings were derived, what the sales were, and what expenses were incurred to generate these sales during a specific time period.

Intangibles: Nonphysical assets of a firm that may be of substantial value (e.g., trademarks and licenses).

Ledger: The file of all the different accounts of the business, and the final product of bookkeeping from which an accountant can analyze, report, and interpret financial data.

Liabilities: Legal obligations that usually take the form of accounts payable (i.e., amounts owed to banks and other creditors that were borrowed for a relatively short period of time) and long-term debt.

Liquidation basis of measurement: A method of listing assets in order of the amount that could be obtained by selling each one.

Liquidity: A firm's ability to meet its short-term obligations.

Long-term liabilities: Longer claims against the fixed assets of the company, usually due after one year from the date on the balance sheet.

Merchandise inventories: Raw materials, partially finished goods, goods still in the process of manufacture, and finished goods ready for shipment.

Net operating income (loss): Gross operating income minus depreciation.

Net sales: Amount received after taking into consideration returned goods and allowances for reduction of prices.

Net worth or owner's equity: The remaining assets, that is, the residual interest in the enterprise after all liabilities are paid to the creditors.

Notes payable: Promissory notes owed to banks or creditors, usually due within a year.

Operating and general administrative expenses: Costs that include everything but raw materials.

Out-of-the-ordinary income: Income not derived from operations, such as dividends and interest received by the firm from savings, investment in marketable securities, or income from sale of a fully depreciated asset.

Payroll, sales, and withheld taxes: Amount owed to the Internal Revenue Service.

Prepayment: An out-of-the-ordinary asset for which one firm has paid in advance (e.g., equipment rental fees, or insurance).

Sources and uses of funds: An explanation of how net working capital (the excess of current assets over current liabilities) has changed *during* a period of time.

Total current assets: Assets that head the list because, if necessary, they can be converted into cash in a relatively short period of time, usually less than 1 year, with minimum loss in the conversion. Current assets include cash, account receivable, and merchandise inventories.

Total fixed assets: The net valuation for balance sheet purposes of the firm's investment in land, buildings, machines, and office furniture and fixtures, minus the depreciation accumulated as of the date of the balance sheet.

Total net income (loss): Out-of-the-ordinary income added to net operating income.

Total net income after taxes: Total net income (before taxes) plus an amount set aside for federal income taxes.

Total net income before taxes: Total net income minus out-of-the-ordinary expenses, such as interest expenses.

Working capital: The current assets remaining after current liabilities and running expenses have been paid: current assets minus current liabilities.

Worksheet: A tool used by many accountants to prepare financial statements, which can include many accounts, usually taking the form of a capital T, called T-accounts.

Review Questions

1. Briefly outline the differences between the bookkeeping and the accounting processes.

2. What are the uses of the balance sheet?

3. What are the uses of the income statement?

4. What are the uses of the sources and uses (cash flow) statement?

5. Briefly discuss the four major financial analysis techniques.

6. What is the difference between the short and the long version of the ROI ratio, and what are its uses?

7. Briefly discuss the fundamentals of building a cash flow pro forma statement.

8. What are the principles of profit analysis?

9. Briefly discuss the break-even analysis and its uses.

Reflections from the Front Lines of LifeGuard America

Like any other start-up business, initial funding is a primary objective. We based our initial request for funding on two strategic principles. The first was that we would target only one round of equity funding to break even and reach profitability. The second was to back up our initial equity funding with a debt instrument that funded 95% of our 3-year contracts with the OPTN organizations. This means that for every 30 organizations that contract for our services, we receive $950,000 in up-front cash to operate and expand. This backup strategy allows us to sell less of the company in the critical start-up mode when valuation of the company is at its lowest point. We worked with several experts who came up with an initial valuation of LifeGuard America at $5,000,000. This translated into needing to sell 30% of the company to raise the required $1,500,000 to get us through break-even and to profitability. Let's now turn our attention to the business plan section titled Financials:

> We have established a sales price of $1,500,000 to acquire 30% ownership in LifeGuard America. We have created a business model that generated our pro forma financials, presented below. This business model allows "what if" scenarios to be run quickly that enable the user to understand important relationships between key business assumptions. Our corporate financial model includes the ramp-up of our services business and the launch, in 2005, of our flight operations.

Use of Funds

First, $500,000 will be used to secure the office space, office equipment, computers, and software required for the development of the 24×7 response center and initial operating expenses. Another $500,000 will be used to launch the sales and marketing effort, acquire the necessary personnel to man the response center, and fund the company's operations for the first year. An additional $500,000 will be used to accelerate the national marketing campaign. The following table lists and describes the key posts of a business organization. It is structured in three parts: Management, Marketing, Money. You may restructure the table to suit your own management style. Customize the task descriptions so they apply to your operation, or add positions and tasks appropriate to your operation. You can also consolidate tasks under fewer positions. Ownership and salary data are optional, and the deployment of our Virtual Private Network extends throughout the entire OPTN.

Assumptions

Our financial model is based on a conservative sales plan that calls for the rollout of our services beginning in UNOS region 4, (Oklahoma and Texas) in the first 90 days. This launch is happening in parallel with our response center development during the first 2 months after the close of funding. Further, we will launch into UNOS region 3 (the Southeast) during the second 90-day period and continue with a quarterly rollouts into the rest of the UNOS regions through 2004. This projection assumes no growth in the number of donors, transplant centers, or transplant programs.

Income Statement

	2003	2004	2005	2006
Revenue	4,570,395	11,026,971	20,534,403	32,516,582
Cost of Service	1,765,503	3,355,585	7,040,168	10,841,761
Gross Profit	2,804,892	7,671,386	13,494,235	21,674,821
GPM	61.4%	69.6%	65.7%	66.7%
Operating Expenses				
Selling/Marketing	1,240,000	965,000	1,092,000	665,000
G&A Expense	1,898,100	3,436,007	5,835,618	5,761,745
Other	68,556	495,134	956,736	1,990,941
Operating Expenses	3,206,656	4,896,141	7,884,354	8,417,687
Operating Income	(401,764)	2,775,244	5,609,881	13,257,135
OPM	−8.8%	25.2%	27.3%	40.8%
Interest	0	—	—	—
Net Income Before Tax	(401,764)	2,775,244	5,609,881	13,257,135
Taxes (35%)	0	971,336	1,963,458	4,639,997
Net Income After Tax	(401,764)	1,803,909	3,646,423	8,617,137
Net Income Margin	−8.8%	16.4%	17.8%	26.5%
EBITDA	(258,664)	2,967,569	5,838,481	13,528,735

Cash Flow

	2003	2004	2005	2006
Operations				
Net Income	(401,764)	1,803,909	3,646,423	8,617,137
Depreciation	143,100	192,325	228,600	271,600
Inventory	0	(100,000.00)	0	(100,000)
Accounts Receivable	(634,777)	(896,747)	(1,320,477)	(1,664,192)
Accounts Payable	147,125	131,988	306,942	316,799
Accruals	100,000	0	0	—
Cash Flow from Operations	(646,316)	1,131,475	2,861,488	7,441,345
Investing				
Capital Expenditures	(715,500)	(515,000)	(175,000)	(215,000)
Aircraft Deposits	(25,000)	—	—	—
Intangibles	(50,000.00)	—	—	—
Retirements	—	—	—	—
Cash Flow from Investing	(765,500)	(515,000)	(175,000)	(215,000)
Financing				
Revolver Debt	—	—	—	—
Term Debt	—	—	—	—
Paid In Capital	1,500,000	—	—	—
Cash Flow from Financing	1,500,000	—	—	—
Change in Cash	88,184	616,475	1,686,488	7,226,345
Beginning Cash	0	88,184	704,660	3,391,148
Ending Cash	88,184	704,660	3,391,148	10,617,493

Balance Sheet

	2003	2004	2005	2006
Assets				
Cash	88,184	704,660	3,391,148	10,617,493
Inventory	—	100,000	100,000	100,000
A/R	634,777	1,531,524	2,852,000	4,516,192

Total Current	722,961	2,336,184	6,343,148	15,333,685
Fixed	715,500	1,230,500	1,405,500	1,620,500
Less: Depreciation	(143,100)	(335,425)	(564,025)	(835,625)
Total Fixed	574,400	895,075	841,475	784,875
Other	50,000	50,000	50,000	50,000
Total	1,345,361	3,281,259	7,234,623	16,168,560
Liabilities				
Accounts Payable	147,125	279,113	586,056	902,855
Other/Accruals	100,000	100,000	100,000	100,000
Total Current	247,125	379,113	686,056	1,002,855
Long Term	—	—	—	—
Total Liabilities	247,125	379,113	686,056	1,002,855
Equity	1,098,236	2,902,145	6,548,567	15,165,705
Total Liabilities + Equity	1,345,361	3,281,258	7,234,623	16,168,560

Discussion Questions on LifeGuard America

1. After reviewing LifeGuard America's financial pro forma statements, do you believe that Mr. Fitzpatrick is raising enough money by offering 30% and $1,500,000?

2. How close does LifeGuard America come to "hitting the ground" under this operational plan? What contingencies are there?

Reference

Stayen, H. T. (1982, October). How to treat your start-up expenses. *Inc. Magazine, 4*(10), 147–148.

8 | Venture Financial Needs: Personal Investment and Additional Funding Needs

Can We Commit?

LEARNING OBJECTIVES

1. To show the diversity of financing options for a new venture.
2. To explore traditional and nontraditional funding sources and techniques.
3. To provide insight in determining the best funding source and technique for a new or existing venture.

TOPIC OUTLINE

Ως εκ τούτου, υπάρχει ανάγκη για χρήματα, ω Αθηναίοι
"Therefore, there is need for money, Oh Athenians!"

(Athenian orator Demosthenes urged the Athenians to exercise fiscal control
to succeed in fending off the military threat from the Macedonian king Philip,
Alexander the Great's father. Not heeding his advice, the Athenians were
defeated by Philip and Alexander in the battle of Chaeronea in 338 B.C.)

——

INTRODUCTION

To ensure success, the funding needs and requirements of the venture must also be satisfied. The fact is, however, that tapping conventional lending sources for the start-up of many new ventures can be virtually fruitless. Even the entrepreneurs who are able to convince their local bankers of the worthiness of a venture find themselves sometimes paying what are considered usurious interest rates. Generally, as interest rates soar, small-business borrowing declines. Thus, increasingly entrepreneurs have to seek funds from many previously untapped sources—funds not only for start-up but also for internal injections at times of depressed sales or cash-flow problems.

Many of the funding options presented here are considered traditional, but other, unorthodox funding mechanisms have also emerged in recent years as traditional sources have increasingly shunned the requests of entrepreneurs. Some confuse borrowing with equity or investment capital: there is a big difference. Equity money does not have to be repaid. It is money accrued from selling a part interest in the business to people who are willing to risk their money in it because they are interested in potential income rather than in an immediate return on their investment. Whether entrepreneurs satisfy their funding needs through borrowing or investment, they need to determine early on specifically what their needs for success are and communicate them clearly and precisely to lenders and/or investors.

VENTURE FUNDING

Accompanying a heightened interest in the general area of small business and entrepreneurship has been increased interest from policy makers, regulators, and academics in the nature and behavior of the financial sources that fund start-up ventures. At the core of this issue are questions about the type of financing growing companies need and receive at various stages of their growth. Particular attention has been focused on private equity financing and the connections between and substitutability among alternative sources of funding because they are so critical for the successful operation of the new venture. In addition to the interest in the micro-foundations of small-business finance, there is also growing interest in the macro-economic implications of small-business finance (Berger & Udell, 1998).

In general, small firms comprise a major economic force that has been the subject of some recent policy initiatives. But not all small firms are alike. The firms that are ultimately able to offer a public listing of their stock are qualitatively different from most small businesses. The small minority of firms with the economic potential to list their stock can be distinguished from the others by their growth potential rather than their size, which is a concern. Because these firms have the potential for rapid growth of at least 20% annually, they are able to attract external suppliers of equity capital and additional venture funds from an initial public offering (IPO) (Freear & Wetzel, 1990). However, while venture funds may be raised from the financial markets through IPOs, these funds are usually available to a start-up company well after its early stages. A more typical and widely recognized source of early-stage capital for high-growth startups is formal venture capital funds. In fact, venture capital funds controlled an estimated $24 billion of assets in the United States in start-up venture funding (Alleva &

Barnes, 1998). This figure increased in 2000 by 80% over 1999 to $68.8 billion, despite an 18% decrease from the third quarter to the fourth quarter of 2000, according to statistics from the PricewaterhouseCoopers (PwC) "Money Tree Survey" in cooperation with VentureOne. However, most of these venture capital funds are now reserved for companies that are already in venture capital portfolios rather than for ventures seeking start-up funding. For example, during the fourth quarter of 2000, only 25.5% of venture capital resources were directed toward start-up funding, while more than double that figure, 52%, were directed to firms already being funded and existing venture capital portfolios (Prince, 2001).

In the mid- to late 1990s, an unprecedented increase in the growth of new start-up companies occurred, especially in the tech sector, in which a very large number of electronic commerce web-based companies emerged. Most of these firms started with funds from friends, family, and/or angel investors rather than the entrepreneurs themselves. Some firms also raised additional funds from other private sources, such as banks and venture capitalists, while others with the greatest potential obtained further funding in the over-the-counter (OTC) financial market through IPOs. The success exhibited by some firms in raising money was usually followed by an extraordinary rise of their stock price in the aftermarket, which led to a rash of IPOs as even more start-up companies scrambled to leap on the bandwagon. Seemingly overnight, investors poured billions of dollars into these companies and their stocks. As stock prices continued to spiral upward, many remained optimistic that stock prices would rise in perpetuity, while others started wondering when the bubble would burst. Instead of blindly following the herd, however, these investors started raising doubts about the manner by which many in their midst chose to ascertain the true value of the start-up ventures and the stocks being offered. Indeed, a recent study in which people were asked in hindsight to rank the causes of dot-com failures, "risky investors" was cited by 67% of respondents, followed by 56% for "poor planning," and 39% for "inexperienced managers" ("Dot-com shakeout," 2001). As mentioned previously, investors must place a great deal of importance on obtaining solid signals from a framework of success and on the overall quality of a venture when evaluating which proposals are worthy of funding.

SOURCES OF CAPITAL FUNDING

Once the framework for success is in place and has been clearly communicated, finding money for seed capital is probably one of the easiest tasks to accomplish; many types of financing are available to the entrepreneur. Building on the agency theory, investors can use the information provided in the venture proposal's framework for success, as well as information on the proportion of the entrepreneur's personal investment of his or her wealth into the project, as an indication of true commitment on the part of the entrepreneur. Thus, the knowledge that a venture's prospects are indeed framed in success and the knowledge that a large proportion of the entrepreneur's wealth is invested in the project may provide a direct signal of value *and* commitment about the project. These factors should be strongly emphasized by the entrepreneur when constructing the business plan for the project, especially because this emphasis has the additional benefit of demonstrating that the entrepreneur is able to analyze the rate of return before making his or her own investment decision in their venture project (Prasad, Bruton, & Vozikis, 2000).

Most new firms, of course, are not eligible for formal venture capital or have the ability to take their company public immediately. However, they have to find some equity capital, and in most cases, after they have depleted their personal savings, entrepreneurs turn to family, friends, and acquaintances. The vast majority of the companies utilize personal savings, family, and friends as sources of capital ("Fastest 50," 2001).

There are various means through which entrepreneurs can obtain financing for their new business venture. Exhibit 8.1 shows the sources of seed capital for the *Inc.* 500; this list reinforces the idea that, after exhausting their personal savings, many entrepreneurs turn to family, friends, and acquaintances for capital (Mangelsdorf, 1992, p. 80; the sources of seed capital do not add up to 100% because some firms used more than one source).

Exhibit 8.1	Sources of Seed Capital for *Inc.* 500			
Personal savings	78.5%	Bank loans	14.4%
Family members	12.9	Employees/partners	12.4
Friends	9.0	Venture capital	6.3
Mortgaged property	4.0	Government guaranteed loans	1.1
Other	3.3		

Exhibit 8.2	Considered Sources of Funding vs. Actual Funding	
Sources of funding	% Firms considering	% Firms actually funded
Personal savings	69%	49%
Bank loans	69	7
Family or friends	12	9
Government agencies	48	9
Venture capital and angels	45	10
University endowments	5	6
Strategic partners	0	6

Exhibit 8.2 depicts the percentage of firms that consider a certain source of funding and contrasts this with the percentage of firms that *actually* securing funding from that source (Van Osnabrugge, 2000, p. 53).

It is interesting to note from this table that a great deal of faith for potential funding is placed in banks, government agencies, venture capitalists, and angels that is not realized, while some funding sources, such as university endowments or strategic partners, materialize without having been seriously considered by venture entrepreneurs.

BOOTSTRAPPING

Bootstrapping occurs when the entrepreneur uses creative financing to get by on as few resources as possible and by using other people's resources as much as possible. This occurs because it may be difficult for a new venture to obtain financing through lenders or investors; therefore, many new ventures have to bootstrap for various reasons. Typically, but not in all cases, new ventures are prone to failure because they lack competitive advantage; proprietary rights, or the founders lack a significant track record in the industry. The vast majority of all firms were started by this method, and most of them are initially financed with less than $10,000. In fact, 94% of new technology-based firms and 80% of the *Inc.* magazine 500 fastest growing privately held entrepreneurial firms in the United States listed bootstrapping sources as their most likely funding source (Van Osnabrugge, 2000). Bootstrapping may include (a) using credit cards and on-line lending agencies that connect borrowers with lenders such as American Express, GE Capital, and others, (b) taking second mortgages, customer advances, and extended terms from vendors or other suppliers, (c) hiring as few employees as possible or using temporary employees, or (d) subcontracting tasks unrelated to the firm's competitive advantage to other firms. Leasing, sharing, or bartering resources or assets also minimizes unnecessary costs and provides an indirect source of funding. Pressing customers for payment, factoring accounts receivables to a bank, or forestalling payment to vendors can also temporarily increase funds.

FRIENDS, FAMILY, COUNTRYMEN (AND FOOLS)

"When a friend deals with a friend, let the bargain be clear and well penn'd, that they may continue friends to the end."

(Benjamin Franklin)

In many instances, borrowing from family, friends, or "fools" is the only available option, but even under the most plausible circumstances, it is usually a no-win situation. This type of financing can be most costly due to the personal and intimate bond that exists in this arrangement. If the venture fails, then the borrower is always to blame. If the venture succeeds beyond anyone's expectations and the loan is repaid in full, the repayment may never be enough, especially if the returns from the venture's success are not shared and/or needed capital is raised without first offering family and friends a funding option. The entrepreneur might encounter the "I remember when . . ." declaration.

> It is safe to say that, in a very large number of instances, relatives and friends play a key role in the financing of new enterprises. Frequently, relatives and friends are the only investors who can be persuaded to participate in the early financing of a business, but too often such investments are made emotionally without the participant having any appreciation of the risks involved. Funds are advanced primarily out of the desire to give a helping hand to someone they know well and to whom they wish the best of luck. However, in such situations, people often lose the objectivity that should always characterize financial dealings and often neglect to shore up agreements and understandings with legal documentations. Entrepreneurs should further satisfy themselves that participating investors invest only those funds that they are in a position to lose comfortably. (Dible, 1986, p. 248)

Another source of funding is preyed upon by "ethically impaired" entrepreneurs who are swindlers or white-collar con artists, better known as "contrapreneurs" (Francis, 1988). Contrapreneurs prey on "fools" who are investing for the wrong reasons, most likely greed. Greed is a very powerful catalyst for foolhardy decisions, and foolish investors get caught up in the hype of a deal when they know very little or nothing about the industry or the individual contrapreneur that they invest in.

"Crowd-funding" websites like Kickstarter.com have also created avenues for creative people to get enough start-up money to get their projects off the ground, even in exotic categories besides technology, such as film, art, design, food, and publishing. Aspiring entrepreneurs can describe their project with a video, a description, and a target dollar amount. If the project takes off, Kickstarter.com takes 5%, and the entrepreneur pays 3–5% to Amazon.com's credit card service, but if the target money is not raised by the deadline, the deal is off, your contributors keep their money, and Kickstarter.com takes nothing (Pogue, 2012).

BANKS

Many small companies depend on bank loans, but in most cases commercial banks are rarely a viable financial option (except for SBA-guaranteed loans), even though, according to the

U.S. Small Business Administration, in the past few years the number and the amount of bank loans to small firms have increased ("Cash Flow," 2001). Some reference, however, should be made to the bank's evaluation of the general creditworthiness of the firm and the entrepreneur. Commercial banks are heavily regulated and have a system to follow when lending called *The Five Cs: character, capacity, collateral, capital,* and *condition.* The Five Cs are the factors that loan officers use to monitor and determine whether a business and their founders are qualified for a loan.

Generally, before approaching a bank with a request for a loan, certain basic information (discussed previously) should be prepared and addressed in quantitative as well as qualitative terms. This helps convince loan officers that the venture firm and their founders are creditworthy. The following points should be thoroughly assessed prior to visiting a bank official:

- Why is the money needed? An ongoing concern with a respectable track record does not need the documentation required for a pre-start-up request. Is the money for inventory, fixtures, salaries, or travel expenses? Specifically, how and when will the funds be deployed? There should be no secrets nor cryptic responses as to how these funds will be applied.

- Has a sophisticated cash budget and payback schedule for the principal and interest been prepared and developed? The venture's management abilities are of utmost concern to the lending institution, and the preparation of such a budget is the acid test.

- Will an extension or a request for more money be submitted at a later date? Planning for contingencies indicates insightfulness, and the possibility of a shortage assessment reveals the many unknowns that the venture may confront.

- What is the overall status of the venture's macroeconomic environment? In general, is business good? Are interest rates currently at a level that makes profitability a formidable objective? A realistic evaluation of the external environment and its impact on the venture's framework for success is critical.

- Is the individual entrepreneur credible? Entrepreneurial characteristics are the most underrated and difficult to discern, and yet the most essential component of the loan request is the competency, ability, and professionalism of the entrepreneur. Not only is it essential to sell the venture's value concept, it is essential that entrepreneurs also sell themselves. Depending upon the loan officer and the financial institution, as many as half of the evaluation criteria might be predicated on the entrepreneur. Understanding of the financial aspects, attitude and character, past experience and personal knowledge, being the "right person at the right time," and, finally, managerial skills are all important criteria to loan officers. With regard to the FAKTS, this is "déjà vu all over again," to paraphrase Yogi Berra.

Once the answers to these questions have been thoroughly and carefully prepared, a determination of the amount of funding the firm needs from the bank can be made. Naturally, no money is ever borrowed from a bank without certain stipulations being placed upon the individual and the firm. This is simply part of any loan agreement, and generally, the bank will place restrictions on the individual and the firm in three different areas: repayment terms, a pledge of some type of security, and periodic reporting.

Obviously, both sides have a vested interest in maintaining an open, cordial, and compatible relationship. The entrepreneur may indeed need to seek additional monies from the lender in the future; at the same time, the bank wants to ensure a systematic repayment schedule that protects its investment in the entrepreneur. In general, there are two types of borrowed money as a source of funds: short-term money (or loans), and term money (or long-term loans).

Short-term bank loans are used for financing accounts receivable for 30 to 60 days or for purposes that take longer to pay off, such as building a seasonal inventory over a period of 5 to 6 months. Usually, lenders expect short-term loans to be repaid after the loan purposes have been served and satisfied. For example, when the borrower's customers have paid the outstanding accounts receivable, or when the inventory has been converted into saleable merchandise, the short-term loan needs to be repaid. Occasionally, banks grant unsecured loans based on an entrepreneur's general credit reputation, or as a secured loan when sufficient collateral is available. In contrast, the secured loan involves a pledge of some or all venture assets as security and collateral for the protection of its depositors against the risks involved, even in business situations in which the chances of success are outstanding.

Term borrowing provides funds that will be paid back over a fairly long period of time. Term loans are broken down into two categories: intermediate loans for longer than 1 year but less than 5 years, and long-term loans for more than 5 years. Term borrowing is also typically the kind of loan that is paid back in periodic installments from the company's earnings. As in the case of secured short-term loans, few entrepreneurs are able to secure term loans on the basis of their signatures alone. Generally, the bank requires some added protection guaranteeing the repayment of the loan. There are many forms of collateral that may be utilized in securing a loan.

Endorsers, Co-makers, and Guarantors

Endorsers are other people whom borrowers get to sign a note to bolster their own credit. Endorsers are contingently liable for the note they sign. If the borrower fails to pay, the bank expects the endorser to make the note good. Sometimes, endorsers may be asked to pledge their own assets or securities. A **co-maker** is one who creates an obligation jointly with the borrower. In such cases, the bank can collect directly from either the maker or the co-maker. Finally, a **guarantor** guarantees the payment of a note by signing a guaranty commitment. Both private and government lenders often require guarantees from officers of corporations to assure the continuity of effective management. Sometimes, a manufacturer acts as guarantor for one of its customers, or the federal government acts as guarantor in the form of an SBA-guaranteed loan.

Lease Assignment

The assigned lease as security is similar to the guarantee. Sometimes it is used when a franchise is involved, for example, when the bank lends the money on a building and takes a mortgage. Then the lease, which the dealer and the parent franchise company agree upon, is assigned so that the bank automatically receives the rent payments and, thus, is guaranteed repayment of the loan.

Warehouse Receipts

Banks also take inventory commodities as security, lending money on a warehouse receipt. Such a receipt is usually delivered directly to the bank and shows that the merchandise used as security either has been placed in a public warehouse or has been left on the premises under the control of a bonded employee in a field warehouse. Such loans are generally made on staple or standard merchandise that can be readily marketed; they are drafted using as security a percentage of the estimated value of the goods.

Trust Receipts and Floor Planning

The only way many small firms can afford merchandise that needs to be displayed in order to be sold, such as automobiles, appliances, and boats, is by borrowing money with loans that are often secured by a note and a trust receipt. This **trust receipt** is the legal paper for floor planning and is used for identifiable, serial-numbered merchandise. A trust receipt signed by the entrepreneur signifies and acknowledges that the merchandise was received that it will keep in trust for the bank, and that, as soon as the goods are sold, the loan will be paid.

Chattel Mortgages

Chattel mortgage loans allow the small firm to buy equipment such as a cash register or a delivery truck using a lien on the equipment as security. The bank evaluates the equipment's present and future market value as well as the protection of the equipment being used to secure the loan, and considers depreciation and insurance issues that may affect its value in case of fire, theft, property damage, and liability.

Real Estate

When taking a real estate mortgage, the bank evaluates and appraises the location of the real estate, its physical condition, its foreclosure value, and the amount of insurance that is needed for the property and/or life insurance for the borrower.

Accounts Receivable

Many banks lend money on accounts receivable. The bank may take accounts receivable on a notification or a non-notification plan. Under the notification plan, the bank informs the firm's customers that the account has been assigned to the bank and that the payment should be directed there. Under the non-notification plan, the borrower's customers continue to pay their accounts to the firm and the firm in turn pays the bank back.

Savings Accounts

Sometimes a savings account is assigned to the bank, which gets to keep the savings account passbook. If the savings account used as collateral is at a bank different from the one that makes the loan, then the lending bank asks the other bank to mark its records to show that the account is held as collateral.

Life Insurance

Another kind of collateral is life insurance, upon which banks will lend up to the cash value of a life insurance policy, and the policy in turn is assigned to the bank. If the policy is on the life of an executive of a small corporation, corporate resolutions must authorize such an assignment. Most insurance companies allow the policy to be signed back to the original beneficiary once the assignment to the bank ends, that is, when the loan is paid off. A bank loan with an insurance policy as collateral is often more convenient to obtain and is usually at a lower interest rate than a loan directly from the insurance company that issued the policy.

Stocks and Bonds

Marketable stocks and bonds can also be used as collateral. As a protection against market declines and the possible expenses of liquidation, however, banks usually lend no more than 75% of the market value of high-grade stock. On the more secure federal government or municipal bonds, banks may be willing to lend 90% or more of market value. The bank may also ask the borrower for additional security or payment whenever the market value of the stocks or bonds drops below the bank's required margin.

While banks impose many stipulations and regulations, they contribute to efficiency and/or effectiveness of businesses through close monitoring and better evaluation, which leads to higher performance. A sample bank loan application can be found at Business

Owner's Toolkit ("Sample Bank Review Form for Loan Applications," http://www.toolkit. cch.com/tools/loan_m.asp).

GOVERNMENT LENDING SOURCES

Although the *Small Business Administration* (SBA) generally captures the limelight where loans to entrepreneurs are concerned, a number of government lending sources, other than the SBA, deserve mention. The federal government injects billions into start-ups, and these monies are available to entrepreneurs through no less than 350 different types of lending programs, in spite of the red tape involved.

SBA Loans

Since 1953, the SBA has helped small firms succeed from start-up through the many stages of growth. Many large firms, whose names are now quite well known, such as FedEx, Intel, Nike, Apple, Compaq, and AOL, all received assistance from the SBA along the way. Their website (http://www.sba.gov) provides valuable information as well as additional related links. The SBA is the highest volume lender (in dollars) to entrepreneurs, accounting for 30% of all loans made ("SBA Loans," 2001, p. 65). The heart of the SBA loan program has two sections, the 7(a) loan, which is targeted to a broad base, and the 8(a) loan, which is targeted toward minorities seeking business funding.

The 7(a) loan program represents the bulk of SBA loans. Under the guidelines of this program, small manufacturers, wholesalers, retailers, service concerns, and other businesses may borrow from the agency to construct, expand, or convert facilities; purchase buildings, equipment, materials; or to obtain working capital. By law, the SBA may not make a loan if a business can obtain funds from a bank or other private source. Therefore, the venture entrepreneur must first seek private financing from a local bank or other lending institution before applying to the SBA. In a large city, one with more than 200,000 people, loan application rejections by two banks are required before applying for a direct SBA loan. Applicants for loans must agree to comply with SBA regulations that there will be no discrimination in employment or services to the public based on race, color, religion, national origin, sex, or marital status. The SBA emphasizes maximum private lender participation in each loan. This policy has made it possible for the SBA to respond to a far greater number of requests for financial assistance than is possible under the direct lending program. When financing is not otherwise available on reasonable terms (effective December 22, 2000), a maximum loan amount of $2 million has been established for 7(a) loans. However, the maximum dollar amount the SBA can guaranty is generally $1 million. Small loans with a gross loan amount of $150,000 or less carry a maximum guaranty of a bank loan to a small firm of 85%. For loans greater than $150,000, the maximum guaranty is 75%. SBA business loans may be for as long as 10 years, except for those portions of loans used for acquiring real property or constructing facilities, which may have a maturity of 20 years. Working capital loans are usually limited to 6 years.

Repayment ability from the cash flow of the business is a primary consideration in the SBA loan decision process, but good character, management capability, collateral, and owner's equity contribution are also important considerations. Additionally, all owners of 20% or more of the firm are required to personally guarantee SBA loans.

If the entire loan is not obtainable from a private lender and if an SBA guaranteed loan is not available, the SBA will then consider advancing funds on an immediate participation basis with a bank. The SBA will consider making a direct loan only when these other forms of financing are not obtainable, and SBA funds are available for direct lending when there are no federal fiscal restraints (U.S. Small Business Administration, 2000).

More than 2,000 companies participate in the SBA's 8(a) loan program, which sets aside government contracts for minority companies. This amount is equivalent to about one third of the total dollar volume of loans made under the 7(a) program. A great fear here, however, is that many of the firms receiving assistance under this program would collapse without it.

There are some relatively simple guidelines for applying for an SBA loan for either a new or an existing venture. For a new venture, the application should include the following:

1. A description, in detail, of the type of business to be established.
2. A list of the entrepreneur's business education, experience, and management capabilities.
3. An estimate of how much the individual entrepreneur or others have to invest in the business and how much they will need to borrow.
4. A current, signed, personal financial statement of the owner(s).
5. A projected profit and loss statement for the first year the business will operate.
6. A list of collateral to be offered as security for the loan, listing the market value of each item.
7. This material should be taken to a bank to apply for a direct bank loan, and if declined, the bank should be asked to make the loan under the SBA's loan guaranty plan. If the bank is interested in an SBA guaranty loan, the bank needs to contact the SBA for discussion of the application. In most guaranty loans, the SBA deals directly with the bank. If a guaranty loan is not available, the first six items need to be sent to the nearest SBA office.

For ongoing ventures, different items are requested:

1. Submission of SBA Form 912 (Personal History Statement) for each person: owners, partners, directors, major stockholders, etc.
2. A signed current personal balance sheet (SBA Form 413 may be used for this purpose) for each stockholder (with 20% or greater ownership), partner, officer, and owner, along with his or her Social Security number.
3. The statements listed below: a, b, and c for the last 3 years; a, b, c, d, dated within 90 days of filing the application; and finally, statement e, if applicable.
   a. Balance Sheet
   b. Profit and Loss Statement
   c. Reconciliation of Net Worth
   d. Aging of Accounts Receivable and Payable
   e. Earnings projections for at least 1 year when financial statements for the last 3 years are unavailable or were requested by a district office. If a Profit and Loss Statement is not available, it needs to be substituted with Federal Income Tax Forms, along with a detailed explanation for its unavailability.
4. A brief history of the company and a paragraph describing the expected benefits it will receive from the loan.
5. A brief description of the educational, technical, and business background of all individuals listed under Management.
6. A list of any co-signers and/or guarantors for the loan, including addresses and personal balance sheet(s).

7. A list of any machinery or equipment along with its documented cost to be bought with the loan proceeds.

8. A detailed list of any officers of the company who have ever been involved in bankruptcy or insolvency proceedings.

9. Details of any pending lawsuits involving the business.

10. An affidavit stating that the applicants or their spouses or any member of their household, or anyone who owns, manages, or directs the business or their spouses or members of their households do not work for the Small Business Administration, Small Business Advisory Council, SCORE or ACE, any federal agency, or the participating lender.

11. The names of any subsidiaries or affiliates and their relationship with the company, along with a current balance sheet and operating statement for each.

12. The name of any concern the firm buys from, sells to, or uses the services of in which someone in the company has a significant financial interest.

13. A copy of any franchise agreement, along with a copy of the FTC disclosure statement supplied by the franchisor (US SBA, 2000).

An applicant for any loan from the SBA may obtain the assistance of any attorney, accountant, engineer, appraiser, or other representative to aid him in the preparation and presentation of his application to SBA. However, such representation is not mandatory.

In the event a loan is approved, the services of an attorney may be necessary to assist in the preparation of closing documents, title abstracts, etc. The SBA allows the payment of reasonable fees or other compensation for services performed by such representatives on behalf of the applicant.

Finally, it is important to note "what's in it for the bank." Why should a lending institution risk making an SBA loan? The answer is simple and profitable for many lenders. The increased opportunity to sell the SBA-guaranteed loans on the secondary market makes them quite attractive to banks, especially since the SBA has cut down the paperwork involved. For example, after a bank makes a $200,000 80% guaranteed loan and collects its loan service charges, it can sell the $160,000 government-guaranteed portion on the secondary market. This leaves the bank with only $40,000 tied up in the loan, making it possible for the bank to make more SBA-guaranteed loans. Such possibilities make a lot of fresh money available to small businesses.

Small Business Investment Companies

The *Small Business Investment Company Act* came into existence in 1958 in an attempt to boost the economy with tax-advantaged capital. Banks, financial institutions, university endowments, and foundations soon became the primary source of capital for the technology industry. In this scheme, the SBA leverages the capital invested with loans of its own, so for every $1 invested by a fund, the *Small Business Investment Company* (SBIC) actually has $3 to invest in a new emerging technology. SBICs thus derive their initial capital from private investors and are normally eligible to obtain funds from the government or from private financial institutions through government-guaranteed loans. SBICs are privately owned and privately operated and are licensed by the SBA to provide equity or venture capital and long-term loans to small firms as well as management assistance to the companies they finance. But these are their only functions. They cannot, for instance, sell insurance, trade in property, or become holding companies for groups of operating businesses.

For SBICs with private capital equal to or in excess of $500,000, the SBA funds an equivalent of 400% of private capital, which becomes available if 65% of the total funds designated for investment are indeed invested or committed to venture capital investments. Minority enterprise SBICs, dedicated solely to assisting socially or economically disadvantaged small business concerns, may borrow from the SBA at a subsidized interest rate (usually 3% below the going cost of money to the US Treasury) for the first 5 years of the loan. They may also sell to the SBA non-voting preferred securities on a one-to-one basis in relation to their private capital or, in some cases, portions of their private capital.

An SBIC finances small firms in two general ways, straight loans and equity-type investments, which give the SBIC actual or potential ownership of a portion of a small firm's stock. In general, financing must extend at least 5 years, except when a borrower elects to prepay indebtedness.

SBICs invest in practically all types of manufacturing and service industries and in a wide variety of other types of businesses, including construction, retailing, and wholesaling. Many seek out ventures offering new products or services about which the SBIC management has special knowledge and because they believe these firms have unusual growth potential. Most SBIC companies diversify and consider a wide variety of investments, but naturally, because SBICs are profit-making ventures, they always seek maximum returns on their investments.

SBA (504) Certified Development Company Program

A long-term credit gap exists for small and medium-size businesses for several reasons: (a) most commercial banks are predominantly short- to medium-term lenders (5 to 10 years), (b) most savings institutions are legally required to be residential lenders, and (c) the majority of insurance companies and pension funds prefer large projects of over $1 million.

The SBA's *504 Certified Development Company Program* was enacted on July 2, 1980, as an amendment to the Small Business Investment Act of 1958. The program's purpose is to help communities by stimulating the growth and expansion of small businesses within a defined area of operation. SBA-certified development companies organized under provisions of Section 504 provide long-term, fixed-asset financing that enables communities to create jobs, to increase their local tax base, to expand business ownership opportunities, and to offer improved community services. In addition, the program is a flexible economic development tool that can be used for other purposes, such as city or regional development, neighborhood revitalization, and minority enterprise development. Through this joint federal government/private sector program, financing for the acquisition of land and building construction, expansion, renovation, and equipment is available to small business concerns for up to 25 years. The Certified Development Company Program allows private lenders to meet long-term credit needs of up to 50% of the project's cost, with a contribution of at least 10% equity from the small firm that is being assisted, and through SBA-supported loans based on subordinate SBA second-mortgage financing, in the form of 100% SBA-guaranteed debentures. The certified development company can provide assistance to small business concerns, under two basic plans.

Re-lend Plan

Under a **re-lend plan**, the small business buys the property being financed, and the certified development company is a conduit through which SBA-guaranteed debentures and non-federal financing flow to the small business concern. Under a re-lend plan, the business has title to the property, and, under the first-mortgage formula, the bank is entitled to make a direct loan to the business in exchange for a second mortgage that is then assigned to the SBA.

Lease Plan

Under a **lease plan**, the development company owns the property and leases it to the small firm. The arrangement can be a lease, lease-purchase, or a lease with an option to purchase.

The development company uses the proceeds from the sale of the debenture along with the funds borrowed from non-federal sources to purchase property, or it constructs or renovates the property for the identifiable small firm.

Other Government Funding Sources

It seems that every government-lending agency attempts to establish its own niche and target market in the small-firm loan business. For example, the *Economic Development Agency* (EDA) controls loans to ventures in socioeconomically disadvantaged areas. Under the auspices of the *Economic Development Administration*, loans and loan guarantees are made to new and ongoing ventures in socioeconomically depressed areas with low- to medium-income populations and high unemployment. As much as 30% of the aggregate EDA funds go to new ventures annually. Loans and loan guarantees can be amortized over a period of 25 years.

The *Farmers Home Administration* (FMHA) concentrates on lending money to ventures bringing non-farm jobs to rural areas. FMHA borrowers need not be rejected elsewhere to apply for a loan. The average FMHA loans are relatively large, and less than 10% of them are direct loans.

The *Department of Housing and Urban Development* (HUD) has a variety of loan programs of value to entrepreneurs. The programs grant monies to cities and towns, which in turn grant funds to entrepreneurs for the construction of buildings or manufacturing facilities. Community development block grant programs are designated for rehabilitation and commercial development in central city areas. Loans from this program are made at a very low interest rate. In cities like Atlanta, Baltimore, and Philadelphia, these loans have proven invaluable to homeowners and entrepreneurs interested in reviving residential and commercial areas.

A comparatively smaller program funded by the National Science Foundation also provides funds to entrepreneurs involved in innovative research and development.

VENTURE CAPITAL

Venture capital is as old as capitalism itself. But organized venture capital in the United States has a relatively brief history. After World War II, several wealthy families, including John Hay Whitney and the Rockefeller brothers, decided to set up partnerships to finance new companies in electronics, communications, and other fields. Their timing was perfect. The combination of rapid technological advances in many fields during the war and pent-up consumer demand for new products created a booming economy in the 1950s, largely fueled by the new technologies the investors backed. Following the Whitney and Rockefeller leads, other wealthy families and individuals in New York, Boston, Chicago, and San Francisco also established venture partnerships during the 1950s. In 1958, their efforts were given a substantial boost when Congress passed the Small Business Investment Act, authorizing the SBA to license and lend money at preferred rates to SBICs. Within 6 years, more than 700 licenses had been granted, and $500 million in private capital was committed to SBICs. Many of venture capital's first generation of professional investment managers learned the ropes while working in these early SBICs. Venture capital's first boom era peaked in 1969. During the succeeding 8 years, new investment activity slowed and the professional community consolidated. During the same period, large institutional investors, particularly pension funds, became the dominant force in the stock and bond markets. By the late 1970s, when lower capital gains tax rates and a new wave of technologies combined to provide a fertile climate for renewed venture capital vigor, financial institutions such as pension funds, banks, and insurance companies had begun to invest in venture partnerships as well. Major corporations also began to test the venture capital waters, both by investing in established firms and by setting up their own venture capital subsidiaries (Leach, 1981).

In the years since its beginning, venture capital has expanded from an informal art practiced by a tiny number of individuals into a formally managed business with carefully defined and controlled risks. It has also become a more active business. Organized venture capital is still concentrated in the cities and regions where it originally grew, such as the East and the West coasts, although some branching out has begun, especially in the Southwest and recently in the Midwest. It is evident that the dramatic increase in venture capital comes not from SBICs or corporate subsidiaries but from independent venture capital firms. Traditionally funded by wealthy individuals, institutions, life insurance companies, and foundations, the independent venture capital market has soared in recent years. A variety of venture capital managers for large corporations have left the comfortable confines of corporation venture capital funds and have initiated their own independent firms. Since most parent groups manage more than one venture capital pool, the number of investing entities is smaller.

Venture capital firms involve a large number of investors. The money contributed by these investors is pooled together to form the fund. These firms are usually structured as *partnerships* or *limited liability companies* (LLC). Employees of the venture capital firm are compensated through annual fees paid by limited partners. Fees are considered quite generous, typically 2% of the committed capital. Within that operating structure, there are specific roles and responsibilities, including the following:

- *General partners/managing members:* Managers of the firm that frequently act as primary investment advisors, too.

- *Limited partners:* Entities that are willing to contribute to the funding of the firm. This includes wealthy individuals, pension funds, university endowments, insurance companies, and even mutual funds.

- *Venture partners:* Members of the firm that are compensated for finding successful investment opportunities.

- *Entrepreneur-in-residence:* Subject matter experts involved in the evaluation and communication of investment opportunities.

- *Principals/associates/analysts:* Mid-level and entry-level positions in the firm that help with the daily operation of the company as well as the evaluation of investment opportunities and emerging technologies.

Most venture capitalists provide management advice and technical help as well as money to the companies in which they invest. Venture capitalists comprise a very small community, but, as the success of many of the high-technology sector and the other small businesses it has spawned indicates, venture capital is a vitally important part of the U.S. capital structure. However, most of these venture capital funds are reserved for companies that are already in venture capital portfolios, rather than for ventures that are seeking start-up funding. **Venture capital** is typically defined as the investment by professional investors of long-term, unquoted, risk-equity finance in new firms in which the primary reward is an eventual capital gain, supplemented by dividend yield (Wright & Robbie, 1998). Capital gains tax cuts have proved to be the catalyst needed for the explosive growth in venture capital pools.

A major problem, however, is that venture capitalists fund only a very small percentage of the potential venture plans presented to them (Zider, 1998). As a group, venture capitalists invest a huge amount of money (almost $124 billion in 2008), but the pace has slowed, and only a tiny fraction of new companies ever get any venture capital money (less than 1% in 2008). Venture capitalists prefer to fund certain industries, such as Internet-specific ventures (40% in 2000), communications companies (21%), software and related services (15%), and semiconductors and electronics products (8%) ("Cash Flow," 2001, p. 76).

The National Venture Capital Association (NVCA) publishes statistics on venture capital deals and funding throughout the year. This information is republished by government agencies such as the *Small Business Advocate* (http://www.sba.gov/advocacy). The NVCA gathers information from more than 400 venture capital firms throughout the United States. According to the 2009 statistics compiled by the NVCA, there were 2,795 VC investment deals worth a total of $17.6 billion. That works out to an average deal of $6.3 million. Over the 5-year period from 2005 through 2009, there were 3,534 VC deals worth a total of $25 billion, or an average of $7 million per deal. In 2009, there were nine deals involving an investment of at least $50 million. The largest investment of the year was $105 million in Silver Spring Networks, Inc., a maker of metering solutions to the utility industry. Venture capital firms involved in this deal included Foundation Capital, Google Ventures, Kleiner Perkins Caufield & Byers, and Northgate Capital Group (Money-Zine, 2011).

Entrepreneurs often develop ideas that require substantial capital to implement, and most do not have sufficient funds to finance these projects themselves. Start-up companies that lack substantial tangible assets expect several years of negative earnings, and their uncertain prospects are unlikely to receive bank loans or other debt financing. Venture capitalists finance these high-risk, potentially high-reward projects, purchasing equity stakes while the firms are still privately held. They normally have access to analysis and research on given ventures and technologies, and some specialize in specific industries where their knowledge is extensive. Thus, valuing the potential return on investment in an entrepreneurial venture is challenging, but there is strong research support to gauge this potential. Venture capitalists have backed many high-technology companies, including Cisco Systems, Genentech, Intel, Microsoft, and Netscape, as well as a substantial number of service firms, such as Federal Express.

As mentioned previously, venture capital funds are generally provided by venture capital organizations, which are usually set up with an elaborate organizational structure, as vehicles for providing capital to generally unproven, and thereby more risky, ventures. Whether the firm is in a high- or low-technology industry, venture capitalists are typically active investors. They monitor the progress of firms, sit on the board of directors, monitor financial decisions, and quite often retain the right to approve the appointment or dismissal of key managers and members of the entrepreneurial team. In addition, venture capitalists can help entrepreneurial ventures by providing them with access to critical networks within a given industry, including contacts with consultants, attorneys, suppliers, buyers, and potential employees.

Typically, the funds that the firm needs are not provided all at once by the venture capitalist; rather, they are disbursed in a series of financing rounds based on the attainment of milestones. Venture capitalists typically exit their successful investments by taking them public, and while they rarely sell their shares at the time of the initial public offering, they frequently sell the shares or distribute them to their investors within 2 years of going public. In the United States, venture capital is also characterized by highly variable capital inflows that affect not only the volume of investments but also the valuations of these transactions (Gompers & Lerner, 2000).

For entrepreneurs, the decision to pursue venture capital includes pros and cons. Some of the concerns surrounding the marriage between entrepreneurs and venture capitalists include the following:

- *Autonomy:* Who retains control? Usually it is the entrepreneur who has difficulty in responding to authority, but in return for funding, a venture capitalist desires some say in the operations of a firm.

- *Financial reporting and regulatory compliance*: Entrepreneurs need to develop sophisticated techniques for maintaining accurate financial records and for complying with mounds of regulatory paperwork in order to make monitoring by the venture capital firm easier.

- *Managing growth:* Often as the firm begins to grow, conflict emerges between the entrepreneur and the venture capitalist in terms of the degree, nature, and direction of that growth.

- *Harvesting:* Similarly, as the venture's profitability rises, there may be conflict between the entrepreneur and the venture capital firm regarding the timing and terms of harvesting the firm.

The venture capital firm and the entrepreneurs may experience serious confrontations and conflict over the management and the future of the firm in relation to these issues. On the other hand and in spite of these potential problems, a number of factors support a relationship between entrepreneurs and venture capital firms:

- *Flexibility:* Most venture capital investments are designed for a long-term return. Immediate production and returns are not demanded or expected, thus allowing the entrepreneur some flexibility in management.

- *Synergy:* As mentioned previously, one of the greatest benefits of venture capital funding is the synergy provided by the venture capital firm. Assistance with networks, market research, industry insight, and cooperative strategic planning are all part of these synergistic effects.

- *Stature and credibility:* The affiliation with venture capitalists increases the overall stature and credibility of the entrepreneurs. In dealing with customers, banks, suppliers, etc., the credibility of an entrepreneur "married" to a venture capital firm is drastically improved.

BUSINESS ANGELS

A more accessible and informal source of private equity for most entrepreneurs is funding from **business angels**, or individuals that invest their own private financial resources in an entrepreneur's start-up business. Financing by business angels is estimated to be much greater than that by venture capitalists (Mason & Harrison, 2000; Freear, Sohl, & Wetzel, 1997). The potential of business angels and the informal venture capital market are enormous, and they have been identified as the largest single source of risk capital for entrepreneurial companies, far exceeding the venture capital industry. In the United States, business angels finance an estimated 30–40 times as many firms as the institutional venture capital community (Van Osnabrugge, 1998). Additionally, entrepreneurs, if given a choice, prefer to seek out financing from sources other than venture capital funds (Amit, Glosten, & Muller, 1990) because business angels usually interfere less in the venture start-up's business operations.

Working with angel investors means acquiring venture capital from individual investors. These individuals look for companies that exhibit high-growth prospects, have a synergy with their own business, or compete in an industry in which they have succeeded. Companies seeking equity capital from angel investors must welcome outside ownership and perhaps be willing to relinquish some control. To successfully accommodate angel investors, a company must also be able to provide an "exit" to these investors in the form of an eventual public offering or buyout from a larger firm. The supply of angel investors is the largest within a 150-mile radius of metropolitan areas, and the more technology driven an area's economy, the more abundant these investors are.

Angel investing is appropriate for early-stage companies with no revenues or established companies with sales and earnings. The best use for angel investing is for companies developing a product or those with an established product or service for which they need additional funding to execute a marketing program. Also, angel investors are appropriate for companies that have increasing product or service sales and need additional capital to bridge the gap between the sale and the receipt of funds from the customer. The cost of capital from angel investors is quite expensive and is likely to cost no less than 10% of a company's equity and, for early-stage companies, it may cost more than 50% for a range of funds between $300,000 and $5 million. In addition, many angel investors charge a management fee in the form of a monthly retainer. The places where angels might be found are universities, business incubators, venture capital funds, and local informal angel groups.

Whereas our understanding of venture capitalists and their activities is reasonably well developed, research on business angels has been limited despite their wide utilization as a source of informal venture capital. This is due, in part, to the absence of a well-defined theoretical base on which to model such financial decisions; such decisions are usually based on the mix of signals that entrepreneurs are sending to potential angel investors (Prasad, Bruton & Vozikis, 2000).

OTHER LENDING SOURCES

Various other obscure types of financing are available to the entrepreneur. The Women's Business Association, for example, aids small firms with their financing in addition to other issues. Certain research grants can be worked out with universities and foundations, and lastly, nongovernmental organizations such as The American Red Cross and Habitat for Humanity are also available to assist with financing. A brief review of a select group of these "hidden" funding alternatives is listed below:

- *International funds:* Not only have these foreign funds invested heavily in U.S. firms, they also provide overseas production, marketing, and distribution networks, in exchange for strategic alliance agreements.

- *Leveraged buyouts:* For an individual or team of entrepreneurs, the leveraged buyout provides the opportunity to acquire all or part of an existing firm for little money down. Generally, once the deal is struck, an initial pool of funds is gathered as a down payment on the purchase price and an additional amount is borrowed for a fixed or, more likely, floating interest rate; these funds include short-term working capital loans. The remainder of the debt to both the lender and the previous owner is paid from future earnings or in stock options over a set period of time. Leveraged buyouts are frequently undertaken in large firms with very small subsidiaries that are not achieving corporate earnings targets. Of great concern is the issue of the subsidiary's ability to stand alone, once the buyout is made.

- *Business development company:* A variation of the venture capital and SBIC themes, Business Development Companies (BDCs) emerged from the 1980 Small Business Incentive Act. This law allows SBICs to go public in seeking investors and concurrently frees them from a number of legal obstacles. One of the real advantages for BDC fund managers is that, unlike traditional venture capital funds that only pay management salaries, BDCs can offer 20% of the profits to its managers. The law increases the leverage capabilities of the fund and allows newly formed BDCs to circumvent certain SEC regulations.

EQUITY SPLITTING

For the entrepreneur seeking funding, there comes a time when the only way to secure financial resources is by offering a "piece of the pie" and surrendering equity to an investor.

When looking for investors, one thing never changes. In attempting to determine the value of the firm and how much equity to yield, no matter what valuation the entrepreneur places on his or her company, the investor always thinks it is worth less. Moreover, the golden rule applies: *He who has the gold, rules.*

For the entrepreneurs who own 100% of their company, the best defense may be to insist on guarding their company's equity and to sell not more than a small percentage of ownership, under any circumstances. In case of an entrepreneurial team, however, it is more difficult to prevent dividing the pie: if the team's equity is too small, the incentives of the team members are diminished.

In placing a value on the entrepreneurial firm and the amount of equity splitting they should share, venture capital firms use different valuation methods depending on the type of business and industry. They generally apply a discounted cash flow to the return of their investment money at the end of 5 years. From a start-up in which the entrepreneurs have very little invested and short track records, they seek a higher discounted cash flow in the neighborhood of 40 to 50%. In a less risky situation, they may use 30% or they estimate the discounted cash flow price/earnings ratio multiples required to apply to 5th-year earnings for example, by differentiating based on the industry and the ownership level, type, and quality. Other venture capitalists firms ask hypothetically how much this company would be worth if it were public today, and, of course, this price is frequently lower than the entrepreneurs accept. Thus, venture capitalists look for a 30–40% compounded return on investment projections when determining the reasonableness of the entrepreneur's request.

Finally, the amount of capital being raised is crucial and the request has to be credible. An accurate method of determining the amount of capital required is projecting cash flow over a 12-month period, showing the accumulated loss at the eventual turnaround when sales pass the break-even level. The sum of the losses, plus a hedge of 20–30%, is the amount of capital needed. Entrepreneurs should indicate in the business plan the amount of ownership they expect to keep, making it a point of potential negotiations. They should remember the plight of the first person ever to have eaten a lobster: he had to convince others that it was good ("Splitting the equity with backers," 1981).

GOING PUBLIC

The goal of achieving financial independence through the transformation of sweat equity into bottom-line earnings is not to be discounted among the various pursuits of the entrepreneur. The use of an underwriter for public offerings can cost a firm a flat 10% fee plus other expenses, which can account for another 10% of the proceeds. In dealing with the Securities and Exchange Commission, creditors, the National Association of Securities Dealers, and the public, underwriters can provide expertise not easily attained by entrepreneurs. Some underwriters who specialize in high-technology stock, for example, process only firm commitment offerings. In these cases, the underwriter buys all of the shares offered by the company and then resells them to the public. Some entrepreneurs, however, choose to "fly solo" with their offerings, whereby issuing costs can be cut by as much as 75%.

Once the decision to go public is made, a company can choose one of four ways to file a registration statement with the Securities & Exchange Commission:

- *S-1:* This is the SEC's general filing registration, but it can be burdensome for small firms, especially start-ups. Its major drawback is that it requires maximum disclosure and reporting in both the offering and quarterly reports. It constitutes a last resort if the firm cannot use any of the other types of filings. It is the only choice, however, for all oil, gas, and mining ventures, which cannot file any other way.

- *S-2:* This is a special filing procedure for start-ups, and it requires different information than other methods, that is, greater detail about what the proceeds of the offering will be used for and the people behind the company. This registration is intended only for companies with no substantial sales or net income for the past 5 years. Few companies choose *S-2* filings.

- *S-18:* This form was designed to help businesses raise relatively large amounts of money without filing with SEC headquarters in Washington, D.C., as required with *S-1.* This type of filing is handled by SEC regional offices closer to the company, and a number of requirements must be met: The securities must be sold for cash; the firm must be incorporated in and must operate principally in the United States or Canada; and it may not constitute an investment company or offer limited partnerships.

- *Regulation A:* This is not actually a filing but an exemption from certain filing requirements, and it works as a type of mini-registration procedure. *Regulation A* offerings can be filed through SEC regional offices, but the company cannot raise more than $1.5 million. Once the company has gone public, it does not have to file *10-K, 10-Q,* or interim *8-Q* forms if the company has fewer than 500 shareholders and less than $1 million in assets (Lindorff, 1980).

In light of the increased number of initial public offerings by smaller firms, the SEC has recently taken a number of steps to reduce the regulatory burden on smaller firms interested in raising capital. This, along with changes in capital gains taxes, might continue to fuel more public offerings.

CONCLUSION

Despite their occasionally considerable potential, entrepreneurial firms quite often have difficulty obtaining outside equity capital. They are often in the early stage of development and have little or no track record or collateral, and are therefore seen as risky investments by banks and other lending institutions (Van Osnabrugge, 1998). Whether venture capitalists or business angels, investors will always be in the same predicament: they must try to ascertain the true potential value of the venture proposal and/or stocks being offered. Can entrepreneurs "stack the deck" in their favor? Can they increase their chances of succeeding? In terms of funding needs and funding sources, one chapter cannot thoroughly review the numerous funding sources available to the entrepreneur. But the key to success lies in the venture's value concept idea, its strategic target market, the original feasibility study, the venture's formal business plan, the financial statements, and the quality of the management of the firm proving the overall ability to execute the vision and accomplish the goals of the firm. Information pertaining to these factors should also be thoroughly examined and re-examined to allay any fears of failure, because entrepreneurs will be doing both themselves and their investors or lenders a tremendous disservice if they enter into any new venture ill prepared. However, once ready, the enormous possibilities and variety of financing options justify a very optimistic outlook about funding the new venture. The ability to obtain money when needed is as necessary to the operation of the business as is a good location, the right equipment, reliable sources of supplies and materials, or a competent workforce. The amount of money requested should always depend on the purpose for which these funds are required, and this amount should be crystal clear to the entrepreneur and relatively easy to communicate to investors and lenders.

Website Information

Topic	Web Address	Description
Venture funding	http://www.vfinance.com	List of websites that offer venture capital funding.
Sources of capital funding	http://www.businessfinance.com	Business loan programs for financing your needs, suggestions for sources of capital funding, links to credit institutions, loan opportunities, and much more.
Bootstrapping	http://www.entrepreneur.com/Your_Business/YB_SegArticle/0,4621,303443,00.html	An article from entrepreneur.com that talks about bootstrapping.
Small Business Administration (SBA) loans	http://www.sba.gov	Home page for the SBA. Valuable information on how to start, manage, and finance your business, as well as links to related business opportunities.
Going public	http://www.sec.gov	Gives information about the SEC, forms to fill out, regulatory actions, investor information, news statements, and litigation reports.
SBA (504) Certified Development Company program	http://www.nadco.org/i4a/pages/index.cfm?pageid=1	The National Association of Development Companies (NADCO) is a trade association of Certified Development Companies (CDCs)— companies that have been certified by the SBA to provide funding for small businesses under the SBA 504 Program. This site contains general information for small businesses who would like to learn more about the SBA 504 loan program as well as information on the 504 industry for NADCO's Certified Development Company (CDC) members and affiliate members.
Venture capital and business angels	http://www.vfinance.com	Helpful website for finding sources of venture capital and business angels. Provides help to entrepreneurs, investors, public companies and institutions.
Small Business Investment Companies	http://www.nasbic.org	Homepage for the national association of SBICs. Acts as the voice for these companies before Congress and the administration. Provides resources and information such as publications for small business investment companies.

Key Terms

Bootstrapping: A type of creative financing in which the entrepreneur uses his/her own resources as little as possible while using other people's resources, such as credit cards, as much as possible.

Business angels: Individuals that invest their own private financial resources in an entrepreneur's start-up business.

Chattel mortgage: Loans that allow small firms to buy equipment such as a cash register or a delivery truck using a lien on the equipment as security.

Endorsers: People who borrowers get to sign a note to bolster their own credit. A **co-maker** is one who creates an obligation jointly with the borrower. In such cases, the bank can collect directly from either the maker or the co-maker. Finally, a **guarantor** guarantees the payment of a note by signing a guaranty commitment.

Five Cs: *character, capacity, collateral, capital,* and *condition*—the factors that loan officers use to monitor and determine whether a business and their founders are qualified for a loan.

Lease plan: A plan in which a development company owns the property and leases it to the small firm.

Re-lend plan: A plan in which a small business buys the property being financed, and the certified development company is a conduit through which SBA-guaranteed debentures and the non-federal financing flow to the small business.

Short-term bank loans: Loans used for financing accounts receivable for 30 to 60 days or for purposes that take longer to pay off, such as building a seasonal inventory over a period of 5 to 6 months.

Term borrowing: Loans that provide funds that will be paid back over a fairly long period of time.

Trust receipt: Legal paper for floor planning, which is used for identifiable, serial-numbered merchandise.

Venture capital: A type of investment typically defined as investment by professional investors of long-term, unquoted, risk-equity finance in new firms in which the primary reward is an eventual capital gain, supplemented by dividend yield.

Review Questions

1. Distinguish between short-term money and term money, and give an example of each.
2. Describe the re-lend plan and the lease plan.
3. Describe two of the three hidden funding alternatives.
4. Select your favorite product innovation related to the agriculture industry and research this product's potential market size and competition. Create a list of the top three bullet points you would emphasize in pitching the idea to a venture capitalist. How would these points be different if you were pitching to a business angel (or would they not be different, and why)?
5. Keeping with the same product above, start researching attorneys who could help you take your idea to market. Search attorneys by both geography and specialty, and generate a list of three potential candidates you'd like to interview for the position. Be sure to list your reasoning for wanting to consider each.

Reflections from the Front Lines of LifeGuard America

Attracting outside investment in any endeavor is tough, and most of the time it is a very frustrating experience. My own drama has played out over the past 2 years as I watched my severance package from Indian Motorcycle Company disappear; our family's short- and long-term savings dwindled, while our debt on our credit cards rose beyond any reasonable level. My personal credit has been trashed, and family and friends have been stretched past their normal operating limits. All because the funding is almost here, just another week; one more day. . . . The bottom line: if you can't stand the heat, don't go in the kitchen; if you don't want to run with the big dogs, stay on the porch. These old sayings are all true. My 6-month plan to raise the necessary funding for LifeGuard America turned into a 2-year plan! Along the way, however, I have attracted some of the most creative and influential people to the venture imaginable. Our legal firm of Johnson, Jones, Dornblaser, Coffman & Shorb has been incredibly helpful during the process. These lawyers worked long hours over the Christmas holidays to create our Private Placement Memorandum, a key document for our fund-raising effort. They also put together a comprehensive Operating Agreement for our limited-liability company. These two documents, with our business plan, serve as the cornerstone for our funding efforts. We made the early decision to sell them an equity position in LifeGuard America for their work to get us to full funding. This is an excellent way for a small start-up to leverage the service it needs to get to full funding.

Lessons learned over the past 2 years:

- If you can afford it, get a professional fund-raising partner. It will be money well spent.

- If not, forget brokers; talk directly to the checkbooks. Nobody, but nobody tells your story like you do.

- Generate a list of potential investors and work that list.

- When it comes to investors, go with your gut. If it does not feel right, it probably isn't. If it looks like a duck, quacks like a duck, waddles like a duck, cook it and eat it for dinner; it was a duck.

- Don't waste time with lenders if you don't have the assets or the ability to offer credible personal guarantees.

- If you are like me, the Small Business Administration Loan Program was a waste of time because we are a service company with very little need for capital equipment and a pre-revenue start-up that equated to HIGH RISK.

- Do not waste precious time hoping or wishing your way into funding. It is time-consuming work that takes an enormous amount of energy that requires you to be always the optimist, always positive, and above all, always honest with others and yourself.

Discussion Questions on LifeGuard America

1. What appears to be the single most important factor to Mr. Fitzpatrick in terms of fund raising?

2. What type of funding source would be the most appropriate for LifeGuard America in your opinion?

References

Alleva, L. M., & Barnes, S. W. (1998). Marrying for money: The venture into venture capital. *Price Waterhouse Review, 32*(2), 42–51.

Amit, R., Glosten, L., & Muller, E. (1990, October). Entrepreneurship ability, venture investments, and risk sharing. *Management Science, 36*(10), 1232–1245.

Berger, A. N., & Udell, G. F. (1998, August). The economics of small business finance: The roles of private equity and debt markets in the financial growth cycle. *Journal of Banking and Finance, 22*(6–8), 613–673.

Cash flow (2001, May 29). *Inc. Magazine, 23*(7), 76–77.

Dible, D. (1986). *Up your own organization.* Reston, VA: Reston.

Dot-com shakeout (2001, April 16). *Newsweek, 137*(16), 52F.

Fastest 50 2001—Part I & II (2001, July 13). *Pacific Business News, 39*(18), pp. 42, 44.

Francis, D. (1988). *Contrapreneurs.* Toronto, Ontario, Canada: MacMillan.

Freear, J., Sohl, J. E., & Wetzel, W. E., Jr. (1997). The informal venture capital market: Milestones passed and the road ahead. In D. Sexton and R. Smilor (Eds.), *Entrepreneurship 2000* (pp. 47–69). Chicago: Upstart.

Freear, J., & Wetzel, W. E., Jr. (1990, March). Who bankrolls high-tech entrepreneurs? *Journal of Business Venturing, 5*(2), 77–89.

Gompers, P., & Lerner, J. (2000, February). Money chasing deals? The impact of fund inflows on private equity valuations. *Journal of Financial Economics, 55*(2), 281–325.

Leach, C. A. (1981, September). The billion-dollar gamble. *Inc. Magazine, 3*(9), 64.

Lindorff, D. (1980, December). New issues boom. *Venture, 2*(12), 38–39.

Mangelsdorf, M. E. (1992, October). Behind the scenes: An inside look at the companies creating jobs and wealth in a recessionary economy. Where did the founders get their seed capital? Who are their heroes? Which are the hot industries? And more. *Inc. Magazine, 14*(10), 72–80.

Mason, C. M., & Harrison, R. T. (2000, July-September). Influences on the supply of informal venture capital in the UK: An exploratory study of investor attitudes. *International Small Business Journal, 18*(4), 11.

Money-Zine. 2011. Venture capital funding. http://www.money-zine.com/Investing/Investing/Venture-Capital-Funding/.

Pogue, D. (2012, January 26). Website helps folks embrace mothers of invention. *The Fresno Bee, 179*(32491), B7–8.

Prasad, D., Bruton, G., & Vozikis, G. S. (2000). Signaling value to business angels: The proportion of the entrepreneur's net worth invested in a new venture as a decision signal. *Venture Capital: An International Journal of Entrepreneurial Finance, 2*(3), 167–182.

Prince, C. F. (2001, May). Setting a new pace: VC investment hit a high note in 2000, but experts anticipate a slowdown. *Entrepreneur, 29*(5), 28.

SBA loans (2001, June). *Entrepreneur, 29*(6), 65.

Splitting the equity with backers (1981, August). *Venture, 3*(8), 19.

U.S. Small Business Administration (2000). *Guide to small business success.* Washington, D.C.: U.S. Government Printing Office.

Van Osnabrugge, M. (1998, Summer). Do serial and non-serial investors behave differently?: An empirical and theoretical analysis. *Entrepreneurship Theory and Practice, 22*(4), 23.

Van Osnabrugge, M. (2000). *Angel investing: Matching start-up funds with start-up companies.* Cambridge, MA: Harvard University Press.

Wright, M., & Robbie, K. (1998, June/July). Venture capital and private equity: A review and synthesis. *Journal of Business Finance and Accounting, 25*(5–6), 521–570.

Zider, B. (1998, November/December). How venture capital works. *Harvard Business Review, 78*(6), 131–139.

9 Venture Infrastructure: Product/Service and Marketing Considerations

Can We Plan the Product and Marketing Infrastructure?

LEARNING OBJECTIVES

1. To understand the complexity of the marketing function.
2. To investigate the product life cycle concept and its importance for marketing.
3. To connect the market segmentation process with the strategic market targeting process.
4. To relate the marketing concept with the marketing mix.
5. To examine the intricacies of market research.
6. To obtain insight into the development of a comprehensive strategic marketing plan.

TOPIC OUTLINE

Introduction

The What and Why of Marketing

The Marketing Concept

The Product Life Cycle

Market Segmentation

The Marketing Mix
- Product or Service
- Price
- Promotion
- Placement

Internet Marketing

Market Research

Strategic Market Planning: Putting It All Together

Conclusion

Website Information

Key Terms

Review Questions

Case Study

References

"If a man can write a better book, preach a better sermon, or make a better mouse trap than his neighbor, though he builds his house in the woods, the world will make a beaten path to his door."

(R. W. Emerson)

INTRODUCTION

It is a scary reality: e-commerce sites turn over their customers at the rate of 60 percent every six weeks (Campanelli, 2001). If this happens to Internet sites where shopping is so easy, imagine how difficult it is for a regular store, shop, or service provider to replace lost customers, especially because lost customers rarely return. The answer to this dramatic issue lies in marketing efforts to build customer loyalty. The venture's infrastructure relating to the product or service and related marketing considerations needs to be designed to develop long-term relationships with customers. The venture's **marketing mix** and its related **Four Ps (Product, Promotion, Place, and Price)** must provide real as well as perceived incentives for customer retention. Before designing this specific marketing mix, however, the entrepreneur needs to know the **venture's niche**, in terms of "why would a customer buys this product or service?" as well as, the **venture's strategic target market**, in terms of "who buys, how many do they buy, when do they buy, how do they buy, and where do they buy" (as discussed previously). This type of information helps entrepreneurs lay the foundation for the venture's product and marketing infrastructure and select the appropriate marketing strategy.

THE WHAT AND WHY OF MARKETING

Recent behavioral research keeps confirming how often people make poor decisions. Humans, it turns out, are impressionable, emotional, and irrational and do not adhere to the classic concept of the *Homo economicus* (the Economic Man): we buy things we don't need, often at arbitrary prices and most importantly quite often for silly reasons, especially if we are in a good mood, when we are much more susceptible to persuasion (*The Economist,* 2011a). Behavioral marketing research discerns what you have bought in the past (purchase history) and how you bought it (purchase behavior). They can then draw a buyer's attention to products they think that you might want in the future (Lindstrom, 2011). It would thus be helpful to revisit Frieda Caplan's. Many years ago, Frieda Caplan started Frieda's Finest, a wholesaler of exotic fruit and vegetables in Los Angeles. She nurtured the business by relying on instinct, simple marketing tools, and her willingness to keep an open mind with regard to her target market—Frieda's Finest became a multimillion-dollar company. She created the right marketing strategy based on a unique design of the venture's product and marketing infrastructure by aiming at just the right strategic market target. Frieda's success factors were as follows:

- *Innovation:* To be successful, you have to be totally open to unique or novel concepts.

- *Convenience:* Market the firm's wares as product lines, not individual commodities, as well as offer the luxury of one-stop shopping for hard-to-get items.

- *Niche:* Frieda took on business that mainstream wholesalers turned away.

- *Know the industry:* Frieda noticed the national trend toward more variety in grocer produce departments.

- *Definition of the target market:* Frieda virtually reinvented vegetables by adding new exotic items.

- *Quality:* Offer a predictable and consistent standard of quality.

- *Research and development:* Freida tested the vegetables in the kitchen before adding a new one into the target market product mix.

- *The use of publicity:* Freida was able to generate excitement and news coverage.

- *Recognize your limitations:* Know that if something takes off, the business will be alone (without competition) for a limited period of time.

- *Position the company as a leader:* Freida conducted retail supermarket seminars, lectures on produce theory, bulletins for retailers, and newsletters for consumers (Larson, 1989).

Frieda Caplan's story is about the ability to evoke the key benefit of the venture's value concept to the customers by effectively implementing a marketing strategy in a competitive environment. It is also about testing this value concept continuously with prospects and customers by defining, redefining, and adapting to the venture's strategic target market. Finally, it is about growing a thriving venture by sticking to a successful and unique product and marketing infrastructure, which not only creates brand identity and customer loyalty but also persuades new prospective customers to buy products and services (such as Frieda's fruits and vegetables) they had never seen or tasted.

Most people relate the word marketing with advertising. There is a great deal more to marketing than that. The American Marketing Association defines **marketing** as the process of planning and executing the conception, pricing, promotion, and distribution of ideas, goods, and services to create exchanges (sales). A different and more specific definition of marketing is that of manipulation, not of customers, but rather of a business. Businesses that are able to reengineer their organizational structures around markets and new market opportunities are in the best position to respond to customer needs and changing market conditions (Best, 1999). Even though the definition as presented here suggests a for-profit environment, most marketers agree that not-for-profit organizations also participate in marketing activities.

Marketing, as an established discipline, is relatively young in the realm of other business disciplines; it has come of age only in the past century. Numerous principles of marketing, however, have generated considerable attention during this period and have guided countless companies to tremendous success. A few of these principles are discussed in this chapter: the marketing concept, the marketing mix, the product life cycle, market segmentation, and marketing research.

THE MARKETING CONCEPT

Like most of the principles that have emerged from the marketing discipline, the marketing concept has not been free from controversy and debate. Because it focuses on the customer's point of view, the marketing concept has stimulated a great deal of research on consumer needs and market characteristics (Turner & Spencer, 1997). In fact, even after all these years, there is no universally accepted definition. Regardless of the controversy, the marketing concept as opposed to marketing per se, can be defined as follows:

> The **marketing concept** is a business philosophy, which requires that all organization members focus their efforts on customer satisfaction, that management emphasizes marketing strategy and planning, and that the organization strives to earn a profit through selectively meeting customer needs. (Peterson, 1989, p. 38)

A firm's marketing concept does not need to have elaborate plans supported by exhaustive studies and well-crafted theories. Rather, the marketing concept needs to be practical; beginning with the product or service itself and the value concept it represents, it investigates its demand- or supply-driven target market and the price that this market can bear; it decides how to best promote the product's value concept in the strategic target market; and finally, it examines how the potential customer will be able to find the business and the product in the marketplace and deal with it. This marketing mix of the *Four Ps* (i.e., *Product, Price, Promotion,* and *Place*) is not difficult to discern and coordinate, but it demands conscientious and considerable efforts in order to deliver the desired outcomes.

It can be argued that, by adopting the marketing concept, American companies have abandoned a previous philosophy that made this country great, namely innovation, because by following the marketing concept of strictly satisfying customer needs, companies have changed from a technological supply–push perspective, to a demand–pull strategy. Emphasizing the importance of adjusting and setting marketing goals for the demand-pull target market that already exists and working tirelessly to satisfy them may stifle new product development and innovation; there is no need to risk trying to satisfy a previously unrecognized supply need by engaging in innovative activities. There are, however, two sides to this debate. Sometimes it is just as important to change course when opportunities arise as it is to pursue existing strategic demand-driven target markets. The reinvention of a firm and a firm's product shows commitment toward a renewal of the venture's competitive advantage edge through productivity enhancements and innovation. It also shows existing customers that the firm is committed and is focused on bringing improvements to their perceived value concept; at the same time, renewal lures prospective new customers who find the newly enhanced value concept appealing, in contrast to the old value concept, which had not been perceived as yielding enough value to make them commit and become customers (Moran, 2000).

Kotite (1989) expands on this idea by suggesting three reasons for success in a venture's *re-inventive* marketing concept:

1. The entrepreneur's ability to recognize niches and move quickly on the opportunity.

2. The small firm's ability to foster more of a team spirit in its marketing efforts, bringing together entrepreneurs, employees, and the customers themselves.

3. The ability of entrepreneurial firms to adapt larger company strategies without the unwieldy management structure and problems.

This also implies that the entrepreneurial sector of the economy is responsible for the creation of a very innovative and *re-inventive* marketing concept that characterizes most new venture opportunities and subsequently creates most of the new employment in this country. For example, in an economy that is shaped more and more by the growing number of working mothers, two-career couples, and less leisure time, the reinvention of existing value concepts in time-saving alternatives and related specialized services will be tremendously successful.

THE PRODUCT LIFE CYCLE

Another marketing principle that has far-reaching implications for the entrepreneurial venture is the **product life cycle** (PLC). This concept is based on the hypothesis that a product or brand or industry passes through a number of stages during its lifetime, namely, introduction, growth, maturity, and decline. These stages are defined by inflection points in the rate of growth of a product's sales, and they typically follow an S-shaped curve. As the new product is introduced and if successful, becomes widely distributed, sales grow slowly first and steeply later, until a point at which sales mature and flatten. Later, sales start to decline slowly at first, then rapidly at the end. The slow introductory growth reflects the difficulty of overcoming buyer inertia, which stimulates trials of the product in the strategic target market. Rapid growth occurs as more buyers rush into the market once the product's value has been proved and/or it is perceived as useful or necessary. Complete penetration of the product's strategic target market and its potential buyers is eventually reached, causing the rapid growth to level off. Finally, growth eventually tapers off as new substitute products appear on the market or as the product becomes and/or is perceived to be obsolete or without purchase value any longer.

Although there have been minor modifications of the PLC concept, such as describing more stages than the four given above, the basic underlying principles have remained constant over the years. The major debate usually has centered on the actual application of the concept. Life-cycle research is one of the best techniques for attempting to predict how a particular product will perform in the market (Modis, 1994). Much of the criticism of the PLC concept, however, has focused on firms that have used the concept as their sole marketing planning tool (Lambkin & Day, 1989). Michael Porter (1980), well known in the area of strategic planning, suggests an even more basic flaw in the application of the PLC concept:

> The real problem with the product life cycle as a predictor of industry evolution is that it attempts to describe *one* pattern of evolution that will invariably occur. . . . Since actual industry evolution takes so many different paths, the life cycle pattern does not always hold. . . . Nothing in the concept allows it to predict when it will hold and when it will not. (p. 162)

The implications for the entrepreneur are very pointed. If adherence to the PLC theoretical concept is accurate and inflexible, then the only place where small firms can be found thriving is in the introduction and early growth stage. Once the entrepreneur has provided the innovation and had tested the waters, confirming that indeed an opportunity exists, larger companies possessing the advantage of economies of scale will force them out.

Entrepreneurs exit during the growth stage because of their personal predilection for the innovation stage (Simurda, 1989). Even though this is often the case, there are notable exceptions. If entrepreneurs, instead, make an effort to emphasize quality and to reinvent their competitive edge as much as they initially emphasized innovation, then their ability to compete increases significantly because their competitive advantage is enhanced.

> You may have given your career to creating a device, but 18 months down the pike somebody else is going to come in and undercut you. Neglecting to keep ahead of the competitors in terms of quality is at least as important as lack of capitalization in the failure of start-up businesses. (p. 127)

MARKET SEGMENTATION

Two general approaches can be pursued in targeting a company's goods and services to consumers. Some companies elect to attempt to achieve a certain level of sales by focusing on the entire population. This mass marketing strategy defines everyone as a potential buyer.

A second approach that is more economical and in line with the capabilities of a small firm is strategic target-market segmentation, which takes advantage of a specific strategic window of opportunity in combination with the venture's strategic competence, as discussed previously. In this approach, the firm focuses its marketing efforts at one or a few closely related elements within the population. Segmentation is a very popular marketing technique because sales in segmented target markets can be generated more efficiently than with mass marketing approaches (Cross, 1999).

To pursue this second approach, the firm generally groups these potential customers into **market segments** of unique customer needs and/or purchase behaviors, or according to some similar demographic, economic, social, or cultural characteristics. Market segmentation also determines the possible multiple target-market strategies and thus leads to a greater efficiencies in marketing strategy implementation. For example, lifestyle influences, such as differences in values, attitudes, and personal interests, contribute to different needs. By identifying a specific target market segment of a particular lifestyle, the marketing strategy may cross into and be implemented in a different demographic age, race, or sex target market segment. Markets, for example, might be segmented on the basis of any of the following characteristics, either individually or coupled into groups that form market segment combinations:

- Age

- Sex

- Race

- Income level

- Education

- Lifestyles

- Geographic location

- Customer concentration density

- Type of product

- Frequency of product use

- Duration of product use

The specific configuration of the target market segment that may emerge from the market segmentation process can be formulated and assessed using the following criteria (Best, 1999):

1. *Need-based segmentation:* Grouping customers under the umbrella of a specific customer or consumption need, benefit, or value concept that solves a specific consumption problem.

2. *Segment identification:* Defining the demographics, lifestyles, and usage behaviors that make a needs-based segment distinct, identifiable, and actionable.

3. *Segment attractiveness:* Using predetermined segment attractiveness criteria, such as volume, customer concentration density, ease of distribution, etc.

4. **Segment profitability:** Calculating the marketing contribution of a target market segment, which can be calculated as follows:

$$[(\textit{Market Share} \times \textit{Market Demand}) \times (\textit{Revenue per Customer} - \textit{Variable Costs per Customer})] - \textit{Marketing Expenses}$$

5. *Segment positioning:* Defining and interpreting the target market segment's value concept proposition into a product-price positioning strategy based on that segment's unique identification.

6. *Segment "Acid Test":* Testing the attractiveness of each market segment's product-price positioning strategy through "market segment" descriptive storyboards on the product's value concept.

> *7. Segment marketing mix strategy:* Expanding the product-price positioning strategy to include all aspects of the marketing mix: product, price, promotion, and place.

Market segmentation, therefore, presupposes that we may be able to distinguish with accuracy relatively homogeneous groups of customers who can be targeted similarly because they share needs and preferences. Market segmentation, however, involves viewing a heterogeneous market as a number of smaller homogeneous markets in response to differing preferences, which are attributable to satisfying the desires of customers. That in itself creates problems in clearly identifying homogeneous groups of customers with extreme accuracy (Wedel, 2001).

THE MARKETING MIX

While the marketing concept provides a philosophical basis for evaluating the direction of the marketing plan, an assessment of the marketing mix helps the entrepreneur to integrate the various components of the total marketing program. Specifically, the marketing mix that satisfies the demands of the firm's chosen market segment can be defined as the blend of the *Four Ps* of marketing: P*roduct,* P*rice,* P*romotion,* and P*lacement* (distribution).

Fitting the four elements of the marketing mix into a strategic marketing plan is a formidable task to the entrepreneur. To satisfy the needs of the strategic target market segment, the entrepreneur must carefully mix the right product, at the right price, with the appropriate amount of promotion and distribution to satisfy the vacillating needs of the target market segment.

In adapting the Four Ps of marketing, some useful guidelines may prove invaluable to the small firm in the development of the venture's marketing infrastructure. The following sections provide a more comprehensive analysis of the marketing mix.

Product or Service

Generally, the first marketing decision confronted by the entrepreneur concerns the product or service offered to consumers in the specific target market. The key here is, of course, to transform the needs and wants of the consumer into a viable product or service of real and/or perceived value to attract and keep customers. Some of the greatest examples of product response to shifting demographics can be seen in the marketing of products and/or services to women. In recent years some unique products and services have been marketed to working women. The Mind Safety Appliances Company offers a "pared down" version of a hard hat for women construction workers. In addition, magazines, starting with *Ms.,* have flooded the market with such titles as *Working Woman, Self,* and *Women Who Work.* A number of factors impact the **product decision**. They include quality, features and options, style, brand name, packaging, and warranty.

Quality

Most people associate quality with price. Injecting quality into a product may or may not, in fact, enhance revenue, but quality always adds to the production cost. However, some studies suggest that quality may not be as related to cost as once thought. Curry and Riesz (1988) and Shoemaker (1986) suggest that quality is not as important as the stage of the product in its life cycle (i.e., introduction, growth, etc.). Other researchers, such as Zeithaml (1988) and Tellis (1988), maintain that quality is just one of the many important influences on price. Mag Instruments illustrates all too well that this is probably the case. Mag Instruments manufactured the best flashlight that could be produced. Initially, the higher selling price was in fact due to the high quality. Years later, when the technology could easily be replicated, and the flashlight could be manufactured more efficiently by imitators, the higher price for a Mag flashlight was not because of the better quality, but to protect Mag's trade secrets and patents (Brown, 1988).

Features and Options

Does the consumer need a microwave oven or a dishwasher with a memory, cars with wipers on the rear window, blenders with 27 different speeds, or a briefcase that is burglarproof? All of these products simply represent variations on a theme designed to entice the consumer with one more feature or one more option. Is this true innovation? Maybe it is, if this is what consumers really need and if they attach value to it.

Style

American society is indeed very conscious of style and status differences. Fashion changes, in particular, force consumers to choose between staying "in" or "out" of style. Are ties too wide? Are lapels too narrow? Are mini-skirts in or out? What about color? This year blue is in, but what about next year?

Brand Name

The power of brand recognition should not be underestimated. Every organization, every product has a brand, which becomes the firm's reputation. Brands are not invented, but rather discovered by customers who match a message to a product's performance. But name alone does not always work. Levi Strauss & Co. tried to utilize its brand name in marketing a line of men's suits; they failed at the venture because they strayed from their primary product/market identification—jeans. On the other hand, the Jordache label has been used very successfully on literally dozens of products, all bearing the very familiar Jordache emblem.

Packaging

Often, the key to successfully marketing a product is not found in differentiating that product, but rather in distinguishing the package. Rather than promoting the quality their dry-roasted peanuts (which are, after all, somewhat generic in size and taste), Planter's Nuts has done an outstanding job of developing marketing campaigns around the packaging of the peanut. Likewise, Avon Cosmetics has relied for years upon the uniqueness of its "limited edition" cosmetic containers in marketing hundreds of cosmetics. Products may not be easily differentiated as such, but packaging can add a real or perceived uniqueness to the product. There are, of course, thousands of examples of packaging innovations (Celestial Seasonings tea, long-neck beer bottles, L'eggs stockings, to name a few) that indirectly admit to the consumer that "our product might not be unique but our package is." Research has shown that color is the most important packaging element, followed by shape, numbers, words as well as graphics on the package, and finally size (Beresford, 1997).

Warranty

One of the greatest consumer fears is to be "stuck" with a lemon. Internationally, Sears has capitalized on this by providing wary consumers with an ironclad warranty. Consumers, of course, do pay extra for the solace of purchasing a worry-free product, but the product's value concept is a combination of value concepts: the value concept of the product per se plus the value concept of peace of mind. Extended warranty programs are a significant proportion of sales of "hard goods," such as appliances, automobiles, etc.

Price

No area within the marketing mix is as devoid of sound scientific explanation and direction as is pricing. This may be even more critical for the new entrepreneur, where even a minor miscalculation can spell disaster. Some researchers recommend using pricing to maximize sales; others call for pricing inventory at such a level as to increase inventory turnover; while still others emphasize pricing levels to ensure profit maximization. There is far more to the pricing concept than any one of these approaches. All too often, price is simply established in reaction to what competitors are charging or what the market will bear. For the entrepreneur to remain successful over time, a more sophisticated approach must be taken because it does small-firm owners a disservice to sell a product or service at the same or lower price than a competitor if they ultimately lose money from the sale. Pricing often remains an art despite claims to the contrary. But in many cases, the price includes sociological and psychological factors that are hard to identify. Thus, the pricing process is sometimes incredibly arbitrary, and, after considering costs and prices of similar products, pricing very often remains a wild guess. Therefore, the first step in setting price is to understand revenues, cost, and profit.

It is absolutely essential to have a profit target during any financial evaluation in setting a product's price. Some business firms hit their profit target more often than others because they never lose sight of this goal. Ending the year with a profit is reserved for firms that strive for outstanding performance. To keep the firm pointed toward profit and to achieve this outstanding performance, some profit analysis principles need to be identified and applied:

- *Know your revenues:* Each revenue source must be identified for each of the product lines and for the operations as a whole.

- *Know your costs:* All cost items must be known in detail, so cost figures can be compared as a percentage of sales and as operating ratios. The costs must be itemized so that the costs that rise or fall can be identified easily and quickly, based on experience and cost figures for the industry. It is important to remember that profit is not only a function of revenues but also a function of the cost level (*Profit = Sales Revenue – Costs*).

- *Know your profit:* The pricing of products or services must provide an adequate profit beyond the costs. Pricing must be monitored closely so prices can be adjusted according to rising costs or to remain competitive. There should be no hesitation to drop a "loser" product from the product lineup.

- *Know the tax implications of your expenses:* Major decisions must be made early to minimize taxable income.

A simple break-even analysis can also provide the owner with a graphic representation of how cost, revenues, and selling price are related. The first element, which is often ignored or underestimated by the entrepreneur, is the fixed costs. How much will it cost to keep the doors open if no sales are made? These costs might include rent, utilities, insurance, administrative salaries, etc. Next, a clear understanding must be established for the variable costs to produce each and every unit, in terms of raw materials, labor, and selling expenses. Once these two cost measures are known, determining the markup of the total cost provides a valuable pricing direction.

Break-even analysis determines how many units need to be produced and sold in order to break even and cover (at least) total costs (fixed and variable costs).

$$\text{Break-even Point} = \frac{\$Total\ Fixed\ Cost}{\$Unit\ Price - \$Unit\ Variable\ Cost} = No.\ of\ BEP\ Units$$

Break-even analysis is a quick-screening device that can determine whether it is worthwhile to employ more intensive and costly analyses, such as discounted cash flow, which requires large amounts of data that are expensive to collect. Break-even analysis also permits the comparison of alternative product designs and specifications with a different cost mix, before the specifications are determined by examining trade-offs. Each product design has its own cost implications, which obviously affect price and marketing feasibility. Finally, break-even analysis also serves as a substitute for estimating an unknown factor in making "go" or "no-go" project decisions; there are always many variables to consider such as demand, costs, price, and other factors. While most expenses can be determined fairly easily, profit and demand are usually the only two unknown variables that remain. Because demand is usually tougher to estimate, by deciding that profit must at least be zero (the **break-even point**), the entrepreneur can fairly simply calculate the demand needed to make the project a reasonable undertaking. Of course, the demand figure at the break-even point needs to be related to the product's estimated future market share to determine the ultimate worthiness of the product or project. This is a matter of careful evaluation and business sense.

The result of this analysis will determine the firm's margins and will serve as a guideline to ensure a tight rein on costs and revenues, resulting in a better control of the consequences of alternative pricing levels. Margin results should be compared with industry peers to gain valuable insight into the venture's performance.

Gross margin = What percentage of sales are/should be the cost of production?

$$\frac{Gross\ Profit}{Net\ Sales\ Revenue}$$

Operating margin = What percentage of sales are/should be the cost of total operations?

$$\frac{Operating\ Profit}{Net\ Sales\ Revenues}$$

Net profit margin = What percentage of every dollar of sales constitutes/should constitute profit?

$$\frac{Net\ Profit}{Net\ Sales\ Revenues}$$

Retail pricing is somewhat different than manufacturing; the two have different sets of margins. Most retail stores use a markup system of pricing, and this usually means that a certain amount of inventory stock will be sold below markup, so an average gross margin will be achieved. Emerging trends in retailing, however, have begun to blur the accuracy of this approach. Many retailers offer their products and services at a premium price, because more people in a specific area, region, or demographic market segment have more discretionary income. Therefore, these retailers succeed in mass marketing at a premium margin (Sheth, 1983).

In addition, shifts toward a service-oriented economy and more home-based businesses have led to a shift in product offerings. One industry affected by this trend is office supplies. A few years ago, manufacturers of office supplies sold to only a handful of wholesalers, who in turn sold to a few retailers in a given market, with only the biggest companies receiving any price break, because of economies of scale. One retailer that has been able to change this setup has been Staples. Tom Stemberg, the founder of Staples, decided to take the office-supply industry into the supermarket arena, even at a less than 3% margin, far below the traditional industry average of 10% (Solomon, 1989).

Another trend that is having a profound influence on pricing policies in the retail sector is direct sales companies. As society becomes more "time poor," the acceptance of higher prices and consequently higher margins when shopping by mail or phone is becoming more prevalent. With no middlemen to include in the pricing formula, margins are sometimes high enough to create price reductions. Thus, this segment of retailing is growing at a rate more than double that of in-store retailing (Peterson, Albaum, & Ridgway, 1989).

Strategically speaking, pricing for a new product can usually be approached in either of two directions. The company can have a goal of building a large initial market share by charging a low price for market penetration purposes. Alternatively, the company can feature a high price directed at making as high a profit as possible, before other competitors enter the market. This strategy is called "market skimming."

One thing to keep in mind, of course, is that small firms are normally limited in their ability to compete against larger companies, which take advantage of their economies of scale capabilities, precisely because of their size. Therefore, the market skimming strategy is a better alternative, at least during the introduction stage.

Promotion

The most exciting aspect of the marketing mix, and the area that receives the most attention, is promotion. **Promotion** can be defined as any communication activity that increases sales activity, either directly or indirectly. Most people relate advertising to promotion, but there are also numerous other opportunities available to promote a product. Promotion involves establishing the strategy for communicating the product/service into the market segment that ultimately leads to a purchase by the consumer. It also involves determining not only the mode of communication but the content as well. The purpose of the communication or information is to influence or encourage each party to enter into the transaction. This is accomplished by providing information regarding the costs and benefits of the transaction; in different words, this is the perception of the performance and the penalty for neglecting its purchase (Yudelson, 1999). This information may include the nature of the expected benefit as well as information that is designed to reduce the perceived Penalty/Price associated with the transaction (e.g., low price, free delivery, knowledgeable sales staff).

The most common method of promotion for a majority of small firms is personal selling. Other categories include public relations, publicity, and sales promotion. A hybrid category and one receiving considerable recent interest is trade shows.

Personal Selling

Personal selling is one area that most small firms rely on to differentiate themselves from their larger competitors. In many situations the only difference between the merchandise carried by a large national chain and that sold by a local small firm is the customized personal selling approach taken by the entrepreneurial firm.

Publicity

Many new ventures introduce their innovation using free and unpaid publicity. Most trade journals, as well as news media shows, provide this type of coverage for the introduction of new products.

Trade shows

Another effective way to promote new products and services is trade shows. Industry statistics suggest that the cost of closing a sale for industrial products can be as much as $1,000 less per sale using trade shows compared to personal selling (Bloom, 1988). In fact, a national survey showed that closing a sale from an exhibition or trade show lead costs on the average $625 and takes 1.3 follow-up phone calls, compared with $1,117 and 3.7 phone calls needed to close a sale in a different way ("Trade Secrets," 1999). Selecting the "right" trade show is important, because different shows have different requirements and promotion goals. Certain issues need to be considered, such as whether typical market segment customers would be attending that trade show, what specific goals need to be accomplished by participating in the trade show, and what kind of pre-show marketing and preparations needs to be done (Anderson, 1998).

Advertising

Without a doubt, the area of promotion that receives the greatest attention is **advertising**, defined as any non-personal promotional activity for which the sponsor pays a fee. If solid market segmentation and reasonable pricing exists, then the foundation for an effective advertising campaign is set. Unfortunately, the problem of deceptive advertising has long received considerable attention in the legal world. In the past, deceptive ads have been placed by reputable companies, such as Campbell's soup, which used rocks in the bottom of the bowl to make the vegetables come to the top, and Listerine, which falsely claimed to cure colds. Today, many of the earlier excesses in the industry have been eliminated. Of even more significance is the criticism that advertising is fostering a society preoccupied with materialism, cynicism, irrationality, selfishness, sexual preoccupation, and loss of self-respect. Others have suggested that advertising forces the masses to purchase products they do not need, or worse, cannot afford, and that advertising has a powerful, detrimental effect on children. Regardless of the negative opinion held by many toward advertising, there can be no denying that because of advertising's effect, sales grow, jobs are created, and the economy in general flourishes. A study by Aaker and Bruzzone (1985) identified several areas as being responsible for the majority of discontent by advertising viewer audiences, and they recommend avoiding several areas of irritation:

- Demonstration of "sensitive" products
- Situations that were contrived, phony, unbelievable, or over dramatized
- Individuals being "put down" because of their appearance
- Important relationships, such as father/son for example, being threatened
- Demonstrations of personal discomfort
- The creation of uncomfortable psychological tension
- Unattractive or unsympathetic characters or poor casting
- Suggestive scenes

The fact that small firms lack name recognition or an established customer base is the very specific reason that small firms should advertise. There are alternatives to the higher-priced national advertising campaigns, such as the Yellow Pages, which can have quite a promotional impact if the ad has enhanced readability, complete information, and a clear focus, as well as colorful and large messages coupled with value-added coupons, which can generate significant response by customers. Regardless of what advertising method or combination of methods is selected, before doing any advertising, some preliminary research is necessary to determine first and foremost what makes a business unique. These unique aspects of the firm and its product should be emphasized over and over in all advertising. Other areas of concern include avoiding too much copy in advertising, getting the audience's undivided attention, and above all, establishing a budget and sticking to it (Huffman, 1988). The creative philosophy behind an advertising campaign's success should be very straightforward: keep it simple, keep it specific, and keep it believable.

Television

In the past, prime-time television advertising by any except the largest national firms was virtually unthinkable, due to the prohibitive cost. Cable television, however, opened some interesting possibilities for smaller firms, either for direct-response advertising in which the viewer picks up the phone to place an order or request information, or for regular retail advertising that generates brand awareness or interest. Access to cable television initially led many small firms to advertise on local independent channels. Even though the target audiences per channel of television viewing may be reduced because of the very large number of channels available, this avenue still offers wide promotional coverage that is quite affordable for a small business. The additional possibilities of reaching even larger audiences during slots allocated for local advertisement on national channels, such as CNN and ESPN, have also become affordable marketing options. Finally, additional opportunities during television station "fire sales" of last-minute advertising spots are available at large discounts to fill unsold advertising time (Cotriss, 1998).

Radio

Radio has long been a means of promotion used by small-business firms. Since the Federal Communication Commission (FCC) relaxed its licensing requirements, the number of stations has been increasing on almost a daily basis, targeting specific market segments and audiences. What this means for the entrepreneur is the ability to reach a more specific target market segment, with messages that can be changed on short notice, at a very affordable price. In addition, because of the competition for air space, radio stations are conducting their own marketing research, which can be very useful to the small firm. One company that used an innovative approach using radio advertising was the architecture and engineering firm of Burt, Hill, Kosar, Rittleman and Associates of Butler, Pennsylvania. While most marketers stress target audiences, this firm decided to use a "shotgun" approach by advertising on an all-news radio station. Marketing research had shown that the audience consisted of individuals who would never hire an architect or be the decision makers in putting up a $20 million building. The commercials were not even formatted as commercials; rather, each spot was a 60-second discussion on general architectural matters. What the firm hoped to do was differentiate the firm from other architectural firms and to gain name recognition. The approach worked, and sales rose significantly as a result of the promotional campaign (Brown, 1988).

Direct Mail

Direct mail is an expensive promotional approach, but sometimes it is worth the high cost. The mailing list is usually designed to include likely prospects for a firm's goods and services in the targeted market segment. However, the obvious disadvantage is that most people regard direct mail as "junk mail" and usually toss it away.

Magazines

Large-circulation magazines offer high-quality reproduction, prestige, and low cost per individual reached. On the other hand, many readers do not belong to the firm's target market segment, and the ad is a waste of money and effort unless the periodical is a special interest publication specifically targeting the firm's market segment. Other ways to advertise inexpensively are local and college newspapers, or other special promotional publications. For print advertising, Meinhardt (1989) suggests the following 10 steps:

1. Set a budget
2. Plan your campaign
3. Choose a publication
4. Find inexpensive help
5. Write customer-oriented copy
6. Use design to reflect your image
7. Decide when to advertise
8. Choose frequency over size
9. Choose the best position in the print medium
10. Test and follow-up

Many elements of promotion other than advertising have direct bearing on the small-firm community. Judging from the amount of online display ad publishers and advertising done by just the top ten largest advertising spenders and the escalating cost of advertising (Exhibit 9.1), many small firms owe their very existence to these alternative ways of promoting, besides advertising.

Most of the promotional opportunities described in marketing books have some limitations for small ventures. Detailed below are some marketing approaches with promotional alternatives that have worked for various small firms. Each approach was successful for a particular business or industry and may not be applicable to all small firms.

Licensing

Sometimes it does not pay to wait until a product gains national recognition and generates the local and regional profits needed to mount a national campaign. One alternative is to let someone else's name do the work, and buying the rights to a nationally well-known name can do this. Licensing works quite simply by having a company purchasing the rights to a name, usually for an up-front fee plus a given percentage on royalties of sales. However, the small firm should exercise caution in applying this strategy because the name must "fit." Even if the brand name or the name itself is well known, this does not mean that the customers will make the association with the small firm's product. That is why the length of the license agreement should be sufficiently long to maximize the worth of the investment into that name, especially when there is a possibility that the licensor may at some point become a competitor.

| Exhibit 9.1 | Top 10 U.S. Online Display Ad Publishers and Advertisers |

Total U.S., Home/Work/University Locations (Q1 2011)		
	Total display ad impressions (MM)	Share of display ad impressions (%)
Display Ad Publishers		
Total Internet: Total audience	1,110,448	100.0
Facebook.com	346,455	31.2
Yahoo! sites	112,511	10.1
Microsoft sites	53,592	4.8
AOL, Inc.	33,454	3.0
Google sites	27,993	2.5
Turner Digital	18,050	1.6
Fox Interactive Media	11,697	1.1
Glam Media	10,207	0.9
CBS Interactive	9,208	0.8
Viacom Digital	9,051	0.8
Display Advertisers		
Total Internet	1,110,448,112	100.0
AT&T Inc.	19,467,236	1.8
Experian Interactive	16,635,360	1.5
Scottrade, Inc.	11,225,895	1.0
Intuit Inc.	10,980,711	1.0
Verizon Communications Inc.	9,687,999	0.9
Netflix, Inc.	8,787,348	0.8
Groupon	7,681,414	0.7
Toyota Motor Corporation	7,043,887	0.6
Progressive Corporation	6,773,297	0.6
Weight Watchers International, Inc.	6,425,473	0.6

Source: comScore's Ad Metrix®.
Note: Display ads include static and rich media ads; excludes video ads, house ads and very small ads (< 2,500 pixels in dimension).

Private labels

Private-label marketing is similar to licensing because the product is sold with someone else's name under private labels through known establishments. Once again, it may be a great promotional strategy, but without additional resources to market the product, the strategy will fail because it will not be able to compete with other national brands and labels, regardless of whose private label is used. By deciding to sell under private-label names, the company is able to shift the costs of marketing to the retailer. The elimination of these costs enables the company to offer the product at a discount, which, in turn, allows the retailer to compete against national brand names.

Franchising

Although similar to licensing in some respects, franchising is quite different because of the control issue. A franchisee does, in essence, purchase a name, but along with this name comes a lack of discretion in operations. As discussed previously, franchising is, however, a very versatile tool for many entrepreneurs getting started; one of the greatest advantages of franchising has always been the marketing support provided by the franchisor, which begins with the instant name recognition of a product or service. Name recognition does not, however, grow simply by having franchised units throughout the country. National advertisement, generally supplemented by advertisement fees paid by the franchisees, provides the continuous exposure necessary to keep the franchise business on everyone's "short list." Subway sandwiches knows exactly how important this is to the franchise, and Fred DeLuca, its founder, attributes much of this success to continuous advertising, which allows Subway to be positioned in the public eye as a fresh alternative to burgers. As a result, Subway has been continually selected by *Entrepreneur* magazine as one of the number-one franchises over the past 30 years, as well as being a VetFran featured franchise since that program's inception.

Placement

The final "P" in the marketing mix is **placement**, or distribution. Transportation is a major factor here, but proper placement of the product also involves decisions about distribution outlets. For example, small-business owners may find that even local "flea markets" provide a relatively inexpensive distribution outlet for their products.

Although most people think "location, location, location" when this final "P" of the marketing mix is addressed, there is much more to consider. Placement is part of a product's or service's value chain and supply chain, in which everyone who has something to do with a product or service adds some value to it. Along the way, the placement channel joins the value chain either in a "fingerprint" manner, just touching a product along its path, or by adding substantial tangible value through the product's placement, because marketing channels create value-added outlets to reach customers. Whether the customers are reached through retailers, wholesalers, or directly from the manufacturer, this is a decision that should be planned carefully in light of the specific transportation, energy, and channel costs.

Sometimes, real placement value is not necessarily found in exclusive partnership channel arrangements, which are based on the notion that value is created in a linear fashion, from idea, to raw materials, to production, to placement, and to final consumption.

Value can also be created by the effective manipulation of *value webs*, temporary alliances which may last only for the duration of a single transaction. They may constitute the placement of the venture's product or service in a hotel's lobby during a popular event, for example (Wacker, 2001).

The placement and distribution of a product or service depends on the strategic competence of the individual venture and the entrepreneur's ability to take advantage of the best placement opportunities that add the most value in the value chain.

INTERNET MARKETING

The World Wide Web is becoming a very important player in the relationship between manufacturers, retailers, and consumers. Although it is actually part of the marketing mix, e-commerce needs to be examined separately, not only because of its importance for the future but also because it constitutes a comprehensive marketing mix on its own. Internet marketing serves as an advertising promotion channel, a placement channel, a product support, and a customer service channel. Additionally, Internet marketing can provide relatively inexpensive information for market research. And finally, Internet marketing has a major influence on product pricing.

The Internet can be used for advertising by providing a "store front" website, where customers can review products. In spite of its advantages, however, the Internet is not as effective for advertising purposes as other advertising channels, such as television, radio, print media, and direct mail. This is because only small banners can be shown on screen; the Web surfer is "out of control" because there is no captive market segment target; consequently, the cost of "per thousand exposure" becomes too high. However, these added elements of interactivity in store-front website applications can collect valuable demographic information; customers can send comments to the Web master, customize their user profiles, etc. The website can evolve from this simple interactive mode to becoming a full-fledged placement channel, where customers can place orders and where customer service and after-sales support can be provided. In essence, a website can replace expensive toll-free telephone numbers, customer service operators, and paper-based documentation, and online information can be updated easily (Chaudhury, Mallick, & Rao, 2001).

The percentage of small companies on the Internet keeps rising, and this is critical because retailers' e-commerce sales increased by 2.1% in 2009. As a share of total retail sales, e-commerce sales was 4.0% ($145 billion) in 2009, up from 3.6% ($142 billion) in 2008. Placement, especially in the form of an e-commerce website, is the most overlooked component of the marketing mix and has not yet received the attention it deserves from researchers and practitioners alike.

MARKET RESEARCH

Market research is essential for any business. It can be defined as the application of scientific method to acquire knowledge and understanding of consumers, buyers, competitors, markets, and marketing. In simpler terms, market research is the process of designing, gathering, analyzing, and reporting information that may be used to resolve a specific marketing problem (Burns & Bush, 2000). This research provides the information necessary to identify the market and to track changes in that market. It includes the monitoring of competitors and consumers alike. Most entrepreneurs rely on their personal experience or their "gut instinct" when evaluating the market for a product or service. Smaller companies really are in a "Catch-22" situation. They need the market research information more than larger companies, yet they are often charged more for it, even though they can afford it less. It is harder for small firms to research their potential niche customers. If a major corporation makes an error in accessing a potential market segment target, it might mean lower dividends for the year, but if a small-business owner makes the same mistake, the consequences can be far more serious. The American Marketing Association defines **market research** as the function that links the consumer, customer, or the public to the marketer through information used to (a) identify and define marketing opportunities and problems, (b) generate, refine, and evaluate marketing actions, (c) monitor marketing performance, and (d) improve understanding of marketing as a process (Anderson & Bennett, 1988). Market research has often been blamed for the historically abysmal rate of new product failures. However, more recent investigations into new product failures tend to exonerate at least some of the benefits of market research. More often, the failures occur because (a) there were inadequate investments in research, (b) the research was ignored, (c) what was researched was not what was launched, (d) there was inadequate marketing and promotional support, or (e) there was inadequate sales or fulfillment support (Neal, 2002).

Market research is not a perfect science; it deals with people and their constantly changing likes and dislikes, which can be affected by a myriad of influences, many of which simply cannot be identified. Market research does, however, try to learn about a specific market scientifically and to gather facts in an orderly, objective way. These data are used to find out how things are, not how we think they are or would like them to be, and what people want to buy, not just what we want to sell them.

Market research can sometimes be a hit-or-miss proposition. Too often research is based entirely on numbers and a quantitative approach that should be prefaced by a qualitative investigation. This implies setting some investigative parameters by examining the industry to determine the trends regarding customers, competition, and the industry itself, as well as the small firm. The results of this investigation at this preliminary stage can make the design of the research as well as the results of the quantitative analysis much more accurate and valuable (Fuller, 1989). Entrepreneurs must ask many qualitative questions when undertaking market research to validate their venture's value concept or to update, adjust, and possibly, *reinvent* their existing value concept. This validation should be done on a regular basis by using a combination of market research techniques, as Frieda Kaplan did in the example given in this chapter. The following questions provide a basic framework of the issues that need to be investigated in a market research project:

- Who are the customers and potential prospective customers?

- What kind of people are they?

- Where do they live?

- Can and will they buy?

- Am I offering the kinds of goods or services they want, at the best place and time, and in the right amounts?

- Are my prices consistent with what buyers view as fair?

- Are my promotional programs working?

- Are my placement channels appropriate?

- What do customers think of my business?

- How does my business compare with my competitors'?

Market research does not have to be fancy and expensive. Data used for marketing research does not always need to consist of the expensive primary data many market research firms recommend. It can often be done with much less expensive **secondary information** data, already collected for other purposes; it can be done sometimes for "peanuts," as one creative discount merchandiser discovered. During a 3-day promotion, the merchant gave away, free to customers, all the roasted peanuts they could eat while shopping in his store. By the end of the promotion, the merchant observed "litter trails" that provided information on the traffic patterns within the store. Trampled peanut hulls littered the most heavily traveled store aisles, and the highest concentrations lay in front of displays of merchandise of special interest to his customers. In short, he learned how they shopped in the store and what they wanted by observing their path and drawing conclusions from what he saw. Thereby, he organized a way of finding objective answers to questions his business had to answer in order to succeed (U.S. Small Business Administration, 1979). A select sample of the numerous statistical sources of secondary data and information that can be used for market research is provided in Exhibit 9.2.

| Exhibit 9.2 | Some Sources of Secondary Data and Information |

Web site	URL
Factiva	http://www.dowjones.com/factiva/
FED World: "FedWorld makes it easy to locate government information"	http://www.fedworld.gov
FedStats	http://www.fedstats.gov/
Lexis-Nexis	http://www.lexisnexis.com/en-us/home.page
U.S. Bureau of Labor Statistics, *Consumer Expenditure Survey*	http://www.bls.gov/cex/
U.S. Business Reporter, *Market Share Reports*	http://www.activemedia-guide.com/mrksh_profile.htm
U.S. Census, *State & County QuickFacts*	http://quickfacts.census.gov/qfd/states/00000.html
U.S. Census, *The 2012 Statistical Abstract: The National Data Book*	http://www.census.gov/compendia/statab/
U.S. Department of Labor, *Statistics*	http://www.dol.gov/dol/topic/statistics/inflation.htm#.UPN1yrakAhM
U.S. Small Business Administration, *Business Data & Statistics*	http://www.sba.gov/content/consumer-statistics
USA.gov, *Data and Statistics*	http://www.usa.gov/Topics/Reference-Shelf/Data.shtml

Sometimes, these no-cost and lower-cost research approaches can be very effective and can make a market research campaign very successful. Numerous low-cost methods are available to the entrepreneur undertaking market research. They can be as simple as counting cars, comparing license plates, coding coupons, or just plain people watching. These simple marketing research methodologies might generate information as valuable as that of market research conducted by professional market research firms or by the 500 federally funded research agencies that make their research available under the Stevenson-Wylcher Technology Innovation Act of 1980.

Existing market information can also be extremely beneficial and, better yet, free. The informational "grapevine" consists of sources such as accountants familiar with important industry-specific ratios; suppliers in the industry who know what is selling and what is not; or trade associations that collect massive amounts of information on their industry and share it through trade publications. When this information network does not provide sufficient information to estimate the economic strength of a specific target market segment to suit a firm's market research needs, and before undertaking expensive market research campaigns, entrepreneurs can still utilize some low-cost market research alternatives. They can do some of the basic market research work themselves, they can allow some latitude in their decision making by using "best guess" information estimates instead of precise numbers, and they can buy specific sections of previously conducted market research studies (Brown, 1988).

More market information is useful only if it can be accurately interpreted and converted into meaningful information. It seems, however, that businesspeople are already overloaded: 62% of them report that the quality of what they do is hampered because they cannot convert the data they already receive into meaningful information. Therefore, there seems to be an overload of data, and this data deluge is expected to grow by more than 40 times by 2020 (*The Economist,* 2011b).

STRATEGIC MARKET PLANNING: PUTTING IT ALL TOGETHER

The preparation of a comprehensive marketing plan is essential for the entrepreneur's long-term success. The plan itself comprises all of the various topics and issues examined so far, and the plan should be *continuously* compared with the initial marketing assumptions and decisions generated by the venture's original feasibility analysis, the original business plan itself, and the venture's original strategic target market analysis. The point of departure for the market plan as well as the overall venture strategic plan lies in determining how the venture itself has evolved over time and keeps evolving, that is, where it came from, where it is now, and where it will be in the future. However, a number of characteristics, when included in the marketing plan, contribute to the venture's success. These elements of an effective strategic marketing plan are outlined in Exhibit 9.3.

Exhibit 9.3   Elements of a Strategic Marketing Plan

1. Current marketing situation
   a. Market
   b. Product
   c. Competition
   d. Distribution channels
   e. Macroenvironment (regulation, social, political, technological, economic)
2. Opportunity and issue analysis
   a. Opportunity/threat analysis
   b. Strength/weakness analysis
3. Qualitative objectives of sales, market share, and profit
   a. Quantitative financial goals of sales, market share, and profit
   b. Quantitative marketing goals of sales, market share, and profit
4. Marketing strategy and action plans
   a. Identification of strategic target market
   b. Identification of strategic target market segment
   c. Product strategy
   d. Price strategy
   e. Promotion strategy (advertising strategy, publicity, and public relations)
   f. Placement/distribution/referral strategy
   g. Customer service strategy
   h. Overall sales strategy
5. Internet marketing strategy
6. Market research strategy
7. Research and development strategy
8. Summary of marketing strategy (what, when, who, where, how, and how much)
9. Projected financial outcomes
10. Marketing strategy evaluation and monitoring controls
11. Appendix and supporting material

Profitable firms seem to have a clear commitment to consumer-oriented goals, sizeable advertising budgets, breadth of services, and most importantly, a very well-defined strategic marketing plan (Peterson & Lill, 1981). Certainly each of these characteristics does not in itself guarantee profitability, but when they are incorporated into a strategic marketing plan, the opportunity and the probability for success is higher.

CONCLUSION

Marketing the venture is one of the most critical entrepreneurial functions because the best product or service in the world will never be recognized or rewarded without a comprehensive market plan. This chapter introduced the multitude of market concerns and activities requiring close attention and response of the entrepreneur.

Website Information

Topic	Web Address	Description
American Marketing Association	http://www.marketingpower. com/	Homepage for the AMA, links to AMA information, how to become a member, topics of interest, articles, and reports, as well as marketing tools.
Product life cycle	http://www.marketingteacher. com/lesson-store/lesson-plc. html	Explains the product life cycle.
Marketing mix	http://www. consultancymarketing.co.uk/ marketing-mix.htm	A brief overview of the marketing mix components, plus links to help create a marketing mix.
Brand name	http://www.levistrauss.com/	Information about the company in general, about the brands, and about products available.
Break-even analysis	http://www. knowledgedynamics.com/ demos/BreakevenFlash/	Explains how to run a break-even analysis through simulations.
Promotion	http://www.amazon.com; http://www.statefarm.com; http://www.geico.com	Home pages for some of the top ten national advertisers in 2012.
Market research	http://www.mrs.org.uk/	Home page for the Market Research Society. Gives links to new information in the research field, how to become a member, conferences and events about market research and networking skills.

Key Terms

Advertising: Any non-personal promotion activity for which the sponsor pays a fee.

Break-even point: The number of units that need to be produced and sold in order to cover (at least) total costs (fixed and variable costs).

$$\frac{Total\ Fixed\ Costs}{Unit\ Price - Unit\ Variable\ Cost} = \#\ of\ Break\text{-}Even\ Units$$

Four Ps of Marketing: Product, Promotion, Place, and Price.

Gross margin: Percentage of sales that constitutes the cost of production: Gross Profit / Net Sales Revenue.

Market research: The function that links the consumer, customer, or the public to the marketer through information used to (a) identify and define marketing opportunities and problems; (b) generate, refine, and evaluate marketing actions; (c) monitor marketing performance; and (d) improve understanding of marketing as a process.

Market segments: The unique customer needs and/or purchase behaviors, or some similar demographics, economic, social, or cultural characteristics segmented on the basis of age, sex, race, income level, educational level, lifestyle, geographic location, customer concentration density, type of product usage, frequency of usage, and/or time of usage.

Marketing: The process of planning and executing the conception, pricing, promotion, and distribution of ideas, goods, and services.

Marketing concept: A business philosophy that requires that all organization members focus their efforts on customer satisfaction, that requires management to emphasize marketing strategy and planning, and that requires the organization to strive to earn profit through selectively meeting customer needs.

Marketing mix: The blend of product, price, promotion, and placement that satisfies the demands of the firm's chosen market segment.

Net profit margin: Percentage of every dollar of sales that should constitute profit: Net Profit / Net Sales Revenue.

Operating margin: Percentage of sales that constitutes the cost of total operations: Operating Profit / Net Sales Revenue.

Placement: Part of a product's or service's value chain and supply chain, in which everyone who has something to do with the product or service adds some value to it.

Product decision factors: Quality, features and options, style, brand name, packaging, and warranty.

Product life cycle: The stages a product passes through during its lifetime, including introduction, growth, maturity, and decline.

Promotion: Any communication activity that increases, either directly or indirectly, sales activity.

Secondary information: Information not directly gathered for a specific business but whose information can reflect on broad business operations.

Segment profitability:

$$[(Market\ Share \times Market\ Demand) \times (Revenues\ per\ Customer) - Variable\ Costs\ per\ Customers] - Marketing\ Expenses.$$

Venture's niche: Why somebody would buy your product.

Venture's strategic target market: Who buys, how many they buy, when they buy, how they buy, and where they buy.

Review Questions

1. Describe some of the main components of each of the four profit analysis principles.

2. Discuss the three reasons for success in a venture's re-inventive marketing concept.

3. In general, discuss the life cycle of a product, brand, or industry.

4. Describe the two approaches that can be used when pricing a new product.

5. Describe some of the ways that a small firm can use television as a means of promotion.

6. Discuss some of the low-cost ways that a firm can conduct marketing research.

Reflections from the Front Lines of LifeGuard America

Let's get right to the business plan's section on marketing and identify the elements that constitute LifeGuard America's marketing strategy:

Market Positioning

Our market niche consists of those organizations interested in increasing their range of organ acquisition, reducing the overall cost of procurement and the simplification of their part in the organ preservation, procurement and transportation process. In short, our market consists of the OPTN, UNOS, the UNOS organ center, 59 OPOs, 259 transplant centers, 871 transplant programs, and any hospital capable of providing a potential for organ donation.

This market currently is underserved and limited in its options due to the lack of attention to the overall organ procurement process. No single nationwide organization is focused on improving the range of organ travel that supports the UNOS Principle of Equitable Organ Distribution. One of our objectives is the elimination of distance as a barrier to equitable organ allocation through the application of advanced communications, computer, and aviation technologies. It is our goal to wrap these advanced technological services into a single, round-the-clock, high-tech response center offering the entire OPTN a single 1–800 hotline for time-critical response to organ preservation, procurement, and transportation services.

Our services can be differentiated in the marketplace on the basis of reduced cost and complexity with increased flexibility of all facets of organ preservation, procurement, and transportation. Our unique positioning will be bringing a high-tech solution to the Organ Procurement and Transplantation Network in a manner that reduces cost, time, and complexity.

By focusing our services on eliminating the need for transplant teams to travel to the procurement surgery to assess organ suitability, we will be positioning the cost of our services against the massive costs associated with air transport and the resulting time lost in the process. The cost of procuring just one organ, where travel is required to obtain it, can easily exceed $25,000, not to mention the strain on those involved that must return after the procurement to participate in the transplant process. Also, if the organ turns out to be unsuitable, the resulting costs are sunk into non value-added overhead. Our job is to create the perception that traveling for organ procurement is a twentieth-century solution that has been replaced by twenty-first-century technology, allowing virtual access to the procurement process. Travel is an expensive and unnecessary means to achieve this end.

Service Pricing

LifeGuard America's pricing strategy satisfies the following prerequisites:

- Services are priced based on perceived value.

- Our pricing creates a sense of exceptional cost/benefit proposition.

- Our pricing relates to OPTN existing cost parameters which highlight our advantages.

- Our pricing structure is based on direct, multi-year contracts with the OPOs, Transplant Centers, the UNOS Organ Center and Transplant Physicians. *(Get your "Average Unit Price" and "Average Revenue per Sale" data from the Sales Forecaster Table in the Financial Planner. See the glossary in Appendix A for definitions.)*

- We are confident that our pricing strategy is realistic, for the following reasons:

_____

_____

_____

_____

_____

(Use/modify/add to statements below to support your pricing strategy in context of your product or market life cycle [see glossary in Appendix A] and your competitive position. Delete statements that do not apply.)

- We are creating a new market segment. No other company offers one-call services similar to ours. The pricing precedent is set by the way the network evolved over the past 20 years. We will test a variety of price points in focus groups over the coming months to refine our initial price points. The suggested pricing structure will be the highest at which they will still be perceived as an excellent value.

- We have received strong support for our pricing structure from several prospective customers.

- The pricing structure allows us to penetrate the network by going in at the same cost structure with additional benefits that enable organ procurement organizations (OPOs) and transplant centers to increase their bottom lines.

- Our pricing structure will also allow us, over time, to reduce prices to create barriers to entry into the market by copycat or knockoff competition after we have established the segment.

We have established a preliminary pricing structure based on a monthly service charge for the OPOs, the transplant centers, and the transplant programs that are distributed across the country. While this monthly service charge is initially dependent on the number of participating organizations, it is targeted at $1,500 per month per organization. This service charge covers the organization's capability to create an on-demand request for ORaccess, VirtualTeam, and/or MedXpress services through the 24×7 Response Center. A contracted, per-event charge will be assessed to the Organ Procurement Organization that hosts the procurement of $1,800. We have also established a pay-per-view option for transplant teams wanting to access the Web-enabled Internet site for the ultimate convenience of viewing and interacting with a procurement surgery from any computer with DSL-level access to the Internet. This service has been established at $495 per team per event.

Our coordination of MedXpress will be included in the monthly service charge for ORaccess. The actual costs associated with the MedXpress air transport will be passed through to the initiating organization as a line item on our existing monthly invoice statements.

The costs associated with VirtualTeam are initially bundled into our start-up costs as we provide training and onsite services to enable Transplant Centers to begin hosting ORaccess events. These teams are planned to transition into a resource available to the Organ Procurement Organizations for coordination of tasks associated with remote multiple organ procurements. It is believed that this service will progress to a high value-added resource for the OPOs as our experience grows over the years, thus adding another revenue potential to the mix of services we provide.

The demand for our services is based on this fundamental fact: anything that will bring more organs to an OPO, transplant center, or transplant program is highly desirable. We have also positioned our services at a price point that has a very attractive payback or break-even, based on organs procured that would have otherwise been wasted. For example, a relatively small OPO such as the Oklahoma Organ Sharing Network, which performed 75 procurements and 230 transplants in 2001, has a break-even point of only 8–10 additional organs procured during that same period. That represents less than 5% increase in the number of organs procured to cover our services for a year.

Marketing Plan

It will be important to establish acceptance of this new approach to organ procurement and transportation from both the medical transplant teams and UNOS. The fundamental thrust of our marketing strategy consists of a focus on reducing wasted organs and costs associated with the organ procurement and transportation process. We will begin with the organizations which ultimately pay the bills, that is, the transplant centers, and the OPOs. We will target these organizations with a full-scale marketing campaign and follow through with on-site presentations that are directed at the executive levels within these organizations. These prospects fall into three different groups:

1. The organizations that begin the organ transplant process
   - The United Network for Organ Sharing (UNOS)
   - Regional organ procurement organizations (OPOs)
2. The organizations that finance the operations
   - Medicare
   - Medicaid
   - Hospitals
   - Insurance companies
3. The organizations that perform the transplants
   - Hospitals
   - Transplant centers
   - Transplant programs
   - Surgeon and physician corporations

Marketing Scenario

The strategic marketing objectives are to educate, demonstrate, and become a key element of the organ procurement and delivery process. The first objective is to educate the organ transplant community about the results that can be achieved when the organ transplant process is redesigned to take advantage of new technological developments. This objective must also clearly illustrate how these results are achieved through a centralized, dedicated organization that responds 24 hours/day, 7 days/week to an OPO's request for remote procurement access and the resulting organ delivery of time-critical organs. The second objective is to demonstrate that this enhanced process of remote organ assessment can be realized by a single dedicated organization: LifeGuard America. This will require demonstrating to the organizations involved not only that this is possible but also that most transplant centers have the necessary infrastructure already in place. This becomes another capability that plugs into their existing network allowing higher utilization of an existing asset. In short, this becomes further validation of the transplant centers' investment in broadband telecommunications technology.

The last objective is to enter into a relationship with UNOS and the participating OPOs that unites LifeGuard America with these organizations at the process level and integrates them at a functional and operational level.

The three phases of the Tactical Marketing Plan will be conducted simultaneously at all levels of designated key organizations. The key organizations in this plan are

- The United Network for Organ Sharing (UNOS)
- Regional OPOs
- Transplant center hospitals
- The medical teams that conduct the transplants
- The governmental organizations that administer the transplants
- The insurance companies and hospitals that pay for the transplants

By simultaneously approaching all key organizations within the organ transplant process, we will effectively establish acceptance from the doctors and hospitals that perform transplants together with those who ultimately pay for the transplants. Approaching the marketing plan this way, we can effectively demonstrate, from a macro perspective, how this application of technology will benefit all those involved with the organ transplant process.

This marketing approach is outlined below, and the actual process maps for the organ transplant process will be developed during the third quarter of 2003. As this marketing plan is successfully implemented, it will create the necessary demand for a single-point service organization that handles activities associated with remote organ procurement and delivery—a demand that LifeGuard America will fulfill. To be successful, our marketing plan must address all levels of the organizations involved; we must gain acceptance of the operational players; and we must show substantial and sustainable competitive advantage for the extended transplant community as a whole. To achieve this, the marketing plan consists of the following tactics:

- Direct marketing to executive management, administrative, and operations personnel of key organizations by phone, mail, and face-to-face presentations clearly outlining the benefits to the bottom line of this new approach.
- Solicitation of direct buy-in at the OPO level as well as the transplant teams, hospitals, and insurance company levels to more clearly understand the current process and its limitations and inefficiencies.

- Demonstration of substantial monetary benefits to the organizations that finance the overall process and offer sustainable competitive advantage to the hospitals that want to grow and expand their organ transplant capabilities.

Discussion Questions on LifeGuard America

1. What approach do you think was taken by Mr. Fitzpatrick when he formulated the pricing model for LifeGuard America?
2. How do you think LifeGuard America could benefit from low-cost market research?
3. Where would you go to get the primary research for LifeGuard America?

References

Aaker, D. A., & Bruzzone D. E. (1985, Spring). Causes of irritation in advertising. *Journal of Marketing, 49*(2), 47–57.

Anderson, L. (1998, August). On with the show: Make the most of your next trade show. *Entrepreneur, 26*(8), 94.

Anderson, P. F., & Bennett, P. D. (1988). *Dictionary of marketing terms.* Chicago: American Marketing Association.

Beresford, L. (1997, March). It's a wrap. *Entrepreneur, 25*(3), 40.

Best, R. J. (1999, November). *Market-based management: Strategies for growing customer value and profitability* (2nd ed., paperback). Upper Saddle River, NJ: Prentice Hall.

Bloom, L. (1988, July/August). Trade show selling tactics. *In Business, 10*(4), 43–45.

Brown, P. B. (1988, February). On the cheap. *Inc. Magazine, 10*(2), 108–110.

Burns, A. C., & Bush, R. F. (2000). *Marketing Research* (3rd ed.). Upper Saddle River, NJ: Prentice Hall.

Campanelli, M. (2001, August). Good incentive. *Entrepreneur, 29*(8), 82–84.

Chaudhury, A., Mallick, N. D., & Rao, H. R. (2001, January). Web channels in e-commerce. *Communications of the ACM, 44*(1), 99.

Cotriss, D. (1998, December). Is cable TV right for you? *Target Marketing, 21*(12), 14.

Cross, L. (1999, June). Segmentation: When less is more. *Graphic Arts Monthly, 71*(6), 124.

Curry, D. J., & Riesz, P. C. (1988, January). Prices and price quality relationships: A longitudinal analysis. *Journal of Marketing, 52*(1), 36–51.

Economist, The. (2011a, December 17). Retail therapy. *401*(8764), 119–123.

Economist, The. (2011b, December 31). Too much buzz. *401*(8765), 50.

Fuller, C. (1989, July). Taking charge. *Entrepreneur, 17*(7), 228–232.

Fuller, C. (1990, January). The year of the hero. *Entrepreneur, 18*(1), 93–94.

Huffman, F. (1988, December). The ad game. *Entrepreneur, 16*(12), 130–138.

Kotite, E. (1989, December). Made in the USA. *Entrepreneur, 17*(12), 69–75.

Lambkin, M., & Day, G. S. (1989, July). Evolutionary processes in competitive markets: Beyond the product life cycle. *Journal of Marketing, 53*(3), 4–20.

Larson, E. (1989, November). Strange fruits. *Inc. Magazine, 11*(11), 80–90.

Lindstrom, M. (2011). *Brandwashed: Tricks companies use to manipulate our minds and persuade us to buy.* New York, NY: Crown Publishing Company.

Meinhardt, S. (1989, January). Put it in print. *Entrepreneur, 17*(1), 54–62.

Modis, T. (1994, September–October). Forecasting the rise and fall of almost anything. *The Futurist, 28*(5), 20–25.

Moran, G. (2000, February). Something different. *Entrepreneur, 28*(2), 40.

Neal, W. D. (2002, Summer). Getting serious about marketing research. *Marketing Research, 14*(2), 24–28.

Peterson, R. A., Albaum, G., & Ridgway, N. M. (1989, Summer). Consumers who buy from direct sales companies. *Journal of Retailing, 65*(2), 273–286.

Peterson, R. T. (1989, January). Small business adoption of the marketing concept vs. other business strategies. *Journal of Small Business Management, 27*(1), 38–46.

Peterson, R. T., & Lill, D. J. (1981, October). An examination of marketing factors related to small business success. *Journal of Small Business Management, 19*(4), 65.

Porter, M. E. (1980). *Competitive strategy: Techniques for analyzing industries and competitors.* New York: The Free Press.

Sheth, J. N. (1983, Fall). Emerging trends for the retailing industry. *Journal of Retailing, 59*(3), 6–18.

Shoemaker, R. W. (1986, February). Comment on "Dynamics of price elasticity and brand life cycles: An empirical study." *Journal of Marketing Research, 23*(1), 78–82.

Simurda, S. J. (1989, May). A call for quality. *Entrepreneur, 17*(5), 127–132.

Solomon, S. D. (1989, June). Born to be big. *Inc. Magazine, 11*(6), 94–101.

Tellis, G. J. (1988, November). The price elasticity of selective demand: A meta-analysis of econometric models of sales. *Journal of Marketing Research, 25*(4), 331–341.

Top ten national advertisers in 1999 (2000, September 25). *Advertising Age, S-2.*

Trade secrets (1999, August 16). *Business Week,* 20.

Turner, G., & Spencer, B. (1997, January–February). Understanding the marketing concept as organizational culture. *European Journal of Marketing, 31*(2), 110.

U.S. Census Bureau E-Stats (2011). www.census.gov/estats May 26, 2011.

U.S. Small Business Administration (1979). *Learning about your market* (Small Business Marketing Aid No. 167). Washington, D.C.: U.S. Government Printing Office.

Wacker, W. (2001, June). A valuable proposition. *Entrepreneur, 29*(6), 20.

Wedel, M. (2001, Winter). Is segmentation history? *Marketing Research, 13*(4), 26–29.

Yudelson, J. (1999, April). Adapting McCarthy's four Ps for the twenty-first century. *Journal of Marketing Education, 21*(1), 60–67.

Zeithaml, V. A. (1988, July). Consumer perceptions of price, quality, and value: A means-ends model and synthesis of evidence. *Journal of Marketing, 52*(3), 2–22.

10 Venture Infrastructure: Organizational and Operational Considerations

Can We Plan the Organizational and Operational Infrastructure?

LEARNING OBJECTIVES

1. To identify the need for an internal team to help achieve the venture's goals.
2. To describe how to recruit and compensate potential partners and internal team members.
3. To discuss the special circumstances at work in a family business and in a "copreneurial" couple.
4. To identify the need for an external support team.
5. To identify low-cost support services available to small businesses seeking help and information.

TOPIC OUTLINE

"The best chance you have of making a big success in this world is to decide from square one that you're going to do it ethically."

(Alan Greenspan, former U.S. Federal Reserve
Bank Chairman, November 13, 2001)

———

INTRODUCTION

The most important consideration for a venture start-up begins with the type of business the entrepreneur wants to start. Is it an income-producing business or a potentially high-growth venture? Many of the business skills, but the most specialized of roles, such as law, accounting, insurance, etc., that an income-producing business requires for success may already be possessed. When other skills or resources are needed, income-producing businesses, such as beauty salons or hardware stores, tend to look for partners among friends or family.

After this initial direction is taken, virtually every business founder has to ask him/herself some additional questions at the beginning of the start-up process: Can I do this venture on my own or will I need help? And if I need help, where do I find it? Who can provide what I need, and at what cost? Part of the answer to these questions depends upon the venture's objectives. Is the objective to make a lot of money? If this is so, will taking on partners dilute the "wealth" to the point that it no longer fits the definition of "a lot of money"? Or will the added resources brought into the venture improve the chances of achieving these financial goals? Is the objective to start a business so that the founder gains independence from a "boss"? If so, how much control will be lost with a partner or partners? How much of the decision-making authority needs to be shared with internal team members. This is especially important because sharing responsibility is almost always a problem for a firm's growth and because most partnerships end up in messy "divorces." Answers to these questions can help determine whether or not internal team partners are needed in a venture.

On the other hand, the complexities of today's business environment virtually require the use of an external team if the venture start-up is a potentially high-growth venture. The demands of the start-up process are simply too difficult for all but a few exceptional individuals, because the breadth of the task is enormous and a larger pool of external experts is needed. Because "Renaissance" people are in short supply, taking on internal partners and/or putting together an external team will provide the venture with the ability to execute the venture idea by bringing in the needed talent and resources to embark upon a high-growth opportunity and thus improve the chances of success. However, it should be noted that advisors help the entrepreneur make better decisions, but they are not the owners and they should not be ceded control of the business.

THE NEED FOR TEAMS

Not every venture needs a team to guide it through the start-up process. Even among those that do, a full team may not be required at the start. Instead, venture teams can build gradually, initially substituting part-time help or professional advisors for full-time expertise. Team members can be added as needed, depending on the business's mix of skills and the demands of the marketplace. Without question, a careful assessment of the venture's need for a team must be made as early as possible.

This decision boils down to two generic concerns: the character of the venture, and the entrepreneur's personality, energy, and ability. To what extent do the venture and the entrepreneurs need help at the start of the firm as opposed to later? Can they get by with what they have now and with part-time outside help, or do they need full-time expert help immediately? Can they perform the work required of a generalist, as well as be proficient and knowledgeable in marketing, finance, management, etc.? Are they willing to share decision-making authority in areas in which they are not comfortable (Baty, 1981, p. 41)?

Today's "common" wisdom holds that there is a strong correlation between success in a venture and the presence of a high-quality start-up team. It is no secret that funding sources, such as bankers, venture capitalists, and others, prefer to invest in a business with a strong founding team rather than an individual founder because experience has taught them that a good team not only contributes a more balanced set of skills and resources, but also provides the venture with greater credibility among the members of the business community. The willingness to work with a team may send a positive signal to potential financial investors regarding the venture's managerial capabilities. On the other hand, think of the signal sent if an entrepreneur is not willing to do this.

The ability to recruit team members to the venture may indicate talent in attracting and managing personnel. But even more important, it signifies that others have "bought in" to the venture idea. They have decided that the venture has potential, and they are willing to sacrifice their current jobs and/or higher incomes for longer-term potential. Furthermore, venture teams can often withstand the loss of a key employee better than a solo entrepreneur, and employees should be able to grow further before new talent is needed in the company.

The attributes possessed by the business founder will also weigh heavily on the decision whether or not to form a team. Certainly, a team provides a larger pool of managerial talent, but at the same time, members need to bring complementary skills to the business. The more of a specialist the entrepreneur is, the greater the need for supporting help in other areas in order to achieve the venture's goals. Are there gaps in knowledge, resources, or skills that could create the kinds of obstacles that might impede the chances for success? Is there a need for someone to share the costs of the business? Is there a need is for a specialized expertise? While it sounds like it makes sense to put together a team or at least look for partners, it does not always make sense to share the venture with other people. At the very least, the founder should retain control at the inception of the venture. However, if sharing ownership with partners is inevitable, the owner should consider the following:

1. Partners need not be equal partners. Common stock makes unequal partnership both feasible and easily quantified.

2. Do not take on a partner if you can hire a person for the same role.

3. Do not take on partners because you think having a balanced team will impress financial backers. Responsible backers will be much more interested in knowing that the people who are *actually* responsible for the company's progress are the ones who hold the motivating stock.

4. Do not allow your normal sense of democracy to cause you to part with more stock than is needed to give your partners a higher degree of motivation. Try to view the situation from the standpoint of what are they doing now, that is, what are their alternative prospects if they do not join the venture.

5. Do not allow the immediacy of your present need, whatever it might be, to bias your judgment in favor of a partner versus an employee.

6. Stay flexible in terms of compensation and motivation. Consider stock options, or preferably, bonus plans instead.

7. Do not approach potential partners with tentative offers to elicit their help in shaping your ideas until you have gone as far as you can go without them. In short, make sure that you have established the company as *yours,* so that anyone joining it will do so on *your* terms.

8. If your analysis shows that you can do it alone, do not be afraid to try it. If you discover, as things progress, that you really do need a couple of partners, it is easier to get them later than to add partners too soon (Baty, 1981, pp. 42–43).

Some experts contend that teams are not necessary. Perhaps they are right in certain cases or if they are talking only about internal teams. But most ventures, whether an income-producing small firm or a potentially high-growth venture, need a team of seasoned professionals to help them through the inevitable "peaks and valleys" faced by every venture. An accountant may be needed to help with bookkeeping and financial records, a lawyer to help sort through legal problems, or a Chief Financial Officer (CFO) whose skills lie more in fund-raising than controlling financial resources. The key question is this: what kind of team will the venture need? There is no easy answer to this question, but it seems that start-up ventures at some point in their early existence need to successfully collaborate with three different sources of help:

1. An **internal team** whose members may participate in the founding of the firm.

2. An **external team** whose members are advisors and other outsiders actively assisting the venture.

3. **Personal contacts or connections**, which although not directly hired for their services, nevertheless interact with and affect the firm's progress (Vesper, 1980, p. 40).

INTERNAL TEAMS

What is an internal team? Many of the issues involved in building a team or simply recruiting partners for an income-producing business or for an entrepreneurial venture are quite similar. However, idiosyncrasies are unique to each type of venture, and these "generic" guidelines can be interpreted differently in various situations.

An **internal team** can include individuals who do not own a share of the venture, as well as those who actually own a share of the firm and are partners in the legal sense. It can also include those who were given stock as part of their compensation when they joined the firm yet are not really thought of as partners, or members of top management. In other words, the founder is the one who determines the nature of the members of an internal team; there are no definitive boundaries regarding who is and who is not a member of the internal team and/or what their roles are.

A **partnership** is one kind of internal team that is popular because it is easy to start and is specifically defined by law. The **Uniform Partnership Act** defines a partnership as "an association of two or more persons to carry on as co-owners of a business for profit." This type of relationship implies the sharing of ownership and responsibility, whether it is a two-person partnership or a giant partnership like those found in the accounting, legal, and consulting professions.

Interestingly, the partnership relationship is often perceived as one of "equality in status," despite differences in capital commitment, expertise, function, personality, motivation, and control (Bird, 1989, p. 215). Although the idea of equality may exist in some form or another, the reality is that partners come to the table with different skills, abilities, and resources, and consequently, they contribute differently to the firm's success. Some may specialize in certain business functions, such as marketing or accounting, while others bring capital or have specific knowledge of the technology of the product or service to be provided. Whatever the differences, the idea of equal ownership and responsibility is frequently violated. In defying this principle, the partnership often encounters a serious form of conflict: *who gets what, how much,* and *why?* Unfortunately, compensation and stock distribution are much more complex than simply splitting the value of the company into equal shares, and consequently, partnerships are fraught with problems, both legal and interpersonal. Unfortunately, prospective partners all too often concentrate on the legal issues without giving enough attention to interpersonal relationships, which tend to generate the most difficult problems because they are loaded with emotion, anxiety, and frustration and often result in the dissolution of the partnership.

Once entrepreneurs have defined what a successful partnership represents in their mind, the decisions and issues awaiting them as they build their venture should be somewhat easier to deal with. Is a successful partnership one that lasts for a long time, one that changes, or one that ends "cleanly," with everyone "winning" and without ill feelings? Is a successful partnership one that sustains a growing organization or one that focuses on the satisfaction of the individual partner's needs? Is a successful partnership one that is evolving or one that remains steady and familiar to the partners? Is a successful partnership one that is acknowledged by outsiders as being "sound" or one that "feels good" to the partners (Bird, 1989, pp. 228–230)?

Putting Together an Internal Team

One popular misconception labels entrepreneurs as "mavericks," or individualists who are intent on building their company in their own way. Often, entrepreneurs are seen as the square peg in the round hole, the persons who could not work for anyone else and thus had to go out and do it on their own. Obviously, this description does not fit well when success in an entrepreneurial venture is dependent on the "ability to execute" which may necessitate the building of a quality management *team*. In fact, the entrepreneur must possess a host of interpersonal skills that include, among others, the ability to recruit good team players, to motivate team members, and to constantly change the team when conditions require it, either by adding or by subtracting personnel, without disrupting the firm's operations.

But where does one start? For what qualities should one look? Who makes a good partner or team member and why? Finding team members has often been considered a convoluted process, idiosyncratic, a crapshoot, and many other names that reflect the uncertain and random manner in which this procedure is conducted. Sometimes the entrepreneur is relatively sophisticated and sets out with a planned and somewhat structured approach to finding team members. Sometimes team members are predetermined by family membership or friendship. And at other times, team members are chosen based on their ability to bring in needed resources, such as money or some type of specialized knowledge.

Each of these team-building approaches has advantages and disadvantages. For example, the ability to bring money into the venture is perhaps the single most important selection criterion used. And yet, it may be the worst, because access to capital does not necessarily indicate good entrepreneurial skills. Another important criterion is whether the individual possesses the experience and expertise needed for the venture to succeed. But these are not guarantees for a successful partnership in an internal team either. Rather, a successful internal team must have chemistry, a shared commitment to the venture, mutual respect and trust, a compatible value system, and an understanding and acceptance of different personalities. Communication among team members or partners is as essential as shared interests and attitudes.

The requirements for a successful internal team are not new or revolutionary, but the excitement, the glamour, and the urgency to get started often preclude a more planned approach to team building. Far too often, the criteria used for determining partners or team members are those of convenience rather than the considerations that should count, and internal teams become "look-alike" teams in which founders disregard the conventional wisdom of adding complementary skills to the team and instead choose partners similar to themselves (Bird, 1989, p. 222). This tendency is easy to understand because as a basic tenet of human behavior, it is easier to work with and trust people with whom we have similarities. At the same time, however, joining forces with clones of oneself seldom brings what is needed to make a venture successful. Thus, one of the hardest tasks in building an internal team is to fight the urge to assemble team members with similar traits and, instead, build an internal team with people with complementary skills that are needed to form a complete team with the needed resources. Complementary qualities and skills bring many more benefits to the venture, in spite of conflicts that may initially arise because of differences of opinion. These differences must be channeled toward productive solutions.

Problems and Pitfalls of an Internal Team

The potential for conflict lies mainly in the split between ownership and operating responsibility, but there are a vast number of areas in which internal team members can run afoul of each other. For instance, most experts contend that, even within equal partnerships, there must be a leader, that is, someone charged with the responsibility for making the important decisions. Yet far too often, partnerships based on friendly or family relationships evolve into a type of "leaderless democracy" (Timmons, Smollen, and Dingee, 1985), in which decision making is paralyzed and ineffective. Such partnerships can also suffer from "double-vision," in which the boundaries between friendship or family and business relationships are so blurred that the same event can be interpreted in two or more different ways. For example, a performance appraisal could be much more complicated when the appraised is not only a member of the internal start-up team but is also a close, personal friend, or a brother, sister, or other relative. It is very difficult to tell a friend or relative they are doing a poor job, and the business or personal relationship may not stand up to tests such as performance appraisals.

How well can the entrepreneur possibly know any partner or internal team member? Certainly, if they have worked together previously, or if they are family members, it may be a different story, but what if they do not know each other well? Will they handle pressure and uncertainty differently than the individual entrepreneur, and if so, will their approaches be acceptable? What if, after all of the checking, rechecking, and interviewing, the entrepreneur finds that the internal team member's ethics or goals are not as compatible as originally thought?

Perhaps the entrepreneur is comfortable with the initial start-up internal team, but over time, people join and leave organizations on a regular basis. Such activities bring new personalities with different interests and expectations, all of which affect the communication and decision-making processes at work in the venture. What if the entrepreneurs suddenly determined that they and their partners can no longer get along? What if the partner goes through an emotional breakup with their spouse and can no longer "carry their weight"? Lines of communication may break down or the level of trust may be affected. To an extent, the breakup of the initial venture team is almost a certainty. The pressures of the start-up process and natural human inclinations virtually guarantee that people will come and go from the firm. What can be done about it?

In a formal partnership, the first line of defense is the partnership agreement. It should contain, in specific language, items such as these and many others: How work is to be divided. How much each partner is allowed to take out of the partnership each year. What is to be done if a partner wants to leave the firm? But what if there is no formal partnership agreement and a stock-owning internal team member's sub-par performance and actions are endangering the success of the venture? Obviously, the working relationship must end, but at the same time, the entrepreneur and the venture need to be protected. Certainly some protection devices, such as stock vesting, stock buybacks, etc. are appropriate, but if they do not work, an equitable offer to buy back the individual's stock needs to be made. The situation must be confronted immediately and resolved, even if it means getting rid of the individual right then and there, instead of allowing bad circumstances to become worse. It is the entrepreneur's responsibility to correct the poor choice of internal team member and/or partner, and it is usually easier to do so at the beginning, when the firm's valuation is lower or nil, than in a later stage when the numbers at stake are much larger.

Where to Find Internal Team Partners and Members

Considering the various problems that can crop up among partners or internal team members, finding good ones can be very difficult, particularly when all there is to start with is an idea, and nothing else. Where can the entrepreneur find candidates for the internal team and/or partnership who have capital or who are specialists in the type of technology the venture needs? Several sources for finding good internal team members and partners are suggested here:

1. *Former business associates:* Entrepreneurs already know whether or not they can work with these people.
2. *Friends:* Even though the pool of possible candidates may be smaller than the entrepreneur would like or need and often does not work for long periods of time, the conventional wisdom is that if it does work, it works splendidly.
3. *Business consultants:* Often hired on a temporary or "trial basis" to test the working relationship. If it works, the consultant is integrated into the firm; if not, the relationship can be easily terminated.
4. *Competitor's "raided" staff:* This may incur some risk of legal action, but such litigation is generally uncommon due to the cost and problems associated with it.
5. *Referrals by friends and associates:* Referral candidates can often fulfill requirements. In some cases, venture capitalists bring people together whom they feel have complementary skills and the ability to form a successful internal team.
6. *Classified advertising:* Two types: those listing people looking for positions or situations, and those listing situations looking for people (Dible, 1986, pp. 73–75).

Managing the Internal Team Formation Process

Much of the discussion on finding team members refers to what Timmons (2001) calls *the natural processes of team formation.* That is, either one individual has the initial idea and several associates join him/her to bring the idea to fruition, or a group of individuals share several features, such as the idea, friendship, money, or experience that bring an entire team or partnership together to fulfill their common goal of building a profitable venture. As Timmons (2001) further points out, naturally formed partnerships seldom last for long because they are usually poorly conceived from the very beginning, and they often struggle with many of the very internal team issues and pitfalls mentioned previously. In response to these misguided "natural" approaches, they advocate a *planned* approach to team formation. To avoid the inevitable crises and conflicts in the early life cycle of the new business, a carefully thought-out process can assist the new venture team to identify its personal needs in a methodical way. Exhibit 10.1 illustrates a conceptual framework for a planned approach to internal team formation.

Exhibit 10.1	Internal Team Formation Process and Issues

1. A planned process, rather than a natural evolution, can reduce the chances of failure.

2. The founder or founders should begin with a self-assessment in terms of:
   - Entrepreneurial orientation.
   - Self-image and expectations.
   - Expertise and management skills.
   - Team skills.

3. Analysis of the venture is needed to determine what skills and expertise it requires in terms of
   - The major goals from start-up through the first three years.
   - The key tasks and action steps.
   - The requisites for success.
   - The firm's distinctive competencies.
   - The required external interfaces.

4. Comparison of the needs of the venture with the founder's existing inventory of capabilities will help to identify needs for other complementary internal team members or outside resources:
   - Partners should be picked as one would pick an ideal spouse, and they should complement the founder's personal and business strengths.
   - A prospective partner's trust and commitment should be carefully calibrated.
   - Aligning a new team member's expectations with the realities of the start-up is crucial, and should begin prior to his/her actual joining the internal team.
   - Supportive reference groups can facilitate the total immersion of a prospective team member.

Compensating Internal Team Partners and Members

One of the most complex and difficult issues that the entrepreneur faces in regard to internal teams is the compensation of team members or partners, especially if the original intention was to share the firm's value and its financial rewards with partners or internal team members. Who gets what, how much, and in what form? How much are these individuals and their contributions worth? How can a specific value be placed on what is commonly called *sweat equity*? And what about the wise recommendation that start-up firms should do everything humanly possible to defer their cash outflows to the last moment possible?

Because cash is frequently the scarcest resource, the more that can be postponed in terms of compensation for internal member contributions, the greater the cash "cushion" to cover unforeseen expenses. Profit sharing or stock distribution plans can also be used to delay part of the cash expenditures typically allotted for employee compensation. Additionally, such incentive plans are popular ways to recruit and motivate key internal team members. Unfortunately, the argument over whether or not to share a firm's equity with internal team members is not a simple one, nor do easy answers exist. Instead, a multitude of good reasons support both sides of the issue. Exhibit 10.2 lists a number of arguments for and against involving internal team members and/or employees in the ownership of a venture.

Even if the decision is made to distribute the entrepreneur founder's stock among internal team members and/or employees, the issue is not over. Subsequent decisions need to be made in regard to who should get it, how many shares should be distributed, whether it should be given freely or provided through an option to purchase, and when the distribution should take place. Obviously, these decisions deal with important issues and should not be taken lightly; they can have a significant impact on the venture's future. Finally, important philosophical questions remain: Should the initial equity-sharing

Exhibit 10.2	Reasons For and Against Involving Internal Team Members and/or Employees in the Ownership of a New Venture

Reasons for Joint Ownership	Reasons against Joint Ownership
Financial and/or Legal Rationale	
1. To provide additional investment capital.	1. To conserve a relatively undervalued resource, namely equity.
2. To defer expense of labor.	2. To avoid future litigation.
3. To support the price of shares.	3. To avoid complications in any future sale of the business.
4. To take advantage of tax provisions.	
Behavioral Rationale	
1. To acquire and hold key personnel.	1. To increase the long-run likelihood of maintaining control.
2. To be fair or to avoid the guilt associated with being unfair.	2. To conserve privacy.
3. To enhance employee commitment and performance.	3. To avoid the conflict caused by increased knowledge of differences in earnings and accumulated wealth.
4. To reward past exemplary service.	4. To avoid future regrets.
5. To forestall future requests and control allotments.	5. To avoid the complexity of issues associated with what, when, how, and who, in formulating a policy for distributing equity.
Strategic Rationale	
1. An important symbol of control and compensation	1. Having many stakeholders distracts management because of internal politics.
2. A way of sharing risk.	2. Difficulties in separating the compensation and control aspects of ownership.
3. Motivates people to undertake innovative activities.	

Source: Adapted from McMullan (1982) and Bird (1989, p. 237).

reflect the best guess of what the internal team member will contribute in the next couple of years, or merely to provide motivation for future actions? Should evidence of past performance be rewarded or not?

Another issue of critical importance during the formation of an internal team for a venture start-up is the valuation of the venture's idea. How much is the idea worth in relative terms? Is it worth more than the effort of a partner who developed the business plan enabling the entrepreneur to raise the necessary capital and get the venture up and running? What if the entrepreneur came up with the idea but had no capital to contribute? Whose stake should be larger, the stake of the idea generator or the stake of the investor who provided the required funding? What is the value of specialized technical skills, reputations, commitment to the venture, etc., and how can technical, managerial, or other skills and intangible factors, such as commitment, be ranked in terms of importance and contributions? In essence, all of these questions boil down to this issue: how can value be assigned to different types of contributions so that compensation proportionate to contributions can be settled among internal team members and partners? The issue becomes more complicated and difficult given the fact that contributions *per se* and team members can change over time, and that perceptions of equitable rewards differ from individual to individual.

In spite of the inherent problems, however, it is possible to develop a customized "earn-in" system (Baty, 1981). Each major task could be assigned a specific value, such as a certain number of shares, in advance of completion. When the task is finished, the shares are allocated to the internal team member or partner responsible for the completion of the task. As the venture progresses, other tasks can be added to the list, and their valuation should be agreed upon in advance. While the above system may sound appealing, it has both strong and weak points, as outlined in the following sections.

Advantages of the "Earn-In" System

- It eliminates the arbitrariness and potential unfairness of simply giving most of the stock to the one or two people who were on board first.

- By relating distribution to actual accomplished tasks, each partner has a special motivation to perform and bring the task to completion.

- Since completed tasks trigger stock distribution, non-performing internal team members or partners can be divested more easily than if they held a share of the firm's equity negotiated and received during the venture's beginning.

Disadvantages of the "Earn-In" System

- It is very hard to correctly gauge the relative difficulty and corresponding value of accomplishing specific goals. For example, the effort needed to write a business plan can be estimated fairly easy, but what is the value of raising capital, especially in a tight market?

- The mere completion of a task is not necessarily the same as outstanding completion. As always, the quality of work is more elusive to measure than quantity.

- It is likely that the future abilities and contributions of individual team members will be quite different in nature and value than the contributions during the start-up phase. The individual who was very good at getting start-up tasks done may prove later to be of much less value than the team member who contributes outstanding managerial skills, yet they may both hold equal amounts of stock (Baty, 1981, p. 45).

The types of compensation available to team members often vary with the stage of development of the firm and its financial position. For example, as mentioned previously, during the earliest stages of development, the firm generally needs to conserve cash outflows; hence, salaries might be lower than those found in comparable but already established firms and bonuses and fringe benefits may be deferred. Once the venture progresses into more mature stages, however, salaries can be raised and bonuses and fringe benefits can be added.

If entrepreneurs wish to use company stock as part of the compensation system, they need to ensure that stock will be available when needed to reward the team member's contributions to the venture, especially if the entrepreneur's philosophy is to reward team members when *future* contributions materialize, rather than for their record of *past* activities, which could be, for all practical purposes, with another firm. As time passes and the venture grows, substantial changes in an internal member's contributions may occur, new team members may be added, outside investors may dilute the equity positions of current team members, team members may exit the venture voluntarily or involuntarily, and divorce or even death may occur. Considering all these possibilities, it is quite obvious that the chances of stock ending up with individuals who no longer work for the venture is relatively high. All of these possibilities need to be reconciled with the belief that internal team members should be rewarded for what they achieve while they are still part of a team, and not when they are no longer with the team.

Timmons (2001) recommends several ways to protect the venture from the possible situations described above, while at the same time providing current team members an incentive for performing well. For instance, to provide an ongoing reward stream, stock can be purchased by the team and placed in an escrow account, to be released over a certain period of time, perhaps 3 or 4 years. A second alternative is to set up a buy-back agreement that will allow the venture to repurchase an individual's stock whenever certain conditions are met.

A third and perhaps the most popular option is to use a stock vesting agreement. Under this agreement, the firm identifies some period of time, such as 3 to 4 years, during which team members deciding to leave the venture are required to sell the stock back to the company at the original price paid for it, which for start-ups is typically nothing.

However, if the entrepreneur feels that some team members should be rewarded for their past performance despite their departure from the firm, a vesting agreement can be written that allows team members to keep a portion of their shares for every month or every year that they were part of the firm. To further ensure fairness, vesting agreements can also be set up placing heavier weight on the more recent years of the vesting period. Such agreements highlight the facts that *venturing* is a long-term process requiring commitment and dedication, and that the reward structure of the venture is based strictly on successfully building the firm and nothing else (Timmons, 2001).

The Family Business: A Special Type of Internal Team

Some of the largest and most prominent public and privately held firms in the country are "family" businesses: Ford, Marriott, Levi Strauss, Playboy, Anheuser-Busch, Coors, and many others. Several of these firms have passed ownership to several succeeding generations, extending back 100 years and more. The visibility of family business as a concept has increased dramatically during the last few years, with classes on operating family businesses offered at universities, family business research institutes being set up, workshops being offered, and consulting experts targeting specialized seminars dealing with topics unique to the family business.

Family businesses comprise a special form of an internal team. Because of their unique characteristics, there is a growing recognition that the "family" part of a family business, with its inherent family dynamics, has a critical influence on the business itself, especially as it relates to succession (Dyer & Handler, 1994). Unfortunately, not much is yet known about family firms, and statistics vary as far as their survival rate is concerned. Research shows that only 3 in 10 family firms make it through the second generation, and only 1 in 10 make it through the third. Furthermore, the average life-span of an entrepreneurial firm is only 24, the usual length of time the founding entrepreneur is associated with the firm (Kets de Vries, 1993).

Despite their importance in the American economy, family businesses have a complex set of problems not completely addressed by classical management theory. One such problem is the effect of conflict within the family due to "family distance." This distance may be a case of in-laws versus blood relatives or cousins versus immediate family (Davis & Harveston, 2001). Tension and conflict are, of course, inevitable ingredients of a successful organization, and the idea is not to live in a perfect world, free of conflict. However, the objective is to prevent the buildup of years of disagreement and anger that, if unmanaged, can burst out and blacken the family and the family firm's future (Hutcheson, 2002).

Exhibit 10.3, identifies three circumstances in which an individual can become part of a family business: launching a venture with a family member(s), joining a family venture early

Exhibit 10.3	Joining the Family Firm: Issues to Consider

1. Launching a venture with a family member (a start-up or buyout).
- Who is the lead entrepreneur?
- What are the specific strengths and weaknesses of each member of the team?
- What are the backgrounds of each member of the team in other areas of the business?
- What are the specific responsibilities of each member of the team?
- How much money will each member of the team contribute, and how will equity be divided?
- Under what circumstances, and on what terms, will non-family members be brought into the venture?

2. Joining a family venture early in its operation.
- What is the exact definition of each family member's area of responsibility and to whom will he or she be responsible?
- What forms of compensation will be used (salary, bonus, equity shares, or a combination)?
- How will conflicts be handled, particularly when they involve non-performing family members?
- What is the initial contribution required, and can it be redeemed if there is a change of mind and heart?

3. Joining a family company as a second- or third-generation member.
- What exactly will the individual's accomplishments be under the family umbrella that could not be accomplished as well somewhere else?
- What will the individual's role be? Dutiful apprentice? Head of an autonomous division? Eventual chairman and CEO?
- Given the present organizational and managerial structure of the family firm, how much leeway will individual newcomers have in advancing ideas, even if they fail?

Source: Adapted from Timmons, 2001.

in its operation, or joining as a later-generation member. Within each of these circumstances, there are both unique and overlapping questions that need to be considered before entering the family business.

Family businesses historically have been characterized by the literature as antithetical to effective management practices and internal team building, because of nepotism and non-rational managerial behavior influenced by the family ties and emotions (Dyer, 1994).

Levinson (1985) suggests the following reasons for the problems common to family-owned businesses:

- *Difficulty in obtaining outside capital:* Investors may be discouraged from joining a closely held family firm because they question the firm's potential for future growth.

- *Complex questions regarding estate planning and tax liability:* Such technical issues frequently require outside advisors and consultants who are typically not trusted by family members. It also means opening up the company's books and the family's individual personal financial records, an unpopular option for many family members, with dire consequences as far as a smooth succession transition is concerned.

- *Dashing the desires and expectations of second- or third-generation members:* Involvement of second- or third-generation family members should be purely voluntary. The family firm should make sure they feel welcome and let them know that they will be supported in whatever they choose to do. Rules should be formulated describing the terms of their participation so they know what the expectations are and how they can progress within the family business. Some experts even recommend that next-generation members be encouraged to first develop their experience with another firm and then come back to the family business.

- *Succession problems:* This is generally considered one of the most difficult issues for family firms and a quick road to failure. Successors need to be identified, trained, and in place before the patriarch or matriarch leaves.

- *Conflicts regarding expenditures:* Family members often oppose needed expenditures that may contribute to greater earnings and constitute an investment in the family firm's future, because they fear they will reduce their dividends and subsequent income from the firm. Sometimes, outside advisors are needed to convince these family members, while some other times it is just a matter of showing them on paper.

- *Family cliques develop rapidly:* Far too many personal situations, such as sibling rivalry, can be played out in the family and transferred to the business arena. They have the potential to rub emotions raw and create warring camps, and conflict quickly spreads to non-family employees, which worsens the situation. One suggestion for combating this problem is to develop a family mission statement or covenant that lays out the ground rules of how the family wishes to work together, and identifies the "game rules" for the family's behavior in case of conflict.

- *Leadership is "fuzzy":* The president of a family firm may not be in charge, but in reality, the "family" as a whole, may be running the daily operations, by imposing for instance, limits on the amount that can be spent for capital expenditures without family permission. One way to combat this situation is to have an outside board providing balance and a better perspective.

- *Non-performing family members:* A family member lacking managerial talent and performance is a potential disaster. The best thing to do is to move him/her into a job that retains their sense of self-worth but does not impact negatively on the firm. If this is not done, other employees, especially non-family employees, lose their respect for the family firm's leadership.

- *High non-family employee turnover:* Sometimes this is a result of relatives who resent outside talent and make their lives miserable, while at other times it happens because promotions are not available to non-family members when only family members occupy most of the firm's top-level managerial positions. If such turnover occurs, it is necessary to find out why, and an exit interview is one way of understanding the roots of this problem.

- *Inequitable compensation:* Complaints about inequitable compensation are not unusual, and it is a problem that never seems to be completely resolved. Compensation should be fair and based on competitive salaries within the local area, with fringe benefits that enable family members to build their personal assets. Above all, pay should be based on the type of work the family member does, not based on the family relationship, which can lead to accusations of nepotism.

Entrepreneurial Couples as an Internal Team

Randi and Debbi Fields of Mrs. Fields Cookies have built a very successful firm. Fred and Gale Hayman built Giorgio Beverly Hills into a multimillion boutique and fragrance line until they divorced in 1983. These are just two examples of the many couples combining "marriage and management" in a special type of family business, involving the concept of an entrepreneurial couple. When their venture is successful, couples claim that their teamwork improves both their home and business lives. If unsuccessful, however, the business and their personal relationship can suffer; hence, the ability to compromise becomes critical if the couple wishes to stay together. Entrepreneurial couples or *copreneurs* also contend that their arrangement cuts down on the politics in the firm, allows for easier communication, and provides for a unique closeness that cannot be experienced in more traditional firms (Carson, Michals, & Baum, 1986).

One of the problems of such an arrangement, however, is the tendency to play and work together, rather than to keep these activities separate. In addition, even though there are assumptions about an egalitarian style of family business ownership, research has shown that copreneurs define their work and home boundaries very differently in terms of sex-role orientation, self-concept at work and home, and marital and business equity. More specifically, copreneurial couples still maintain a conceptual boundary between work and home, and they rely on gender differences to define their roles within the domains of love and work (Marshack, 1994). Another issue is the question of who is in charge. Almost overwhelmingly, these couples recommend that one partner be in charge and that clear lines of labor be set up. If there is any uncertainty in this area, problems quickly develop. Responses to the Work-Home Identity Scale (Friedlander, 1990), indicate however, that typically the husband is the leader and decision maker at work and at home, while the wife is consistently the support person.

Divorce: The Internal Team's Nightmare

Ann Bass, former wife of Texas millionaire Sid Bass, received a divorce settlement valued at $200 million. Other spouses have received large chunks of equity from their spouse's business as part of their divorce settlements. And yet, only a few years ago, the idea of one-half of a married couple taking control of the other's business through a divorce decree was virtually unheard of. Today's legal system supports the belief that both parties to a marriage make contributions, such as financial and otherwise, to form marital assets, which can include a company. If one or both spouses owned an interest in a business that was started, acquired, or gained value during the marriage, it should be part of the distribution of property (Wojahn, 1986, p. 55). While it is rare that a settlement ends with a spouse displacing the business founder, it is not without precedent. Generally, the position of the court is that a divorce should end a relationship, not keep the couple together in a shared investment. Thus, most divorce settlements result in an exchange of cash or other non-business assets.

Frequently, it is not the cash settlement, however, that causes the entrepreneur the greatest trouble. Instead, if the case goes to court, it is the subpoenas, depositions, expensive litigation, and the possibility of having to open the company's books that represents the most trouble. It disrupts work, distracts employees, and can give the company a reputation for instability with lenders, customers, and investors. It is therefore advisable to resolve the dispute and settle through negotiations and compromise, before it goes to litigation and the family's dirty linen gets aired in front of employees and tax authorities, while suppliers and customers get nervous and may look elsewhere (Nelton, 1991). Furthermore, if business valuators are called in to appraise the company and assign it a value, the nightmare only gets worse. Valuations of small start-up firms are difficult to make and open to highly subjective judgments. It is no wonder that pre- and post-nuptial agreements are becoming popular among today's entrepreneurs; they serve to protect the firm's assets from being used as part of a settlement in a messy divorce, and most importantly, they protect against the dilution of the firm's ownership.

EXTERNAL TEAMS

"An expert is someone who knows more and more about less and less. . . ."

(Unknown)

The venture start-up process has become so complex that it virtually necessitates the use of part-time, one-time, or periodic advisors in a variety of areas. Bankers, lawyers, accountants, insurance agents, specialized consultants, outside board members, and venture capitalists are all part of an **external team**. These experts can help the venture remain up to date on the latest technology, with changes in the law, tax consequences, help obtain financing, protect the firm's assets, and they can provide a number of other specialized services. Knowing how to find good professional advisors, what roles they can fulfill, how to select the best ones for a particular situation, and how to cultivate long-term relationships with them can be invaluable during the early stages of the venture's development. At the same time, using these experts wisely can lower the company's requirements and costs for full-time, in-house expertise.

The Lawyer

One of the most difficult tasks facing entrepreneurs may be finding a good lawyer. Unfortunately, this decision is not always optimal, because entrepreneurs frequently do not know how or where to look for a good lawyer. They follow shortcuts; they use well-meaning but ill-conceived recommendations, they hire lawyers on the basis of low fees, or they use lawyers lacking competence in the specific areas needed because they know them personally or have used them successfully for another purpose. Often they end up receiving poor advice, and subsequently they develop a lack of faith in their lawyer's professional judgment.

Most entrepreneurs know little about the law in general, and they probably know even less about the specific rules and regulations affecting their particular ventures. Yet, there are so many important areas in which a good lawyer can aid a budding entrepreneur, such as setting up partnership agreements or incorporating, electing corporate officers, writing and negotiating contracts, examining leases, creating effective non-compete agreements, protecting intellectual property through patents, trademarks, and copyrights. They can also assist by consulting on tax issues, participating in stock underwriting agreements as well as other functions involved in public and private stock placements, helping to distribute stock, developing stock vesting agreements, locating potential investors, defending the entrepreneur against lawsuits, providing answers to legal questions, and many other areas of much-needed advice. Perhaps a better way of looking at this issue is how much a poor lawyer can cost the entrepreneur beyond the legal fee.

It is unrealistic to expect most entrepreneurs to have a detailed knowledge of many of the venture's legal considerations, but on the other hand, lawyers, no matter how much they are trusted, cannot be given unlimited decision-making power and authority to make decisions for the owner. Good legal expertise is critical, but it must also be carefully managed. This means that at least a working knowledge of the areas of law most relevant to the firm is a resource well worth having. It allows the entrepreneur to understand the lawyer's thinking process and ask the right kind of questions.

Small income-producing businesses may have limited needs for legal representation, but the potentially high-growth venture needs to invest considerable time and energy into a search for good legal representation. That is why many experts suggest that growing firms are better off using larger, more prestigious law firms, even though given the particular business and the existing financial resources, a good small law firm may make more sense. Certainly cost is important, but it should not be the sole or even the most important criterion in choosing legal representation. Larger law firms generally have greater prestige, which can influence or intimidate opponents in your favor. They have greater resources and more internal experts from whom to draw advice and expertise, and they have probably had a greater exposure to a variety of different legal cases and issues. On the other hand, large law firms are often criticized as being less creative, shunting smaller accounts to junior partners, having higher costs, and seldom referring clients to outside experts if in-house help is available, with no consideration of the quality of inside versus outside expertise (Rollinson, 1985).

The best time to choose an attorney is when one is not needed. Most people wait until they have a problem big enough that they cannot handle on their own before thinking of contacting an attorney. They will be in a panic and in a rush. However, when choosing the person that they may have to rely on to save their business, entrepreneurs do not want to be in a panic or in a rush. The entrepreneur might opt for Yellow Pages advertisements, advertisements on television, radio, etc., or the local bar association attorney referral system, where attorneys provide information about their areas of specialization, which is rarely verified, in the hope of increasing their business. Additionally, many attorneys have websites providing an abundance of information about their location, how many attorneys are in the firm, the different backgrounds and areas of practice of the attorneys, e-mail access, etc. The fact that the law firm has a website is a positive sign that the firm is comfortable with technologically up-to-date methods of communication.

Unless the choice is limited to a family member or a friend, the search for good lawyer should begin with a source found in most libraries, namely, the *Martindale-Hubbell Law Directory*. It is the most comprehensive directory of lawyers available, and it includes ratings on a limited number of those listed from confidential surveys of attorneys and judges who have worked with them. This way, entrepreneurs can find out how the attorneys on their list are viewed by their peers. If a lawyer is not rated, it should not be viewed negatively. It could simply mean that he/she just has not been rated yet. The ratings are as follows:

- *AV:* Legal ability is very high to preeminent.

- *BV:* Legal ability is high to very high.

- *CV:* Legal ability is fair to high.

Another good approach is to ask for recommendations from other entrepreneurs, bankers, accountants, and others who come into contact with the legal profession. Usually people who do a great job running their businesses expect only the best from the people they hire. If they demand the best and they are satisfied with their attorney, this should be the first name on the list of attorneys to interview. However, individuals tend to refer lawyers based on their own experiences and needs, many of which might be quite different from those at hand.

Another way to find a good attorney is to contact a law school and/or the state's bar association to determine whether they have continuing legal education departments. Attorneys have to take a certain number of credit hours each year, under *continuing legal education* (CLE) programs, to maintain their licenses to practice law. Law schools and bar associations frequently sponsor these CLE seminars, which means that they hire attorneys who are experts in their areas of specialty as speakers or instructors. A seminar usually involves five or six expert attorneys who speak about various aspects of a particular legal topic, such as employment law, business law for the entrepreneur, legal issues for the family-owned business, etc. To find a seminar on a topic closely related to the owner's specific business needs, some law school and bar association CLE departments have websites, and if not, they can be contacted by phone.

Finally, another way to find a good attorney is to actually go to the courthouse. The clerks at the courthouse have a great deal of "inside" information on lots of attorneys, because they deal with them every day. Although officially they are not supposed to do so, many civil litigation clerks often give recommendations, if asked, on who has a good reputation for representing businesses and who is respected around the courthouse (Boyd, 2001).

Once a list of possible legal representatives has been identified, appointments should be set with the most likely candidates. When calling for an appointment, entrepreneurs should explain that they are seeking an attorney with whom they want to establish a business relationship, and that they need to set a 15-minute, free, get-acquainted visit. If attorneys do not agree to an interview for a few minutes without charge, they should be crossed off the list, because their legal fees are probably too high. If they cannot incorporate the interview into their schedule within 2–3 days, unless they are in the middle of a trial, they should also be crossed off the list, because they are probably too busy.

The entrepreneur should go into the interview with a set of questions developed in advance, such as: Who are their current clients? Have they been dropped by any small firms, and if so, why? How much time will they be able to spend with the owner? In the event they are not available, how much time will their partners or assistants be able to spend with the owner? What kinds of relevant experiences have they had? What is their specific expertise? Some sample questions and their rationale are suggested below (Boyd, 2001).

How long have you been in practice? What types of legal issues have you handled?

Clients mistakenly believe that attorneys already know how to handle every legal issue. They do not. The reason is that the body of law is so huge that no one can be an expert on everything. So, attorneys specialize. The first time they handle a certain type of case or legal question, it takes them longer because they are learning on the job. This is a problem for the entrepreneur if the attorney is paid by the hour, yet gets training and education through research at the entrepreneur's expense. Therefore, a better choice is someone who has been practicing law for a few years already, has gained experience, and has had the opportunity to handle a number of different legal matters, and specifically the ones that concern the entrepreneur.

Do you represent other entrepreneurs, family-owned businesses, and small businesses?

The entrepreneurial venture's legal needs will be different from those of an older, established business or a giant corporation. Entrepreneurs need attorneys with a similar mindset and a vision toward innovation, creativity, and fresh ways of doing business. If an attorney has represented only large corporations, he or she may not understand the small venture's financial constraints or the need for fast-paced decisions. A like-minded attorney will be identifying legal issues that the entrepreneur may not even have thought of yet, because he or she has worked already with a number of other similar firms and can help predict problems and mistakes that should be avoided.

How quickly do you respond to telephone calls? Do you have e-mail access? Do you have a pager/cell phone?

One of the biggest complaints that clients make about their attorneys is inaccessibility. If attorneys cannot promise to return phone calls within 24 hours, or immediately in case of an emergency, they should be crossed off the list. The attorney's office staff must be able to reach him or her anytime, anywhere, whether by pager or cell phone. There is an old story about the founder of a giant fast-food chain that wanted to talk to an attorney when he was getting started on a Saturday. He tried calling a number of attorneys, and he finally found one working on Saturday. That business was not very big at the time, but it grew into one of the largest hamburger restaurant chains in the world, and that attorney was certainly glad that he was both working that Saturday and willing to take on that small client.

How much do you charge?

Legal fees are obviously of paramount importance. In fact, fear of expensive legal fees is probably the biggest reason that people avoid using attorneys. However, a clear understanding of the timing and the amount of the legal charges makes contacting an attorney much easier. An attorney should be willing to create different types of fee arrangements, depending on the venture's needs and cash flow. The following are some common fee arrangements.

Hourly rate. Most attorneys charge by the hour. One of the best reasons for interviewing more than one attorney is to get a basis for comparison within the legal community. People often assume that the rate quoted is set, but it may be negotiable. Many lawyers will consider a reduced rate for a venture start-up with the idea that when the firm reaches success, it will become a valuable client that can later be charged the standard rate. An attorney can also offer a discount for repeat business for clients with an ongoing relationship, and a long-term commitment, or agree for a legal fee payment to be spread over 2 to 3 months or more. The attorney should also be able to give an estimate of the number of hours a particular job will take. This way a cap can be placed on the job, and a limit set on the amount of money the entrepreneur spends, to determine whether the attorney will do the job for that amount, or an associate will do the work under the direction of the partner. The rate should be less for an associate and significantly less for a legal assistant.

Contingency fee. If an attorney is representing a client in a case that may generate money damages or payments due the client from the other party, attorneys may agree to take a percentage of whatever damages, payments, etc. that they obtain for their client. The percentage varies according to how much action the attorney is required to take and is negotiable, especially if some of the legal research was done by the entrepreneur.

Flat fee. Sometimes attorneys charge fixed rates for specific services, such as a standard will for example, no matter how many hours of work are involved. If they already have a standardized form of a will on the computer, it does not take much time to make the specific changes pertaining to the specific individual and circumstances. So, it does not hurt to ask for a price break especially when a client pays bills on time, or as part of a fee arrangement that includes other services being billed on an hourly basis or contingency fee.

Annual retainer. Attorneys sometimes ask for a retainer, and what they mean is a deposit toward work they will begin in the future. This is different than an annual or monthly retainer, which clients who have a fairly predictable amount of legal work each month or year pay to keep an attorney "on retainer." This means that the attorney and the client have determined a monthly or yearly fee that the client pays for all specified work, no matter how much or how little time it takes. This helps a client budget an exact amount for routine legal work, but there are certain services that are excluded and are charged separately. Having an attorney during a venture start-up on a small monthly retainer makes him or her available to answer questions, which can prevent expensive mistakes. Many attorneys welcome a consistent, even though small, monthly income, particularly if the venture has the potential of becoming a steady and permanent client.

After the interviews, the selection must be made based on the outcome of the interview, recommendations, ratings from *Martindale and Hubbell,* and recognition of the importance of having trust and faith in this person's judgment; therefore, the personal chemistry must be right. Entrepreneurs need to feel relaxed and comfortable with the attorney since he or she will play an important role in the venture's future. Entrepreneurs need to keep looking until they find the attorney who is accessible, will work with them on rates, and makes them feel welcome and respected. Rollinson (1985) offers some other suggestions:

1. *Avoid moonlighting lawyers:* They may be violating an obligation of loyalty by the very act of moonlighting, and they may not be able to provide timely services.

2. *Avoid hiring the first attorney you talk to:* Attorneys should be considered like any other employee. Before a new employee is hired, several applicants are interviewed to select the best one for the job.

3. *Avoid waiting until you have a huge legal problem before finding an attorney to work with:* Attorneys can save the venture money by consulting them *before* taking action.

4. *Avoid lawyers willing to take equity for services:* Exchanging stock for services is tempting because it conserves much-needed cash and it ties the recipient attorney to the best interest of the venture. However, it is generally preferable to be in a position where, if needed, lawyers can be changed without incurring problems because they are also part owners. A lawyer should be offering dispassionate advice, not as an owner, but as a truly independent external advisor.

5. *Negotiate the legal fee:* If attorneys are convinced that the firm will be a dependable paying client, they will usually give a price break while the business is getting started.

6. *Pay bills on time:* Maintaining a good relationship with attorneys means paying them on time, which also provides them with a good incentive to possibly give the venture a price break at some later date.

7. *Avoid verbal fee agreements:* Fee agreements should always be in writing. This written agreement should clearly state for what services and for how much the venture will be charged, including items such as, photocopies, filing fees, etc.

8. *Preparing for meetings with the attorney:* The more of the attorney's time the entrepreneur wastes, the higher the cost. Therefore, in preparing for a meeting with an attorney, the entrepreneur needs to write down every question that needs to be asked, bring all documents that relate to the specific case, and finally provide an outline of the facts that led to the case, in the order in which they occurred.

9. *Tell the attorney the truth:* Because the attorney is on the entrepreneur's side, it makes no sense to leave important information and details out. The attorney is the one who should decide whether the information is relevant.

10. *Establish a long-lasting relationship with the attorney:* The best type of relationship for an entrepreneur getting started is one in which the attorney not only provides legal services, but also acts as a mentor and confidant, in which case there is a

need to candidly discuss whether and how much the firm will be charged for the part of the relationship that involves mentoring and brainstorming. That part of the attorney's services may be the most valuable.

Of course, the best way to handle problems is to prevent them, and most problems with attorneys stem from lack of communication. Entrepreneurs need to make clear what they expect from their attorney, and they should not assume that the attorney already knows what the expectations are. If attorneys were hired only to tackle a specific legal problem or to act as business advisors and mentors, they need to be explicitly told about the role they need to play in the venture's business.

If, in spite of doing all this, an entrepreneur still encounters a problem with attorneys, he or she needs to discuss it very frankly with them, and if the choice of an attorney has been undertaken with care, any problems can be comfortably communicated and openly tackled. The attorney should be given a chance to correct a troublesome situation, and if the problem ultimately cannot be resolved, all attempts to resolve the matter with the attorney first have failed, and it *does* seem that the attorney has acted inappropriately, a serious step can be taken—the attorney can be reported to the state bar association. The state bar association will investigate the matter and can take action, if necessary, to discipline the attorney. On the other hand, if the problem ultimately cannot be resolved, all attempts to resolve the matter with the attorney first have failed, and it *does not* seem that the attorney has acted inappropriately to warrant a report to the state bar association, it is time to terminate the relationship and hire a new lawyer. But a new lawyer cannot accept the entrepreneur as a new client until the relationship with the former attorney has ended and the important documents from the former attorney's files have been retrieved.

Finally, one of the ways entrepreneurs can save some money on legal fees is to do research on their own, but even though it is fairly easy to find what the law says, an attorney is still needed to apply it to the specific situation. A good tip to remember is that there are federal laws and there are state laws. Federal laws apply to all of us as individuals and businesses, while state laws apply only to the individuals and businesses within a particular state. State laws can vary from state to state, and they are valid only if they are not in conflict with federal laws. A quick review of the different parts of the American legal system is listed here (Boyd, 2001):

- *U.S. Constitution:* The federal Constitution is the foundation of the American legal system. Every other law is valid only if it does not conflict with the United States Constitution. It would be unusual for a business to have a legal issue involving the federal Constitution, but if it does, an attorney definitely needs to be hired. (For a copy of the Constitution, see http://www.law.cornell.edu: 80/constitution/constitution.)

- *State constitutions:* Each state has its own constitution, but it should not be in conflict with the U.S. Constitution.

- *Federal treaties:* These are agreements between the United States government and other countries. States cannot make their own treaties. Again, it would be unusual for a business to have a legal issue involving treaties, but if it does, it needs to hire a lawyer specializing in this area.

- *Statutes:* These are laws written by the legislature and are what we normally think of when we talk about "the law." The United States Congress creates federal statutes, while state statutes are created by state legislators. These statutes will definitely affect any type of business.

- *Ordinances:* Laws passed by local municipalities that also affect a business.

- *Administrative regulations:* These are rules created by federal administrative agencies. Depending on the type of business, they will have either a great deal of impact or almost no impact at all.

- *Case law:* These are the decisions made as a result of lawsuits and court cases. Since statutes are applied and interpreted to reach a decision, case law is very helpful in understanding statutes, which are usually not very clear and are ambiguous. Sometimes it takes a judge in a court case to decide what the legislators really meant when they wrote the statute. An example occurred when a state legislature was writing a law to create a pedestrian–traffic-only area in a state park. What they actually wrote was that, *"no four-wheeled vehicles"* would be permitted in the designated area. The problem was with that particular language which *did not* exclude motorcycle traffic, which the legislators meant to do, and it *did* exclude parents pushing baby strollers (technically a "four-wheeled" vehicle), which they did not mean to do. What brought the problem to the attention of the court was that a veteran's group wanted to put a monument in the designated area of the park, and the monument they had in mind was a World War II army jeep, a "four-wheeled" vehicle prohibited by the statute. It took a lawsuit and the court's application and interpretation of the statute to make its meaning clear.

Although many do-it-yourself guides advise individuals to start with a trip to the local law library, there are numerous law libraries on line, and most have links to others. A good place to start is www.law.cornell.edu/. This is the Legal Information Institute of Cornell Law School, which in addition to providing federal law also has the state statutes from all fifty states. It also has links to many other legal sources and websites. See Exhibit 10.4 for other great resources.

The Venture Capitalist

The great majority of professional venture capitalists are in the business of "building businesses." They are not looking to make a quick buck; they are generally in it for the long haul. Certainly there are times when they must exit from a losing proposition, but their investments are usually made with the belief that it will take a long time before they begin to pay off. Therefore, even though the main role of venture capitalists is to raise capital for potentially high-growth ventures, this is only one aspect of their job, albeit the most important. They recognize that they must be an active part of an external team, providing contributions wherever they can, not only to safeguard their financial investment but also to help a venture grow and achieve its goals.

Gorman and Sahlman (1986, p. 426) identified the following additional roles fulfilled by venture capitalists:

1. Providing additional financing
2. Strategic planning
3. Management recruiting
4. Operational planning
5. Resolving compensation issues
6. Introducing potential customers and suppliers
7. Recruiting board members

| Exhibit 10.4 | Compliance-oriented Website Information |

Website	URL
Copyright website	http://www.benedict.com
Nick Szabo, Smart Contracts (good discussion of "smart contracts")	http://szabo.best.vwh.net/smart.contracts.html
The Institute of International Commercial Law (Pace University) (information on contracts for international sale of goods)	http://cisgw3.law.pace.edu/
The Center for Internet and Society (Stanford University) (studies law and policy around the Internet and emerging technologies)	http://cyberlaw.stanford.edu/
The U.S. Consumer Product Safety Commission (CPSC) (online versions of CPSC publications)	http://www.cpsc.gov/
The LawEngine.com (online legal research source)	http://thelawengine.com/
Findlaw (directory of law-related websites offers numerous links to all aspects of contract law)	http://www.findlaw.com/
The Federal Trade Commission	http://www.ftc.gov/
The International Revenue Service (information about limited liability corporations)	http://www.irs.gov/Businesses/Small-Businesses-&-Self-Employed/Limited-Liability-Company-%28LLC%29
Hoover's Online (collection of data on U.S. corporations)	http://www.hoovers.com
Cornell University Law School's Legal Information Institute (information on agency law)	http://www.law.cornell.edu/wex/agency
USA.gov (A-Z Index of U.S. government departments and agencies)	http://www.usa.gov/directory/federal/index.shtml
LawGuru.com (links to more than 400 legal search engines and indices from a single location)	http://lawguru.com
The Internet Law Library (sponsored by the U.S. House of Representatives) (offers links to legislative and regulatory materials)	http://www.lawguru.com/ilawlib/
The 'Lectric Law Library's Legal Lexicon (legal encyclopedia)	http://www.lectlaw.com/d-a.htm
The 'Lectric Law Library's Business & General Legal Forms	http://www.lectlaw.com/formb.htm
U.S. Equal Employment Opportunity Commission (Federal Equal Employment Opportunity Laws)	http://www.eeoc.gov/facts/qanda.html
The University of Waterloo's Scholarly Societies Project (information on professional standards for various professional organizations)	http://www.lib.uwaterloo.ca/society/standards.html
The Occupational Safety & Health Administration (OSHA) (information related to workplace health and safety)	http://www.osha.gov/
The U.S. Small Business Administration (information on forming, financing, managing, and operating a business)	http://www.sbaonline.sba.gov/
The U.S. Bureau of Labor Statistics (data on employment)	http://stats.bls.gov/blshome.html
The Library of Congress (federal/congressional information)	http://thomas.loc.gov/
World Intellectual Property Organization	http://www.wipo.int/portal/index.html.en
The U.S. Patent and Trademark Office (online access to U.S. and international trademark and patent resources)	http://www.uspto.gov/

8. Managing the investor group

9. Helping entrepreneurs find professional services such as accounting, law, consultation

10. Providing a sounding board for the entrepreneur

Professional venture capital firms specialize in providing seed capital for a person walking in with a yellow notepad and the "seed" of an idea, but with no business plan and no prototype, just an idea. Others focus on a combination of seed, start-up, or later-stage financing, or leveraged buyouts, having several different funds for which they raise money for different stages of financing, or they may simply provide capital to a variety of firms at different stages of development. Regardless, venture capital firms cannot be all things to all people. In other words, their financing activities may favor certain industries in which they possess a modicum of expertise, such as high-tech ventures, or they may favor certain geographic areas. What this means is that entrepreneurs must do their homework to find out which venture capital firms specialize in the industry of their interest. They must seek out advice and referrals by networking with those acquainted with these venture capital firms, such as other entrepreneurs, lawyers, bankers, etc. Directories, such as the one published by the National Venture Capital Association or regional associations, such as the Oklahoma Investment Forum, can also be very helpful.

Timmons (2001) made the following suggestions for contacting venture capital firms. First, the nature of the venture capital industry dictates that the idea or the venture proposal must be presented to multiple potential investors, but not in a mass-mail fashion. Rather, with proper referral and introduction, the venture proposal should be presented to 5–10 firms that have been identified as potential investors in the venture. These firms need to have enough financial resources to fund the venture to completion, barring any unforeseen circumstances, and they need to know what it takes to bring a product to market in a specific industry, both in terms of time and money. Finally, the venture capital firm must also have experienced personnel, knowledgeable in the specific industry and willing and able to help with the start-up process. Frequently, the first contact with venture capitalists is over the phone, and this may be the first and last chance entrepreneurs have to persuade them of the feasibility of the venture idea and to express enthusiasm and commitment for it. If the entrepreneur is successful, however, the venture capitalist will ask to see the business plan, and the process begins. But the typical funding rate by venture capitalists is 2–3% of the business plans they review, so many obstacles must be overcome. Venture capitalists want to see well-thought-out business plans with a strong management team and a manageable and business-oriented entrepreneur willing to work with the venture capital firm. They look for a novel technology with a strong intellectual property position, potential for quick and short-term cash flow (preferably less than 12 months), possible technology applications in multiple markets, a clear path to exit, and finally an adequate venture fund "burn rate" (Paiva, 2003).

On the other hand, rejection by a venture capitalist is not the kiss of death. A study of rejected ventures by Bruno and Tyebjee (1983) found that 70% of them were operating within 3 years of their initial denial by venture capitalists.

The Accountant

Years ago, an accountant was synonymous with the bookkeeping function of a small business, but no longer. Today, accounting firms are aggressively competing for the business of new ventures with the belief that they can be a member of a start-up's external team and that they can help the venture grow into a lucrative big-business client. The plethora of services offered by accountants is a far cry from the past, when they merely helped with bookkeeping and setting up an initial accounting system.

Virtually every medium- and large-sized accounting firm offers some variation of the following services: cash control, establishing and maintaining an effective accounting system, auditing, tax consultation, personal financial planning, deal making by helping to secure financing, and many other services. Frequently, these are offered to entrepreneurial ventures with high growth potential at a substantial discount or with deferred payments. Some of the larger accounting firms even provide rent-free office space, software that helps write a business plan, and contacts and referrals with equipment lessors, banks, and other sources of capital. These areas are only one small part of the services offered by today's accounting firms. In fact, many of the services they offer to emerging ventures emanate from their consulting departments rather than their more traditional accounting functions.

Unfortunately, these services are not typically available for small, income-oriented businesses. Given their limited resources and growth potential, and the sizeable fees commanded by larger accounting firms, most small, income-oriented businesses often opt to use smaller accounting firms or independent CPAs to do their taxes or to help them set up bookkeeping and/or accounting systems.

Some issues of concern in selecting an accountant as a member of the venture's external team should be the nature of the legal relationship between the venture and the accountant, and the nature of their liability if errors or omissions are made on the venture's financial statements. Mistakes can be made which affect the venture's future, and the entrepreneur should be able to recover all or part of any damages caused by the accounting firm's negligence.

Given the extensive number of services offered by accountants today, how should entrepreneurs choose an individual accountant or an accounting firm that will give them the kind of help they need during the start-up stage and later, as the firm progresses and the problems change? The answer lies in identifying the specific tasks with which help is needed, such as closing books to complete the financial statements, preparing tax filings, developing a more effective control system, etc. Once the most pressing needs have been identified, the question becomes whether a national, regional, or local firm can best serve the venture. Regardless how big or what type of firm is chosen, some overwhelming considerations apply when selecting an accountant as a member of the venture's external team:

1. Look for previous experience with start-up ventures.

2. Make sure they communicate clearly, because not every entrepreneur understands the language of accounting.

3. Look for someone or a firm that has broad expertise and can give advice not only on accounting but also on managerial, marketing, financial issues, and on all general aspects of the venture.

4. Consider the cost of these services versus the level of service provided. Who exactly will be handling the accounting services? How often they will be available? If they are not, who will take their place?

5. Check out the firm's reputation, particularly if dealing with a branch office. Interview the individuals that will be dealing with the venture and ask for recommendations from a variety of sources, such as other accounting clients, the venture's customers, lawyers, bankers, etc.

6. Make sure they can service not only present needs but also those of the future, as the firm develops over time.

The Banker

Unlike the external team members discussed previously, entrepreneurs should establish a working relationship with a banker long before one is needed. If they wait until they actually need to borrow money, it may be too late. The worst time to ask a bank for money is when the financial need already exists; that tells the bank that the firm has already poor money management practices and is unable to forecast specific cash needs before they arise. Given the typical bank's risk-averse nature, their response to the loan request under these circumstances will probably be a resounding "no." Therefore, one of the first decisions of aspiring entrepreneurs should be to identify and secure a banking partner as an external team member that can offer a variety of services to an emerging venture, which range from lines of credit to help with other forms of financing, contacts, referrals, credit checks, tax advice, etc.

Shopping around will reveal just how different some banks are. Some banks are reluctant to deal with start-ups, while others are aggressively seeking out small firms by offering services that separate them from the run-of-the-mill commercial banks. Interestingly, while the different services available to entrepreneurs are certainly a factor for selecting a bank, the most important criterion may be the bank's philosophy toward small business and entrepreneurship, evidenced by making resources available and by working with new ventures providing a good fit for their needs. Entrepreneurs should identify that kind of philosophy by seeking prospective banking firms that do the following:

- Develop a long-term relationship with the venture.

- Exhibit a professional attitude toward the entrepreneur.

- Realize that money is just a commodity and can be had from many sources.

Entrepreneurs should also seek recommendations and references from other existing small firms by asking them to describe their experiences with specific bankers, as well as recommendations from accountants, lawyers, and other professionals. Building and maintaining a good relationship with a bank based on trust and good faith is a critical task. This good relationship needs to be maintained to formulate a successful external team partnership with that bank. Baty (1981) and Bennett (1987) offered a few common-sense suggestions for developing a healthy and mutually beneficial relationship with a bank as an external team member:

1. Financial and other information should be shared as if the banker were a full partner.

2. Make certain that the banker is never faced with surprises, because they literally hate surprises.

3. Keep the banker informed about and interested in the venture's progress by regularly sending a copy of the financial statements, press clippings, news articles, releases, and anything else that will let the bank know that the venture is doing well.

4. Never allow the firm's banking account to become overdrawn or past due on a payment.

5. When visiting or negotiating a loan, always go in prepared, with written documentation, numbers, and if available, collateral.

6. Start borrowing as soon as possible, even when there is an excess of cash, because paying off borrowed funds establishes a line of credit and builds goodwill.

The Insurance Person

Providing the venture with a comprehensive insurance package is critical in today's business environment. It is necessary to protect the firm's assets to guarantee continued operations and to ensure that any unacceptable risks are covered at affordable costs. Rising insurance costs can cause some small firms to go out of business. In some cases, insurance protection is simply unavailable. Given these difficulties and the range of services a good insurance firm can offer, it is critical to get the right insurance person on the external team, one who can provide a cost-effective insurance program that minimizes the firm's exposure in the areas in which the firm can least afford to have them exposed to potential disaster.

Perhaps not surprisingly, the insurance function involves an interesting paradox that will affect the design of insurance coverage program and its cost. The goal of a venture's management is to select an insurance firm that will help alleviate the company's exposure to risks, which if successful, theoretically reduces the insurance premiums. In contrast, an insurance firm's revenues are typically based on the total premiums paid. With this in mind, it becomes quite clear why a good insurance agent is well worth the effort put forth to find one.

Insurance firms generally provide the basic fire, liability, automobile, and worker's compensation insurance services, which are the essential kinds of insurance coverage. Sole proprietors, for example, need life insurance protection to ensure that their dependents or heirs will be safely cared for, and/or that the business will continue after the owner's death. In case of a partnership, there is a need for insurance coverage to help protect against dissolution at the time of the death of a partner. In a corporation, there may be a need for stockholder insurance. However, not all insurance firms and all agents are well versed in the specific types of life insurance coverage needed for a particular situation much less their intricate details. Additionally, other more complex and uncommon types of insurance coverage may or may not pertain to the venture's unique situation: business interruption insurance, renter's insurance, group life, group health, disability, retirement, key-man insurance, and many others. Experience suggests that the entrepreneur will be confronted with a variety of insurance questions and issues, and a good insurance agent, as part of the venture's external team, is necessary to provide the right answers.

The first step in selecting an insurance firm is to decide what type of firm to use, such as an independent agency, an insurance broker, or a direct writer. *Independent agents* can place or "broker" insurance policies with a third party because they represent several insurers at once, and they have the following advantages:

1. They are independent and not under the control of any one insurer.

2. They usually offer a greater variety of policies and insurers.

3. They usually provide better services, since they have a financial incentive to serve clients in a customized fashion.

4. They usually have better claims representation.

5. They have greater knowledge since they must be well versed in many types of insurance ("Selecting the Right Insurance Agency," 1986, pp. 62–65).

Brokers are similar to independent agents in some ways but very dissimilar in others. For instance, they may be able to provide services that an independent agent cannot, or at least not in a cost-effective way, such as technical advice. Frequently, brokers are used once a firm gets to a size large enough to require a "risk manager."

Direct writers do not always use a sales force. Instead, they may use direct mail, salaried personnel, or commissioned salespeople to contact customers. The business belongs to the insurer, who maintains control over their activities, and they often offer policies at a discount; thus, they are an attractive option for many cash-starved start-up firms. For growth-oriented companies, however, price should be a secondary consideration to expert advice and good asset coverage. Their advantages may include the following:

- Lower premiums.
- Better service since a direct writer is often a specialist in a given field.
- Centralized administration and mass advertising ("Selecting the Right Insurance Agency," 1986, pp. 62–65).

The roles fulfilled by insurance firms may differ somewhat from situation to situation. In general, however, the entrepreneur should look for the following qualities among insurance candidates as members of the venture's external team:

1. Ability to handle difficult or unusual types of coverage if the situation warrants it.
2. Responsiveness to questions, answering quickly and accurately.
3. Innovativeness, always looking for ways to improve the venture's risk management program.
4. Stability of the insurance firm.
5. Communication in easy-to-understand terms rather than industry jargon.
6. Periodic review of the venture's account and coverage needs.
7. Ample professional liability coverage.
8. Reasonable premium cost with manageable deductibles.
9. Identification and differentiation of coverage that is essential, coverage that is desirable but not absolutely necessary, and coverage best suited for the firm, the individual entrepreneur, and the firm's employees.
10. Customization of policies to meet the firm's specific exposures, financial situation, and needs ("Selecting the Right Insurance Agency," 1986, pp. 62–65).

Once an entrepreneur has identified the type of insurance firm he or she wishes to use and has obtained referrals, a preliminary investigation should be completed. Then formal written proposals should be requested. These documents frequently contain a general outline of the agency's offices, both national and local, a brief resume for each of the key agents in the office, their products and services, a description of how the agency proposes to handle the venture's needs for insurance, and finally, references. Entrepreneurs should invite potential insurance agents to discuss their individual programs in person with the management team who will be affected. It is very helpful to provide details ahead of time about which physical assets are exposed to loss and need to be protected and where other potential liability losses can be incurred to give the insurance agent clear information on which to develop final proposals.

As mentioned previously, cost should not be the overwhelming factor, since the issue here is buying a service, not just a commodity product called insurance. Besides, low cost may be a sign that the firm has unusually tight claim policies, insufficient loss reserves, or low commissions, which may reduce the quality of service provided. It may be advisable to try to maximize the venture's bargaining leverage by either contracting with only one insurance agency or by dividing the coverage of the venture's insurance needs into two or three different categories (e.g., property and casualty, life, and health) split among two or three different insurers. Depending on the size of the insurance firm and its premiums, this may provide the venture with better service, but at the same time, it may mean giving up certain discounts gained by using only one firm.

For very small businesses and/or self-employed individuals, the costs of employee benefits purchased through an insurance agent may not be financially feasible. Sometimes, the local Chamber of Commerce or a small business association in a specific region may offer group coverage. Often, their large numbers and combined purchasing power enable their group members to get more reasonable rates.

The Consultant

Depending on how they are used, consultants may or may not be part of the venture's external team, but they have the potential to be one of the most important resources. Typically, consultants are hired when in-house specialists cannot be hired, when the need for their expertise is only part time, or when danger signals indicate that the venture is not performing up to expectations.

Consultants come in an array of sizes, from multinational firms to sole practitioners, and with many specialties: accounting, computer systems, personnel, inventory control, etc. Some sell advice and some sell equipment. Consultants can be very expensive, yet it is frequently hard to judge whether or not their services were or will be beneficial. Unfortunately, there are no easy ways to identify the skilled from the unskilled consultant, but a few recommendations can be made.

First, the entrepreneur should check to see whether the prospective consultant is certified by a professional management consulting association. While this is no guarantee of quality, it at least suggests that they have a baseline of skills. Recommendations from satisfied clients are usually the best way to select a consultant, as well as the chemistry and personality match with the owner. The Institute of Management Consultants and the Association of Management Consulting Firms offer free referral services and consultant directories that can be found in libraries. Articles written by the consultants themselves in business periodicals are also good sources by which to gauge their competence and background.

Once several potential consultants have been identified, the entrepreneur should try to determine their advantages and disadvantages within the context of what needs to be done and in terms of providing advice and/or information or solving a specific problem. Candidates need to be interviewed, and written proposals, references, and cost estimates should be obtained. It should never be assumed that because they are consultants they are always right, because when they are finished, they can walk away from the firm, and the entrepreneur may be stuck picking up the pieces.

Another opinion on consultants advocates never hiring them unless there is highly specialized work that cannot be done in-house. Consultants may not be venture-oriented and seldom think like an entrepreneur. Most are technicians or specialists, bogged down in the details of their specialized interests, and most importantly, they are not accountable for bottom-line profitability. Instead of using consultants, the venture might attempt to develop the capabilities needed in-house, by rewarding risk-taking employees and by creating a climate conducive to change (Samuels, 1983).

The Outside Board Members

Outside board members focus on advising the entrepreneur. Unfortunately, in many smaller businesses, outside board members are often one of the more unappreciated and under-utilized assets, because having outside board members often runs counter to the very autonomy that many entrepreneurs and small-business people so desire. Outside board members require the owner to disclose details about the firm's operations, finances, and plans for the future. Trust is critical, and if the owner feels comfortable sharing this type of information, outside board members can play an important role in improving the venture's chances of succeeding in the following ways:

1. Helping to develop leadership and professionalism within the firm.
2. Critically examining the owner's decision-making process.
3. Providing the firm with a sense of credibility to the business community.
4. Helping when a change in management is required.
5. Providing needed expertise in a wide variety of fields.

Without question, good board members can provide a sense of perspective and a view from outside the firm. But at the same time, they must use their influence subtly, knowing when to push and when to back off. In some companies, selecting outside board members is simply not done, and for many small businesses, or income-oriented firms, using outside board members is not an option because of their cost, or because management sees them as being focused on growth rather than on income-producing goals. Thus, many small businesses choose to use inside board members only, such as family, friends, key employees, and others who share similar personal and business goals.

In some start-ups funded by venture capital, the outside board may be dominated by the lead venture capitalist, who, as part of the conditions of funding, may have insisted on a majority of the board's seats for co-investors or other individuals. In situations in which there is some choice, however, deciding whom to choose is a difficult question, especially given the trend of increasing litigation against directors and officers. Directors' and officers' (D&O) liability insurance has become a virtual necessity given the increasingly large number of lawsuits being filed in which board members are charged with neglecting their fiduciary responsibility to the stockholders. Because of the need for the expertise that these board members can bring to the table, many firms have had to offer incentives, both monetary and non-monetary, to attract competent board members, which can add up to quite an expense for a small firm with scarce resources. The task of finding effective outside board members is difficult because the entrepreneur needs individuals who will bring a breadth of skills, experience, and diversity to the venture. Ideally, members of the board should have backgrounds and contacts that differ from but complement the entrepreneur's background and those of the other directors. Additionally, as the company grows and changes, the governing board also needs to evolve to meet changing needs and circumstances (Online Women's Business Center, 1997).

Advisory Boards

By law, every corporation needs a board of directors. However, more and more entrepreneurial ventures are supplementing their directors with an advisory board. Typically, their use depends on the needs of the firm, but they tend to be less expensive than a formal board, and supposedly, less liable for the decisions they make.

Furthermore, advisory boards may not provide the needed counterbalance to the management decisions made by the owners because unlike a formal board of directors, they have no formal control over management. Still, the use of advisory boards is a viable option for many firms, particularly those with a technological thrust, which are in need of an advisory board with technical capabilities to help management solve problems that may exceed their current skill level.

Personal Contacts, Connections, and Other Sources of Help

The third category of people and organizations offering supporting services to the entrepreneur as external team members seems to include just about everyone else in the business world. Although this is an obvious overstatement, the list of contacts, connections, and other networking sources is quite extensive. In fact, some aspiring entrepreneurs contend that one of their initial problems is sorting through the multitude of people and organizations offering help and advice.

The best recommendation for those with ideas, prototypes, small business goals, or those who are just short of capital, is to first use whatever sources of help that are free or relatively inexpensive, keeping in mind that the quality of free services and sources varies extensively. If they are not completely satisfied or if there is need for more information, other more expensive sources can be consulted. Numerous contacts and sources of information should be utilized not only during the venture's early stages but also later, depending, to a great extent, on the type of venture and the kinds of skills and resources needed. These valuable contacts, information sources, and services are listed below, not in any particular sequence or priority. They are characterized mostly by the fact that they are free or relatively inexpensive. However, as mentioned previously, the quality of information from these sources varies.

- Government publications such as Census Reports (Census of Business, Census of Population, etc.) are particularly helpful for gathering demographic data and identifying trends in potential target markets.

- The local chamber of commerce frequently offers workshops and seminars. Perhaps even more important, chambers of commerce offer opportunities to meet and network with other entrepreneurs and the professionals that help support them, such as, accountants, lawyers, bankers, etc. Most chambers of commerce for example, host a "Business After Hours" social gathering once a month for networking, that is, to get people together to talk over similar problems, meet new clients, new customers, etc.

- People you already know who have their own business can provide information regarding who use for various services.

- Local universities or colleges provide various services that can include internships for students, having a class group do a research study, arranging a student group to do a "consulting" project, among others. Faculty members are also frequently looking for field projects that they can fit into their curriculum. Some schools have idea evaluation programs at minimal costs to the aspiring entrepreneur. Business plans are often presented to classes in exchange for constructive criticism by students who compensate for their lack of experience with enthusiasm and youthful energy.

- Local Small Business Development Centers (SBDC) or Small Business Advancement Centers (SBAC) connected with the local university, offering free or inexpensive consulting, sometimes done by students, faculty, or professional consultants.

- The local office of the U.S. Small Business Administration (SBA) or www.sba.gov. They conduct conferences, workshops, and educational programs on a variety of small-business topics. They also offer services regarding actual funding, how to participate in federal government procurement opportunities, information on grants through the Small Business Innovation Research (SBIR) Program, import/export data, and many other topics of interest.

- The local SCORE (Service Corps of Retired Executives) chapters have consultants who are retired executives who wish to give something back to the business community that helped them succeed in their careers.

- Local and state government offices offer information, particularly with regard to cutting red tape, finding available funds, and numerous other services.

- For minorities, opportunities for networking may be available through Black, Hispanic and Asian Chambers of Commerce. Workshops and funding opportunities may also be available through the local Minority Business Development Center (MBDC).

- The newspaper lists events of interest, meetings, speeches, etc. of people actively working in the industry of interest. They can help by providing information about the industry, the competition, or the typical problems encountered by entrepreneurial firms.

- Trade associations as well as trade journals offer valuable industry and marketing information.

- The popular press, such as *Inc. Magazine, Entrepreneur, Black Business, Working Woman, Business Week, Fortune,* and others, have ideas, suggestions, and first-rate articles describing entrepreneurial experiences, along with excellent practical advice on a number of topics pertinent to entrepreneurs.

- Organizations such as the Toastmasters Club help improve skills in areas critical to entrepreneurial success, such as negotiating or better speaking skills.

- Entrepreneurs who are already in the same industry or business may be willing to help, even those who may be eventual competitors. They are always interested in developing new suppliers and customers, and therefore they are frequently very helpful sources of information.

- Newsletters on products or services offer valuable industry and marketing information.

- Product-licensing services publish information on products available for licensing.

- Patent brokers can be contacted to see what is available for purchase or license.

- The National Technical Information Service (NTIS) maintains a huge database that can be accessed to locate information on recent research projects funded by the federal government.

- Dissertations are on file at university libraries.

- Some reference books are dedicated to helping small businesses.

- And last but not least, of course, the Internet offers access to valuable industry and marketing information.

This list just scratches the surface of the personal contacts, connections, and other sources of help that exist to help the entrepreneur. However, in addition to the obvious differences in the quality of assistance, not everyone has the entrepreneur's best interests at heart. The entrepreneur needs to get referrals and recommendations whenever possible, to check references, to talk to former clients, and to take time to sort them out. Even if the time available to do the required homework for the process of forming an external team may be limited, a little time, money, and energy spent on that now should be viewed as an investment in the future for a bigger payoff later. Some will be well worth the cost, and some will not even be worth the time. Exhibit 10.5 lists 26 sources of information from a 1983 study done in metropolitan Atlanta (Franklin & Goodwin, 1983). Even though this

Exhibit 10.5	Ranking of Important Sources of Information		

Source	Mean	Rank
Other business people	1.928	1
Accountants	1.957	2
Suppliers	2.037	3
Trade associations	2.043	4
Business managers	2.084	5
Customers	2.107	6
Attorneys	2.253	7
Manufacturing representatives	2.258	8
Bankers	2.267	9
Distributors	2.426	10
Newspapers	2.445	11
Conferences	2.532	12
Chamber of Commerce	2.548	13
College Courses	2.757	14
Better Business Bureau	2.957	15
Small Business Associations	3.000	16
National Federation of Independent Business (NFIB)	3.017	17
Credit Associations	3.019	18
State Dept. of Industry & Trade	3.148	19
U.S. Economic Development Administration	3.207	20
City Regional Commission	3.259	21
City Development Authority	3.274	22
College Professors	3.278	23
City Private Industry Council	3.281	24
State Employment Security Agency	3.399	25
State Dept. of Minority Business Entrepreneurs	3.416	26

Source: Franklin & Goodwin, 1983.

study was conducted before the advent and convenience of research through the Internet, it gives a pretty good idea about the relative value of the many sources of information, most of which can still be accessed through the Internet.

CONCLUSION

The entrepreneur needs an internal team to achieve success. Decisions need to be made as to who should be on this team, what issues need to be considered regarding recruiting, responsibilities, compensation, changes in the internal team's composition, etc. Team members or partners bring skills, resources, and knowledge to a firm, along with their own emotional baggage from previous experiences. The latter can take too much of the founder's time and energy and can impede progress toward goals. This can be minimized to some extent by identifying, either through a conscious or unplanned process, the right individuals who share the commitment, the vision, and certain interests and chemistry with the founder. Team members or partners can also fill in the gaps that prevent the fulfillment of the venture's goals by bringing the skills needed to get a product or service to market and to create the kind of growth required for future success. They can bring money and other resources—they may be the last piece of the success puzzle. Therefore, they should be allowed to share in the venture's success by being rewarded accordingly. The entrepreneur needs to make certain decisions about which member of that internal team should share in the rewards, how rewards should be distributed, in what form, and at what point of time. These questions are critical in ensuring the recruitment and the successful tenure of good partners and internal team members. Having a good external support system is also critical. Knowing where to go for help, putting together effective external teams, connections, and other sources of help are also essential for the entrepreneur. However, difficulties arise in trying to recruit competent external team members and in trying to determine what they need to do for the venture. In many specialized areas, the typical entrepreneur's working knowledge is limited, which implies that there will be situations in which explicit and implicit trust must be placed on these external advisors in addition to gut instincts. The level of trust must be extraordinarily high, and the quickest way to establish that type of confidence and faith is first to make the best selection possible, and second, to work closely together. For many entrepreneurs, this is a difficult task because it runs counter to their ideas of independence and autonomy. However, there is no other choice.

Website Information

Topic	Web Address	Description
Internal teams/family business	http://www.marriott.com/culture-and-values/core-values.mi	Information on the history, family business, and organizational culture of the Marriott hotel chain.
Divorce and the internal team	http://www.inc.com/magazine/19980901/998.html	Dramatic stories of famous entrepreneurial couples and their divorces.
External teams: The lawyer	http://mansfieldlaw.com/	A legal group that offers services directed specifically to the legal needs of entrepreneurs.
External teams: The banker	http://www.start-upjournal.com/financing/loans/20020625-mancuso.html	*Wall Street Journal* article on how to deal with banks, what banks to use, including a quiz to test how well you know your banker.

Key Terms

Internal team: Members participating in the founding of the firm.

External team: Members, advisors, and other outsiders actively assisting the venture.

Personal contacts or connections: Members not directly hired for their services, they nevertheless interact with and affect the firm's progress.

Uniform Partnership Act: A partnership as an association of two or more persons to carry on as co-owners of a business for profit.

Review Questions

1. What are some things that an owner should take into consideration when facing the reality that he or she must share ownership with a partner or partners?

2. Discuss three of the six sources for finding good internal team members and partners.

3. With regard to financial and/or legal rationale, what are the reasons for joint ownership? What are the reasons against it?

4. What are two advantages and two disadvantages of the "earn-in" system?

5. How should family-owned businesses deal with second- or third-generation members, and with succession problems?

6. When interviewing a potential lawyer for your firm, why is it important to ask if they represent other entrepreneurs, family-owned businesses, and small businesses?

7. What is the paradox in the insurance function that affects the design of an insurance coverage program and its cost?

8. Differentiate between an independent insurance agency, an insurance broker, and a direct writer.

Reflections from the Front Lines of LifeGuard America

The concept of a team is probably the most central element to any start-up endeavor. Think about it. No, I mean really stop and think about it. Every successful venture I have ever heard about started with a core team of three or four people. Usually, they all had a very different perspective of the venture and the ability to "speak their minds." It is this nucleus that is the epicenter for every great endeavor. Of the many entrepreneurial skills I learned from the corporate world, the most important were the understanding of what composes a great team, how to build one, and how to keep a great team together.

From the corporate halls of Bell Canada came the method by which a great team is assembled. If you worked in the process improvement group within Bell Canada back in the late 1980s and early 1990s, you had already taken a personality traits survey like Meyers-Briggs and were classified as to your personality type (A, B, C, etc.). It had been discovered at Bell Canada that the composition of a strong team depended on getting a mix of left-brain and right-brain thinkers, drivers and listeners, numbers and graphic thinkers in the right combination. In short, Bell Canada spent many hours working on the composition of the team's "personality" before they ever had their first meeting. The output required from the team was the driving force behind the elements of the composition of the team. I was so impressed by this approach that it has driven my every move in putting together any team in my business life since and certainly affected my assembly of the management team for LifeGuard America. From within the four walls of Harley-Davidson's Kansas City Plant, I learned how to build an effective team and how to keep any team (Harley refers to them as natural work groups) together. The main component of attracting people to any endeavor is clearly articulating what the team's objectives are and what the individual brings to the team in the form of skills and experience. It is not enough for me to understand the primary objective at LifeGuard America. I must also clearly understand why I am here and what I bring to the endeavor. It all sounds very simple, but so often companies that flounder do so because they have lost sight of the fundamentals of business practices. Once you have identified the players and have created a shared vision of what success looks like, the way you keep the team together is to get out of the way and let them figure it out. This is what allows great talent to grow. If I feel that I am indeed growing in my knowledge and experience and I believe my efforts within the team are making a difference, I am in it for the long run. Teams stay together because the individuals are growing at least as fast as the team. It is a dynamic that any leader must identify and nurture. I have found that it is just that simple. Business is not usually that difficult. We just make stuff up and artificially insert it to make it look like it is.

Through my ongoing studies and reviewing the disasters that have plagued giants in the business community over the past 3 years, it has become evident to me that a healthy business is based on strong ethical standards, and therefore, corporate governance must be a core competency of the endeavor. Harvard Business School Press is still the primary source of reading material for me, and I have modeled our corporate governance out of the pages of some of the best minds of the past decades. For starters, even though I am a primary unit holder of LifeGuard America and sit on the Board of Directors, I am not the Chairman and I am the only "management insider" on the board. As President and CEO, my responsibilities are clearly outlined in our Operating Agreement. I am responsible for the day-to-day activities of the company, and my primary goal is directing the company to meet the next 12-month goals and objectives. It is the responsibility of the Board to hold the management team accountable for its primary business objectives and to concern themselves with the 10-year strategic plans. Our board consists of experts in the fields of legal, finance, technology, medical operations, organ transplantation, and hospital administration. Most importantly, five of the six members of the board of directors are from outside the company. This way we have a truly objective board that is positioned to be as effective when we are a large company because we started with the end in mind.

This section reflects on the personnel and infrastructure required to get any business off the ground and into an operational status that is self-sustaining. First, we will look at the management team of LifeGuard America and then transition to Article VI of our Operating Agreement.

First we will review the business plan section on the Management Team:

President and CEO: John R. Fitzpatrick, III
Mr. Fitzpatrick has over 15 years of experience managing high-performance organizations. He is an expert in business re-engineering; aligning processes and practices to reflect corporate vision and mission. Mr. Fitzpatrick is also an influential leader skilled in inspiring peak performance and team cohesion through an empowering management style. Mr. Fitzpatrick has, for the last 10 years, been a visionary senior executive driving exponential performance improvement spanning all organizational areas in the consumer products and service industries. Most recently he was President, CEO and Director on the Board of Indian Motorcycle Company, where he provided strong leadership through a challenging transition to a revised business plan. Mr. Fitzpatrick headed an 11-person senior management team and 740 employees generating $94 million annual revenue. Mr. Fitzpatrick also is highly experienced in start-up companies where, at Harley-Davidson Motor Company, he had senior leadership responsibilities at the newly established Kansas City Sportster facility. Mr. Fitzpatrick has held various management positions in both military and civilian organizations with broad experience in Business Process and Organizational Design. Mr. Fitzpatrick holds a Bachelor of Science in Electrical Engineering and a diverse career spanning the software, computer, aircraft, automotive, and motorcycle industries.

Chief Financial Officer: Parker L. Strickland
Mr. Strickland's business experience covers the areas of financial management as well as commercial banking. He has served as Chief Financial Officer for companies in the manufacturing and service distribution industries. Most recently, he held the position of Chief Financial Officer for a $100 million manufacturing company. In this position Mr. Strickland was part of a five-person management team that led the company through a 50% growth in revenue in a 4-year time period. Mr. Strickland also held a lead position in the sale of the company to a publicly traded entity where he identified the buyer and acted as liaison between financial consultants and the company. In addition to financial management skills, Mr. Strickland's commercial banking experience includes 7 years in lending and credit administration positions with multiple regional banks. Mr. Strickland has a Bachelor of Science in Agricultural Economics from Oklahoma State University and a Masters in Business Administration from Southern Methodist University.

Chief Technology Officer: J. Calvin McClure

Mr. McClure is responsible for the Strategic Planning and Technology Implementation at LifeGuard America. Mr. McClure comes to LifeGuard America from Hewlett Packard where he had senior program management responsibilities in HP Operations, the outsourcing services group of HP Services. Mr. McClure has held various program-level responsibilities for technical design, security consulting, and business modeling of some of HP's largest outsourcing contracts to date. This list includes Ford Motor Company, the joint venture between HP and the Canadian Imperial Bank of Commerce (CIBC) known as Intria-HP as well as having provided both technical design and implementation of Hewlett Packard's first external customer Operations Services Center in Atlanta, Georgia. Mr. McClure brings a broad range of experience in process development, computer technology and support services, having provided services in seven countries in North America, Europe, and the Far East. Mr. McClure has over 10 years of experience in Hewlett Packard's legendary Management by Objective (MBO) business management environment and is skilled in all facets of human resource management. Mr. McClure holds a Bachelor of Science in Mechanical Engineering from the University of Florida, with graduate level studies at the College of Business Administration from the University of Tennessee.

Director of Operations: Richard W. Poplin

Rick is responsible for all aspects of flight operations. He will direct all operations related to mission execution based on the schedules generated by the logistics group. Mr. Poplin has over 4000 hours of flight time in T-37, T-38, F-16, Boeing 727, 737, 757, 767, Airbus A319, and A320 aircraft. Mr. Poplin currently holds both an Airline Transport Pilot Certificate and a Flight Engineer Certificate. As an F-16 Instructor Pilot, Mr. Poplin currently serves as a Supervisor of Flying, Mission Commander, and Officer in Command of Quality Assurance for the 138th Fighter Wing, Oklahoma Air National Guard in Tulsa, Oklahoma. Supervising the Quality Assurance office, Mr. Poplin oversees 20 maintenance personnel that ensure the safe operation of over $300 million worth of combat aircraft. Mr. Poplin is skilled in the development and integration of Aircraft Mission Planning and Electronic Briefing systems. Mr. Poplin initiated an Electronic Briefing system in Tulsa that has become the standard for F-16 Squadrons worldwide. Mr. Poplin holds a Bachelor of Science Degree in Business from Oklahoma State University, majoring in Management Science and Computer Systems.

Vice President of Business Development: Ron Bertanzi

Mr. Bertanzi has more than 30 years of healthcare experience. He has spent the last 18 years developing and implementing telecommunications and information technologies as a means of addressing the problems relating to quality, cost, and access to care that now afflict many healthcare systems. Prior to joining LifeGuard America he was Vice President of Worldwide Enterprise Solutions for PictureTel. His responsibilities included managing the sales and marketing efforts to the Fortune 100 corporations as well as the vertical markets of healthcare and education. In addition, he was the principal liaison between PictureTel engineering group and Cisco development team for their internal video communications network. Mr. Bertanzi earned his Bachelor degree in Pre-Med from the University of Mainz in Germany. He was a practicing Physician Assistant and Certified Cardiovascular Perfusionist and is a fellow of the American and International Academy of Extra-Corporeal Technology.

The operational structure of a company is the key to its ultimate success. We have put together a comprehensive set of checks and balances in our corporate governance that represents the best of twenty-first-century thinking. What follows is LifeGuard America's corporate governance philosophy put into practice.

Article VI

Management and Operation of Business

Section 6.01. Directors

Strategic direction and oversight of the Company shall be vested in a Board of Directors comprised of seven individuals, one of whom shall be the President of the Company. As vacancies occur on the Board, new members of the Board shall be nominated by a majority of the remaining members of the Board and elected by a Majority Vote of the Members. The Chairman of the Board shall be appointed by a majority of the members of the Board (which majority must include the President).

The Board of Directors currently consists of six individuals who have been appointed by the original Members of the Company, and who shall serve until their successors are elected and qualified. An additional member of the Board shall be nominated by a majority of the members of the Board and elected by a Majority Vote of the Members following the Company's completion of its offering of an additional 30,000 Units (anticipated to be closed on or before June 1, 2003).

In the event that hereafter all members of the Board of Directors have resigned or been removed from office, the business of the Company shall be under the exclusive management of the Members, and in such case, a Majority Vote of the Members shall be necessary for all decisions affecting the Company.

Section 6.02. Responsibility of Directors

It shall be the responsibility of the Board of Directors to provide the overall strategic direction of the Company, and in such role the duties of the Board of Directors shall include, but not be limited to: (i) approving long-term objectives and goals for the Company, including potential areas of business expansion; (ii) selecting of the chief executive and senior officers and overseeing the mentoring of such officers; (iii) approving compensation and retirement policies for executive officers; (iv) delegating administrative authority to the chief executive and subordinate officers; (v) approving policies related to capital needs and financing, including distribution of Cash Available for Distribution; and (vi) implementing a formal review process in the form of a strategic audit, using such criteria and time-line as the Board may determine.

Section 6.03. Compensation of Directors

Each Director will be compensated for his or her services as a Director, in the form of a Director's fee equal to $_____ per meeting of the Board attended by such Director. In addition, each Director will be entitled to reasonable expense reimbursements incurred in connection with the performance of his or her duties as a Director of the Company.

Section 6.04. Restrictions on Directors

Notwithstanding any other provision hereof, the Board of Directors shall not, without consent or ratification of the specific act by a Majority Vote of the Members:

    a. Sell all or substantially all of the Company's Property;

    b. Admit a Person as a Member, except as otherwise provided in this Agreement;

    c. Knowingly perform any act that would subject a Member to personal liability; or

    d. Do any act, which would make it impossible to carry on the ordinary business of the Company.

Section 6.05. Term and Qualifications

Each Director shall hold office until his or her successor shall have been appointed. Directors need not be Members of the Company.

Section 6.06. Outside Activities

Each Director and such Director's Affiliates may have business interests and engage in business activities in addition to those relating to the Company, for such Director's or such Director's Affiliates' own account or for the account of others, and no provision of this Agreement shall be deemed to prohibit such Director or such Director's Affiliates from conducting such businesses and activities. Neither the Company, the Members, the Directors nor any officer of the Company shall have any rights by virtue of this Agreement or the relationship contemplated herein in any business ventures of the Directors or the Directors' Affiliates.

Section 6.07 Limitation on Liability of Directors

No member of the Board of Directors shall be liable to the Company or its Members for monetary damages for breach of fiduciary duty as a Director; provided, however, that nothing contained herein shall eliminate or limit the liability of a Director: (i) for any breach of the Director's duty of loyalty to the Company or its Members; (ii) for acts or omissions not in good faith or which involve intentional misconduct or a knowing violation of the law; and (iii) for any transaction from which the Director derived an improper personal benefit.

Section 6.08. Authority of Board of Directors to Confirm Officers of the Company

a. The Board of Directors, by a majority vote of the members thereof, shall elect the executive officers of the Company, and shall authorize each such officer to act on behalf of the Company with such authority as set forth in this Agreement or as such officer may be granted in writing at the time of his or her appointment; provided that no such appointment shall relieve the members of the Board of Directors of the ultimate responsibility imposed by applicable law for the overall supervision of the Company.

b. Initially, the Board of Directors has elected the following to serve as officers of the Company:

John R. Fitzpatrick	President (Chief Executive Officer)
Parker L. Strickland	Vice President of Finance (Chief Financial Officer)
J. Calvin McClure	Vice President of Technology (Chief Technology Officer)
Richard W. Poplin	Vice President of Operations (Chief Operations Officer)
Ron Bertanzi	Vice President of Business Development (Chief Marketing Officer)

Subject at all times to the direction of the Board of Directors, and subject further to the same restrictions that apply to the Board of Directors as set forth in *Section 6.04,* the officers shall have the following general authority:

President and CEO

The President shall be the Chief Executive Officer of the Company and a member of the Board of Directors. In the absence of the Chairman of the Board, the President shall preside at the meetings of the Board. The President shall attend and preside at all meetings of the Members and, subject to the overall control of the Board of Directors, shall have general authority to see that all resolutions of the Board of Directors are carried into effect. The President will nominate individuals that he or she feels are qualified to fill the roles of the executive vice presidential offices identified above, and shall submit such nominations to the Board for the Board's approval. The President shall have authority to make decisions affecting the normal business operations of the Company, and to act on behalf of the Company in executing documents in the name of the Company and to contractually bind the Company except where required or permitted by law to be otherwise signed and executed and except where the signing and execution thereof shall be expressly delegated by the Board of Directors to some other officer or agent of the Company. The President shall be responsible for the active management of the day-to-day business operations of the Company.

Vice President

Each Vice President shall make all day-to-day decisions in their respective area of responsibility affecting the Company, subject to the direction and control of the President. In the absence or disability of the President, the Vice Presidents, in the order listed above, shall be authorized to perform the duties and exercise the powers of the President and shall perform such other duties and have such other powers as the Board of Directors may from time to time prescribe.

Section 6.09. Compensation of Officers

Officers shall be compensated for his or her services as an officer of the Company in such amounts as shall be established from time to time by the Board of Directors. In establishing the compensation of any officer other than the President, the Board of Directors shall seek the input and guidance of the President.

Section 6.10. Limitation on Liability of Officers

No officer of the Company shall be liable to the Company or its Members for monetary damages for breach of fiduciary duty as an officer; provided, however, that nothing contained herein shall eliminate or limit the liability of an officer: (i) for any breach of the officer's duty of loyalty to the Company or its Members; (ii) for acts or omissions not in good faith or which involve intentional misconduct or a knowing violation of the law; and (iii) for any transaction from which the officer derived an improper personal benefit.

Discussion Questions on LifeGuard America

1. What do you think is meant by the term "speak their minds" and why do you think Mr. Fitzpatrick believes it to be an important characteristic of a successful venture?

2. Do you believe that the personality makeup of individual team members can have an effect on the performance of a team? How?

3. How is LifeGuard America's Board of Directors elected? How are the executives selected?

4. What is the primary role of the Board of Directors at LifeGuard America?

5. What is the primary role of the CEO? How is it different from the Chairman of the Board? Do you agree with this separation of powers in a small start-up company?

6. What group within LifeGuard America has the ultimate and final say in any matter?

References

Baty, F. (1981). *Entrepreneurship for the eighties.* Reston, VA: Reston.

Bennett, T. E. (1987, February). How to choose a bank. *Inc. Magazine, 9*(2), 110–112.

Bird, B. (1989). *Entrepreneurial behavior.* Glenview, IL: Scott, Foresman.

Boyd, S. (2001). *How to select an attorney.* Unpublished manuscript, University of Tulsa, Tulsa, OK.

Bruno, A., & Tyebjee, T. (1983). The one that got away. In J. A. Hornaday, J. A. Timmons, & K. H. Vesper (Eds.), *Frontiers of entrepreneurship research* (pp. 289–306). Babson Park, MA: Babson College.

Carson, T., Michals, D., & Baum, L. (1986, September 15). Honey, what do you say we start our own company? *Business Week,* 115–118.

Davis, P. S., & Harveston, P. D. (2001, January). The phenomenon of substantive conflict in the family firm: A cross-generational study. *Journal of Small Business Management, 39*(1), 14–30.

Dible, D. (1986). *Up your own organization.* Reston, VA: Reston.

Dyer, W. G., Jr. (1994, June). Potential contributions of organizational behavior to the study of family-owned businesses. *Family Business Review, 7*(2), 109–131.

Dyer, W. G., Jr., & Handler, W. (1994, Fall). Entrepreneurship and family business: Exploring the connections. *Entrepreneurship Theory and Practice, 19*(1), 71–84.

Franklin, S. & Goodwin, J. (1983, April). Problems of small business and sources of assistance: A survey. *Journal of Small Business Management, 21*(2), 5–12.

Friedlander, F. (1990). *Work home identity scale.* Unpublished manuscript, The Fielding Institute.

Gorman, M., & Sahlman, W. (1986). What do venture capitalists do? In R. Ronstadt, J. Hornaday, R. Peterson, & K. H. Vesper (Eds.), *Frontiers of entrepreneurship research* (pp. 414–436). Babson Park, MA: Babson College.

Hutcheson, J. O. (2002, August). The fires of family business. *Financial Planning, 32*(8), 82–83.

Kets de Vries, M. F. R. (1993, Winter). The dynamics of family controlled firms: The good and the bad news. *Organizational Dynamics, 21*(3), 59–72.

Levinson, R. E. (1985). *Problems in managing a family-owned business* (Management Aid No. 2004). Washington, DC: U.S. Small Business Administration.

Marshack, K. J. (1994, Fall). Copreneurs and dual-career couples? Are they different? *Entrepreneurship Theory and Practice, 19*(1), 49–70.

McMullan, W. E. (1982). In the interest of equity: Distributing equity among new venture employees. In K. Vesper (Ed.), *Frontiers of entrepreneurship research 1982* (pp. 396–414). Wellesley, MA: Babson College.

Nelton, S. (1991, July). Avoiding "business divorce" court. *Nation's Business, 79*(7), 34.

Online Women's Business Center (1997, June). *The management institute.* Dallas, TX: Author. Retrieved November 11, 2002, from http://www.onlinewbc.org.

Paiva, W. D. (2003, April). *New VCs focus in Oklahoma.* Paper presented at Oklahoma Investment Forum Private Enterprise Presentation, Tulsa, OK.

Rollinson, M. (1985, November/December). Small company, big law firm. *Harvard Business Review, 63*(6), 6–14.

Samuels, T. W. (1983, May). Advice to business: Stop listening to advisors. *Inc. Magazine, 5*(5), 17–18.

Selecting the right insurance agency: Key to effective coverage (1986, June). *Small Business Reports, 11*(6), 62–65.

Timmons, J., Smollen, L., & Dingee, A., Jr. (1985). *New venture creation.* Homewood, IL: Richard D. Irwin.

Timmons, J. (2001). *New venture creation* (5th ed.). New York: Irwin/McGraw-Hill.

Vesper, K. (1980). *New venture strategies.* Englewood Cliffs, NJ: Prentice Hall.

Wojahn, E. (1986, March). Divorce: Entrepreneurial style. *Inc. Magazine, 8*(3), 55–64.

11 Venture Infrastructure: Legal Considerations

Can We Plan the Legal Infrastructure?

LEARNING OBJECTIVES

1. To assess the legal options available to the entrepreneur in structuring the new venture.
2. To ensure that the legal structure is the most appropriate for the venture's staying power.
3. To be able to evaluate some alternative legal structure options as the ventures grows and evolves.

TOPIC OUTLINE

Introduction

Issues to Consider in Selecting the Right Legal
   Organizational Form
- The Sole Proprietorship
- The Partnership
- The Corporation
- Some Other Legal Organizational Form
   Options

Conclusion

Website Information

Key Terms

Review Questions

Case Study

References

INTRODUCTION

Entrepreneurs engage in a contest of strategies governed and structured by unique rules and laws for the purpose of profit. In addition to skill, entrepreneurs need the true experience provided by professional counsel, or training, to be able to gain insight into these rules of the game. More specifically, the legal form of a business is no longer something that can be casually fashioned. The long-run success of a business is due almost as much to the systematic preparation and professional advice regarding the "correct" legal formation of the business as it is to providing a unique product or service.

ISSUES TO CONSIDER IN SELECTING THE RIGHT LEGAL ORGANIZATIONAL FORM

Prior to examining the various legal options available concerning the appropriate legal form of business organization, it is critical that a series of simple, yet fundamental questions be posed and carefully evaluated. The following issues should guide the decision-making process:

1. *Ownership:* Will there be one or more owners? Will ownership be 50–50? An entrepreneur's initial concern is fear of loss of control, since one of the primary motivations for starting a business is to avoid the burden of working for someone else. Generally, partnerships and corporations imply that other principals will be involved in ownership, management, and decision making.

2. *Management:* Is the composition of management different from that of ownership? The key issue here is the extent of the entrepreneur's day-to-day involvement in running the organization. In the case of partnerships, are the role of management and the identity of the manager and decision maker clearly defined in the partnership agreement?

3. *Financing:* How much capital is required for start-up and operations, and where will it come from? For ventures that require large quantities of funding, the sacrifices made by the entrepreneur in terms of managerial and decision-making control of the venture during the acquisition of investors through partnerships or incorporating must be carefully weighed.

4. *Liability:* In many cases, personal assets should be separated from those of the firm. The increasing fear of lawsuits, prolonged litigation, and uncertain economic conditions necessitate the examination of incorporation to limit personal legal liability.

5. *Incentives:* What types of long-term financial incentives are provided to the entrepreneur, as well as to the partners, other key managers, and employees of the firm?

6. *Taxation:* Recognizing that tax avoidance is legal but tax evasion is not, what legal organization form enables entrepreneurs to minimize their tax burden?

7. *Income objectives:* Are the entrepreneur's personal financial objectives short-term and income oriented or long-term and growth oriented?

8. *Continuity:* Are legal provisions made for the protection of the venture in the event of illness or death of the principal(s), so the venture's life is extended and continues?

It should be noted that the choice of legal form does not have to be final. The usual progression is to start as a sole proprietorship or a partnership and to evolve into a *limited liability company* (LLC) or a corporation, when the venture's growth establishes that the advantages of being a corporation outweighs its disadvantages. The main feature of LLCs and corporations that attracts small firms is the limit they provide on their owners' personal liability for business debts and court judgments against the business, as well as a range of fringe benefits to both employees the owners and the deductibility of the cost as a business expense. It is obvious that professional advice is essential in choosing any legal entity for the venture.

The Sole Proprietorship

The **sole proprietorship** is unquestionably the simplest legal form to create, the least expensive in terms of legal fees, and the most prevalent in the business world. If this legal structure is chosen, then legally speaking, the owner and the business are one and the same, as long as the owner obtains a business license to do business (if this is required under state laws or local ordinances). Sole proprietorship business income and losses are reported on the owner's federal tax return (Form 1040, Schedule C). Business loss may offset income generated from other sources. The **advantages of a sole proprietorship** are the following:

- *Ease of creation:* The formation of the sole proprietorship is relatively simple, less formal, and generally less expensive than other business structures. Other than obtaining local operating and license permits, tax and employee identification numbers, and other related employee forms if required, there are few legal hurdles. Even the registration of the name of the venture can be handled at the local city hall or courthouse with relative ease and speed.

- *Single beneficiary for profits:* The sole proprietor assumes all the risks and receives all the rewards. Profits, as well as losses, are based upon the proprietor's performance and are not shared with anybody.

- *Total control:* One of the most appealing characteristics of the sole proprietorship is the fact that the control and responsibility of the venture resides with one person, the entrepreneur. No opinions need to be heard or debated, no advice needs to be taken, and all decisions rest squarely on the shoulders of the entrepreneur.

- *Maximum flexibility:* There is no board of directors to consult, no restricting policies, no rules to constrain the actions and decisions of the entrepreneur. The sole proprietorship can respond adequately and expediently to changes in the business and economic environment when action is deemed necessary. This definitive advantage is the one that has enabled many small firms not only to be able to compete with larger firms but also, quite often, to stay a step ahead of their larger counterparts.

- *Minimal burden of local, state, and federal regulation:* Regulation is more easily avoided by a sole proprietorship because government, in general, finds the regulation and policing of small sole proprietorships too cumbersome and of little benefit. Additionally, "special taxes" often are levied only to larger firms and are sidestepped by proprietorships.

The **disadvantages of the sole proprietorship** are the following:

- *Unlimited liability:* Unlimited personal liability on all business debts and court judgments related to the business is clearly the most troublesome disadvantage of sole proprietorship. Entrepreneurs are obligated for all debts incurred during the course of doing business, which may exceed their total investment. This liability extends not only to the entrepreneur's personal bank account but also to any personal valuable property, such as a house, car, etc.

- *Restricted participation in ownership:* The entrepreneur cannot offer managers an equity position in the firm. This makes it difficult for the venture to attract competent managers who know that their long-term future with the firm is restricted and that rewards for their personal contributions toward the firm's profits are limited to their salary.

- *Limitations in raising funds:* For entrepreneurs requiring continuing infusion of capital during the formative years of the venture, the sole proprietorship restricts the sources and the amount of capital that can be raised, usually to the entrepreneur's personal savings or a small bank loan. To make matters worse, these limited financial resources and savings are quite often required by a lender to be used as collateral for that small loan, anyway. This predicament may prevent the sole proprietorship from meeting the challenges of changing competitive or environmental trends.

- *Over-reliance on a "one-man show":* The venture faces an unstable and limited life if the entrepreneur becomes ill, suffers serious injury, or dies. Generally, the greatest asset of the sole proprietorship is the entrepreneur himself or herself.

- *Cumbersome tax records:* A sole proprietor can deduct day-to-day business expenses the same way an LLC, corporation, or partnership can. The IRS has strict rules for tax-deductible business expenses, which need to be documented if challenged. Thus, one good approach is to keep separate checkbooks for business and personal expenses and pay for all business expenses out of the business checking account.

- *Limited perspective:* Finally, one of the most unrecognized limitations of the sole proprietorship is the restricted access to opinions, suggestions, and information of others. Too often, the "I can do it myself" philosophy can prove detrimental to the venture, because it incorporates all the biases and limited perspectives of the owner, which may not be appropriate anymore as the business evolves.

The Partnership

The **Uniform Partnership Act**, adopted by many states, defines the partnership as "an association of two or more persons to carry on as co-owners of a business for profit." Though not specifically required by the act, the best way to form a partnership is indeed to draw up and sign a partnership agreement and to have these *Articles of Partnership* customarily executed. These articles outline the contribution by the partners into the business, whether material or managerial, and generally delineate the roles of the partners in the business relationship. The partnership certificate may need to be filed with a public office to register the partnership name, as well as obtain the business licenses that would have been needed if the partnership were a sole proprietorship. But even if the choice is made to not form a formal partnership, the law may view the firm as a partnership as de facto partnerships, regardless of the lack of a stated intention or lack of a formal partnership business organization form, because the Uniform Partnership Act is considered to be a part of the partnership agreement, as if it had been written into the contract already. The following are some examples of articles contained in partnership agreements:

- The names of the partners

- The name of the partnership

- The purpose and duration of the partnership

- The financial contributions of each partner

- The method of sharing profits and losses

- The salaries, if any, to be paid to and by the partners

- The fiscal year

- The accounting method used to calculate profits

- The rights and liabilities of the partners upon the withdrawal or death of a partner

- The dissolution procedure

- The settlement of disputes

- The managerial authority of individual partners

Some of the characteristics that distinguish a partnership from other forms of business organization are the limited life of the partnership, the unlimited liability of at least one partner, the co-ownership of the assets, the mutual ownership "agency," sharing in the management of the partnership, and sharing its profits. Some additional important provisions that should govern partnership agreements:

1. *The buy-and-sell provision:* Problems arising from the withdrawal or the death of a partner can be resolved by the establishment of a buy-and-sell provision, either as part of the partnership agreement or as a separate contract. The buy-and-sell provision provides an orderly system for purchasing the interests of departed or deceased partners. Generally, the agreement will also contain provisions for determining the value of the departed or deceased partner's share, as well as the time and method of payment.

2. *Name provision:* Partnerships cannot employ the words *company, incorporated, corporation,* or any other language implying the existence of a corporation. Additionally, if the name of the partnership differs from that of the partners, public notice must be given revealing the true identity of the partners. The name of the firm becomes an asset, which can be sold, assigned, etc., in any way the partners deem appropriate.

3. *Goodwill provision:* If the partnership is dissolved, the goodwill of the firm must be taken into account, since it implies that the name and reputation of the firm will continue to attract customers. Goodwill, like the partnership name, can be bought and sold.

4. *Profit and loss provision:* Unless clearly outlined in the partnership agreement, each partner has the right to share equally in the firm's profits. Likewise, losses are to be allocated like profits, unless otherwise specified. The partnership must also indemnify each partner's payments made and liabilities incurred in the normal operation of the business.

5. *Partnership capital provision.* Partnership capital represents the total credits to the capital accounts of the individual partners. These credits represent the monies and the proportions of the total partnership capital to be returned to the various partners in the event of the dissolution of the business as a whole, as

outlined in the partnership agreement. For example, if a partner's contribution in a restaurant partnership was the land upon which the restaurant was built, the land, upon dissolution of the partnership, belongs to the partnership as a whole, unless otherwise stated. The contributing partner is only entitled to the share of the partnership's total capital credits, as outlined in the partnership agreement.

There are a number of different types of partners; a partner is not always a "partner":

1. **Ostensible (declared) partner:** Active and known as a partner.

2. **Active partner:** May or may not be ostensible as well.

3. **Secret partner:** Active, but not known or held out publicly as a partner.

4. **Dormant partner:** Inactive, but not known or considered publicly as a partner.

5. **Silent partner:** Inactive, but known or considered publicly as a partner.

6. **Subpartner:** A partner who, even though not a member of the partnership, has contracted with one of the partners to participate in the interest of the contracting partner in the firm's management and profits.

7. **Limited or special partner:** Assuming compliance with the statutory formalities and legalities, limited partners risk only their agreed investment in the business, and are generally not responsible to the same extent for liabilities as general partners, as long as they do not actively participate in the management and control of the partnership or in the conduct of its business.

8. **Partner by *estoppel*:** Partnership liability can be predicated in the legal premise of *estoppel*. These are not true partners in any sense, since they are not a party to the partnership agreement. However, they hold themselves out as partners, or permit others to make such representation by the use of their name or in any other similar manner. Therefore, *estoppel* partners are liable, as if they were full partners, to creditors who provided credit to the partnership based and relying on the reality of such representation. The use of *estoppel* also applies to a legal partner for the actions of another partner who acted beyond his or her contractual authority.

The **advantages of partnerships** are as follows:

- *Ease of creation:* Like the sole proprietorship, partnerships are legally simple formalities and relatively inexpensive.

- *Allocation of profits:* Partnership members are motivated by knowing that the success of the partnership is in part due to their personal efforts, and that as the business prospers, all partners will be rewarded either equally, or as agreed upon in the partnership agreement. This encourages the partnership members to always place the success of the business above their own self-interest, and this is why providing employees the chance to become a partner, as an inducement and incentive, makes good business sense.

- *Accessibility to capital:* The negotiating ability to obtain additional capital from bankers or venture capitalists is enhanced because of the combined financial resources of all the general partners.

- *Flexibility:* Like a sole proprietorship, the partnership has a great deal of flexibility in responding to changing environmental threats and opportunities. Though not as responsive as a sole proprietorship, a partnership can generally respond much quicker than a corporation.

- *Lighter burden of regulation and taxation:* A partnership, much like a sole proprietorship, is subjected to a lesser amount of regulation than its corporate counterparts, and its partners are taxed on their own individual incomes, rather than the double taxation that a corporation has to endure. Additionally, under certain conditions, a partnership of 10 or fewer persons can incorporate to achieve corporate benefits but still retain the right to dividing partnership income among the partners, as if it were a partnership rather than a corporation.

The **disadvantages of partnerships** are presented below:

- *Unlimited liability:* All the partners, except limited or special partners, are ordinarily liable for the actions of each other in a joint liability, which applies even if one or more of the partners were totally unaware of the acts of another.

- *Tenuous life:* The partnership is subjected to many eventualities, which may terminate its existence or disrupt its operation. A partnership may be terminated voluntarily, legally, or terminated involuntarily by the death, or the declaration of insanity or incapacity of a partner. A serious disagreement between or among partners may affect the proper conduct of the business, but the disagreement per se may not necessarily result in the actual dissolution of the partnership.

- *Management harmony and coordination are difficult to achieve:* The equality of the partners is simple in theory but much more difficult in practice. Partners may not agree, leading to power plays and politics. Division of work assignments may prove awkward, and, consequently, essential activities for the operation of the business can be easily neglected. The principle of equality among partners does not predicate management harmony and coordination, because a strong leader must emerge in a partnership, with followers who are willing to compromise.

- *Problems in disposing the partnership interest:* A partner's share is not easily disposed except by agreement with the other partners, and then most likely to one or more of the remaining partners. Attempting to sell a partnership share to an outsider without proper valuation or consent by the remaining partners can and should be met with strong opposition.

- *Limitations in raising funds:* Although the ability of a partnership to acquire capital generally exceeds that of a sole proprietorship, compared to a corporation, partnerships are simply not capable of obtaining the same levels of equity or financing.

The Corporation

The corporation is by far the most complex form of legal business structure and may be categorized in a number of different ways. There are public corporations, privately held corporations, corporations for profit, not-for-profit corporations, foreign corporations, and *de jure* and *de facto* corporations. Classifying the corporation at the outset is important. If a choice is made for a closely held corporation and stock is sold only to a few friends or family members, normally this type of corporation will be exempt from all but the most routine requirements of federal and state securities laws. But if stock in the corporation is sold to outside investors, the requirements of the securities laws, and primarily state, not federal, law will control the corporation.

As defined by Chief Justice Marshall in a famous decision in 1891, a **corporation** "is an artificial being, invisible, intangible, and existing only in contemplation of the law." In other words, a corporation is a distinct legal entity, separate from the individual or individuals who own it, and it may own property or be sued as if it were a physical person. Its main advantage is that, as a legal entity, the corporation is not affected by the departure or death of an individual member.

A corporation is usually formed by the authority of a specific state's government. If they do business in more than one state, they must comply with the federal laws regarding interstate commerce as well as the state laws of each state in which they operate. These state laws and the related terminology may vary considerably from each other. Most state laws generally require that a number of adult persons, generally at least three, who are U.S. citizens and one of whom is a citizen of the state of incorporation, file for the charts of incorporation. The application for incorporation generally includes the names of the principals, the name of the corporation, the reasons for forming the corporation, the proposed life of the firm, the location of the corporate office, the total amount of capital stock, and the number of the shares to be issued, including the value per share. People involved in a corporation traditionally play different legal roles: incorporator, shareholder, director, officer, and employee.

Generally, the incorporators file the application in a specific state with that state's secretary of state, who subsequently issues a corporate charter and assesses a fee for the application. Once the charter has been received and filed, a meeting of the incorporators is held during which the board of directors is elected with the further responsibility to ratify the original corporate bylaws. In addition to approving the original corporate bylaws, the board of directors also has the power at a later date to alter, amend, or revoke these bylaws. However, if such subsequent changes affect the rights of the stockholders, the board is limited in its action. The bylaws provide rules for the operations of the corporation and deal with such issues as the corporate seal, the stock certificate, the numbers of officers and directors, the method for electing these officers and directors, and the time and place of board and stockholder meetings. While bylaws are certainly of great importance to the incorporators, they are of equal and at times greater importance to prospective investors, who want specific insight into the operating procedures of the corporation.

The corporate charter, operating within the legal bounds defined by the incorporating state, outlines the powers of the corporation. Along with the general power of conducting corporate business, most corporations enjoy the following additional powers:

- To have perpetual existence

- To sue and be sued

- To have a corporate name and corporate seal

- To own, use, convey, and deal in both real and personal property

- To borrow and lend money

- To purchase, own, and dispose securities

- To enter into contracts of any kind

- To make charitable contributions

- To establish and pay pension plans

- To have any other power necessary or convenient to pursue any other legal purpose

As stated earlier, corporations can sell their stock or securities, and state and federal government laws have regulated these sales since the 1930s. Federal security laws are administered by the *Securities and Exchange Commission* (SEC) and are designed to protect prospective investors. Securities laws cover not only stocks and bonds but also every kind of investment in which the investor relies on the activities of others to generate investment profit. Securities laws are covered by two general statutes: the *Securities Act of 1933* and the *Securities Exchange Act of 1934*, under the legal heading of "Blue Sky Laws," so called because they provide protection for the public against investments and securities sales activities into the "deep blue sky." The Securities Act of 1933 is, in actuality, a disclosure law. This law requires the registration of securities and publication of a prospectus for investors, and it focuses on securities sales to the general public. The Securities Exchange Act of 1934 in contrast, is concerned with the trading of securities after the primary offering; it also regulates stockbrokers and the stock exchange markets. This act calls for the registration of certain stock sales with the appropriate stock exchange, such as the New York Stock Exchange or *NASDAQ*. As a general rule, all equity securities held by 500 or more owners must be registered if the issuing firm has more than $1 million in gross assets.

The **advantages of incorporating** are the following:

- *Limitation of the stockholder's liability:* The corporate liability limitation is a fixed amount, usually the amount of investment, and should not be confused with regular liability insurance considerations. There is no limited liability when the corporation breaks the law, for failing to deposit taxes withheld from employees' wages, for example.

- *Legal entity:* As mentioned earlier, the corporation is an entity separate and distinct under the law, with ownership represented by shares of stock. It may own property, is not affected by the death or withdrawal of any of its stockholders, and is protected, as a physical person would be, with "due process and equal protection" covered by the Fourteenth Amendment of the U.S. Constitution.

- *Ease of transferability of ownership:* The shares of stock can be sold or transferred without difficulty, as long as there is a buyer.

- *Obtaining capital:* Forming a new corporation with a "saleable" idea can provide opportunities to sell stock to a variety of investors. Later, as a corporation achieves growth, stability, and credibility, it can usually bargain more effectively for a substantial amount of equity or borrowed capital than can either a proprietorship or partnership.

- *Employee benefits:* The corporation has a better chance to create incentives for employees and minor stockholders. Fringe benefits may include stock ownership and bonuses, pension plans, insurance programs, such as group term life insurance and health and disability insurance, reimbursement of employee medical expenses not covered by insurance, and death benefit payments. And other "fringe" benefits can be designed and offered more readily because they generate tax advantages for the corporation. In some cases, these advantages can also benefit the owners of a family-owned or a "closely held" corporation.

- *Tax savings:* Once the business becomes profitable, doing business as a regular corporation allows a degree of flexibility in planning and controlling federal income taxes that is unavailable to partnerships and sole proprietorships. A regular corporation may not have to pay any corporate income tax even though it is a separate taxable entity if it is a closely held corporation where the owners are usually the employees. They receive salaries and bonuses as compensation for the services they perform for the corporation, and the corporation then deducts this "reasonable" compensation as a business expense. This may eat up all corporate profits, so there is no taxable income left for the corporation to pay taxes on.

- *Stability and relative permanence of existence:* In the case of illness, death, or other cause for loss of a principal or officer, the corporation continues to exist and do business.

- *Delegated authority:* Centralized control is secured when owners delegate authority to hired managers who act as their "agents," although they are sometimes one and the same.

- *Better management:* The corporation usually has the ability to draw on the expertise and skills of many individuals, and therefore has better chances of attracting competent management than either a proprietorship or partnership.

- *Favorable legal status:* Certain laws, such as those relating to usury, are not applicable to corporations. Additionally, many tax laws make special provisions for corporations.

The **disadvantages of incorporating** are as follows:

- *Activities limited by the corporate charter:* Often, it becomes exceedingly complicated for corporations to operate in other states without having to refile copies of their charter in every state in which they want to do business.

- *High incorporating costs:* Forming and maintaining the corporate form, corporate license fees, and franchise taxes can be very expensive.

- *Double taxation of corporate income:* Corporate profits are taxed first as corporate income and then as personal income tax, when they are distributed as dividends to the individual stockholders. However, in case of closely held corporations this can be avoided fairly easy.

- *Excessive regulation:* Corporations in general are subject to many more government regulations and reporting requirements than other business legal forms.

- *Manipulation of minority stockholders:* At times, minority stockholders find themselves powerless at the mercy of majority stockholders.

Some Other Legal Organizational Forms

A variety of other incorporating options is available to entrepreneurs. They include: S corporations, professional service associations, not-for-profit corporations, cooperatives, limited liability corporations, and joint ventures.

The S Corporation

As mentioned earlier, a regular corporation (sometimes also called a C corporation) is treated as a tax-paying entity separate from its investors, and it must pay corporate federal income tax. By contrast, the **S corporation** is a hybrid between a partnership and a corporation, and a corporation that chooses S corporation status does not pay federal income tax, but instead, the corporation's owners pay income taxes. Thus, an S corporation status has the advantage for the stockholders to be treated as if in a C corporation with the limited personal liability of a corporate shareholder, but with the possibility of using corporate losses to offset other taxable income on the same basis as a sole proprietor or a partner. Among other things, this means that as long as the owner actively participates in the business of the S corporation, business losses can be used to offset income from other income-producing sources, effectively reducing or maybe even eliminating the tax burden. Losses from an S corporation on a personal return are deducted only to the extent of the investors' stock and money they personally loaned to the corporation. A few states, however, tax an S corporation the same as a regular corporation. If the stockholder did not work actively in the S corporation, there are potential problems with the deductibility of losses, because they might be considered losses from passive activities. Shareholders pay income tax on their share of the corporation's profits, regardless of whether they actually received the money or not.

To be treated as an S corporation, all shareholders must sign and file IRS Form 2553. The S corporation may not have more than 75 shareholders and can receive no more than 20% of its income from rents, interest, royalties, or dividends. It files an informational tax return notifying the IRS on each shareholder's portion of corporate income, but, as mentioned earlier, it does not pay corporate taxes itself, as well as certain other taxes. For instance, the S corporation does not deduct, nor pay Social Security taxes on the income of an owner who works for the firm, unlike regular corporations that must deduct Social Security taxes on income paid to owners employed by the company.

The greatest advantages of the S corporation are for businesses expecting to operate for a given time period at a loss and the unlimited reliance of S corporations on passive income from rents, royalties, interest, etc. This explains the growing popularity of this corporate form in recent years, even though S corporations have somewhat lost their appeal because of passive activity loss tax limitations for individual income tax returns and because states have been passing laws favoring another non-traditional corporate form, the *limited-liability company* (LLC), which also offers its owners greater flexibility in allocating profits and losses. There are also other advantages, such as the possibility of raising additional capital without losing control of the company by being allowed to issue two classes of common stock: voting and non-voting. This however, may limit equity financing in some cases, because venture capitalists are not particularly fond of this situation.

From a tax point of view, the S corporation loses its appeal once the company grows and starts generating a great deal of profits, at which time it is advisable to drop S corporation status with the possibility of picking it up later, during an expansion period. Some other disadvantages of the S corporation include the fact that all shareholders must be individuals who are U.S. citizens or permanent residents, estates, or some type of trust. Corporations, partnerships, or foreign investors are not allowed to invest in the company, thereby limiting the ability of an S corporation to raise additional investment capital.

The Professional Service Association

Since the Internal Revenue Service recognized the status of professional corporations in 1969, the traditional notion of the professional/client relationship has changed, at least in terms of tax treatment. Today, every state has a statute pertaining to professional associations generally noted by the letters *S.C.* (service corporation) or *P.C.* (professional corporation). Furthermore, tax laws often give favorable treatment to fringe benefits for corporate employees in professional corporations. These corporate hybrids provide professional proprietors, such as lawyers, doctors, engineers, etc., with the same pension and profit-sharing plans that are available to corporations but are not available to sole proprietorships or partnerships. Much professional incorporation activity followed the passage of H.R. 10, or the Keogh pension plan provision.

Nonprofit Corporations

Today, according to Internal Revenue Service figures, there are more than 800,000 **nonprofit organizations** in the United States. Increasingly, this has been a unique route for entrepreneurs entering the start-up stage of their business operation. Many religious, educational, or charity-oriented organizations obtain exemption under section 501(c)(3) of the tax code. Not only is a nonprofit organization free from paying taxes on its income, individuals and organizations that contribute to the nonprofit corporation can also take a tax deduction for their contributions. However, an investor who "invested" assets into a nonprofit corporation must give up any ownership or proprietary interest in those assets, and in the case of the dissolution of a nonprofit corporation, any remaining assets must be transferred to another nonprofit. For many entrepreneurs, however, tax protection is not the only motive for pursuing a nonprofit legal status. Some of the reasons offered by entrepreneurs for opting for a **nonprofit legal form** include the following:

Reduced postal rates for mailings. Sometimes, it is more difficult to maintain tax-exempt status with the Post Office than with the IRS. Indeed, both the Sierra Club and the National Rifle Association, as well as some church-affiliated and other nonprofit organizations, have lost their tax-exempt status with the U.S. Post Office. For instance, even the appearance of any C corporation's direct or indirect advertising in a nonprofit's mailing will disallow the nonprofit's reduced rate by the U.S. Post Office.

Exemption from most taxes. U.S. Federal law, state laws, and many local laws exempt nonprofits from most taxes, but they are also very clear on what the status of the tax-exempt groups organized under Section 501(c)(3) of the Internal Revenue Service Code should be. In light of this, the *Branch Ministries v. Rossotti* case ruling has revoked the tax exemption of churches that engage in partisan politics. This case began in 1992 when the Church at Pierce Creek, a Binghamton, New York, congregation, bought political advertisements in *USA Today* and *The Washington Times*. Adding to the legal implications of the church against a tax-exempt status was a line at the bottom of the advertising page that said, "Tax deductible donations for this advertisement gladly accepted" (Conn, 2000).

Instant credibility. Nonprofit status seems to provide companies with instant credibility and respectability in the corporate world.

Accessibility to grants. Nonprofit status often facilitates the acquisition of federal and foundation grants.

The Federal Tax Code lists at least 26 different categories of tax-exempt organizations. But the letter of the law and its interpretation is always changing and is subject to frequent review. The option to "go" nonprofit is an unusual one, but certainly worthy of consideration for a new venture with special circumstances and a unique mission.

Limited-Liability Corporations (LLCs)

Since 1977, an increasingly growing number of states has been authorizing the formation of another nontraditional form of corporation, namely **limited-liability corporations** (LLCs) for entrepreneurs, and **limited-liability partnerships** (LLPs) for professional groups that are similar to the LLCs, discussed below. The LLC is the newest form of business entity, and it is often a very attractive alternative to the traditional legal forms of doing business. The state laws specifying how an LLC is created and the federal tax regulations determining how an LLC is taxed are still evolving. The advantages of an LLC are similar to the advantages enjoyed by the S corporation, allowing the entrepreneurs the benefit of limited liability provided by the corporation, even if they participate in management. Additionally, LLCs provide the advantages of the avoidance of double taxation enjoyed by the partnership, without the special eligibility requirements and restrictions of the S corporation. However, not all states have authorized LLC provisions, and that poses some problems when the venture is involved in interstate commerce. Furthermore, the *Securities and Exchange Commission*

(SEC) has joined the states to ensure that LLCs are not formed to avoid U.S. securities laws. Many states now also permit the formation of *professional limited liability companies* (PLLCs), whose members also will not be personally liable for other business debts, such as obligations owed to business creditors, lenders, or landlords (Emshwiller, 1994). The decision to be organized as an entity that limits personal liability for business debts should be further analyzed by comparing the choice between forming a LLC and a C corporation, and it should be weighed according to the following factors.

Limited personal liability. As with a corporation, all owners of an LLC enjoy limited personal liability. This means that being a member of an LLC does not normally produce personal legal liability for business debts and court judgments against the business, and generally speaking, LLC members risk only their share of capital paid into the business. By contrast, owners of a sole proprietorship or general partnership have unlimited liability for business debts, as do general partners in a limited partnership, and limited partners who take part in managing the business, as discussed below.

Number of owners. In most states, if the sole owner of a business wishes to limit personal liability, he or she has no choice but to form a corporation or an LLC. If the state of residence still requires two or more members for a valid LLC, the married owner can meet that requirement by inviting his or her spouse to be an LLC member. If this is not a possibility, and the owner still wants limited personal liability for the one-person business, there is no choice but to form a corporation.

Tax flexibility. A single-member LLC will not be taxed as a separate entity, like a regular corporation, unless the single LLC member elects to have it taxed in this manner. Similarly, an LLC with two or more members will be treated as a partnership for tax purposes, with each partner reporting and paying income tax on his or her share of LLC profits, unless they elect to have the LLC taxed as a corporation. Occasionally, the members of an LLC may determine that there is an advantage to being taxed like a corporation, with two levels of tax—one at the business-entity level for company profits, and another at the owners' personal income tax level for salaries and dividends. This way, they are able to split taxable profits between the business owners and the business itself, resulting in some situations in significant overall tax savings. Electing to have the LLC taxed as a corporation can also be advantageous for receiving tax-free fringe benefits from the business. If the LLC is not taxed as a separate entity like the corporation is taxed, then the LLC's business owners, unlike other employees, will pay taxes on the value of the fringe benefits they receive from the LLC.

Management structure flexibility. The LLC can be managed jointly by the entrepreneur and other LLC members, by a single member, an outside manager, or by a management group consisting of some LLC members, some nonmembers, or both. No matter how it is done, all LLC members must sign an operating agreement that spells out exactly how the business will be managed.

Flexible distribution of profits and losses. The LLC members can decide to apportion the LLC profits and losses in any way they wish.

Overall, for the majority of small firms, the relative simplicity and flexibility of the LLC makes it a better choice than a corporation. As discussed above, some circumstances tip the balance in favor of a corporation: (a) when the entrepreneur wants to set up a single-member LLC but lives in a two or more member state, (b) there is a need to provide extensive fringe benefits to owner-employees, or (c) to entice or keep key employees by offering stock options and bonus incentives.

Limited Liability Partnerships

In a few states, laws or professional ethics rulings prevent accounting or law firms from doing business as corporations or LLCs. Available in some but not all states, a *limited liability partnership* can be formed as a general partnership whose partners enjoy some protection from personal liability. Most limited partnerships are formed to invest in real estate because of tax advantages for passive investors. The passive investor is often able to personally write off depreciation and other real estate deductions. There must be one or more *general partners* with the same basic rights and responsibilities as in any general partnership, and one or more *limited partners,* who are usually the passive investors. The general partner is personally liable for the obligations of the partnership, but the limited partner is not. Typically, general partners in an LLP are personally liable only for their own negligence or that of a directly supervised employee, but they are not personally liable for the negligence of anyone else in the firm. However, a general partner in an LLP is still personally liable for a large variety of partnership debts. To maintain limited liability, a limited partner may not participate in the management of the business, with a very few exceptions. The advantage of a limited partnership as a business structure is that it provides a way for business owners to raise money from passive investors without having either to take in new partners who will be active in the business or to engage in the intricacies of creating a corporation and issuing stock. However, doing business as a limited partnership can be at least as costly and complicated as doing business as a corporation.

The Joint Venture

A **joint venture** is a form of temporary partnership whereby two firms join forces to undertake a venture such as land development or research, for profit that is taxed as if the two firms were a partnership. When the profit targets have been reached or the joint venture's viability is no longer necessary or desirable, the joint venture is dissolved. A joint venture makes a lot of sense, especially in the case of two firms with complementary strengths, such as one providing financial clout and the other research and development capabilities, or one providing an innovative product and the other a strong marketing network. These alliances are quite common in the high-tech and communications industries, and they occur frequently in both domestic and multinational joint ventures. This legal form may also be appropriate for ventures in countries that possess vast resources and inexpensive labor but lack capital and technology, such as Russia, China, and the former Eastern European countries, such as Poland, Hungary, Romania, Bulgaria, etc.

The Cooperative

A **cooperative** is a business formed by independent producers, wholesalers, retailers, or consumers that act collectively in selling and/or buying products and services. Cooperatives pay no taxes and distribute any residual profits after their operating expenses back to the members of the cooperative at the end of each year. Federal and state governments regulate and impose certain requirements in order for a firm to qualify as a cooperative form of business. Cooperatives are usually associated with the production, processing, and marketing of agricultural and farm products, but they can also appear as utility cooperatives with the recent deregulation of the utilities industry. For example, several residents of the island of Kauai in Hawaii, where the cost of electricity is among the highest in the nation, recently decided to form a cooperative called the Kauai Island Utility Co-op. They announced their intention to buy the local utility company Kauai Electric from its owner, Citizens Utilities, hoping that in the long run they will be paying less for their electric bills ("Kauai Electric," 2000, p. A5).

CONCLUSION

An evaluation of the best choice for the legal form of the venture needs to be performed, as well as periodic reviews to make sure that the legal framework of the new venture is the appropriate one. It is imperative to seek and receive the very best advice available from lawyers, accountants, bank officers, consultants, etc., on this critical matter. Olmi and the U.S. Small Business Administration (1977, Management Aid #231) summarized this quest in eight straightforward questions:

1. What is the size of the risk? What is the amount of the investors' liability for debts and taxes?

2. Given a specific legal organizational form, what would the continuity of the life of the firm be if something happened to the principal or principals?

3. What legal structure would ensure the greatest flexibility and adaptability for the management and administration of the firm?

4. What is the impact of the applicable laws?

5. Given a specific legal organizational form, what are the possibilities of attracting additional capital?

6. What are the needs for and possibilities of attracting additional expertise?

7. What are the costs and procedures in launching the enterprise under different legal structure alternatives?

8. What is the ultimate goal and purpose of the enterprise, and which legal structure can best serve its purposes?

Website Information

Topic	Web Address	Description
Sole proprietorship	www.irs.gov/Businesses/ Small-Businesses-&-Self- Employed/Sole-Proprietorships	IRS guide for sole proprietorships.
S corporation	http://www.irs.gov/Businesses/ Small-Businesses-&-Self- Employed/S-Corporations	IRS guide for S corporations.
Non-profit corporations	http://www.njnonprofits.org/	Gives some information on how the New Jersey non-profit corporations are organized.

Key Terms

Active partner: May or may not be ostensible as well.

Advantages of a nonprofit legal form: Reduced postal rates for mailings, exemption from most taxes, instant credibility, and accessibility to grants.

Advantages of incorporating: Limitation of the stockholder's liability, legal entity, ease of transferability of ownership, obtaining capital, employee benefits, tax savings, stability and relative permanence of existence, delegated authority, better management, favorable legal status.

Advantages of partnerships: Ease of creation, allocation of profits, accessibility to capital, flexibility, lighter burden of regulation and taxation.

Advantages of sole proprietorship: Ease of creation, single beneficiary for profits, total control, maximum flexibility, and limited local, state, and federal regulation.

Cooperative: A business formed by independent producers, wholesalers, retailers, or consumers acting collectively in selling and/or buying products and services.

Corporation: A distinct legal entity, separate from the individual or individuals who own it, and may own property or can be sued as if it were a physical person.

Disadvantages of incorporating: Activities limited by the corporate charter, high incorporating costs, double taxation of corporate income, excessive regulation, manipulation of minority stockholders.

Disadvantages of partnerships: Unlimited liability, tenuous life, management harmony and coordination are difficult to achieve, problems in disposing the partnership interest, and limitations in raising funds.

Disadvantages of sole proprietorship: Unlimited liability, restricted participation in ownership, limitations in raising funds, over-reliance on a "one-man show," and a limited perspective.

Dormant partner: Inactive, but not known or considered publicly as a partner.

Joint venture: A form of temporary partnership whereby two firms join to undertake a venture such as land development or research, for profit that is taxed as if the two firms were a partnership.

Limited-liablility corporation (LLC): A type of legal entity whose members have some degree of protection from personal liability.

Limited-liability partnership: A general partnership whose partners enjoy some protection from personal liability.

Limited or special partner: A partner who risks only his or her agreed investment in the business, and generally not responsible to the same extent for liabilities as general partners.

Nonprofit organizarions: A business free from paying taxes on its income. Individuals and organizations that contribute to the nonprofit corporation can take a tax deduction for their contributions.

Ostensible partner: Active and known as a partner.

Partners by estoppel: These are not true partners in any sense, since they are not a party to the partnership agreement; *estoppel* partners are liable to creditors as if they were full partners.

S corporation: A hybrid between a partnership and a corporation, the S corporation does not pay income tax, but the corporation's owners pay income taxes.

Secret partner: Active, but not known or held out publicly as a partner.

Silent partner: Inactive, but known or considered publicly as a partner.

Sole proprietorship: The owner and the business are one and the same.

Subpartner: A partner, who even though not a member of the partnership, has contracted with one of the partners to participate in the interest of the contracting partner in the firm's management and profits.

Uniform Partnership Act: An association of two or more persons to carry on as co-owners of a business for profit.

Review Questions

1. Discuss three of the eight issues to consider in selecting the right legal organizational form.

2. Discuss the advantages and disadvantages of each type of legal organization: sole proprietorships, partnerships, and corporations.

3. What are some other legal organizational forms open to the entrepreneur?

4. Discuss the reasons for deciding for or against the LLC legal form.

Reflections from the Front Lines of LifeGuard America

LifeGuard America is a limited liability company. We chose this type of company for several of the pros listed above, but mainly because it offered us the most flexibility based on not fully knowing what future investors might require in their term sheets. That, while short-sighted, does not limit us in any way. If an investor had come to us and said, "Here's the cash, but our terms include the element that LifeGuard America needs to be a C corporation," we would have been able to reverse the board's election of a limited liability company (LLC) the very next day. The fact is that we believed that there are several key elements of the LLC form that met our needs, and it has proved to be even more beneficial for the angel investors that want to flow their earnings out of LifeGuard America and into their favorite charity.

Our structure allows them to assign their unit ownership to any entity they want, and we flow the profits out to that entity in the same manner as any other unit-holder. The structure is an important facet of the company, no doubt, but no matter which structure you choose you need to make sure that you build in flexibility to change if it becomes necessary.

Discussion Questions on LifeGuard America

1. What is important in the selection of the structure in Mr. Fitzpatrick's opinion? Do you agree or disagree?

2. What are the specific advantages and disadvantages of the structure selected? Would LifeGuard America have been better served with a better structure?

References

Conn, J. L. (2000, June). Judgment day. *Church and State, 53(6),* 11–12.

Emshwiller, J. R. (1994, March 31). SEC sets sights on certain limited liability companies. *The Wall Street Journal,* p. B2.

Kauai Electric faces rough road (2000, February 16). *The Honolulu Advertiser,* p. A5.

Olmi, A. M., & U.S. Small Business Administration (1977). *Selecting the legal structure for your firm* (Management Aid No. 231). Washington, DC: Small Business Administration.

Venture Management

12 Venture Ability to Execute: Organizing, Staffing, and Management Considerations

Can We Execute the Management and Leadership of People?

LEARNING OBJECTIVES

1. To determine the ability of entrepreneurial ventures to recruit and retain qualified employees.
2. To investigate the recruitment process for employees with specific skills.
3. To investigate methods of selection process and their legal implications.
4. To emphasize the importance of compensation and benefits to the small firm, and discuss various options available for providing competitive compensation packages.
5. To examine how the importance of management and leadership increases as the venture develops.
6. To examine the importance of delegation in managing the venture.
7. To emphasize the importance of conflict resolution to the venture.

TOPIC OUTLINE

*"One reason why the big apples are at the top of the basket
is because a lot of little apples are keeping them up there. . . ."*

(Unknown)

———

INTRODUCTION

It has been documented over and over again that small firms with less than 100 employees create more than half of all new jobs (Johnston & Packer, 1987). This trend is expected to continue as the economy experiences a decline in manufacturing and an increase in service firms, which usually tend to be smaller than manufacturers. However, attracting and retaining qualified, competent workers is one of the major problems facing small firms because of the disadvantages small firms face in competing with large businesses in such areas as salaries, benefits, and working conditions. Regardless, attracting and keeping qualified workers should be as high a priority for small businesses as attracting and retaining customers. The purpose of this chapter is to investigate the areas of organization design, staffing, and compensation for the small venture, which fulfill a number of unique organizational needs. Ventures have distinctive characteristics that influence the way start-up and ongoing businesses are managed, such as instability in the markets they serve, the existence of close family and kinship ties within a firm, the educational and occupational experiences of their owners and managers, and their patterns of management training and development (Deeks, 1976). In addition, small firms provide the initial training for people just entering the labor force, and they absorb all of the expected costs resulting from employee errors (Berney, 1981). The success of the small firm may ultimately depend on the quality of the people who work for it (Eckert, Ryan, & Ray, 1989).

When studying the staffing and organizing function of a small firm, some issues that apply to large organizations are not applicable to small firms; small firms should not be viewed like children who are not "little grown-ups." The venture's organizing, staffing, and management should be custom-made for the organizational system at hand (Dandridge, 1979). McGuire (1976) accuses management researchers of neglecting organizational research on small firms, which is perceived to be too simplistic and trivial to warrant serious study:

> To the sophisticated organizational theorist, the small business enterprise is too simple and too obvious: it contains no long hierarchical chains; no Machiavellian power machinations; no complex shifting interpersonal relationships; no large and confused communications network; and no need to develop yet one more theory of leadership. To most scholars in these disciplines, then, the small company does not appear to promise the research challenge provided by the giant corporation. Rather, the problems of the small company seem to be uncomplicated and the solutions, in many cases, self-evident. . . . (p. 115)

The experience of many entrepreneurs reflects that of many in similar situations who have been successful in starting new ventures only to find out later that the start-up was the easy part (Hyatt, 1989). It has been suggested that the start-up of a new venture progresses through steps or stages; these include evaluating the opportunity, developing the business concept, assessing required resources, acquiring needed resources, and managing and harvesting the business (Stevenson, Roberts, & Grousback, 1985).

This chapter focuses on the last step: managing the venture. In the early stages of business development, the entrepreneur typically thrives on the "hands on" involvement required in building a successful enterprise. However, growth in the business generally requires a shift in management style (Dolan, 1989). Is it possible for an entrepreneur to also assume the role of manager? Results from years of reviewing entrepreneurial successes are contradictory. But as mentioned earlier, the fact is that the conditions under which the entrepreneur operates are different from those of the large corporation (Andrews, 1983). Although the management tasks may be different for the entrepreneur, management skills are essential (March, 1984).

JOB DESIGN

A venture's prospective should have appropriate and well-defined job roles. The owner entrepreneur should make sure that an employee being recruited is not subjected to conflicting roles, or repeating the activities that an existing employee already performs (Feldman, 1980). Job design and job descriptions set rules and are therefore very important, especially in a new venture. Job descriptions and personnel manuals are quite often absent from a work situation, which increases the possibility of problems between the entrepreneur and prospective employees.

Research has shown that employees are more satisfied and less confused when they have clear job titles, ranks, and career paths, and when there are no "gray" areas in job design. In contrast, role ambiguity consistently shows a moderate to high correlation with employee job burnout (Maslach, Schaufeli, & Leiter, 2001). Failure to create and maintain comprehensive job descriptions that clearly define the expectations of the company for an employee can lead to employee dissatisfaction, which in turn can lead to customer dissatisfaction, hampering a new venture's chances of success. Brief job descriptions convey the essence of the job and are flexible as the specifics of the job evolve (Joinson, 2001). Using the typical job description catch phrase *"and other duties as assigned"* can be a trap, causing entrepreneurs to neglect job descriptions. To help with these descriptions, the typical manner in which companies create job descriptions needs to be redefined. Instead of focusing on the skills required for a particular position, job descriptions in an entrepreneurial firm revolve around the role the position has within the company. Because skills do not often define the success of an employee within a role, role-based job descriptions focus on behavioral competencies that are essential to job success. This is accomplished by considering and implementing four key management principles (DeLong, 1982):

- All employees have job descriptions and titles that accurately reflect their roles and ranks in the venture.

- All employees have logical career paths within the venture that are clearly defined.

- Employees are encouraged to take responsibility for their own career development.

- Employee performance is undertaken through consistent evaluation and performance standards.

A good **job description** should be carefully designed to include the following (Evered, 1981):

1. *Job title:* The job title should actually read exactly as it will later appear in employment advertising and personnel records.

2. *Basic job function:* The fundamental job function should be stated clearly in one sentence.

3. *Relationships:* The interrelationships of the job should be described in terms of defined lines of communication to other jobs and individuals.

4. *Responsibilities:* All the duties for which the employee is responsible should be indicated clearly and narrowly, avoiding the phrase "other duties, as assigned," which is often viewed as a manager's license to exploit employees.

5. *Authority:* The job's authority should be delineated in terms of clearly defined limits of decision-making power legislated by the organization and limits of delegation to other employees.

6. *A "Standards of Performance" statement:* This statement should clearly state how well the employee is expected to accomplish each of the primary responsibilities in the job description. Completing the following sentence for each responsibility creates a well-defined set of standards: "Your work will be deemed completely satisfactory, when. . . ."

7. *Accountability:* The employee is accountable for every responsibility and duty listed in the job description.

RECRUITMENT

The average cost of recruiting talented employees can be high because expenses related to advertising, telephone calls, travel, relocation, recruiting agency fees, training, and administration should also be included in the direct cost of recruiting. Indirect recruiting expenses result from operational delays caused by the vacant position and the time required to interview job candidates. Therefore, finding and keeping good people is of critical concern to small-firm owners.

Recruitment is more than the mere act of hiring someone. It is often viewed as a form of business competition, as firms try to identify, attract, and hire the most well-qualified individuals (Lord, 1989). This part of the employment process matches applicants with the necessary abilities, skills, aptitudes, and attitudes to fill the needs of the organization. In spite of major differences, the job of recruiting employees for a small firm is in many respects the same as for a large one. It is important that the entrepreneur first establish specific objectives and goals for staff selection which cover such issues as the importance that the venture places on its workforce, the philosophy regarding "buying" expertise versus developing talent from within the venture, the hiring of minorities and the disadvantaged, and levels of authority responsible for employment-related decisions. It is also helpful to keep a record of expenditures and the results of the recruitment advertising alternatives to evaluate the success of the recruitment strategy ("How to Recruit," 1981).

Recruitment can be viewed as a marketing problem. When an advertisement is placed in the classified section of a newspaper, certain factors have to be kept in mind:

• The target audience of the ad

• How to best reach the target audience

• The projected image of the job

• The projected image of the firm

Another very effective recruitment device can be a referral program that offers incentives and rewards when someone recommends a successful job candidate (Lord, 1989). For such a program to be successful, entrepreneurs must promote the idea by informing partners, internal and external team members, and current employees of openings as they occur; employees should be made aware of the qualifications required. Documentation of all recruitment-related information is critical, as all recruitment materials, applications, and resumes must be retained for at least 1 year after the employment decision has been made (Lesonsky, 2001).

Recruiting for Specific Skills and Employee Categories

A venture should seek the specific types of skills that are essential to the survival of the firm. It should be quite obvious that different types of skills and different categories of employees require different recruiting methods and approaches.

Sales Representatives

Smaller firms face two major disadvantages compared with larger firms in hiring salespeople: difficulty offering competitive salaries and difficulty providing the necessary sales training ("Promotion from Within," 1987). Consequently, the average turnover rate for sales personnel in small firms has been estimated to be as high as 50% the first year and nearly 80% within the first 3 years ("Building the Sales Force," 1986, p. 71). Identifying potentially successful salespeople is a difficult and challenging job because education and experience may not always predict future sales success. Therefore, individuals should be identified who possess the right combination of personal traits, skills, and experience to best fulfill the firm's needs. Personality traits that should be brought to the job include personal drive, focus, empathy, judgment, the ability to learn, self-discipline, creativity, adaptability, and honesty. Job-related skills include product knowledge, analytical skills, selling, and communication skills. While these traits and skills may be difficult to measure, a variety of testing methods exist to help in the process, including biographical analyses, in-depth multiple interview techniques, checklists, multiple choice tests, psychological tests, and assessment-center approaches. The choice of the procedure to be used depends upon the type of job being filled, the availability of testing facilities and qualified administrators, the time allotted, the number of job candidates, and the training programs available ("Building the Sales Force," pp. 71–77). When screening for good sales candidates, firms should attempt to discover the communication, negotiation, and people skills of the candidate. According to the five-factor model of personality, referred to as the Big Five (see page 294), salespeople that display the personality dimension of extraversion are sociable, outgoing, and assertive (Robbins, 2001).

Temporary Workers

The use of temporary workers is now as important to small firms as to large firms because this option provides a good way to control staffing expenses. Another reason for using temporary help is that it is possible to match a special type of skill to a customized temporary project, particularly if the task is boring or repetitive, such as filing. When the special project is over, the firm releases the temporary worker without having to carry unemployment benefit costs. However, the use of temporary workers is not without its liabilities under certain tax and labor laws, unless the firm gives up the day-to-day control of temporary employees. In addition, temporary workers, regardless of the duration of employment, are always protected by anti-discrimination laws, workers' compensation laws, and the Occupational Safety and Health Administration's workplace safety regulations (Manley, 1988). Thus, it is advisable to always weigh the costs versus the benefits carefully when making the decision to use temporary workers.

Outside Contractors

Another alternative available to small firms is the use of self-employed individuals who work only on a project-by-project basis, that is, outside contractors, when extra help is needed to complete special projects requiring a particular expertise. One way to identify contractors who meet the firm's particular needs is keeping track of former associates and soliciting referrals (Posner, 1989b).

Teenage Workers

Many labor-intensive ventures, such as the fast-food industry in particular, depend upon teenage workers. For most of these young people, such a job is their first experience with the real world of work, which may include difficulty adjusting to work discipline, ethics, and reliability. Even though it probably takes only a day or two to train a new employee to a level of reasonable competence, high turnover still costs the owner money in terms of training, employee errors, and lost customers. However, the number of young people will decline in the future in both relative and absolute terms, and as a result, employers may have to pay higher wages, hire other types of workers, such as older workers, and/or invest in labor-saving technology (Johnston & Packer, 1987, p. 82).

MBA Graduates

Most small firms feel they cannot afford to pay a new MBA whose average starting salary expectation is quite high. In addition, entrepreneurs feel that MBAs cannot provide the firm with immediate value usually stemming only from "hands-on" experience, which they consider essential for their line of operations. Despite this negative outlook, MBA students at major accredited business schools such as the University of Tulsa, rush to take entrepreneurship courses, not only because they want to pursue employment by entrepreneurial ventures, but also because they see themselves as following the entrepreneurial path one day. As a University of Virginia MBA running a 33-employee firm puts it: "It all boils down to one word: Freedom!" ("Labor Letter," 1978, p. 1).

Corporate Executives

Sometimes, by offering the right incentives rather than high salaries, it is feasible to attract the skills and talents of executives from larger corporations. Depending upon the particular needs of the firm, it often pays to recruit a seasoned executive who can complement the venture's managerial assets with a different style of aggressiveness or creativity. Executives in their fifties, who have already paid their dues in the corporate world, as well as their mortgages and their children's education, may be looking for the kind of job satisfaction that a smaller firm can offer. Bringing in outside experience may be necessary for various reasons, most notably to facilitate the growth of the enterprise to the next level. Venture capitalists may prefer "bench strength" as a qualification for financing to be extended to the firm (Paris, 2001). Administration, creativity, inspiration, and diversity may be other reasons. Critical to this decision is a clear understanding of the values and culture of the firm, the leadership style, and teamwork expectations (Lynn, 2001). Making personal decisions and seeing that they are carried out is something new to a corporate executive used to top-to-bottom strategic planning. Entrepreneurs also appreciate the immediate results, rather than credentials and promises for the future, that these skilled individuals can offer. However, the chances of an incompatible marriage between a small firm and a corporate executive may be quite high, because the entrepreneur is usually reluctant to give the new executive enough authority to get the job done, while executives may resent being told what to do or having the owner looking over their shoulders. The unwillingness of the entrepreneur to relinquish control is quite understandable, because in a large company, one must really make a large mistake with huge dire consequences to get fired, but in a small firm, something quite minute may produce drastic consequences, perhaps even fatally wounding the venture. Some other reasons for possible incompatibility between the owner and the executive are the lack of rapport and common frames of reference, as well as the unwillingness of owners to divulge information about their own companies, especially if they are privately held. In situations such as these, a better alternative to hiring a former corporate executive is to hire the services of a consultant.

Recruitment from Within

When staffing vacant managerial and supervisory positions, one source of potential candidates is the company's own employees, partners, or internal and external team members. By adopting a policy of promoting from within, it is possible to attract and retain productive employees, while providing the firm with continuity. The use of this method of filling management positions provides employees with the opportunity for advancement, more challenging assignments, and the chance for a more rewarding career. Promotional methods used by firms include job posting, nomination, and career counseling utilizing resource charts ("Promotion," 1987). A policy of promotion from within is very helpful in recruiting inexperienced but potentially dependable employees, since someone already affiliated with the venture provided references for the newly hired individual (Posner, 1989a).

SELECTION

The process of personnel selection involves numerous steps and processes through which a firm can hire and maintain effective personnel. The greater the number of formal selection methods and steps used, the better the selection choice. When choosing the best combination of selection methods, the entrepreneur must weigh the potential costs, in terms of time and money, against the anticipated gains or benefits to the venture. However, research has documented that objective biographical information is one of the most reliable predictors of successful work performance, while the employment interview is one of the least reliable, though it is one of the most popular methods (Hakel, 1989). The following steps are among those used in the venture's employee selection process:

1. Preliminary screening interview
2. Completion of biographical data form or application
3. Employment tests
4. Formal employment interview
5. Background and reference checks
6. Physical examination
7. Employment decision

During the preliminary screening interview, some common sources of selection bias may emerge, such as

1. Nepotism or preferential hiring of relatives.
2. Physical characteristics, such as height, weight, beauty, hair, etc.
3. Projection of personal traits, self-identification onto the interviewee, producing generalizations of two types:
   - **"Halo Effect"** when the interviewer perceives nothing but good traits.
   - **"Devil's horns"** when the interviewer perceives nothing good at all.

Relying too heavily on interviews alone has not proved successful in the past. Multiple studies have been done to analyze the results of the various selection techniques available to potential employers. The following results provide evidence of the changing trends in the techniques used for selection:

- Studies have shown only a 14% correlation between the ability to deliver well in an interview and the ability to perform on the job.

- Assessments of personality characteristics improved the successful-hire percentage to 38%.

- When adding an ability assessment on top of a personality assessment, the percentage rose to 54%.

- With the addition of an interest assessment, this percentage increased again, up to a 66% success rate.

- The latest technique, integrated assessment, attempts to match the candidate to those who are successful in a similar role; it has been shown to further increase the percentage of successful hires to 75%, from 1 in 7 by interviewing alone to 3 of 4 (Sirbasku, 2002).

These statistics indicate the shortcomings of the interview process alone as well as the trend toward assessment based personnel selection. Therefore, the completion of biographical data forms, application forms, along with possible employment tests are designed to improve the selection decision choice after the formal and final employment interview takes place. This information based on objective evidence gives the decision maker as many facts as possible to assess the potential candidate, along with the candidate's qualitative or personality factors and the possible selection biases that might have emerged during the preliminary screening interview. Furthermore, when it comes to filling jobs that require specific, measurable abilities, after the preliminary screening interview, companies must often rely upon the use of objective employment tests. However, because the testing industry is unregulated, entrepreneurs should be skeptical when purchasing standardized tests to be used in employment screening (Simurda, 1989). Most personality assessments focus on traits such as the following:

- *Adjustment:* Upbeat, calm under pressure, patient with others, receptive to feedback, not likely to constantly complain.

- *Ambition:* Energetic, competitive, driven, good leader, take initiative.

- *Interpersonal sensitivity:* Easy to work with, service oriented, helpful, friendly, relationship builder.

- *Conscientiousness:* Dependable, trustworthy, rule-following, careful, detail-oriented, good organizational citizen.

- *Openness:* Creative, strategic, big-picture oriented, open to change, interested in learning.

Additionally, paper and pencil tests designed to determine honesty and integrity have increased in popularity in recent years, particularly since federal law has banned the use of polygraph tests in screening potential employees (Simurda, 1989, p. 174). In using tests to determine honesty, it is important to look to the publisher of the test for evidence of continuing research with regard to validity. In addition, if an applicant scores poorly on such a test but has good qualifications and recommendations, it is important to recheck references or the scoring of the test to ensure that a mistake has not been made (Cascio, 1987). Again, such tests should be used with caution; they have been the focus of much litigation related to charges of discrimination when their use has resulted in disparate impacts on certain minority groups (Hakel, 1989). It is important that the material covered in the selection test is related as directly as possible to the job being filled. Although recent Supreme Court decisions have made it tougher for employees to prove racial bias using statistics (Wermiel, 1989), it is important to be aware that there may be sources of bias in certain types of tests, such as

1. *Lack of reliability* or consistency in scores.

2. *Lack of validity* of the degree to which the test measures what it is intended to measure. There are several types of validity of concern in employment testing:

    - **Construct validity:** The extent to which a test measures a specific trait considered necessary for successful job performance, such as intelligence.

    - **Content validity:** The extent to which a test includes reasonable or representative samples of the behavior or skills needed to successfully perform the job.

    - **Predictive validity:** The extent to which a test predicts successful performance on the job measured by testing a group of applicants and then comparing their scores on the test to a measure of performance after hiring and training.

    - **Concurrent validity:** Obtained by testing current employees, correlating their scores with measures of their performance, and using these criteria for selection of future employees (Werther & Davis, 1989).

In summary, employment assessments need to determine how well prospective good performers are identified, how well prospective poor performers are screened out, and how defensible these determinations are in court, because even unintentional discrimination based on "race, color, religion, sex, or national origin" is prohibited under Title VII of the Civil Rights Act of 1964 and the Civil Rights Act of 1991.

Finally, an increasing number of companies are testing both employees and job applicants for drug and alcohol use. Although critics of drug testing charge that it is a violation of the individual's civil rights, there is presently no legal prohibition against drug testing. If the decision is made to utilize drug testing in the screening of prospective employees, steps should be taken to limit legal liability. For instance, applicants should be informed in writing of the company's intention to use drug testing in the screening process. It is also important that each applicant understands the company's policy regarding drug use and that routine testing by a reliable laboratory, which should be carefully selected, will be a part of their employment (Cascio, 1989).

After information on a prospective employee has been gathered from the preliminary screening interview, the biographical and application forms, and possibly from employment tests, the formal employment interview may take place. This process requires planning and careful preparation to conduct it to produce the desired results.

Preparation of the Interview

1. Identify and assign duties and responsibilities of the specific job to be filled, in writing.

2. Identify the skills, experience, personality, and training needed from the prospective employee.

3. Identify a list of related items to be covered during the interview, stemming from the preliminary screening interview, the biographical form, the application form, or possibly from the results of the employment tests.

The Interview

1. Allocate sufficient time.
2. Allow no interruption whatsoever.
3. Put the interviewee at ease by being pleasant and courteous.
4. Show enthusiasm about the job and its prospects.
5. Listen to what interviewees say, and especially what they do not say.
6. Observe dress and manners.
7. Take notes during the interview.

Interview Questions

Ask the candidate probing open-ended questions with no single "right" answer, along with very narrow questions, such as "What was your selling technique in your previous job?" that do have a "right" answer. Both types of questions can help assess the candidate's operating style on both technical competence and personal contribution to the firm, and at the same time force the candidate to reflect and organize an answer, instead of making prepared statements. Questions asked or remarks made during job interviews may get the interviewer in trouble because of equal opportunity issues. Most of the issues that usually come up during employment interviews are issues that are perfectly legal to discuss, some may weigh against the interviewer if other additional factors point to discrimination, and some are just plain illegal. There are three categories of questions during a job interview according to the *Fair Employment Practices Guidelines* ("The Interview," 1982, pp. 2–4).

What Cannot Be Asked

There are some absolute prescriptions, but not many:

- *Applicant's race:* During either personal or telephone interviews an applicant cannot be asked to state his or her race or color.
- *Applicant's sex*
- *Applicant's national origin*
- *Applicant's marital status:* This might be allowed if the practice is to always ask all candidates regardless of sex, and nothing else in the selection process and record points to potential discrimination against one particular sex.
- *Applicant's religion*

What Should Not Be Asked

Any inquiries on the following subjects could reveal information that should not be gathered during a job or even promotion interview. Any of this information that is required, for insurance purposes for example, can be gathered after the candidate is hired. Asking for the following information before hiring is just asking for trouble:

- *Former name*
- *Parents' names*
- *Place of birth*

- *Second language:* Unless the job requires the use of a second language.

- *Arrest record:* Conviction record is justified to get if the job opening requires an applicant with no conviction record and the business necessity for this requirement can be proved.

- *"Who will take care of the children while the applicant works?":* This might be allowed if the practice is to always ask all candidates regardless of sex, and nothing else in the selection process and record points to potential discrimination against one particular sex.

- *Occupation of spouse:* This might be allowed if the practice is to always ask all candidates regardless of sex, and nothing else in the selection process and record points to potential discrimination against one particular sex, as well as there is no unfair impact on one sex or the other that appears to be based on the answers.

- *Name of religion or clergy*

- *Religious clubs or organizations*

- *Date of birth*

- *Age*

- *Educational background:* Unless it can be proved that it is job related.

- *Physical disabilities:* Unless they would affect performance on the job.

What Can Be Asked

The interviewer is free to ask many questions of any applicant for any job to elicit more information that applies to the job:

- "Do you understand what this job entails?" A discussion of the job can lead to interesting observations about the applicant's abilities, experience, enthusiasm, etc.

- "Why do you think you are suited for this particular job?"

- "Have you ever had any hobbies that would help you do this job?"

- "Do you have any outside activities giving you experience and opportunities that would help on this job?"

- "Have you done any jobs like this before?"

- "What can you tell me about yourself that makes you think you would be good at this job?"

- "From what I have told you about the company and the job, do you think you would like working here?

- "Can you give me any particular reasons?"

- "How do you feel about our hours of business?" As long as this question does not delve with issues of religious holidays or Sabbath hours that might be in conflict with the applicant's religion.

- "Do you have any other information about yourself or about your interests that you think would help me make a decision about filling this job?"

These are all "safe" areas because they are closely job-related. The key to success in interviewing without being accused of discrimination is to concentrate on the job itself as the subject under discussion, rather than personal information about the applicant. This job-related interviewing technique should be used with all applicants, not just minorities, women, and those over 40; practice will perfect the interviewer's performance and prevent any inadvertent blunders or bad interviewing habits ("The Interview," 1982).

After the Interview

Impressions should be recorded immediately after the interview so important details will not be forgotten. These impressions should be compared with the notes made during the actual interview, the initial screening interview, and the results of any employment tests. They should be evaluated on the basis of three factors only: technical competence, personal contribution that the candidate could make to the venture, and the results of reference checks on the candidate.

Background checks attempt to authenticate the identity and accuracy of the candidate's employment and personal information. An estimated 95% of U.S. corporations use background checks, with the most commonly verified areas being legal eligibility for employment, prior employment, military service, education, and identification (Dessler, 2000). The value of reference checks on a person's past performance or integrity is a subject of debate. However, some guidelines on how to approach reference checks are helpful to avoid the possibility of legal challenges:

1. Obtain written permission from the candidate before checking job references.
2. Organize the questions to be asked and keep them job specific.
3. Consider the credibility of the source of the information.
4. Ask for and organize the information obtained in written form to prove that the employment decision was based upon relevant information.
5. As long as the information asked and provided is related to work behavior and/or the reasons for leaving a previous job, the courts have ruled that reference checks do not violate an applicant's civil rights (Cascio, 1989).

In contrast, if asked to provide reference information on a former employee, the following guidelines should be considered:

1. Obtain written consent from the employee before providing any information.
2. Do not blacklist former employees.
3. Keep a written record of all information provided.
4. Avoid subjective statements, such as, "The employee had a bad attitude." Keep information specific and job related.
5. When responding to requests by phone, typically do not provide any information. Instead, simply verify whether or not the information the caller has is correct.
6. The following types of information are always appropriate for release, subject to the written consent of the employee: dates of employment, job titles of positions held and the time spent in each position, promotions, demotions, attendance, salary, and reason for termination without details (Cascio, 1989).

There are no fail-safe formulas guiding the employment decision, because even the best interview and selection techniques do not guarantee that the person hired will work out in the long run. Choosing selection techniques involves weighing costs and benefits, because a procedure that may be high in predictive ability may also be too expensive to administer. The choice of techniques depends upon the relative importance placed upon the objectives of selection, such as the costs of development and administration, validity, acceptability to applicants, and legal defensibility (Rynes & Milkovich, 1986). Once the employment decision has been made, it is important to legally verify the identity and work eligibility of the individual before hiring, whether the position is full-time, part-time, temporary, or seasonal. Acceptable documents include U.S. passports or "green cards" for resident aliens (Cascio, 1989); under the Immigration Reform and Control Act of 1986, employers who do not comply with the law and its verification requirements are subject to stiff fines and possible jail sentences if they hire undocumented workers (Yoshihashi, 1989). Appropriate paperwork must always be kept on file, documenting that the employee is eligible to work in the United States.

COMPENSATION AND BENEFITS

It is very hard for small companies to compete with large firms in the job market, because it is difficult not only to attract quality people but also to retain them, since many employees are motivated by creative and rewarding jobs as well as salary and benefits. As a result, smaller firms fight a constant bidding war for qualified people, especially on the lower end of the salary and skill spectrum, where jobs are difficult to enrich and are evaluated by employees solely on the basis of the salary or wage rates paid. Timmons (1990) extensively discussed reward systems in the venture context, and he contended that individuals joining a venture with a clearly recognized lead entrepreneur, in addition to salaries and fringe benefits will usually consider other benefits, such as title, ownership, and power, which will be awarded to them based on what they contribute or according to how hard they bargain.

The first consideration in determining wage and salary is establishing what the venture can afford, because the firm's ability to pay is constrained by its ability to compete. In other words, if the entrepreneur cannot raise prices without suffering a loss in income or revenue because of decreased sales, then the ability to raise wages and salaries is also decreased (Cascio, 1989). Thus, the small firm must first evaluate its external competitiveness as it relates to its ability to pay competitive wages. A second consideration involves evaluating salaries and wage rates of competing firms as well as the added value that the venture will receive from the individual hired at a salary comparable to, lower than, or higher than the prevailing rates. Three types of wage and salary information are prepared by the Bureau of Labor Statistics:

1. Area Wage Surveys with data broken down by geographic area.

2. Industry Wage Surveys with data on job categories within specific industries.

3. National Survey of Professional, Administrative, Technical and Clerical pay with data categorized by geographic area and company size ("Taking the Guesswork Out of Salary Setting," 1981).

Local labor market conditions must also be evaluated. In areas where the cost of living is high relative to other parts of the country, salary and wage rates may have to be adjusted upward to attract qualified individuals. The information from the Bureau of Labor Statistics surveys, in combination with careful job definition and requirements obtained from job descriptions, can give the entrepreneur a good idea of the median salary offered for a specific occupation, at a specific level, in a specific industry, in a specific geographic area, and for a specific firm size. In addition to government statistics, there are many specialized salary surveys available from trade associations, professional journals, management consulting firms, and periodicals.

Fringe benefits are another area in which it is difficult for the small firm to compete with larger corporations, especially during labor shortages, when there is the perception that an employee's base pay bears no relationship to the level of performance. Often, employees perceive that they will earn the same amount of money whether they work hard or whether they give their job a minimal amount of effort. However, regular fringe benefits such as health insurance or pension plans for example, are costly and often become a major component of overall operating expenses and overhead. It has been estimated that benefits may exceed 39% of the total compensation costs for each employee (Tannenbaum, 1989).

Most companies provide group health insurance coverage for their employees, but the rising cost of health care has resulted in annual premium increases of 20% to 40% in recent years. Often small companies are offered reasonable first-year rates followed by increases of 60% or more if an employee files a major claim (Saddler, 1989). Thus, most small firms must resort to various cost-containment and cost-sharing strategies to manage these costs effectively: (a) **cafeteria plans** in which the employee uses a credit to "purchase" options from a menu of benefits, (b) the use of **preferred provider organizations (PPOs)** in which a network of physicians and hospitals agrees to a fee schedule that represents a discount over usual charges, and (c) **health maintenance organizations (HMOs)** in which a set annual fee is paid for each enrollee, through the use of higher deductibles, or by requiring the employee to contribute more to the cost of the premium (Solomon, 1989). Beyond these increasing benefit costs, legislation has brought about important changes in the management of health insurance benefits. **The Consolidated Omnibus Budget Reconciliation Act of 1986 (COBRA)** requires firms with at least 20 employees to offer the same group health benefits offered to current employees to workers who have been fired, are on leave, or whose hours have been reduced, as well as to widowed or divorced spouses of employees (Cascio, 1989). In addition, Section 89 of the 1986 Tax Reform Act requires that employers who provide primarily tax-free health and life insurance benefits to employees distribute them fairly, and if the employer fails to comply, benefits paid to employees may be considered taxable (Manley, 1989). An important part of the health benefit package is the way in which it is communicated to employees because they not only need to know what kind of health insurance coverage is provided, but they also need to be aware of how much costs have increased, and how much the company spends on health insurance premiums on behalf of the employees. Then efforts at cost containment will be much more successful (Carroon & Black, Inc., 1989).

A pension plan as a fringe benefit should be one that is affordable and provides visibility and perceived value to its participants. Employers who want to provide retirement benefits to employees have many options available, and their contributions, as well as vesting requirements, are governed by the regulations of the *Employment Retirement Income Security Act of 1974* (ERISA). Most firms provide defined-benefit plans in which the employer promises to pay the employee a stated pension determined according to a formula. Defined-contribution plans provide a fixed rate for employer contributions to the fund, such as group incentive bonuses, gain sharing, profit sharing, and employee stock ownership plans to supplement the base wages of employees, and future benefits are determined by how fast the fund grows. They are attractive because the employer never owes more than the amount that was contributed (Cascio, 1989).

Profit sharing is appealing to most small firms because of the absence of predefined, fixed commitments and the positive psychological effect on the employees when they see that they benefit from the success of the firm. The percentage of profits to be contributed to a profit sharing plan is usually determined by the owner-manager or board of directors. Normally, if no profits are given in a year, there will be no contributions to the plan.

Employee Stock Ownership Plans (ESOPs) as fringe benefit plans, allow the firm to create an employee trust and to make fund contributions in its own stock as well as in cash. The advantage is that the stock and cash stay within the company, and although issuing new shares of stock may dilute the founder's ownership in the company, ESOPs create an inexpensive and convenient market for the company's stock. As with pension plans, the *Employee Retirement Income Security Act* (ERISA) regulations regarding contributions and vesting requirements apply to ESOPs.

A small firm considering the implementation of any incentive program should seek professional advice to ensure that the end result meets the requirements of ERISA. The documented benefits derived from these fringe benefit programs include increased commitment and productivity, as well as decreased turnover and absenteeism ("The Staff Role," 1987). ERISA (1974) regulates pension funds; it determines who qualifies for benefits, vesting qualifications, and what kind of pension fund investments are considered prudent. Many small firms often decide to turn the management of their pension fund over to a bank or trust company to avoid the time and expense of keeping up with and complying with ERISA requirements.

AFTER THE HIRE

All new recruits undergo a socialization process when they enter an organization. How well they adapt or accept this socialization will make the difference between the success and failure of the recruiting and selection process. The socialization process, however, is a two-way street, because the organization has almost as much to lose as the individual. When there are well-defined policies and procedures and they are communicated clearly, organizational values are instilled in the new hire, and the locus of control resides within the individual. When new recruits willingly adopt the venture's value system, their individual personal goals will be closer to the organizational goals. The socialization process eliminates extremes, rather than forces the new recruits to conform to the existing organizational values, by gently nudging them in the direction the organization is heading. This direction is a result of good working relationships and communication that has been established by existing organizational members who have worked together for a long time and already get along (Eisenhardt & Schoonhoven, 1990).

Bird (1989) considered factors that may draw entrepreneurial teams together: likeability, proximity, alikeness, complementarity of attributes, and mutual enjoyment. Similarly, Kamm and Nurick (1993) noted that prospective entrepreneurial team members and employees may be attracted to others with similar beliefs and interests or who have qualities judged to be desirable. The socialization process therefore really succeeds when the chemistry of people attracted to each other is the right one.

Performance, high morale, prevention of disagreements, and possible litigation avoidance can be achieved if the venture develops a carefully written handbook that specifically outlines policies and procedures, such as a personnel manual. This manual keeps all employees informed about the venture's policies and regulations, and at the same time, it provides the entrepreneur owner and other managers in the venture with support in enforcing them during the process of managing the venture (Ellman, 1981).

THE MANAGEMENT TEAM

After organizing and staffing the venture, the most essential ingredient contributing to its success or failure is the management team. A management team is more than a mere group because it involves a sense of shared commitments (Guzzo & Dickson, 1996). One way to ensure effective teamwork is to learn about the venture's team members, partners, and employees. Team members like to be informed and feel that they should be making a real contribution to the success of the organization. Small group meetings and retreats away from the office provide the right environment in which team members and employees may be more willing to speak freely about issues that are important and real to them:

- Why do I work here and not somewhere else?
- What do I get out of my work here?
- What are my aspirations for the long run?
- What are the behaviors, actions, or circumstances that make me motivated, energized, and happy with my work?
- What are the things that people do that dampen my enthusiasm and make me angry or depressed? (Bernstein, 1988)

While these issues seem rather simple and straightforward, the owners of rapidly growing ventures often overlook them. Successful entrepreneurial ventures are attentive to these perceived problems and complaints, which should be treated with respect, out of loyalty to the individuals that make things happen, namely the internal team members and employees. "People who feel good about themselves produce results. The best minute I spend, is the one I invest in people." These words from the *One-Minute Manager* reflect the importance of building commitment and a team atmosphere by taking time to listen to the management team's perceived concerns to achieve success and effectiveness (Blanchard & Johnson, 1982).

LEADERSHIP AND MANAGEMENT

The manner in which entrepreneurs behave toward their management team, partners, and subordinates to obtain desired objectives determines their leadership style. In the case of the new venture, the entrepreneur is the founder, leader, motivator, and manager, in addition to being one of the employees. Miner's (1996) research suggested a relationship between personality types and entrepreneurial success, with entrepreneurs being classified as personal achievers, real managers, empathetic "super-salespeople," and expert idea generators. His findings indicated that those entrepreneurs who combine multiple types are the most successful leaders for their venture. While a plethora of leadership theories have developed over the years, ranging from trait theory to situational or contingency theory, many are simply not applicable to the new-venture setting. However, one of the classical theorists, Douglas McGregor (1960), provides some insight into the entrepreneurial process of managing subordinates. McGregor rose from service station attendant to college president, and his concepts of "Theory X" and "Theory Y," while they always included among the most influential leadership theories, are too often superficially dismissed. McGregor brought unique insight into leading and motivating subordinates, and his theory touches upon management practices that are indeed universal in content and scope.

In *The Human Side of Enterprise*, McGregor (1960) introduced two perspectives to explain the task of transforming human energy through leadership and motivation into goal-directed behavior. The first, Theory X, comprises four basic propositions:

1. It is the responsibility of management to organize the elements of productivity for economic ends.

2. To fit the needs of the organization, the behavior of people must be directed, motivated, controlled, and modified, or else they would be passive or even resistant to organizational needs.

3. Employees must be persuaded or punished, at times, to achieve organizational objectives.

4. Finally, the average employee is lazy, lacks ambition, dislikes responsibility, is self-centered, resistant to change, gullible, dumb, and prefers to be led.

McGregor (1960) assailed these conventional notions of human behavior and argued that this behavior is not a consequence of man's nature. Rather, it is the consequence of the nature of the industrial organization *per se* and its distorted assumptions about employee behavior, which are a result of misguided corporate managerial philosophies, policies, and practices. Unhappy with these assumptions, McGregor developed the dimensions of a new theory of management, Theory Y, which is also described in terms of four basic propositions:

1. It is the responsibility of management to organize the elements of productivity for economic ends.

2. People become passive and resistant to organizational needs as a result of their past experiences.

3. It is the responsibility of management to provide employees the opportunity to assume responsibility, to develop, to excel, and to be rewarded within the organizational setting.

4. By managing organizational conditions and methods of operation, management's task is to allow people to achieve their own goals by directing their own best efforts toward organizational objectives.

What McGregor (1960) described typifies much of the frustration encountered by prospective entrepreneurs in the traditional organizational setting. The key is for the entrepreneur to learn how to lead and motivate others by utilizing methods different from those previously experienced. The McGregor theorem places an intrinsic value on an employee's worth, who in turn, takes his or her cues from the role model of the entrepreneur. In leading others, McGregor implies that the entrepreneur/manager must provide an example of what to do, how to do it, when to do it, and how to reward outstanding performance. Leadership by example can indeed be a very effective management technique.

Entrepreneurs quite often do not seriously consider what it means to be a good manager, because everything they do as managers usually results from their own previous experience as employees. Their shallow commitment to management may not survive the pressures of running a successful and growing company, and unless they begin to listen to their employees and accept their input, they will soon find not only that there is no "quick fix" for poor management practices but also that the attitude of the people at the top is what makes a difference. What Hambrick (1994) termed "behavioral integration" is essential for many entrepreneurial managerial teams because of the critical need to manage under shared information exchanges, collaborative behaviors, and joint decision making. Ultimately, the importance of a positive attitude, high level of empathy, and actively listening can be a businesses' greatest source of competitive advantage; people matter.

DELEGATION AND MANAGEMENT

Delegation is simply the art of a manager getting things done through other people. One of the most taxing decisions confronting the entrepreneur is the delegation of authority and responsibility within the organization. For the entrepreneur who is wedded to the venture, the act of sharing control with subordinates is not only difficult but also at times impossible. Too many entrepreneurs have built great ventures only to see them collapse because of the inability to delegate. Roberts (1991) referred to a "founder's disease," noting that some entrepreneurs were inadequate managers from the start, while others manage only the initial stages competently but not later stages, when the need for delegation becomes more prominent.

Delegation as a principle of effective management has been an important topic for thousands of years. One of the most insightful looks at the role of an entrepreneur as a manager is provided in the biblical "Book of Exodus" as it relates the story of Moses, the world's first manager, leading the Israelites out of Egypt to the Promised Land. Any study of the length of this trip on any modern map reveals that the distance from Egypt to Israel is not that great and that it should not have required 40 years of walking. Moses quickly recognized that the management of his organization was responsible for not achieving his objective.

Moses turned to Jethro, his father-in-law, probably the world's first management consultant, for advice. Once these two biblical figures settled upon an equitable fee, Jethro began his analysis. Jethro's first comment to Moses did little to remedy the situation. Jethro said, "Moses, what you are doing is not good." Aware of the overall scope of the problem, Jethro continued, "Moses, you sit by the people from dawn to dusk and from dusk to dawn, day in and day out, listening to their problems." Although he commended Moses for his concern, he quickly indicated that once organizational objectives and strategies have been developed, it is incumbent upon the chief operating officer to structure the organization in a manner that ensure the achievement of organizational goals. Top management must be free to evaluate organizational performance and to develop innovative short-term plans that guarantee a gradual movement toward these goals. Thus, Jethro suggested, "Moses, look out among you and you will find leaders of men (managers). From these men, select leaders and place them over thousands (top management), hundreds and fifties (middle management), and tens (first-line supervisors). Should a minor family problem arise, then allow your first-line supervisors to handle the problem themselves. By delegating authority, you become free to contemplate broader concerns." Jethro did indeed have a strong argument, and by following his advice, Moses finally managed to get the Israelites into the Promised Land, even though he himself never did.

The recommendation to delegate managerial authority and responsibility evolved and was applied to a very traditional organizational setting by Frederick Taylor, the "father" of scientific management. It was included in the fourth of his four principles of scientific management; the plainest of them all, it involves a complete "re-division" of an organization's work. Under the old scheme of management, the workers did almost all of the work. Under the new scheme, the work to be done, which was formerly done by the workers alone, is divided into two large parts and one of those parts is handed over to management. This real cooperation, this genuine division of the work between the two sides, more than any other element accounts for the fact that Taylor became convinced that there would never be any labor strikes under his ideal scientific management scheme. The "best way of getting things done" becomes true teamwork when the workers realize that there is hardly a thing they do that does not have to be preceded by some act of preparation on the part of management, and also when they realize that when the managers fail to do their part, the task of "getting things done" is not done, and it is not the workers that are punished, but the managers. That is the characteristic of scientific management, and it represents democracy, cooperation, and a genuine division of work, which never existed before Taylor's time (Taylor, 1916).

One of the primary factors preventing managers from delegating effectively is the fear of losing control. Entrepreneurs, who have built their organization from the ground up, often hang on to too many tasks for fear that nobody else can do the job right, or even worse, for fear that someone else may do it better. The following steps have been proposed for effective delegating:

1. Plan before you delegate.
2. Know what you want to accomplish.
3. Decide who will do the project.
4. Choose the person best for the job.
5. Communicate your decision.
6. Explain the task.
7. Manage and evaluate.
8. Follow up.
9. Reward or rework.
10. Respond to the person's performance (McLaughlin, 1989).

Delegation in new and growing ventures is a critical managerial skill that must be practiced and mastered. The new enterprise needs professional style management, because as the venture grows and evolves, the entrepreneur realizes that time is limited and that only so much can be accomplished by one individual. Delegation, if done effectively, frees time and allows the entrepreneur to focus on the challenges and areas that need to be confronted by the venture.

CONFLICT AND MANAGEMENT

There are many sources of conflict within an organization. It can arise from the structure of the organization itself, from communication distortion, or from interpersonal and behavioral factors. While politics and conflict in large, established organizations are viewed as part of normal business operations, conflict in new ventures may often have a negative impact; it is typically viewed as something that should be suppressed and eliminated (Labovitz, 1988). Entrepreneurs often overlook the potential benefits of conflict altogether, which can be healthy for the venture and may produce an atmosphere in which quality innovative decisions can be made ("Management by Conflict," 1989).

The Nature of Conflict

"Whenever human beings compete for scarce resources or share different goals and time perspectives, conflict is likely to exist" (Labovitz, 1988). Conflict can be defined as a divergence or incompatibility of values or behaviors within oneself or between two people (Paranica & Fuchs, 2001). Through the normal course of business, it is inevitable that conflicts with suppliers, customers, and employees will occur. A key supplier might have all of a customer's orders in a state of perpetual backorder. A certain large customer may continue to short-pay every invoice. And some employees just cannot seem to coexist. All of these situations eventually reach a point at which the conflict must be addressed. Often, this results in difficult circumstances for the entrepreneur.

Conflict within organizations has been described in terms of a corporate battleground, complete with a barrage of threats and innuendos against the opposition. In contrast, traditional entrepreneurial settings typically resolve conflict by throwing partners and subordinates out of the venture. The lead entrepreneur must take responsibility for establishing and maintaining shared values and goals within the venture team. Doing so helps avoid unnecessary conflicts created by the pursuit of peripheral goals that may waste resources critical to the new venture's primary goals (Watson, Ponthieu, & Critelli, 1995). Early organization theorists viewed conflict as inevitable, with both positive and negative consequences for organizational effectiveness. They felt that a highly structured, centralized organization could remedy most sources of conflict. Generally, researchers have identified four types of conflict:

1. *Conflict within an individual:* While this does not fit the literal definition of conflict, it can be dysfunctional to the organization, especially when it takes the form of role conflict, which is the most common type of individual conflict. Such role conflict can arise when there is a contradiction between tasks and job expectations or when an individual is asked to perform a task that requires compromising personal values or ethics.

2. *Conflict between individuals:* This is the most widely recognized form of conflict and often results from personality differences, different attitudes, values, or beliefs. This is particularly evident in entrepreneurial environments, because it is not unusual for the entrepreneur to hold strong opinions about what is "right." This creates conflict among entrepreneurs, partners, and subordinates, as well as a high degree of turnover, unless the management team has been carefully selected.

3. *Conflict between the individual and the group:* Such conflict arises when an individual does not conform to group norms. This is the situation confronted by the "rate buster" entrepreneur, for example, who insists on maximizing productivity despite warnings by internal and external team members to "take it easy" or "slow down."

4. *Conflict between groups:* Group versus group conflict is often manifested in the form of clashes between line and staff departments, or between internal and external venture team members who feel that, as conflict arises out of overlapping responsibilities, their authority and the venture's operations are jeopardized ("The Staff Role," 1987). As ventures develop, the effective utilization of internal and external team members and their effective contribution to the firm is a very difficult task confronting the entrepreneur, which must be continuously reassessed.

Although a variety of factors can incite conflict in organizations, three causes of conflict are most visible in entrepreneurial ventures:

1. *Differences in perceptions and values:* We all tend to perceive a given situation only from our own personal perspective, which is a function of our own objectives, value system, and needs. This perspective is often in conflict with others who may not hold the same beliefs or have the same objectives. The values of the entrepreneur are, in many instances, unique, and although the careful selection of a management team may enable entrepreneurs to identify candidates whose value systems are compatible with theirs, this process is far from perfect. While conflict can still create some beneficial benefits by avoiding "tunnel vision," serious value differences can erode both morale and productivity in new ventures.

2. *Individual differences in social background, values, education, length of service, and age:* It is wise to undertake orientation programs that socialize newly

hired employees by introducing them to the existing organizational culture, ideas, attitudes, and objectives as defined by the organizational participants. However, this luxury is simply not affordable for many new ventures. Therefore, the impact of individual differences between existing and incoming participants needs to be preventively minimized through careful selection and professional training.

3. *Poor communication:* When individuals or groups do not fully understand a particular situation or action and cannot or are not willing to communicate with each other to iron out their differences, conflict often results. Research on trust in established venture teams found that members had more trust in their leaders when they know that their input was considered (Korsgaard, Schweiger, & Sapienza, 1995).

The dysfunctional consequences of conflict can create havoc within the enterprise and sometimes have lasting negative results:

1. Dissatisfaction, low morale, increased turnover, and decreased productivity.
2. Less cooperation and contributions in future endeavors.
3. Loyalty to one's own group, rather than the organization.
4. Unproductive competition and rivalry between groups within the organization.
5. Perceiving the other party as the "enemy."
6. Decreased interaction and communication between the conflicting parties.

As stated earlier, however, conflict does have redeeming values and creates some positive consequences for the organizations, as well as negative ones, as long as

1. Problem resolution is an acceptable goal to all motivated parties.
2. Groups are more cohesive and therefore more inclined to cooperate.
3. Conflict overcomes the "yes man" problem.
4. Conflict reduces the incidence of "groupthink," the phenomenon that encourages consensus in a group and inhibits conflicting but potentially more productive opinions and suggestions.

Managing Conflict

Conflict needs to be managed not only to avoid its dysfunctional consequences but also to enhance the benefits that some level of constructive conflict can produce for the entrepreneurial venture. Traditional methods of managing conflict can be grouped into two categories: the use of structural techniques and the use of alternative interpersonal styles. Structural techniques for managing conflict can reduce conflict by

1. Clarifying what each individual and group is expected to accomplish.
2. Using the chain of command as a coordinating mechanism, such as a common superior, committees, task forces, etc., that can often remedy the situation.
3. Establishing superordinate objectives, thus directing the efforts of all individuals and all groups to a common objective, rather than concentrating on narrow individual or group objectives.
4. Using a coordinated reward system that encourages behavior consistent with organizational objectives, for example by rewarding salespeople, not for sales to

their individual wholesalers or retail outlet personal customers, but for the total volume sold to the ultimate consumers.

Similarly, Labovitz (1988) suggests the use of alternative interpersonal management styles that can be used to deal with organizational conflict in some very effective ways:

1. *Avoidance:* Denial, or withdrawal from the conflict situation.

2. *Smoothing:* Suppressing anger, discontent, and conflict by appealing to solidarity.

3. *Forcing commitment:* Having one's view accepted at any cost, even though this may suppress initiative and create resentment.

4. *Compromising:* Resolving an issue, sometimes without fully investigating all available alternatives, and risking having the best possible option overlooked.

5. *The problem-solving approach:* Confronting emotion, encouraging candor, acknowledging the existence and inevitability of differences of opinion, which leads to better decisions and increased organizational effectiveness.

Other conflict management experts believe that when a manager/entrepreneur is faced with a difficult conversation to settle a conflict, things can be better managed if the conflict management process is properly understood as being comprised of three concurrent conversations. These three simultaneous conversations can be summarized as follows:

- *What happened?* This is the most obvious one, and it relates to the actual circumstances that have caused the conflict.

- *Feelings:* Why does one party feel the way they do and what can be done about it?

- *Identity:* Anxiety about conflict is often the result of how someone believes they will be perceived (Tiffany, 2000).

Each of these methods of conflict resolution may effectively succeed in managing conflict, but the last approach dealing with problem solving as the way to handle conflict is the most promising. The following section elaborates upon a specific applied conflict-resolution technique, based on problem solving, that has been both theoretically developed and empirically applied to specific situations, namely the *Conflict Perception Resolution method* (CPR).

CONFLICT PERCEPTION RESOLUTION (CPR)

The **Conflict Perception Resolution method** (CPR) is a simple, straightforward technique developed from actual applications in small firms that can be extremely useful in resolving internal sources of conflict. It is specifically targeted toward ventures that survived the initial period of inception and development and reached a new stage at which expansion, reorganization, or simple maintenance of existing operations are creating dysfunctional conflict situations (Vozikis & Mescon, 1979). These dysfunctional conflict situations emerge and fester, because most employees in entrepreneurial ventures (or non-family members in a family-owned business) are either reluctant to or have no incentive whatsoever to offer real suggestions to the real problems confronting the firm because they do not perceive this to be part of their job.

The advantages of CPR stem not only from the fact that the owner receives "bottom-up" feedback from the individuals "in the trenches" of the business but also from the fact that this feedback is the true story of the causes and sources of conflict as perceived by the disgruntled members of the venture team, which the owner would have never received otherwise. Additionally, the fact that the employees implement the solutions to the problems that they themselves identify, ensures the positive outcomes of motivation, satisfaction, effort, and organizational commitment on their part, which makes the entrepreneurial owner's managerial job much easier in the long run. The implementation of the CPR method must be undertaken by an individual outside the realm of the organization, and it involves a three-stage process that usually extends over a 6-month period. These three stages involve (a) the identification of the perceived conflict, (b) the implementation of its proposed resolutions, and (c) a follow-up stage to examine the progress of the implementation and to confirm that the source of conflict has been indeed addressed, resolved, and eliminated. Before the CPR process is initiated, the entrepreneur owner must make certain concessions, such as

- Paid release time for CPR group meetings.
- Guaranteed anonymity of conflict-related comments.
- Non-interaction between and among the participants and management concerning the CPR method per se or issues that may emerge during the 3-month period.

Once these conditions have been met and agreed upon, stage one of the CPR process can be initiated. At a designated neutral site away from the company's premises, all key internal team venture members, excluding the entrepreneur owner, meet on company time or during off hours at the expense of the company. During this initial meeting and after an introductory "ice melting" session by the outside facilitator, the purpose and the objectives of the CPR meeting are explained, and identical notebooks and pens are distributed to the participants. An assistant to the facilitator tabulates and enters into an electronic document the emerging issues and suggestions submitted by the participants. He or she then proceeds by dramatically shredding the handwritten comments in their presence to ensure the participants' faith in the guaranteed anonymity of their input. This process is repeated until all input is gathered and tabulated electronically, and all handwritten sheets are shredded in the presence of the participants.

CPR Stage I involves four elements to identify the source of the perceived conflict, namely (a) the identification of the perceived specific problems, (b) the ranking of these perceived problems, (c) identification of in-depth suggestions for the resolution of these perceived problems, and (d) the ranking of the offered suggestions for the perceived problem resolution.

CPR Stage I: Identification of the Perceived Conflict

Identification of Specific Problems

Participants are asked to list the problems they encounter on their job. A problem is defined as something that impedes their flexibility in managing or that they find frustrating because it prevents them from accomplishing their job. Participants are given 30 minutes to complete their lists.

Ranking of Problems

The various sheets are collected from the participants by the CPR administrators, who immediately begin the task of generating a non-overlapping list. The list of problems is tabulated, printed, and distributed to the participants. As mentioned earlier, the original handwritten sheets received from the participants are shredded in front of them, to enhance the credibility of the process, and to further enhance the perception that all responses are guaranteed to remain anonymous. The participants are then given 15 minutes to rank the top five or six problems from the list. This is also done anonymously, with the results tabulated by the CPR administrators and the original handwritten sheets ceremoniously shredded. The most frequently mentioned five or six problems are then identified in a ranking order, tabulated, and distributed back to the participants.

In-Depth Suggestions for Problem Resolution

This stage requires 30 minutes and is also crucial to the CPR process. At this point, the participants are asked to utilize all of their creative abilities to develop specific solutions for the problems they have identified. They are also instructed to avoid simplistic solutions and to describe each of their proposed solutions, together with their impacts on the organization. In accordance with the law of physics that "for every action there is an equal and opposite reaction," the participants are instructed to fully consider the possible effects that their suggested solutions could have upon ongoing business operations. They are given a 15-minute break during which time the administrators tabulate the various solutions offered for each of the top five or six problems. These are printed and presented to the participants, while the original handwritten sheets are again shredded.

Ranking the Suggestions for Problem Resolution

This time, the participants are given 30 minutes in which to rank (once again, anonymously and with no interaction) the most frequent suggestions for the resolution of each of the ranked problems. These are tabulated in a ranking order, printed, and distributed to all participants, and the actual handwritten sheets are shredded. This last task concludes the 2-hour introduction stage of the CPR method that identified the perceived sources of conflict.

CPR Stage II: Conflict Resolution Implementation

The administrators can now initiate the indirect employee–management interaction stage of the CPR process. During a visit with the entrepreneur owner, the top five or six identified problems as perceived by the internal venture team members as a group are presented in ranking order, as well as the suggested solutions related to each of these problems. Working closely with the administrators, owners determine the specific problems they wish to initially tackle. At the same time, they select from the collective list of the proposed problems and solutions the ones with which they agree the most, and they begin their implementation.

CPR Stage III: Evaluation of the Conflict Resolution Implementation

At 4 weeks, 8 weeks, and 12 weeks, the CPR administrators meet independently with the internal team members, as well as with the owner. The implementation process toward the resolution of the perceived conflict is reevaluated and modified if necessary. These meetings are critical because they ensure that the identified problems have indeed been resolved and will never resurface. Also, the meetings implicitly ensure that there is a standing agreement between the entrepreneur owner and the employees or the internal team members. If problems emerge from perceived conflict in the future, they will be approached and resolved in a similar fashion.

SPORT UNIVERSE, INC.: A CPR APPLICATION

Sport Universe, Inc., has five specialty shops, with three located in the metropolitan Tulsa area and two in Kansas City. The stores employ a total of 25 full-time employees, and they primarily offer five basic item classifications in each of the stores: golf clothing, tennis clothing, golf hardware and bags, tennis hardware and accessories, and shoes. The owner does all of the purchasing centrally, with some participation by the store managers.

Compensation Programs

All employees are compensated on a base salary plus commission of 1% on hard goods and 2% on soft goods. The profit margin is greater on soft goods, so the incentive there is higher. Managers also receive a base salary plus commission, as well as a year-end bonus based upon the increase over the previous year's gross margin. There is also a comprehensive benefit program, including 2 weeks of vacation, 1 week of paid sick leave, and medical/dental coverage.

Cyclical Nature of the Recreation Industry

By specializing in golf and tennis equipment and accessories, the business must be content with a minimum of 5 months slack in sales. Ideally, the business strategy for the long run is to smoothen this cyclical fluctuation by offering winter sporting goods or non-seasonal goods such as bowling equipment.

Owner's Management Philosophy

"Managers are not sophisticated enough to handle part-time people. . . . If I can get 2 years out of them, I'm happy. . . ."

Organizational Structure

The owner handles all product-line purchasing, accounting, and advertising centrally. Store managers are allowed to hire salespeople with the approval of the company's vice presidents, but basically, no sophisticated responsibilities are delegated to managers, who lack personal discretion on the job, even though an existing policy manual implies that managers can offer the owner a good bit of "support" advice. Vice presidents meet with store managers on an informal basis to discuss store operations, but no regularly scheduled meetings are held for managers to exchange ideas and opinions. Additionally, in recent months, two managers have been fired, and it appears that in both cases emotional factors overwhelmed objective performance criteria.

CPR Implementation

With the owner's cooperation, the store managers and the assistant managers, as well as the support staff, met in a conference room in downtown Dallas. Under conditions of guaranteed anonymity and non-interaction to avoid interpersonal bias, the seminar participants listed many perceived problems. These problems were tabulated, and 15 issues were identified. These issues were then ranked according to severity and importance. The results of the top six ranked problems are as follows:

1. The managers are not involved in the company's overall planning.
2. The managers are not involved in product selection and new product orientation.

3. There is no communication among the store managers.

4. There is inequitable pay among different managers and stores.

5. Severe inventory problems require frequent inter-store transfers.

6. There is irregular employee evaluation and minimal opportunity for advancement.

The managers were then asked to generate solutions to these problems by playing the dual roles of the subordinate and the superior. Examples of their comments aimed at the specific problems above are as follows.

The Managers Are Not Involved in the Company's Overall Planning

- Schedule regular meetings.

- Ask for the opinions of managers.

- Have meetings monthly or quarterly, especially when changes in policy are being considered.

- Make key people in the organization aware of major decisions and solicit their opinions.

- Owner should discuss company planning with managers.

- To ensure a sales force that is truly successful, company participation is necessary. Informal conversations on future expansion or developments involving all employees and would give them a sense of worth and importance, especially when their feedback is applied to the final decision.

The Managers Are Not Involved in Product Selection and New Product Orientation

- Have sales reps demonstrate products and inform everyone regarding new products.

- Talk over new products in regular meetings. Ask for opinions regarding new products.

- Store managers should have copies of all new catalogs and should meet with the sales reps to learn more about new products.

- Send every store manager a complete copy of prices, pictures, etc., of all new merchandise being considered and ask their opinion before ordering.

There Is No Communication Among the Store Managers

- Conduct regularly scheduled meetings.

- Have manager meetings on a regular basis to go over problems. If anyone has a complaint, let it be known.

- Managers should also meet on their own to discuss problems, as well as things that are working well or badly in their stores.

- It is imperative that the individual stores communicate with one another.

There Is Inequitable Pay Among Different Managers and Stores

- There should be a minimum salary with regular increases.
- The owner should reevaluate each of his managers regarding duties and pay. Then he should discuss this information with each manager.
- Everyone in the company is unhappy with the money he or she is making. In some cases, it is fair or enough, and in other instances it is not.
- Kansas City employees earn more than Tulsa employees in general.
- More "work" is done in the original store than in any other store.
- Managers should have equitable pay.
- Bonuses should be evenly distributed to all full-time employees as an incentive to sell and not stagnate.

Severe Inventory Problems Require Frequent Inter-Store Transfers

- Keep a constant supply of products that sell well in stock and on order.
- Order the same merchandise for stores in sufficient quantities.
- Set up transfers on a regular basis.
- Order before "we are out of something."
- Store managers should communicate their inventory problems to the buyers.
- One person should be in charge of inventory.
- Employees other than managers should put transferred merchandise in stock immediately. This will help familiarize them with the merchandise.

Irregular Employee Evaluation and Minimal Opportunity for Advancement

- Because different employees have different capabilities and personalities, the owner needs to be flexible in evaluations without showing favoritism.
- Set up a time for evaluations, for example, every 4 to 6 months, and do it!
- Employees should be told that they are to be evaluated at certain periods of time.
- The managers should evaluate employees every month. An evaluation sheet should be developed jointly by the managers and the owner.
- Advancement opportunities should be evaluated every 3 months among managers and owner.
- Is there room for advancement, and if so, to what degree or capacity and when can it be expected?

- New jobs should be implemented and positions available, such as an inventory control person.
- Keep employees informed about planning and future decisions.

Based on the recommendations by Vozikis and Mescon (1979), the owner tackled the issue of inequitable pay among different managers and stores. First, the owner implemented the suggestion most frequently mentioned by the CPR participants as the one that would resolve the perceived conflict, namely, establishing a minimum salary for store managers along with regular increases. This resolved a great deal of conflict. For example, because managers were on commission basis along with everybody else, when a merchandise order arrived, no one, not even the managers, was willing to take time to store the inventory because of the real possibility of losing sales and commissions.

Many CPR applications in both small and large organizations and in a variety of industries have demonstrated that the CPR technique is both theoretically sound and pragmatically appealing, especially to small-business owners and entrepreneurs where interpersonal conflict can do the most damage. Simple in nature, yet revealing in its content, CPR proves to be a viable mechanism for the resolution of the many types of interpersonal problems and overall conflict that emerges in growing ventures.

CONCLUSION

Attracting and retaining good employees is of critical concern to the small firm. This chapter examined such issues as recruitment, selection, and compensation as they relate to the entrepreneur owner. It is always important to study socioeconomic and demographic trends that affect the firm's ability to recruit and retain qualified employees in the future and to tap the best possible pool of applicants. The use of effective interviewing techniques and the appropriate selection tests help assure that the best person for the job is selected. However, it often is not only difficult to attract good employees, but it can also be difficult to retain quality people once they have been hired. Compensation and fringe benefits play an important role in employee retention. In addition, it is important that employees know and understand their wage and benefit package. Finally, personnel manuals and job descriptions are important in socializing the employee into the organization, as well as maintaining performance, morale, and preventing disagreements and possible litigation. By communicating critical job-related information to the employees, unnecessary turnover can be easily prevented. The growth of a business generally requires the development of managerial skills on the part of the entrepreneur. It is important that the entrepreneur provides an example of what to do, how to do it, when to do it, and how to reward the resulting performance. In many cases, it is critical for an entrepreneur to realize that his or her managerial style is often affected by past experiences as an employee and therefore may not be appropriate or effective. Delegation, or the art of getting things done through other people, is an important concept in learning to manage the venture effectively. While many entrepreneurs fear losing control, the proper use of delegation frees up precious time to focus on the challenges faced by the venture. Finally, the development of conflict management skills is important to the entrepreneurial manager. Conflict has both functional and dysfunctional consequences, and several structural and interpersonal methods are available for managing conflict. The Conflict Perception Resolution (CPR) method of conflict management has been presented as a simple problem-solving mechanism to be used in resolving internal sources of organizational conflict. Successful companies that show loyalty to members of the management team, as well as employees, are attentive to their problems and complaints, and treat them with respect. The development of effective managerial skills on the part of the entrepreneur ultimately promotes both teamwork and commitment for the internal team members and employees.

Website Information

Topic	Web Address	Description
Job descriptions	http://www.hrvillage.com/jobdescriptions.htm	Gives information on how to structure a job description as well as more than 30 typical job descriptions for certain professions.
Recruiting	http://www.recruiting-online.com/	Offers advanced online recruiting training, how to fill job openings through recruiting, provides outsourced candidate sourcing, and career counseling.
Drug testing	http://www.drugtestingnews.com/	Provides the most comprehensive source for up-to-date news and information on the drug and alcohol testing industry including legislation, legal issues, business, and technology.
Interviews	http://www.job-interview.net/	Gives tips on how to answer tough questions, provides a sample interview question bank, mock interviews, and more.
Benefits and compensation	http://www.intel.com/jobs/bencomp/	Compensation and benefits Intel offers to its employees.
Conflict management	http://www.iacm-conflict.org/	The International Association for Conflict Management encourages scholars and practitioners to develop and disseminate theory, research, and experience useful for understanding, managing, and resolving conflict situations in family, organizational, societal, and international settings.

Key Terms

Cafeteria plan: A benefits option in which the employee uses a credit to "purchase" options from a menu of benefits.

Concurrent validity: Obtained by testing current employees, correlating their scores with measures of their performance, and using these criteria for selection of future employees.

Conflict Perception Resolution method (CPR): A simple, straightforward technique developed from actual applications in small firms that can be extremely useful in resolving internal sources of conflict.

The Consolidated Omnibus Budget Reconciliation Act of 1986 (COBRA): This act requires firms with at least 20 employees to offer the same group health benefits offered to current employees to workers who have been fired, are on leave, or whose hours have been reduced, as well as to widowed or divorced spouses of employees.

Construct validity: The extent to which a test measures a specific trait considered necessary for successful job performance, such as intelligence.

Content validity: The extent to which a test includes reasonable or representative samples of the behavior or skills needed to successfully perform the job.

"Devil's horns": The interviewer perceives nothing good at all.

"Halo effect": The interviewer perceives nothing but good traits.

Health maintenance organizations (HMOs): A health care option in which a set annual fee is paid for each enrollee, through the use of higher deductibles, or by requiring the employee to contribute more to the cost of the premium.

Job description: A good job description is carefully designed to include a job title, basic job function, relationships, responsibilities, authority, a "standards of performance" statement, and accountability.

Preferred provider organizations (PPOs): A health care option in which a network of physicians and hospitals agrees to a fee schedule that represents a discount over usual charges.

Predictive validity: The extent to which a test predicts successful performance on the job measured by testing a group of applicants and then comparing their scores on the test to a measure of performance after hiring and training.

Problem-solving approach: An alternative interpersonal management style which confronts emotion, encourages candor, acknowledges the existence and inevitability of differences of opinion, and leads to better decisions and increased organizational effectiveness.

Review Questions

1. Describe the four key management principles and their relationship to job design.
2. Describe some of the biases that may emerge during the preliminary screen interview.
3. List some questions that can be asked of an applicant during an interview.
4. Discuss the four parts of Theory X and Theory Y.
5. What are some of the advantages of the CPR method of conflict resolution?
6. This chapter discusses many strategies to evaluate and resolve conflict, and the source of conflict can be internal or external to the organization. While farms can certainly experience conflict between employees or management, they also may experience conflict with neighboring farms, families, and other businesses. Read this pamphlet on communicating with neighbors published by the State of New Jersey Ag Department: http://njsustainingfarms. rutgers.edu/PDF/Farmer_to_Farmer_Advice_for_Avoiding_Conflicts.pdf. How can you apply the strategies for conflict resolution from this book to the situation discussed in the pamphlet?

Reflections from the Front Lines of LifeGuard America

Since I have stated before that any endeavor's ultimate success is determined by the quality of people the leadership hires, it stands to reason that how you recruit and manage these highly motivated people is also key to its success. We spent 3 months on a hands-on read and assemble test, a physical examination, and three separate interviews before we hired a new employee at the Harley-Davidson Kansas City Plant. I learned from that experience how important it is to get it right the first time. In a start-up company, it is crucial to maintain the entrepreneurial integrity as the company grows. Senior leadership must spend a great deal of time and energy recruiting and maintaining the "Right Stuff" in the organization. This is not easy in a high-performance workplace such as Harley-Davidson or LifeGuard America. The senior leadership must be exceptionally good at identifying the right person or sometimes a person that is not right for the organization and making the right call early. I have seen it happen all too often when someone says, ". . . well he/she is certainly technically qualified, but I don't think that they are a right fit for the organization. Maybe we should overlook that because. . . ." It does not work. Having a person with the wrong personality type is as bad as having someone who does not add value to the company.

We have put together two extensive questionnaires that a prospective employee fills out online. One is an assessment of basic skills and the other is a behavior assessment. From one of our standard job descriptions (one of which is shown below), we created a specific set of online questionnaires that allow a person to walk into the interview process with a good basic understanding of the person being interviewed. In this way, we help ensure that we have a good chance of doing it right the first time without wasting anyone's time. These questionnaires cost about $100 to administer and are well worth the investment up front in the process. The following is a job description/requirements/skills with a profile for our Response Center Manager:

> Successful candidate will be responsible for the operation of a Tier II Help Desk (24x7 availability and 5x8 manning with on-call support) providing consolidated, comprehensive technical assistance for medical logistics services. Responsibilities include understanding and managing automated logistics request tickets, customer call tracking and resolution/escalation, customer liaison, coordination with the software engineering team, reporting, staff management, and ensuring work is performed consistent with budgetary goals. Also responsible for tracking system configuration control/management, interfacing with Flight Services Tier I Help Desk to ensure proper categorization of service request tickets, problem escalation, and resolution follow through. Oversee development and maintenance of Standard Operating Procedures to assure that contract terms are met, staff training/monitoring/scheduling, maintenance and growth of Help Desk knowledge base, and develop strategies for improving customer service and quality of service delivery. This position reports to the Director of Logistics. Education: Required: Bachelor's degree or equivalent experience (min. 6 years) Desired: Master's.

Requirements:

- At least 5 years of progressive experience in Help Desk or Network Operations Center operations, with at least 3 years at a managerial level.

- Demonstrated accomplishments in promoting customer satisfaction; development, motivation, and retention of employees.

- Experienced with task and project management.

- Proven leadership skills, with the ability to act decisively and handle pressure during resolution of critical problem situations.

- Must be available for on-call response 24x7 during scheduled periods.

- Desired Skills: Experience with flight scheduling; video conferencing.

I have also come to understand that if you intend to build a high-performance work environment, you had better build in a method for managing conflict. High-performance workplaces, by their very nature, tend to produce conflict. In the best case, it is referred to as "creative tension," and in the worst case, it manifests as nonproductive behavior that has no place in the workplace. Here again, it is up to senior leadership to provide not only the "rules-of-engagement" for the workplace but also to demonstrate behavior that is expected from everyone involved in the company. This also includes outside partners and suppliers who ultimately influence the success or failure of the company. In my experience, it all boils down to basic respect. Respect for each other, respect for the company, respect for the customer and respect for self. It is important to have a respectful manner to disagree and resolve a conflict. At Harley-Davidson, it was a simple matter of asking the person "if they were open to feedback" or "here is my push-back." These were simple, respectful key words that announced, "I do not agree with you, but I am asking you if this is the right time to offer my opinion and my views on the subject." The entire endeavor at Harley-Davidson was based on establishing a "shared vision" among everyone involved. That meant that everyone had the responsibility to be a participant in the process, not a bystander, and a method of reaching consensus on major elements of the business was required. There are many other details to creating the right environment, but they all revolve around respect and trust. Below is the benchmark for the Response Center manager that outlines the optimum attributes of a candidate. The candidate then fills out our online questionnaire, and his/her results are compared to the benchmark to see how well the candidate's traits match our benchmark (see Exhibit 12.1). It is just one facet of the interviewing process that allows us to choose the best among a list of very good prospects.

Exhibit 12.1   Response Center Manager: LifeGuard America

Thinking Style (shaded = benchmark range)

Trait	Benchmark range (shaded)
Learning index	5, 6, 7
Verbal skill	7, 8, 9
Verbal reasoning	8, 9, 10
Numerical ability	4, 5, 6
Numeric reasoning	1, 2, 3

Occupational Interests

Trait	Benchmark range (shaded)
Enterprising	7, 8, 9
Financial/administrative	8, 9, 10
People Service	8, 9, 10
Technical	4, 5, 6
Mechanical	6, 7, 8
Creative	4, 5, 6

Behavioral Traits

Trait	Benchmark range (shaded)
Energy Level	6, 7, 8
Assertiveness	3, 4, 5
Sociability	8, 9, 10
Manageability	4, 5, 6
Attitude	1, 2, 3
Decisiveness	4, 5, 6, 7
Accommodating	7, 8, 9
Independence	2, 3, 4
Objective judgment	6, 7, 8

(Each trait is rated on a scale of 1 to 10.)

The bottom line, however, is that no amount of data can take the place of good interviewing instincts. I always interview an individual with the thought, "Would I want to spend 48 hours non-stop with this person working on a project with a serious deadline?" If the answer is no, say good-bye.

My father taught me early in life that the world would not need unions if companies treated their employees well. It is a lesson that I have taken to heart. There are many ways to build employee loyalty to a company. Williams Companies, headquartered in Tulsa, Oklahoma, is an excellent example of a company that has invested heavily in its employees' ongoing education, with programs that build teamwork in a diverse workplace. They send all of their people through a ropes course designed to build trust and respect, and what they got out of it in return is an employee base that is loyal to the end. As they have been downsizing like almost every other large company lately, it is interesting to note that those leaving have nothing but good to say about the company, and they hope that they can return when the economy improves. It is tough to get that kind of loyalty these days. My goal is to have a corporate condo at a lake resort 1 hour north of Tulsa. We will allow the employees to manage the schedule and pay for someone who has vested in the company with a certain time and performance to take their family to spend a long weekend, company paid, at the condo. The idea: work hard—play hard. Support the family because a happy home makes for focused employees during the workday. Take care of people and help them meet their goals and they will help you meet yours. Sounds familiar? It should.

Discussion Questions on LifeGuard America

1. Why is it important to have job descriptions in a small start-up company?

2. What can you conclude about the person LifeGuard America is looking for in their search for a Response Center Manager?

3. Do you believe that it is important to have "rules-of-engagement" that are published in a start-up company? Why or why not?

References

Andrews, K. R. (1983, January/February). Letter to the editor. *Harvard Business Review, 61*(1), 1.

Berney, R. E. (1981, May). Evening the odds. *Entrepreneur, 9*(5), 22.

Bernstein, J. E. (1988, November). How to get your people working like a team. *Inc. Magazine, 10*(11), 167–169.

Bird, B. J. (1989). *Entrepreneurial behavior*. Glenview, IL: Scott, Foresman.

Blanchard, K., & Johnson, S. (1982). *The one minute manager*. New York: Berkley Books.

Building the sales force (1986, November). *Small Business Reports, 11*(11), 71–77.

Carroon & Black, Inc. (1989, March). Benefits: Are your employees in the dark. *Inc. Magazine, 11*(3), 119.

Cascio, W. F. (1987). *Applied psychology in personnel management* (3rd Ed.). Englewood Cliffs, NJ: Prentice Hall.

Cascio, W. F. (1989). *Managing human resources: Productivity, quality of work, life, profits* (2nd ed.). New York: McGraw-Hill.

Dandridge, T. C. (1979, April). Children are not "little grown-ups": Small business needs its own organizational theory. *Journal of Small Business Management, 17*(2), 35–37.

Deeks, J. (1976). *The small firm owner-manager*. New York: Praeger.

DeLong, D. (1982, April). Tell employees where they stand. *Inc. Magazine, 4*(4), 61–62.

Dessler, G. (2000). *Human resource management* (8th Ed.). Englewood Cliffs, NJ: Prentice Hall.

Dolan, C. (1989, May 15). Entrepreneurs often fail as managers. *The Wall Street Journal*, p. B1.

Eckert, L., Ryan, J., & Ray, B. (1989, April). Owning the store. *Entrepreneur, 17*(4), 48.

Eisenhardt, K. M., & Schoonhoven, C. B. (1990, September). Organizational growth: Linking founding team, strategy, environment, and growth among U.S. semiconductor ventures, 1978–1988. *Administrative Science Quarterly, 35*(3), 504–529.

Ellman, E. S. (1981, October). How to write a personnel manual. *Inc. Magazine, 3*(10), 70–72.

Evered, J. (1981, April). How to write a good job description. *Supervisory Management, 26*(4), 14–19.

Feldman, D. C. (1980, March/April). A socialization process that helps new recruits succeed. *Personnel, 57*(2), 11–23.

Guzzo, R. A., & Dickson, M. W. (1996). Teams in organizations: Recent research on performance and effectiveness. In J. T. Spence, J. M. Darley, & D. Foss (Eds.), *Annual review of psychology* (Vol. 47) (pp. 307–338). Palo Alto, CA: Annual Reviews.

Hakel, M. D. (1989). Merit-based selection: Measuring the person for the job. In W. F. Cascio (Ed.). *Human resource planning employment and placement* (pp. 135–158). Washington, DC: Bureau of National Affairs.

Hambrick, D. C. (1994). Top management groups: A conceptual integration and reconsideration of the "team" label. *Research in Organizational Behavior, 16,* 171–213.

How to recruit the best troops (1981, January). *Inc. Magazine, 3*(1), 90–91.

Hyatt, Joshua (1989). Rewriting the Book on Entreprenuership. *Inc. Magazine,* (August 1). http://www.inc.com/magazine/19890801/5755.html

The interview (1982, May). *Fair employment practices guidelines, 202,* 1–8.

Kamm, J. B., & Nurick, A. J. (1993, Winter). The stages of team venture formation: A decision-making model. *Entrepreneurship Theory and Practice, 17*(2), 17–28.

Korsgaard, M. A., Schweiger, D. M., & Sapienza, H. J. (1995, February). Building commitment, attachment, and trust in strategic decision-making teams: The role of procedural justice. *Academy of Management Journal, 38*(1), 60–84.

Johnston, W. B., & Packer, A. E. (1987). *Workforce 2000: Work and workers for the 21st century.* Indianapolis, IN: Hudson Institute.

Joinson, C. (2001, January). Refocusing job descriptions. *HR Magazine, 46*(1), 66–71.

Labor letter: Small is beautiful (1978, January 31). *The Wall Street Journal,* p. 1.

Labovitz, G. H. (1988). Managing conflict. In J. L. Gibson, J. M. Ivancevich, & J. H. Donnely, Jr. (Eds.), *Organizations close-up: A book of readings* (p. 201). Plano, TX: Business Publications.

Lesonsky, R. (2001). *Start your own business: The only start-up book you'll ever need* (2nd ed.). Irvine, CA: Entrepreneur Press.

Lord, J. S. (1989). External and internal recruitment. In W. F. Cascio (Ed.), *Human resource planning employment and placement* (pp. 2–73). Washington, D.C.: BNA.

Lynn, J. (2001, April). New exec on the block [Electronic version]. *Entrepreneur, 29*(4), 92–93. Retrieved May 5, 2001, from http://www.entrepreneurmag.com/Your-Business/YB_PrintArticle/0,2361,287753-----,00.html

Management by conflict (1989, June). *Entrepreneur, 17*(6), 152.

Manley, M. (1988, December). The pitfalls of employee leasing. *Inc. Magazine, 10*(12), 154–156.

Manley, M. (1989, January). Who benefits? *Inc. Magazine, 11*(1), 112.

March, J. (1984, February). Entrepreneurship: Teaching the right stuff. *Harvard Business School Bulletin, 60,* 66.

Maslach, C., Schaufeli, W. B., & Leiter, M. P. (2001). Job burnout. In S. T. Fiske, D. L. Schacter, & C. Zahn-Waxler (Eds.), *Annual review of psychology* (Vol. 52) (pp. 397–422). Palo Alto, CA: Annual Reviews.

McGregor, D. (1960). *The human side of enterprise.* New York: McGraw-Hill.

McGuire, J. W. (1976, Spring). The small business enterprise in economics and organizational theory. *Journal of Contemporary Business, 5*(2), 115.

McLaughlin, D. (1989, July). The art of delegation. *Entrepreneur, 17*(7), 84–86.

Miner, J. B. (1996). Evidence for the existence of a set of personality types defined by psychological tests that predict entrepreneurial success. In P. D. Reynolds, et al. (Eds.), *Frontiers of entrepreneurship research* (pp. 62–76). Wellesley, MA: Babson College.

Paranica, K., and Fuchs, T. (2001, June). Training orientation and conflict theory: Transforming our understanding of conflict. *Mediate.com.* Retrieved July 8, 2001, from http://www.mediate.com/articles/Paranica.cfm

Paris, E. (2001, March). Relief wanted: Hiring a CEO could save your business [Electronic version]. *Entrepreneur, 29*(3), 33. Retrieved April 7, 2001, from http://www.entrepreneur.com/37732.

Posner, B. G. (1989a, June). Growing your own. *Inc. Magazine, 11*(6), 131–132.

Posner, B. G. (1989b, August). Inside out. *Inc. Magazine, 11*(8), 120–121.

Promotion from within (1987, January). *Small Business Reports, 12*(1), 44–48.

Robbins, S. P. (2001). *Organizational behavior* (9th ed.). Englewood Cliffs, NJ: Prentice Hall.

Roberts, E. B. (1991). *Entrepreneurs in high technology: Lessons from MIT and beyond.* New York: Oxford University Press.

Rynes, S. L., & Milkovich, G. T. (Eds.) (1986). *Current issues in human resource management: Commentary and readings.* Plano, TX: Business.

Saddler, J., (1989, October 30). Cheaper health insurance for small firms carries catch. *The Wall Street Journal,* p. B2.

Simurda, S. J. (1989, July). The screen test. *Entrepreneur, 17*(7).

Sirbasku, J. (2002, January). Secrets of finding and keeping good employees. *USA Today Magazine, 120*(2680), 32–34.

Solomon, S. D. (1989, December). Help wanted. *Inc. Magazine, 11*(12), 140–153.

The staff role today: Helping managers manage effectively. (1987, April). *Small Business Reports, 12(*4), 53.

Stevenson, H. H., Roberts, M. J., & Grousback, H. I. (1985). *New business ventures and the entrepreneur.* Homewood, IL: Irwin.

Taking the guesswork out of salary setting (1981, April). *Inc. Magazine, 3*(4), 122.

Tannenbaum, J. A. (1989, September 20). Small firms hack away at expensive fringe benefits. *The Wall Street Journal,* p. B2.

Taylor, F. (1916, December). The principles of scientific management. *Bulletin of the Taylor Society, 2, 20.*

Tiffany, L. (2000, May 15). Conflict management expert Sheila Heen. *Entrepreneur, 28,* Retrieved June 6, 2000, from http://www.entrepreneurmag.com/article/28044.

Timmons, J. 1990. *Entrepreneurship in the 1990s* (3rd ed.). Boston: Irwin.

Timmons, J. A. (2001). *New venture creation.* New York: Irwin/McGraw-Hill.

Vozikis, G. S., & Mescon, T. S. (1979). Conflict perception resolution (CPR): Getting to the heart of small business interpersonal problems. In International Council for Small Business (Eds.), *Proceedings of the 24th Annual Conference of the International Council for Small Business, Quebec City, Quebec, Canada* (pp. 35/1–35/14). Montreal, Canada: Federal Business Development Bank.

Watson, W. E., Ponthieu, L. D., & Critelli, J. W. (1995, September). Team interpersonal process effectiveness in venture partnerships and its connection to perceived success. *Journal of Business Venturing, 10*(5), 393–411.

Wermiel, S. (1989, June 6). Standards for providing bias charges are toughened by high court ruling. *The Wall Street Journal,* p. A24.

Werther, W. B., Jr., & Davis, K. (1989). *Human resources and personnel management* (3rd ed). New York: McGraw-Hill.

Yoshihashi, P. (1989, May 26). Employer sanctions and illegal workers. *The Wall Street Journal,* p. B1.

13 Venture Ability to Execute: Financial Management Considerations

Can We Execute the Management and Control of Money?

LEARNING OBJECTIVES

1. To realize that the success of the small firm relies on strong financial management and control.
2. To understand the importance of cash flow management, the "blood" of the venture.
3. To learn how to evaluate, monitor, and control the four critical areas of financial management: cash flow, capital funding sources, taxes, and financial performance.

TOPIC OUTLINE

Introduction

Cash Flow Management
- Cash Inflow Management
- Cash Outflow Management
- Accounts Receivable and Credit Policy
  Management
- Depository Practices and Investment
  Management

Capital Funding Management
- Debt Financing
- Equity Financing
- Internally Generated Funds

Tax Liability Management
- Balance Sheet Items
- Cash Flow Items

- Profit and Loss Items
- Deduction Items

Financial Performance Management
- Inaccurate Financial Performance Measures
- Inadequate Financial Performance Strategies

Conclusion

Website Information

Key Terms

Review Questions

Case Study

References

INTRODUCTION

Financial management and control in small firms is without doubt the most important determinant of the success of the business. The financial environment is always characterized by turbulence caused, among other things, by fluctuations in interest rates, stiff competition from domestic and foreign businesses, and a continuous struggle to procure future funds as well as secure existing ones. The very size of a venture creates a condition of almost permanent state of resource poverty that requires a special treatment. Resource poverty is the result of small income-producing firms clustering in highly fragmented industries, such as services, retail, job-ship manufacturing with a great deal of cutthroat pricing competition and slim margins, and many high-growth ventures clustering in a "dotcom" format that compete for increasingly scarce venture seed capital, as well as later-stage financing and financial viability. Poor accounting, bookkeeping, and financial management practices that result in many small firms not being able to survive unforeseen misfortunes and miscalculations in this area further accentuate this handicap. This is especially true for entrepreneurs who are not used to such controls at the high-paying jobs they left to start their own ventures (DeCeglie, 1998). For the venture manager, effective control and management of the financial resources is crucial to the survival of the venture. This can be accomplished using the following methods:

- Cash flow management, to ensure a continuous positive cash flow position:
  - Cash inflow management to accelerate cash inflows and receipts.
  - Cash outflow management to decelerate cash outflows and payments.
  - Account receivable and credit policy management to minimize bad debt.
  - Depository practices and investment management to maximize the venture's return on idle financial resources.
- Capital funding management to determine the firm's future short-term and long-term capital needs, as well as to evaluate and select low-cost sources of funds.
- Tax liability management to avoid tax liabilities as much as possible.
- Financial performance management to ensure the venture's long-term financial viability.

CASH FLOW MANAGEMENT

The source of cash is a key indicator of venture success because liquid funds must be generated mainly from internal sources, rather than always relying on outside sources. In a *Dun and Bradstreet* survey, 33% of small-business owners admitted that they have problems managing their cash flow as they are in the process of building their ventures ("Help! My Firm," 1996). Young companies, especially, have been compared to "cash sponges," soaking up every available dollar and always hungry for more; that is why cash management should be the entrepreneur's concern from day one (Fraser, 1998). However, very few entrepreneurs deal diligently with cash flow management and even fewer use formal techniques for tracking their cash balances (McMahon & Holmes, 1991).

To manage cash effectively, a small firm must create an ongoing program to provide a steady flow of cash from within the company, because an indication of profit in the bottom line is not enough for a business to survive. Even though profit is the most common measure of business performance, positive cash flow is more critical than profit because it ensures that the firm can meet critical short- and long-term payments as they come due. Focusing only on profits or assets may be extremely dangerous because too much money may be tied up in assets and not available to pay bills (Fisher, 1998). Survival can be prolonged without profits, but when cash, the "blood" of the firm, dries out, the firm dies an instant death. Successful cash flow management must involve the entire organization. Everyone must shift mindsets from operating income and earnings to free cash flow (Moore, 2002). The entrepreneur should take the following factors into serious consideration as far as cash flow management is concerned:

- Remember that "Cash is King," meaning that, if the balance sheet is correct, most if not all current assets should be easily convertible into cash.

- Keep your assets working for you, and do not keep obsolete inventory or equipment.

- Make sure your business is properly financed.

- Have a financial plan with its goals matching the balance sheet (Weinstein, 1995).

A firm's cash flow refers to the stream of cash inflows (receipts) and outflows (disbursements) over a certain period of time. Cash includes cash at hand or deposited in a bank in the form of checking accounts. Near-cash items include other negotiable instruments such as money orders, cashier's checks, bank drafts, and lines of credit. Banks mediate these transactions by converting the near-cash items into real cash and by safely depositing the firm's valuable cash assets in a business account. By adding up the deposits during a particular period and then subtracting the withdrawals during that period, the firm can determine its net cash flow position at the end of the period.

The first step in developing an effective cash flow management system is understanding (a) the venture's cash flow cycle, (b) the time lag between paying suppliers for merchandise and supplies and receiving payment from customers, and (c) the development of a corresponding strategy that incorporates the venture's specific cash flow patterns (Bak, 1993). Therefore, an alert cash flow manager not only monitors cash receipts and cash payments as average amounts but also monitors these amounts as a function of the calendar and the dates when cash flows in or out (Mamis, 1993). A positive net cash flow is accomplished by ensuring that customers make prompt payments for the goods and services they receive from the firm, by making sure the size of current expenditures and bills are low, and by paying financial obligations only when they become due to realize the benefit of having extra cash at hand or in the bank. Herein lies the difference between profit and cash flow. Profit is positive when sales revenues exceed expenses, regardless of whether these sales are on a cash or credit basis, and regardless of whether any of the customers paid or not. On the other hand, cash flow is positive only when customers make payments in cash and the firm does not have any bills falling due.

A firm's *cash flow position* is therefore, the outcome of the calculation of *net cash receipts* minus *net cash expenditures*. To manage inflows and outflows of cash in a "checkbook" fashion, the current assets and liabilities of a firm must be monitored and managed with utmost care. For example, managing accounts receivable that will be converted into cash at a future date is an integral part of cash management. The same should be said for inventory, the sale of which generates cash inflows, but in the meantime, it has generated cash outflows in the form of purchase invoices that are due in the near future. Cash management, therefore, is the planning, monitoring, and management of current assets (assets that can be converted into cash easily) and current liabilities (liabilities and obligations that are due within a normal operating cycle, usually the next 12 months). More specifically, the objectives of cash flow management are the following:

1. *Planning* what levels of assets and liabilities should be maintained to generate sales and income for the business.

2. *Monitoring* the levels of primarily current assets and liabilities and their activity flow and trends to determine which are contributing to positive cash flow and which are not.

3. *Managing* all assets and liabilities based on the results of planning and monitoring to ensure that the firm is always pointed in the direction of positive cash flow and subsequently profit.

Cash flow management, therefore, involves planning and setting targets for what kind and what level of assets and liabilities are needed for the business to operate successfully. Once these targets have been established, monitoring must be undertaken to ensure that the selected targets were accurate and that the activity of assets and liabilities contributes to a positive cash flow. The final integral part of the cash flow management process is the management and control of assets and liabilities given the information gathered during the planning and monitoring stages, by improving positive cash flow asset and liability contributions, and by minimizing the impact of negative asset and liability cash flow outlays to ensure that inflows are always greater than outflows.

As mentioned previously, the primary obligation of the entrepreneur is to meet cash needs with internally generated funds rather than continuously with externally borrowed funds, which can be disastrous when interest rates are high. However, according to a survey of 440 small-company executives, the function of management that small firm managers believe needs the most improvement is managing cash. Pricing strategy, internal controls, and cost reduction came next in importance ("Small Business: What Function," 1982, p. 27).

Most entrepreneurial managers do not generally understand the importance of modern cash management methods, nor do they think they are really applicable to their businesses. The lack of use of outside advice and the lack of simple internal management controls further accentuate the problem and result in cash being controlled on the basis of *ad hoc* opinions by the entrepreneurs. Annual budgets are customarily prepared instead of cash budgets or sales forecasts, even if there are cash flow problems. A majority of respondents believed expending time or money to reduce "cash float" would have little or no effect, because they believed that they were at the mercy of customers in receiving payment. Few of the small firms in the survey had formal lines of credit, used quantitative methods to determine the amount of cash reserves needed, or invested in excess cash. To ensure effective planning and control of cash flow, the entrepreneurial manager should periodically but consistently prepare a statement of cash flows reflecting the sources and uses of cash for three distinct activities:

- Operating activities

- Investing activities

- Financing activities

Cash flow from operating activities comprises "cash flow in" from sale of merchandise and services to customers, and "cash flow out" to realize sales, such as inventory purchases, distribution, expenditures, labor wages, etc. Cash inflows from investing activities include proceeds from the sale of property, plant, or equipment, and from sale of investment securities, as well as from loans obtained. Cash outflows from investing activities include expenditures on new plant, property, real estate, purchases of new investments, loans, etc. Cash inflows from financing activities consist of proceeds from newly generated equity capital, short-term or long-term debt, and cash outflows from financing activities; these are payments to retire debt obligations and payments and withdrawals to the entrepreneur/ owner. Therefore, before effective and comprehensive cash management plans can be implemented, preliminary data about the business must be gathered encompassing the following:

- Firm financial statements for the past 3 years.

- Accounts receivable and accounts payable aging schedules, as of the end of last month.

- Sales, by month and by product category, for the past 24 months.

- A 12-month collection history, determined by dividing each month's total collections by the account receivable balance on the last day of the prior month.

- A schedule and a monthly average of general ledger cost items, except purchases and direct labor, for each of the previous 7 months.

- A list of all loans, including the name of the lender, balance due, interest rate, monthly payments, collateral, due dates, and present status.

- A roster of all non-direct labor employees, including name, salary, and position (Durkee & Sharlit, 1983).

Exhibit 13.1   Cash Flow Budget, XYZ Company

Month/Quarter/Year	Pre–Start-up		1		2		3	
	Estimate	Actual	Estimate	Actual	Estimate	Actual	Estimate	Actual
1. **Cash on Hand** (Beginning of the month)								
2. Cash Receipts								
• Cash sales								
• Collections from A/R								
• Loan or other cash infusion								
3. Total Cash Receipts								
4. Total Cash Available (1 + 3)								
5. Cash Paid Out								
• Operations								
• **Subtotal**								
• Loan principal payment								
• Capital purchases								
• Reserve and/or escrow								
• Owner's withdrawal								
6. Total Cash Paid Out								
7. **Cash Position** (4–6) (End of month)								

Thus, the cash flow statement provides a comprehensive summary of the operating, investing, and financial activities of the venture, and it serves as a very useful information base for making important future financial decisions. A typical statement of cash flows is shown in Exhibit 13.1. Effective cash management should be viewed as a critical administrative function that should always give special consideration to the process of generating, managing, and controlling the following important elements:

- Cash inflow management
- Cash outflow management
- Accounts receivable management
- Depository practices and investment management

Cash Inflow Management

This aspect of effective cash management deals with the issue of accelerating the cash inflows and revenue collections. Cash inflows should be steady and without seasonal fluctuations or administrative bottlenecks that may create cash inflow "lows" that require emergency cash infusions ("Solving the Cash Crunch," 1981). To this end, the following areas need to be carefully examined and monitored:

- *Invoice processing:* Invoices need to be mailed and processed as soon as possible. Outdated billing procedures are usually responsible for cash inflow delays due to invoice processing bottlenecks. A careful study of the activity flow of the billing process may identify and remedy these bottlenecks.

- *Mail flow:* Mail needs to be picked up and deposited in an efficient and expeditious manner, because some cash inflow delays may well be attributed to outgoing or incoming mail procedures.

- *Remittance processing:* The firm needs to study how long it takes to physically process a payment. A diagram of the activity flow in this area will also help identify any hidden backlogs (Tompkins, 1982).

Cash Outflow Management

Accounts payable are what the venture owes to others; they are probably the most current of all outstanding liabilities and cash outflow items. There are two ways to account for them (a) on a cash basis and (b) on an accrual basis. The accounting basis employed depends upon the business itself and the specific type of the rest of the firm's accounting system.

Cash basis accounting is very simple because a payment is not recorded until it is actually paid out. On the other hand, accrual basis accounting is recorded when the invoice arrives. *Due date recognition invoices* should not be processed as soon as they are ready for payment. If a supplier offers credit terms for early payments, it is often wise to take advantage of them. *Trade credits* or accounts payable are generally set up to be paid within 30 days. If they are paid within this 30-day period, there is no service charge, making trade credit a very inexpensive method of financing the purchases of the business. However, if the accounts are not paid during this 30-day period, a service charge of typically 1.5% of the balance is charged. This 1.5% per month, however, results in an annual rate of 18%, which may be more expensive than short-term financing from a commercial bank or other financial institution. If the account cannot be paid within the 30-day limit, then the 1.5% per month service charge should be compared to the short-term interest rate at the commercial lending institution to see which alternative is less expensive (White & Jahera, 1980).

Small companies that are short on cash often delay paying accounts payable. Tactics include sending unsigned checks that must be returned, scrambling envelopes so somebody else gets the firm's check, or paying the wrong amount. Then there is the missing invoice ploy, which can buy a week or two while a duplicate is being sent, or a demand for proof of delivery, which can gain another month's reprieve while the trucking firm digs out a copy of the delivery slip. Another stalling tactic is blaming the computer as often as the mail. A broken computer or a "missing" account payable file can be worth a delay of a week, a month, or more (Jackson, 1981). Stalling and delaying payment as part of a cash outflow management strategy and its "collect early, push out the product, and pay late" attitude squeezes both customers and suppliers and, in the long run, may have a negative effect. Firms using their financial muscle to hold off paying smaller suppliers as long as possible through stalling techniques cannot last long (Hall, 2002). The best policy is to talk to the suppliers honestly and up front because most of the time a partial or delayed payment is acceptable, especially since the biggest supplier of credit for small firms is not the banks, but other small firms ("Business Bulletin: Small Companies," 1980, p. 1).

Finally, many small firms should examine their accounts payable and cash outflow process because they often write 10 to 15 checks per month to the same supplier, instead of consolidating all the payments and paying just once per month (Tompkins, 1982).

Inventory purchases are also part of cash outflows and represent money invested in the business, whether they have been paid for already or are currently being paid. A large number of small firms often find themselves in a cash flow shortage, even when their sales are in very good shape, and in many cases, it is because of lack of inventory management. Managing these inventories translates into managing the cash flow of the business because obsolete, damaged, or otherwise unsalable merchandise not only is not helping the business revenue, but it is also making the financial statements look better than they really are by overstating the current assets (White & Jahera, 1980).

Inventory should be reduced as much as possible as long as it does not affect customer service. Inventory-related management issues should take the form of the following questions:

- What kind of inventory can the firm live without, when, and for how long?

- What can the firm do differently in ordering inventory and when?

- What kind of inventory contributes most toward overhead and profit?

Idle inventories, for whatever reason, like unsalable inventories, are not productive assets, because they are not generating any income. Inventory should be listed in descending dollar amounts and each item should be classified into three categories: current usage, excess usage, and obsolete dollar amounts. Management should aim to achieve an inventory ratio of approximately 80/20, or 80% of the inventory dollar amount to 20% of the inventory items. If there is seasonality in the business, knowing what items are expected to sell or which ones are selling can help in the ordering of new stock that will turn over quickly and produce immediate cash inflows to offset the cash outflows of the inventory ordered. By keeping accurate records of what items sell best, and in what part of the year, it is possible to plan the purchases for any season, thereby minimizing the amount of idle or unsalable inventory on hand at any given time. Once products not contributing sufficiently to overhead and profit are identified, each should be examined to determine which action or series of actions can solve the problem. Here is a partial list of the options to explore:

- Increase prices

- Decrease overhead costs

- Improve labor productivity

- Reduce material costs through value engineering techniques or improved purchasing practices

- Discontinue the product

- Do not maintain an inventory of a product, but instead make only to order

- Have the product manufactured by another firm.

- Redesign the product to improve market acceptability, thus allowing higher prices

- Strengthen sales effort without decreasing prices (Durkee & Sharlit, 1983, pp. 17–18)

Some additional insights regarding the impact of inventory on cash flow can be derived from the following aspects of financial analysis:

- *Total number of days inventory was held:* Date last item was sold *minus* the date all items were received.

- *Number of days before first item was sold:* Date first item was sold *minus* the date all items were received.

- *Total number of days an inventory batch was held:* Batch of sold units (as a percentage of the total inventory received) *times* the number of days the batch of sold units was held from the date when the total inventory was received.

- *Average number of days inventory was held:* Sum of days held for each of the sold inventory batches that represent the total inventory.

- *Gross profit margin:* Price of the item *minus* the cost of the item.

- *Gross profit margin for an inventory batch:* Batch of sold units (as a percentage of the total inventory received) *times* the gross profit margin for that particular sale.

- *Average gross profit margin for total inventory:* Sum of gross profit margins for each sale of inventory batches that represent the total inventory.

Another way to contribute to an efficient cash outflow management plan is through exchange transactions or through bartering. Bartering is very attractive for small firms because it unloads surplus inventory, and most importantly it does not involve cash transactions. A business can barter its goods at fair market value for trade credit, and at the same time, a small firm can reach broader markets without extra advertising or distribution costs. Bartering, however, must be treated as income or cost and taxed or deducted accordingly ("Using Barter," 1980).

Accounts Receivable and Credit Policy Management

Three areas relating to accounts receivable contribute to an effective cash flow management process:

1. A sound credit policy
2. The establishment of an account receivable system
3. The evaluation of the current accounts receivable

Credit Policy

A sound credit policy should incorporate three elements:

- A proper classification of credit customers

- The determination of appropriate credit limits for each account

- The development of a proper system of collection and evaluation for each account

Credit customers do not ask for or need the same amount of credit as other customers, and neither can they pay in the same manner. Therefore, credit customers need to be classified according to how much credit they need, how much they are capable of handling, and for how long (Christy & Roden, 1976). The venture's bank can also help create this classification because banks usually know when a firm seeking credit is headed for trouble before credit reporting agencies do. Banks can pass such information to other banks, even though they are not supposed to, and they often reveal details of banking transactions ("Small Business: Should You Extend," 1983). Additionally, a key financial ratio for checking a customer's credit is **times interest earned**, which measures how many times required interest payments are covered by pretax earnings. A low ratio, for example *two times* interest, reveals that the firm is overextended credit-wise compared to other firms in the industry. The nature of the potential customer's loan agreements, the repayment schedule, and interest fluctuations also help to properly classify a credit customer (Abelson, 1983).

Setting proper credit limits is a protection for both the venture and its customers, in that the customer's chances of getting the account out of line is reduced, while the venture has limited the chance of having a bad debt account. Therefore, for marginal customers, it is wise to grant only token or trial credit first, because, as mentioned, all customers are not alike.

Finally, the venture needs to absolutely adhere to the set credit terms and limits, insist that all customers pay their bills when due, and constantly evaluate and reevaluate the credit-worthiness of its customers and the current account receivables. Economic cycles are often not taken into consideration when setting credit policies, but common sense dictates that if it is hard to get credit from the suppliers, credit should not be extended to customers, either! Ultimately, the success or failure of any sound credit policy program lies on the firm foundation established by credit rules and policies and on their faithful implementation in the accounts receivable system.

Establishment of an Accounts Receivable System

The key to an effective accounts receivable management system is, of course, success in collection. Accounts receivable is a very liquid asset that contributes a great deal to cash inflows, and the key word is liquid when describing accounts receivable, and unless they are regularly turning over, this asset could become a drain on the business. Therefore, a systematic way of collecting accounts is necessary to make receivables regularly contribute cash inflows.

However, few small firms use more than one or two of the simplest credit control techniques taken for granted by larger firms, and consequently, small firms typically have bad debt rates far exceeding those experienced by larger firms (Grablowsky, 1976).

Collecting receivables requires an early start and dogged determination. That means keeping timely accounts receivable records and recognizing that receivables are older than they may seem. For merchandise shipped at the beginning of a month, accounts listed as "current" at a month's end are already 30 days old. As receivables get older, collection attempts must get progressively tougher. A polite "please pay" for an amount 30 days past due should escalate when it gets to be 45 days past due, to a warning that shipments will be stopped if the amount due is not paid in 15 days. If the amount becomes 60 days old, shipments should be halted as threatened and immediate payment demanded. Fifteen days later, when the bill is 75 days old, collection or legal action should be threatened if payment is not received in 15 days. Then, when the account payable is 90 days old, the threatened action should be carried out ("Timely Advice," 1981).

Collection of accounts receivable is a test of good management. Strict collection policies and an established accounts receivable system will enable the venture to hold the line on accounts receivable delinquency. Regular weekly readings on the aging of accounts should be taken, with the first collection letter going out at 30 days, and the first phone call on the 45th day ("Bite the Bullet," 1982). Each firm is different, but some general rules should be followed in establishing an accounts receivable system:

- Billing should take place at the time of shipment, because a lag in paperwork can hold up collection almost as much as slow-paying customers.

- Receivables more than 45 days old are a clear sign of trouble, and an investment in a special collections staff is worth consideration.

- Personal contact can sometimes speed response, by discussing business in a friendly manner first and socializing later.

- Customers need to be called immediately after a past due notice goes out, and in case of a long-standing relationship, the entrepreneur needs to handle the collection calls in person.

- As mentioned earlier, the risk of a big bad debt is minimized by setting a maximum limit to any bill a customer can run up and a maximum number of days that bill can be overdue before shipments are stopped.

- Established policies need to be faithfully followed because customers soon learn to recognize empty threats.

If an account receivable remains overdue, there are three options that are not mutually exclusive: (a) cut off shipment, (b) call a collection agency, and/or (c) sue. Negotiations may be preferable to an unbending stance in cases where the customer seems to be in danger of being pushed into bankruptcy, because then chances of recovery may be nil. Abusive tactics in collecting overdue accounts are out of the question because courts and legislation have backed down on practices such as:

- Subjecting the debtor to repeated phone calls at inconvenient times.

- Threatening the debtor with a jail term or loss of a job.

- Embarrassing the debtor by communicating news of the debt to neighbors and relatives.

- Calling the debtor a "deadbeat" or worse.

- Falsely telling the debtor that a judgment has been entered (Steingold, 1982).

Collection of the account receivable can be made easier if there are incentives for the customer to pay off on time or early. Offering a finance charge only on unpaid balances to encourage a larger payment may help. Or if payment should be in the form of one lump sum, discounts are helpful ways of encouraging early payment. And once again, because all credit customers are not equal, different credit policies should be set for different customer groups, with the highest volume accounts classified in an "A" group that receive maximum service and incentives at no cost or penalty regardless of the size of the invoice. Medium-to-small accounts with growth potential should be classified in a "B" group and receive regular service and incentives with a penalties for small orders or past due accounts. Small accounts should be lumped in a "C" category and receive no service or incentives with substantial penalties for small order or past due accounts (Ketchum, 1982).

Even the government is not immune from collection efforts. Under the *Prompt Payments Act* unanimously passed by the House of Representatives in March 1982, federal agencies are forced to pay private contractors on time or face interest penalties. The bill sets a 45-day limit for payment of most bills. If bills remain unpaid, interest is charged from the 31st day. Shorter time periods are set for contracts for meats and vegetables. In case of court actions against the government, the *Equal Access to Justice* law allows small firms to recover expenses if they prevail in court action involving the federal government. Under the law, a small firm might be reimbursed for attorney fees and court costs if it is the prevailing party and the government is unable to prove to the satisfaction of the court that it was "substantially justified" in its actions. The *National Federation of Independent Business* (NFIB) made passage of these laws one of its top priority goals to correct an extreme imbalance of power that had created "horror stories" for small firms that could not afford to fight the government's unlimited legal resources for their rights (National Federation of Independent Business, 1982).

Evaluation of Accounts Receivable

In evaluating a small firm's accounts receivable the use of ratios is always a good place to start. To evaluate the turnover rate of the current accounts, the **accounts receivable turnover ratio**, which is the net credit sales divided by the average net receivables, indicates approximately how fast accounts were recorded and collected during the year. Utilizing effective collection methods through an established accounts receivable system, the average accounts receivable turnover ratio is increased. This keeps accounts receivable liquid and cash flow free.

A second equally important ratio is the average age of receivables ratio, which is the accounts receivable turnover ratio, divided into the number of days in the year. This indicates approximately how long it takes to collect these accounts.

Finally, the concept of evaluating accounts receivable through their *net realizable value* provides a sharper picture of the history of accounts receivable. Because certain past due accounts receivable have a higher ratio of uncollectibility than others, "aging" them can indicate when these accounts are falling into the areas of uncollectibility. These account balances can then be recorded on the balance sheet as being an *allowance for bad debt,* which follows the accounts receivable amount as a credit figure. The difference becomes the *net realizable value,* and allows the posting of a lower figure on the financial statements at the end of the year (Welsch & Anthony, 1977, p. 213). The actual value of these ratios and evaluation methods is relative and needs to be compared to the ratios of similar businesses and industry standards. These figures can be found in trade journals and can be used as comparisons for the assessment of the venture's current collection and accounting processes.

Depository Practices and Investment Management

The depository practices of the small firm must be structured to take advantage of the cash deposited as well as earlier collections. In many cases, depository practices are dictated by agreements with local banks limiting or expanding this kind of possibilities. Most banks offer automated cash management system service that provides customers not only with draft deposits and payments but also with timely information on their bank account's activity and the current status of their cash flow. Either online through the Internet or through a phone linked to the bank's computer with an assigned code number, a small-firm manager can receive up-to-date information regarding delinquent and collected balances, number and total amount of checks cleared, total number of deposits, and outstanding ("floating") checks. By having a target balance of cash to be maintained, the firm knows exactly how much idle cash is available to invest (Tangorra, 1982).

Floating checks, writing checks against cash already deposited in the bank, is quite beneficial because one can invest the deposited funds for a few days, until the checks clear. This floating activity, however, should be monitored closely and regularly to know exactly how much cash reserves are available. Striking a balance between appropriate liquidity and credit reputation with financial institutions while trying to get a return on investment of idle cash, can become almost a full-time job. There are many options for putting idle cash to work:

1. Establishment of a checking account "sweeping" at the close of the bank's business day, moving any amount over a target balance into a money market fund, where it earns daily interest until it is needed back in the checking account.

2. Establishment of a checking account with a money market fund, which incidentally is not guaranteed by the *Federal Deposit Insurance Corporation* (FDIC), especially for big-ticket accounts with minimum draft amounts of $250 or $500.

3. A repurchase agreement or **"repo"** with a bank that agrees to sell the firm a government security from its portfolio and agrees to buy it back at a later date, specified or unspecified, at the same price plus interest.

4. A **"lockbox" arrangement** where customers of a small firm mail payments to a post office lockbox number operated by a bank, which picks up the payments and immediately credits the firm's account and/or invests the money.

5. Investment in a bank *certificate of deposit* (CD) issued for terms ranging from 14 days to several years, insured up to $100,000, and paying interest usually at maturity. The longer the maturity the higher the interest.

6. Investment in commercial paper of the financial branch of major corporations like GMC of General Motors. Terms depend on length of investment and amount, and yields may vary depending on the risk factor evaluation of the borrowing company and maturity.

7. Investment in a large company's commercial paper, similar to the CD concept, serves to finance a large firm's short-term borrowing needs.

8. Investment in a money market fund exclusively in government-backed Treasury Bills. However, less risk is usually accompanied by a lower yield.

9. Investment in a tax-free money market fund with a checking account but with a yield lower than that of a taxable fund.

10. Investment in tax anticipation notes issued by state and local authorities against future collection of taxes. Maturities for these notes range from 30 days to a year and usually produce tax-free income.

11. Investment in Treasury Bills directly purchased from the Federal Reserve Bank free of state and local taxes but not federal taxes, and with the interest on them discounted, i.e., subtracted from par at the time of purchase (Mamis, 1982, pp. 158–159).

The key concern in depository practices and cash investment management is to strike a balance among the following aspects: the liquidity target, the security of investment, the investment yield, and the ease of management of the investment.

CAPITAL FUNDING MANAGEMENT

Even during the best of times, small firms have more trouble raising capital funds than large firms do. Economic and business trends dictate the need for concise guidance on types and sources of finance, their appropriateness for particular projects, and how to "present a case" to finance providers. Because new ventures are usually too small initially to tap the public stock and bond markets, they largely depend on bank credit, and they usually find themselves last in line. Banks would much rather handle a $2 million line of credit than a measly $20,000 credit line. A *Fortune* 500 company can generally borrow as much as four times the amount of its deposits at a bank, but for smaller firms, the ratio often sinks to as low as one-to-one (Pauly, Manning, & Thomas, 1979).

Small firms derive about two thirds of their operating funds from debt sources, and more than 50% of this debt is short-term in nature. Only 15% of all funds sources are in the form of mortgages, notes, and bonds. Bank lending accounts for only 16.5% of all fund sources and 30% of all debt. Trade credit supplies more than 17%, and this type of business financing is very important to small firms. Large firms recognize the reliance of small firms on trade credit, and they make a point of offering such a financing method as an important selling tool, usually with generous terms. Furthermore, during tight money or slow economic periods, small firms may stretch out their payments to large suppliers, resulting in some sort of intermediation by which small firms borrow from large firms through trade credit and large firms, in turn, finance themselves in the credit markets (Eisemann & Andrews, 1981). There are basically three types of capital funding:

1. Debt financing
2. Equity financing
3. Financing from internally generated funds

Debt Financing

Debt financing is the type of financing in which the business borrows money for a certain length of time and must then pay back the principal amount plus interest. Sometimes high interest rates create a great deal of hardship for small firms, and they are usually a symptom of bad economic conditions created by the federal government. Government deficits creating excessive public funding demands on the capital markets in competition with the private sector help push interest rates to high levels. Because the government is insensitive to the interest rates it pays, it can borrow billions of dollars, while consumers and businesses have to divide up what is left, and in essence are "crowded out" of the credit pool. When borrowing costs climb, as they did during the 1980–1981 period when they exceeded 20%, small-sized firms showed signs of economic distress.

When money is tight, smaller borrowers have to pay rates scaled up from the prime rate. According to *Webster's New Collegiate Dictionary,* **prime rate** means the "lowest commercial interest rate available at a particular time and place." But the largest banks in the nation apparently do not adhere to any set definition of prime rate. Morgan Guarantee Trust, for example, has defined the prime rate as "the rate of interest publicly announced by the Bank in New York City from time to time as its prime rate" (Rock, 1982, p. 53). Even though the *Robinson-Patnam Act* makes discriminatory pricing of goods and commodities illegal, small firms, which seldom get loans at prime anyway, whether this is the lowest commercial lending rate available or not, have every right to feel discriminated. What sounds like a good deal at a prime rate plus two points may not be so good after all, especially when the small venture's large competitor may be paying two points under prime. Furthermore, the rates banks are permitted to charge borrowers on loans guaranteed by the Small Business Administration are, by regulation, tied to the prime rate "printed in *The Wall Street Journal* that was published on the date the SBA received the application" ("What Does Prime Rate Mean," 1981).

Are bankers wrong to hold smaller businesses to the same capitalization standards they set for big business? Do they fail to look for the real strengths of a venture beyond debt-to-equity ratios? Should they be willing to take more of a chance on entrepreneurial ventures? On the other hand, fewer than 10% of prospective small borrowers come to a bank prepared with an adequate loan application package and/or business plan. And of these well-prepared entrepreneurs, some believe their bank wants perfection, so they try to hide bad news, even though, as mentioned repeatedly earlier, when dealing with banks, mutual trust and honesty is the best policy (Jacobs, 1981, p. 25).

The relationship between bankers and small firms, as mentioned in earlier chapters, is clouded with some kind of conservative bias. Banks favor much more collateralized consumer loans or large firm loans secured by a history of profitable operations. In an independent study, *Inc. Magazine* interviewed 150 large and regional banks on how bankers view small firms and on the reasons why very few ventures are financed by bank loans. Bankers cited the main reasons for rejecting small venture loans: signs of undercapitalization or too much debt, lack of collateral, inability to demonstrate source of repayment, poor credit history, inadequate financial information, weak management, lack of experience in the field of business, poor track record or poor profitability, insufficient cash flow, and unprofessional financial statements (Howitt, 1981, p. 50).

Venture start-ups therefore, are not a favorite with the banks, and as a result, many solid growth ventures needing funding often cannot qualify for unsecured bank loans on the mere strength of their financial statements. That is why a growing number of entrepreneurial ventures have discovered aggressive asset-based lending banks as a last resort, which make secured loans based on a careful review of the venture's asset liquidation value (Stevens, 1982, p. 108).

There are two forms of debt financing: short term and long term. A **short-term loan** is a loan in which the principal is usually due within 1 year.

Short-term Financing

There are many sources of short-term loans with trade credit, as mentioned earlier, being one of the most common.

- **Trade credit** is short-term credit extended by a supplier to a buyer in connection with the purchase of goods for ultimate resale. The supplier lends the purchasing firm inventory rather than cash, and this can be a very inexpensive source of funds if the supplier has a repayment policy of, say, net 30 and offers no discount for early payment. However, this could also turn out to be a very expensive source of credit in case of not paying on time, with high corresponding annual interest rates similar to credit card charges.

- **Bank overdrafts** are also considered short-term loans, but payment may be demanded on a very short notice, although many businesses assume that this will never happen. Overdrafts tend to be unsecured, are available primarily to companies that are financially strong, and their cost is usually less than all types of debt financing.

Long-term Debt Financing

A **long-term debt** is a loan of 1 year or longer. There are several sources of long-term debt:

- **Unsecured loans** are loans that are usually obtained from a bank and do not require collateral. If the loan is not paid back on time, then the bank will attempt to draw on the company's assets to have the loan repaid. Obtaining one of these loans can be difficult, because the decision to grant an unsecured loan results from a favorable evaluation of the entrepreneur's character, and the firm's reputation, condition, capital reserves, and creditworthiness.

- **Installment-type loans** are long-term loans that usually extend from 2 to 15 years. This type of loan is amortized with regular payments required to pay the interest and to gradually reduce the outstanding principal of the loan. Installment loans are often used to finance plant and equipment and can be obtained from banks, equipment suppliers, or government agencies.

- **Equipment leasing** is another type of long-term debt. The company that leases a piece of equipment from another company has the utility of the use of that equipment without having to pay full price for it, or get stuck with an obsolete technology by purchasing instead of leasing. Along these same lines, a company can sell a piece of equipment to another company and then lease it back, thus providing additional capital to the lessee.

- A **mortgage** is a very common conventional long-term credit arrangement, usually maturing in 10 to 30 years after being issued. A mortgage will have equipment, plant, or land pledged as security in case the payments are not paid when due.

- **Small business investment corporations (SBICs)** are privately owned financial corporations that are licensed, regulated, and promoted by the Small Business Administration (SBA), an agency of the federal government. SBICs can only lend to or invest in companies that meet the definition of a small business as defined by the SBA. When SBICs invest in small companies, they are not allowed to gain control of those small companies, but instead provide management counseling and assistance to protect their investment. These investments can be in the form of purchasing the businesses convertible debentures, capital stock, and debt securities. Long-term loan financing to the venture by the SBICs must be for at least 5 years and may be as long as 20 years.

- The **Small Business Administration (SBA)** is a federal agency that also provides direct loans, economic opportunity loans, guarantees on loans by private lenders, as well as other types of financial assistance to small firms.

Equity Financing

Equity financing entails the sale of a company's stock. This can be done in two ways: through the sale of preferred stock or through the sale of common stock. Selling preferred stock gives the buyers first rights to the residual profits of a company after creditors get paid and before common stockholders receive dividends, but this does not turn over any control to the buyers in the form of voting rights. Small companies are leery about selling any type of stock to outsiders because the control of the company is diluted, but if it becomes necessary to sell equity to raise funds, then the sale of preferred stock is preferable to the sale of common stock. The sale of common stock is unpopular in entrepreneurial circles, because common stockholders may be able someday to assume control of the venture.

The *Entrepreneur Access to Capital Act* passed by the U.S. House of Representatives in November 2011 allows first-time ordinary investors to put up to $10,000 in small businesses through what is called "crowd funding." Small firms that are not registered with the Securities Exchange Commission can post information about their developmental business plans in an attempt to attract investors, especially since many banks are not exactly keen on lending funds to even well-established businesses (*The Economist,* 2011).

Internally Generated Funds

This form of financing has as its source the retained earnings that the venture does not pay to its shareholders and/or owners after interest and taxes, but rather plows them back into the company to finance future growth, or weather lean economic times, or simply bad luck. Internally generated funds are also the result of funds generated from an ongoing, sound cash management system that implements cash-tracking and cash-saving procedures for the most advantageous purchasing techniques and the shortest billing and collection cycles.

One valuable liquid asset that is internally generated and can be quickly turned into cash and retained earnings is the accounts receivable. These accounts can be turned into cash quickly not only through collection but also through their use as collateral against a loan, or "factoring." **Factoring** is the act of selling accounts receivables for cash to another financial entity, which represents the finance charge for the seller, usually at a sizeable discount, depending on how much legal recourse against the debtor exists. The discount also lowers the risk for the factoring purchaser, who assumes the risk that these account receivables may ultimately never be collected and end up being worthless, especially if collection is attempted by an entity other than the original creditor.

TAX LIABILITY MANAGEMENT

State and local governments are becoming more sensitive about creating and maintaining a favorable tax climate for businesses. On the federal level, the formation of new enterprises and the creation of new jobs are stifled by the high capital gains tax, which discourages inventors, scientists, engineers, marketers, and entrepreneurs from putting their ideas to work for themselves. Instead, because of the burden of the capital gains tax, these "idea" people sell their talents to large corporations for a salary. When Congress reduced the maximum tax on capital gains from 49% to 28% in 1978, new equity offerings for firms with net worth of less than $5 million jumped 135% in a 5-year period. This is a clear sign of the correlation between small firm creation and growth with capital gains tax reduction.

Accelerated depreciation and beneficial liberal depreciation rules probably do not make much difference for small retailers, construction, or service companies. By their nature, many small firms are labor intensive and not capital intensive, and they gain no direct benefit at all from liberal depreciation schedules, which are clearly aimed at rewarding companies that invest heavily in capital goods.

Inventory reporting for tax purposes generally has worked against small firms. During inflationary times *the last-in, first-out* (LIFO) inventory accounting method prevents a business from paying taxes on paper profits caused by the inflated value of inventory. However, switching to LIFO and maintaining the bookkeeping the tax law requires is so complicated and costly that many small firms avoid switching methods (Jacobs, 1981, p. 29)

Constant changes in the tax law also create problems for owners of small concerns especially in terms of new, different, or additional paperwork required. Only careful planning can assure that the firm did not pay more income tax than necessary and every possible deduction was claimed, but in reality, most entrepreneurs seem to be oblivious of how new tax rules can help or hurt them. Owners are so consumed with running a business that they do not see how tax law changes can affect decision making (James, 1982, p. 27).

Even though it is hard to generalize about what kind of tax structure would benefit entrepreneurial ventures, the following suggestions are offered, keeping in mind that production processes differ from firm to firm:

- Taxes on net profit are preferable to taxes on sales or gross receipts for new and rapidly expanding firms whose sales are usually growing more rapidly than their profits.

- A corporate income tax with a progressive rate structure like Wisconsin's, Kentucky's, or Arizona's is preferable to one that takes a fixed percentage of profits, like California's, New York's, or Minnesota's, since a growing firm's profits are likely to be lower than those of its established competitors.

- The value-added tax does not discriminate between labor-intensive and capital-intensive firms, so it is preferable to payroll or property taxes.

- A personal property tax that does not include inventories greatly benefits smaller retailers and wholesalers, who tend to be inventory intensive (Berney, 1981, p. 16).

The bottom line is that tax law is simply too complex, and as mentioned earlier, tax considerations and implications for the venture should be assigned to a member of the external or internal team, the accountant. Tax management implies not only staying out of trouble with the IRS but also saving money by avoiding legally (as contrasted to evading illegally) paying taxes, especially when there are new tax laws or changes in tax rates.

The expert assistance of the venture's tax accountant should be given serious consideration, especially given the fact that the tax preparation fees are deductible. Moreover, the Internal Revenue Service, in a celebrated case, imposed a negligence penalty on a taxpayer who underpaid his taxes on the grounds that his return was too complex to complete without professional help, which means that there is absolutely no excuse for not seeking professional tax assistance for the venture's tax management affairs ("How to Pick a Tax Accountant," 1981, p. 142).

Tax management and year-end tax planning is an "always-win" situation and as a general guideline the following checklist is recommended for year-end tax planning. The basic assumption behind this checklist is that the firm wants to reduce reportable income as much as possible. If the owner expects to be in a higher tax bracket the following year or if there is a loss carryover that is about to expire, the reverse of many of these suggestions should be considered:

Balance Sheet Items

Many of the best opportunities for controlling profits for tax purposes occur during the review of the balance sheet. Here are some important points:

- All bad debts should be written off.

- Consideration should be given to whether the allowance or reserve for bad debts should be increased.

- Obsolete inventory should be sold or given away, so it can be written off.

- Damaged, old, or obsolete merchandise should be valued at its market price if this is lower than its original cost.

- Inventory levels and inventory location should be where state and local property taxes are minimized.

- If inflation kicked up the value of inventory and created phony, but taxable, profits the LIFO method of inventory accounting should be used.

- If equipment becomes obsolete, it should be abandoned so the remaining book value can be deducted, sold, or traded in. Trade-ins are advantageous if their market value exceeds their book value, since a capital gains tax is avoided.

- Property acquisition should be carefully planned and timed to coincide either before or after year-end, depending on which point of time will maximize the benefits of first-year depreciation and the investment tax credit.

- All loans, particularly to owners, stockholders, or officers, need to be formalized with notes at fair interest rates, and with the interest paid when due.

- All expenses due to a holder of more than 50% of the company's shares need to be paid within 2.5 months of year-end so they will be deductible.

- Investments that show a loss need to be sold, so the loss can be applied to offset extraordinary profits.

- In case of expiring loss carryovers, some successful investments need to be sold to realize profits that can be offset by the expiring past losses.

- All excess and idle cash needs to be invested in taxable securities, tax-free municipal bonds, or dividend-paying stock of domestic corporations, depending on the tax implications.

- The level of excess cash needs to be evaluated because this may make the IRS conclude that too many earnings have been accumulated and require the venture to declare a dividend.

- Dividends must be timed to produce the best tax advantages to the stockholders by generally declaring them at year-end and paying them the following year.

- Every asset and liability needs to be checked and reevaluated to determine if anything can be done to move income into the year that will be most favorable to the company.

Cash Flow Items

The following suggestions are offered to increase cash flow resulting from tax issues:

- Expenses due can be paid with notes.

- If an automatic 90-day extension for filing a return is requested, contributions to a pension or profit-sharing plan can also be delayed for 90 days. Payments can still be deducted in the current year, but the actual payments need not be made until 5.5 months after the year ends.

- If the firm overpaid its estimated tax, a refund claim needs to be filed immediately.

Profit and Loss Items

The following are possible ways to decrease reportable income on the profit-and-loss or income statement:

- Shipping of products sold can be delayed.

- End-of-the-year shipments are always shipped to the point of their destination in terms of *Free-on-Board* (F.O.B), so the title sometimes does not pass to the buyer until after the end of the year.

- Sales are made on consignment or based on approval to delay posting.

Deduction Items

The following ideas can increase tax deductions:

- Bonuses to employees and to a controlling stockholder are made within 2.5 months after the year's end.

- Qualified pension or profit-sharing plans are established, large contributions are made under existing discretionary plans, or benefits under a defined benefit plan are enhanced.

- Donation of profits to charity.

- Benefits that will be received by employees the following year are declared at year-end, so they can be deducted as liabilities in the present year.

- Supplies that will be needed later are purchased at year's end.

- Needed plant and equipment repairs are made.

- Whenever possible disputed amounts are paid at year's end to deduct the payments, but the final settlement of the dispute is reserved for later.

- All items on the P&L statement need to be reviewed carefully to determine whether any additional deductions can be taken (Blackman, 1981).

FINANCIAL PERFORMANCE MANAGEMENT

Most people would conclude that the purpose of accounting and financial management is to answer the fundamental question of whether the venture made any money in the final analysis. Financial data, especially income statement data, are essential in answering this question, and quite too often, entrepreneurs rely only upon what they see or hear to determine whether or not their business is doing well.

However, certain aspects of the business are not anticipated and cannot always be accurately sensed. Changes in customer preferences, changes in the national and local economy, changes in the market, and gradual but seemingly irreversible changes in the cost structure of the firm can develop into a financial crisis, unless they are detected at an early stage and effective action is taken. Therefore, financial performance management should be based on comprehensive and well-documented facts, not upon piecemeal or random observations, so out-of-line financial conditions can be detected early and corrective action can be taken promptly, to get a clear picture on the value added to the firm from the financial operations (Aguilar, 2003).

Monitoring "how well" the firm is doing, as well as the development of a working operating profit plan, entails the following actions:

1. *Continuously evaluating financial results:* Each time an income statement is prepared, actual sales and costs are compared with those projected in the original profit plan to detect areas of unsatisfactory performance so that corrective action can be taken.

2. *Continuously establishing whether there is a need for fewer or additional resources, such as plant, equipment, or personnel:* For example, the profit plan may show that a sharp increase in expected sales will overload the company's billing personnel. A decision can then be made to add additional invoicing personnel, to retain a billing or collection service, or to pursue some other alternative.

3. *Carefully planning purchasing requirements and related costs:* The volume of expected sales may be more than the firm's usual suppliers can handle, or expected

sales may be sufficient to permit taking advantage of purchasing quantity discount savings.

4. *Anticipating and planning additional financing needs:* With planning, the search for needed additional funds can begin as early as possible, so financial crises are avoided and there is enough time allotted to arrange financing on the most favorable terms.

5. *Delegating and highlighting financial responsibilities:* With a working operating profit plan, personnel are readily aware of their responsibility and most importantly, they are accountable for meeting sales objectives and profit targets, as well as controlling costs.

6. *Developing cost sensitivity:* When the cost sensitivity of alternative decisions is determined and comparatively analyzed, cost excesses can quickly be identified and planned expenditures can be compared with original budgets before they occur, thus reducing unnecessary costs and overspending.

7. *Developing a disciplined approach to problem solving:* A profit plan should permit early detection of potential problems so that their nature and extent are known through a disciplined preventive maintenance problem-solving approach, so that alternative corrective actions can be more easily and accurately evaluated.

8. *Continuously thinking about the future:* Thinking about where the venture is today, where it could be, should be, and will be next year, or the year after, ensures that opportunities are not overlooked. At the same time, seemingly unforeseeable events crises may be anticipated and avoided.

9. *Securing the confidence of lenders and investors:* A realistic working operating profit plan, supported by a description of specific steps proposed to achieve the sales and profit objectives, inspires the confidence of potential lenders and investors. This confidence not only influences their judgment on the entrepreneur as a business manager, but also on the prospects of the venture's success and worthiness for a loan or an investment (U.S. Small Business Administration, 1980, pp. 1–2).

Because profit plans and subsequent financial performance are based upon estimates, inevitably, many conditions expected to materialize when the plan was prepared do change. In a year, any number of factors can change, many of them beyond the control of the entrepreneur. The economic fortunes of customers may decline, the prices of materials may increase, or the suppliers become unable to deliver on their promises. All of these eventualities may disrupt profit plans and overall financial performance, and consequently, adjustments must be made from time to time to meet changing conditions. There is no point in trying to operate a business according to a financial plan that is no longer realistic because conditions have changed. Some common problems with the management and control of financial performance include the following:

Inaccurate Financial Performance Measures

Unless they are built on discounted cash flow budgets, conventional accounting methods assume a stable monetary unit of measure, and they may not incorporate the impact of inflation in measuring financial performance. Especially during times of high inflation, a firm's adjusted net income may artificially increase, increasing for all practical purposes the effective tax rate also. In essence, this artificial increase clouds the true picture of the venture's financial performance, because the firm will not be able to retain enough earnings to maintain capital investment and high productivity levels. At best, total sales volume is a very crude measure of financial performance. At worst, it is misleading, because it says nothing about the financial "quality" of the gains or losses. A better measure of performance is comparative business sales. But even this measure may be misleading because what looks like a solid sales increase may not have corresponding comparable profits to go with it. The reason is that sales might have been built up in a costly way with expensive promotions and markdowns, especially during recessionary times. Another measure of financial performance widely used by retailers is sales per square foot, which can help in some comparisons of different kinds of stores. But it is nearly impossible to define what to include as sales space, and any big gains made by a growing store are diluted by the increasing floor space. A combination of sales information such as comparable regional (instead of national) sales figures, sales per square foot of existing stores without including any added floor space or new stores, changes of holidays from one reporting period to another, and sales analysis according to product category can portray a much more accurate picture of financial performance (Weiner, 1980).

Inadequate Financial Performance Strategies

There are three principal areas of misguided strategies toward financial performance:

1. *Growth for growth's sake:* Sales growth is not the solution to all problems, because growth is expensive, and almost always, it is accompanied by an increase in overhead except in the short run.

2. *Inadequate product analysis and cost allocation:* Direct costs can easily be attributed to a particular product or activity. Indirect costs, however, are not easy to allocate, and an easy way out is to charge the same proportionate amounts of indirect costs to both old and new products alike. This is not reasonable, because a new product line costs far more to start up. The inadvertent outcome of such an inexact product analysis and cost allocation is to encourage costly new projects, downgrade the financial performance of old "cash cow" products, and artificially upgrade that of new expensive ones. Using the Japanese concept of *kaizen costing,* cost targets can be accurately set in advance for all aspects of new product design, development, and production (Monden & Lee, 1993).

3. *Lack of concern for the balance sheet in favor of the income statement:* As mentioned earlier, typically entrepreneurs tend to show lack of concern for the cash flow and the productivity of the employed assets. Instead, they would rather seek new funds to improve the income statement, rather than make a better and more efficient use of the funds and assets they already have (Woodward, 1976).

These accuracy problems as well as misguided strategies toward financial performance make a firm of any size highly susceptible to financial errors. These errors may develop into pitfalls from which a venture is not able to extricate itself, with disastrous consequences for the firm's future prospects. Exhibit 13.2 identifies 14 pitfalls in financial management that smaller companies are often guilty of committing, which may eventually become serious problems and not only deprive the venture of its original competitive advantage but also may eventually lead to bankruptcy if left unchecked.

Whenever any of these pitfalls occur or an inadequate financial performance strategy is pursued on a permanent basis, it is time to consider a firm's "peaceful death" through bankruptcy proceedings. The point of no return is reached when all parties concerned, customers, suppliers, creditors, stockholders, internal and external team members, with the possible exception of the owner, realize that the following decisive factors have been established:

1. The inability of management to recognize there is a pitfall.

2. Failure to realign and reform a declining business from a pitfall in the belief that soon everything will return to "the good old days."

Exhibit 13.2	Financial Pitfalls for Entrepreneurial Ventures

1. Insufficient capital from the start.
2. Insufficient capital for growth and expansion.
3. Overdependence on debt.
4. Inadequate financial planning.
5. Inadequate cash management.
6. Emphasizing sales volume at the expense of return on investment (ROI).
7. Overlooking the risk-return trade-off.
8. Withdrawing too much money out of the business for personal compensation and perks.
9. Confounding cash and net income, since net income may not necessarily be cash.
10. Ineffective bank relations.
11. Too liberal credit policies.
12. Inadequate billing, accounts receivable, and collection system.
13. Inadequate handling of accounts payable.
14. Inadequate overall accounting system

Source: Abdelsamad, DeGenaro, & Wood, 1977.

3. A disorganized management who never knows where it stands, constantly "extinguishing fires" of continuous profitability and cash crises.

Instead, if a comprehensive but simple network of gathering financial performance information to develop an accurate picture of how well the firm is doing is permanently in place, an effective financial performance management system is feasible. This does not mean that the effective financial control of the business should lack sophistication, but rather that the items used to gauge financial performance should be simple, straightforward, well organized, and result oriented. Such an organized approach to financial analysis and control leads to a better understanding of how the firm is doing and how the financial return can be increased. For example, as mentioned in an earlier chapter, calculating a company's or a division's *return on investment* (ROI) is an excellent way to measure financial performance in a simple and efficient way:

$$ROI = \frac{\textit{Profit before taxes}}{\textit{Total equity}}$$

A better expression of the same formula is as follows:

$$ROI = \frac{\textit{Profit before taxes}}{\textit{Net sales}} \times \frac{\textit{Net sales}}{\textit{Total assets}} \times \frac{\textit{Total assets}}{\textit{Total equity}}$$

$$(\textit{Profitability}) \times (\textit{Activity}) \times (\textit{Leverage})$$

The long version of ROI gives a better financial performance picture because it directly identifies the "culprit" family ratio that was mainly responsible for good or bad return performance. The important issue is to be consistent and use the same measures of profit (customarily, before taxes), net sales (customarily, sales after returns and allowances for bad debt), assets (customarily, net, year-end book value assets), and equity/investment when figuring ROIs for different periods and/or divisions. The ROI ratio and its variation, *the Dupont formula* (asset turnover times margin), are used to gauge financial performance as outlined below:

- Measure current performance overall
- Compare different companies
- Compare different divisions of individual companies
- Compare future potential profitability among divisions
- Evaluate future investment opportunities
- Evaluate alternative capital expenditure types and levels
- Measure the effect of cost reductions
- Measure the effect of changes in inventory levels
- Measure the effect of changing asset utilization
- Evaluate new product development
- Provide framework for pricing decisions
- Rate managerial effectiveness among divisions
- Provide the basis for determining management promotions and rewards

However, it should be noted that different companies, divisions, and products require different levels of investment, and differences in managerial effectiveness also create different levels of ROI. Return on investment and *productivity* (output divided by input; O/I) improve when managers do the following:

- Increase sales (output) and reduce expenses (input)
- Increase sales proportionately more than the increase in expenses
- Reduce sales proportionately less than the reduction in expenses
- Retain level of sales steady, while reducing expenses
- Increase level of sales, while retain expense level steady
- Increase sales proportionately more than the increase in investment
- Reduce sales proportionately less than the reduction in investment

The ROI and Dupont formulas provide a useful and comprehensive analytical model that avoids piecemeal approaches, such as simply "cutting costs," or "increasing sales" in evaluating financial performance and in developing strategies to improve it. Rather, their approach helps entrepreneurs to see the interactions and trade-offs involved among the important financial variables in terms of a cause–effect relationship.

The ROI formula is superior to the Dupont formula because the latter has certain inherent limitations. In spite of the benefits of gradually moving from financial measure to measure to gauge financial performance, it considers only the effects of operations to calculate the earning power of a firm (margin multiplied by asset turnover) and ignores asset financing, that is, the composition of the firm's investment.

However, the proportions of debt versus equity, as well as long-term debt versus current liabilities or current assets versus fixed assets, have a direct bearing on financial results and performance, and these questions are answered directly from the balance sheet. Unlike the

ROI methodology illustrated previously, the original Dupont formula does not have a direct balance sheet orientation; rather, it has an indirect one in the asset turnover section. As Van Voorhis (1981) indicated, the breakdown of the orientations of the Dupont formula into the two categories of an income stream and an investment stream enables the small-firm owner to trace the reason for any financial performance decline. For example, by backtracking in both streams, the causative factor may be an operating element, or an investment element such as the mix between current and long-term debt. Each ratio at each stage of the model can be further subdivided and broken down into its components of more and more sub-indicators, until the problem or weakness is identified. By comparing the current figures to composite statistics for similar firms and to historical records, the tracking process becomes even more valuable and real for the small firm.

Konstans and Martin (1982) further modified and improved the original DuPont formula as well as the Van Voorhis (1981) version. They claim that the both formulas have a monolithic orientation toward *profitability* (return on investment) and their three components: *margin, turnover,* and *leverage*. An equally important consideration should be given to the *stability* of profits. The measures of such stability are these:

1. *Vertical balance:* The extent of the commitment of assets to uses that will potentially produce revenue as opposed to commitment of assets to non-productive uses, such as loans to the owner (current and fixed assets/total assets).

2. *Horizontal balance:* The extent to which equity capital is committed to non-liquid, long-lived assets (fixed assets/stockholders' equity and long-term liabilities).

3. *Liquidity:* The ability to meet currently maturing obligations.

4. *Solvency:* The ability to service long-term debt, for both interest and principal.

The model of Konstans and Martin contains 18 ratios, which are classified as either primary or secondary, depending on whether they focus directly on problems or indirectly on symptoms of problems. Liquidity and solvency do not have primary ratios associated with them.

Another technique for financial performance management and control is the Z value formula developed by Edward I. Altman of New York University (Ball, 1980). Altman studied 33 manufacturing companies with assets averaging $6.4 million, all of which had filed Chapter X bankruptcies. As controls, he looked at 33 other randomly selected manufacturing firms with assets between $1 million and $25 million. He found five weighted ratios that proved a pretty accurate guide to a company's financial state. His system of multiple discriminant analysis, or "bankruptcy indicator" as it is less formally known, is used by stockbrokers to determine whether a company is a good investment. *The Z formula* is as follows:

$$Z = 1.2x_1 + 1.4x_2 + 3.3x_3 + 0.6x_4 + 1.0x_5$$

where

x_1 = working capital divided by total assets (what someone would pay for the company if it were for sale)

x_2 = retained earnings divided by total assets

x_3 = earnings before interests and taxes divided by total assets

x_4 = market value of equity divided by book value of total debt

$x_5 =$ sales divided by total assets

$Z =$ the overall index of corporate fiscal health

By inserting a company's numbers into the formula, a number between −4 and +8 is produced. The higher the number, the healthier the company, and more specifically, according to Altman, financially strong companies have Zs above 2.99, while companies in serious trouble have Zs below 1.81. Those in the middle could go either way. The closer a company gets to bankruptcy, the more accurate the Z value is as a predictor. In his group of 33 failed companies, Altman reports an accuracy of 95% using a single year's numbers. The other 5% fall in the bottom of the gray area. Numbers from 4 years, however, would predict bankruptcy for only 36% of companies.

It should be obvious by now that there is no sure method or technique for financial performance management and control, but with diligent application of any of these models, owners and entrepreneurs will develop a dynamic and relatively simple means of reacting quickly when the numbers start going in the wrong direction.

CONCLUSION

Financial management consists of careful overview, supervision, and analysis of four critical financial areas: cash flow, taxes, capital sources, and overall financial performance of the firm. Cash flow shortages create critical operational problems and serious doubts about the viability and ultimately survival of a small enterprise. Tax planning and tax avoidance (not evasion!) helps cash flow and ensures that every legitimate deduction is claimed, so the least possible tax is finally paid. Capital management and the determination of how operations, as well as growth and expansion, will be financed are also of primary importance. How much debt a business should carry and its risk level, cost, and availability depends on the industry, economic conditions, the competitive structure, as well as the value system and the preference of the owner. Finally, the purpose of an overall financial performance review may uncover hidden problems not detected by the financial controls that are in place, so corrective action can be undertaken. Additionally, a financial performance review can determine whether the conditions and the financial health of the firm are solid, so growth and development can be planned for the future.

Website Information

Topic	Web Address	Description
Cash flow budget	http://www.toolkit.cch.com/text/P06_4300.asp	Gives a brief description of what a cash flow budget is and the purpose of it. Gives four basic steps to preparing a cash flow budget, and provides a worksheet that lets you make your own budget.
Credit policy	http://www.jpg.com/creditpolicy.htm	This website gives the current credit policy for Pegasus Imaging Corporation.
Long-term debt financing	http://sbinfocanada.about.com/cs/financing/g/debtfinance.htm	Lists characteristics of a long-term loan, describes types of loan agreements, and lists tips on how to approach long-term debt lenders.

Key Terms

Accounts receivable turnover ratio: The measurement of net credit sales divided by the average net receivables.

Bank overdrafts: Also considered as a short-term loan although payment can be demanded on a very short notice.

Equipment leasing: Another type of long-term debt when the company that leases a piece of equipment from another company has the benefit of the use of that equipment without having to pay full price for it.

Equity financing: The sale of a company's stock, either in the form of preferred stock or common stock.

"Factoring": The act of selling accounts receivables for cash to another financial entity, usually at a sizeable discount.

"Floating" checks: Writing checks against cash already deposited in the bank.

Installment-type loans: Long-term loans that usually extend from 2 to 15 years. This type of loan is amortized with regular payments required to pay the interest and to gradually reduce the outstanding principal of the loan.

"Lockbox" arrangement: An arrangement in which customers of a small firm mail payments to a post office lockbox number operated by a bank, which picks up the payments and immediately credits the firm's account and/or invests the money.

Long-term debt: A loan of 1 year or longer.

Mortgage: A common conventional long-term credit arrangement usually maturing in 10–30 years after being issued.

Prime rate: The lowest commercial interest rate available at a particular time and place.

"Repo": A repurchase agreement.

Short-term loan: A loan where the principal is usually due within 1 year.

Small business investment corporations (SBICs): Privately owned financial corporations that are licensed, regulated, and promoted by the SBA.

Times interest earned: A measurement for how many times required interest payments are covered by pretax earnings.

Trade credit: Short-term credit extended by a supplier to a buyer in connection with the purchase of merchandise or services.

Unsecured loans: Loans that are usually obtained from a bank and do not require collateral. If the loan is not paid back on time, the bank usually puts a lien on the company's assets.

Review Questions

1. Effective control and management of financial resources is crucial to the survival of a venture. According to your text, how this can be accomplished?

2. What are the objectives of cash flow management?

3. Briefly describe the three key areas relating to accounts receivable that contribute to an effective cash flow management process.

4. Identify and briefly discuss at least three ways to put idle cash to work.

5. Briefly discuss the three basic types of capital funding available to new ventures.

6. What is trade credit? What are bank overdrafts?

7. Identify and discuss at least three methods described by your text that are used to monitor how well the firm is doing from a financial perspective.

8. What are two common problems associated with the management and control of financial performance, according to your text?

9. Identify at least four of the most common financial pitfalls faced by entrepreneurial ventures.

10. The *Z* formula was developed by Edward Altman. Explain how it is used in financial performance management and control.

11. Capital funding management is critical to any business, and especially in agricultural businesses given their equipment-intensive nature. Not every type of financing is appropriate for every situation. Assume you are managing a medium-sized family almond farm. Do a search for long-term debt financing options that are available for this industry (bank options—secured and unsecured, SBICs, SBA, etc.). What common requirements do you see? Are there a variety of long-term debt financing options available for medium-sized family almond farms?

Reflections from the Front Lines at LifeGuard America

There is nothing like hard times to bring out the lessons in business. My experience at Indian Motorcycle Company was unlike anything I had ever experienced before. Most of my early experience was with high performance companies like FlightSafety and Hewlett Packard and start-ups like Advanced Graphics Systems or my own consulting business that led me to Harley Davidson. All the companies that I worked for or with were growing and expanding. Indian Motorcycle was my first experience with a company whose historical past was bigger than its current capabilities. When I got to Indian, the company was expanding and growing like there was no tomorrow. It had grown from 60 employees to almost 800 in less than 1 year. It had a million-dollar annual marketing budget for a company that had made 2,000 motorcycles in its second year. It had positioned itself against the giant in the industry, Harley Davidson. It was only after a very strong review of the business plan that we came to the conclusion that there was no way we would be able to produce 8,000 units during our third year and absolutely no way we could produce and sell 16,000 in the fourth year. There were a whole host of issues that would keep the company from reaching its projections, but the bottom line was clear: the company would not reach the performance levels and worse yet, it would not even come close. This threw the company into a major reevaluation mode, and it was out of this that I learned some very important lessons. My work ethic had always dictated honesty, but I got to witness first-hand how important this single trait is during times of trouble. Be honest with your suppliers; tell them where you are and what your plans are to recover. They are in it with you, and if you lose their trust, the end will come far faster. We could not build motorcycles without engines, and we could not afford the negative cash flow of paying for them without terms that allowed us to build, ship, and invoice for the motorcycles. Be honest with your employees; you can't deliver product or services without them. Spend as much time as needed to keep them in the loop. Get ahold of the checkbook and create a plan that reviews it daily. Nothing is paid that is not reviewed. Cash is King and Cash is Life, period. All of the education and spreadsheets in the world do not replace a simple cash management policy. The main takeaway from all of this is *don't wait for a crisis to get your financial management procedures in place, do it while you are just beginning*. It will serve you well as you expand and grow.

Discussion Questions on LifeGuard America

1. How would you explain the term "Cash is King"?

2. What would you say to an investor in your company if things went bad and expenses (cash out) exceeded revenues (cash in)?

References

Abdelsamad, M. H., DeGenaro, G. J., and Wood, D. R., "14 Financial Pitfalls for Small Businesses," *Advanced Management Journal*, Spring, 1977.

Abelson, H. R. (1983, January 1). Brainstorming on financial management. *Boardroom Reports 12*(1), 15.

Aguilar, O. (2003, January). How strategic performance management is helping companies create business value. *Strategic Finance, 84*(7), 44–50.

Bak, W. (1993, October). I owe, I owe. *Entrepreneur, 21*(10), 56.

Ball, M. (1980, December). Z factor: Rescued by the numbers. *Inc. Magazine, 2*(12), 48.

Berney, R. E. (1981, October). Taxes aren't high unless you have to pay them. *Inc. Magazine, 3*(10), 16.

Bite the bullet on collections (1982, January). *Inc. Magazine, 2*(1), 114.

Blackman, I. L. (1981, December). A year-end checklist. *Inc. Magazine, 3*(12), 105.

Business bulletin: Small companies short on cash use the big stall to delay paying bills (1980, March 27). *The Wall Street Journal*, p. 1.

Christy, G., & Roden, P. F. (1976). *Finance, environment and decisions* (2nd ed.). New York: Harper & Row.

DeCeglie, P. (1998, March). Reality check. *Business Start-ups, 10*(3), 12.

Durkee, J., & Sharlit, I. (1983, Winter). Proper cash flow planning can make any business more successful. *SAM Advanced Management Journal, 48*(1), 15–18.

Economist, The. (2011, November 19). Many scrappy returns. *401*(8760), 36–37.

Eisemann, P., & Andrews, V. L. (1981, August). The financing of small business. *Economic Review—Federal Reserve Bank of Atlanta, 66*(5), 16–19.

Fisher, A. (1998, March 30). Starting anew. *Fortune, 137*(6), 165.

Fraser, J. A. (1998, October). The art of cash management. *Inc. Magazine, 10*(10), 124.

Grablowsky, B. J. (1976, October). Mismanagement of accounts receivable by small business. *Journal of Small Business Management, 14*(4), 23–26.

Hall, C. (2002, November/December). "Total" working capital management. *AFP Exchange, 22*(6), 26–32.

Help! My firm is hemorrhaging cash (1996, April–May). *Your Company, 6*(3), 10–11.

How to pick a tax accountant (1981, November 9). *Business Week,* 142.

Howitt, D. (1981, November). Step to the head of the line. *Inc. Magazine, 3*(11), 50.

Jackson, B. (1981, August 12). Having problems paying your bills? Buy a computer to blame it on. *The Wall Street Journal,* p. 23.

Jacobs, S. L. (1981, June 29). Best ties with banks build from a base of mutual trust. *The Wall Street Journal,* pp. 25–29.

James, F. (1982, February 8). Many companies don't know how tax changes help them. *The Wall Street Journal,* p. 27.

Ketchum, B. W. (1982, July). Make small accounts count. *Inc. Magazine, 4*(7), 103.

Konstans, C., & Martin, R. P. (1982, January–March). Financial analysis for small business: A model for control. *Business, 32*(1), 21–26.

Mamis, R. A. (1982, May). Put your idle cash to work. *Inc. Magazine, 4*(5), 158–163.

Mamis, R. A. (1993, March). Money in, money out. *Inc. Magazine, 15*(3), 98.

McMahon, R. G., & Holmes, S. (1991, April). Small business financial management practices in North America. *Journal of Small Business Management, 29*(2), 21.

Monden, Y., & Lee, J. (1993, August). How a Japanese auto maker reduces cost. *Management Accounting, 75*(2), 22–26.

Moore, M. (2002, January). Cash flow management in a leveraged environment. *Strategic Finance, 83*(7), 30–34.

National Federation of Independent Business (1982, June). Agencies to pay a price for overdue bills. In *Mandate 403* (p. 1). Washington, DC: Author.

Pauly, D., Manning, R., & Thomas, R. (1979, November 26). Small business blues. *Newsweek, 94*(22), 87.

Rock, M. (1982, March). A small businessman challenges the big banks. *Inc. Magazine, 4*(3), 53.

Small business: Should you extend credit to Company X? (1983, January 31). *The Wall Street Journal,* p. 27.

Small business: What function. (1982, April 26). *The Wall Street Journal* (Western ed.), p. 27.

Solving the cash crunch (1981, December). *Management Review, 70*(15), 71.

Steingold, F. B. (1982, June). Bad debts can cost you more than you think. *Inc. Magazine, 4*(6), 101.

Stevens, M. (1982, January). Lenders of last resort. *Inc. Magazine, 4*(1), 108.

Tangorra, J. (1982, April). It's 9 a.m. do you know where your cash is? *Inc. Magazine, 4*(4), 48.

Timely advice on accounts receivable (1981, January 12). *The Wall Street Journal,* p. 21.

Tompkins, T. J. (1982, June 7). Effective cash management is option to tax increases. *Dallas/Fort Worth Business,* 3.

U.S. Small Business Administration, Office of Management Assistance (1980). *Business basics: The profit plan.* Washington, DC: Author.

Using barter as a way of doing business (1980, August 4). *Business Week,* 57.

Van Voorhis, K. R. (1981, April). The DuPont model revisited: A simplified application to small business. *Journal of Small Business Management, 19*(2), 45–51.

Weiner, S. (1980, July 21). Retailers are looking to some store sales and other data as tests of performance. *The Wall Street Journal,* p. 6.

Weinstein, B. (1995, March). Balancing act. *Entrepreneur, 23*(3), 56–61.

Welsch, J., & Anthony, L. (1977). *Fundamentals of financial accounting.* Homewood, IL: Irwin.

What does prime rate mean? Congressman asks (1981, August). *Inc. Magazine, 3*(8), 18.

White, L. R., & Jahera, J. S. (1980). *Cash flow management for the small business.* Athens, GA: University of Georgia, Small Business Development Center.

Woodward, H. N. (1976, January/February). Management strategies for small companies. *Harvard Business Review, 54*(1), 113–121.

Venture Development

14

Venture Growth Management and Development

Can We Grow?

LEARNING OBJECTIVES

1. To understand the concept of stages of growth and development in the venture's life cycle.
2. To learn the organizational characteristics of each stage of development.
3. To understand the necessity of deploying different functional strategies at different growth stages of development.
4. To realize that occasionally a voluntary or involuntary exit may be inevitable.
5. To learn the implications of a successful harvesting or sellout strategy.
6. To understand the consequences of bankruptcy.
7. To realize the significance of succession for a business enterprise, and especially a family firm.

INTRODUCTION

Like living organisms, business organizations are subject to a life cycle. They have a period of youth, a period of growth, a period of maturity, and a period of decline. The life cycle of an organization, however, represents a mere potential, not necessarily an actuality. Survival to a mature stage does not just happen, and if performance is to match opportunity, such a result must be *made* to happen. Growth and development must be planned, controlled, and managed in such a way that various problems that will inevitably emerge do not stifle the venture's development, causing premature stagnation or decline.

Even larger and much older organizations are not immune from the stagnation and decline. Eastman Kodak is a picture-perfect example. Founded in 1880, it had long been known for its pioneering technology and innovative marketing, and in 1976 accounted for 90% of film and 85% of camera sales in America. Eastman Kodak even built one of the first digital cameras in 1975, but its culture of complacent monopoly and mentality of perfect products, instead of "make it, launch it, and fix it," ushered its bankruptcy filing in early 2012, and like many other companies before it, it simply ran its course (*The Economist,* 2012). The entrepreneurship literature has finally reported that significant differences exist between venture start-ups and growing ventures, and that most government and other assistance programs directed to start-ups have limited value for assisting a venture's growth (Harrell, 1992).

THE ORGANIZATIONAL LIFE CYCLE

A typical *organizational life cycle* consists of four stages: *early growth, accelerated development, maturity,* and *decline* (McCammon, 1973). New entrepreneurial ventures and business organizations, in general, typically generate high rates of growth and attractive profitability ratios during their initial stages of development. Some organizations achieved such extraordinary results during their formative years: the department store in the late 1800s, the supermarket in the 1930s, and the discount department store in the late 1950s and early 1960s (Stern & El-Ansary, 1977, p. 48).

As organizations and institutions mature, however, they are increasingly confronted by new forms of competition and are forced to compete in increasingly saturated markets. As a result, price competition intensifies, usually accompanied by declines in market share and profitability. Ultimately, mature organizations enter the declining stage of their life cycle, where they invariably become disadvantaged participants in the marketplace. Thus, from this perspective, department stores, variety stores, and supermarkets are, for all practical purposes, already mature and/or declining institutions, and they represent ways of doing business that no longer ordinarily produce high rates of growth or extraordinary rates of return on investment (McCammon, 1973, pp. 2–3).

More important for theorists and managers, however, is the knowledge that organizational life cycles within particular industries have accelerated over the years. For example, it has been estimated that the time to reach maturity has declined in retailing from approximately 100 years, in the case of department stores, to approximately 10 years, in the case of catalog showrooms (McCammon, 1973). It seems that life cycle of the "dotcom" retailing format is becoming even shorter. Many contemporary organizations and institutions now in their initial stages of development, such as software and e-commerce firms, will soon face the same problems and challenges that confronted department stores and supermarkets in the recent past.

Several theories have been formulated to describe the process of institutional change and the basic forces underlying organizational development:

- Cycle theories
- Dialectic processes
- Vacuum theories
- Crisis-change model theory

Cycle Theories of the Organizational Life Cycle

Cycle theories of organizational change may be either partial or complete. Partial cycles describe the rise and fall of an organization, while complete cycles describe the resurgence of an organization as well as its rise and fall. Perhaps the best-known partial cycle theory is the *wheel theory*. According to this theory, a new and innovative organization appears, generally as a low-status, low-margin, low-price operation, to take advantage of a competitive weakness in an established organization. This new organization gains acceptance and attracts emulators. Then to differentiate itself from its emulators, it begins to trade up by acquiring elaborate facilities, increasing services, and thus widening its margin. Eventually, this organization matures as a high-cost, high-margin operation and thus becomes vulnerable to innovative competitors that emerge in the institutional structure. These competitors, in turn, go through the same pattern (McNair, 1958). In essence, the wheel portrays an organization's evolution from a low-price, low-margin, efficient operation to a high-price, high-margin, inefficient one.

An example of a full cycle theory is provided by the so-called *accordion theory* of institutional development, which postulates that American institutions have gone back and forth between extremes of product lines (Hollander, 1966). For example, the wide-line general store was followed by the limited-line specialty shop, followed by the introduction of the department store with its wide line of merchandise, followed by the specialized discount store, finally followed by "megastore" supermarkets carrying an enormous variety of both grocery store and general merchandise items.

Additional evidence for the accordion theory is supplied by the fact that the number of establishments in the apparel, furniture, and general merchandise categories of retail trade has shown a tendency to fluctuate over time, due to cyclical redistribution of the customer base among these three merchandise groups (Dalrymple & Thompson, 1969), which have been consolidated in recent years by the megastores.

Dialectic Processes

It is also possible to view institutional change as a **dialectic process** where there is a thesis, or an established institutional form, an antithesis, or an innovative institutional form, and a synthesis, or a hybrid new form that emerges drawing positive characteristics from the other two (Gist, 1971, pp. 370–372). For example, in the past, the department store, characterized by high margins, low turnover, full service, and a downtown location, represented a thesis. The antithesis was represented by the discount store, characterized by low margins, high turnover, low service, and a suburban location.

The competition between these two institutions has resulted in the development of general merchandise retailers with average margins, average turnover, a moderate service level, and a suburban location. Also, in wholesaling, the general-line, full-function merchant wholesaler provides a thesis, the cash-and-carry wholesaler represents the antithesis, and the limited-line full-function specialty wholesaler can be viewed as the result of the interaction between the two.

Vacuum Theory

The **vacuum theory** advocates that innovative organizations come into being when there is a void in the institutional coverage of a specific market (Gist, 1971, pp. 370–372). The dynamics of such movements as well as the identification of a void can be explained by a development that can be broken into three stages representing various levels of complexity in the product cost and the product service and, consequently, the product mix offered by a firm. Product cost is used as a configuration of product quality, while service cost is used as a surrogate for the level of service provided by the firm.

The most primitive stage of institutional development is the **simplex stage**. Here the firm offers one level of product quality and a corresponding level of service. Thus, a firm offers one of the following combinations: high quality–high service, average quality–average service, or low quality–low service. To attract new customers, and thus increase sales and profits, however, firms need to expand into a **multiplex stage**. This is accomplished by either holding the level of product quality constant while the firm offers more than one level of service, or by holding the service level constant while offering the consumer alternative levels of product quality. The final stage of development is the **omniplex stage**, during which all possible quality–service combinations are offered (Alderson, 1957). Like the *multiplex* stage, the *omniplex* stage is reached as the firm increases its product mix in an attempt to expand its market.

However, once a firm establishes a market niche for a product offering or what is commonly referred to as a "cash cow," this niche provides a haven for the firm during periods of trouble with other product offerings. The niche's value concept core is that part of the firm's core competency environment that is best suited to the operations and the strategic resources of the firm, and where the firm has built a sustained competitive advantage. The fringe elements of the niche provide some resistance to attack, thus insulating the niche's value concept core. If a firm fails in the attempt to diversify its operations in a *multiplex* or *omniplex* fashion, it can always fall back on its "cash cow" products to weather the storm, while it regroups and develops new overall or marketing and product strategies.

The vacuum theory is useful in predicting the diversifying market behavior of firms in terms of thrusts made by both established and non-established firms, as they seek to move into areas unfamiliar to them beyond their market niches. However, because of their strong strategic commitment to the particular market niches where their cash cow products lie, even firms with sustained competitive advantages ultimately become vulnerable to innovative strategic thrusts of other firms seeking to penetrate the niche's fringes and eventually the value concept core. The very commitments on the part of established firms to specific ways of doing business by exploiting their niches allow voids to develop in the marketplace, and thus create opportunities for new innovative firms to fill these voids.

The Crisis-Change Model

Perhaps the most useful model for describing the organizational life-cycle change is the crisis-change model that identifies four distinct phases through which organizational systems pass as they adapt to crisis situations (Fink, Beak, & Taddeo, 1971). According to this theory, adaptation begins with an initial period of *shock,* when any factor critical to the viability of the total environmental system, of which the organization is a part, is threatened. Consequently, as survival becomes the paramount objective, a *defensive retreat* phase follows, when the established organizational system mobilizes its forces by imposing controls designed to reduce the threat. It is succeeded by the *acknowledgment* phase, in which the established organizational system begins to doubt the validity of its own traditional strategic beliefs, assumptions, and value systems. It therefore begins to experiment with new alternatives, but in a rather cautious manner, using structure in an attempt to reorganize and facilitate the performance of its tasks and functions, rather than attempting to fit tasks and functions into the existing structures.

Finally, a process of *adaptation and change* reflects effective coping of the organizational system and adaptation of tasks, functions, and structures that represent a rebirth into an ongoing evolutionary developmental stage. By the time the organizational system has reached this phase, it has, to a large degree, disposed of task, function, and structural dysfunctional behavior and is finally beginning to work interdependently, complementing the larger environmental system. It would appear that the "adaptation and change" phase would terminate the cycle, but in reality, it typically triggers a "shock" phase for the larger environmental system that posed the original threat, and now it is that system's turn to be in crisis as it adapts to the organizational changes.

The crisis–change cycle continues as a chain of actions and reactions, with innovation, progress, and efficiency being the final outcome for whole industries, as long as cost-effective technological and marketing innovation continues to become available to induce productivity improvements and the creation of new value concepts in the marketplace.

ORGANIZATIONAL STAGES OF VENTURE DEVELOPMENT

Clearly, organizational change is the product of a vast number of forces and circumstances. All of these forces, as well as the relationships and linkages among firms, must be included in an analysis of organizational change and of the simultaneous alterations in organizational functions and structures that such changes induce, as the venture evolves through distinct stages of development. Not all organizations progress through the same stages of growth nor do they exhibit exactly the same characteristics in each stage of development. Sexton and Bowman-Upton (1991) warn of the danger of drawing close analogies between natural phenomena and social phenomena when describing organizational stages of development, because in a chaotic and extremely diverse business world exact, continuous, and time-dependent constructs of a seamless stage of development process cannot exist. Nevertheless, the importance of successfully managing the complexity that accompanies the realization of growth through organizational size, number of employees, increased revenues and profits, and scope of operations demands a focus on the organizational transitions to different stages of development to better understand the complexity that growth brings to organizations (Covin & Slevin, 1997).

Managerial Knowledge and Venture Stages of Development

For many years, society as well as academicians ignored the impact, problems, and importance of small firms and venture start-ups, arbitrarily defined by some magical cutoff point. This neglect had resulted, until recently, in a lack of theory regarding the internal organization of a small enterprise. Thus, small enterprises, in the eyes of society, chambers of commerce, and the academic community, were analogous to "plain girls and acne-ridden boys at a high school dance, who are present in large numbers, but they usually are unnoticed" (McGuire, 1976, p. 115). McGuire further advocates that the crucial factor that causes the small company to grow and that eventually limits its growth is entrepreneurial expertise. He defines it as follows:

> The entrepreneur's stock of knowledge about both the operations of the firm and the present and future internal and external environments in which it exists at any

moment of time. Although entrepreneurial expertise is defined as a stock rather than a flow concept, it is evident that changes in this stock do occur over time. Thus, while knowledge is not depleted through use, it can be reduced through neglect. The stock of entrepreneurial knowledge also may be enlarged in basically three ways: through formal or informal educational processes; through the utilization of external advisors or consultants; and through the addition of "experts" (in the form of personnel) to the population of the enterprise. (p. 122)

The stage of development that a particular small business finds itself in, is therefore determined by how, where, and to what extent the entrepreneurial knowledge was amplified.

Managerial Roles and Venture Stages of Development

There is a very important relationship between the stages of venture development and the managerial knowledge stages of development of the entrepreneur, which are essential for the longevity and prosperity of the firm, because "managerial capability and skill depreciate over time" (Kroeger, 1974). Major managerial functions must be executed, and different roles must be assumed at each stage, so the organizational life cycle continues sequentially to the next stage. Megginson (1961) further explains the problem of role growth in small business:

> There appears to be a built-in dilemma in small business management. First, if the owner proves to be inefficient and if his initiative or his abilities are not sufficient, the organization will flounder and eventually become one of the casualties included among the statistics called "business failures." Second, if the owner-manager is mediocre, the organization will continue to be a small business and will be constantly plagued with the problems associated with smallness. Third, if the manager proves to be efficient and capable in the exercise of his initiative and is able to succeed and grow, he runs the risk of losing the very things he seeks from the business. For the very act of growing means losing some of the autonomy and the control that he is seeking. If nothing else, he now must please a larger number of people: his/her customers, the public, and his/her employees. There is then the problem of controlling other people, that is, exercising the thing that he has resented himself in others. (p. 7)

Ventures need a systematic program of organizational development as they grow in order to achieve a professionally managed status. This transition from a personal entrepreneurial status to an impersonal, professionally managed status requires change in three organizational aspects: the firm's culture, its management systems, and its management team per se.

Change of Culture

A firm's culture is its value system and the beliefs held by its people. The culture of an entrepreneur tends to be based upon the informality of relationships, the lack of accountability, and the lack of systematic planning. Individuals are relatively free to do what they want on an *ad hoc* basis, although important decision making tends to be centralized. The value system of a professionally managed firm emphasizes the importance of planning, developing a mission for the firm, and controlling efforts to meet the original business plan's objectives and goals. To develop commitment to the venture's plans, accountability and discipline, the beliefs in the value of participation of people, and the value of effective communication and coordination, need to be sheltered, enhanced, and developed.

Change of Management Systems

The transition to a professionally managed status also requires developing or modifying the three basic managerial systems in the firm: *planning, the organization of jobs or roles,* and *controls.* The venture must develop the original intent of the business plan into an annual planning process that produces incremental plans. It must also restructure and formally rationalize its organizational chart by specifically redefining in detail jobs and responsibilities, which in an entrepreneurial informal organization structure have overlapping and undefined responsibilities. Finally, it must develop a control system, including planned series of meetings, management reports, performance appraisal systems, and a budgetary control system.

Change of Management Team

The creation of a sound management team is accomplished through the recruitment of skilled managers and a formal program of managerial development. This process will create the distinctiveness of a professional management status that is essential for the successful transition from the existing entrepreneurial management status.

In a professionally managed firm, profit is an explicit goal, and it is planned rather than being left as a residual or an aside thought. A professionally managed firm operates with formal operating plans, and the practice of informal, superficial, and *ad hoc* planning is replaced with regular planning cycles, which become a way of life. The firm begins to regularly develop a strategic plan for what it wants to ultimately become, operational plans for all levels and functions of the organization, as well as contingency or "what if" plans and scenarios for contingency situations.

A professionally managed firm has a set of written role descriptions that clearly state responsibilities and are mutually exclusive and exhaustive. As the venture grows, the very act of moving from an informal, unstructured organization to one that is based on formal planning and control represents a fundamental shift in the managerial roles and values of the firm.

Crises and Venture Stages of Development

In an insightful study of the small furniture store industry in Great Britain, Deeks (1976, pp. 77–80) developed a model of the life cycle of small firms and arrived at an interesting description of the fragmentation of the development of a furniture company over a period of 13 years:

1. 1956–59: A period of *initial struggle,* during which the new business was established as a *financially viable concern.*

2. 1959–61: A period of *rapid growth* in sales turnover following the purchase of new premises.

3. 1961–65: A period of *consolidation* with little increase in sales turnover.

4. 1965–68: A *further period of rapid growth* in sales turnover accompanied by additions to existing premises and purchase of more property.

Therefore, as Greiner (1972) pointed out, growing small organizations move through distinguishable phases of development, each involving a relatively calm period of growth that ends with a crisis. More specifically, he identifies five phases of growth:

1. A growth phase generated by creativity during the venture's embryonic stage of development, ended by a crisis of leadership.

Exhibit 14.1	Characteristics of Stages of Venture Development

Stage I

1. General Management
    *   "One-man show"
    *   Non-routine, and informal decisions
    *   Good communication
2. Operations
    *   Reliance on unique personal skills, unique product, or unique market
    *   Diseconomies of scale
3. Finance
    *   More concern with survival and break-even, than rate of return
    *   Limited resources
    *   No cushion to absorb bad luck
    *   Emphasis on historical cost
4. Marketing
    *   Risk concentrated on few products, markets, and people
    *   No reputation outside of the immediate vicinity
    *   Stable market environment

Stage II

1. General Management
    *   Delegation of operating decisions to "lieutenants" or "assistants to."
    *   Formal consideration of growth
    *   Direct control and direction
2. Operations
    *   Improvement of skill, method, or market niche
    *   Production problems
    *   Technical specialization
3. Finance
    *   Attention to industry standards
4. Marketing
    *   Attention to competition
    *   Attention to market feedback

Stage III

1. General Management
    *   More management levels and more delegation
    *   Utilization of staff analysts
    *   Increased emphasis on management skills and techniques
    *   Formal written policies and procedures
    *   More planning time
2. Operations
    *   Economies of scale
3. Finance
    *   Lower rate of return
    *   Emphasis on future costs
    *   Emphasis on short-run performance measures
4. Marketing
    *   Heavy investment in product and market development
    *   Drop unprofitable products
    *   Increased dependence on marketing distribution
    *   Better equipped to fight competition

Source: Vozikis, 1979.

2. A growth phase through *direction*, if and when the crisis of leadership is successfully resolved, ended by a crisis of autonomy.

3. A growth phase through *delegation*, if and when the crisis of autonomy is successfully resolved, ended by a crisis of control.

4. A growth phase through *coordination*, if and when the crisis of control is successfully resolved, ended by a crisis of red tape.

5. A growth phase through *collaboration*, if and when the crisis of red tape is successfully resolved, ended by a new crisis. (pp. 40–44)

These intermittent series of crises lead to organizational growth that tends to be nonlinear and passes through the five discrete stages with varying growth rates. Periods of profound organizational development in managerial, financial, and operational terms often occur between periods of growth. These slower periods often are viewed with alarm, but they are essential because they force entrepreneurs and managers to reexamine the firm's direction and evolution. These periods of development are the transition periods, which appear to be less dramatic because of the slow growth, but they may be more crucial to a firm's preparation for the future. The apparent floundering and inertia can provoke useful learning once the firm's leadership begins to adopt and encourage new practices and procedures (Greiner, 1972).

A typical management response to crises and transitional strains is a total or partial reorganization of the company. This sometimes helps shake up old habits and inefficiencies but rarely resolves a transition crisis if taken lightly and if only cosmetic changes are introduced. Time is needed for the social and political systems of the firm to realign themselves into new norms and relationships and new strategic thinking (Barnes & Hershon, 1976).

Growth Phases and Venture Stages of Development

The growth pattern of a small business can also be viewed in a slightly different way, as a chain reaction. First, there is growth, which leads to new responsibilities, which leads to the search for executive talent to undertake the new responsibilities since the existing entrepreneurial skills that helped launch the venture are no longer adequate. A successful executive search leads to professional management, which leads to a better business, which leads to more profits. At this point, the firm reaches decision-making crossroads and a decision must be made regarding whether to expand further or not. Then the cycle is repeated. If the attempt to find skilled professional managers is unsuccessful, growth will wane. Consequently, somewhere along the line, the entrepreneur ceases being the venture's owner-manager and has to either be transformed from an entrepreneur into a full-blown manager with its associated implications, or recruit professional management, which transforms the venture into a professionally run firm with a new set of challenges (Stewart, 1956, p. 41). These small firm growth phases and transformations can also be viewed along a success continuum:

1. The survival firm

2. The attractive growth potential firm

3. The underachieving firm

4. The high success growth firm (Susbauer, 1979)

Cooper (1978) presented a simple but sensible typology of the growth stages of development of the small firm, describing the challenges the venture faces as it makes transitions:

1. *Start-up stage:* Includes the strategic decisions to found a firm and position it within a particular industry with a particular competitive strategy.

2. *Early-growth stage:* The initial product-market strategy is tested, and the entrepreneur/owner maintains direct contact with all major activities. Many entrepreneur/owners make a conscious decision to stabilize at this stage and grow no more, out of fear of losing control and direct contact with all aspects of the venture's operations.

3. *Later-growth stage:* Often characterized by multiple sites for retail and service businesses and by some diversification for manufacturing firms. Organizationally, the firm usually has one or more levels of middle management and at least some delegation of decision making.

Vesper (1979) makes a valuable contribution to the growth stage development theory for small firms by pointing out a fallacious *a priori* assumption of most researchers. He observes that most development theories seem to imply that the start-up stage or the early-growth stage is generally followed by more growth. In fact, very few of the "Mom and Pop" firms are destined for growth, because either they tried to grow but found they could not, or they could grow but just did not. With this caveat in mind, Vozikis (1979) summarized in Exhibit 14.1 a relevant portion of the theoretical framework discussed so far, and the characteristics of each stage of venture development, using Cooper's (1978) general typology of three stages of development.

TO GROW OR NOT TO GROW? THAT IS THE QUESTION!

It has been taken as an article of faith that the growth of a venture start-up is the realization of the "American Dream." Consequently, growth is both normal and desirable. Growth makes sense in terms of economies of scale, increases in market share, sale revenues, and profits. In most instances, however, growth is taken for granted by the entrepreneur or as something that occurs by itself automatically and therefore will take care of itself without due diligence. As a consequence, systematic growth management is a widely neglected area from both theoretical and practical perspectives as far as entrepreneurial ventures are concerned.

However, as mentioned previously, not all venture start-ups with growth potential are growth oriented. Some firms may have growth potential but do not know it, and some may know it but consciously choose not to grow. On the other hand, some firms want to grow, even try to grow, and cannot (Vesper, 1990). Conscious underachievement is based on the basic character of the entrepreneur, recognizing his or her limited capability to grow, a desire to keep the enterprise privately held and under control, or a value system in which leisure occupies a prominent place. Unintentional underachievement, however, has nothing to do with the entrepreneur's values. In this case, growth potential in unintentionally thwarted by actions or lack of action on the part of the entrepreneur (Susbauer, 1979). Research has also shown that lack of contacts with outside expert advisors is an obstacle to the expansion of a small firm and perpetuates both unintentional underachievement and conscious underachievement (Larsson, Hedelin, & Garling, 2003). Interestingly, when it comes to the consequences of growth, non-economic concerns and beliefs, such as the well-being of the employees, the preservation of the work atmosphere, etc., seem to be more important than the possibility of personal economic gain or loss. These salient beliefs are considered to predispose entrepreneurs regarding the positive or negative consequences of growth (Wiklund, Davidsson, & Delmar, 2003).

Growth, therefore, should be given careful consideration, and the entrepreneur must recognize that certain personal, internal, and external conditions must be present for growth to be achieved. Quite often, entrepreneurs find it difficult to find the time to make the conscious decisions and to think systematically about business growth. Consequently, this indecision and inertia on the issue of growth actually overwhelms the venture's operational prospects and places the firm in financial jeopardy because of seriously and steadily diminished administrative control (McKenna & Oritt, 1980).

Growth planning and management should also take into consideration the personal and professional values of the entrepreneur, in conjunction with the strategic competence of the firm and the evolution of the strategic window of opportunities in the venture's environment and strategic target market. The decision to grow should be made with the venture's future viability and economic performance in mind, not because bigger is necessarily better. In the process of answering this fundamental question and haunting dilemma regarding the venture's growth, entrepreneurs should elaborate and formulate answers to the following questions:

1. How large do they wish the venture to become?
2. What financial, human, and operational resources do they have at their disposal?
3. Are they willing to and capable of going public?
4. Do they wish their competitive edge to be production or marketing based?
5. To what extent are they constrained by financing, management expertise, and experience, as well as employee skills, knowledge, and productivity?
6. Are there stockholders, investors, or other stakeholder demands to satisfy by pursuing growth? (Van Auken, Sexton, & Ireland, 1982, p. 13).

Similarly, the following guidelines and considerations are suggested when entrepreneurs try to decide between growth and no growth, always keeping in mind that this decision should be made for the sake of the venture's future viability and not just for the sake of getting bigger:

1. *Why is the growth of the business important?* Does it make sense in terms of the state of the economy and local competition, or would it simply reflect the expectations and ego of the owner?
2. *What should this business ultimately become?* Is the owner capable of administering and managing a larger operation? Should he or she step aside from active management or perhaps seek further management education to ensure the venture's success?
3. *Is the current management capable of growing with the business?* What does the owner see as the ultimate goal of the business? At what point should growth be curtailed? While the answers to these two questions may evolve and change, they are still important for the owner to consider.
4. *At what rate should the business grow?* How quickly should the business grow? Too much growth too soon can be disastrous to the survival of the organization. If the growth of the business is to be successfully managed, its rate must be predetermined and continually kept in check.
5. *What type of resources and commitment will the growth process require?* What resources does the entrepreneur have available to assist with the growth process? While fiscal matters are usually given highest, if not sole, priority, it is equally

important to determine what human resources are available, and whether the entrepreneur or others in the venture's internal or external teams have the knowledge to handle the challenges of growth, such as new technology for example (McKenna & Oritt, 1981).

A small firm determined to grow in size, market share, and other vital dimensions therefore, must consciously and strategically put together the "right" combination of the essential conditions for growth in all functional aspects of the venture. The successful entrepreneur must recognize that to maintain success and growth, he or she must experience a change in attitudes and perspective that is absolutely critical for real growth to occur, and which will be expressed and articulated in a carefully planned transition from an entrepreneurial to a professional growth management system, because growth not only constitutes a change *per se*, but also brings changes to the physical, structural, managerial, and financial aspects of the business. The essential elements in this transition from an entrepreneurial to a professional management style require, therefore, not only a commitment to growth but also a subsequent commitment to all the necessary structural and procedural issues necessary for a successful transition to higher level of growth and development. Once the answer to the question "to grow or not to grow" has been answered in favor of growth, the entrepreneur's commitment to changing attitudes and management style should equal the amount of commitment to growth. The successful transformation of a "one-man show" to a professionally managed organization involves trade-offs in flexibility, direct control, and informal communication in exchange for coordination, delegation of responsibility, and decentralized decision making and a well-developed, broad-based formal management information and communication system. These commitments to changing attitudes and perspective should exhibit the following characteristics:

- Explicit and enduring commitment to growth
- Development of a definite and distinct hierarchical structure
- Increased delegation of authority
- Increased emphasis on management skills and techniques
- Freedom from dependence on one or more key individuals
- Formal written policies and procedures
- Utilization of formal information analyses especially through staff personnel
- Increased formal control through documentation and budgets (Vozikis, 1979, p. 48)

Throughout the transition process from an entrepreneurial to a professional growth management system, a constant evaluation and reevaluation of the entrepreneur's emotional and psychological frames of reference should be juxtaposed with the constant monitoring of the outcomes and performance of the ongoing growth process, in order to ensure a successful and smooth transition.

Many businesses, however, favor staying small because it allows far more flexibility, is less bureaucratic, is more efficient and profitable, and generally is more fun for the entrepreneur. This flexibility stems from the ability to make internal decisions quicker, from the avoidance of the immediate liquidity problems that growth requires, and finally from the ability to use a wider array of alternative strategic decisions quickly and efficiently if a course of action does not produce the desired outcomes. Additionally, by staying small, entrepreneurs have more direct client contact and have typically better profit margins than their larger counterparts. After all, they may already be making more money than they had originally planned (Jansson, 1977). Making the conscious decision not to grow should begin not with a fear of what can be lost or at least not gained, but rather with a vision of what can be gained by not growing. Then the decision not to grow becomes a matter of choice, not a matter of circumstances. Rather than blaming external forces, luck, fate, or government regulation, the no-growth future of the firm should rest in the hands and mind of the entrepreneur. Recognition of the ultimate responsibility and accountability for the venture's future is a sign of true entrepreneurial leadership.

The decision to remain small should not diminish by any means the quality of the organization or personal growth for the entrepreneur. The decision and the process toward a purposeful and positive no-growth future simply means that the firm is seeking to realize an optimal size of conviction rather than convention. Another positive implication of the conscious decision not to grow is that the entrepreneur remains an entrepreneur, and is not transformed into a manager. The entrepreneurial strength and the specific skills that transformed an idea into a thriving business are therefore not lost by the decision not to grow (Williams, 1983).

EFFECTIVE FUNCTIONAL GROWTH MANAGEMENT

Numerous entrepreneurial ventures suffer from the underlying weaknesses of being small, which lead to mistakes that can adversely affect their return on investment and their prospects for future growth. These weaknesses and management problems tend to become more glaring when the business starts to grow and, consequently, is beginning to extend itself beyond its current managerial and resource limitations, or beyond what the venture's entrepreneur/owner can cope with. Major difficulties occur, especially when

1. Growth of sales is commonly seen as the solution to all problems, when in reality the problems are managerial in scope.

2. Inadequate cost/product analysis blinds entrepreneurs to the losses incurred by indiscriminately adding new products.

3. Operations are geared to the income statement outcomes while ignoring the balance sheet (Woodward, 1976).

It is therefore imperative for the effective overall management of the venture's growth that each business function area of management, marketing, operations, and finance be carefully monitored and managed, while at the same time, the entrepreneur's attitudes toward growth and professional management also undergo major adjustments, committing the venture toward an effectively planned and managed path toward growth.

General Management and Organizational Growth Management

As the venture grows, it enters areas of increasing market complexity, far from the safety of the relative monopoly of the original niche, perhaps a well-known neighborhood or regional market. In the niche of the neighborhood monopoly, there were probably no product substitutes, and the firm's reputation, as well as the quality of its product or service, constituted sufficient barriers to protect it from new entrants.

When a venture enters the growth stage, it may expand its scope of operations in the much more competitive environment of an oligopoly. In this market environment, relatively few firms with close substitutes generally compete on combinations of non-price variables such as advertising, customer loyalty, etc., which creates a great deal of differentiation among product offerings. Of course, if the nature of the product's or service's value concept is absolutely unique, a firm may grow and still enjoy a monopolistic market environment.

Growth can create big gains that may arrive as firms find better ways to use new technologies. Process innovation may be as valuable as the inventions themselves. Henry Ford did not invent the car, but his moving assembly line led to dramatic declines in car prices and a surge in American car sales from 64,000 in 1908 to 3.6 million in 1923. Experimentation with new technologies can produce new combinations of man and machine that are fruitful and profitable (*The Economist*, 2011).

The level of management effort is very high in the embryonic stage, but it declines during the growth stage as a result of benefits stemming from the learning curve of experience. These benefits produce the following outcomes:

1. *Increased competence level:* As entrepreneurs and their employees become familiar with the required tasks, the level of competence and expertise regarding the product and service increases.

2. *Increased economies of scale:* Economies of scale are materialized, as the total fixed cost of the productive capacity is allocated among a larger number of product or service units.

3. *Material substitution:* Expensive materials used originally in the production process are substituted now with less expensive materials.

4. *Innovation and value engineering:* Innovation, productivity enhancements, as well as value engineering in methods and procedures further reduces the level of managerial effort (Rowe, Mason, & Dickel, 1982, p. 150).

As the small firm grows even further and enters maturity, it may well enter a monopolistic competitive environment far more complex than either oligopoly or monopoly. This market structure is now composed of many competitors offering products considered close substitutes and competing not only on promotion, quality of the product and the like, but also on price. Because there are differences between mature and new industries, it follows that firms in mature industries grow slower than firms in new industries, especially in manufacturing. A fit between competitive strategy and structural administrative mechanisms, such as managerial skills and organizational structure, is therefore absolutely essential to superior performance and continued growth in a mature industry (Barth, 2003). The monopolistic competitive environment is by far the largest segment of the economy that leads to further new discoveries and innovations. Additionally, the level of management effort rapidly starts increasing during this stage due to the following market complexity factors, which typically require a more complex organizational structure:

- The need to further differentiate the market offerings from competitors with respect to value concept and product attributes.

- The need to differentiate with respect to quality and services.

- The need to make appropriate price adjustments (Gibson & Wald, 1983, p. 28).

The starting point as well as the level of management effort for a venture therefore, depend on the evolution of the complexity of its competitive market environment. The closer to monopoly, the lower the initial level of management effort. As the firm grows, the level of management effort required falls due to the experience curve, but as the venture enters the maturity stage, it rapidly rises in importance and effort expended. Consequently, the younger the firm, the safer it is under monopolistic market conditions. Only when the firm becomes mature and savvy in management and organizational development should it venture into the highly complex market environment. During growth and decline, monopoly and oligopoly are the most appropriate market environments for a small firm, because during the final stage of decline the firm may want to retrench to less complex market environments. Due to the threat to its overall survival, however, the demands on the level of management effort reach their peak.

Marketing Growth Management

As the firm grows, certain key elements of marketing-related growth factors have to be carefully determined, readjusted, and well managed:

- *Retaining, broadening, or narrowing the range of product and/or service package offered:* Some small firms diversify into related products and services, while others basically stick to a single or identical format.

- *Geographic scope:* Growth can take a firm from a regional to a national and even to an international scope of activities, with corresponding requirements for marketing adjustments.

- *Quality standards and service streamlining:* Real quality and exceptional service are very expensive to maintain, but on the other hand, quality generates sales and profits, which in turn finance growth. To grow, the entrepreneur must determine what kind and what level of quality is needed to ensure continued adequate sales without jeopardizing profits.

- *Market research:* Growth requires reliable, current, and accurate information not only about the venture's existing markets but also about related or potential new strategic target markets, to determine their size, growth rates, market segments, customer needs, competitive trends, technology trends, and sales forecasts (Granger, 1977).

Operations Growth Management

Increased sophistication of methods and techniques of the operation's business function is a must during the growth stage of a firm's life cycle.

- *Cost accounting detailed determination:* This is necessary in order to know the difference between estimated and actual costs, and to optimally allocate costs among the firm's divisions and products. Additionally, in conjunction with cost allocation data, revenue comparisons and revenue contributions by type of product, customer, and location need to be undertaken on a continuing basis to measure productivity enhancement possibilities in terms of outputs and inputs.

- *Automation:* Growth requires significant improvements in production and operations, as well as computer data handling, information storage, and data retrieval for more efficient flow of operations.

- *Quality control.* In conjunction with the conscious marketing decision regarding the improvement in the kind and level of quality standards embodied in the venture's products and services, steps must be taken to ensure that the operationalization and the quality control of these quality standards are maintained so the planned pace of growth is sustained and does not falter because of substandard quality control in operations.

Financial Growth Management

Financial standards and close examination and reevaluation of financial factors are essential for successful growth management if the venture wants to remain on track with the financial goals and objectives that were set in the original business plan.

- *Commitment to the "right" pace of growth:* Growth can "seduce" the small business owner. The firm needs commitment to a growth rate that will not impose undue strain on the physical, financial, and human elements of the enterprise, because growth is expensive. A growth rate lower than the planned rate may constitute a missed opportunity. But a growth rate faster than planned may entail an excessive financial burden, lower product quality, inadequate quality control, excessive overtime, undue training expenditures, and many other undesirable financial outcomes.

- *Consistent operating profit:* The "right" pace of growth must be coupled with the preservation of the "right" operating profit target. Profit objectives imply a pricing strategy and a pace of growth that reflects not only the absolute *amount or stock* of costs but also the *rate of growth* of the rising costs as the firm grows in sales revenues. The rate of profit growth depends on the rates of growth of both revenues and costs.

- *Capital sources for growth financing.* During growth it should be realized that the traditional sources of capital that gave birth to the venture, such as personal savings or sources from friends and family, are no longer adequate to finance rapid growth. New funding sources, in addition to retained earnings, have to be traced and tapped. The risk and the cost of risk capital are inversely related to the firm's life cycle, because, as the firm and sales grow, the risk for the creditor and/or investor and consequently the cost of capital decrease.

HARVESTING THE VENTURE

In agriculture, harvesting involves reaping the crop at the end of the growing season. Similarly, growing businesses, like growing crops, need to be "harvested" to collect terminal after-tax cash flows on the investment that was initially "planted." Unlike agricultural crops, however, when a business is harvested, in most cases it continues to exist, since the entrepreneur or the initial investor may not necessarily leave the company.

Instead, through harvesting, the ownership mix of the venture is changing in such a way that harvesting or exiting owners or shareholders extract tangible value from their investment in the form of money, stock, or other cash flow to be used for other purposes. In the case of parent entrepreneurs passing the business to their children without any financial benefits, the intangible value of succession can be rewarding in itself (Fry, 1993, p. 432). If the goal of the venture is not just to provide a living for the entrepreneur but instead to create and extract value from a growing and profitable business for the owner and other stockholders, a "harvesting" strategy is absolutely mandatory (Petty, 1994, p. 379). The initial investors, whether they are family members, other private informal investors, or even professional venture capitalists, are critically interested in a mechanism that will allow them to exit the venture, liquidate their investment, and maximize their after-tax cash flows. These cash flows will determine the return earned on their investment to be used for other investments or purposes.

But how can one determine the business performance of a start-up about to be harvested through an IPO? Groupon, the online coupon giant, recommends that investors willing to invest in them use something called *ACSOI,* an acronym that stands for *adjusted consolidated segment operating income.* It is essentially operating profit minus the company's large online marketing and acquisition expenses, a highly unorthodox methodology to say the least. But without it, Groupon, LinkedIn, Facebook, Twitter, and other firms not necessarily only in the social networking business would appear to be drowning in losses. Liberties taken with valuation methods that prompt investors to look only at the positive aspects of a hot company have been labeled by Lynn E. Turner, a former chief accountant with the U.S. Securities Exchange Commission, as *EBBS,* or *earnings before bad stuff* (De La Merced, 2011).

One such exit mechanism of harvesting a growing and profitable business is going public—selling the stock in the open market through an **initial public offering (IPO)**. This is the preferred choice for harvesting a firm as opposed to the direct sale of the firm, employee stock option plans, management buyouts, leveraged buyouts, mergers, liquidations, or bankruptcy. An IPO, if successful, usually provides higher valuation for the stockholders who decided to exit the venture; at the same time, an IPO may generate a major infusion of cash for the firm's future growth, benefiting the stockholders who decided to stay with the venture. Exiting shareholders who want to sell their stock and incoming investors who want to buy stock in the firm use the marketplace, as the ultimate valuing mechanism, to determine the final outcome.

However, taking the company public through an IPO is a complex, tedious, and expensive proposition, and its success depends on two factors. One relates to the agreement with the price underwriter regarding the amount and type of stock to be offered, especially since there is strong evidence to suggest that investment bankers tend to underprice new offerings, possibly to provide their customers buying the stock a better deal (Petty, 1994, p. 407). The other factor relates to the amount of the retained, non-cashed-out proportion of equity funding that will be added, providing the firm the resources necessary for quantum leaps in venture growth. Most firms that later grow to become national and international companies could not have achieved that dramatic growth without having gone public. "Underpricing" has been well established for common stock initial public offerings (CSIPOs). Earlier empirical studies found that the average firm goes public with an offering price lower than the price that prevails in the immediate aftermarket. As noted by Ritter and Welch (2002, p. 1803), these firms signal their high quality by "throwing money away" in the form of leaving money on the table. Theoretically, they anticipate that they will recoup this cost at a subsequent time (Daily, Certo, Dalton, & Roengpitya, 2003). However, the extent of underpricing varies from firm to firm.

Most earlier studies examined the underpricing of CSIPOs without regard to the type of offering, even though an examination of the prospectuses of different firms reveals that the mode of, and motivation for, going public varies from firm to firm. Prasad (1990, 1994) pointed out that, in practice, there are three types of offerings. The first type is a **pure primary offering**, in which only the company offers shares to the public. In other words, funds are raised by the firm through the issue of new shares to outside investors, and all the new, supplemental funds from the issue go to the firm after adjusting for the floatation costs. The purpose of this type of offering may be to expand operations, pay off debt, etc. Most CSIPOs are primary offerings. The second type is a **pure secondary offering**, in which where only some of the existing shareholders exit the firm and offer some or all of their shares to outside investors in the public offering. The motivation for the firm going public, in this case, appears to be "harvesting" by these exiting shareholders, who are cashing in their investments. Presumably, through divestment of their personal shares, the selling shareholders expect to make a profit by selling the offered shares at a price higher than the price they paid at their initial investment. In this case, no new funds become available to the firm through the public offering. These secondary offerings, however, are not common. The third type of offering is **simultaneous primary and secondary offerings, or mixed offerings**, in which both new shares of the company and the shares of some exiting shareholders are simultaneously made available for purchase by outside investors in the same public offering. This third type of offering is very common.

A number of questions arise relating to whether incoming investors will distinguish among these three types of offerings (i.e., primary offerings, secondary offerings, and mixed offerings) while making their pricing and investment decisions. Are these incoming investors indifferent between the choice of buying into a firm through the issuance of new shares by the firm or through the shares offered by exiting shareholders (primary offerings versus secondary offerings)? Will the investors be indifferent to whether the shares are offered by the firm alone or by the firm and exiting shareholders simultaneously (primary offerings versus mixed offerings)? Or, while incoming investors may consider the selling of stock by the firm necessary, will they consider the sale of shares by exiting shareholders a "red flag" since the latter's "harvesting" reduces the proportion of equity retained by the firm? Will the incoming investors ask why the exiting shareholders are selling out, if the growth prospects for the firm are so great? Has the value of the stock already reached its peak?

The answers to all these questions reflect the extraordinary perspective on the issue of harvesting being about more than money, involving personal and non-financial aspects of the harvest as well, especially from the entrepreneur's perspective (Petty, 1997). Entrepreneurs do not usually heed conventional wisdom, which dictates the need for a harvest strategy before the actual event. Various studies report that only a scant 15% had a written harvesting strategy as part of the original business plan (Holmburg, 1991), while in another study roughly 60% of the CEOs surveyed gave some advance thought to the harvest, either formally or informally, but only 20% were serious in their efforts (Hyatt, 1990).

Finally, even 10 years after the IPO, founding family owners may continue to exercise considerable control on the firm. Thus, the influence of family shareholders on their firms can usually be preserved, despite the exit through an IPO, especially when only cash-flow rights are sold, instead of a complete sale of corporate stake (Ehrhardt & Nowak, 2003).

EXITING THE VENTURE VOLUNTARILY OR INVOLUNTARILY

For many entrepreneurs, their business is their own creation or their own "baby," and they hang on to it until they reach retirement age, when their younger heirs can possibly take over. However, nearly half of all entrepreneurs eventually sell out. Another 10% seek a buyer at any price when their interest fades or their health fails (Butrick, 1980). While the sale of a business is more desirable than liquidation, it is often hard to find individuals with the entrepreneurial savvy, capital, and dedication necessary to buy the present owner out. This is why advanced planning for the future development of a business is so important for the owner who is considering retirement, quitting the business, harvesting, or even going bankrupt due to unforeseen circumstances.

In case of the positive development of an acquisition possibility, the firm's owner must make provisions for facilitating the sale of his business. Some owners find and train their successors, who eventually buy them out, and in many cases they remain available as consultants to ensure a smooth transfer. In the case of the negative development of bankruptcy, an equal amount of care and painstaking management should be exercised so that such a business disaster does not translate into an equally personal disaster for the entrepreneur.

Voluntary Exit: Selling the Business

Howard Head developed the metal ski, and in 1969, AMF Corp. acquired his Head Ski Co. for $16 million. He then developed the oversize tennis racquet, and in 1982, he sold his

Prince Manufacturing Company to Cheesebrough-Pond's Inc. for $62 million in exchange for Cheesebrough-Pond stock. "The fact is that I had no plans for the skis," Head said. "They just happened. After that, I had no plans for a tennis racquet. It just happened. I have no plans now, but who knows what will happen?" ("Howard Head Sells," 1982, p. 5H).

Such extraordinary developments may sometimes happen by themselves. However, small companies do not always deal with glamorous innovations, technology, or energy. Even the mundane businesses of retailing or service can have "charms" that may lure investors and buyers. From the investor's point of view, buying a small company is a good idea, especially when, in addition to such tangibles as cash reserves, the company has already suffered and evolved successfully through its growing pains. When there is shortage of capital, larger, more prosperous companies digest many small firms whose owners are not very happy with the thought of having their venture being acquired and disappearing. The hard facts, however, are that they are unable to obtain the capital they need from normal sources, and sometimes these companies have to be sold out of necessity (Gilligan, 1977). Especially when the economy is bad or when the interest rates cut into the earnings of small firms, the acquisition process accelerates significantly "not just because the big fish is gobbling up the small fish but also because the little fish wants to swim right into the big fish's mouth" ("Business Slump," 1981). A poor business climate can also create a situation in which more owners are trying to unload their companies than there are actual prospective buyers, creating a glut of sellers and a shortage of buyers. Smaller companies typically can sell for about four times their net earnings, however, when high interest rates or a bad economy erodes earnings, want to sell their firms may have to settle for less.

There are also serious tax considerations involved in the sale of a business. The owners can take full cash payment at once and have a big tax obligation, or they can sell the business in installments and hope that the new owner can meet these obligations. If the small company is bought with stock from a large company, tax can be deferred until the stock from the sale is sold (Rausch, 1975).

Whether they sell willingly or reluctantly, owners must follow a careful valuation of the firm that will reflect the true value and potential of the firm. They must adopt a sales strategy that will not only bring the best price for the company but will also ensure its further success and development. A company dependent on the owner's know-how and contacts, for example, is not worth as much as one whose success can be transferred readily to someone else in a similar or different competitive setting, while a firm with declining earnings in the past few years is worth less than one with a rising profit trend. Some owners cling to valuation methods used in their lines of business, even if these valuations do not make much sense. As discussed previously, assets and earnings are a better guide to a company's worth. Assets can be assessed several ways: by their replacement, liquidation value, or book value. Earnings, too, have different values. Someone who wants a 20% return on investment will place a lower value on a company based on its profits than someone who will accept 8%. Earnings of $100,000 a year are worth $500,000 at a 20% rate of return and $1,250,000 at 8% ("Putting a Price on Your Firm," 1982). Even if a small-business seller decides to use a broker for the company's sale, it is difficult to find one who will understand the company's true worth and potential or will recommend the right way to package the firm's sale. Five basic guidelines for selling a business are offered below:

1. *The decision to sell needs to be carefully determined:* A business should not be sold out for ridiculous reasons such as curiosity over an offer or "the ego trip of being courted." A list of likely buyers from personal contacts, such as customers, suppliers, competitors, and larger firms with related operations are among the best candidates.

2. *Plan ahead:* A realistic projection of sales and earnings, an up-to-date audit of the company's financial records, and scrupulously honest books before a planned sale, even if this costs extra in income taxes, will prevent unnecessary explanations and financial reconstructions.

3. *Package the company:* The package should include the company's history, a production process description and outline, data about the product or service development, a summary of the company's marketing program, a profile of the key company people, and financial statements for the last 5 years.

4. *Negotiate effectively:* Listening carefully, being able to trade off less essential items for more critical ones, and most importantly, being flexible when discussing financing are musts in effective negotiations, since most sales are financed to some degree by the seller.

5. *Assess an accurate asking price:* Hidden value in a business, such as real estate carried in the books at less than market value, a long-term renewable lease, a valuable customer list, or the relative absence of strong competition, can increase the value of the firm. A comparative analysis of similarly sized firms can also help in assigning the right value to the firm ("Selling Your Business," 1981).

When the entrepreneur follows a conscious developmental strategy of selling to big companies that want to acquire the venture to launch a new product line, open up new markets, or just increase the present level of sales, a plan of action must be undertaken to convince the larger company that a merger is in the best interest of both parties involved. Sellers should investigate prospective acquirers with the same diligence that they are investigated by buyers. Future benefits must be assured not only for the acquirer but also for the seller. The following are certain basic questions that need to be answered before the two firms merge:

1. Can the acquisition be financed? In case of an installment plan, can the acquirer secure future payments?

2. Will the firm be a viable entity and efficiently integrated into the acquiring firm?

3. Can the acquirer's management administer effectively the seller's firm?

4. What are the acquirer's *true* future intentions for the seller's firm?

5. What kind of policies and procedures will the acquirer implement after the acquisition?

6. What is the acquirer's past financial performance and its future profitability potential?

7. What do the customers think about the acquiring firm? (Spilka, 1982).

However, small firm development by acquisition is not always smooth or voluntary. Big firms have voracious appetites for small, innovative companies, quite often simply for tax breaks specifically designed for firms over a certain size. As a result, small firms cannot easily acquire other small firms as an investment and for development, and they themselves may be the victims of hostile takeover by larger firms.

Another area of concern is what happens even after a friendly acquisition, when both firms seem to have the best of all possible worlds. Entrepreneurs got a hefty settlement, and their cash problems are over, while the acquiring larger firm has added a dynamic business to its folds. As time goes by, the honeymoon may be over, and entrepreneurs may find themselves competing with other divisions for funds, dealing with superiors that have little knowledge of their business, feeling an enormous amount of peer pressure to which they are unaccustomed, saddled with reporting requirements, or having to meet strict corporate financial goals. Failure to personally adapt and failure to meet these goals may elicit corporate pressure on the entrepreneur to leave. From the corporation's point of view, the end of the "honeymoon" brings problems that result from the lack of understanding on the part of the entrepreneur of the necessity to meet corporate financial goals and objectives, as well as lack of understanding regarding the need to conform to a more participative and professional management style ("How to Manage," 1981).

Finally, another area of concern may be the idea of foreign firms interested in acquiring smaller American firms. When the dollar is weak, foreign investment in the United States goes up, even though in many respects the exchange rate is just the trigger, and the acquired US firm's long-term profits are the ultimate incentive for the international acquisition. Nevertheless, when exchange rates fluctuate broadly, foreign companies can make an inexpensive investment in their currency, while the US small firm can still recover a healthy amount in dollars (Rosenbaum, 1981, p. 124).

Involuntary Exit: Bankruptcy

Bad economic times or merely bad luck push many small firms into bankruptcy, a quite negative perspective in the firm's development that most likely will arrest its growth. High interest rates or inflation result in bankruptcies that result in large employment losses and worsen an economic downturn. There are many reasons that a healthy business runs aground. Gary Goldstick and George Schreiber, both management consultants, after years of business troubleshooting, have summarized many recurring reasons that send companies to bankruptcy (Banaszewski, 1981b):

1. Changes in the marketplace and management being out of touch.
2. Changes in technology and products, which suddenly become obsolete or less competitive.
3. Increased cost of debt and lack of flexibility for strategically shrinking the business as necessary.
4. The *Peter Principle syndrome* as applied to entrepreneurial firms, when they grow beyond the skills and the expertise of their management.
5. Development of a location disadvantage in productivity or labor costs.
6. Management short of guts to cut expenses or fire "sacred cow" employees when necessary.
7. Company becoming hostage to others, such as bankers, or suppliers.
8. Limited financial resources to remain competitive.
9. Drastic changes in a product's distribution system in terms of economic or legal constraints.
10. Internal conflicts and "bad blood."
11. Business grows beyond its working capital sources.
12. Deliveries fall continuously behind schedule.
13. The firm's goodwill evaporates.
14. Inadequate control systems resulting in poor merchandise quality.
15. Overdependence on a single customer.

Robert Donaldson, who watched his father's 46-year-old automobile dealership go bankrupt, offers some tongue-in-cheek advice about how to go bankrupt:

- *Rule 1:* Delegate all authority and learn to pass the buck by becoming an absentee owner.

- *Rule 2:* Focus on sales and totally disregard such mundane things as profits, inventory levels, and customer service.

- *Rule 3:* Keep all financial matters strictly your business. Those bankers or factory representatives are always full of advice and don't know how to run your business. It is your money anyway.

- *Rule 4:* Think short-run because long-range goals are for pencil-pushing idiots with college degrees, probably in statistics.

- *Rule 5:* Expand. (This one is for your ego.) There is a joke about two country boys who took a shot at the produce business. They took their goods to market in a run-down pickup truck and sold their merchandise at cost. At the end of their first day in business, realizing that they had only broken even, one said to the other, "Golly! Guess we're gonna have to get a bigger truck!" (Donaldson, 1982).

When the situation becomes desperate and it seems that the firm has lost battle after battle, some drastic decisions are in store for the owner, who has to select among various unpleasant choices.

Give It One Last Chance

Charles "Red" Scott has helped in turning around small companies that were nearly dead, and he has developed an eight-step plan to help a crumbling organization in its last stand before it becomes a casualty (Banaszewski, 1981a):

- *Step one:* Take personal control of cash, the firm's lifeblood.

- *Step two:* Listen carefully to bankers, employees, and customers and pay attention to what they have to say.

- *Step three:* Stop the hemorrhaging by selling, disposing of, and eliminating losing propositions in products and people.

- *Step four:* Find the positives in products and people, because "eagles don't flock, you find them one at a time."

- *Step five:* Make a plan of action that takes advantage of the positives identified in step four, and minimize the losers.

- *Step six:* Raise new cash the easiest ways first: by collecting receivables, by liquidating inventory, by selling and leasing back real estate, etc.

- *Step seven:* Establish credibility by making only promises you can keep and keep comfortably.

- *Step eight:* Improve attitudes and morale by building an enthusiastic and cohesive management team.

If, despite all turnaround efforts, the company still does not show a profit, it is time to consider other final closing options.

Sell the Business

An ongoing concern, especially with a long-term lease, may be a good opportunity for somebody, despite the fact that it is losing money. People have all kinds of reasons for buying "dogs" or "puppies," especially if they are the kind of entrepreneur that thrives in small-scale fixing and turning small companies around ("Puppy Catcher," 1981).

Give It Away

There might be an employee, an associate, a relative, or a friend that may be willing to assume both assets and liabilities with a written agreement.

Disappear into the Sunset

Departing without notice is probably not a viable option from a moral or even realistic standpoint, because regardless of despair or distress, the consequences of running away from debts may be severe and permanent.

Liquidation

With a **liquidation sale**, the creditors at least get some cents on their loaned dollar, and they may deem this preferable to declaring bankruptcy. This involves converting all assets to cash by selling them privately under a contract after a court hearing, submitting the contract to the scrutiny of creditors, or holding an auction in the courtroom. Private sales are unusual because they involve only perishable items or very small sales. Submission of a liquidation sales contract to the scrutiny of the creditors is the most typical and most widely used. The creditors receive notice of the sale at least 20 days before the proposed date of the sale. If no creditor requests a court hearing, the sale materializes. In liquidation through a court auction, the best price of the highest bidder buys the liquidating firm's auctioned assets. If no hearing is requested by any creditors in regard to any objections that they may have concerning questions about the fairness of the price, the bidder's ability to pay, or the terms of the sale, the sale is final (Morrison, 1982).

Bankruptcy

Bankruptcy proceedings are like getting involved in a nasty divorce. In addition to nervous creditors, there may be outraged stockholders, disgruntled workers, lawsuits and counter lawsuits among principals and purveyors, and a host of other problems. There are two general types of bankruptcy: *voluntary*, which is instigated by the debtor, usually called Chapter 11 bankruptcy, and involuntary, which is initiated at the request of the company's creditors, known as Chapter 7 bankruptcy. In the case of the very small firm, the creditors themselves are not generally well enough informed or adequately organized to force Chapter 7 bankruptcy proceedings (Smith, 1982, p. 25).

Despite the fact that the bankruptcy route is being recognized more and more as an acceptable business practice, it is a course of action that should not be taken lightly because closing down a business is embarrassing, heartbreaking, and stressful, to say the least. Therefore, any option or alternative considered when the business must close should be carefully discussed with the firm's attorney and accountant.

In addition to asset liquidation, bad publicity, and the complete managerial and financial control by a creditor's committee, declaring bankruptcy requires generally more ready cash than the insolvent business possesses, especially for legal and consulting fees that understandably must be paid up front. Additionally, bankruptcy proceedings can be extremely lengthy, complicated, and loaded with applications, complaints, responsive pleadings, court hearings, court transcripts, and court auctions.

THE BANKRUPTCY CODE

The Bankruptcy Code that took effect in October 2005 has proved to be an obstacle to businesses seeking bankruptcy protection from the courts. Under the old bankruptcy code, businesses were encouraged to seek protection from creditors when they needed a period of time in which to reorganize the operations and obligations of the company. Very few businesses sought complete liquidation under Chapter 7 of the Bankruptcy Code because Chapter 11 Reorganization was preferable as a means to keep assets while being able to discharge certain debts. Reorganization allowed the business to come up with a new business strategy that was protected by the courts. Congress strategically organized Chapter 7 and Chapter 11 bankruptcies this way so that the businesses would have an incentive to continue in their business instead of throwing in the towel and liquidating the company and its assets. The intent of Congress in this strategic benefit for Chapter 11 reorganization was protection of the capital markets of the United States. The revised Bankruptcy Code has proven to be an obstacle to both the small business and the intent of Congress of avoiding liquidation and promoting reorganization of companies in bankruptcy because more small businesses will ultimately fail at reorganization and will be forced into liquidation as a result.

High numbers of bankruptcy filings and abuses of the system have led to changes in the Bankruptcy Code that make it more difficult for businesses, and particularly small-business owners, to successfully complete a Chapter 11 reorganization. The changes in the Bankruptcy Code stem from excessive abuses seen in cases such as Enron and Worldcom, where the principals and officers of these corporations walked away with large salaries and severance packages right before bankruptcy was filed, leaving the shareholders with empty coffers and worthless stock in their hands. After bankruptcy, the shareholders stand to lose millions of dollars to pay off creditors, whereas the large sums of money that the officers leave with are, in essence, taken as a preference for the departees instead of being kept by the corporation as part of the bankruptcy estate. Taking money and cashing in stock when the officers know that the corporation is about to lose stock price and file bankruptcy is, in essence, an illegal shifting of assets that belong to the corporation. The officers are privy to inside information and act on this to first and foremost protect and expand their personal assets, leaving the shell of the corporation to file bankruptcy and leaving its creditors in dire financial straits.

The result of all this greed and malfeasance is a hardship on the capital markets. When a corporation as highly leveraged as Enron or Worldcom uses bankruptcy as a financial planning tool to escape paying large institutional investors while personally lining their own pockets, the outcry from the public and the investors is overwhelming. Not only do the little guys such as investors and small creditors get burned, because of the size of the debt, the secured creditors also do not get paid—there simply are no assets for distribution under the reorganization plan. Congress has changed bankruptcy laws to make it more difficult for petitioners to meet the criteria to reorganize, which, in essence, will force them into liquidation after they cannot meet the tougher reorganization standards and time frames.

Bankruptcy Provisions

The key elements in Chapter 11 filings are these:

- Getting a plan confirmed
- Obtaining post-petition financing
- Management control
- Retention of key employees
- Small business debtors (Bohn, 2006).

The bankruptcy provisions that went into effect in October 2005 have made it much more difficult to restructure debt, assets, management, and financing options. Creditors who stand to lose in reorganization can make it very difficult for a petitioner to get his or her proposed plan for reorganization approved by the creditors. The goal of reorganization is to keep the business operating as a going concern so that the capital markets do not suffer as much as if there was an outright liquidation. To help the petitioner restructure and continue on in the business, Congress has traditionally given the petitioner help to keep creditors at bay while continuing operations and incurring new debt that gets to be paid before the other secured and unsecured creditors. Congress has also traditionally given the petitioner the ability to restructure its management and operations while being protected from the provisions of financing arrangements that in the normal course of business would constitute a default on obligations, allowing the creditor to reclaim its investment. In contrast, with the protection of a bankruptcy filing, the ordinary default provisions in contracts and financing arrangements may not be enforced by the courts if an executory contract is assumed by the estate on the theory that it is burdensome on the bankruptcy estate under §365 of the Bankruptcy Code. These traditional protections of the petitioner that are afforded to keep businesses operating have given way to fraud and greed, and many of these provisions are being taken away or are being changed under the new revisions.

The Plan

A petitioner traditionally had a period of 120 days after filing for bankruptcy in which to file a reorganization plan and then had to have the plan approved no later than 180 days from filing. This provision was based on the assumption that the petitioner knew the extent of the business better than anyone else and would be able to propose a fairer plan better than any one creditor who would be looking out for his or her own interest at the expense of the other creditors. The petitioner could be (and usually was) granted unlimited extensions on these time periods for cause at the discretion of the court. When the case involved a company of substantial size, extensions were often necessary to do the due diligence to put together a confirmable plan. "As a recent example, it took American Airlines nearly 3 years to confirm its plan in 2003" (Bohn, 2006, p. 44).

In contrast, the revised Bankruptcy Code has an 18-month deadline for the non-small-business petitioner to exclusively file a plan and a period of 20 months from filing to get the plan approved, with no extensions of time granted. For small businesses, the time frames are even shorter. The petitioner has an exclusive period to file a plan that is in effect on the date of filing and can be extended by the court on motion to a maximum of 10 months for both filing and confirmation. The only way that the small business debtor can avoid this short time frame is for the petitioner to demonstrate a preponderance of the evidence that it is more likely than not to have a plan confirmed. In either event, the shortened time frames for the petitioner to exclusively propose and confirm a plan for reorganization require that strides toward preparing for bankruptcy must be made prior to filing to have the reorganization proceed according to the wishes of the business. If a petitioner cannot meet these deadlines, then the creditors can propose and have adopted a competing plan for reorganization.

Post-Petition Financing

The ability to gain financing while a debtor-in-possession is in the process of bankruptcy is critical to the survival of the business as a going concern. Obviously, the petitioner does not have any assets to put up as collateral because they are all part of the bankruptcy estate and are subject to a stay of the court. For a petitioner to be able to gain financing post-petition, the cash flows from the continuing business are the source of repayment guarantees for the creditor. For the creditor to get repaid, the business has to survive and maintain its cash flows. Four changes in the Bankruptcy Code make post-petition repayment riskier:

- The ability of utility providers to cut off service if the debtor provides adequate assurance of future payment that is satisfactory to the provider within 20 days of filing under 11 U.S.C. §366;

- Debtors' vendors have 45 days to reclaim goods sold to the insolvent debtor under 11 U.S.C. §546(c)(1).

- Debtors have a shorter time to pay tax claims—now a maximum of 5 years to draw out payments as compared to the previous 6 years under 11 U.S.C. §1129(a)(9)(c).

- Debtors now have a limit on the amount of time they have to decide if they will keep or reject commercial leases of 210 days; whereas previously there was no limit on time extensions to make this decision (Bohn, 2006, pp. 45–46). These factors have a negative impact on cash flows because they require the debtor-in-possession to stay current on these expenses and to take away any preferential purchases that would have been settled through the estate instead of operating funds. With the lower levels of cash flow to ensuring that the business remains a going concern, the post-petition financiers are fewer and farther between. The risk of non-payment is too high. This translates into the debtor having less success at reorganization. If the debtor fails at reorganization, the court transfers the Chapter 11 reorganization into a Chapter 7 liquidation.

Management and Key Employees

After filing for reorganization, the petitioner can continue to operate its business with either the petitioner continuing to manage its operations or with a trustee appointed by the court. The duties of these two distinct parties are the same as they pertain to managing the business, but the goals are drastically different. The debtor-in-possession wants to keep the business running, while the trustee may or may not. The trustee is appointed by the court to manage the business after there has been a bad act by the debtor-in-possession that places its intentions in doubt with the court. Typically, a court will appoint a trustee upon the showing of fraud or dishonesty that rises to the level of incompetence or intentional fraud. However, under the revised Bankruptcy Code (11 U.S.C §1104(3)), the situations in which a court will intervene and appoint a trustee have expanded so that it just has to be in the best interests of the estate or the creditors to have a trustee appointed. A trustee can also be appointed when there are reasonable grounds to suspect that management has "participated in actual fraud, dishonesty, or criminal conduct in the management of the debtor or the debtor's public financial reporting." (Bohn, 2006, p. 47).

Another new area that is regulated by the revised Bankruptcy Code, 11 U.S.C. §503(c), places limits on compensation and benefits that can be given to insiders of the company after filing a petition for bankruptcy. The compensation given to management cannot be more than ten times the compensation given to non-management employees; severance packages must be available to all full-time employees and meet the same compensation threshold; and retention payments to insiders can occur only when another company has placed an offer of the same or more amount for the insider's services.

Small Businesses

Small businesses that are filing for Chapter 11 reorganization face even more stringent hurdles to complete the reorganization plan. If the small-business debtor cannot clear all of these hurdles, the reorganization plan will not be completed. The stakes are high for a failed reorganization. When reorganization under Chapter 11 fails, the court can dismiss the case or transfer it to a Chapter 7 liquidation. The debtor then faces no protection of the Bankruptcy Code from its creditors or a straight Chapter 7 liquidation. This is not what the debtor wants, but if the debtor cannot clear the hurdles, this is the result. With the revised Bankruptcy Code, small-business debtors face shorter deadlines to submit financials, to propose a reorganization plan, and to get that reorganization plan approved by its creditors.

The revisions that affect small-business debtors protect employees who lost insurance coverage within 180 days prior to the filing and creditors whose collateral is not exempted from the bankruptcy estate as an asset necessary to maintain the business. Small-business debtors and creditors will see shorter time frames for the completion of the plan, and therefore shorter time until they see recovery of their secured collateral. The specific changes and additions to the Bankruptcy Code for small-business debtors are these: (a) a shorter time frame of 10 months to exclusively propose and have approved a reorganization plan; (b) a maximum of 7 days to file financials and federal tax returns from date of petition (debtor must also keep current with timely payment of taxes); (c) management must attend the meeting of creditors (this was optional before); and (d) the maintenance of appropriate insurance (Bohn, 2006, p. 47).

Other Issues

Other revisions to the Bankruptcy Code are general in nature and affect all reorganizations. Under §548 of the Bankruptcy Code, a trustee can recover fraudulent transfers made 2 years prior to the filing of the petition. The prior benchmark was 1 year prior to filing. Fraudulent transfers are transfers that are made with an intent to delay or defraud the bankruptcy estate. This often occurs when a debtor knows that bankruptcy is inevitable and pays a debt owed to a favored creditor (such as one that the debtor wishes to continue to do business with) before other creditors that are due payment first.

If the debtor is the lessee in a commercial lease, the provisions for assumption or rejection of a commercial lease have been revised. Under the prior code, the assumption or rejection of non-residential leases could be extended for cause indefinitely until the plan was confirmed. The revised code deems commercial leases rejected if it is not assumed upon 120 days after the filing of the petition or by the date of plan confirmation. The initial 120-day period can be extended by the court for cause, but only for an additional 90 days (Gregg & Mears, 2005, p. 24). Upon rejection of the lease, the property must be surrendered to the landlord. If the debtor chooses to assume a commercial lease, the debtor must cure all monetary defaults and provide the landlord with adequate assurance of continued future performance. Any nonmonetary defaults are deemed cured upon the assumption of the lease by the tenant, but the tenant must reimburse landlord for all pecuniary losses that he has suffered.

Retail leases often pose a larger problem for both tenant and landlord in the event of bankruptcy filing. If the tenant chooses to assume the lease or assign it to a third party, the tenant must provide the landlord with adequate assurance that it or the third party can continue to fulfill both the monetary and non-monetary obligations of the lease. Congress has been pressured to enact the revised Bankruptcy Code because it favors landlords who are faced with tenants holding retail spaces hostage while going through the lengthy bankruptcy process. The new code allows the shorter time for assumption or rejection of the lease, and it also gives the landlord more discretion regarding the use of the space if it is assigned to a third party. Prior, a third party could assume the lease if there was adequate assurance only of the financial performance of the lease; now the third party must also adhere to the operating provisions of the lease so as not to violate use, exclusivity, or radius restrictions, or to upset the current tenant mix of the property. For example, previously, Barnes and Noble could assume a lease in bankruptcy from a retailer of women's clothing in a mall where there was already an existing local bookstore. The existing bookstore almost always has an exclusivity clause saying it can be the only book retailer in the mall. This was a way of getting around the exclusivity clause in the existing bookstore's lease, and the bankruptcy court would strike this non-compete clause from the women's clothing retailer's lease because it was held to be detrimental to the bankruptcy estate. This was a huge problem for the landlord, who usually got sued for violating this provision. Now, the new code (11 U.S.C. §365(b)(3)(A)) does not allow a violation of these clauses that result in a disruption of the tenant mix of the shopping center.

The revisions to the Bankruptcy Code are an attempt to rein in the corruption of the system that has been practiced by individuals who are able to drain the company coffers and leave the creditors and shareholders holding the bag for fraud. However, the provisions go too far in caving to pressures from lobbyists to make all bankruptcy filings subject to impossible time frames and hurdles. This allows a reorganization failure to result in a straight liquidation, which is precisely in opposition to the stated purpose of Congress because it enacts the original Bankruptcy legislation allowing the honest but unfortunate debtor a fresh start. Now, a fresh start is much harder to come by if you cannot meet the high standards put in place, which limits the number of firms and owners able to take advantage of this legislation.

SUCCESSION MANAGEMENT

One of the most severe problems that entrepreneurial firms and especially family-owned businesses face is the problem of succession. Often, the younger generation cannot hold out until the older generation quits. The wait is long, filled with frustration, and young persons are torn between loyalty and logic. The consequences of not thinking about retirement, disability, or succession to the helm of the small firm can be much greater than ever imagined. What is needed is an orderly and clear plan for succession with the main goal being not only to ensure that the business continues in good health but also that the entrepreneur owner's spouse and children are well provided. In the struggle to survive, entrepreneurs typically solve problems by trial and error, usually doing things on their own and not training someone else. At the owner's death or severe disability, there are sometimes no trained successors. Without the entrepreneur's personal knowledge of suppliers, customers, and working procedures, the business generally is worth only the liquidation value of its tangible assets.

While there is merit to self-reliance and independence, creating managerial back-up could contribute to the ability of the business to sustain its growth (Bulloch, 1978). Succession management therefore involves the management of personal and financial matters so that the entrepreneurs may pass the business on to their children and others without unnecessary taxation or interference from outsiders.

The succession of the chief executive of any organization is an important event, and studies have revealed that it is one of the major causes of all business failures. McGivern (1978) introduced a model for analyzing succession situations based on five variables that influence the process through a cycle of stages before, during, and after the succession itself:

1. The stage reached in the firm's development

2. The motivation of the owner-manager

3. The extent of family, internal team, or external team domination

4. The organizational climate within the firm

5. The business environment

Succession planning is a difficult commitment for a busy owner, especially because it may take a year or more and because it needs to be reviewed every few years. Succession management can be successful and financially rewarding to the owners and their family or partners if it deals with both the complex managerial and complex financial issues, such as the following:

1. *Slowing down of the growth of the owner's estate:* Without slowing down the growth of the business, so upon the owner's death the estate tax does not reduce much the capital of a business, which is probably already undercapitalized.

2. *Recapitalization:* Reorganizing the capital structure and issuing a voting preferred stock, which the owner keeps, and common stock with minimal value assigned to it. The common stock is given as a gift to the family, with minor gift tax liability (Schultz, 1982).

3. *Maintaining control:* Periodically reviewing the shareholders list to buy out inactive shareholders that may cause problems in a succession process, by creating voting and non-voting classes of shares, and by requiring that voting shares must be offered first to the company before they are offered for sale to an outsider.

4. *Buy–Sell agreements:* These are the most common means of providing for succession when the business is jointly owned and succession takes place at a predetermined point of time (death, retirement, etc.), with a predetermined formula for valuing the stock for estate purposes (book value at date of death, etc.) and predetermined restrictions on the sale of stock to outsiders to satisfy Internal Revenue Service regulations for estate tax purposes. This way, a buy-sell agreement addresses three key concerns: succession in the business, continuation of income during retirement or disability, and provision of funds to pay estate taxes.

5. *Management development:* Bringing younger managers and family members into positions of responsibility with incentive programs such as bonuses paid in stock and profit sharing.

6. *Family partnership:* Parents as individuals (not as a company) form a partnership with younger family members. Parents are general partners and younger family members are limited partners receiving the flow of earnings directly from their parents and not from the firm, where those earnings would be subject to double taxation (Muchin & Banoff, 1983).

7. *Joint venture with trusts:* Especially when the children are still minors, trusts are set up in which the trusts, not the children, are the partners. Thus, the parents can

still make decisions on the business while having cash contributions flowing to the children. Since each trust is considered a separate taxpayer, the new joint venture can be split among the children's trusts, minimizing income tax liabilities. In all cases, however, gift tax liabilities still exist.

8. *Creation of independent capital sources outside the business:* The owner is less dependent upon the business for retirement and health insurance purposes, and thus will be more willing to let go of the helm of the business and seriously plan succession.

9. *Solving personal estate problems:* Consider the owner's remaining active years, retirement, possible disability, protection of surviving spouse and children, maximum flexibility for changing conditions, and of course, the owner's unique personal situation, objectives, and lifestyle (Moffitt, 1982).

10. *Balancing the pressures and interests of insiders and outsiders in both family and business:* Family and business, though separate, remain tied together. Family managers (inside the family and inside the business) face different pressures and concerns from the employees, who are inside the business and outside the family; the relatives, who are family members not active in the management of the business; and the outsiders, such as creditors, customers, vendors, accountants, etc., who are neither inside the family nor inside the business, but are connected to the firm through business practices and activities.

11. *Drawing prenuptial agreements:* Worries about a son- or daughter-in-law ending up with a chunk of the family business, especially true in community property states, have created conditions of respectability for these sensitive prenuptial agreements, in which the in-law to be is asked to give up any marital rights to the family firm. Prenuptial agreements are not valid unless those signing them are fully informed of the value of the assets to which they are waiving their marital rights, so owners must be willing to disclose financial information regarding the family venture ("Small Business: Prenuptial Accords," 1982, p. 25).

The duality of both family and business transitions lies at the heart of any succession management. Facing the future and the inevitability of death or retirement, older entrepreneurs must learn how to make the passage from directing and controlling, to advising, guiding, and teaching. Healthy confrontation can make the transition from conflict to problem solving and from name-calling to concentrating on issues, facts, and numbers. Mediation through periodic family meetings, outside boards of directors, or any other third party can also help soften hardened positions, because managerial succession problems are not strictly business problems. Ultimately, however, and despite the problems with succession by a son or daughter, one of the things that can kill a thriving business is nepotism, that is, pushing a family member through the ranks even though he or she is not capable. Nepotism or unwillingness on the part of young family members to undertake the job will not guarantee that the business will stay in the family or that the family will stay in business (Barnes & Hershon, 1976).

CONCLUSION

The small-business life cycle needs to be tied with the individual convictions and aspirations of the entrepreneurs or their family traditions in the case of a family business. These factors are extremely important in determining the venture's specific stage of development at a particular point of time, and they should be considered in conjunction with the traditional criteria of employee number, asset size, organizational characteristics, and so on. When entrepreneurs are convinced that their managerial practices and strategies are no longer adequate, and/or growth is absolutely necessary for the survival of the small firm, they should take appropriate actions to move into the next developmental stage by applying new strategies to the venture's development. The management problems, issues, strategies, approaches, and style particular to each stage are quite different, and if entrepreneurs are either unaware of the need for change or are unwilling to adjust and adapt to the venture's growth requirements, they will be unable to exploit the venture's potential. The form of an organization is the result of the laws of growth up to that point, and a lack of understanding of these laws and what must be done to take advantage of the situation will result in entrepreneurs' becoming mere caretakers of the enterprise. The fundamental issue is to recognize the operational and organizational implications of change. Managing change is an inevitable necessity in a growing enterprise and is the major challenge to making growth happen. The inability or lack of desire to recognize and act upon this challenge is the major cause of a business failing or not living up to its expectations. Finally, it is quite obvious that exiting the enterprise, whether voluntarily or involuntarily, is not just an event, but is rather a process that has to be planned far ahead and managed properly. The managerial and financial considerations of the transition into the sale, bankruptcy, or succession of a firm can be devastating if this transition is allowed to happen in a haphazard manner rather than in a well-planned and organized fashion.

Website Information

Topic	Web Address	Description
Dialectic life cycle processes	www.Nordstrom.com, www. Walmart.com	The thesis and the antithesis; home pages for Nordstrom and Wal-Mart show the differences in life cycles of these two retail giants.
Voluntary exit: Selling the business	http://www.inventionatplay.org/ inventors_hea.html	Gives the story behind the Head Ski and the Prince racquet.
Cash cow	http://www.bcg.com/publications/ publication_view.jsp?pubID=222	Article about the "anatomy of the cash cow"—what it is, and potential for investors and owners of a business.
Marketing growth management	http://www.smallbusinessmarketi ngmanagement.com/12steps.asp	The "12-Step Business Growth Plan" gives an alternate view of how to plan the growth of a small business.
Succession management	http://maxa.maf.govt.nz/mafnet/ rural-nz/people-and-their-issues/ social-research-and-welfare/ farm-succession/succn98.pdf	A real-world application of succession management. This website explains the succession problems faced by family farmers in New Zealand.

Key Terms

Cycle theories of organizational change: May be either partial or complete; partial cycles describe the rise and fall of an organization, while complete cycles describe the resurgence of an organization as well as its rise and fall.

Dialectic process: A view of institutional change in which a thesis, or an established institutional form, an antithesis, or an innovative institutional form, and a synthesis, or a hybrid new form emerges, drawing positive characteristics from the other two (Gist, 1971, pp. 370–372).

Initial public offering (IPO): A mechanism of business growth in which the business "goes public" and sells its stock on the open public market.

Liquidation sale: The conversion of all assets to cash by selling them privately under a contract after a court hearing, submitting the contract to the scrutiny of creditors, or holding an auction in the courtroom.

Multiplex stage: The stage of institutional development established by holding the level of product quality constant while the firm offers more than one level of service, or by holding the service level constant and offering more than one level of product quality.

Omniplex stage: The stage of institutional development in which all possible quality–service combinations are offered. This stage is reached as the firm increases its product mix offerings in an attempt to expand its market.

Pure primary offering: Shares to the public are offered only by the company itself.

Pure secondary offering: Only some of the existing shareholders are exiting the firm and offer some or all of their shares to outside investors in the public offering.

Recapitalization: The reorganization of capital structure and issuance of voting preferred stock, which the owner keeps, and common stock with minimal value assigned to it.

Simplex stage: The most primitive stage of institutional development in which the firm offers one level of product quality and a corresponding level of service.

Simultaneous primary and secondary offerings (mixed offerings): Both new shares of the company and existing company shares are simultaneously made available for purchase by outside investors in the same public offering.

Vacuum theory: This theory advocates that innovative organizations come into being when there is a void in the institutional coverage of a specific market.

Review Questions

1. Briefly describe the three organizational changes required of a venture as it changes from a "personal" entrepreneurial status to an "impersonal" professionally managed status.

2. Define and describe the five basic guidelines for selling a business.

3. What are the outcomes that occur as a result of the decline in the level of management effort?

4. What is meant by the following statement: "To grow or not to grow, that is the question"?

5. Briefly discuss the critical issue of succession management for a family business.

6. Research a local agriculture-related venture. Using the "Characteristics of Stages of Venture Development" from this chapter (Exhibit 14.1, page 360), assess at which stage of

development this venture is operating. Provide a short summary of the venture and your key points of rationale for this assessment.

7. Exiting an agricultural venture creates a unique set of challenges, especially given that many are family run. Read Ohio State University's fact sheet titled "What should I do with the farm?" available at http://ohioline.osu.edu/ae-fact/pdf/AEDE_13_09.pdf.

Reflections from the Front Lines of LifeGuard America

Begin with the end in mind. It is a great strategy. Always know where you are going because direction is more important than the destination. Flexibility is the key to thriving in today's business environment. Change is inevitable, and those who create a business environment that embraces change will ultimately fare better than those who don't. There are many growth opportunities for us that include international expansion into a LifeGuard Canada, LifeGuard Europe, LifeGuard Brazil, or LifeGuard Japan. It will be imperative for us to remain flexible as to how we expand into other markets because of the nationalistic approach to organ transplantation. The main point to make here is that we have made the decision upfront that growth is a long-term objective of the company. It is important also to formulate a clear exit strategy and have it in place from the beginning, even if it is not an IPO into the world of publicly traded companies. An investor always wants a strategy that generates a ROI commensurate with the perceived risk. LifeGuard America is an excellent example of a company that is not suitable for an IPO, and as a result, certain venture capital investors are not players for our initial funding efforts. We are looking for smaller, "angel" investors who are equally interested in the humanitarian aspect and a solid return on their investment. We have put together a dual-track funding strategy that uses both equity and debt as key elements to get us started and allow us to rapidly grow based on successful sales. The equity capital of $1,500,000 gets us through start-up to cash-flow-positive and the break-even point, while the financing of our 3-year contracts produces upfront cash to grow the business based on selling our service contracts to our primary market, the organ procurement and transplantation organizations across America. The financing of our long-term contracts basically gets us up-front access to roughly $950,000 for every thirty contracts we close. That equates to about $3 million in just 1 of the 11 regions in the United States. That becomes our safety net and our growth capital fueled by success. What is the end we have in mind? Our vision is a direction, not a destination, so our end is a private company that offers payback to its investors and a 39% ROI in the same third year of its operation and a company that creates spin-off opportunities from the intellectual property it creates doing business in the field of medical logistics. Certainly a mouthful, but ours is a simple model that collaborates with higher educational institutions to produce new ideas that can be incubated into small companies that extend our market and our presence in it.

Discussion Questions on LifeGuard America

1. How would you explain the strategy of "begin with the end in mind"?

2. Is there a perfect investor for every venture? If so, what business elements are the fundamentals to each type of investor?

References

Alderson, W. (1957). *Marketing behavior and executive action.* Homewood, IL: Richard D. Irwin.

Banaszewski, J. (1981a, February). Nine steps to save troubled companies. *Inc. Magazine, 3*(2), 43–47.

Banaszewski, J. (1981b, September). Thirteen ways to get a company in trouble. *Inc. Magazine, 3*(9), 97–100.

Barnes, L. B., & Hershon, S. A. (1976, July/August). Transferring power in a family business. *Harvard Business Review, 54*(4), 105–114.

Barth, H. (2003, April). Fit among competitive strategy, administrative mechanisms, and performance: A comparative study of small firms in mature and new industries. *Journal of Small Business Management, 41*(2), 133–147.

Bohn, E. 2006. Time to reorganize: But how? *Business Law Today, 15*(4): 43–47.

Bulloch, J. F. (1978, Summer). Problems of succession in small business. *Human Resource Management, 17*(2), 1–6.

Business slump spurs sellouts and mergers (1981, July). *Inc. Magazine, 3*(7), 26.

Butrick, F. (1980, December). Sell your company on the installment plan. *Inc. Magazine, 2*(12), 70.

Cooper, A. C. (1978). *Strategic management: New ventures and small business* [Mimeographed Paper No. 656]. West Lafayette, IN: Institute for Research in the Behavioral, Economic, and Management Sciences, Krannert Graduate School of Management, Purdue University.

Covin, J. G., and Slevin, D. P. (1997). In D. L. Sexton & R. W. Smilor (Eds.), *Entrepreneurship 2000* (pp. 99–126). Chicago: Upstart.

Daily, C. M., Certo, S. T., Dalton, D. R., & Roengpitya, R. (2003, Spring). IPO underpricing: A meta-analysis and research synthesis. *Entrepreneurship Theory and Practice, 27*(3), 271–295.

Dalrymple, D. J., & Thompson, D. L. (1969). *Retailing: An economic view.* New York: The Free Press.

De La Merced, M. J. (2011, June 21). Start-ups rewrite the book on valuation. *International Herald Tribune,* 18.

Deeks, J. (1976). *The small firm owner-manager.* New York: Praeger.

Donaldson, R. (1982, November). How to lose $1 million without even trying. *Entrepreneur, 10*(11), 72–73.

Economist, The. (2011, January 14). The last Kodak moment? *402*(8767), 63–64.

Ehrhardt, O., & Nowak, E. (2003, April). The effect of IPOs on German family-owned firms: Governance changes, ownership structure, and performance. *Journal of Small Business Management, 41*(2), 222–232.

Fink, S. L., Beak, J., & Taddeo, K. (1971, January–February). Organizational crisis and change. *Journal of Applied Behavioral Science, 7*(1), 15–37.

Fry, F. L. (1993). *Entrepreneurship: A planning approach.* St. Paul, MN: West.

Gibson, C. K., & Wald, R. A. (1983). A macro-model for guiding the entrepreneurial plan. In R. Peterson (Ed.), *Proceedings of the Southwestern Small Business Institute Association* (pp. 24–39). Las Cruces: New Mexico State University.

Gilligan, J. J. (1977, January). The coming boom in mergers. *Credit & Financial Management, 79*(1), 26–27.

Gist, R. R. (1971). *Marketing and society.* New York: Holt, Rinehart & Winston.

Granger C. H. (1977, April). Growth strategies in service businesses. *Management Review, 66*(4), 10–11.

Gregg, J. & Mears, P. (2005, November/December). What congress hath wrought: Provisions of the bankruptcy abuse prevention and the consumer protection act affecting interests in real estate. *Probate and Property,* 24. www.americanbar.org/publications.

Greiner, L. (1972, July/August). Evolution and revolution as organizations grow. *Harvard Business Review, 50*(4), 37–46.

Harrell, W. (1992). Foreword. In D. Sexton & J. Kasarda (Eds.), *The state of the art of entrepreneurship* (pp. xiii-xiv). Boston: PWS-Kent.

Hollander, S. C. (1966, Summer). Notes on the retail accordion theory. *Journal of Retailing, 42*(2), 29–40.

Holmburg, S. (1991). Value creation and capture: Entrepreneurship harvest and IPO strategies. In N. C. Churchill, et al. (Eds.): *Frontiers of entrepreneurship research* (pp. 191–204). Wellesley, MA: Babson College.

How to manage entrepreneurs (1981, September 7). *Business Week,* 66–69.

Howard Head sells another success story (1982, July 4). *The Dallas Morning News,* p. 5H.

Hyatt, H. (1990, June). The dark side (of going public). *Inc. Magazine, 12*(6), 46–56.

Jansson, S. (1977, February). The enduring appeal of staying small. *Institutional Investor, 11*(2), 76–78.

Kroeger, C. V. (1974, Fall). Managerial development in the small firm. *California Management Review, 17*(1), 41–47.

Larsson, E., Hedelin, L., & Garling, T. (2003, April). Influence of expert advice on expansion goals of small businesses in rural Sweden. *Journal of Small Business Management, 41*(2), 205–212.

McCammon, B. C., Jr. (1973, April). *The future of catalog showrooms: Growth and its challenges to management.* Working paper. Cambridge, MA: Marketing Science Institute.

McGivern, C. (1978, Spring). The dynamics of management succession. *Management Decision, 16*(1), 32–42.

McGuire, J. W. (1976, Spring). The small enterprise in economics and organization theory. *Journal of Contemporary Business, 5*(2), 115–138.

McKenna, J. F., & Oritt, P. L. (1980, Spring). Small business growth: Making a conscious decision. *SAM Advanced Management Journal, 45*(2), 45–53.

McKenna, J. F., & Oritt, P. L. (1981, Spring). Growth planning for small business. *American Journal of Small Business, 5*(4), 25–27.

McNair, G. (1958). Significant trends and developments in the postwar period. In A. B. Smith (Ed.), *Competitive distribution in a free high-level economy and its implications for the university* (pp. 1–25). Pittsburgh, PA: University of Pittsburgh Press.

Megginson, L. C. (1961). *Providing management talent for small business* [Small Business Management Research Reports series]. Baton Rouge, LA: College of Business Administration, Louisiana State University.

Moffitt, P. (1982, Autumn). A question for business owners: "Are you prepared for success?" *SAM Advanced Management Journal, 47*(4), 4–11.

Morrison, R. (1982, March). Shopping for bankruptcy bargains. *Inc. Magazine, 4*(3), 126–129.

Muchin, A., & Banoff, S. (1983, February). The family cache. *Inc. Magazine, 5*(2), 132.

Petty, W. J. (1994). Harvesting. In W. D. Bygrave (Ed.), *The portable MBA in entrepreneurship* (pp. 377–409). New York: John Wiley & Sons.

Petty, W. J. (1997). Harvesting firm value: Process and results. In D. L. Sexton & R. W. Smilor (Eds.), *Entrepreneurship 2000* (pp. 71–94). Chicago: Upstart.

Prasad, D. (1990). An asymmetric information approach to forecasting project quality (Doctoral dissertation, University of Oklahoma, 1990). *Dissertation Abstracts International, 51*(06), 2075A. (UMI No. 9029874).

Prasad, D. (1994, Spring). Is underpricing greater for mixed offerings as compared to pure primary offerings in the OTC market. *Journal of Financial and Strategic Decisions, 7*(1), 25–34.

Puppy catcher (1981, October 19). *Fortune, 104*(8), 16.

Putting a price on your firm (1982, September 20). *The Wall Street Journal,* p. 23.

Rausch, B. I. (1975, October). Small business: How marketable is it? *The Woman CPA, 37*(4), 16–17.

Ritter, J. R., & Welch, I. (2002, August). A review of IPO activity, pricing and allocation. *Journal of Finance, 57*(4), 1795–1828.

Rosenbaum, M. (1981, September). The new owners speak German. *Inc. Magazine, 3*(9), 123–124.

Rowe, A. J., Mason, R. O., & Dickel, K. (1982). *Strategic management and business policy: A methodological approach.* Reading, MA: Addison-Wesley.

Schultz, T. J. (1982, November). The transfer of ownership ought to pay off. *Inc. Magazine, 4*(11), 146.

Selling your business. (1981, March). *Management Review, 70*(4), 4–5.

Sexton, D. L., and Bowman-Upton, N. B. (1991). *Entrepreneurship: Creativity and growth.* New York: MacMillan.

Small business: Prenuptial accords: All in the family (1982, December 6). *The Wall Street Journal* (Western ed.), p. 25.

Smith, I. (1982, November/December). Is there life after business failure? *In Business, 4*(6), 25.

Spilka, G. M. (1982, January). How a seller can predict the success of an acquisition. *Entrepreneur, 10*(1), 38–39, 144–145.

Stern, L. W., & El-Ansary, A. J. (1977). *Marketing channels.* Englewood Cliffs, NJ: Prentice Hall.

Stewart, N. (1956, January). Building to-morrow's management. *Dun's Review and Modern Industry, 67*(1), 40–41.

Susbauer, J. C. (1979). Commentary. In D. E. Schendel & C. W. Hofer (Eds.), *Strategic management: A new view of business policy and planning,* (pp. 327–332). Boston: Little, Brown.

Van Auken, P. M., Sexton, D. L., & Ireland, R. D. (1982, Fall). Increasing small business through situational management. *Wisconsin Small Business Forum, 1*(1), 11–20.

Vesper K. H. (1979). Commentary. In D. E. Schendel & C. W. Hofer (Eds.), *Strategic management: A new view of business policy and planning* (pp. 332–338). Boston: Little, Brown.

Vesper, K. H. (1990). *New venture strategies.* Englewood Cliffs, NJ: Prentice-Hall.

Vozikis, G. S. (1979). *A strategic disadvantage profile of the states of development of small business: The experience of retail and service small business in Georgia.* Unpublished doctoral dissertation, University of Georgia, Athens.

Wiklund, J., Davidsson, P., & Delmar, F. (2003, Spring). What do they think and feel about growth? An expectancy-value approach to small business managers' attitudes toward growth. *Entrepreneurship Theory and Practice, 27*(3), 247–270.

Williams, H. (1983, January/February). Growing smaller may be your best strategy. *In Business, 5*(1), 52–53.

Woodward, H. N. (1976, January/February). Management strategies for small companies. *Harvard Business Review 54*(1), 113–121.

15

Venture International Growth Management

Can We Grow Internationally?

LEARNING OBJECTIVES

1. To understand the importance of exporting and international growth for the venture's development.

2. To recognize that there are stages of development in the exporting process.

3. To investigate the sources of export trade assistance.

4. To develop the foundations for an effective exporting strategy.

TOPIC OUTLINE

INTRODUCTION

The United States came out of World War II virtually unchallenged economically, politically, militarily, and technologically, and it overwhelmed other countries with resources and wealth. Times have changed since then. Although the United States has continued to engage in some degree of international business, most U.S. firms, especially small firms, have ignored global markets in favor of a constantly growing U.S. market. Since the 1950s, not only has the United States run up the largest trade deficits in its history by importing hundreds of billions of dollars of foreign trade goods, but the American consumer has also come to perceive many American produced goods as inferior to many foreign products, and the U.S. market has become saturated with foreign-made products. The significant changes in circumstances in the world in the past decades require that small firms not be hesitant in looking for growth opportunities abroad, because expanding a venture's business beyond domestic borders may actually enhance overall performance by growing faster and earning more from operations ("International Incentive," 1992). Additionally, businesses can no longer consider themselves purely domestic companies when global competition can be as direct and threatening as a competitor six blocks away (Miller, 1991). Failure to cultivate global markets, especially through exporting and/or an e-commerce configuration, can be a critical mistake for ventures and businesses of any size. Globalization is not a future event, it is already here. Therefore, successful growth requires innovation and competitive moves not only for domestic consumption but also for the satisfaction of foreign customers' unique requirements: 96% of the world's population and 67% of the world's purchasing power lie outside the borders of the United States (U.S. Small Business Administration, Office of International Trade, 1999, p. 1). Exhibit 15.1 presents the U.S. Export Profile from 1992 to 2012.

International entrepreneurship can be defined as "new and innovative activities that have the goal of value creation and growth in business organizations across national borders" (McDougall & Oviatt, 1997, p. 293). It encompasses such diverse forms of international involvement by venture firms as *foreign licensing, international franchising, countertrade and bartering, international cooperative alliances,* which reflect the new restructuring of business as firms adapt to compete in the global economy (Hara & Kanai, 1994). International entrepreneurship also includes *new joint ventures* and *IPOs,* when entrepreneurial undertakings require resources from multiple countries because venture financing, markets, internal processes, and competition span national borders (Timmons & Sapienza, 1992). In addition, *exporting,* according to Czinkota (1994), is very well-suited to small firms successfully entering the international marketplace. This last mode of international entry for entrepreneurial ventures is the most prevalent and will be the main focus of the pages that follow.

THE REALITIES OF INTERNATIONAL TRADE

Up to now, no one has managed to change the way most people think about the trade balance, as a kind of scoreboard in a game of "us against the world." It is easier to ride with the tide and pretend that the trade account is the pure and simple truth about how the economy is doing internationally.

The **trade balance** is a familiar concept; it is the measure of the balance between a country's merchandise exports against its imports. The **balance of payments (BOP)** in contrast, can be defined as the balance that reflects not only the *visible merchandise trade* balance of exports and imports, which is the largest single component of total international payments, but also the *invisible trade* of all of a country's transactions. These transactions include the merchandise trade balance to which the balance on services is added, that is, receipts from and expenditures for travel, transportation, and insurance as well as the net flow of international investment and earnings flows. The BOP is often misunderstood as a balance sheet, when in reality, it is a

Exhibit 15.1	U.S. Export Profile in 1992–2012

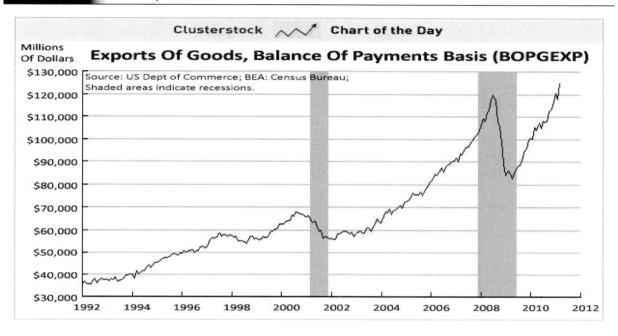

Source: U.S. Department of Commerce; U.S. Bureau of Economic Analysis; U.S. Census Bureau.
Note: Shaded areas indicate recessions.

country's cash flow statement over a period of time. These cash flows are measured in terms of real asset transactions or **current account** of income inflows and outflows during the current period for goods, services, official grants and foreign aid from one country to another, private remittances to and from foreigners, and investment income to and from foreign sources, as well as in terms of financial asset transactions or **capital and financial account** of inflows and outflows of direct investment for purchases or sales of companies, and portfolio investment for exchanges of financial claims on stocks, bonds, loans, in exchange for other financial claims or money (Czinkota, Ronkainen, Moffett, & Moynihan, 1998).

From these definitions, it is evident that the relationship between the various accounts is not only complex but also tightly knit. Without pushing matters further, their interconnections suggest that a rise or fall in the trade balance or balance on the current account cannot be disassociated from the financial side.

But the temptation is always there to present changes in the trade balance or in the current account as if they were self-propelled events, isolated from financial and monetary pressures. Yet when these accounts are presented in such terms, the effect is to obscure the complexity and scope of what is happening to the balance of payments as a whole. Deficits and surpluses in the current account affect a nation's economy in many ways. Money supply, prices, national income, employment, interest rates, foreign exchange rates, and foreign exchange reserves are all affected by current account disequilibria, and in turn they affect domestic businesses as well. Additionally, the forces that change a country's trade balance may be grouped under two headings. The first is the growth of its exports relative to imports, measured in volume terms. The second is its terms of trade, which are expressed as a ratio, obtained by dividing its export-price index by its index of import prices. A decrease in the ratio signifies that the country must export more to get the same volume of imports.

Projections of the trade and the current account balances hinge on general assumptions about the course of monetary policy. Since the overall balance of payments weighs financial flows against the real flows shown in the current account, it reflects the net impact of monetary pressures, that is, the net effect of U.S. monetary expansion relative to money growth abroad, as well as the extent of central bank intervention to influence the dollar's exchange rate.

INTERNATIONAL TRADE AND SMALL FIRMS

Although the international business scene is dominated by larger companies, mere size does not exclude a firm from seeking opportunities in foreign markets. The overseas opportunity most frequently encountered by smaller firms is the unsolicited order from a foreign country. This opportunity represents a demand for some of the firm's products or services for which a particular return may be expected. Considering also the possibility of future business from the overseas customer, the question becomes a very simple one, "Is the return worth the effort?" Many smaller firms will not fill an unsolicited order, believing it not worth the effort, while others will and act to develop future overseas business. The management of these firms reach opposite conclusions about the merit of investing resources to develop overseas opportunities. Either decision may be correct for a particular firm, but the decision should be based on facts rather than assumptions.

Given the ease of globalization nowadays and the **proliferation of e-commerce** where "a company can ship all over the place from all over the place" (Williams, 1990), why do so many American businesses, particularly small-to medium-size companies, shy away from exporting? There are two main reasons: The comfort of a vast home market and fear of the unknown (Finlay-Mulligan, 1981).

The North American market, with its highly organized distribution system and a common language, keeps most entrepreneurial operations more than busy. That tends to inhibit adventure into the unfamiliar, possibly risky, overseas markets. What are the main problems with overseas markets? Well, for one thing, these markets are populated by "foreigners" and many of them do not speak English. They do not think "the way we do," and some of them have "peculiar ideas" about adhering to contract and settlement terms. Additionally, in Europe they operate on a metric system, which makes their manufactured spare parts incompatible with American ones. There is also a problem with the translation of user manuals and sales and technical literature. For the European market alone, new literature would have to be printed in at least German, French, Italian, and Spanish.

Some foreign governments (and in some instances the U.S. government, too) are not exactly cooperative. They impose red tape and customs duties on imported goods and services to make prices of imported good less competitive, and thus, protect domestic production. This creates the headaches of developing and maintaining an export market all but insurmountable. In spite of all these problems, the development of a healthy export market can add a lucrative and dynamic dimension to any small firm with a competitive product to sell. Studies by the U.S. Small Business Administration determined that small firms that engage in international trade are 20% more productive and 9% more likely to stay financially strong than firms that are not involved in international trade ("International Incentive," 1992). As the export market continues to open globally, more and more small- and medium-sized firms will enter. They will find problems not as large as they first imagined, as well as sizeable profits to be made. Some important reasons and factors in favor of U.S. entrepreneurs entering the exporting business include the following:

1. The economic cycle, which is crucial for economic downturns, almost invariably hits the United States a year or 18 months before it reaches foreign countries,

giving a cushion to companies with business in the United States and abroad, thus sale declines in the domestic market can be offset by selling abroad.

2. Foreign firms are often more hesitant to make innovative changes in production, styling, and overall product lines, enabling American companies to come out with more up-to-date and innovative products.

3. Pay scales are now close to being the same here as they are in several foreign nations, especially considering U.S. worker productivity, which is much higher.

4. Increased sales and profits by expanding abroad means that small firms do not have to depend on the domestic market alone, which may not be enough in the long run for survival (Mulhern, 1998).

5. Entering foreign markets can produce economies of scale gains, because fixed costs can be spread over a larger number of units, thus lowering production cost per unit. This is especially true for fixed cost and capital-intensive firms.

6. Entering foreign markets can help a small firm hone its competitive skills and position by being forced to raise quality levels to world-class standards, thus becoming more customer oriented with a greater sensitivity toward the different tastes, customs, and unique preferences of both domestic and foreign customers.

7. Entering foreign markets allows firms to discover through exporting the use of new competitive approaches, new channels of distribution, and even new product ideas, which they are able to apply later to their domestic target markets with great success.

8. Entering foreign markets allows small firms with products that have already reached the maturity stage of their product life cycle domestically to rejuvenate themselves in foreign markets and possibly start a brand new product life cycle all over again.

An international trade order should almost never be ignored. If it is not to be filled, a very clear and definite reason should be given, such as an inability to service the product in foreign countries, for example. Even in these cases, the courtesy of a reply giving the reason for not being able to fill the international order is important to make sure that the international contact will remain intact and on good terms, because the firm's situation may change later and international trade may be by then a viable option. Entrepreneurs who enter foreign markets, at least initially by exporting, can indeed easily recoup their initial investment of analyzing foreign markets and visiting them, of providing promotional material and sample products and, of course, of their risk investment in receivables that are exposed to the same or even lower bad debt risk as domestic markets. Exporting provides the initial valuable international experience after which, if the initial experiment with exporting is met with success, a more elaborate strategy for further expansion and growth into foreign markets can be developed.

INTERNATIONAL GROWTH STRATEGIES FOR SMALL FIRMS

An international growth strategy is a challenge not only for large firms but also for small ones as well. There are many ways to enter the international trade arena.

Launching an E-Commerce Web Site

This is probably the least expensive and the simplest way of "going global." Basically, it is small- and medium-sized companies with more customized and innovative products and cheaper and more flexible computer-based technologies, such as a well-designed website, that can reach customers anywhere in the world, not the large vertically integrated giants of yesteryear driven by standardized mass markets and rigid mass-production (Howard, 1990). Unfortunately, nearly half of all U.S.-based websites are not set up to process international orders, costing millions of dollars of exporting opportunity cost (Grossman, 2000). Most small firms, however, tend to have an innovative spirit and a "let's give it a try" attitude, something that many larger, more cautious corporations lack, because layers of management make it difficult for new export ideas to percolate up through the various levels to the person who can decide to "Just do it!" (Emery, 1980).

Joint Ventures

Joint venture—the domestic or foreign alliances of two or more small firms for the purpose of exporting goods and services abroad—provide clout and important connections in foreign countries. In the development of export trading companies (ETCs), a domestic joint venture, the *Export Trading Act of 1982* also provides immunity from antitrust legislation. With a joint venture, the small firm shares not only the costs of getting export licenses and permits, distribution and transportation costs, but, of course, the joint venture's profits. In the case of foreign joint ventures, the key to success is choosing the right foreign partners and establishing common objectives with them. Unfortunately, the success rate for joint ventures is very poor, reaching just 43%, with the average life barely exceeding 3 years (Burroughs, 1991).

Foreign Licensing

Some small firms enter foreign markets by licensing patents, trademarks, and copyrights, as well as by transferring turnkey technology processes to customers overseas in return for royalties (Lado & Vozikis, 1997). **Foreign licensing** enables a small entrepreneurial firm to enter foreign markets quickly, easily, and virtually, with no capital investment whatsoever. But the risk of losing control over the quality of the manufacturing and marketing processes, as well as the risk of patent, copyright, and trademark "piracy" cannot be underestimated.

Countertrade and Bartering

Methods of international trade, such as countertrading and bartering, usually occur in countries whose currencies are virtually worthless outside their borders, or that do not have sufficient cash flow to pay for imported goods (Gilbert, 1992). Countertrade is a transaction in which a company selling goods in a foreign country agrees to promote investment and trade in the same foreign country through its connections and strategic alliances, a difficult, time-consuming, and complicated task for a small firm. Bartering, in contrast, is the exchange of goods and services for other goods and services with countries lacking convertible currencies, as in the case of countertrade, but in a much less cumbersome and much simpler transaction.

International Franchising

More than 20% of the 4,000 U.S. franchisers have outlets in foreign countries, according to the International Franchise Association (Tomzack, 1995). This is a great way to boost sales and profits when the domestic market gets saturated with franchise outlets and margins get thinner and thinner. In most cases, products and services are identical to those sold in the domestic market, but as every good international trader knows, adjustments to foreign cultures, tastes, and customs are a must. McDonald's sells "lambburgers" in India, beer in its German outlets, and Cadbury chocolate sticks in Great Britain.

However, the prevailing way in which a small firm enters a foreign market is exporting. The following sections concentrate on this very effective global strategy, which can provide an entrepreneurial firm with a great source of increased sales and profits. But unfortunately, only 1% of all small- and medium-sized businesses do export (Grossman, 2000; U.S. Small Business Administration, Office of International Trade, 1999, p. 6).

EXPORTING

Like all things, natural resources do not last forever; they are being depleted at an alarming rate in the United States. Oil, copper, iron, and many other minerals are being used up, but U.S. industries and consumers depend more and more on other countries for the tin, mercury, platinum, rubber, nickel, titanium, and manganese they need. Each of us consumes imported tea, coffee, cocoa, and spices. Therefore, every year the United States must increase imports to supply domestic needs, to provide the materials for factories and homes, and in turn, through the remittances of payments for these imports, help the nations that sell to us survive and prosper, by providing them with hard currency to buy goods and services from the United States and other countries. Thus world trade creates jobs, and the more trade takes place, the more domestic and international jobs are created.

There are many reasons why U.S. firms should export:

- A decline in the exchange rate of the dollar, resulting in increased purchasing power in many export markets.

- Available productive capacity in the United States to handle manufacturing expansion and a ready supply of workers.

- Lower costs for transportation and communications.

- Reduction in trade barriers.

- Increase in sales and profit.

- Reduced dependence on the domestic market alone.

- Extension of the sales potential and product life of existing products.

- Stabilization of seasonal market/sales fluctuations (U.S. Small Business Administration, 2011).

One cannot conclude, however, that although the United States has a negative trade balance once in a while, this should be a cause for concern. But continuous and significant trade deficits and a suffering export market are major problems, not only because trade deficits increase U.S. international debt that needs to be eventually repaid but also because, even more importantly, large trade deficits create job losses for domestic workers; it has been estimated that $1 billion in exports creates approximately 22,800 jobs (Davis, 1989).

When the dollar declines against most major currencies on a price-adjusted basis and after compensating for country differentials in inflation rates, the United States gains a competitive price advantage because of the dollar's depreciation. Over the same period, exports increase and the U.S. share of world-manufactured trade also increases. A close look at the movement of these two variables over time suggests that there is indeed a causal relationship between the fall of the price-adjusted dollar and an increase in the share of U.S. world trade. An annual inflation rate of 4–6% can cause a price-adjusted currency to remain below parity levels against other currencies.

During the latter part of the 1980s, the falling dollar acted to reduce the trade deficit in two ways: (a) by raising the dollar price of imports and thus slowing domestic demand for foreign products and (b) by lowering the price of U.S. exports in foreign markets. But in the initial stage of this process, the trade balance actually tends to deteriorate temporarily. Economists term this phenomenon the **J-curve effect**. It stems from the fact that import prices respond relatively rapidly to a sustained drop in the dollar, while volume is unaffected. Thus, the import bill, measured in dollars, goes up. Only after the higher tabs begin to slow domestic demand does lower import volume combine with a rise in exports to place the trade balance on an upward course. The initial negative stage of the *J-curve effect* is normally felt over a period of 3 months or so, after a country's currency depreciates significantly, whereas the positive impact on trade flows may be felt only gradually over another 6 to 9 months. Others note that the beneficial effect may be delayed even longer. For example, a 20% drop in the value of the dollar against the yen will probably aggravate the U.S. trade deficit vis-à-vis Japan for at least another quarter before things start getting better (Wolner, 1977, p. 23). The reverse effect or a *reverse J-curve effect* happens when there is an appreciation of the dollar against the euro, for example, because U.S. exports to Europe will continue to rise for at least another quarter before they start slowing down. The appreciated dollar value renders U.S. exports more expensive relative to the period before the dollar's appreciation (Rosenzweig & Koch, 1988).

There is a market somewhere for every product. For every surplus of $1 million in overseas sales, 25 new jobs are created in the United States. Furthermore, some 25% of all exports come from small businesses (Hogan, 1989). Moreover, exports can reduce domestic inflation and unemployment in addition to increasing sales and profits.

The immediate and long-term attractiveness of opportunities overseas has drawn the attention of small firms to foreign markets. These foreign markets often promise a greater return on the invested resources than would be obtained from investing equivalent resources in the U.S. market, especially because the United States is highly competitive in the global export market. More specifically, in spite of the fact that the United States lags behind other countries in terms of the *absolute volume* of exports and imports, a comparison of the dollar value of exports and imports as a *per capita ratio* relative to other countries, indicates that the value of U.S. exports for each person in the country is lower than that of many other countries (International Monetary Fund, 1996). As economists say, the incremental investment is made where it will earn the greatest incremental return. Too few U.S. manufacturers are actively engaged in exports, thus allowing world market volume to go untapped.

Many businesses think they are too small to compete in the world market. In fact, 97% of all exporters are small firms. While 96% of the world's customers reside outside the United States, most U.S. companies do not realize that foreign sales opportunities are now well within reach (U.S. Small Business Administration, 2011).

THE STAGES OF THE EXPORTING PROCESS

A basic theoretical question is whether a firm's export behavior should be considered a multi-activity development process keyed to the firm's position and perspective in this learning process, or whether export behavior should be considered in terms of a single activity model at any given point of time. Most empirical studies illuminated this question by analyzing export data without consideration of possible differences in the firm's export stages. Consequently, cross-sectional studies focusing on perceived serious obstacles or barriers to exporting found seemingly contradictory results: Alexandrides (1971), De la Torre (1972), Simpson (1973), Rao and Weinrauch (1974), Bilkey and Tesar (1975), State of Minnesota (1975), and Tesar (1975) found that non-exporting firms perceived significantly more serious obstacles to exporting than did exporting firms. Others found no relation (Doyle & Schommer, 1976), or an inverse relation, meaning that non-exporters perceived fewer obstacles to exporting than did exporters. The former have no basis for realizing obstacles related to exporting *per se*, and therefore non-exporters listed fewer problems with exporting than did exporting firms (Bilkey, 1978).

In a recent study that examined the perceptions of small-firm owners regarding the *North American Free Trade Agreement* (NAFTA), significant differences in involvement with exporting were reported to depend on the firm's strategy, performance, experience, and size. In other words, small-firm owners with favorable perceptions of NAFTA seem to be associated with significantly different firm characteristics compared with managers with unfavorable perceptions. For example, a differentiation strategy and decentralized structure were more closely associated with favorable perceptions than a cost leadership strategy or a centralized structure, and overall better firm performance is also more closely associated with favorable NAFTA perceptions than with unfavorable ones. These notions might suggest that favorable or unfavorable perceptions toward NAFTA and consequently toward exporting to NAFTA countries and exporting in general, are part of a small firm's institutionalized belief system that dramatically affects their attitude toward investigating the possibilities of exporting and overall export behavior (Pett & Wolff, 2003).

Export models depicting a firm's export behavior as a multi-activity process have generally concentrated on three issues: (a) identifying the major variables involved, (b) specifying the relationship among these variables at any given time, and (c) specifying the dynamics of this relationship. Some have also suggested that the internationalization process of firms follows a learning curve, similar to a series of incremental decisions made when stimuli induce a firm to move to a higher export stage. The experience and learning gained from that stage alters the firm's perceptions, expectations, managerial capacity, profitability, etc., until new stimuli induce a firm to move to a higher stage. This evolution of the exporting process has also been described as follows:

> The exporting process usually begins with an unsolicited inquiry about a company's product. The inquiry often comes from either a domestic export intermediary or directly from a prospective foreign buyer. If the inquiry leads to a profitable sale, it usually leads to sales with other foreign buyers. Then, the manufacturer must decide whether to actively develop his or her export business and appoint an export manager with a small staff. If export sales continue to grow, the next step is to establish a full-service export department similar in structure to the domestic sales department. With more sales growth, the manufacturer may look for additional ways to lower transportation and/or tariff costs such as establishing overseas sales branches and assembly operations (Root, 1977).

The U.S. Small Business Administration, Office of Management, Information and Training and Office of International Trade (1977, pp. 8–9) has similarly identified the following levels of the export development process:

- *Level 1: Export of surplus.* The firm is interested only in overseas sales of surplus products, or lacks resources to fill overseas orders for most products on an ongoing basis.

- *Level 2: Export marketing.* The firm actively solicits overseas sales of existing products and is willing to make limited modifications in its products and marketing procedures to accommodate the requirements of overseas buyers.

- *Level 3: Overseas market development.* The firm makes major modifications in products for export and in marketing practices to better be able to reach buyers abroad.

- *Level 4: Technology development.* The firms develop new products for existing or new overseas markets.

Bilkey & Tesar (1975) formulated a "stage" model to which the following generalized multiple regression equation was applied:

$$A = a + bE - cI + dF + eM$$

Where:

A = the firm's export behavior for the stage in question

E = management's expectations regarding the benefits of exporting after it has been developed

I = the inhibitors (mainly serious infrastructural and institutional obstacles) that management perceives to initiating exporting

F = the facilitators (unsolicited orders, information, subsidies, infrastructural and institutional aids, etc.) that management perceives to initiating exporting

M = the quality and dynamism of the firm's management and organizational characteristics that affect exporting

Lowercase letters are coefficients, and differ at each stage because of the experience gained from the preceding stages. Their model used the following export stages, derived from Rogers's (1962) stages of the export adoption process:

- *Stage One:* The firm is unwilling to export. It would not even fill an unsolicited export order because of apathy, dislike of foreign activities, busy doing other things, etc.

- *Stage Two:* The firm fills unsolicited export orders but does not explore the feasibility of exporting.

- *Stage Three:* The firm explores the feasibility of exporting. This stage may be bypassed if unsolicited export orders are received.

- *Stage Four:* The firm exports experimentally to one or a few markets.

- *Stage Five:* The firm is an experienced exporter to those markets.

- *Stage Six:* The firm explores possibilities of exporting to additional markets.

After classifying 32 small exporting firms into three stages of export development, Vozikis (1981) found significant differences in the overall export problems of small exporters depending on their stage of export development. Furthermore, there were no significant differences in the number of financial export problems that small exporters experience, regardless of their stage of export development. Thus, small exporters always encounter problems with financing their exports, regardless of their stage of export development. Export Stage I comprised non-exporters or exporters who exported by responding to unsolicited orders. Export Stage II included exporters who formally explored the feasibility of exporting or exported to limited markets, while finally, export Stage III comprised experienced exporters.

The research findings outlined in this section lead to a major conclusion regarding the export behavior of firms, namely, that exporting is essentially a developmental process. This process may be conceptualized as a learning sequence involving feedback loops from one stage of the exporting process to another, suggesting that export profiles can be formulated for each stage of exporting development, with potentially great usefulness both theoretical and practical. For example, government export stimulation programs can be tailored to the specific export development stage of the firms to be stimulated, such as experienced exporters versus non-exporters or firms that are just beginning to experiment with exporting.

SMALL-FIRM EXPORTING PROBLEMS

As emphasized above, export management should be keyed to the firm's stage and positioning in the export development process and should also be viewed as a learning process. A firm that has never exported, for example, should first concentrate on gaining basic export learning and experience rather than abruptly undertake major international ventures. A theoretical and practical implication here is that profiles of successful or unsuccessful exporters can serve as a guide to determine an effective export behavior of non-exporters during their export developmental process. This is because international trade involves many administrative problems that have often been obscured by the broader problems of international relations.

Less attention has been given to the specific exporting problems of entrepreneurs and managers, who must try to carry on their business whether political, financial, or economic conditions are entirely to their liking or not. While it is essential that for greater success an exporter should know the nature of these conditions and the progress of government political and trade development overall, the immediate problems of a business enterprise are those involved in attaining the purposes of every business enterprise, that is, making a profit. Following the example of the effective export behavior of successful exporters while avoiding the export behavior of unsuccessful ones at specific stages of export development allows ventures pursuing exporting to prevent problems usually associated with international trade.

The problems of exporting include, of course, all of the problems of domestic trade complicated by the fact that every foreign transaction must comply with the laws of two jurisdictions. Therefore, adjustments must be made to accommodate the greater differences between buyer and seller than those in domestic transactions. These differences and problems could be exaggerated for exporters who are in relatively early exporting stages of development. The export problems that small firms usually encounter throughout their export development process are listed in Exhibit 15.2 and are classified according to their functional area (Vozikis, 1981).

The most frequently encountered problem that small exporters experience regardless of function or stage of development is that of *foreign market research,* a marketing problem reported by 97% of the firms surveyed. A close second was *lack of export contacts,* a management problem for 94% of the firms. The least frequently mentioned problems overall were *lack of product modification capacity* and *lack of product service/parts capacity,* both operations problems, as well as, *"insurance,"* a marketing problem. Only 19% of the surveyed firms experienced these three problems (Vozikis, 1981).

In another study that investigated the elements necessary to stimulate small business exporting, Pricer (1980) surveyed 329 manufacturing firms, representing 14 standard industrial classification (SIC) codes. The results indicated that the greatest barrier to exporting was the fact that owners and managers of these firms had little or no knowledge of international trade and the potential benefits that might be derived from it. The second greatest barrier to exporting was the inability to overcome the fear of risk and loss. Pricer's study recommended insurance legislation that directly lessens the risk to small exporters when marketing abroad.

Perritt and Prakash (1980) also studied the many reasons that small firms lag in exports. They found that small-firm exporters have had very few foreign experiences that serve to stimulate exports. They are usually bewildered by export regulations, lack information on foreign markets, and, typically, have not had profitable exporting attempts previously. For most of the entrepreneurs surveyed, the decision to export was not part of the strategic plan of their firm. Rather, if exporting was undertaken at all, it was initiated by chance, through an unsolicited order, through a plant visit by a vacationing prospective foreign customer, or through a contact made during a foreign vacation. The study also found that conferences and seminars trying to attract small-firm owners who are already involved in foreign trade do "preach to the

Exhibit 15.2   Small-Firm Functional Export Development Problems

Management
1. Lack of previous export experience/apathy
2. Lack of export contacts
3. Lack of export personnel training
4. Legal problems

Production/Operations
1. Lack of product modification capacity
2. Lack of product service/parts capacity
3. Lack of adequate production capacity

Marketing
1. Foreign market research
2. Pricing
3. Sale terms and documentation
4. Distribution
5. Promotion
6. Competition
7. Shipping
8. Packaging
9. Insurance

Finance
1. Lack of export capital
2. Lack of working capital
3. Payment terms problems

choir" and do not appear to stimulate additional exports by new exporting firms. Similarly, banks with international trade departments have a rather passive role in international trade development by focusing their efforts on current, rather than potential, exporting customers. Moreover, the dismal state of international trade involvement by small firms is also due to the fact that the personnel required to staff international trade efforts are not available in great numbers and because few universities offer international business programs (Perritt & Prakash, 1980). Finally, another study investigating foreign trade opportunities for small firms found that the major reasons that many small firms do not attempt to market their product overseas are, in order of importance: lack of market information, lack of qualified marketing people, and lack of resources and capital. Despite efforts by federal and state governments to implement numerous programs for promoting exports, the evidence clearly indicates that these programs have not been successful (Sood, 1980).

However, although small firms are usually at a disadvantage when competing for exports because of a lack of expertise involving complex government regulations and financial transactions, and because managerial and technical expertise is lacking, they also have certain advantages in serving foreign markets. Potential exporters do not have to be on the *Fortune* 500 list before they can be effective exporters; the same factors that enable the small firms to compete effectively with larger firms domestically are also present in exporting, in terms of greater market sensitivity and faster response time. Competition overseas is no tougher than competition in the United States, and small firms enjoy the same advantages over large firms there as they do here. In fact, many of the barriers to exporting are not insurmountable, especially because small firms can get free, but expert, advice from the *Department of Commerce's* (DOC's) *International Trade Administration* (ITA) field offices, or from trade and industry associations, which can answer most inquiries about how to get started or problems with exporting.

EXPORT TRADE ASSISTANCE

A small firm's limited capacity to acquire information and use sources to explore its potential for exporting is a major factor explaining the low involvement and performance of small firms in the export markets. Effective small-business export performance is determined by the firm's general competitive strategy, which in turn is explained by the ability of the specific firm to acquire and manage foreign market information and assistance (Julien & Ramangalahy, 2003). A very effective and efficient source of export assistance is the DOC. For a small fee per country, the DOC will produce a survey of the market potential for a particular product and a list of possible contacts, suppliers, or retailers (Watterson, 1981). However, exports would increase if the government would do more for small firms and develop an "export-oriented mentality" among small firms, rather than just hold foreign trade seminars and distribute brochures and publications. A single positive export experience by entrepreneurs produces a shift to a more positive view of the export risk factors and the fears of non-payment, the pirating of technology or process, or other possibly negative outcomes of export activity (Roy & Simpson, 1981).

Given a national policy that seeks to expand the export activity of small- and medium-sized manufacturing, the reorganization and consolidation of federal export efforts into the DOC has created an information and advisory system that is actually, not just theoretically, useful to small- and medium-sized U.S. firms trying to compete in the world market. With the help of the *Foreign Commercial Service*, the *Trade Opportunities* program, and the computerized *Worldwide Information and Trade System*, U.S. firms have a chance to obtain a share of the market in international government procurement business opened up by multilateral trade negotiations (Pattison, 1981).

State governments also recognize the importance that exporting has for their local economies. Every state has responded by creating an international trade division that promotes internationalization of small- and medium-sized firms. For example, while the federal government provides a 15% exemption on profit earned from exports for small businesses, the state of Delaware also offers special incentives for small businesses to become involved in exporting through EMCs. Export assistance activity at whatever level—federal, state, and/or local—must focus on the decision-making process in the small firm, concentrating on acquainting the CEO with actual export experience. Too often, the presumption is that by familiarizing the CEO with the mechanics or the "how to" aspects of exporting, the entrepreneur's decision to export has been positively affected. Dealing effectively with the attitudinal factor, however, should provide more substantive results, because after the initial export experience, it is quite common for risk to abate: costs become apparently lower than anticipated, and profits generally become higher than anticipated, thus creating positive experiences and motivating circumstances for entrepreneurial firms to continue their further experimentation with exporting.

To succeed in exporting, the most profitable international markets for the firm's products or services must first be identified. Without proper guidance and assistance, however, this process can be time-consuming and costly, particularly for a small firm. The U.S. federal government, state governments, as well as private-sector trade associations, exporters' associations, and even foreign governments, offer low-cost and easily accessible resources to simplify foreign market research.

Federal and State Government Resources

Many government programs and staff are dedicated to helping the small-business owner assess whether the product or service is ready to compete in a foreign market.

The U.S. Small Business Administration (SBA)

Many new-to-export small firms have found the counseling services provided by the SBA's *Service Corps of Retired Executives* (SCORE) particularly helpful. Two other SBA-sponsored programs are available to small firms needing management and export advice: *Small Business Development Centers* (SBDCs) and *Small Business Institutes* (SBIs) affiliated with colleges and universities throughout the United States. SBDCs offer counseling, training, and research assistance on all aspects of small-business management, while the SBI programs provide small-business owners with intensive management counseling from qualified business students who are supervised by faculty. They provide advice on a wide range of management challenges facing small businesses, including finding the best foreign markets for particular products or services.

The U.S. Department of Commerce

The U.S. DOC *International Trade Administration* (ITA) is a valuable source of advice and information. In ITA offices throughout the country, international trade specialists can help a small firm locate the best foreign markets for its products. Oklahoma exporter OK-1 Manufacturing Co. has found the foreign market research available through the ITA extremely useful: "The Oklahoma District ITA office prepared a market research study to determine whether we should export our fitness accessory items to Japan," according to Sherry Teigen, export manager at OK-1 Manufacturing Co. Today, the company exports to Japan in addition to 20 other countries. Since it began exporting, the company staff has grown by 75, and Sherry's husband, OK-1's President, Roger Teigen, won the SBA Exporter of the Year award.

District Export Councils (DECs)

These councils are another useful ITA-sponsored resource. The 51 *District Export Councils* located around the United States are comprised of 1,800 executives with experience in international trade who volunteer to help small firms export. Council members come from banks, manufacturing companies, law offices, trade associations, state and local agencies, and educational institutions. They draw upon their experience to encourage, educate, counsel, and guide potential, new, and seasoned exporters in their individual marketing pursuits.

The U.S. and Foreign Commercial Service (US&FCS)

The U.S. and Foreign Commercial Service (US&FCS) helps U.S. firms compete more effectively in the global marketplace, with trade specialists in 69 U.S. cities and 70 countries worldwide. US&FCS offices provide information on foreign markets, agent/distributor location services, trade leads, and counseling on business opportunities, trade barriers, and prospects abroad.

The U.S. Department of Agriculture (USDA)

In case of an agricultural product, the USDA *Foreign Agricultural Service* (FAS), with posts in 80 embassies and consulates worldwide, can obtain specific overseas market information for the product. It also maintains sector specialists in the United States to monitor foreign markets for specific U.S. agricultural products.

State Commerce and Economic Development Offices

State commerce and economic development offices also have international trade specialists to provide export assistance.

Port Authorities

Port Authorities are also offer a wealth of export information. Although traditionally associated with transportation services, many port authorities around the country have expanded their services to provide export training programs and foreign-marketing research assistance. For example, the New York–New Jersey Port Authority provides extensive services to exporters, including XPORT, a full-service export trading company.

Online Resources

- "Take your Business Global: An Introduction to Exporting" is a free comprehensive training course is available at www.sba.gov/training.

- Exporting experts and successful small business exporters share their knowledge via podcasts and videos available at www.sba.gov/tools/audiovideo/index.html.

- Resources from across the U.S. government including market research, trade leads, and information about export finance are available at www.export.gov.

Private-Sector Resources

In addition to government-supported resources, private-sector organizations can also provide invaluable assistance. *Exporters' associations, world trade centers, import-export clubs,* and organizations such as the *American Association of Exporters and Importers* and the *Small Business Exporter's Association* can all help with foreign market research.

Trade Associations

The National Federation of International Trade Associations lists more than 150 organizations in the United States to help new-to-export small firms enter international markets. Many of these associations maintain libraries, databanks, and established relationships with foreign governments to assist in exporting efforts. More than 5,000 trade and professional associations currently operate in the United States; many actively promote international trade activities for their members. For example, the Telecommunications Industry Association is just one association that frequently helps members obtain leads for overseas trade missions and monitors the pulse of foreign market conditions around the globe. Whatever the product or service, a trade association probably exists that can help the small firm obtain information on domestic and foreign markets.

Chambers of Commerce

State chambers and local chambers of commerce, especially those located in major industrial areas, often employ international trade specialists who gather information on markets abroad (U.S. Small Business Administration, 2001).

Other Sources of Information and Assistance

Other sources of information in general are the following:

1. *Commerce America Magazine,* published by the U.S. Department of Commerce, prepares bi-weekly reports on current activity and developments in foreign and domestic commerce.
2. Banks with international departments.

3. Marine insurance brokers.

4. Foreign trade zones.

5. U.S. export factors.

6. Overseas travel assistance is available for American business travelers through the U.S. Department of Commerce and U.S. Foreign Service posts overseas.

EXPORT STRATEGY DEVELOPMENT

The development of an effective export strategy should consist of the following interrelated steps that will sequentially contribute valuable input to the successful implementation of a firm's exporting plans:

1. Analyze export potential by evaluating the firm's exporting strengths and weaknesses.

2. Analyze export foreign market research by evaluating the exporting environment's threats and opportunities.

3. Locate export intermediaries, foreign representatives, and foreign buyers.

4. Qualify potential foreign representatives and buyers.

5. Evaluate export financial considerations.

6. Evaluate export legal considerations.

7. Evaluate export shipping and documentation considerations.

EXPORT POTENTIAL ANALYSIS

A determination of the product's export potential is the first step in the process of identifying an effective export strategy. A clear understanding of the firm's and the product's export strengths and weaknesses will enable the entrepreneur to select the types of information that are essential for a clear assessment of the firm's export potential. This is undertaken by taking the following steps:

1. Understanding the significance of exporting as an alternative to domestic activities.

2. Assessing the ability to undertake export activities by taking stock of the firm's resources and their current and projected rate of utilization.

3. Laying a foundation for isolating and evaluating overseas sales opportunities by analyzing product lines, product functions, features, and designs related to customer needs and characteristics, as well as the cases when the product or service may have to be modified.

Only by careful assessment of the firm's export strengths and weaknesses is it possible to evaluate the potential of overseas opportunities. A relatively small number of firms may find out through such as assessment that there is no point in looking for opportunities abroad, while most others may wish to move further toward fully exploring their export potential abroad. The firm's analysis of exporting in terms strengths and weaknesses that will subsequently determine its export potential should include the factors listed by business function in Exhibit 15.3.

Exhibit 15.3 Small-Firm Export Potential Analysis Factors

Finance
1. Availability of capital
2. Cash flow

Production
1. Product uses
2. Product features (color, quality, dimensions packaging, uniqueness)
3. Available production capacity
4. Product manufacturers (domestic, foreign)
5. Product modification capacity
6. Location
7. Product training/maintenance

Marketing
1. Pricing
2. Packaging
3. Transportation
4. Risk Insurance
5. Quotation
6. Terms of sale: cost, insurance, freight (CIF), free on board (FOB), etc.
7. Method of payment
8. Preferred distribution channels

Previous export management experience
1. Export contacts
2. Trade organization involvement
3. Export agency contacts
4. Export literature knowledge

FOREIGN EXPORT MARKET RESEARCH

The objective of foreign export market research is the selection, from among potential customers located in the many countries throughout the world, of a small group of attractive markets and finally one or two markets to be considered for more detailed analysis. This selection is important because it helps ensure that the exporter is considering the most attractive opportunities at the very outset. A detailed analysis is necessary before a final decision can be made to sell and a marketing strategy can be planned. Careful selection helps to ensure that this detailed analysis will not be wasted on a market that later turns out to offer only limited opportunities. The U.S. Department of Commerce suggests the following guidelines and kinds of information to be determined before a small firm seeks export assistance from government sources:

1. Accurate classification of the product or service in Standard Industry Classification (SIC) codes.

2. Identification of the largest and fastest growing markets and countries for the firm's product.

3. Identification of the most penetrable markets for the firm's product.

4. Identification of specific export markets.

Product Classification

The **Standard Industrial Classification** (SIC) **code** is the system by which the United States government classifies its goods and services. Knowing the proper code for a product or service can be useful in collecting and analyzing data available in the United States. Data originating from outside the United States or information tabulated by international organizations are organized under the *Standard International Trade Classification* (SITC) system, or the *Harmonized System* (HS)—which is another method of classifying products for export—which may assign a different code to the same product or service. Knowing the HS classification number, and the SIC and SITC codes for the product, is essential for obtaining domestic and international trade and tariff information. DOC and USDA trade specialists can assist in identifying the codes for your products. The *U.S. Bureau of the Census* (USBC) can help identify the product's HS number.

Identification of the Largest and Fastest Growing Markets and Countries

At this stage of the research, the entrepreneur should consider where the firm's domestic competitors are exporting. Trade associations can often provide data on where companies in a particular industry sector are exporting their products. The three largest markets for U.S. products are Canada, Japan, and Mexico. Yet these countries may not be the largest markets for the firm's product.

Three key U.S. government databases can identify those countries that represent significant export potential for a product: the SBA's *Automated Trade Locator Assistance System* (SBAtlas), *Foreign Trade Report* (FT925), and the *U.S. Department of Commerce's National Trade Data Bank* (NTDB).

SBA's Automated Trade Locator Assistance System (SBAtlas)

The **SBA's Automated Trade Locator Assistance System** (SBAtlas) database is offered only by the U.S. Small Business Administration and provides current market information to SBA clients on world markets suitable for their products and services. This valuable research tool supplies small business exporters with information about where their products are being bought and sold and which countries offer the largest markets. The Country Reports detail products imported and exported by various foreign nations. Data are supplied by the DOC's Census Bureau, as well as by member nations of the United Nations. This information can be obtained through a SCORE counselor at the SBA District and Regional Offices and at SBDCs and SBIs. This service is free to small businesses.

Foreign Trade Report FT925

The **Foreign Trade Report FT925** is a database that gives a monthly, country-specific breakdown of imports and exports by SITC code. Available by subscription from the Government Printing Office, the FT925 can also be obtained through DOC's ITA offices.

National Trade Data Bank (NTDB)

The **National Trade Data Bank (NTDB)** is a database that contains more than 100,000 U.S. government documents on export promotion and international economic information. With the NTDB, the entrepreneur can conduct databank searches on country and product information. The NTDB can be purchased by subscription and used with a CD-ROM reader, or it can be used at Federal libraries throughout the United States. DOC's ITA offices also conduct specific NTDB searches to meet a firm's foreign market research needs.

Once the largest markets for a firm's products are identified, the fastest growing markets need to also be determined, in terms of demographic patterns and cultural considerations that will ultimately affect market penetration. Several publications provide geographic and demographic statistical information pertinent to a firm's product: *The World Factbook,* produced by the Central Intelligence Agency; *World Population,* published by DOC's Census Bureau; *The World Bank Atlas,* available from the World Bank; and the *International Trade Statistics Yearbook* of the United Nations. Volume Two of this U.N. publication, which is available at many libraries, lists international demand for commodities over a 5-year period.

Identification of the Most Penetrable Markets and Countries

The few prospective foreign markets for the firm's product that were identified and targeted as the largest and fastest growing need to be examined in detail in terms of their degree of penetrability. At this stage the following questions need to be asked:

- How does the quality of the product or service compare with that of goods already available in the strategic target foreign markets?

- What is its value concept?

- How competitive is the firm's price in the strategic target markets that are being considered?

- Who are the major customers?

- Who buys, how many, when, how, and where?

Answering these questions may seem overwhelming at first, but many resources are available to help select which foreign markets are most conducive to selling the firm's product. The ITA can link the firm with specific foreign markets. ITA offices are part of the US&FCS and communicate directly with FCS officers working in U.S. embassies worldwide. FCS staff and in-country market research firms produce in-depth reports on selected products and industries that can answer many questions regarding foreign market penetration.

A firm can also order a comparison-shopping service report through ITA district offices. The report is a low-cost way to conduct research without having to leave the United States. Additionally, SBA's and DOC's *Export Legal Assistance Network* (ELAN) provides new exporters with answers to their initial legal questions. Local attorneys volunteer on a one-time basis to counsel small businesses to address their export-related legal questions. These attorneys can address questions pertaining to contract negotiations, licensing, credit collections procedures, and documentation. There is no charge for this one-time service, available through SBA or DOC district offices.

The *Trade Opportunities Program* (TOP) of the DOC can also furnish U.S. small businesses with trade leads from foreign companies that want to buy or represent their products or services. These trade leads are available in both electronic or printed form from the *DOC.* Participating companies must pay a modest fee to gain access to this service. Other important issues about the target foreign markets need to be explored:

- Political risk considerations.

- Cultural environment considerations.

- Product modification needs, such as packaging or labeling that will make the product more "exportable."

- Market barriers, such as tariffs or import restrictions.

Identifying market-specific issues is easily accomplished by contacting foreign government representatives in the United States. Commercial posts of foreign governments located within embassies and consulates can assist the firm in obtaining specific market and product information.

American Chambers of Commerce (AmChams) abroad can also be an invaluable resource. As affiliates of the United States Chamber of Commerce, 61 AmChams, located in 55 countries, collect and disseminate extensive information on foreign markets. While membership fees are usually required, the small investment can be worth it for the information received. Another fundamental question to ask country-specific experts is what market barriers, such as tariffs or import restrictions (sometimes referred to as non-tariff barriers), exist for the firm's product. Tariffs are taxes imposed on imported goods, and in many cases, they raise the price of imported goods to the level of domestic goods. Often tariffs become barriers to imported products because the amount of tax imposed makes it impossible for exporters to profitably sell their products in foreign markets. To determine the rate of tariff duty, the firm needs to identify the *Harmonized Tariff* section, which corresponds to the product to be exported. Each country has its own schedule of duty rates corresponding to the section of the *Harmonized System of Tariff Nomenclature, I-XXII.*

Non-tariff barriers in contrast are laws or regulations that a country enacts to protect domestic industries against foreign competition. Such non-tariff barriers may include subsidies for domestic goods, import quotas, or regulations on import quality. Specialists at *U.S. Trade Representative* (USTR) should be consulted on trade barriers.

Identification of the Specific Export Target Markets

Once the largest, fastest growing, and most penetrable markets for the product or service have been identified, the firm must then define its export strategy by not choosing too many markets, but rather two or three foreign markets. One market may be the test case, and then the firm can move on to secondary markets as its export learning curve develops. Focusing on regional, geographic clusters of countries can also be more cost effective than choosing markets scattered around the globe (U.S. Small Business Administration, 2001).

LOCATING EXPORT INTERMEDIARIES, FOREIGN REPRESENTATIVES, AND BUYERS

The objective of locating export intermediaries, and/or foreign representatives, and buyers, is to guide the firm through the necessary steps for establishing proper export channels of distribution. A poor selection of distribution channels undermines all of the careful work that has preceded this step. A basic distinction should be made between direct and indirect exporting. Direct exporting places the firm in direct contact with customers and channels of distribution located in foreign countries. Indirect exporting involves the use of intermediaries who assume responsibility for all or part of the firm's export sales. A combination of direct and indirect exporting is possible and sometimes desirable.

A variety of intermediaries and representatives are available to assist small firms with indirect exporting. They have the networks of contacts, extensive knowledge of local customs and markets, and experience in international trade to market products effectively and efficiently, and account for roughly 10% of all U.S. export activity.

Export Management Companies (EMCs)

For commissions ranging from approximately 10 to 20% of sales, an EMC provides a wide variety of services, including market research, distribution, financing, advertising, shipping, translation, and documentation. Basically, they leave little for the manufacturer to do except get the product to the dock or airport for shipment overseas. There are more than 1,000 EMCs, mostly located near seaports or other major exporting centers, and they typically specialize in one or two types of products, such as consumer goods, computer products, or machine tools. A number of EMC local associations can help entrepreneurs find an EMC for their needs, as can the *Federation of International Trade Associations* (FITA) website at www.fita.org/emc_list_all.html.

Export Trading Companies (ETCS)

The *Export Trading Company Act* was signed into law on October 8, 1982, in an attempt to duplicate the success of important vehicles throughout the history of international trade, such as the Hudson Bay Company and the East India Company in the 1600s. The underlying purpose of this act was to promote and encourage the increase of exports of United States products and services to foreign markets by allowing the banding together of small- and medium-sized U.S. firms to form export trading companies to buy and sell products in a number of countries and offer a variety of services to their clients, so they can enter the international arena. Under the act, certificates are granted to export trading companies that provide them with protection against U.S. antitrust laws for certain export activities that do not affect domestic commerce. However, U.S. exporters are not exempted from foreign antitrust laws ("Interim Regulations," 1983).

Manufacturer's Export Agents

Manufacturer's export agents act as international sales representatives in a limited number of markets for non-competing domestic firms on a commission basis, for a short term and for a specific market.

Export Brokers

Export brokers operate a little like a real estate broker, receiving a fee only after a sale is generated, usually about 10% of the overseas delivery price. Unlike *EMCs* and export research firms, however, the broker assumes all up-front marketing costs and does not charge a retainer in advance.

Export Merchants

In contrast, **export merchants** buy and obtain title of goods from domestic manufacturers and then market them in foreign markets, often carrying competing lines from a variety of manufacturers.

Resident Buying Offices

These offices are set up by foreign governments or foreign privately owned companies as a means to open up shop on U.S. soil so that they can buy U.S. goods for distribution in their own country. Selling to them is like selling to a domestic firm because the resident buying office handles all the details of exporting.

Some firms may find that the nature of their products is such that it will be difficult, unnecessary, and/or costly to use intermediaries on a continuing basis. For such firms, an export program may be carried out through direct exporting using the domestic sales force, or foreign distributors and representatives. Foreign distributors and representatives handle all the marketing, distribution, and service functions in a foreign country, typically under an exclusive contract giving them distribution rights. For domestic small firms who export directly to the foreign distributors, this provides the benefits of intimate knowledge and expertise of the foreign market, as well as sales and service support.

The efforts to identify foreign representatives and foreign buyers should center on implementing the original export strategy and marketing plan developed during the detailed analysis of the target export market. The need for continuing evaluation, research, periodic visits, and close support of the activities of the distributors and/or representatives cannot be stressed enough. Foreign export representatives and distributors as well as direct buyers can be located through the following avenues.

Advertisements in Trade Journals

Many small businesses report that instead of them looking for foreign buyers, foreign buyers often find them. An ad placed in a trade journal or a listing in the DOC's *Commercial News USA* can often yield innumerable inquiries from abroad. *Commercial News USA* is a catalog-magazine featuring U.S. products, and distributed to 125,000 business readers in more than 140 countries around the world and to more than 650,000 *Economic Bulletin Board* users in 18 countries. Fees vary according to the size of the listing. Many U.S. companies have had enormous success in locating buyers through this vehicle.

Participation in Catalog and Video/Catalog Exhibitions

Catalog and video/catalog exhibitions are another low-cost method of advertising a firm's product abroad. The firm's products are introduced to potential partners at major international trade shows, and the entrepreneur may never have to leave the United States. For a small fee, US&FCS officers in embassies can show a firm's catalogs or videos to interested agents, distributors, and other potential buyers. A number of private-sector publications also offer U.S. companies the opportunity to display their products in catalogs sent abroad. They include *Johnston International's Export Magazine*, *The Journal of Commerce*, and the *Thomas Publishing Company's American Literature Review*.

Pursuit of Trade Leads

Rather than wait for potential foreign customers to contact the firm, another option is to search out foreign companies looking for the particular product the firm produces. Trade leads from international companies seeking to buy or represent U.S. products are gathered by US&FCS officers worldwide and are distributed through the DOC's *Economic Bulletin Board*. There is a nominal annual fee and a connect-time charge. The leads also are published daily in *The Journal of Commerce* under the heading *Trade Opportunities Program* and in other commercial news outlets. Another source of trade leads is the *World Trade Centers* (WTC) network, where a firm can advertise its product or service on an electronic bulletin board transmitted globally. If the product is agricultural, the U.S. Department of Agriculture (*USDA*) Foreign Agricultural Service (*FAS*) disseminates trade leads collected by their 80 overseas offices. These leads may be accessed through the *AgExport FAX* polling system, the *AgExport Trade Leads Bulletin*, *The Journal of Commerce*, or on several electronic bulletin boards.

Exhibits at Trade Shows

Trade shows also are another means of locating foreign buyers. DOC's *Foreign Buyer Program* certifies a certain number of U.S. trade shows each year. DOC commercial officers actively recruit foreign buyers, and special services, such as meeting areas and translators, are provided to encourage and facilitate private business discussions. International trade shows are another excellent way to market a firm's product abroad, and going to a foreign trade show just once is not enough. Through a certification program, DOC also supports about 80 international fairs and exhibitions held in markets worldwide, where U.S. exhibitors receive pre- and post-event assistance. The *USDA FAS* sponsors approximately an additional 15 major shows overseas each year.

Participation in Trade Missions

Participating in overseas trade missions is yet another way to meet foreign buyers. Public/ private trade missions are often organized cooperatively by federal and state international trade agencies and trade associations. Arrangements are handled for the firm so that the process of meeting prospective partners or buyers is simplified. *Matchmaker trade delegations* are DOC-sponsored trade missions to select foreign markets. A company is matched carefully with potential agents and distributors interested in the company's product. Being properly prepared for the kinds of inquiries a firm might encounter on overseas trade missions is important. The *SBA* offers pre-mission training sessions through its district offices and the SCORE program, labeled "How to Participate Profitably in Trade Missions."

Contacts with Multilateral Development Banks

In developing countries, multilateral development banks such as the World Bank, the African, Asian, Inter-American Development Banks, and the *European Bank for Reconstruction and Development* often fund large infrastructure projects. *Multilateral Development Bank* (MDB) projects often represent extensive opportunities for U.S. small businesses to compete for project work. Development bank projects can be an excellent way to start exporting, and DOC estimates that MDB projects could amount to at least $15 billion dollars in annual export contracts for U.S. businesses. Many U.S. small-business exporters have benefited from large MDB projects through subcontracting awards from larger corporations. From their Washington, D.C., headquarters, many MDBs hold monthly seminars to acquaint businesses with the MDB procurement process. Additionally, the DOC's *Office of Major Projects* can be of assistance in identifying contracting and subcontracting opportunities (U.S. Small Business Administration, 2001).

QUALIFYING POTENTIAL FOREIGN REPRESENTATIVES AND BUYERS

Once a potential foreign buyer or representative is located, the next step is to qualify them by reputation and financial position, and as much information as possible needs to be obtained. The following are a few sample questions that need to be asked:

- What is the company's history and what are the qualifications and backgrounds of the principal officers?
- Does the company have adequate trained personnel, facilities, and resources to devote to the business?
- What is their current sales volume?
- What is the size of their inventory?
- How will they market and promote the firm's product: retail, wholesale, or directly to the consumer?
- Which territories or areas of the country do they cover?

- Do they have other U.S. or foreign clients?
- Are any of these clients competitors?
- Can references be obtained from several current clients?
- What types of customers do they serve?
- Do they publish a catalog?
- What is their sales force?

When this background information is collected and the entrepreneur feels comfortable about proceeding with the individual representative or buyer, then a credit report needs to be obtained about the representative's or buyer's financial position. DOC's *World Trade Data Reports* (WTDRs) compiled by *US&FCS* officers are available from local district ITA offices. A WTDR can usually provide an in-depth profile of the prospective company under investigation.

There are also several commercial services for qualifying potential partners, such as *Dun & Bradstreet's Business Identification Service* and *Graydon* reports. U.S. banks, their correspondent banks or branches overseas, and foreign banks located in the United States can also provide specific financial information (U.S. Small Business Administration, 2001).

EXPORT FINANCIAL CONSIDERATIONS

The financial considerations of international trade should include the following:

1. Methods of receiving payment
   - Cash in advance
   - Open account
   - Sight and time drafts
   - Letters of credit
2. Checking on the financial standing of foreign firms
   - World Traders Data Reports available through the U.S. DOC
   - The firm's bank
   - Commercial credit reporting agencies
3. Insurance
   - Marine insurance to protect goods in transit
   - *Overseas Private Investment Corporation* (OPIC), a self-supporting government agency offering political risk insurance and financial services to U.S. firms interested in investing in developing countries
   - *Foreign Credit Insurance Association* (FCIA), commercial and political risk insurance on U.S. exports
4. Financing
   - Export–import bank assistance with financing U.S. exports

EXPORT LEGAL CONSIDERATIONS

The legal considerations of international trade should concern

1. Special legal treaties and legal provisions

   - *Western Hemisphere Trading Corporation (WHTC):* Corporate tax reduction for exporting in countries of the Western Hemisphere.

   - *Possessions corporation*: Tax relief for firms establishing operations in U.S. possessions, primarily Puerto Rico or American Samoa.

   - *Webb-Pomerene Act*: Provides a limited exemption from antitrust laws for export associations.

2. Sales and agency agreements

3. Patents and trademarks

EXPORT SHIPPING AND DOCUMENTATION CONSIDERATIONS

Information on shipping and documentation can be obtained from the following sources:

1. *Ocean carriers and airlines:* Data on freight rates, packing, schedules. Some lines offer worldwide marketing services.

2. *Foreign freight forwarders:* Experts in documentation and shipping that handle all details of movement of goods from the manufacturing plant to the foreign destination and licensed by the Federal Maritime Commission.

3. *District offices of the U.S. Department of Commerce:* These offices provide

   - Export licenses
   - Shippers' export declaration
   - Foreign trade regulations

4. *American International Traders Register (AITR):* A computer registry of American firms engaged in or interested in exporting and used to channel marketing and other useful information matching the interests of the registrant.

5. *Preparation of quotations and terms of sale*: This involves

   - Pro-forma invoice
   - Foreign trade definitions
   - Steps in handling an order

6. *Preparation of the commercial invoice and other export documents.*

CONCLUSION

Many small firms first become involved in exporting by receiving unsolicited orders from overseas. The decision to become involved in exporting is one of managerial viewpoint: does management view the unsolicited order as an opportunity or a problem? Many small firms are content with their domestic markets and do not wish to accept the challenge that export markets offer. There are exporting stages of development the same way there are organizational stages of development. Each stage is characterized by differing problems relating to the stage of development *per se*, and the culture and business practices of the foreign country where exporting takes place, but through each stage of development, the exporter becomes more involved and more experienced with exporting. Compared to large international firms, small exporters have the advantage of flexibility with which they meet a changing market and react faster by quickly adapting to foreign client needs. The small exporter also has the advantage of extensive federal government and private sector assistance. Additionally, through intermediaries and foreign representatives, they can develop a very effective indirect exporting strategy if a direct one is not feasible. Finally, small exporters should develop an exporting strategy to identify the following:

- The firm's exporting strengths and weaknesses
- The exporting environment's threats and opportunities
- Export intermediaries, foreign representatives, and foreign buyers
- Qualified potential foreign representatives and buyers.
- Financial considerations
- Legal considerations
- Shipping and documentation considerations.

It is quite obvious that elaborate market research and preparation is the best way for a small firm to target an export market. Some additional international trade definitions are presented in Appendix A.

Website Information

Topic	Web Address	Description
Export trade assistance	http://www.ita.doc.gov/	Home page for the U.S. Department of Commerce.
Small-firm exporters	http://www.sbea.org/	The homepage for the Small Business Exporter's Association. Gives many sources of exporting information for small firms.
International growth strategies for small firms: e-commerce websites	http://export.gov/sellingonline/eg_main_020795.asp	Gives types, categories, and examples of e-commerce websites.

Key Terms

Balance of payments (BOP): The balance that reflects not only the visible merchandise trade balance of exports and imports, which is the largest single component of total international payments, but also the invisible trade of all of a country's transactions.

Capital and financial account: Financial asset transactions of inflows and outflows of direct investment for purchases or sales of companies, and portfolio investment for exchanges of financial claims on stock, bonds, loans, in exchange for other financial claims or money.

Current account: Real asset transactions inflows and outflows during the current period for goods, services, official grants, and foreign aid from one country to another, private remittances to and from foreigners, and investment income to and from foreign sources.

Export brokers: They assume all up-front marketing costs and do not charge a retainer in advance.

Export merchants: Export merchants buy and obtain title of goods from domestic manufacturers and then market them themselves in foreign markets.

Foreign licensing: Entering foreign markets by transferring turnkey technology processes to customers overseas in return for royalties.

Foreign Trade Report FT925: A database that gives a monthly, country-specific breakdown of imports and exports by SITC code.

International entrepreneurship: New and innovative activities that have the goal of value creation and growth in business organizations across national borders.

J-curve effect: Raising the dollar price of imports and thus slowing domestic demand for foreign products, by lowering the price of U.S. exports in foreign markets.

Joint ventures: Domestic and foreign alliances of two or more small firms for the purpose of exporting goods and services abroad.

Manufacturer's export agents: They act as international sales representatives in a limited number of markets for non-competing domestic firms on a commission basis.

National Trade Data Bank (NTDB): A database that contains more than 100,000 U.S. government documents on export promotion and international economic information.

Proliferation of e-commerce: A company can ship everywhere from anywhere.

SBA's Automated Trade Locator Assistance System: This database provides current market information to SBA clients on world markets suitable for their products and services.

Standard Industrial Classification Code: The system by which the U.S. government classifies its goods and services.

Trade balance: The measure of the balance between a country's merchandise exports against its imports.

Review Questions

1. Explain some of the potential problems with operating in overseas markets.

2. List and briefly explain the four levels of the export development process.

3. Why is foreign market research considered to be one of the determining factors when deciding to export goods to foreign markets?

4. Briefly discuss some financial, legal, and shipping and documentation considerations impacting international trade.

5. Identify some strengths and weaknesses of small firms as far as their export potential analysis is concerned.

6. Exporting agricultural products is blossoming into a huge industry. For example, many California farms are beginning to explore exportation of nuts since the international demand is continually growing. Many companies have begun brokering export (freight forwarding) services catered to agricultural exports. Please identify three such companies who handle the exportation of agricultural products to markets other than the United States. What are the primary crops they are exporting? Where are they export the products? Are there any common destinations or products?

Reflections from the Front Lines of LifeGuard America

We have created an element of our long-term strategy for international expansion. As mentioned previously, we will need to spend significant research and development activity to completely understand all the implications that come with moving offshore. The most notable are the government laws and regulations associated with organ transplantation and the structure an American company must have to provide medical logistics services in foreign countries.

We have a primary goal to explore the franchise potential of LifeGuard America worldwide. LifeGuard Canada, LifeGuard Europe, Asia, and South America are all potential extensions as these countries continue to develop and refine their own national organ transplant programs. Looking further ahead, we feel that by the first quarter of 2007, LifeGuard America will be in a suitable position for expansion into Canada and possibly Europe using the experience gained during its first 4 years. We must make it work first at home and we must understand all the peculiarities and possible pitfalls before we begin to think in terms of expanding outside the four walls of the United States.

Discussion Questions on LifeGuard America

1. Do you believe there is an international market for LifeGuard America?

2. How would you go about finding out what the best next step would be for LifeGuard America, internationally speaking?

In 2011, John Fitzpatrick left LifeGuard America and returned to his engineering roots by accepting the position of Chief Executive Officer and President of US Highland, Inc., located in Tulsa, OK. US Highland is a premier developer and manufacturer of high-performance, single-cylinder, and V-twin powertrains. According to the company's website, "Our engineers and executives are racers. It is no wonder why they have been quietly designing the fastest and most innovative motors and chassis for the largest motorcycle companies in the world for the past 12 years. Now you can ride the purebred bikes they have designed for their intense and competitive riding pleasure." Another innovative value concept credited to this remarkable serial entrepreneur!

References

Alexandrides, C. G. (1971, May). How the major obstacles to expansion can be overcome. *Atlanta Economic Review, 21*(5), 12–15.

Bilkey, W. J. (1978, Spring/Summer). An attempted integration of the literature on the export behavior of firms. *Journal of International Business Studies, 9*(1), 42–43.

Bilkey, W. J., & Tesar, G. (1975, July). *The export behavior of smaller-sized Wisconsin manufacturing firms.* Paper presented at the European Meeting of the Academy of International Business, Fontainebleau, France.

Burroughs, D. L. (1991, June 3). Lifting off with exports. *U.S. News & World Report, 110*(21), 65.

Czinkota, M. R. (1994). Executive insights: A national export assistance policy for new and growing businesses. *Journal of International Marketing, 2*(1), 91–101.

Czinkota, M. R., Ronkainen, I. A., Moffett, M. H., & Moynihan, E. O. (1998). *Global business* (2nd ed.). Fort Worth, TX: Dryden Press.

Davis, L. A. (1989). *Contribution of exports to U.S. employment: 1980–1987*. Washington, DC: U.S. Government Printing Office.

De la Torre, J. R., Jr. (1972). Marketing factors in manufactured exports from developing countries. In L. T. Wells (Ed.), *The product life cycle and international trade* (pp. 225–256). Cambridge, MA: Harvard University, Graduate School of Business Administration.

Doyle, R. W., & Schommer, N. A. (1976). *The decision to export: Some implications* [Study commissioned by the Minnesota District Export Council]. St. Paul: Minnesota District Export Council.

Emery, J. C., Jr. (1980, October). For exporters, company attitude is more important than size. *Management Review, 69*(1), 45.

Gilbert, N. (1992, May). The case for countertrade. *Across the Board, 29*(5), 43–45.

Grossman, W. M. (2000, October). Go global. *Ziff Davis Smart Business for the New Economy, 13*(10), 110–117.

Finlay-Mulligan, D. J. (1981, August 18). Export marketing: The cure can work. *The Dallas Morning News,* p. 3D.

Hara, G., & Kanai, T. (1994, November). Entrepreneurial networks across oceans to promote international strategic alliances for small businesses. *Journal of Business Venturing, 9*(6), 489–507.

Hogan, B. (1989, May/June). The export boom. *D&B Reports, 37*(3), 44–45.

Howard, R. (1990, November/December). Can small business help countries compete? *Harvard Business Review, 68*(6), 88–103.

Interim regulations and guidelines cover export certificates. (1983, April 19). *Peat Marwick Executive Newsletter, 9,* 3.

International incentive [Business bulletins]. (1992, June). *Small Business Reports, 17*(6), 5.

International Monetary Fund. (1996, August). *IMF international statistics.* Washington, DC.

International Monetary Fund. (2001). *Director of trade statistics.* Washington, DC.

Johanson, J., & Vahlne, J. (1977, Spring/Summer). The internationalization process of the firm—A model of knowledge development and increasing foreign market commitments. *Journal of International Business Studies, 8*(1), 23–32.

Julien, P. A., & Ramangalahy, C. (2003, Spring). Competitive strategy and performance of exporting SMEs: An empirical investigation of the impact of their export information search and competencies. *Entrepreneurship Theory and Practice, 27*(3), 227–245.

Lado, A., & Vozikis, G. S. (1997, Winter). Transfer of technology to promote entrepreneurship in developing countries: An integration and proposed framework. *Entrepreneurship Theory and Practice, 21*(2), 55–72.

McDougall, P. P., & Oviatt, B. M. (1997). International entrepreneurship literature in the 1990s and directions for future research. In D. L. Sexton & R. W. Smilor (Eds.), *Entrepreneurship 2000* (pp. 291–320). Chicago: Upstart.

Miller, T. (1991, November). Can America compete in the global economy? *Kiplinger's Personal Finance Magazine, 45*(11), 81.

Mulhern, C. (1998, May). Going the distance. *Entrepreneur, 26*(5), 129.

Pattison, J. E. (1981, March). Solution to U.S. trade imbalance: Unleash the exporters. *Inc. Magazine, 3*(3), 19.

Perritt, G. W., & Prakash, A. J. (1980). *The status of opportunities of small business in foreign trade.* Washington, DC: U.S. Small Business Administration, Office of Advocacy, Economic Research Division.

Pett, T. L., & Wolff, J. A. (2003, April). Firm characteristics and managerial perceptions of NAFTA: An assessment of export implications for U.S. SMEs. *Journal of Small Business Management, 41*(2), 117–132.

Pricer, R. W. (1980). *Incentives for increased small business exporting.* Washington, DC: U.S. Small Business Administration, Office of Advocacy, Economic Research Division.

Rao, C. P., & Weinrauch, D. D. (1974, Spring). *External problems to export expansion: Perceptions of exporters and potential exporters.* Paper presented at the Midwest meeting of the Academy of International Business, Chicago, IL.

Rogers, E. M. (1962). *Diffusion of innovation.* New York: The Free Press.

Root, F. R. (1977). *Entry strategies for foreign markets: From domestic to international business.* New York: AMACOM.

Rosenzweig, J. A., & Koch, P. D. (1988, July/August). The U.S. dollar and the "delayed *J-curve.*" *Economic Review—Federal Reserve Bank of Atlanta, 73*(4), 2–16.

Roy, D. A., & Simpson, C. L. (1981, April). Export attitudes of business executives in the smaller manufacturing firm. *Journal of Small Business Management, 19*(2), 16–22.

Simpson, C. L., Jr. (1973). *The export decision: An interview study of the decision process in Tennessee manufacturing firms.* Unpublished doctoral dissertation, Georgia State University, Athens.

Sood, J. H. (1980). *Opportunities for foreign trade: A proposal to increase small business exports.* Washington, DC: U.S. Small Business Administration, Office of Advocacy, Economic Research Division.

State of Minnesota, Department of Economic Development (1975). *Minnesota export survey summary.* St. Paul: Author.

Timmons, J. A., & Sapienza, H. J. (1992). Venture capital: The decade ahead. In D. L. Sexton & J. D. Kasarda (Eds.), *The state of the art of entrepreneurship* (pp. 402–437). Boston: PWS Kent.

Tesar, G. (1975). *Empirical study of export operations among small and medium-sized manufacturing firms.* Unpublished doctoral dissertation, University of Wisconsin, Madison.

Tomzack, M. E. (1995, April). Ripe new markets. *Success, 42*(3), 73–77.

U.S. Department of Commerce. (1997, July). *Survey of current business.* Washington, DC: U.S. Printing Office.

U.S. Small Business Administration, Office of Management, Information and Training and Office of International Trade (1977). *Export marketing for smaller firms* (4th ed.). Washington, DC: Author.

U.S. Small Business Administration, Office of International Trade (1999, November). *America's small businesses and international trade: A report.* Washington, DC.

U.S. Small Business Administration (2001, July 5). *Breaking into the trade game: A small business guide to exporting* (3rd ed.). Washington, DC: Author. http://www.sba.gov/oit/info/Guide-To-Exporting/ (accessed August 18, 2001).

U.S. Small Business Administration, Office of International Trade (2011). *Take Your Business Global.* Washington, DC.

Vozikis, G. S. (1981). A strategic disadvantage profile of the stages of development and the stages of the exporting process: The experience of the small business exporters in Georgia. In *Selected abstracts of completed research studies* (pp. 86–90). Washington, DC: U.S. Small Business Administration, Office of Advocacy, Economic Research Division.

Watterson, T. (1981, August 18). Small businesses trade overseas, with a little help. *The Christian Science Monitor,* p. 11.

Williams, M. J. (1990, April 23). Rewriting the export rules. *Fortune, 121*(9), 89–91.

Wolner, W. (Ed.). (1977, December 26). Economic diary/Dec. 5–Dec. 9: The dollar, women, and Carter's deficit. *Business Week,* 23.

Appendix A

Definitions of International Trade Terms

Acceptance: Draft payable at a fixed or determinable future date upon the face of which has been acknowledged the unconditional obligation of the person or bank upon which it is drawn to pay it at maturity by writing the word "accepted" across the face of it, followed by the date and signature of the acceptor.

Beneficiary: The party in whose favor a letter of credit is opened.

Bill of Lading (Ocean or Railroad): A document issued by the captain, agent, or owner of a vessel or by a railroad, furnishing written evidence for the conveyance of merchandise sent by sea or rail to a certain destination. It is both a receipt for the merchandise and a contract to deliver it as freight.

Certificate of Origin: A special document required in connection with shipments to certain countries for tariff purposes in which certification is made as to the country of origin of the merchandise. The signature of the consul of the country of destination is sometimes required.

Clean Credit: A letter of credit available to the beneficiary against presentation of only a draft or receipt.

Clean Draft: A draft to which no documents are attached.

Commercial Invoice: An invoice from the seller of goods to the buyer with a description of the goods, price, charges, etc.

Consular Invoice: A detailed statement regarding the nature, etc., of the merchandise shipped on a form provided and certified by a consul of the country from which shipment is made, to a consul of the country of destination.

Customs Entry: U.S. Customs requires an entry to be made by a customs house broker, along with the attached bill of lading and consular invoice describing the shipment and the nature of the articles, prices, and country of origin so that the customs authorities can determine any duty payable.

Date Draft: A draft drawn with maturity on a fixed date, irrespective of the time of acceptance of the trade contract.

Delivery Order: Written instructions from the recorded owners of merchandise to warehouses, steamship companies, railroads etc., to release a specified shipment or part shipment to the party named in those instructions.

Documentary Credit: A letter of credit available to the beneficiary against presentation of a draft and other specified documents.

Documentary Draft: A draft with trade-related attached documents released either on payment or on acceptance of the draft.

Draft: An unconditional order in writing often referred to as bill or bill of exchange, addressed by one person to another, signed by the person making it, and requiring the addressee to pay at a fixed or determinable future date a certain sum of money to the order of a specified person.

Inspection Certificate: A document usually issued by an impartial party, certifying as to the quality of the shipped merchandise.

Insurance Policy or Certificate: A document issued by an insurance company, usually to the order of the shipper, to cover the expenses of the shipment of merchandise. The rights, interests, and the title thereafter under this document are transferred to the party who is the final owner by the shipper's endorsement.

Irrevocable Credit: This is a credit issued by a bank of an importing country in favor of an exporter in a foreign country and usually forwarded or advised to the beneficiary through a corresponding bank abroad. Under this credit, the importer and his/her bank irrevocably undertakes to honor the beneficiary's drafts and documents provided they are drawn and negotiated in accordance with the terms of the credit. The credit may not be cancelled or amended in any manner without the consent of the beneficiary, and because of the irrevocable feature, a fixed expiration date must be set.

Revocable Credit: This is a credit issued by a bank of an importing country in favor of a foreign bank, usually with a fixed expiration date. The credit may be cancelled or amended at any time without the consent of the beneficiary. However, it is customary to include a clause in the revocable credit document to the effect that any draft negotiated by the bank abroad prior to the receipt of a notice of revocation or amendment will be honored by the bank of the importing country.

Sight Draft: A draft payable upon presentation to the drawee.

Time Draft: A draft that matures after a fixed date or time after presentation or acceptance.

Trust Receipt: A document signed by a bank's customer to whom the bank releases merchandise for the purpose of manufacture or sale under the terms of which, however, the bank retains title. The customer is obligated to maintain the identity of the goods or the proceeds thereof distinct from the rest of other assets, and hold them subject to repossession by the bank in case of non-payment.

Warehouse Receipt: A document issued by a warehouse furnishing written evidence that merchandise has been stored in that specific warehouse. These documents may be either negotiable or non-negotiable.

Weight List: A document usually prepared by the shipper, giving details of the weight of each case or package comprising a shipment.

Appendix B

Financial Analysis Essentials

LEARNING OBJECTIVES

1. To understand the fundamental premises of the **accounting process**.
2. To learn the purposes and uses of **financial statements**.
3. To provide a general framework for the **financial evaluation** of a venture or an organization.

OUTLINE

Financial Analysis

The Accounting Process

- Bookkeeping
- Accounting

Financial Statements

- The Balance Sheet
- The Income Statement
- Accumulated Retained Earnings Statement
- Sources and Uses of Funds (Cash Flow Statement)
- Analysis of Changes in Working Capital

Financial Analysis Techniques

- Ratio Analysis
- Profit Analysis
- Cash Flow Analysis
- Break-even Analysis

Conclusion

FINANCIAL ANALYSIS

- Financial Analysis refers to the **systematic study of the current or potential performance** of a business enterprise.

- It **provides guidelines** for all asset and liability accounts, so that actual balances and performances can be compared regularly with the planned or estimated balances and performance.

- It **identifies gaps between planned and actual performance** so that problems can be detected early and corrective measures can be taken promptly, effectively, and efficiently.

THE ACCOUNTING PROCESS

- The Accounting Process consists of **bookkeeping** and **accounting** as the means to provide an overview of the firm's progress toward a financial goal.

- It is a **common language** among owners, managers, investors, and accountants.

- Managers **translate these general decisions into the daily activities** in the everyday course of the business.

- By examining a financial report, owners can **improve their decisions**, managers their activities, and investors their investment allocations, all for better results.

Bookkeeping

Bookkeeping is the function of keeping books, including:

- **Identify transactions** originated during the course of conducting business.

- Bring all pieces of information and documents pertaining to each business transaction to a central location, **sort, file** them into transaction categories, and arrange them in chronological order.

- **Record** each business transaction in terms of the **increase and decrease** in the business accounts that it involves.

- **Update the balance** of the accounts.

- File all accounts in the **ledger**.

Increase in Merchandise $1,000   *Decrease in Cash $1,000*

Cash Account

Date	Description	Increase	Decrease	Balance
July 30	Investment by owner	$10,000		$10,000
July 31	Merchandise purchase		$1,000	$9,000

Merchandise Account

Date	Description	Increase	Decrease	Balance
July 31	Merchandise purchase	$1,000		$9,000

Accounting

- Accounting is the function of **planning and controlling** aspects of the managerial process.

- It categorizes, analyzes, interprets, and processes "raw" financial data into **meaningful managerial information** to reach a sound decision.

- The **fundamental accounting equation** represents all that the firm owns (ASSETS) is owed to the creditors first (LIABILITIES), and what is left, the residual, belongs to the owner(s) (OWNER'S EQUITY).

$$\text{TOTAL ASSETS} = \text{TOTAL LIABILITIES} + \text{OWNER'S EQUITY}$$

FINANCIAL STATEMENTS

Financial statements use *worksheets* that can include many accounts in the form of a capital T, consequently called *T-accounts*.

- For ASSETS, an increase (inflow) is shown as debit, on the left side of the T, and a decrease (outflow) is shown as credit, on the right side.

- For LIABILITIES, an increase is shown as credit on the right side of the T-account and a decrease is shown as debit on the left side.

- For OWNER'S EQUITY, an increase is also shown as credit on the right side of the T-account (goes *into* the owner's pocket) and a decrease is also shown as debit on the left side (goes *out of* the owner's pocket).

- REVENUE accounts increase owner's equity and therefore have credit balances. EXPENSE accounts, are negative components of ownership since they decrease owner's equity, and therefore have debit balances.

Table of Debit and Credit Entries

Account type	Account increase	Account decrease	Typical balance
Asset	Debit	Credit	Debit
Liability	Credit	Debit	Credit
Equity/Capital	Credit	Debit	Credit
Revenue Income	Credit	Debit	Credit
Expense	Debit	Credit	Debit

The Balance Sheet

- The Balance Sheet is the **representation of the fundamental accounting equation**: total assets equal total liabilities plus total owner's equity.

- It represents the adjustments to the balances of all the T-accounts that were included in the worksheet, and is the firm's financial position as a **"snapshot"** statement on a *specific* date.

- The balance of these accounts can be listed on a *liquidation* basis of measurement or on a *historical* basis. Using this approach, asset balances are measured at their **historical cost** (i.e., cost of acquisition of the asset at the time it was acquired). Liabilities and owner's equity balances are measured at the amounts invested to date by creditors and owners.

Balance Sheet, XYZ Co.
December 31, 2xx1

ASSETS	2xx1	2xx0
CURRENT ASSETS	$ 450,000	$ 300,000
Cash		
Marketing securities at cost	850,000	460,000
(market value: 2xx1, $890,000; 2xx0, $480,000)		
Accounts receivable		
(Less: Allowance for bad debt: 2xx1, $100,000		
2xx0, $ 95,000)	2,000,000	1,900,000
Inventories	2,700,000	3,000,000
TOTAL CURRENT ASSETS	6,000,000	5,660,000
FIXED ASSETS		
Land	$ 450,000	$ 450,000
Buildings	3,800,000	3,600,000
Machines	950,000	850,000
Office Equipment	100,000	95,000
(Less: Accumulated depreciation)	1,800,000	1,500,000
NET FIXED ASSETS	3,500,000	3,495,000
PREPAIDS	100,000	90,000
INTANGIBLES	100,000	100,000
TOTAL ASSETS	**$ 9,700,000**	**$ 9,345,000**

Balance Sheet, XYZ Co.
December 31, 2xx1
(Continued)

LIABILITIES	2xx1	2xx0
CURRENT LIABILITIES		
Accounts payable	$ 1,000,000	$ 940,000
Notes payable	850,000	1,000,000
Accrued expenses payable	330,000	300,000
Taxes payable	320,000	290,000
TOTAL CURRENT LIABILITIES	2,500,000	2,530,000
LONG-TERM LIABILITIES		
First mortgage bonds (5% interest, due 2xx5)	2,700,000	2,700,000
TOTAL LIABILITIES	5,200,000	5,230,000
OWNER'S/STOCKHOLDER'S EQUITY		
CAPITAL STOCK		
Preferred stock, $5 cumulative, $100 par value each authorized, issued, and outstanding 6,000 shares	600,000	600,000
Common stock, $5 par each, authorized, issued, and outstanding 300,000 shares	1,500,000	1,500,000
CAPITAL SURPLUS	700,000	700,000
ACCUMULATED RETAINED EARNINGS	1,700,000	1,315,000
TOTAL OWNER'S/STOCKHOLDER'S EQUITY	4,500,000	4,115,000
TOTAL LIABILITIES AND EQUITY	$ 9,700,000	$ 9,345,000

Uses of the Balance Sheet

1. **Determine the overall health of the firm** through the equation of assets and liabilities and owner's equity.

2. **Identify trends** in terms of increases or decreases in assets, liabilities, or owner's equity by comparing the balance sheets of successive months, or years.

3. Determine the ability of the firm to meet its obligations by **checking its working capital**. Moreover, this year's working capital should be larger than last year's.

4. Provide information to owners and managers for **planning and budgeting**.

5. Provide information to creditors, investors, and government agencies for **tax disclosure**, and overall control.

6. Provide additional information to owners and investors through the **calculation of financial ratios**, such as current ratio or inventory turnover ratio.

7. **Determine the net book value** (i.e., net asset value) of a corporation's securities of preferred stock, common stock, or long-term debt (bonds).

8. Determine the capitalization ratios for each of the corporation's securities in terms of proportion of capital provided by each kind of security issued by the corporation; for example, bonds, common stock, or preferred stock.

The Income Statement

The income statement (sometimes referred to also as a profit and loss statement) reflects what happened *during* a period of time, unlike the balance sheet, which shows the fundamental soundness and health of the company at a *specific* point of time.

- It shows the **record of operating activities**, how the firm's earnings were derived, what the sales were, and what expenses were incurred to generate these sales during the time period.

- Of utmost importance is the **historical record** of a series of years, quarters, or months of income statements which tells the owner, the IRS, the potential creditor or investor how the business has done in the past, in the present, and how it might do in the future.

- The final outcome of this comparison is **net profit or net loss** for a particular time period. This outcome is carried to the balance sheet where profit increases the owner's equity in terms of proprietor's capital or corporate retained earnings and distributed in terms of owner's withdrawals or corporate dividends. This is how the income statement and the balance sheet are integrated.

Income (P&L) Statement
XYZ Co., 2xx1

	2xx1	2xx0
NET SALES REVENUES	$ 11,000,000	$ 10,200,000
COST OF SALES AND OPERATING EXPENSES		
Cost of goods sold	8,200,000	7,684,000
GROSS PROFIT	**2,800,000**	**2,516,000**
Depreciation	300,000	275,000
Selling and administrative expenses	1,400,000	1,325,000
OPERATING PROFIT	**1,100,000**	**916,000**
OTHER INCOME		
Dividends and interest income	50,000	27,000
TOTAL PROFIT/INCOME	**1,150,000**	**943,000**
LESS: INTEREST ON BONDS	135,000	135,000
PROFIT BEFORE FEDERAL INCOME TAX	**1,015,000**	**808,000**
PROVISION FOR FEDERAL INCOME TAX	480,000	365,000
NET PROFIT/INCOME AFTER TAXES	$ **535,000**	$ **443,000**
COMMON SHARES OUTSTANDING	**300,000**	**300,000**
Net earnings per common share	**$1.68**	**$1.38**
(2xx1:		

Uses of the Income Statement

1. To determine whether the **firm met its goals** for sales and profit.

2. To determine how **efficient** the firm's production has been, by calculating its *gross margin* (gross profit over sales) over the years.

3. To determine how **effective** the firm's operations have been by calculating its *operating margin* (operating costs over sales) over the years.

4. To determine how **profitable** the firm has been by calculating its *net profit margin* (net profit over sales) over the years.

5. To determine how **volatile** the firm's profitability is by calculating the *ratios of various expense items* (constant, rising, or falling) in relation to sales.

Margins

GROSS MARGIN = What percent of sales are the costs of production?

$$\frac{Gross\ Profit}{Net\ Sales\ Revenues}$$

OPERATING MARGIN = What percent of sales are the costs of total operations?

$$\frac{Operating\ Profit}{Net\ Sales\ Revenues}$$

NET PROFIT MARGIN = What percent of every dollar of sales finally constitutes profit?

$$\frac{Net\ Profits}{Net\ Sales\ Revenues}$$

Margin results should be compared with industry peers in order to gain valuable insight into the company's performance.

Accumulated Retained Earnings Statement
XYZ Co.

		2xx1		2xx0
Balance January 1	$	1,315,000	$	1,022,000
Net Profit for the Year		535,000		443,000
TOTAL		**1,850,000**		**1,465,000**
Less: Dividends Paid on:				
Preferred stock		30,000		30,000
Common stock		120,000		120,000
Balance December 31	$	**1,700,000**	$	**1,315,000**

Accumulated Retained Earnings Statement

- Should a firm **always pay dividends** regardless of whether it made money or not, as a stability and confidence policy?

- Should a firm **pay the same amount of dividends** as a consistent policy, or should it alter the amount according to each year's earnings?

- Should a company **pay out a higher proportion** of a year's increased earnings as dividends, **or should it pay less** in the hope that the retained earnings will be reinvested?

- Should stockholders prefer to have these **"surplus" earnings** in their pockets, or should they leave them in the firm's "pockets"?

- Are companies more careful with **money borrowed from outside sources,** where they subject themselves to the scrutiny of financial markets, or will they be disciplined enough to put those retained earnings to good use and reinvest that capital wisely?

Sources and Uses of Funds (Cash Flow Statement)

- The Sources and Uses of Funds statement shows the **financing of the investment activities of the firm**; that is, where the funds came from, and what they were used for.

- Another name for this financial statement is **statement of changes in financial position**.

- The Sources and Uses of Funds statement shows how the enterprise works. Like the income statement, it is an explanation of how net working capital **(the excess of current assets over current liabilities) has changed during a period of time.**

- It provides **direct information on the inflow and outflow of funds** that could not have been obtained without tedious and makeshift analysis and interpretation of the balance sheet and the income statement.

Sources and Uses of Funds
(Cash Flow Statement)
XYZ Co., 2xx1

Funds were provided from:				
Net Income		$	535,000	
Depreciation			300,000	
TOTAL				$ 835,000
Funds were used for:				
Dividends on preferred stock		$	30,000	
Dividends on common stock			120,000	
Plant and equipment			305,000	
Sundry Assets			10,000	
TOTAL				$ 465,000
INCREASE IN WORKING CAPITAL				$ 370,000

Analysis of Changes in Working Capital
XYZ Co., 2xx1

Changes in Current Assets		
Cash	$ 150,000	
Marketable securities	390,000	
Accounts receivable	100,000	
Inventories	(300,000)	
TOTAL		$ 340,000
Changes in Current Liabilities		
Accounts payable	$ 60,000	
Notes payable	(150,000)	
Accrued expenses payable	30,000	
Federal income tax payable	30,000	
TOTAL		$ (30,000)

Cash Flow? It isn't always what it seems

- Few things matter more than cash inflows and outflows.

- If core operations are not generating enough cash, sooner or later the firm needs to load up on either debt (payment of which will reduce earnings) or equity (which involves undesirable dilution).

- If a firm is not growing, negative cash flow can signal unsustainable cash burn, but what really matters is what the cash is used for: investment or "frivolities"?

- One common method to make cash flows look better is to sell or securitize accounts receivable, but thus sacrificing future operating cash flows for a one-time boost of these flows.

Source: Henny Sender, "Sadly, These Days Even Cash Flow Isn't Always What It Seems to Be," the *Wall Street Journal*, May 8, 2002, C1.

Focus on Stock Price OR on the Business?

- Determine whether the "goodwill" line item is increasing considerably every year.

- Determine whether the firm overpaid for acquisitions. It is extremely difficult to grow a business just by acquisitions, unless they are part of a sound overall strategy.

- Check for other red flags, such as accounts receivable trends and inventory levels, to see if they increase faster than revenues.

Financial Statement Footnotes

Watch for Financial Statement Footnotes, an integral part of a financial report, relating to the following:

- Changes in the company's **method of depreciation**;
- Changes in the value of the stock outstanding due to **stock splits**;
- Details of **stock options** granted to company officers and employees;
- Employment **contracts, profit sharing, pension and retirement plans**;
- Contingent liabilities representing **claims or lawsuits pending**;
- Definition of **"revenue recognition policies"** to determine when a SALE really becomes REVENUE. A sale may immediately become revenue, "*evolve*" into revenue over the life of a contract, or be "*deferred,*" meaning there is no revenue whatsoever yet. (Lucent Technologies and some other companies were recently forced by the SEC to post lower revenues to correct aggressive accounting in the past, when they "booked" sales as revenue before getting any money.)

FINANCIAL ANALYSIS TECHNIQUES

Financial Analysis Techniques help owners and managers **establish targets in sales and profits**, as well as helping them make **periodic evaluations** of the firm to make sure they never lose sight of these targets.

The major Financial Analysis Techniques are:

- Ratio Analysis
- Profit Analysis
- Cash Flow Analysis
- Break-even Analysis

Ratio Analysis

Ratio analysis is one of the most important financial analysis techniques for **assessing the strength** of a firm in the past and the present, as well for **comparing its performance** with that of the industry.

- **Managers** use ratio analysis to determine how well the firm is doing.
- **Investors** use it to determine whether the firm will provide an adequate return on their investment.
- Finally, **creditors** use financial ratio analysis to determine whether the company is a good credit risk.

Typically, the balance sheet and the income statement are the sources of information for the ratio analysis.

There are **four "families" of ratios** that can provide four different, but equally meaningful conclusions about the firm:

- Liquidity ratios
- Profitability ratios
- Activity ratios, and
- Leverage ratios

It should be noted that the ratios by themselves do not produce any meaningful information about the firm, unless each ratio or ratio family is compared in a graphic form:

- With the same **ratio of past years** to detect a certain trend.
- With the other **families of ratios** to draw conclusive information about all aspects of the firm's operations.
- With the **industry average** for the same ratio, since each industry has its own operational characteristics.
- With the **direct competitor(s)' average** for the same ratio, to develop benchmarks.

Liquidity Ratios

Liquidity ratios demonstrate a firm's **ability** to meet its short-term obligations, i.e., current liabilities and currently maturing long-term debt, through its current assets.

$$Current\ Ratio = \frac{Current\ assets}{Current\ liabilities}$$

(The extent to which the claims of short-term creditors are covered by short-term assets.)

$$Quick\ Ratio\ or\ Acid\text{-}Test\ Ratio = \frac{Current\ assets - Inventory}{Current\ liabilities}$$

(The firm's ability to pay off short-term obligations without having to sell inventory.)

$$Inventory\ to\ Net\ Working\ Capital = \frac{Inventory}{Current\ assets - Current\ liabilities}$$

(The extent to which the firm's working capital is tied up in inventory.)

Profitability Ratios

Profitability ratios demonstrate a firm's effectiveness in generating profit, as a result of its sales, and operations.

$$Gross\ Profit\ Margin = \frac{Sales - Costs\ of\ goods\ sold}{Sales}$$

(Total margin available to cover operating expenses.)

$$Net\ Profit\ Margin = \frac{Profits\ after\ taxes}{Sales}$$

(Rate of return on sales.)

$$Return\ on\ Assets = \frac{Earnings\ before\ income\ and\ taxes\ (EBIT)}{Total\ assets}$$

(Rate of return on the total investment from both stockholders and creditors.)

$$Return\ on\ Equity = \frac{Profits\ after\ taxes}{Total\ equity}$$

(Rate of return on the owner's or stockholders' investment.)

The "Cash King" Margin

This margin essentially measures profitability like the net profit margin; however, it circumvents the possibly dubious "revenue recognition policies," which can be manipulated.

- Instead of using net income (from income statement), it uses the more "honest" number of operating cash flow.

- $$\frac{Operating\ cash\ flow - Capital\ expenditures}{Sales\ for\ the\ same\ period}$$

- Operating cash flow = Actual net cash provided by, or used by, operating activities (from sources and uses of funds).

- Capital expenditures = Additions to, or subtractions from, property and equipment (from sources and uses of funds).

- Desirable results over 10%—or even better, 15%—mean that for every sales dollar, 10 or 15 cents of cash were received.

    (*Source:* Motley Fool's online Rule Maker Portfolio, January 13, 2002.)

Activity Ratios

Activity ratios demonstrate a firm's efficiency and productivity and how well its productive capacity is being used.

$$Inventory\ Turnover = \frac{Sales}{Inventory}$$

(The amount of inventory used by the company to generate its sales volume.)

$$Fixed\ Asset\ Turnover = \frac{Sales}{Fixed\ assets}$$

(The firm's fixed-asset productivity and plant utilization to generate its sales volume.)

$$Average\ Collection\ Period = \frac{Accounts\ receivable}{Average\ daily\ sales}$$

(The firm's average length of time that is required to receive payment on its accounts receivable.)

Leverage Ratios

Leverage ratios demonstrate a firm's source of capital, that is, owners/stockholders or outside creditors, and at what proportion.

$$Debt\ to\ Assets\ Ratio = \frac{Total\ debt}{Average\ daily\ sales}$$

(The extent to which borrowed funds are used to finance the firm's operations.)

$$Debt\ to\ Equity\ Ratio = \frac{Total\ debt}{Total\ equity}$$

(Ratio of funds from creditors to funds from stockholders; that is, how much equity the firm has to support its debt.)

$$Long\text{-}term\ Debt\ to\ Equity\ Ratio = \frac{Long\text{-}term\ debt}{Total\ equity}$$

(The balance between debt to equity that usually determines the firm's additional debt capacity, in case it seeks additional outside financing.)

Financial Ratio Profile

A consolidated view of all four ratio families for reporting purposes could use the following sample format below:

Liquidity	Very tight	About right	Slack	Too slack

Profitability	Very low	Average	High	Very high

Activity	Too slow	Slow	About right	Fast

Leverage	Too much debt	Balanced	Too much equity

Industry Ratio Comparison

A very useful resource to compare and contrast a firm's financial ratios with those of the industry is the reference source *Risk Management Associates (RMA) Annual Statement Studies & Financial Ratio Benchmarks*, which publishes industry data using the following:

- NAICS/SIC Code
- Asset size
- Typical **financial statements as percentages** of total assets, total liabilities, and total net sales, according to asset size
- Typical **financial ratios** according to asset size
- Typical **comparative historical data** for previous years, according to asset size

Return on Investment (ROI): The "Queen" of Ratios

Calculating a company's, or a division's ROI is an excellent way to measure performance:

$$ROI = \frac{Profit\ before\ taxes}{Total\ equity}$$

A better expression of the same formula is as follows:

$$ROI = \frac{Profit\ before\ taxes}{Total\ equity} = \frac{Net\ sales}{Total\ assets} = \frac{Total\ assets}{Total\ equity}$$

$$(Profitability) \times (Activity) \times (Leverage)$$

- The **long version of ROI** is better because it directly identifies the "culprit" family ratio that was mainly responsible for good or bad return performance.
- The important issue is to be **consistent** and use the same measures of profit (customarily, before taxes), net sales (customarily, sales after returns and allowances for bad debt), assets (customarily, net, year-end book value assets), and equity/investment when figuring ROIs for different periods and/or divisions.

Uses of the ROI Ratio

- Measure current performance overall.
- Compare different companies.
- Compare different divisions of individual companies.
- Compare future potential profitability among divisions.
- Evaluate future investment opportunities.
- Evaluate alternative capital expenditure types and levels.
- Measure the effect of cost reductions.
- Measure the effect of changes in inventory levels.
- Measure the effect of changing asset utilization.
- Evaluate new product development.

- Provide framework for pricing decisions.
- Rate managerial effectiveness among divisions.
- Provide the basis for determining management promotions and rewards.

An ROI Example

It is possible to have two companies or divisions with the same level of sales, expenses, profit, and liabilities, but with different ROIs:

Division I

Sales	$500,000	Current assets	$125,000
Expenses	−400,000	Fixed assets	+ 500,000
Profit	$ 60,000	Total assets	$625,000
		Total liabilities	−25,000
		Total equity	$600,000

Division I ROI = Profit/Equity = $60,000/$600,000 = 10%

Division II

Sales	$50,000	Current assets	$100,000
Expenses	−440,000	Fixed assets	+ 225,000
Profit	$60,000	Total assets	320,000
		Total liabilities	−25,000
		Total equity	$300,000

Division II ROI = Profit/Equity = $60,000/$300,000 = 20%

ROI Afterthoughts

- Different companies, divisions, and products require **different levels of investment**.
- **Differences in managerial effectiveness** create different levels of ROI.
- **ROI and Productivity (O/I) improve** when managers:
  - ☐ Increase sales (output) and reduce expenses (input)
  - ☐ Increase sales proportionately more than the increase in expenses
  - ☐ Reduce sales proportionately less than the reduction in expenses
  - ☐ Retain level of sales steady, while reducing expenses
  - ☐ Increase level of sales, while retaining expense level steady
  - ☐ Increase sales proportionately more than the increase in investment
  - ☐ Reduce sales proportionately less than the reduction in investment

What Is a Firm's Worth?

- It depends on its **EBITDA** (Earnings Before Interest Taxes Depreciation and Amortization) level and multiples thereof that a buyer is **WILLING** to pay, given the firm's **future potential for growth and profitability**, as well as its "strategic fit" with the buyer's existing operations.

Business Value EBITDA Multiples

		Growth potential		
	Low	Moderate	High	Strategic acquisition
Low	Net assets / 2x	2x / 3x	4x / 5x	6x / 7x
Moderate	2x / 3x	4x / 5x	5x / 6x	7x / 8x
High	4x / 5x	6x / 7x	8x / 9x	10x / ?
Strategic acquisition	6x / 7x	8x / 9x	10x / ?	?

Profitability potential (left axis label)

Business Valuation

Multiple ratings of a business	*Key to rating scale (0–5)*
1. Risk Rating (Steady profitability growth)	_____
2. Competitive Rating (Relative competitiveness in their market)	_____
3. Industry Rating (Industry and "industry pie" growth)	_____
4. Company Rating (Long record of solid operations and reputation/goodwill)	_____
5. Growth Rating (Market share slice of the "industry pie")	_____
6. Attractiveness Rating (EBITDA profitability and growth potential multiples)	_____
7. Liquidity Reserve Rating (Retained earnings amount in reserves)	_____
Total Rating Points	_____
Divided by 7 Ratings	
Firm's Total Multiple Average	_____

Profit Analysis

- During the financial evaluation, it is absolutely essential to have a **profit target**. Some business firms hit their profit target more often than others, because they keep their operations aimed in that direction, never losing sight of it.

- Ending the year with a profit is reserved for the firms who always strive for outstanding performance. To keep the firm pointed toward profit and achieve this outstanding performance some **profit analysis principles** need to be identified and applied.

- It is absolutely essential during the financial evaluation to have a **profit target**. Some business firms hit their profit target more often than others, because they keep their operations aimed in that direction never losing sight of it.

- Ending the year with a profit is reserved for the firms who always strive for outstanding performance. To keep the firm pointed toward profit and achieve this outstanding performance some **profit analysis principles** need to be identified and applied.

Profit Analysis Principles

- **Know your revenues.** Each revenue source must be identified for each of the product lines and for the operations as a whole.

- **Know your costs.** All cost items must be known in detail, so cost figures can be compared as a percentage of sales (operating ratios). The costs must be itemized so that the ones that seem to be rising or falling can be identified easily and quickly, based on experience and cost figures for the industry. An important thing to remember is that profit is not only a function of revenues, but also a function of the cost level

$$(Profit = Sales\ Revenues - Costs).$$

- **Know your profit.** The pricing of the products or services must provide an adequate profit to cover the costs. Pricing must be monitored closely to be alert in adjusting prices due to rising costs or to remain competitive. There should be no hesitation in dropping a "loser" product from the product lineup. Pricing often remains an art despite claims to the contrary. But in many cases, the price includes hard to identify sociological and psychological factors. Thus, the pricing process is sometimes incredibly arbitrary, and, after considering costs and prices of similar products, it very often takes the form of a wild guess.

- **Know the tax implications of your expenses.** Major decisions must be determined early to minimize taxable income.

Cash Flow Analysis

- The **cash flow cycle** defines the period of time beginning with the initial cash outlay for inventories, raw materials or services, and ending with the collection of funds from the sale of the finished product. That is, in any business there is usually some time lag before cash is actually received for the goods or services sold. This time lag creates the need for sound cash planning.

- The **length of the cash flow cycle** for the firm must be determined. If actual production takes 4 weeks, for example, while payment is made 4 weeks after delivery of the goods to the customer, the cash flow cycle is 8 weeks. The firm incurs expenses to produce these goods at the onset of production and receives cash from the sale 8 weeks later.

- A **cash flow projection** is a forecast of cash receipts that the firm anticipates receiving, as well as cash expenditures it anticipates expending during a given period of time, and the resulting anticipated cash position at specific times during the period being projected.

- The **purpose of preparing a cash flow projection** is to determine deficits or surpluses in cash from that level necessary to operate the business during the time for which the projection is prepared.

- If **deficits** are revealed in the cash flow, financial plans must be altered either to provide more cash from more equity capital, loans, or increased selling prices of products; from reduced expenditures including inventory; or from less credit sales, until a proper cash flow balance is obtained.

- If **surpluses** of cash are revealed, this may be an indication of excessive borrowing or idle money that could be "put to work."

- The objective is to finally develop a plan, which, if followed, will provide a **well-managed flow of cash**. These projections become more useful when the estimated information can be compared with actual information as it develops.

Essential Operating Data

- To ensure credibility and validity, the cash flow projections (pro forma) need to be constructed on a **discounted cash flow basis**, taking into consideration that the present value of money is more than the value of tomorrow's money.

- Before the cash flow projections are compiled, the end-of the-month amount of some **essential non-cash flow operating information** needs to be pre-determined:

  ☐ Sales Volume

  ☐ Accounts Receivable

  ☐ Bad Debt

  ☐ Inventory on Hand

  ☐ Accounts Payable

  ☐ Depreciation

A Monthly Cash Flow Projection Form

Year 2xx3	Month:	Pre-Start Up		1		2		3		4....	
XYZ, Co.		Estimate	Actual	E	A	E	A	E	A	E	A....
1. Cash on hand (beginning of month)											
2. Cash receipts											
Cash sales											
Collections from A/R											
Loan or other cash infusion											
3. Total cash receipts											
4. Total cash available											
5. Cash paid out											
Operations											
Subtotal											
Loan principal payment											
Capital purchases											
Reserve and/or escrow											
Owner's withdrawal											
6. Total cash paid out											
7. Cash position (end of month)											

Break-even Analysis

Break-even analysis determines how many units need to be produced/sold in order to break even and cover at least total costs (fixed and variable costs).

$$Break\text{-}even\ analysis = \frac{\$Total\ fixed\ costs}{\$Unit\ price - \$Unit\ VC} = \#\ BEP\ Units$$

Uses of Break-even Analysis

- Break-even analysis is a **quick-screening device** that can determine whether or not it is worthwhile to employ more intensive and costly analysis such as discounted cash flow, which requires large amounts of expensive-to-get data.

- Break-even analysis also permits **comparison of alternative product designs and specifications** with a different cost mix, and before the specifications are determined, by examining trade-offs, since each product design has its own cost implications that obviously affect price and marketing feasibility.

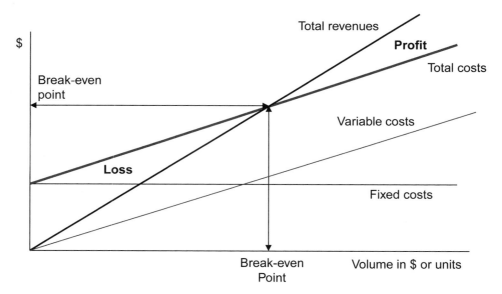

- Break-even analysis also serves as a substitute for estimating an unknown factor in making "go" or "no–go" project decisions, since there are always many variables to consider such as, demand, costs, price, and other factors. While most expenses can be determined fairly easily, profit and demand are usually the only two unknown variables that remain. Since demand is usually tougher to estimate, by deciding that profit must at least be zero (the break–even point), the demand that is needed to make the project a reasonable undertaking can then be fairly simply calculated. Of course, this demand figure at the break–even point needs to be related with the project's estimated future market share to determine the ultimate worthiness of the project, and t39/his is a matter of careful evaluation and business common sense.

CONCLUSION

- The final outcome produced through financial analysis is the reflection of **the true financial condition of an enterprise:**

  - ☐ What business is the company in? Is it in a growing, profitable industry? Is it a leader in the field? What is the business model (that is, how does the business make money)? Are its profit margins and ROE healthy and growing?

  - ☐ What is the firm's track record, and how does it compare with its competitors?

  - ☐ What do the financial statements really tell you? Is the firm growing? Are there any "red flags" or "hidden messages" requiring further investigation?

  - ☐ What are the present and future risks that the company and its investors are facing? Is the stock valued appropriately and attractively?

- Financial analysis is also used by individuals both inside and outside the enterprise to **make decisions** about whether to invest, lend, buy or sell to the firm or not, and about the venture's performance and the performance of the entrepreneurs, managers, and their employees.

- Finally, if the enterprise's accounting system and the resulting financial statements and analysis are sound and trustworthy, this will have a **positive reflection on the firm's management.**

Index

Italic page references indicate charts and tables.

About the Authors

Dr. George S. Vozikis is currently teaching at Chaminade University of Honolulu and retired as the Edward Reighard Chair in Management from California State University, Fresno where he was also the Director of the Institute for Family Business. Prior to joining California State University at Fresno, he taught at the University of Tulsa where he was the Davis D. Bovaird Endowed Chairholder of Entrepreneurial Studies and Private Enterprise, and the Founding Director of the Family-Owned Business Institute, as well as, the Tulsa University Innovation Institute. In addition to numerous journal publications, conference papers, and books, he has conducted executive development seminars and taught in China, Greece, Panama, Mexico, Singapore, Samoa, Cyprus, Russia, Saudi Arabia, and Canada. Vozikis has served as a consultant for many organizations, such as LG (formerly Goldstar), McDonnell-Douglas Corporation, GTE, the Medical University of South Carolina, the U.S. Army Missile Command, the Williams Companies, and many family firms.

Dr. Timothy S. Mescon has been President and Professor of Management at Columbus State University (GA) since 2008. Previously, for eighteen years, he was Dinos Eminent Scholar of Entrepreneurship and Dean of the Coles College of Business at Kennesaw State University. Mescon served as the inaugural chair of the Entrepreneurship Division of the Academy of Management, Vice-President of the U.S. Association for Small Business and Entrepreneurship (USASBE) and as a co-founder of The Edge Connection (Georgia). He previously coauthored four books. His work has appeared in publications as varied as the *California Management Review* and *The Wall Street Journal*. He received his PhD from the Terry College at the University of Georgia; his MBA from Southern Methodist University; and a BA from Tulane University.

Dr. Howard D. Feldman is the Director of Nonprofit Management Programs for the Pamplin School of Business at the University of Portland. He teaches entrepreneurship, social entrepreneurship, strategic management, and social responsibility. Professor Feldman's work has been published in *The Journal of Business Venturing, The Journal of Small Business Management, The Case Research Journal,* and others. He has taught and lectured at graduate business schools in Madrid, Seville, Tel Aviv, Haifa, and Chernivtzi (Ukraine).

Dr. Eric W. Liguori is an Assistant Professor of Entrepreneurship in the Craig School of Business at California State University, Fresno. Dr. Liguori is a nationally recognized experiential entrepreneurship educator, with work featured in *The Entrepreneurship Educator* and on www.3e-learning.org. His research interests include entrepreneurial self-efficacy, entrepreneurial ecosystems, and entrepreneurship education, and his work has been published in *The Journal of Small Business Management, Leadership & Organization Development Journal, The Journal of Managerial Issues,* and *The Encyclopedia of New Venture Management.*